P9-DHE-482

Seven principles

pg 17 - 20.

1 99
PARK PLACE
BOOKSTORE
$61.95

CREATING READING INSTRUCTION FOR ALL CHILDREN

Second Edition

Thomas G. Gunning
Southern Connecticut State University

Allyn and Bacon

Boston / London / Toronto / Sydney / Tokyo / Singapore

hildren, Alex and Paige, whose formal
reading and writing has just begun, but who
happy hours listening to their mom and dad,
vingly read to them.

Series Editor: Virginia Lanigan
Development Editor: Ann Greenberger
Editorial Assistants: Nicole DePalma, Nihad M. Farooq
Editorial Production Manager: Elaine Ober
Editorial Production Service: Lifland et al., Bookmakers
Text Designer: Melinda Grosser for *silk*
Composition Buyer: Linda Cox
Manufacturing Buyer: Megan Cochran
Cover Administrator: Linda Knowles

Copyright © 1996, 1992 by Allyn & Bacon
A Simon & Schuster Company
Needham Heights, MA 02194

All rights reserved. No part of the material protected by this copyright notice may be
reproduced or utilized in any form or by any means, electronic or mechanical, including
photocopying, recording, or by any information storage and retrieval system, without
written permission from the copyright holder.

Library of Congress Cataloging-in-Publication Data

Gunning, Thomas G.
    Creating reading instruction for all children / Thomas G. Gunning.
 -- 2nd ed.
      p.   cm.
    Includes bibliographical references and index.
    ISBN 0-205-16999-6
    1. Reading (Elementary)   I. Title.
 LB1573.G93   1996
 372.4'1--dc20   95-20966
                                                   CIP

Printed in the United States of America

10   9   8   7   6   00   99   98

CONTENTS

Preface   xix

C H A P T E R   The Nature of Reading and Today's Children   1

1   **Anticipation Guide**   1

Using What You Know   2

The Nature of Reading   2

    Importance of Language   3

    Role of Cognitive Development   4

    Importance of Experience   6

    Importance of the Students' Culture   7

The Reader's Role in the Reading Process   9

Approaches to Reading Instruction: Whole Versus Part Learning   10

    Bottom-Uppers   10

    Top-Downers   11

    Interactionists   11

Importance of Literacy Models   12

Approach Taken by This Text   13

Stages of Reading Development   13

    Stage 1. Emergent Literacy (Birth to 5 Years)   13

    Stage 2. Beginning Reading (Grades K–1)   14

    Stage 3. Growing Independence (Grades 2–3)   15

    Stage 4. Reading to Learn (Grades 4–6)   15

    Stage 5. Abstract Reading (Grades 7 and Up)   17

A Reading and Writing Program for Today's Students   17

Summary   21

Classroom Applications   21

Field Applications   22

C H A P T E R

2

Children's Emergent Literacy   23

Anticipation Guide   23

Using What You Know   24

Understanding Emergent Literacy   24

Readiness Versus Emergent Literacy   25

Essential Skills and Understandings for Emergent Literacy   26

Creating a Literacy-Rich Environment   27

Fostering Emergent Literacy   29

Making Reading and Writing a Part of Classroom Activities   30

Reading to Students   30

Emergent Storybook Reading   39

Using the Language Experience Approach   44

A New Concept of Writing   45

Planned Instruction of Essential Understandings   54

The Role of the School in Fostering Language Development   65

Issues in Emergent Literacy Instruction   67

Use of Commercial Materials   67

Reading in Preschool   67

Working with Parents   68

Monitoring Emergent Literacy   69

CAP (Concepts About Print)   72

Informal Assessment Measures   73

Other Measures of Emergent Literacy   75

Using the Assessment Results   75

Summary   75

Classroom Applications   76

Field Applications   76

C H A P T E R

3

Teaching Phonics   77

Anticipation Guide   77

Using What You Know   78

Rationale and Approaches for Phonics Instruction   78

Basic Principles of Phonics Instruction   79

Approaches to Teaching Phonics   79

Stages in Decoding   81
    Logographic Stage   81
    Alphabetic Stage   81
    Orthographic Stage   81
Phonics Elements   82
    Consonants   82
    Vowels   94
    Using an Integrated Approach   111
Phonics and Spelling   112
Strategy Instruction   115
    Incorporating Phonics Strategies with Context   116
    Building Independence   116
Summary   118
Classroom Applications   119
Field Applications   119

C H A P T E R
4

Sight Words; Syllabic, Morphemic, and Contextual Analyses; and Dictionary Usage   120

Anticipation Guide   120
Using What You Know   121
Word Recognition Strategies for Novice and Advanced Readers   121
Sight Words   122
    Sources of Sight Words   122
    Teaching High-Frequency Words   124
    Achieving Automaticity   127
    Using Children's Books to Build Sight Vocabulary   128
    Integration of Sight Words with Other Word Recognition Skills   132
Syllabication   132
    Generalization Approach to Teaching Syllabication   133
    Pattern Approach to Teaching Syllabication   135
    Using the Pronounceable Word Part and Analogy Strategies   137
Morphemic Analysis   137
    Compound Words   138
    Prefixes   139
    Suffixes   141

Root Words   141

Contextual Analysis   146

Processing Context Clues   146

Types of Context Clues   147

Presenting Context Clues   148

Subsequent Lessons in the Use of Context Clues   150

Supplying Corrective Feedback   150

Applying a Corrective Cues Hierarchy   151

Using Prompts   152

Dictionary Usage   153

Using Predictionaries   153

Using Dictionaries   153

The Dictionary as a Tool   159

The Need for an Integrated Approach   160

Summary   161

Classroom Applications   161

Field Applications   161

C H A P T E R

5

Building Vocabulary   162

Anticipation Guide   162

Using What You Know   163

The Need for Vocabulary Instruction   163

Stages of Word Knowledge   164

Seven Principles of Developing Vocabulary   165

Building Experiential Background   165

Relating Vocabulary to Background   166

Building Relationships   166

Developing Depth of Meaning   166

Presenting Several Exposures   167

Creating an Interest in Words   168

Promoting Transfer   168

Techniques for Teaching Words   169

Graphic Organizers   169

Dramatizing   174

Exploring Word Histories   176
Enjoying Words   176
Discovering Sesquipedalian Words   178
Labeling   179
Feature Comparison   180
Using Word-Building Reference Books   180
Using Technology   181
Predicting Vocabulary Words   181
Wide Reading   183
Reading to Students   184
A Planned Program   184
A Balanced Blend   185
Remembering Vocabulary   185
Key Word Approach   186
Teaching Special Features of Words   187
Homophones   188
Homographs   188
Figurative Language   189
Multiple Meanings   189
Connotations   190
Summary   191
Classroom Applications   191
Field Applications   191

C H A P T E R   Comprehension: Theory and Strategies   192

6

Anticipation Guide   192
Using What You Know   193
The Process of Comprehending   193
Schema Theory   193
Mental Models   194
Propositional Theory   195
Comprehension Strategies   196
Preparational Strategies   197
Organizational Strategies   198

Elaboration Strategies   214

Monitoring   224

Putting It All Together: Applying Strategies   230

Reciprocal Teaching   230

Learning Environment   234

Summary   235

Classroom Applications   235

Field Applications   236

C H A P T E R

7

Comprehension: Text Structures and Teaching Procedures   237

Anticipation Guide   237

Using What You Know   238

Nature of the Text   238

Narrative Text and Story Schema   238

Expository Text   242

The Role of Questions in Comprehension   248

Planning Questions   248

Placement of Questions   249

Types of Questions   249

Number of Questions   250

Using Wait Time   250

Classroom Atmosphere   251

Techniques for Asking Questions   251

Frameworks for Fostering Comprehension   255

Directed Reading Activity   255

Directed Reading-Thinking Activity   261

The Cloze Procedure   264

Classic Cloze   264

Scoring Cloze   265

Discussion for Comprehension   265

Constructing Cloze Exercises   265

Variations on Cloze   266

Critical Reading   267

Scope and Sequence of Critical Reading Skills   268

Importance of the Learning Environment   274

Summary   275

Classroom Applications   276

Field Applications   276

C H A P T E R
8

Reading and Writing in the Content Areas and Study Skills   277

Anticipation Guide   277

Using What You Know   278

Overall Goals of Literacy Instruction in the Content Areas   278
    The Teacher's Role   278
    Higher-Order Thinking Skills   279
    Building on Students' Strengths   279

Using Content Area Textbooks   280
    Choosing Textbooks   281

Literature in the Content Areas   286

Instructional Techniques   287
    Before Reading   288
    During Reading   292
    After Reading   300
    KWL Plus: A Technique for Before, During, and After Reading   304

Teaching Content Area Knowledge   306
    Reading for Conceptual Change   307
    Using Children's Books and Periodicals   308

Writing to Learn   311
    Learning Logs   312

Reading to Remember   313

Fostering Retention   314
    Principles of Memory   315
    Memory Devices   315
    Metacognitive Awareness   318
    Distributed versus Massed Practice   319

SQ3R: A Theory-Based Study Strategy   319
    Principles of SQ3R   319
    Teaching SQ3R   321

Test-Taking Strategies   322

Test-Taking Tips   322
Study Habits   323
Expressive Study Skills   324
Taking Notes   324
Outlining   326
I-Charts   327
Metacognitive Study Strategies   329
Summary   330
Classroom Applications   331
Field Applications   331

CHAPTER
9

Reading Literature   332

Anticipation Guide   332
Using What You Know   333
Experiencing Literature   333
Reader Response Theory   335
Principles of Teaching from an Aesthetic Stance   341
Developing Aesthetic Judgment   341
Types of Literature   343
Folklore   343
Poetry   346
Chapter Books and Novels   350
Drama   355
Nonfiction   359
Voluntary Reading   361
Determining Interests and Attitudes   362
The Classroom Library   362
Setting Aside Time for Voluntary Reading   363
Modeling the Process of Selecting and Discussing Books   364
The Importance of Sharing and Instruction in Developing Avid Readers   364
Activities for Motivating Voluntary Reading   365
Summary   367
Classroom Applications   368
Field Applications   368

CHAPTER 10   Approaches to Teaching Reading   369

Anticipation Guide   369

Using What You Know   370

Characteristics of Effective Reading Approaches   370

Basal Approach   371

Advantages of Basals   372

Disadvantages of Basals   372

Using Manuals Flexibly   374

Selecting a Basal   374

Adapting Basals   374

Making the Transition to a Literature-Based Approach   376

Holistic Materials   377

Literature-Based Approach   378

Core Books   379

Text Sets   379

Thematic Units   380

Self-Selection   383

Shaping the Program   383

Creating Literature Guides   383

A Sample Program   384

Choosing Materials   385

Advantages and Disadvantages of a Literature-Based Approach   386

Adapting a Literature-Based Approach   386

Individualized Reading   387

Materials   387

Organizing the Program   388

Implementing Individualized Reading   388

Advantages and Disadvantages of Individualized Reading   394

Adapting Individualized Reading   395

Reading Workshop   395

Preparation Time   396

Self-Selected Reading and Responding   396

Using Dialogue Journals   396

Student Sharing   398

Advantages and Disadvantages of Reading Workshop   398

Adapting Reading Workshop   398

Language-Experience Approach   399

Personalizing Group Stories   402
An Individual Approach   402
Introducing Skills and Strategies   403
The Language-Experience Approach and ESL Students   404
Variant Dialects   404
The Language-Experience Approach in the Content Areas   405
Other Uses for the Language-Experience Approach   405
A High-Tech Language-Experience Approach   405
Advantages and Disadvantages
of the Language-Experience Approach   406
Adapting the Language-Experience Approach   406

Linguistic Approach   406
Advantages and Disadvantages of the Linguistic Approach   407
Adapting the Linguistic Approach   407

Whole Language   408
Basic Principles of Whole Language   408
Conditions of Language Learning   408
Whole Language Activities   409
Making the Transition to Holistic Teaching   410
Advantages and Disadvantages of Whole Language   411
Adapting Whole Language   411

Combining Approaches   411
Summary   412
Classroom Applications   413
Field Applications   413

CHAPTER **11**   Writing and Reading   414

Anticipation Guide   414
Using What You Know   415
The Roots of Writing   415
Process Approach to Writing   416
Prewriting   416
Composing   420
Revising   422
Editing   424

Publishing   427
Conferences   428

Writing Workshop   431
Mini-Lesson   431
Writing Time   432
Group Sharing   432
Management of the Writing Workshop   432

Interactive Writing   433

Keeping Track   435

Technology and Writing   436
Word-Processing Programs   436
Desktop Publishing   438

Teaching Form   439
Skills Lessons   442

Reading Helps Writing   443

A Full Menu   445

Summary   446

Classroom Applications   447

Field Applications   447

C H A P T E R

12

Diversity in the Classroom   448

Anticipation Guide   448

Using What You Know   449

Teaching All Students   449

Multicultural Education   450
Content Integration   450
Knowledge Construction   451
Prejudice Reduction   452
Equitable Pedagogy   452

Students at Risk   452
Economically Disadvantaged Students   453
Linguistically and Culturally Diverse Students   456
Bilingual Learners   459

Students with Disabilities   464
Students with Learning Disabilities   464

Students with Attention Deficit Disorder   467

Students with Mental Retardation   469

Slow Learners   472

Students with Physical Disabilities   473

Students with Other Physical Impairments   478

Gifted or Talented Students   479

Characteristics of Gifted and Talented Students   479

Features of Gifted Programs   479

Inclusion   480

Title 1 and Remedial Programs   481

Early Intervention Programs   481

Reading Recovery   482

Other Early Intervention Programs   482

Lessons from Early Intervention Programs   483

Summary   484

Classroom Applications   485

Field Applications   485

CHAPTER

13

Evaluation   486

Anticipation Guide   486

Using What You Know   487

The Nature of Evaluation   487

The Starting Point   487

Three Perspectives of Evaluation   488

Authentic Assessment   488

Product Versus Process Measures   489

Questions to Be Asked   490

Placement Information   490

Informal Reading Inventory   491

Running Records   499

Norm-Referenced Versus Criterion-Referenced Tests   500

Norm-Referenced Tests   500

Criterion-Referenced Tests   502

Judging Assessment Measures   502

Reliability   502

Validity   503

Reporting Performance   503

   Norm-Referenced Reporting   503

   Criterion-Referenced Reporting   504

Functional Level Assessment   506

Tests in Basal Series   506

Other Methods of Assessment   507

   Retelling   507

   Think-Aloud Protocols   509

   Observation   511

   Anecdotal Records   511

   Ratings   512

   Questionnaires   513

   Interviews   514

Self-Evaluation   514

   Logs and Journals   515

Evaluating Writing   516

   Holistic Scoring   516

   Analytic Scoring   516

   Using a Combination of Techniques   517

Portfolios   518

   Types of Portfolios   518

   Writing Samples   518

   Reading Samples   519

   Reviewing Portfolios   519

Summary   522

Classroom Applications   523

Field Applications   523

C H A P T E R

14

Constructing and Managing a Literacy Program   524

Anticipation Guide   524

Using What You Know   525

Constructing a Literacy Program   525

   Setting Goals   525

   Choosing Materials   526

Selecting Techniques and Strategies   526
Building a Sense of Community   527

Managing a Literacy Program   530
Using Time Efficiently   530
Providing for Individual Differences   532
Continuous Monitoring of Progress   535
Involving Parents   536
Working with Other Professionals   537

Literacy and Technology   537
Computers   537
Other Technologies   540
Hypermedia and Hypertext   542
Literacy in Today's and Tomorrow's World   543

Professional Development   544
Summary   547
Classroom Applications   548
Field Applications   548

References   549

Index   569

SPECIAL FEATURES

Lessons

Elkonin phonemic segmentation technique   62

Analytic-synthetic introduction of initial consonant correspondence   84

Vowel correspondence   99

Word-building pattern   103

A Making Words lesson   107

Sorting beginning consonant sounds   114

Sight words   125

Using predictable books to build sight vocabulary   128

A drastic strategy   131

Syllabication using the generalization approach   134

Syllabication using the pattern approach   135

Prefixes   139

Context clues   149

Semantic mapping   170

Semantic feature analysis   172

Key word approach   186

Determining the main idea and its supporting details   203

Determining important details   207

Introduction to summarization   212

Making inferences   217

Presenting QAR   219

Reciprocal teaching   231

Retelling   241

ReQuest procedure   253

A sample DRA   259

A DR-TA   262

Using PReP   288

Using an anticipation guide   289

Think-alouds   295

Introducing simple outlining   326

Reader response   338

Group language-experience chart   400

Children's Book Lists

Recommended read-alouds   37

Alphabet books   56

Rhyming books   59

Alliterative books for reinforcing beginning consonants   64

Recommended alphabet books for reinforcing initial consonants   88

Children's books that reinforce vowel patterns   100

Books reinforcing sight words   129

Books containing high-frequency words   129

Books that reinforce compound words   139

Word histories   176

Word play   177

Figurative language   189

Math puzzles and riddles   310

Myths, legends, and hero tales   345

Poetry   349

Drama   357

Biographies   360

Books for young writers   426

Multicultural books   451

People with disabilities   478

Student Strategies

Applying the variability strategy to consonant correspondences   93

Applying the variability strategy to vowel correspondences   110

Word recognition   116

Attacking multisyllabic words   137

Constructing the main idea   201

Following directions 209

Judging sources 272

Using ALERT 274

Applying SQ3R 320

Taking notes 325

Reinforcement Activities

Alphabet knowledge 57

The concept of rhyme 61

The concept of beginning sounds 64

Consonant letter-sound relationships 89

Phonics 117

Building a sight vocabulary 132

Morphemic analysis 144

Dictionary usage 159

Main idea construction 205

Determining importance of information 207

Extending the concept of facts
and opinions 270

After-reading strategies 303

Folktales 344

Poetry appreciation 350

Chapter books and novels 355

Exemplary Teaching

Building a bridge from home to school 8

Helping children feel competent 20

Extension activities 33

Shared reading with big books 42

Writing in kindergarten 51

Singing initial consonants 112

Building a sight vocabulary 131

Fostering self-correction 152

How to create an interest in words 180

Developing vocabulary and confidence 190

Using imaging 221

Using literature in the content areas 287

From basals to books 346

Teaching a multicultural unit 382

Implementing individualized reading 395

Writing in kindergarten 422

Making the switch to writing process 427

Building self-esteem 454

Understanding cultural differences 456

Making observations 512

Building a sense of community 529

PREFACE

This book will not tell you how to teach reading. Teaching reading is in large measure a matter of making choices: Should you use basal readers or children's books, or both? Should you teach children to read whole words or to sound out words letter by letter, or both? Should you have three reading groups or four, or no groups? There are no right answers to these questions. The answers depend on your personal philosophy, your interpretation of the research, the level at which you are teaching, the kinds of students you are teaching, community preferences, and the nature of your school or school district's reading program.

What this book *will* do is help you discover approaches and techniques that fit your teaching style and your teaching situation. Its aim is to present as fairly, completely, and clearly as possible the major approaches and techniques that research and practice have indicated to be successful. This book also presents the theories behind the methods, so you will be free to choose, adapt, and/or construct those approaches and techniques that best fit your style and teaching situation. You will be creating reading instruction.

Although approaches and techniques are emphasized in the text, methods are only a portion of the equation. Reading is not just a process; it is also very much a content area. What students read *does* matter, and, therefore, recommendations for specific children's books and other reading materials have been provided. The basic premise of this book is that the best reading programs are a combination of effective techniques and plenty of worthwhile reading material.

Because children differ greatly in their backgrounds, needs, and interests, a variety of suggestions are provided for both techniques and types of books to be used. The intent is to provide you with sufficient background knowledge of teaching methods and children's books and other materials to enable you to create effective instruction for all the children you teach, whether they are rich or poor; bright, average, or slow; whether they are students with disabilities or without; urban or suburban; or from any of the diverse cultural and ethnic groups that comprise today's classrooms.

This book also recognizes that reading is part of a larger language process; therefore, considerable attention is paid to writing and the other language arts, especially as these relate to reading instruction. Whether reading or writing is being addressed, emphasis is on making the student the center of instruction. For instance, activities are recommended that allow students to choose writing topics and reading materials. Approaches that foster a personal response to reading are also advocated. Just as you are encouraged by this text to create your own reading instruction, students must be encouraged to create their own literacy.

Pedagogical and Enrichment Features of the Second Edition

The second edition has expanded coverage of the following essential areas: whole language; literature-based instruction; the changing face and role of basals; use of alternative or authentic assessment, with emphasis on portfolios; various kinds of grouping and individualization, including cooperative grouping and reading and writing workshops; integration of the language arts and all subjects through a unit or theme approach; and advances in technology affecting literacy curriculum and instruction.

To assist you as you construct a framework for teaching reading and writing, a number of features that readers and reviewers found most valuable have also been expanded.

- Each chapter begins with an **Anticipation Guide,** which invites you to take inventory of your current ideas and opinions about chapter topics. Review your answers to this guide after reading the chapter, and note how your ideas may have changed.
- **Using What You Know** is a brief introduction to each chapter that helps you relate your prior knowledge and the information presented in *previous* chapter(s) to the chapter you are about to read.
- Additional model teaching lessons have been provided. Set off by the heading **Lesson,** they now encompass nearly every area of literacy instruction.
- Discussion and practical strategies for helping elementary school students become independent learners have also been expanded. A number of reading and writing strategies that elementary school students can apply *on their own* are described in the text. Key strategies, such as analyzing unknown words or summarizing a paragraph, are outlined step by step and highlighted by the heading **Student Strategy.**
- Because students learn to read by reading, the number of listings of recommended children's books has been increased. Under the heading **Children's Book List,** titles are suggested for virtually every area in reading and writing. Emphasis has been placed on titles that will appeal to students from a wide variety of backgrounds.
- Additional practice and application activities have been added and identified as **Reinforcement Activities.** Activities that involve reading and writing for real purposes have been stressed.
- To help make the descriptions of teaching techniques come alive, examples of good teaching practices have been placed throughout the book in a feature entitled **Exemplary Teaching.** All are true-life accounts; many have been drawn from the memoirs of gifted teachers, while others were garnered from newspaper reports or the author's own observations.
- **Marginal annotations** throughout the text provide the reader with interesting, practical, handy advice and guidance. Because of the movement toward inclusive classrooms, suggestions for teaching students of varying abilities—including students with reading or learning disabilities—are presented in the body of the text and in marginal annotations with the heading **Adapting Instruction for . . . .** Also, **key terms** are highlighted in the text and appear, with their definitions, in the margin.
- Each chapter concludes with a brief summary and two types of activities: **Classroom Applications** are to be done on your own or with your classmates; **Field Applications** are designed for your use in an elementary school classroom.

Organization of the Text

The text has been organized in an attempt to reflect the order of the growth of literacy. Chapter 1 stresses constructing a philosophy of teaching reading and writing, and Chapters 2 and 3 discuss emergent literacy and early reading strategies, including phonics. Chapters 4 and 5 complement the discussion of phonics, presenting additional word-recognition skills and strategies and techniques for teaching vocabulary. Chapters 6 through 8 are devoted to comprehension: Chapter 6 emphasizes comprehension strategies that students might use; Chapter 7 focuses on text structures and teaching procedures; Chapter 8 covers application of comprehension skills in the content areas and through studying. Chapter 9 takes a step beyond comprehension by focusing on responding to literature and fostering a love of reading.

Chapters 2 through 9, which emphasize essential reading strategies, constitute the core of the book. Chapters 10 through 14 provide information on creating a well-rounded literacy program. Chapter 10 describes approaches to reading. Chapter 11 explains the process approach to writing and discusses how reading and writing are related. Chapter 12 suggests how previously presented strategies might be used with children from diverse cultures and those with special needs. Chapter 13 presents techniques for evaluating individuals and programs. Chapter 14 pulls all the topics together in a discussion of principles for organizing and implementing a literacy program. Also included in the final chapter is a section on technology and its place in a program of literacy instruction.

This text, designed to be *practical,* offers detailed explanations, and often examples of application, for every major technique or strategy. Numerous suggestions for practice activities and reading materials are also included. It is hoped that this book will furnish you with an in-depth knowledge of literacy methods and materials so that you will be able to construct lively, effective reading and writing instruction for all the students you teach.

Acknowledgments

I am indebted to Virginia Lanigan of Allyn and Bacon, who provided support, encouragement, and perceptive suggestions, and to Ann Greenberger, Development Editor, whose many valuable suggestions and patient guidance helped me reorganize, reshape, and expand material from the first edition of the text into its present form. I am also grateful to Nicole DePalma and Nihad M. Farooq, editorial assistants at Allyn and Bacon, for their timely and capable aid.

The following reviewers provided many perceptive comments and valuable suggestions. They challenged me to write the best book I could, and for this I am grateful. For the first edition:

Cynthia Gettys, University of Tennessee at Chattanooga

John Beach, University of Nevada, Reno

Barbara Lyman, Southwest Texas University

Audrey D'Aigneault, Pleasant Valley Elementary School

Joyce Feist-Willis, Youngstown State University

Jack Bagford, University of Iowa

H. Jon Jones, Oklahoma State University

For the second edition:

Steven Stahl, University of Georgia

Suzanne Barchers, University of Colorado at Denver

Lea McGee, Boston College

Judith Scheu, Kamehama Schools, Honolulu, Hawaii

Joanna Jones, Grand Canyon University

Janet W. Lerner, Northeastern Illinois University

Shela D. Snyder, Central Missouri State University

Jean A. McWilliams, Rosemont College

Donna Croll, Valdosta State University

Doris J. Walker-Dalhouse, Moorhead State University

My wife, Joan, offered both thoughtful comments and continuous encouragement. I deeply appreciate her loving assistance.

T. G.

The Nature of Reading and Today's Children

Before reading this chapter, complete the anticipation guide below. It will help to activate your prior knowledge so that you interact more fully with the chapter. It is designed to probe your attitudes and beliefs about important and sometimes controversial topics and issues. Often there are no right or wrong answers; the statements will alert you to your attitudes about reading instruction and encourage you to become aware of areas where you might require additional information. The anticipation guide will work best if you discuss responses with classmates before plunging into the text. At the end of the chapter, you might respond to the anticipation guide again to see if your answers have changed in light of what you have read.

For each of the following statements, put a check under "Agree" or "Disagree" to show how you feel. Discuss your responses with classmates before you read the chapter.

Agree		Disagree
✓	1. Before children learn to read, they should know the sounds of the letters in the alphabet.	
	2. Reading should not be fragmented into a series of subskills.	✓
	3. Oral reading should be accurate.	✓
	4. The best time to teach phonics is after children have learned to read.	✓
✓	5. Reading short passages and answering questions about them provide excellent practice.	
✓	6. Mistakes in oral reading should be ignored unless they change the sense of the passage.	
	7. The secret of becoming a good reader is to read, read, read.	✓
	8. The young reader's job is to put aside his or her own thoughts on the subject and get the author's message.	✓

Using What You Know

This chapter provides a general introduction to reading instruction in the elementary school. Before reading the chapter, examine your personal knowledge of the topic so that you will be better prepared to interact with the information. Sometimes you may not realize what you know until you stop and think about it. Think over what you know about the nature of reading. What do you think reading is? What do you do when you read? What do you think the reader's role is? Is it simply to receive the author's message, or should it include some personal input?

How would you go about teaching reading and writing to today's students? What do you think the basic principles of a literacy program should be? What elements have worked especially well in programs with which you are familiar?

THE NATURE OF READING

When I was an elementary school reading consultant in Hartford, Connecticut, teachers would often invite me into their classrooms to hear a student read. This was usually a child who had just cracked the alphabetic code or who was making encouraging progress after a long struggle with the rigors of learning to read. After the child proudly read a passage, we would briefly discuss it, just to make sure she or he had understood it.

These are some of teaching's magic moments. Despite having witnessed hundreds of children, including four of my own, make the passage from emergent reader to apprentice reader, the accomplishment never fails to fill me with a sense of awe and mystery. Bells should toll; trumpets should sound—the torch of **literacy** has been passed on! The best I could do at the time to mark the moment was to offer my heartiest congratulations.

One day, the fourth-grade teacher sent Maria to my office with a note explaining that the child was going to read for me from her basal reader. I was surprised. Maria had transferred to the school just three weeks earlier, her family having recently moved to Hartford from Puerto Rico. Since it was my responsibility to test all new students and recommend a program for each of them, I had interviewed Maria as best I could, given my limited Spanish. I had determined that Maria could read in her native tongue but not in English, and she was placed in an English-as-a-second-language (ESL) program.

I wondered how she could have learned to read English so quickly, and my sense of wonder grew as I listened to the child read aloud from a beginning reader. Although she read with an accent, as was to be expected, she was able to pronounce each word. Then I noticed something—Maria's intonation was off. Her sentences lacked the proper stress patterns, a sign that she may not have been comprehending what she read. When I asked her to tell me about the story she

> **Literacy** commonly refers to the ability to read and write on a functional level but may also encompass the abilities to do math; to engage in higher-level thinking, reading, and writing; and to take part in the visual arts.

had read, she was unable to do so. Nor could she tell me the meanings of the words. In fact, Maria had not really been able to read the book at all. Because she was just beginning to learn English, she was unable to derive any meaning from the words she pronounced. Superior phonics skills enabled her to sound out the words, but the words were meaningless to her. It was a dramatic reminder of the true nature of reading.

Above all else, reading is meaning. You cannot tell from listening to someone read orally whether that person can read. The ultimate test is whether the person can tell you what he or she has read or answer questions about the selection.

Many people have an intuitive, nearly unshakable belief that the essence of reading is pronouncing the sounds represented by printed symbols. There can be no reading without meaning. Although Maria was pronouncing words, she wasn't really reading.

IMPORTANCE OF LANGUAGE

Reading is very much a language activity, and, ultimately, our ability to read is limited by our language skills. Before a student like Maria can read a text in English with understanding, most of the words in the text must be part of the student's listening vocabulary. Progress in learning to read in English is governed by the child's speed in acquiring spoken English. Conversely, learning to read in English fosters overall development of English language skills. As it turned out, Maria learned to understand and speak English rapidly. Because she had excellent reading skills in Spanish, she was able to transfer these skills to English. Within two years, she was reading in English at grade level. Her comprehension of written English had caught up with her superior word-attack skills.

DEVELOPING LANGUAGE

Reading and writing have their roots in a child's earliest attempts to communicate and make meaning. Far from being merely passive recipients of care, babies are "born with a drive to make sense of their experience and with certain effective strategies for doing so" (Wells, 1986, pp. 33–34). Although they use crying to signal their most basic needs, babies also have a drive for social contact. Through cooing, smiling, and a variety of nonverbal gestures and movements, they elicit responses from their caregivers. Predisposed to see meaning and purpose in a baby's features and babblings, a caregiver responds as though the baby were actually talking. As Baron (1992) explained, humans are imbued with a conversational imperative. In the presence of another human, we feel compelled to talk:

> The conversational imperative does more than feed delusions of being understood. As we raise young children, the conversational imperative leads to a self-fulfilling prophecy: The very act of talking to infants as if they understand us is the single most important thing we do to help children become full-fledged participants in a language community. The main reason children succeed in learning language is that they are born into social groups in which language is the medium of exchange. Infant cooing and babbling increase when adults verbalize back. Toddlers imbibe the sounds, words, and phrases they hear around them. (p. 27)

Learning language, however, is not simply a matter of imitating adults. Although imitation is a factor, learning language is an interactive, constructive process. If children were mere imitators, they would only be able to repeat what they hear. But they construct sentences such as "Mommy goed work," which is something that an adult would not say. Creating a hypothesis about how language works, young children note that *-ed* is used to express past action and then overapply this generalization. With feedback and experience, they revise the hypothesis and ultimately learn that some action words have special past tense forms.

SOCIAL INTERACTION

Social interaction is an absolute requirement for language development. In order to learn language and progress from one stage to another, children must interact with others. Both the quantity and quality of the interaction are important. In a longitudinal study of children in Bristol, England, Wells (1986) found that children exposed to the most language heard ten times as many words as those exposed to the least amount. As might be expected, those exposed to more language were generally at a higher level of development.

However, the quality of the interaction is more important than the quantity. Children did best in one-to-one situations in which an adult discussed matters that were of interest and concern to the child or the two talked over a shared activity. It is also essential that the adult adjust his or her language so as to take into consideration and compensate for the child's limited linguistic ability, something which parents seem to do intuitively.

In his extensive study, Wells (1986) found that some parents intuitively provided maximum development for their children's language. Far from being directors of what their child said, these parents were collaborative constructors of meaning. Careful listeners, they made genuine attempts to use both nonverbal and verbal clues so as to understand what their child was saying. Through careful listening and being actively involved in the conversation, parents were able to help the child extend his or her responses so that both knowledge of the world and linguistic abilities were fostered. In this book, high-quality social interactions of the type conducted by the best parents are emphasized.

ROLE OF COGNITIVE DEVELOPMENT

Many of the practices advocated in this text are based on the work of Jean Piaget and L. S. Vygotsky. Piaget, a Swiss psychologist, stressed stages of cognitive development and the unique nature of children's thinking. Vygotsky, a Russian psychologist, stressed the social nature of language and learning and the important role that adults play in both.

JEAN PIAGET

Piaget discovered that children's thinking is qualitatively different from the way adults think and that it evolves through a series of hierarchical stages. Noting that children in the same age range seem to engage in similar cognitive behaviors, even making the same kinds of misjudgments, Piaget concluded that children pass through four periods of cognitive development: sensorimotor, preoperational, concrete operations, and formal operations.

Sensorimotor Stage.   The **sensorimotor stage** lasts for approximately two years. During this time, children's thinking is limited by what they can sense or physically explore. Children in this stage learn primarily through sensory stimulation.

Subsequent research suggests that the average child may pass through some of these stages at an earlier age than Piaget indicated. Depending upon environment and rate of development, children enter the stages at different ages. However, the order of the stages remains the same, regardless of the child's rate of development.

The **sensorimotor stage** is the period from birth to 2 years when a child's cognitive development is primarily a product of sensory and motor activities.

They explore their world and form rudimentary concepts by touching, looking, hearing, smelling, and tasting. Children also learn object permanence—that objects and people still exist even if they cannot be seen. For children up to about 6 months of age, objects cease to exist if they cannot be seen; "Out of sight, out of mind" is literally true. As children grasp the concept of object permanence, peek-a-boo becomes a favorite game.

Preoperational Stage.   In the **preoperational stage**, which lasts from about the age of 2 to 7, children's thinking is not limited by sensory stimulation or motor activities. Capable of representational thought, children at this stage can make a word, drawing, or object represent something not physically present. However, they are captives of their visual perceptual processes. They are unable to **conserve**—to reverse an operation mentally, to imagine what things were like before it occurred. For instance, if liquid is poured from a short round container into a tall container, children in the preoperational stage believe that the tall container holds more. Children are unable to reverse the operation and realize that the short, round container once held just as much as the tall one now holds.

The **preoperational stage** is a period of cognitive growth, occurring between 2 and 7 years of age, in which the child learns to use symbols to represent reality. Symbols used can be words, drawings, or one object representing another object.

Conserve means to realize that an attribute retains its basic property under changing perceptual conditions, e.g., the quantity of a liquid is the same whether it's put in a large, round container or a tall, thin one.

Children in this stage are also **egocentric.** They tend to believe that everyone else sees the world the way they do. In writing or telling a story, they might leave out identifying details because they assume that if they know these details, the listener or reader must also know them.

In this stage, children focus on the central or dominant aspect of a situation. For example, Susan understands who her father is but may have difficulty understanding that her father is her grandmother's son and her uncle's brother. She centers on the father aspect, which is dominant, but is unable to **decenter,** or let go of that dominant idea, and also see her father as someone's son or someone's brother. Children who lack the ability to decenter may have difficulty realizing that words are made up of sounds. They might center on the word *cat* as symbolizing the creature that goes "meow" but are then unable to decenter in order to focus on the concept that *cat* is a word composed of sounds. If children are unable to decenter, they may have difficulty with formal reading instruction. Ironically, formal reading instruction is initiated for many children while they are moving from preoperational to concrete thinking. As Douglas (1989) noted,

Egocentric means to be unable to take on another's point of view because one only sees the world from one's own perspective.

Decenter means to note two or more aspects of a situation or object.

> This means that the learning to read process is being instituted at a time when the child does not reason well logically in the sense concrete operational thinking allows. Thus we must consider in planning for teaching . . . whether the tasks we place before the child are ones that are understandable, or whether they require thought patterns and processes that make little sense to the child, reasonable as they may seem to adults. . . . (p. 78)

This does not mean that we should wait for a child to reach a more cognitively advanced level—true learning is active and constructive. It does mean that we need to observe the child carefully and present activities and materials that fit in with his or her way of understanding the world.

Concrete Operations Stage.   Spanning the age range from about 7 to 11, the **concrete operations stage** is marked by children's ability to decenter, to focus on several aspects of a situation, and to think logically. They are better able to organize

The **concrete operations stage** is the period of cognitive development that spans the approximate age range from 7 to 11 and in which the child is able to focus on more than one aspect of a situation and think logically, using an underlying system to group concrete stimuli.

information and identify causes and effects. They can classify objects by color, shape, size, or other characteristics.

Formal Operations Stage. Beginning at about age 12, the **formal operations stage** is marked by the ability to think abstractly, to reason hypothetically, and to use formal systems of organization and logic. Students would understand and be able to use the scientific system for classifying plants and animals, for instance.

L. S. VYGOTSKY

In L. S. Vygotsky's (1962) view, cognitive development begins on the social level and then is internalized. For instance, a concept or process is demonstrated or explained to a child by an adult. Through interaction with the adult, the child tries out the process or discusses the concept and eventually internalizes it. For young children, the process might be stacking cups or assembling puzzles. For school-age children, the process might be working math problems or learning to use strategies to comprehend a passage. For instance, if a student is having difficulty deriving a main idea from a story being read, the teacher might supply prompts, such as "What is the author trying to say here?" or "What are all the sentences in this paragraph talking about?"

Actual and Potential Development. In a theory that has become a keystone for instruction, Vygotsky distinguished between actual and potential development. Actual development is a measure of the level at which a child is developing. In a sense, it is a measure of what the child has learned up to that point. Potential development is a measure of what the child might be capable of achieving. The difference between the two is known as the **zone of proximal development.** As explained by Vygotsky (1978), the zone of proximal development is "the distance between the actual developmental level as determined by independent problem solving and the level of potential development as determined through problem solving under adult guidance or in collaboration with more capable peers" (p. 84). In other words, the zone of proximal development is the difference between what a child can do on his or her own and what the child can do with help.

Focusing on the importance of interaction with adults or knowledgeable peers, Vygotsky's theory is that children learn through expert guidance. In time, they internalize the concepts and strategies employed by their mentors and so, ultimately, are able to perform on a higher level. The support, guidance, and instruction provided by an adult is known as **scaffolding** (Bruner, 1975, 1986).

Ideally, instruction should be pitched somewhat above a child's current level of functioning. Instruction and collaboration with an adult or more capable peers will enable the child to reach the higher level and ultimately function on that level. Instruction and interaction are key elements. The overall theories of evaluation and instruction presented in this book are grounded in the concepts of actual and potential development and the zone of proximal development.

IMPORTANCE OF EXPERIENCE

Although based on language, reading is also experiential. One second-grade class was reading a story that took place in a laundromat. None of the children had

The **formal operations stage** is a period of cognitive growth, occurring between 11 and 15 years of age, in which the child develops the ability to reason abstractly.

The **zone of proximal development** is the difference between what a child can do on his or her own and what the child can do under the guidance of an adult or more capable peer.

Scaffolding refers to the support and guidance an adult or knowledgeable peer provides to help a student function on a higher level.

Adults clarify and extend children's ideas and provide additional information and advanced vocabulary, lifting children's thinking to higher levels (Raines & Isbell, 1994).

Collaboration with more knowledgeable peers enables students to function on a higher level.

ever been to a laundromat or even heard of one, so they found the story confusing. Reading is not so much getting meaning from a story as it is bringing meaning to it. The more the reader brings to a story, the more she or he will be able to take away. For example, the child who plays on a Little League team will get much more out of one of John Tunnis's reissued tales or one of Matt Christopher's works from having actually been there. Such a child can empathize with the main character who makes a crucial error. In this instance, reading evokes an emotional response as well as an intellectual one.

IMPORTANCE OF THE STUDENTS' CULTURE

All children come to school with some experience in reading and writing; however, the nature of the experience varies from child to child and from community to community.

STUDY OF RURAL AND SMALL TOWN LITERACY

For nine years, teacher-turned-anthropologist Shirley Brice Heath (1983) intensively studied the language environments of three communities in the Piedmont Carolinas: two working-class communities known as Tracton and Roadville, and a middle-class group called the Townspeople. In Tracton, reading was a community event. Letters and articles from the newspaper were read aloud to family and friends. Those who gathered commented on the written piece and together "negotiated" its meaning, which resided not in the printed words but in the experience of the group. Solitary readers were thought to be peculiar, "losers" who read rather than participating actively in life. For Roadville and the Townspeople, reading was seen more as an individual activity. Children were led to construct their own interpretations of selections that were read to them. The Townspeople read for pleasure and also because their jobs demanded it. Their children observed them completing paperwork brought home from the office, and reading novels and magazines for recreation.

However, reading and writing did not play much of a role in the recreational and vocational lives of the parents of Roadville and Tracton. Magazines piled up unread until they were tossed out. Neither group had jobs that required any significant amount of reading or writing. A gap also existed between the literacy experiences and expectations of the children of Roadville and Tracton and those of their school. Tracton students were used to seeing reading and writing performed for real purposes. Workbook and other artificial activities were new to them. Although the Roadville students had experience completing school-type literacy activities at home, they had less experience with abstract, academic, and vocational uses of language and so experienced difficulties as they progressed to higher grades.

STUDY OF URBAN LITERACY

A group of impoverished urban families studied by Taylor and Dorsey-Gaines (1988) also revealed some unique patterns in the uses of reading and writing, as well as a mismatch between children's experiences with literacy and the way it was being taught in the schools. Reading and writing were important survival tools for the families, and they engaged in a full range of literacy activities, from filling out forms to reading and writing poetry. Unfortunately, a gap existed between the academic literacy activities of the school and the personalized, often shared literacy activities of the home. Ironically, although the home incorporated school literacy activities—homework was discussed, school books were read—the school did not incorporate the literacy activities of the home.

Exemplary Teaching

Building a Bridge from Home to School

In her study of a working-class community in southeastern United States, Heath (1983) observed a first-grade teacher who used her understanding of the community to bridge the gap between the informal literacy activities her students had experienced and the demands of the school's more formal program. Wisely, the teacher defined literacy in terms of the reading and writing that her students had experienced in their homes and in their community. Students could start making connections among the signs, labels, bills, and other functional materials with which they were familiar and the books they would soon be encountering. Here is what the teacher told her students:

Reading and writing are things you do all the time—at home, on the bus, riding your bike, at the barbershop. You can read, and you do every day before you ever come to school. You can also play baseball and football at home, at the park, wherever you want to, but when you come to school or go to a summer program at the Neighborhood Center, you get help on techniques, the gloves to buy, the way to throw, and the way to slide. School does that for reading and writing. We all read and write a lot of the time, lots of places. School isn't much different except that here we work on techniques, and we practice a lot—under a coach. I'm the coach. (p. 23)

McLane and McNamee (1990) commented:

> Not all people read and write with equal ease and fluency or use writing and reading in the same ways or for the same purposes. In the long run, it may be useful to think of "multiple literacies." The notion of multiple literacies recognizes that there are many ways of being—and of becoming—literate, and that how literacy develops and how it is used depend on the particular social and cultural setting. Literacy is a social and cultural achievement, as well as a cognitive one. . . . Learning to read and write is a difficult and lengthy undertaking, and children and adults often work hard at mastering it. Their uses for doing so are tied to their uses for writing and reading, and to the meaning of these activities in their everyday lives. (p. 3)

Living as we do in a multicultural, pluralistic society, it is important for us to explore and understand the literacy histories of our pupils. We have to ask such questions as these: In students' culture(s), how are reading and writing used? What values are placed on them? What are the ways in which the students have observed and participated in reading and writing? Is literacy in their environment primarily a group or an individual activity? Given this information, the school should build on the children's experiences and develop and reinforce the skills and values important to their culture(s) as well as those important to the school.

Teaching children how to read and write is not enough. We must help them explore the why of what they read and write. We must encourage children to read for a wide variety of purposes: to be entertained, to be inspired, to be informed, and to learn. We must help them see some of the many purposes of writing: to keep in touch with others, to inform, to conduct everyday business, and to express themselves.

How is literacy used in the culture in which you were raised? Read one of the books on the uses of literacy. *Growing Up Literate, Learning from Inner-City Families* (Taylor & Dorsey-Gaines, 1988) is especially valuable if you have limited experience with inner-city families and plan to teach in the inner city.

THE READER'S ROLE IN THE READING PROCESS

What is the reader's role in the reading process? In the past, it was defined as being passive, getting the author's meaning. "The good reader was the reader who could recognize or apprehend the author's intent in a text" (Straw & Sadowy, 1990, p. 23). Today, reading requires a more active role—the reader must construct meaning from text. The model of transmission of information in which the reader was merely a recipient has given way to **transactional theory**, a two-way process involving a reader and a text:

> Every reading act is an event, or a transaction, involving a particular reader and a particular pattern of signs, a text, and occurring at a particular time in a particular context. Instead of two fixed entities acting on one another, the reader and the text are two aspects of a total dynamic situation. The "meaning" does not reside ready-made "in" the text or "in" the reader but happens or comes into being during the transaction between reader and text. (Rosenblatt, 1994, p. 1063)

In her study of how students read a poem, Rosenblatt (1978) noted that each reader was active:

> He was not a blank tape registering a ready-made message. He was actively involved in building up a poem for himself out of his responses to text. He had to draw on his past experiences with the verbal symbols. . . . The reader was not

Transactional theory is the view of reading as a two-way process between the reader and the text in which each is conditioned by the other.

Stance refers to the position or attitude that the reader takes. The two stances are aesthetic and efferent.

An **efferent stance** refers to the kind of reading in which the focus is on obtaining or carrying away information from the text.

An **aesthetic stance** refers to the type of reading in which the focus is on experiencing the piece—"the rhythm of the words, the past experiences these call up" (Rosenblatt, 1978).

What has been your role as a reader? Were you encouraged to construct meaning? Were you free to create personal interpretations of poems and stories?

only paying attention to what the words pointed to in the external world, to their referents; he was also paying attention to the images, feelings, attitudes, associations, and ideas that the words and their referents evoked in him. (p. 10)

The type of reading being done, of course, has an effect on the transaction. The reader can take an efferent or an aesthetic **stance.** When reading a set of directions, a science text, or a math problem, the reader takes an **efferent stance** with the focus on obtaining information that can be carried away (*efferent* is taken from the Latin verb *efferre,* "to carry away"). In the **aesthetic stance,** the reader pays attention to the associations, feelings, attitudes, and ideas that the words evoke.

Does it make any difference whether reading is viewed as being transmissional, transactional, or somewhere in between? Absolutely. If reading is viewed as transmissional, students are expected to stick close to the author's message. If reading is viewed as transactional, students are expected to put their personal selves into their reading, especially when encountering literature. From a transactional perspective, building background becomes especially important because it enriches the transaction between reader and text. Personal response and interpretation are at the center of the reading process. The reader's role is enhanced when a transactional view prevails.

 ## APPROACHES TO READING INSTRUCTION: WHOLE VERSUS PART LEARNING

The **holistic approach** to learning advocates the completion of whole tasks rather than fragmented subskills and fragments of reading and writing.

Just as there are philosophical differences about the role of the reader, there are differences in approaches to teaching reading. On one end of the continuum are those who espouse a subskills, or bottom-up, approach, and on the other end are those who advocate a **holistic approach,** that is, a top-down, whole language approach. In between are the interactionists. Where do you fit on the continuum? Go back to the anticipation guide at the beginning of the chapter. Take a look at how you answered the first six statements. If you agreed with only the odd-numbered ones, you are a bottom-up advocate. If you agreed with only the even-numbered statements, you are a top-downer. If your answers were mixed, you are probably an interactionist.

BOTTOM-UPPERS

A **bottom-up approach** relies on a kind of processing in which meaning is derived from the accurate, sequential processing of words. The emphasis is on the text rather than the reader's background of knowledge or language ability.

In the **bottom-up approach,** children literally start at the bottom and work their way up. First, they learn the names and shapes of the letters of the alphabet. Next, they learn consonant sounds, followed by simple and then more complex vowel correspondences. The most eloquent spokespersons for this method are Carnine, Silbert, and Kameenui (1990): "Our position is that many students will not become successful readers unless teachers identify the essential reading skills, find out what skills students lack, and teach those skills directly" (p. 3).

Bottom-up procedures are intended to make learning to read easier by breaking complex tasks into their component skills. Instruction proceeds from the simple to the complex. In essence, there are probably no 100-percent bottom-uppers among reading teachers. Even those who strongly favor phonics recognize the importance of higher-level strategies.

TOP-DOWNERS

A **top-down approach,** as its name indicates, starts at the top and works downward. A student learning to read might first memorize a whole story and later learn to deal with the individual words in the story (McCracken, 1989). Phonics might not be taught until after the student has begun to learn to read (F. Smith, 1988). Learning to read is seen as being similar to learning to speak; it is holistic and natural through immersion. Subskills are not taught because it is felt they fragment the process and make learning to read more abstract and difficult (K. Goodman, 1986).

WHOLE LANGUAGE

One of the most influential models of reading is that proposed by Ken Goodman (1994), the father of **whole language.** Goodman defines reading as "a process of meaning making . . . a psycholinguistic guessing game. . . . Readers use the least amount of available text information necessary in relation to existing linguistic and conceptual schemata to get to meaning" (p. 1114).

In constructing meaning, readers use their background knowledge and knowledge of language to predict and infer the content of print. Readers "use their selection strategies to choose only the most useful information from all that is available" (Goodman, 1994, p. 1125). When reading the sentence "The moon is full tonight," the reader can use his or her knowledge of the moon, context clues, and perhaps the initial consonants *f* and *t* to reconstruct *full* and *tonight*. It is not necessary for the reader to process all the letters of *full* and *tonight*. However, in order to make use of background knowledge, context clues, and initial consonant cues, the reader must consider the whole text. If the words *full* and *tonight* were read in isolation, the reader would have to depend more heavily on processing all or most of the letters of each word. As Goodman notes, "Perception does indeed depend on selecting highly significant and distinctive features and inferring the wholes they relate to. . . . It is only in the context of the whole that the features are significant or distinctive" (p. 1125). Given his conception of the reading process, it is easy to see why Goodman stresses the reading of whole texts, which is the cornerstone of whole language.

INTERACTIONISTS

Most practitioners tend to be more pragmatic than either strict top-downers or dyed-in-the-wool bottom-uppers and borrow practices from both ends of the continuum. These **interactionists** teach skills directly—especially in the beginning—but they avoid overdoing it, as they do not want to fragment the process. They also provide plenty of opportunities for students to experience the holistic nature of reading and writing by having them read whole books and write for

A **top-down approach** focuses on deriving meaning by using the reader's background knowledge, language ability, and expectations. The emphasis is on the reader rather than the text.

Whole language is an approach to teaching that advocates holistic teaching strategies, the reading of whole texts (rather than excerpts or workbook exercises), and writing for real purposes. Integration of reading, writing, listening, and speaking with all subject matter areas is also stressed.

In Goodman's model, students use three cueing systems to process text: semantic, syntactic, and graphophonic. Semantic, or meaning, cues derive from one's past experiences and knowledge of the world; syntactic cues derive from one's knowledge of how the structure of language works; graphophonic cues refer to the ability to sound out words or recognize them holistically. All three cue systems interact during reading.

Interactionists hold the theoretical position that reading involves processing text and using the reader's background knowledge and language ability.

Bottom-up theorists claim that readers process nearly every word and virtually every letter in the words. Samuels (1994) concludes that novice readers process words letter by letter but experienced readers may process words holistically or break a word down into its components. Samuels also notes that context fosters both speed and accuracy of word recognition.

real purposes. As Gough (1985), a leading advocate of a phonics or deciphering approach, described the reading process,

> Linguistics knowledge is skillfully combined with visual information to reconstruct the meaning intended by the author. But skilled readers, when seriously reading, not only succeed in extracting meaning from the printed page, they can (and I believe do) also succeed in accurately recognizing virtually every single word on that page . . . for while highly predictive context can and does facilitate word recognition, proving a strictly "bottom-up" model wrong, most words are not predictable and so can only be read bottom-up. (p. 688)

Whereas Gough agreed with Goodman that higher-level processes should be used when reading, Gough also believed that readers process virtually every letter of nearly every word. This is much different from Goodman's idea that the reader uses mostly context and as little letter information or phonics as possible. In a sense, Goodman and Gough have articulated the great debate in reading instruction for the 1990s: Do readers decode by prediction or by processing nearly every letter of almost every word, or do they do both?

The answer to this question has important practical implications. If you believe in a predictive theory, you will encourage students to predict upcoming words. If you believe that students process nearly every letter, you will emphasize phonics and related decoding skills. And if you believe that reading is a combination of predicting and letter-by-letter processing, you will teach students to use both context and phonics.

This book takes the position that all sources of information—semantic, syntactic, background knowledge, and letter-sound relationships—are essential when processing text and emphasizes the use of both context and phonics.

IMPORTANCE OF LITERACY MODELS

Why is it important to be aware of different models of teaching reading? For one thing, it is important that you formulate your own personal beliefs about reading and writing instruction. These beliefs will then be the foundation for your instruction. They will determine the goals you set, the instructional techniques you use, the materials you choose, the organization of your classroom, the reading and writing behaviors you expect students to exhibit, and the criteria you use to evaluate students. For instance, whether you use children's books or a basal, how you teach phonics, and whether you expect flawless oral reading or are satisfied if the student's rendition is faithful to the sense of the selection will depend upon your theoretical orientation (Deford, 1985).

Having a theoretical orientation helps in another way. It provides a means of examining what you do in your teaching. You may find that you are not walking your talk—your practices might not fit in with your beliefs. According to Ross (cited in Deford, 1985), the ability to implement your beliefs is dependent upon the clarity of those beliefs and your ability to see a connection between them and what you do in your classroom.

APPROACH TAKEN BY THIS TEXT

This book draws heavily from research in cognitive psychology, combining an interactionist point of view with a whole language orientation. Reading is considered an active, constructive process, with the focus on the reader, whose experiences, cultural background, and point of view will determine her or his comprehension of a written piece. The emphasis is on cognitive processes or strategies used to decode words and understand and remember text: using context to decipher unknown words, activating one's knowledge of a topic, predicting meaning, summarizing, and visualizing. Stress is also placed on teaching strategies in context and holistically applying them to children's books, periodicals, ads and other real-world materials, and content area textbooks. There is also an emphasis on integrating reading, writing, listening, and speaking with content areas and the performing and visual arts.

STAGES OF READING DEVELOPMENT

Reading is a continuously developing ability which emerges from a child's experience with oral language and print. Proficiency grows and expands as the child progresses through the grades. New experiences, vocabulary, and constant interaction with print enhance reading ability throughout the child's lifetime.

Reading emerges gradually and develops continuously, so it is somewhat artificial to segment the process into stages. This is done, however, to provide greater understanding of the reading process. By having a sense of what readers have accomplished, what stage they are in now, and what stage they are headed for, you should be better able to understand and plan for their needs. Describing literacy in terms of stages should also provide you with a sense of the scope of reading instruction in the elementary grades.

The stages described below are based on the work of Ames, Gillespie, Haines, and Ilg (1979); Ames, Ilg, and Baker (1988); Chall (1983b); Cook (1986); Erikson (1963); Huck, Helper, and Hickman (1993); Piaget (Flavell, 1963); Purves and Monson (1984); and Sulzby and Teale (1991). They are designed to characterize the average child. Slower-to-learn children of the same age may be at an earlier stage, brighter children of the same age might be at a more advanced stage, and, of course, much variability will be seen even among children who are average.

Reading and writing development is a continuous process. For the sake of better understanding how children grow in reading and writing, the process has been artificially divided into stages, which are not as discrete as they might seem. A child may move back and forth from stage to stage, and development, although predictable, is not steady. Children may reach a plateau, stay there for an extended period of time, and then suddenly leap ahead.

STAGE 1. EMERGENT LITERACY (BIRTH TO 5 YEARS)

In the *emergent literacy* stage, children move from learning primarily through direct sensory contact and physical manipulation to using an intuitive kind of logic to form concrete concepts. They draw conclusions based on perceptions and experience difficulty putting them into words. Language growth is rapid. Toward the end of this stage, children may be able to read signs and labels and may explore writing in the form of scribbles, letterlike forms, or invented spelling. One or two children out of a hundred will learn to read before starting kindergarten; however, all will have some experience with reading and writing.

Children at this stage are egocentric and so cannot appreciate another's point of view. They love being read to and cannot hear their favorite tales often enough. They have a poorly developed concept of causation and so enjoy stories that involve magic and personification. They also like the elements of rhyme, repetition, and alliteration.

STAGE 2. BEGINNING READING (GRADES K–1)

In the stage of *beginning reading*, children are able to manipulate objects and ideas mentally and can reason logically in a concrete way. However, they have difficulty comprehending underlying principles, especially abstract ones.

A key characteristic of this stage is an evolving grasp of the alphabetic principle. Students begin using their knowledge of letter-sound relationships and context to decode printed words. Children taught through a bottom-up approach will rely heavily—perhaps, too heavily—on phonics but will later integrate phonics and context clues. Children who are taught through a top-down approach tend to overrely on context. Later, they, too, will integrate phonics and context cues. Children should be given lots of easy books at this stage so that they have ample opportunity to practice their developing skills. The easiest reading material consists of brief, heavily illustrated selections: Sentences are short and uncomplicated; vocabulary consists of easy words that have a high frequency of appearance in print. Here is an excerpt from *Henry and Mudge,*

The **alphabetic principle** is the idea that letters represent sounds, and thus words may be read by saying the sounds represented by the letters and words may be spelled by writing the letters that represent the sounds.

Novice readers should be given lots of easy books so that they have ample opportunity to practice their developing skills.

the First Book (Rylant, 1987), which is typical of the material read at this stage:

> Henry searched for a dog.
> "Not just any dog," said Henry.
> "Not a short one," he said.
> "Not a curly one," he said.
> "And no pointed ears." (p. 9)

STAGE 3. GROWING INDEPENDENCE (GRADES 2–3)

The main characteristic of the stage of *growing independence* is children's evolving fluency. As the process of decoding becomes automatic, they are able to concentrate on meaning. For many, this stage is also marked by extensive reading of both fiction and nonfiction. Reading becomes one of their preferred activities. They especially like humorous tales. Students may begin to read easy chapter books and show an increased interest in informational books. They still enjoy fantasy but may also appreciate biography; as they become less egocentric, they are able to become more appreciative of stories involving the lives of others. They judge their reading affectively and personally rather than by using standards; however, they may have difficulty explaining why they like a selection.

As students pass through the primary grades, their reading selections grow longer and more complex. Sentences are lengthier and more complicated, and a wider range of words is used. By the end of the third grade, children are encountering many thousands of different words in their reading, most of which average third-graders know if they hear them spoken out loud. A major task is to sound out, or "decode," words that are in students' listening vocabularies but that they may be seeing on a page for the first time. A text frequently read in grade 2 is *Katy No Pocket* (Payne, 1944):

> Big tears rolled down Katy Kangaroo's brown face. Poor Katy was crying because she didn't have a pocket like other mother kangaroos. Freddy was Katy Kangaroo's little boy and he needed a pocket to ride in.

A text typical of the type that an average third-grader might read is *Miss Rumphius* (Cooney, 1983):

> All that summer Miss Rumphius, her pockets full of seeds, wandered over fields and headlands, sowing lupines. She scattered seeds along the highways and down the country lanes. She flung handfuls of them around the schoolhouse and back of the church. She tossed them into hollows and along stone walls.

STAGE 4. READING TO LEARN (GRADES 4–6)

The stage of *reading to learn* is marked by the wide application of word-attack and comprehension skills. This is not to suggest that students have not been reading for meaning or have not been learning from their reading. From about grade 4 on, however, much greater emphasis is placed on grasping informational text;

Many children do well in reading until they hit this stage. Carried along by strong decoding skills and the relative ease of reading mostly narrative material, they experience difficulty when faced with concept-laden expository text. Early experience with a variety of informational materials and instruction in strategies that promote comprehension of expository text should ease the transition.

From your reading, observations, and past courses in psychology or child development, what do you know about child development in general and Piaget, Vygotsky, and Erikson in particular? How would you relate this information to the stages of development in reading?

vocabulary and conceptual load increase significantly. Students are required to comprehend numerous concepts, many of them quite abstract, in science and social studies. Reading material is longer and more complex. Students must not only comprehend the material but also be able to carry out complicated sets of directions or form mental maps of concepts.

How-to, hobby, mystery, and sports books become popular, as do series books. Students are able to put themselves in the places of characters and verbalize their judgment about selections, including evaluations of stylistic devices and personal reactions. Increasingly, the interests of boys and girls diverge. Intense absorption in a single topic—sports, horses, or cars, for instance—also manifests itself. Preceding the turmoil of adolescence, this is a stage of industry (Erikson, 1963) in which students have the most energy to devote to their school work. For many, it is a time of peak involvement in reading.

From grades 4 through 6 and beyond, reading material becomes more complex and sophisticated. Informational material is increasingly prevalent as such texts are a prominent part of science and social studies instruction. A major task at this stage is to cope with a burgeoning vocabulary. Students are now faced with large numbers of words that are not part of their listening vocabularies.

A popular novel in fourth grade is *Charlotte's Web* (White, 1952):

Fern came almost every day to visit him. She found an old milking stool that had been discarded, and she placed the stool in the sheepfold next to Wilbur's pen. Here she sat quietly during the long afternoons, thinking and listening and watching Wilbur. (pp. 14–15)

A sample passage from a fourth-grade social studies text reads as follows:

Another new industry, meat packing, developed in Chicago at the same time as the flour-milling industry grew in Minnesota. Located at the southern tip of Lake Michigan, Chicago had become the transportation center of the country. (Armento, Nash, Salter, & Wixson, 1991d, p. 180)

Typical fare for fifth-graders would include the following two excerpts:

In his twelve years Aaron had seen all kinds of weather, but he had never experienced a snowstorm like this one. In a short time their path was completely covered. The wind became as cold as ice. The road to town was narrow and winding. Aaron no longer knew where he was. He could not see through the snow. The cold soon penetrated his quilted jacket. (Singer, 1966, p. 81)

The Boston Tea Party enraged the British. To punish Boston, Parliament passed what colonists called the "Intolerable Acts." These acts ended town meetings. They took away some of the power of the Massachusetts assembly. (Armento, Nash, Salter, & Wixson, 1991a, p. 252)

Excerpts from texts typically read in sixth grade include the following:

I had been in what is called a maze, a device to test the intelligence and memory. I was put in it many times again, and so were the others. The second time I got through it a little faster, because I remembered—to some extent—which corridors had electric floors and which did not. (O'Brien, 1971, p. 114)

Diocletian began by making a number of decisions. First he reorganized the government. He appointed a co-emperor and two junior emperors. Each of these men ruled a portion of the empire. In this way a local problem could be quickly brought to the attention of one of the rulers. This same system would help ensure a peaceful transfer of power at the end of an emperor's reign. (Armento, Nash, Salter, & Wixson, 1991c, p. 483)

STAGE 5. ABSTRACT READING (GRADES 7 AND UP)

Between 11 and 14 years of age, students enter the stage of formal operations, in which they think abstractly. Rather than simply learning systems of information by rote—classification of animals or grammar, for example—they are able to understand the systems as systems; that is, they can grasp the underlying organizational principles. They can construct multiple hypotheses, consider several viewpoints, and mull over logical alternatives. Evaluations of readings become more elaborate and reflect an evolving set of standards for judging. At this point, much of their school learning is conveyed by texts that are longer, more complex, and more abstract. Reading interests are even more varied and individualized. Caught up in adolescence and the need to be involved actively with peers, students typically do the least amount of reading at this stage. Even television takes a substantial dip for most adolescents.

Approximately one elementary or middle-school student out of three will not reach this stage (Chall, 1983b). In fact, some children grow into adults without ever attaining this level of reading development.

A READING AND WRITING PROGRAM FOR TODAY'S STUDENTS

What kind of program will help meet the literacy needs of today's students? That is a question that the remainder of this book will attempt to answer. However, when all is said and done, the seven principles discussed below, if followed faithfully, should make a difference in determining such a program.

1. *Children learn to read by reading.* Learning to read is a little like learning to drive a car—instruction and guidance are required. In addition to instruction and guidance, novice readers, like novice motorists, require practice. They must read a variety of fiction and nonfiction books, newspapers, and magazines to become truly skilled. In a way, each book or article makes a child a better reader. As Hirsch (1987) pointed out, children must have a broad background in a variety of areas in order to be able to understand much of what is being written and said in today's world. For example, a child who has read the fable *The Boy Who Cried Wolf* will have the background necessary to understand a story that includes the sentence "Frank cried wolf once too often." Reading is not simply a matter of acquiring and perfecting skills, it also requires accumulating vocabulary, concepts, experiences, and background knowledge.

To provide the necessary practice and background, children's books are an essential component of a reading program. According to results of the 1992

National Assessment of Educational Progress, students taught through a literature-based approach reached a higher level of proficiency than those taught in traditional programs (Mullis, Campbell, & Farstrup, 1993).

Unfortunately, large numbers of students are aliterate: They can read, but they do not, at least not on a regular basis. According to a questionnaire administered to a representative sample of third-graders who participated in the 1986 National Assessment (Applebee, Langer, & Mullis, 1988), nearly 14 percent indicated that they never read for fun on their own time. Fewer than one-half reported reading for pleasure on a daily basis, and only three-quarters engaged in recreational reading weekly. A study of 155 fifth-graders yielded equally discouraging results (Anderson, Wilson, & Fielding, 1988). Although above average in achievement, the typical child in the group spent fewer than five minutes per day reading on his or her own. In a more recent study, only 44 percent of a large sample of fourth-graders reported reading on a daily basis; however, 60 percent of these same children watched three or more hours of television each day (Mullis, Campbell, & Farstrup, 1993).

It is not surprising that those who do the most reading on their own are the most proficient readers (Anderson, Wilson, & Fielding, 1988; Applebee, Langer, & Mullis, 1988; Mullis, Campbell, & Farstrup, 1993). While it is true that better readers read more partly because reading is easier for them, Anderson, Wilson, and Fielding's (1988) analysis of data suggests a cause-effect relationship. Students are better readers because they read more.

The case for using children's books to teach reading is a compelling one. First, as just noted, those who read more, read better. Second, research suggests that students who read widely and are given some choice in what they read have a more favorable attitude toward reading (Cline & Kretke, 1980). In addition, all types of students—able readers, at-risk children, bilingual students—benefit from an approach that incorporates children's books. Based on their review of research, Tunnell and Jacobs (1989) concluded that programs using children's books achieve stunning levels of success and are particularly effective with disabled and uninterested readers.

Using children's books in the reading program not only leads to an opportunity for a greater enjoyment of reading, but also builds skill in reading. In addition, allowing some self-selection should produce students who can and do read. To assist you in choosing or recommending books for your students, lists of appropriate books are presented throughout the text.

2. *Reading should be easy—but not too easy.* Think about it this way: If children find reading difficult, they will acquire a distaste for it and will simply stop reading except when they have to. Because of inadequate practice, they will fall further behind, and their distaste and avoidance will grow. Also, if the text is too difficult, they will be less likely to take part in the lessons. In an extensive study in which children were videotaped during their reading lessons, the researchers noted that inattention increased as the books grew harder. When the text was difficult, students paid attention only 20 percent of the time. When an easier text was provided, their attention more than doubled to 50 percent of the time. When students with poor ability were given material that was one level below their grade, they performed as well as average students (R. Anderson, 1990).

Giving the child the right level of text is critical. If texts are too difficult, children will be unable to apply the strategies they have been taught, and learning will be hampered (Clay, 1993a). As Fry (1977a) put it years ago, make the match. Give students a book that they can handle with ease. Research by Berliner (1981) and Gambrell, Wilson, and Gantt (1981) suggested that students do best with reading materials in which no more than 2 to 5 percent of the words are difficult for them.

3. *Instruction should be functional and contextual.* Do not teach skills or strategies in isolation—teach a word-attack skill because students must have it to decipher words. For example, teach the prefix *pre-* just before the class reads a selection about prehistoric dinosaurs. Students learn better when what they are being taught has immediate value. Suggestions for lessons that are both functional and contextual are presented throughout this book.

4. *Make connections.* Build a bridge between children's experiences and what they are about to read. Help them see how what they know is related to the story or article. Students in Arizona reading about an ice hockey game may have no experience either playing or watching the sport. However, you could help create a bridge of understanding by discussing how hockey is similar to soccer, a sport with which they probably are familiar. You should also help students connect new concepts to old concepts. Relate reading, writing, listening, and speaking—they all build on each other. Reading and talking about humorous stories can expand students' concept of humor and remind them of funny things that have happened to them. They might then write about these events. Also build on what students know. This will make your teaching easier, since you will be starting at the students' level. It will also help students make a connection between what they know and what they are learning.

5. *Build self-esteem.* According to Bloom's (1976) estimates, how students feel about themselves as learners could account for 25 percent of what they learn: Improve their self-concepts, and they will learn more. Athey's (1985) overview of the research suggested that affective factors may play an even greater role. The message is clear: Value your students. Expect the best from them, and they will give you their best. Expand both their minds and their spirits with a wealth of stories and books. Welcome them into the literacy club. Value their spoken and written contributions. Put them at the center of all you do.

6. *Promote independence.* Whenever you teach a skill or strategy, ask yourself: How can I teach this so students will eventually use it on their own? How will students be called upon to use this skill or strategy in school and in the outside world? When you teach students how to summarize, make predictions, or use context, phonics, or another skill or strategy, teach so that there is a gradual release of responsibility (Pearson & Gallagher, 1983). Gradually fade your instruction and guidance so that students are applying the skill or strategy on their own. Do the same with your selection of reading materials. Although you may discuss ways of choosing books with the class, ultimately, you want students to reach a point where they select their own books.

7. *Believe that all children can learn to read and write.* Given the right kind of instruction, virtually all children can learn to read. There is increasing evidence

Helping Children Feel Competent

Mrs. Hanna is a first-grade teacher, but her approach to building self-esteem is a model for teachers in all grades. Knowing that self-esteem is based on how competent a child feels intellectually, socially, and physically, she matches tasks to each student's level of competence and chooses activities in such a way that each child excels in at least one activity. In the words of Fields, Spangler, and Lee (1991),

She is quick to call attention to the accomplishments of each child. She focuses her comments on how good the child feels about the feat. Helping children tune into the intrinsic rewards of doing well, whether at pumping a swing or completing a puzzle, provides a base for gaining personal satisfaction from accomplishments rather than relying on the judgments of others. . . . She uses praise sparingly since she wants children to be self-motivated rather than rely on her judgments of their behavior. (p. 18)

that the vast majority of children can learn to read at least on a basic level. Over the past two decades, Clay (1993b) has shown that Reading Recovery, an intensive 12- to 15-week early intervention program, can raise the reading levels of between 85 and 95 percent of the lowest achievers to that of average achievers in a class. Surprisingly, Reading Recovery uses an inclusive model:

> The program is designed for children who are the lowest achievers in the class/age group. What is used is an inclusive definition. Principals have sometimes argued to exclude this or that category of children or to save places for children who might seem to "benefit the most," but that is not using the full power of the program. It has been one of the surprises of Reading Recovery that all kinds of children with all kinds of difficulties can be included, can learn, and can reach average-band performance for their class in both reading and writing achievement. Exceptions are not made for children of lower intelligence, for second-language children, for children with low language skills, for children with poor motor coordination, for children who seem immature, for children who score poorly on readiness measures, or for children who have already been categorized by someone else as learning disabled. (Clay, 1991, p. 60)

According to Fry (1993) and Kibby (1993), today's students are reading better than ever, certainly better than their parents or grandparents read. In a sense, however, today's students are further behind. Literacy levels that were adequate a few decades ago are no longer sufficient in our complex, high-tech society.

Using highly trained teachers and one-on-one instruction, Reading Recovery is costly in terms of money and personnel. Many school districts simply have too many needy students to be able to provide one-on-one assistance. However, carefully planned, conscientiously implemented early intervention programs have also been shown to work with small groups of youngsters. Working with the lowest 20 percent of first-grade readers, teachers were able to raise the achievement of approximately 75 percent of the students to a level where it was felt that they could function adequately in second grade (Hiebert & Taylor, 1994). An important aspect of these efforts is that supplementary assistance is complemented by a strong classroom program. These results demonstrate the power of effective instruction and the belief that all children can learn to read.

Although a great variety of topics will be covered in later chapters, the seven primary principles just discussed are emphasized throughout. Teaching suggestions and activities are included for fostering wide reading, keeping reading reasonably easy, keeping reading and writing functional, making connections of various kinds, and, above all, building self-esteem and promoting independence. This book is based on the premise that virtually all children can learn to read and write.

[handwritten margin notes: agree — Phonetics. Grammer. Learning Alphabet. Spelling. Emphasis should be placed on meaning. discagreed reader must put aside all personal thoughts about a passage & take author's view.]

SUMMARY

1. Reading is an active process in which the reader constructs meaning from text. Reading and writing are rooted in language. Although imitation is a factor in learning language, the process is constructive and interactive. Intuitively, parents extend and support their children's attempts to communicate. The school should build on the language and literacy skills that the child has learned at home. For maximum language development, schools should attempt to construct the same warm, accepting environment that is present in nurturing homes.

2. According to Piaget, the child passes through four main stages of cognitive development: sensorimotor, preoperational, concrete operations, and formal operations. To develop to their fullest, elementary-age students need an environment in which they can interact with concrete stimuli.

3. In Vygotsky's view, social interaction is an important factor in children's cognitive and language development. Through scaffolding, adults or knowledgeable peers can help students operate on a higher level of development.

4. Living as we do in a pluralistic society, it is important to be aware of the value that different cultures place on reading and writing and the ways in which reading and writing are used in these cultures. It is also important for the school to build on the literacy activities that are prominent in students' cultures.

5. The type of reading being done can help determine whether the reader takes primarily an efferent or an aesthetic stance. With an efferent stance, the reader comes away from reading with information. With an aesthetic stance, the reader responds to the material in a personal way. A reader may take both stances.

6. Reading can be viewed as being holistic, which is a top-down approach. The best known of the top-down approaches is whole language, which advocates engaging in real reading and writing for real purposes. Reading also can be viewed as being composed of a number of subskills, or from a bottom-up approach. A third approach is to describe reading as being an interaction between top-down and bottom-up processes, which is the position that this book takes. Interactionists emphasize cognitive strategies rather than subskills, which tend to fragment the process. It is important for teachers to explore their personal beliefs about reading and writing instruction so that they can implement a program rooted in their beliefs and consistent with their philosophy.

7. The development of reading may be arbitrarily divided into five stages: emergent literacy, beginning reading, growing independence, reading to learn, and abstract reading.

8. Widespread reading and functional instruction that is commensurate with children's abilities are essentials of an effective reading program. Also necessary is instruction that helps students make connections, enhances their self-esteem, and fosters independence. Believing that virtually every child can learn to read is an important factor in an effective literacy program.

[handwritten: Embrace other cultural perspective by incorporating multicultural reading material. Reading material is Eurocentric. Teachers should include multicultural material in their lessons.]

CLASSROOM APPLICATIONS

1. Analyze your beliefs about teaching reading. Make a list of your major beliefs. Are you a top-downer, a *[handwritten: into classroom curriculum]* bottom-upper, or an interactionist? Now make a list of your major teaching and reinforcement activities. Do

they fit your philosophy? If not, what changes might you make?

2. Whole language has swept the country. Find out more about whole language by reading one of the following sources:

Goodman, K. (1986). *What's Whole in Whole Language?* Portsmouth, NH: Heinemann.

Goodman, K. (1992). I Didn't Found Whole Language. *The Reading Teacher, 46,* pp. 188–199.

Goodman, K., Bird, L. B., Goodman, Y. M. (1991). *The Whole Language Catalog.* New York: American School Publishers.

Smith, F. (1988). *Understanding Reading* (4th ed.). Hillsdale, NJ: Erlbaum.

3. Analyze several reading lessons in a recent basal series. What is the role of the reader in the lessons? Is the reader expected to simply tell what the author's message is? Is the reader expected to interpret and provide a personal response? How would you characterize the approach: transmissional, transactional, or somewhere in between? Does the approach differ for fictional and informational selections?

FIELD APPLICATIONS

1. Conduct a discussion with a small group of children who are about to read a selection. Ask questions designed to probe their attitudes and experiences as they relate to the material. Note how attitudes and experiences differ. After the selection has been read, discuss it and note how students' interpretations are influenced by their attitudes and experiences.

2. Analyze your activities as you teach a reading lesson or observe a class being taught. Classify the instructional activities as being top-down, bottom-up, or interactive. Also, note the reactions of the students to the activities. Do they find them interesting? Do they seem to be learning from them?

c h a p t e r 2

Children's Emergent Literacy

ANTICIPATION GUIDE

Agree

For each of the following statements, put a check under "Agree" or "Disagree" to show how you feel. Discuss your responses with classmates before you read the chapter.

Disagree

1. An informal, unstructured program works best in kindergarten. ✓ (Disagree)

✓ (Agree) 2. Reading books to young children is an excellent use of instructional time.

3. Anyone who has learned to speak should be able to learn to read with no difficulty. ✓ (Disagree)

4. Workbooks have no place in a kindergarten classroom. ✓ (Disagree)

✓ (Agree) 5. To foster emergent literacy, the classroom should have a generous supply of books, writing instruments, posters, and signs.

6. The best way to learn reading is through writing. ✓ (Disagree)

✓ (Agree) 7. Children have to be taught how to form the letters of the alphabet before they can be expected to write.

8. Copying short sentences and favorite stories is a good way to learn to write and read. ✓ (Disagree)

✓ (Agree) 9. For young learners, children's books and teacher-constructed materials and activities are superior to commercial programs.

Using What You Know

Chapter 1 explored the nature of reading, discussed the reading status of children today, and presented seven basic principles for teaching reading. This chapter on emergent literacy is based on those seven principles. The word *literacy* encompasses both writing and reading; *emergent* indicates that the child has been engaged in reading and writing activities long before coming to school. Putting the two concepts together, Sulzby (1989) defined *emergent literacy* as "the reading and writing behaviors that precede and develop into conventional literacy" (p. 84).

Before reading this chapter, reflect on your personal knowledge of emergent literacy. Have you observed young children as they explored reading and writing? How did they do this? What did their writing look like? What did they learn about reading and writing from their homes and the larger environment? How would you go about fostering emergent literacy?

UNDERSTANDING EMERGENT LITERACY

Emergent literacy consists of the reading and writing behaviors that evolve from children's earliest experiences with reading and writing and that gradually grow into conventional literacy.

Children begin developing literacy long before they enter school. According to Sulzby and Teale (1991), this **emergent literacy** "is seen as taking place in home and community settings, in out-of-home care settings, and in school settings such as Head Start, prekindergarten, and kindergarten" (p. 728). Unless they are disabled, all school-age children have acquired a fairly extensive oral language vocabulary and a sophisticated syntactic system. They have seen traffic signs and billboard advertising, printed messages on television, and printing on cereal boxes. They can tell McDonald's logo from that of Burger King and distinguish a box of Fruit Loops from one of Captain Crunch. They have seen their parents read books, magazines, newspapers, letters, and bills and have observed them writing notes or letters, filling out forms, and making lists. They may also have imitated some of these activities. Their parents may have read books to them and provided them with crayons, pencils, and other tools of literacy.

Whereas spoken language "takes much of its meaning from the real situation in which it occurs . . . written language . . . must carry the total load of meaning without ambiguity. This is the main reason why [it] is more formal, more complete and more textured than spoken language and . . . has distinctive structures" (Meek, 1982, p. 33).

All children, no matter how impoverished their environment may be, have begun the journey along the path that begins with language acquisition and ends in formal literacy. The teacher must find out where each child is on the path and lead him or her on the way. As Laminack (1990) noted:

> Children come to the preschool and primary school settings with a wealth of language competence. They have used language and continually use language in all its forms (speaking, listening, writing, and reading), even if only at the exploratory level, for various functions as determined by their individual needs and purposes. (pp. 538–539)

READINESS VERSUS EMERGENT LITERACY

Before the concept of emergent literacy took hold, first-grade teachers and, more recently, kindergarten teachers asked whether their students were ready to read. The feeling was that if children were rushed into reading, they would experience difficulty or failure, would grow discouraged, and would turn against reading or become behavior problems (Hildreth, 1950). This concept has some merit; Elkind (1981) warned about the damage done by hurrying children into reading.

Some experts see **readiness** as primarily a maturational process, thanks to the work of Gesell (1925), whose studies emphasized motor development. Ames (1986) has continued to champion this concept and has warned against having children start school before they are ready. In one study, she and a colleague found that a large percentage of children are thrust into academics too early (Ilg & Ames, 1964). Adherents of this view stress giving the child time to mature—for example, keeping a child who has a late birthday home for an additional year before starting school. Proponents of the maturational approach set up **transitional classes** for students who do not seem ready for first grade by the end of kindergarten and thus require an extra year of preparation to move up.

Interventionists, on the other hand, emphasize the need to set up programs to foster readiness; that is, they focus on nurture rather than nature. Carnine, Silbert, and Kameenui (1990) recommended that disadvantaged children be given formal reading instruction in kindergarten to enable them to catch up to their more privileged peers, suggesting that careful teaching will enhance the learning process for such students. "Since younger students are more instructionally naive, the instruction provided to kindergarten students must incorporate sound instructional design principles" (p. 159). These theorists put their faith in intensified, carefully planned, step-by-step instruction rather than the maturation process.

Over the years, many experts have espoused a middle ground that includes both nature and nurture (Durkin, 1993; Gates, 1937; MacGinitie, 1976). They recognize that some cognitive abilities require maturation but believe that providing instruction and opportunities to learn enhances the process.

For many professionals, the concept of readiness has been replaced by the theory of emergent literacy. Read (1971) reported on a study of early spellers who had learned to spell "spontaneously" in an informal manner. The early spellers were preschoolers who were given help in spelling when they asked for it but were otherwise allowed to spell however they wanted. What surprised Read was that these young children, who had no contact with each other, created spelling systems that were remarkably similar and that, although not correct, made sense phonetically. For instance, *er* at the end of a word such as *tiger* was typically spelled with just an *r*, as *tigr*. In this instance, *r* is syllabic; it functions as a vowel and so does not need to be preceded by an *e*. For long vowels, children generally used the letter name, as in *sop* for *soap*, where the name of the letter *o* contains the sound of the vowel. Commenting on his findings, Read stated, "We can no longer assume that children must approach reading with no discernible prior conception of its structure" (p. 34). Landmark studies by researchers in several countries echoed and amplified Read's findings in both reading and writing (Clay, 1972; Ferreiro & Teberosky, 1982; Teale & Sulzby, 1986).

Readiness is the adequacy of ability in relation to the demands of the task (Ausubel, 1959)

Transitional classes are classes composed of students who have completed kindergarten but who are judged not to be ready for first grade so they are given an additional year of instruction.

Adapting instruction for a variety of cultures

Different cultures might value different literacy activities. Therefore, it is important for the teacher to know what kinds of writing and reading activities are stressed in the children's homes and communities so that these activities can be built on in the classroom. Doing so affirms each child's culture and builds confidence.

Until recently, writing was viewed as being more difficult and advanced than reading; so children were taught to write after they learned to read. However, reading and writing are now seen as developing simultaneously and being interrelated. Writing fosters reading development, and vice versa.

In the past, words and letters were copied and eventually memorized. Literacy was learned from the outside in. However, according to the emergent literacy concept, the child constructs concepts of writing internally by exploring written language.

Concepts of print refer to understandings about how print functions—that printed words represent spoken words, have boundaries, are read from left to right, and so on.

These revelations about children's literacy abilities have a number of implications. First and foremost, we must build on what children already know. In their five or six years before coming to us, they have acquired a great deal of insight into the reading/writing process. Instead of asking whether they are ready, we have to find out where they are and take it from there. We must value and make use of their knowledge.

Recent research suggests that children are active constructors of literacy. They learn a great deal by hearing stories read aloud; attempting to read signs, labels, and storybooks; talking with parents and peers; watching parents read and write; and experimenting with writing and reading materials. Teachers have to continue these activities in their classrooms. Research also indicates that literacy does not develop in a linear fashion. Until recently, it was thought that listening developed first, followed by speaking, followed by reading. Writing was not introduced until students had a good start in learning to read. However, emergent literacy research suggests that writing and reading develop simultaneously and that each encourages growth in the other (Teale & Sulzby, 1986).

As children observe parents and peers read and write and as they themselves experiment with reading and writing, they construct theories about how these processes work. For instance, based on their experience with picture books, children may believe that pictures rather than words are read. In time, they discover that it is the printed marks on the pages that are read. As they explore writing, children may initially believe that the marks they make are like drawings, representing objects. In time, they develop the understanding that the written symbols represent letters and words. Ultimately, they discover the alphabetic principle, that letters represent speech sounds (Ferreiro, 1990). Children's explorations of reading and writing gradually evolve into conventional reading and writing in which they use their overall background of experience, knowledge of language, knowledge of letter-sound relationships (phonics), store of memorized words, and context.

ESSENTIAL SKILLS AND UNDERSTANDINGS FOR EMERGENT LITERACY

The activities described in this chapter have been designed to help emergent readers and writers further develop essential understandings about literacy. The most basic concept concerns the nature of reading and writing. Students need to broaden their understanding of how and why we read and write. They also need to become more familiar with the types of language used in books and to acquire a deeper sense of how stories develop. On a more formal level, they need to construct basic concepts of print, if they have not already learned them. These **concepts of print** include the following:

- What we say and what others say can be written down and read.
- Words, not pictures, are read.
- Words are made up of letters, and sentences are made up of words.
- Reading goes from left to right and from top to bottom.
- A book is read from front to back.
- What we say is divided into words. (Some students may believe that "How are you?" is a single word, for example.) Students must also grasp the concept

of a word. Of course, they use words in their oral language, but understanding what a word is is on a higher level of abstraction, a **metalinguistic awareness,** or **metacognitive awareness.** This means that they must be able to think about language as well as use it.

- Space separates written words. Students must be able to match words being read orally with their written counterparts. Hearing the sentence "The little dog ran," the student must focus on *The, little, dog,* and *ran* as each word is read.
- Sentences begin with capital letters.
- Sentences end with periods, question marks, or exclamation marks.
- A book has a title, an author, and sometimes an illustrator.

Students must also develop phonological awareness and arrive at an understanding of the alphabetic principle. Phonological awareness involves being able to detect rhyming words, to segment words into their separate sounds, and to perceive beginning sounds; understanding the alphabetic principle means grasping the concept that certain letters represent certain sounds.

Because the development of various children follows different paths, a few will enter kindergarten reading conventionally. However, most will still be developing emergent literacy in kindergarten and possibly into first grade; a few may make very slow progress and may still be developing emergent literacy beyond first grade. The activities and procedures explored in this chapter apply to any students who might benefit from them, whether they are in kindergarten, first grade, or beyond. These activities and procedures might even be used with preschool children who are making very rapid progress.

CREATING A LITERACY-RICH ENVIRONMENT

Regardless of where children are in terms of literacy, an essential step in further development is to create an environment that promotes active reading, writing, listening, and speaking. In Hamburger Haven, a chain of restaurants in the Washington, D.C. area, table settings include crayons, and diners are invited to draw on the large paper tablecloth as their meals are being prepared. If they wish, they can hang their creations on the wall. Most children and a surprising number of adults accept the invitation.

Getting children to engage in literacy activities is partly a matter of providing an appealing environment. One means of encouragement is simply to have readily available writing instruments, paper of various kinds, and books and periodicals. The materials should be easy to get to and to use. The more attractive and appealing the display, the greater the participation. Durkin (1966) found that the presence of reading and writing materials in the home was an important element in the development of early readers. However, it was not enough for the materials to be present; they also had to be accessible.

In a classroom environment that fosters literacy, print is everywhere. Bulletin boards include words as well as pictures. There is a calendar of students' birthdays and other important upcoming events. Aquariums and terrariums are labeled with the names of their inhabitants. Most important of all, students' stories and booklets are displayed prominently. The classroom might have a student-run

Metalinguistic awareness is the ability to reflect about language. **Metacognitive awareness** is the ability to reflect upon one's thought processes, or think about thinking.

For a time, children's concepts of letter-sound relationships may be very specific. For instance, at age 4, my granddaughter Paige told me that she had a school friend named Paul, and then she explained, "He has my letter." She had noticed that Paul's name begins with a *P,* like hers. However, she regarded the letters of her name as being personal and specific. The *P* in *Paige* identified her. She had not yet reached the point where she realized that *p* represented /p/ and could be used in any word containing a /p/ sound (see Ferreiro, 1986).

post office so that children can correspond with each other. If computer equipment is available, students might even make use of E-mail.

Although a classroom can be arranged in many ways to induce children to take part in literacy activities, Morrow (1989a) recommended that a variety of centers be set up, including areas for writing, math, social studies, science, music, blocks and other manipulatives, dramatic play, and a library. A listening/viewing center and a computing center are also possibilities. If the classroom is small, some of these centers could be combined.

The writing center should contain the upper- and lower-case alphabets in manuscript form. Letters, stories, lists, and other models of writing can also be displayed. The materials should be posted at a level at which students can make use of them. A selection of writing instruments and paper should be available. Paper should come in various colors and should be unlined so that students are not unduly concerned with spacing. Small memo pads of paper are also recommended. Writing instruments should include crayons and magic markers, the lat-

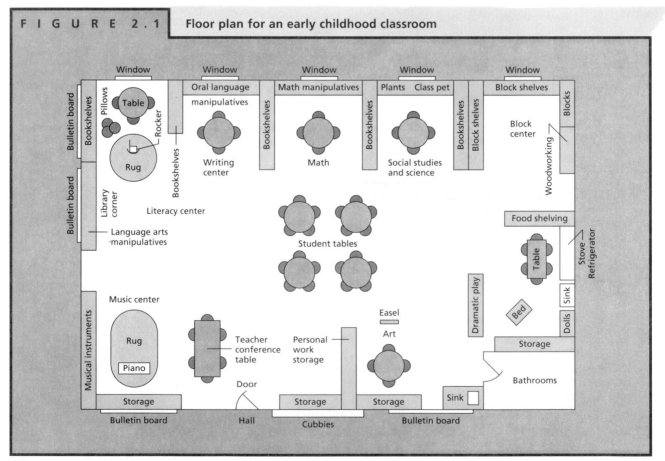

FIGURE 2.1 **Floor plan for an early childhood classroom**

From Morrow, L. M., *Literacy Development in the Early Years*, 2nd ed., Copyright 1993 by Allyn and Bacon. Reprinted by permission.

ter being the choice of most children (Bauman, 1990). If pencils are provided, students should be instructed in using them safely. Other useful items for the writing center are chalkboards, magnetic letters, printing sets, a typewriter, and a computer with an easy-to-use word-processing program. Paste, tape, scissors, and staplers are also useful. Reference materials are important. For kindergarten children, such materials could consist primarily of picture dictionaries, both commercially produced and constructed by students.

The library or book corner should feature a wide selection of reading materials attractively displayed, including both commercial and student-written books. Extra copies of a book currently being read by the teacher or other books by the same author or on the same theme should be given a place of prominence. Rockers, cushions, bean-bag chairs, and pieces of rug will give students comfortable places to read. The listening/viewing center should have a wide variety of audiotaped books and videotapes or, if available, CD-ROM versions of favorite stories so that students can follow the text as the story is being read (see Chapter 14 for a listing of CD-ROM software). Several audiotapes of favorite books will allow small groups of students to listen to a book together. The dramatic play and housekeeping centers should be stocked with order blanks, note pads, signs, bills, and other realia of literacy.

In a classroom that fosters literacy, the tools and products of writing and reading abound. A sample floor plan of a literacy-rich environment is presented in Figure 2.1.

FOSTERING EMERGENT LITERACY

An environment that fosters literacy is both physical and attitudinal. Attitudinally, the teacher believes that literacy is a broad-based, naturally occurring process that takes place over a long period of time. Although it can and should be taught, literacy can also be fostered by "setting the scene" and through subtle encouragement. The teacher should lose no opportunity to reinforce literacy concepts. For example, after the class's pet gerbil has been named George, a label containing his name is attached to the cage. While preparing the label, the teacher explains what is being done and shows the class that the letters *G-e-o-r-g-e* spell "George." When students are running software on the computer, the teacher points to the RETURN key and explains what the printing on it means. After turning a page on the calendar, the teacher indicates the name of the new month and asks the class to guess what the word is. When a notice is being sent home, the teacher reads it aloud to the class first. If students see any familiar words in the notice, they are encouraged to read them.

Students are also encouraged to write or draw, and the emphasis is on expression and exploration rather than on conventional spelling or handwriting. There is plenty of time for that later. The class library is an active place. Students read books in school and are allowed to take them home. The inevitable torn pages and jelly-stained covers and the occasional lost books are a small price to pay for the development of literacy skills.

MAKING READING AND WRITING A PART OF CLASSROOM ACTIVITIES

Dramatic play refers to a type of activity in which students play at being someone else: a doctor, a teacher, a firefighter, and so on.

Fostering literacy growth among young children is sometimes simply a matter of making reading and writing a natural part of their classroom activities. One way to increase early literacy experiences is to stock play centers with the tools of writing and reading that might naturally appear there. Children can make use of these as they take on the roles of adults whom they see in their everyday lives. They also are more likely to role-play literacy tasks if the appropriate materials are available. In one study, children engaged in 290 distinct literacy tasks when writing materials were provided for them to use (Hall, May, Moores, Shearer, & Williams, 1987). Christie (1990) recommended that dramatic play centers be supplied with pens, pencils, note pads, diaries, cookbooks, telephone books, picture books, magazines, catalogs, and newspapers—in other words, the kinds of materials that might be found in the typical home. Opportunities for **dramatic play** that can stimulate reading and writing include the following:

1. Grocery store—creating signs, writing checks or food lists
2. Bank—writing deposit and withdrawal slips and checks
3. Doctor's office—writing prescriptions, making appointments
4. Restaurant—writing and reading menus, taking food orders, creating signs (Christie, 1990)

In planning dramatic play centers, find out what kinds of experiences the children have had and how they have seen literacy function in their environment. For instance, if they are more familiar with fast-food eating places than with restaurants having servers and individual menus, create wall-type menus characteristic of fast-food establishments.

Playing with print is an important part of literacy development through which children can explore the uses of the medium. After scrawling letterlike figures on a piece of paper, one child pretended he was reading a weather report (McLane & McNamee, 1990). Others have been police officers writing tickets, restaurant owners creating menus, store owners writing receipts, parents writing shopping lists, and authors writing books. Children have also pretended to read books to dolls, teddy bears, friends, and younger siblings. "Through play, children may come to feel that they are writers and readers before they actually have the necessary skills to write and read" (McLane & McNamee, 1990, p. 19).

As children learn about literacy skills through playing and observing how members of their family and community use these skills, they become motivated to learn more about reading and writing so that they can make fuller use of these skills. In learning literacy, function fosters form. Students learn the what and the why of reading and writing as a prelude to learning the details of how to read and write.

READING TO STUDENTS

One of the best ways to develop students' emergent literacy is to read interesting books to them. As the Commission on Reading noted (Anderson, Hiebert, Scott, & Wilkinson, 1985), "The single most important activity for building the knowledge required for eventual success in reading is reading aloud to children" (p. 23).

One of the best ways to develop students' emergent literacy is to read to them.

Unfortunately, there is incredible variation in the amount of experience children have in being read to. In his study of language development of children, Wells (1986) found that one child, Jonathan, had been read to six thousand times. His parents had read an average of four stories a day to him. On the other hand, Rosie had never had a story read to her before entering school. Not surprisingly, at age 10, Jonathan was doing quite well in school, whereas Rosie ranked last out of thirty-two children studied. Being read to was the most important predictor of later reading achievement.

Why is being read to so important? Being read to develops children's vocabulary, expands their experiential background, makes them aware of the language of books, introduces them to basic concepts of print and how books are read, and provides them with many pleasant associations with books. Perhaps most important is the power of books to help children create worlds based on words and story structures (Wells, 1986).

In conversation, the child can use context to help construct the meaning of a situation. For instance, if someone is pointing to a ball and making a throwing motion while saying, "Throw me the ball," then the context of the statement—the pointing, the ball, and the throwing motion—aids understanding. However, in a story, there is no context except for, possibly, illustrations. The child must therefore use language to construct meaning. As parents read storybooks to their children, they provide a bridge between conversation with all its support and the more abstract, noninteractive experience of hearing a story read. Intuitively, parents use the illustrations as well as explanations, gestures, and discussion to help children understand the storybook.

Initial readings are highly interactive. Over time, as the child becomes a more sophisticated listener and assimilates the format of storybook reading into her or his own schema or conceptual background, less support is offered by the reader.

In your read-aloud program, include both fiction and informational books. Reading narrative texts is important. As Dorion (1994) points out, "Narrative is the principal mode through which children understand the world around them. . . . Children experience their world and find meaning in their lives through the narratives inherent in their daily interactions with the world and in those captured in children's literature" (p. 616). Informational texts can also be enjoyable, and, in addition to building students' background, they arouse their curiosity.

Reading to students helps them comprehend literary language, which is quite different from conversation. Conversation is concrete, immediate, and contextual. The object being talked about might be physically present. The person with whom the child is conversing gears the conversation to the child's level of understanding and can supply additional information should it be needed. However, in storybook reading, there is no physical context or clarifying interchange between author and reader or listener.

In the process, however, the child learns invaluable lessons about the language and structure of written text. As they read to their children, parents explain new words and expressions that crop up in storybooks. They also discuss unfamiliar concepts, intuitively relating new concepts to the child's background. Parents do not deliberately set out to teach their children new concepts and words; this happens as a natural part of reading to children. As a result of these interactions, children who are read to the most have the most highly developed language skills. They have larger vocabularies and are better able to narrate an event, describe a scene, and understand the teacher (Strickland & Taylor, 1989).

Even children who have not been read to should still have adequate language for instruction in reading and writing. However, they might lack the motivation to read and write. If they have not experienced the joy of hearing stories or witnessed the purposes of reading and writing, they may have little motivation to learn to read and write. What should be done to help motivate these children? First, it is important to make no judgments. And, of course, you should read to them. While being read to as part of a group is a good start, it is not adequate. Much of the value that accrues from listening to stories is the discussion in which reader and child engage. Often books become the springboard for rich conversations. Wells (1986) found book reading to be one of the most productive situations for developing language.

What kinds of books should be read to children? Nearly any book that they can understand and relate to will do. Nursery rhymes and books with repetitive patterns, such as *Are You My Mother?* (Eastman, 1960) or one of the versions of *The Three Little Pigs* or *The Three Billy Goats Gruff*, readily lend themselves to preparation for reading.

Before reading a selection aloud, ask students questions that enable them to make connections between their personal backgrounds and the story. For instance, before reading *All the Way Home* (Segal, 1973), which is a humorous tale about a little girl who falls and hurts herself and then cries all the way home, ask students to tell about a time when they fell and hurt themselves. In preparation for reading Eric Carle's (1973) *Have You Seen My Cat?*, discuss experiences that they have had with a lost pet. Such discussion will build essential concepts and background.

Hold up the book that is to be read. Point to and discuss the title. If it lends itself to it, use the title as a predictive device. Have students think about the title and guess what the story might be about. For example, before reading *The Very Busy Spider* by Eric Carle (1985), ask them to tell what a very busy spider might do.

Point to the author's name. Show a picture of the author, if there is one on the book jacket, and read the author's biography. When reading *Have You Seen My Cat?* show Carle's picture with his two cats and discuss how the pets may have given him the idea for the book and may also have been models for the drawings. Talk about the methods the author may have used to write the book—for example, did the author write it in pen on pads of paper or type it? Emphasize the fact that stories can be written down and then read by others.

Sometimes preparation for a story goes beyond mere discussion. Personal experience can often be the key to understanding a selection that otherwise would be incomprehensible. "Playing outside in the snow and making 'angels' gives meaning

Exemplary Teaching

Extension Activities

Jim Trelease (1989), a staunch proponent of reading aloud to children of all ages, recounted the following incident:

> When my friend Anne Marie Russo of Holy Cross School in Springfield, Massachusetts, saw how fascinated her kindergartners were with the book *My Teacher Sleeps at School,* by Leatie Weiss, she scheduled a classroom "sleep-over." On the appointed day, students came to school equipped with bathrobes, slippers, teddy bears, toothbrushes, and sleeping bags. Then they went through the usual sleep-over ritual—movie, snacks, a read-aloud book [*Ira Sleeps Over* (Waber, 1972)], prayers, tooth brushing, and sleep before the buses arrived to end the day. (p. 89)

to Ezra Jack Keats's *The Snowy Day,* picking blueberries adds to a reading of Robert McCloskey's *Blueberries for Sal*" (Fields, Spangler, & Lee, 1991, p. 97).

As you read a book, stop periodically to review what has happened, and encourage children to make some predictions; after you have finished reading, talk over whether their predictions came true. For example, when reading *Too Many Books* (Bauer, 1984), a story of a girl who accumulated a houseful of books, you might ask, "What do you think Marylou will do with all those books?" Encourage students to modify predictions, if necessary, and make new ones.

Hold the book so that students can see the illustrations as you read the selection. Discuss and ask questions about them. Looking at a picture in *Too Many Books,* you might ask, "What is different about Marylou's house?"

After reading the book, follow it up with some extension activities. Students might enjoy drawing a picture of the story's main character or composing a related story. They might also want to have you read more by the same author. After hearing and discussing Russell Hoban's (1964) *Bread and Jam for Frances,* they might enjoy listening to another book in the Frances series.

DEVELOPING STORY STRUCTURE

Reading to children develops a sense of story, as they become familiar with plot development and the interaction of plot, characters, and setting. This familiarity bolsters comprehension, the ability to discuss stories, and the ability to compose stories.

To develop a sense of story structure, discuss with the class literary language, or words and phrases that are frequently used in stories: *once upon a time, lived happily ever after, many years ago,* and so on. Point out that most stories have a main character, who may be an older person, a young person, or even an animal who talks and acts like a human. Have students identify the main characters in stories they know. Discuss how setting, too, may be an important element.

After students have grasped the concepts of story language and characters, point out that the main characters usually have problems to solve. Give examples from familiar stories. Discuss how Marylou's problem with having too many books and the old man's problem in Wanda Gág's (1928) *Millions of Cats* are similar. Problems are usually solved in some way; talk over how that occurred for Marylou and the old man. These kinds of questions not only build comprehension, discussion, and composing skills, they also develop and lay the groundwork for an understanding of literary techniques.

BUILDING COMPREHENSION

In your discussions about books, ask students a variety of questions, including those that involve important details, sequence, and drawing conclusions or making inferences and that provide a foundation for reading comprehension (Feitelson, Kita, & Goldstein, 1986). Do not use the questions primarily as a technique for gauging depth of understanding, but as means for drawing attention to important details or relating details so that a conclusion can be reached or a main idea constructed. For example, after you have read *The Snowy Day*, ask students how Peter felt about the snow. Then ask them how they know that Peter liked the snow. Go back over the story if children have difficulty supplying details that back up the conclusion. Think of your discussions as a way of sharing so that books can be more fully understood and enjoyed.

Make sure that questioning is a two-way street. From the very beginning, you want students to learn that reading is supposed to make sense. Encourage students to ask about anything they do not understand in a story, including confusing words, concepts, or events (Salinger, 1988). "Children failing to gain this insight while they are still at the listening stage may encounter difficulties later when they themselves begin to read" (p. 208). Do not hesitate to develop vocabulary and concepts, build background, or explain unfamiliar processes or events. This information will enable students to bring more to the reading they do in the future and so will prepare them to be better readers.

MAKING PERSONAL CONNECTIONS

Students will not fully appreciate reading unless the stories touch their lives. Ask questions that involve personal reactions, such as how a story made them feel, what they liked best, whether they have ever met anyone like the main character, or whether they would like to hear a similar book. After reading *Whistle for Willie* by Ezra Jack Keats (1964), have students describe how Willie felt at the end, and ask them about a time when they may have been happy and proud themselves.

Students have to take responsibility for their interpretation of a story and understand that their response counts. It is important to encourage them to venture judgments. After reading the first part of *Frog and Toad Are Friends* (Lobel, 1970), ask the students how they feel about the way Frog tricked Toad, and encourage them to express their true feelings. "When conflicting opinions are solicited and respected, children learn that they can come to their own opinions about what they read rather than accepting whatever is in print" (Fields, Spangler, & Lee, 1991, p. 97).

After discussing a story, you may want to provide follow-up or extension activities. Students might listen to a taped version, or they may pretend to read the story to a partner. Pretend reading provides them with the opportunity to use book language. Fields, Spangler, and Lee (1991) recommended careful observation of children as they "read" a storybook to other students:

> Listen, and you will hear the more formal and complete form of written language rather than the ambiguous oral forms the child usually uses in speech. Careful listening also demonstrates that children haven't merely memorized the story and aren't merely imitating adults. Their story reenactments focus on the personal meanings of the story, using the child's own immature speech patterns. This is important evidence of how children learn by constructing their own knowledge. (p. 96)

Follow-up activities include illustrating a portion of the story; watching a videotape, CD-ROM, filmstrip, or motion picture version; or carrying out some activity suggested by the book. After reading *The Gingerbread Boy* (Galdone, 1975), students might have a hunt for a gingerbread man; reading *The Carrot Seed* (Krauss, 1945) might lead to the planting of seeds. Another excellent follow-up is reading another book by the same author.

Mason, Peterman, and Kerr (1988, Fig. 1) suggested using the following general plan when presenting narrative materials:

Before reading the narrative

Show the cover of the book to the children. Encourage discussion about the book's content.

Discuss the author and illustrator of the book.

Allow children to discuss their own experiences which are related to those raised in the book.

Discuss the type of text the children will be hearing (folk tale, repetitive story, fables, fantasies, etc.).

Introduce children to the story's main characters, the time and place in which the story occurs.

Set a purpose for the children to listen to the story, usually what happens to the main character.

During the reading of the narrative

Encourage children to react to and comment on the story.

Elaborate on the text, when appropriate, in order to help children understand the written language used in the story and story components, such as the main character's problem, attempts to resolve the problem, and its resolution.

Ask questions, occasionally, to monitor children's comprehension of the story or relevant vocabulary.

Rephrase the text when it is apparent that children are having difficulty with the words or phrases.

At appropriate points in the story, ask children to predict what will happen next.

Allow children to share their own interpretation of a story.

After reading the narrative

Review the story components (the setting, problem, goal, and resolution).

Help children make connections between the events of the main character and similar events in their own lives.

Engage children in some kind of follow-up activity, such as a discussion of other books by the same author or illustrator, an art activity, perhaps as simple as drawing a picture about the story, or some other means of active involvement with the story.

For informational books, Mason, Peterman, and Kerr (1988, Fig. 2) recommended the following general plan:

Before reading the text

Determine children's level of understanding of the topic presented in the text. Do this by discussing the pictures in the text and having them describe their experiences with the topic.

Provide demonstrations and in-context explanations of difficult concepts.

Discuss the relationship between the title and the topic to be addressed.

Set a purpose for listening. This might include finding the answers to questions the children raised in their discussion of the topic.

Provide a link between their experiences with the topic and what they will be learning from the text.

During the reading of the text

Ask questions periodically to check their understanding of the text. Questions that actually appear in the text might provide excellent opportunities for discussion and demonstration of the topic.

Through comments about the pictures and through carefully selected questions, help children identify pictures which might represent unfamiliar concepts.

Provide suggestions about activities children might engage in later which will encourage them to further explore the topic.

After reading the text

Allow children to ask questions about the text.

Help them see how informational texts can be used to learn more about their own world.

Offer activities that will tie text concepts to children's experiences.

Whatever specific steps are used, the important point is to interact with students and build bridges of understanding before, after, and during the reading of both fiction and nonfiction selections. Research by Dunning and Mason (cited in Mason, Peterman, & Kerr, 1988) suggested that students comprehend better when stories that are read to them are discussed. Extension activities are also important. Students who participate in follow-up activities, such as dramatizing a story that has been read to them or drawing illustrations for it, also have improved comprehension and a more highly developed sense of story structure

When choosing informational books, use children's interest and curiosity as your guide. What kinds of questions do they have? Do they want to know where fog comes from or where dinosaurs lived? Are they curious about rainbows or clouds or cows?

Adapting instruction for adult volunteers

In Maxie Perry's urban pre-kindergarten, being read to is a favorite activity. Realizing the value of one-on-one reading and personalized interaction between adult and child, Perry has enlisted the services of volunteers and aides to read to individual children. Because some of the volunteers have limited reading skills themselves and lack confidence in their ability to read aloud, she supplies sensitive guidance and suggestions (Strickland & Taylor, 1989).

(Morrow, 1985). However, do not overdo these discussions and activities, as that might detract from the children's enjoyment of being read to.

See the Children's Book List for a number of books that are recommended for reading aloud.

Children's Book List
Recommended read-alouds

Angelou, M. *My Painted House, My Friendly Chicken, and Me*. New York: Clarkson N. Potter. (1994). An eight-year-old Ndebele girl tells about life in her village in South Africa.

Barnes-Murphy, F. *The Fables of Aesop*. New York: Lothrop. (1994). A collection of fables retold from Aesop, including "The Hare and the Tortoise" and "The Ant and the Grasshopper."

Brett, J. *Town Mouse, Country Mouse*. New York: Putnam. (1994). A lovely retelling of the classic fable. After trading houses, the country mouse and the town mouse discover there is no place like home.

Brown, M. *The Three Billy Goats Gruff*. New York: Harcourt. (1957). The troll meets his match when he threatens the third goat.

Canon, J. *Stellaluna*. San Diego: Harcourt. (1993). After she falls headfirst into a bird's nest, a baby bat is raised like a bird until she is reunited with her mother.

Curtis, G. *Grandma's Baseball*. New York: Crown. (1990). Having Grandma around is not much fun until her grandson discovers an autographed baseball from Grandpa's days with the Monarchs.

dePaola, T. *Favorite Nursery Tales*. New York: Putnam. (1986). Presented in this attractive book are thirty well-known traditional tales and poems by the Brothers Grimm, Hans Christian Andersen, Aesop, Robert Louis Stevenson, and others.

dePaola, T. *Strega Nona*. New York: Simon & Schuster. (1975). When Strega Nona leaves him alone with her magic pasta pot, Big Anthony is determined to show the townspeople how it works.

Dorros, A. *Abuela*. New York: Dutton. (1991). While riding on a bus with her grandmother, a little girl imagines that they are carried up into the sky and fly over the sights of New York City.

Eastman, P. D. *Are You My Mother?* New York: Random House. (1960). After falling out of its nest, a small bird searches for its mother.

Fox, M. *Koala Lou*. San Diego: Harcourt. (1988). A young koala, longing to hear her mother speak lovingly to her as she did before her siblings came along, plans to win her mother's attention.

Greenfield, E. *Honey, I Love*. New York: Harper. (1978, 1995). Young girl tells about the many things in her life that she loves.

Hoban, R. *Bedtime for Frances*. New York: Harper. (1960). Frances uses a variety of delaying tactics to put off bedtime.

Hong, L. *Two of Everything*. New York: Whitman. (1993). A poor Chinese farmer finds a magic brass pot that doubles whatever is placed inside it, but his efforts to make himself wealthy lead to unexpected complications.

Howard, E. *Aunt Flossie's Hats (and Crab Cakes Later)*. New York: Clarion. (1990). Two girls share tea, cookies, crab cakes, and stories about the past when they visit their favorite aunt.

James, S. *Dear Mr. Blueberry*. New York: Macmillan. (1991). A young girl and her teacher correspond about the whale she has discovered in her pond.

Keats, E. J. *The Snowy Day*. New York: Viking. (1962). A small boy has fun in the snow.

Krauss, R. *The Carrot Seed*. New York: Harper. (1945). After the little boy plants a carrot seed, everyone predicts that it will not come up. The little boy's faith is rewarded with a giant carrot.

Martin, B., Jr. *Brown Bear, Brown Bear, What Do You See?* New York: Holt. (1983). A brown bear, blue horse, purple cat, and other creatures are asked what they see in this easy-to-read text.

McCloskey, R. *Make Way for Ducklings*. New York: Viking. (1941). With the assistance of a kindly police officer who halts traffic so that they may safely cross the street, a mother duck and her brood waddle from the Charles River to the pond in Boston's Public Garden.

McPhail, D. *Pigs Aplenty, Pigs Galore!* New York: Dutton. (1993). Pigs galore invade a house and have a wonderful party.

Numeroff, L. *If You Give a Mouse a Cookie*. New York: Harper. (1985). This funny book comes full cycle and takes the reader through a young child's day along the way.

Zion, G. *Harry the Dirty Dog*. New York: Harper. (1956). Sick of baths, Harry buries the hated bath brush and takes off. However, he gets so dirty that his family fails to recognize him when he returns.

Literally thousands of books make enjoyable, worthwhile read-alouds. An excellent source of both titles and techniques for reading aloud is Trelease's (1989) *The New Read-Aloud Handbook* (New York: Penguin). Other sources of read-aloud titles include the following:

Bishop, R. C. (Ed.). *Kaleidoscope: A Multicultural Booklist for Grades K–8*. Urbana, IL: NCTE. (1994).

Kimmel, M. M., & Segal, E. *For Reading Out Loud! A Guide to Sharing Books with Children* (rev. ed.). New York: Delacorte. (1988).

Kruse, G. M., & Horning, K. T. *Multicultural Literature for Children and Young Adults*. Madison: Wisconsin Department of Public Education. (1991).

Libson, E. R. *Parent's Guide to the Best Books for Children* (rev. ed.). New York: New York Times Books. (1991).

Liggett, T. C., & Benfield, C. M. *Reading Rainbow Guide to Children's Books*. New York: Carol Publishing Group. (1994).

HELPING STUDENTS WHO HAVE LIMITED EXPERIENTIAL BACKGROUNDS

If students seem to have limited experiential backgrounds, you may want to stress informational books and traditional tales. Future reading will build on their knowledge of the world and their ability to recognize the names *Cinderella, Big Bad Wolf, Goldilocks,* and *The Three Bears* and other allusions to traditional tales (Hirsch, 1987). However, keep in mind that listening to selections, whether they are fictional or informational, should be fun.

If students have not been read to on a regular basis, schedule extra read-aloud sessions. Trelease (1989) estimated that only 20 percent of parents regularly read aloud to children. For poor children, the percentage is even lower. When heads of households with incomes at or below $10,000 were surveyed about the amount of time they spend reading to their children, 90 percent reported reading to them once a month or less (Morrow, 1988). When read to systematically on a one-to-one basis, economically disadvantaged preschoolers demonstrate a greater involvement with stories and increase the number and complexity of their questions and comments. Together with fostering a sense of story, the sessions apparently develop oral language and social skills.

EMERGENT STORYBOOK READING

On one visit with my four-year-old granddaughter Paige, she took me aside and whispered, "I can read." Sitting on the sofa, she "read" *Are You My Mother?* (Eastman, 1960) as she leafed through the pages. Although she was not actually reading the words on the pages—her retelling was guided by the pictures—her voice had the tone and expression of one who is reading aloud rather than of one who is telling a story. Paige was engaged in the emergent reading of a storybook, a widespread phenomenon in homes and classrooms where children are read to frequently.

As Holdaway (1979) pointed out, children who have been read to imitate the process and engage in reading-like behaviors. As a result of being read to, children play with books, often for long periods of time, and gradually learn to reconstruct the stories conveyed in the books that have been read to them. Holdaway commented:

> The most important discovery we made was that the much-lauded bedtime story situation is only half the picture: practice of reading-like behavior and writing-like behavior completes the picture. . . . Both activities are complementary aspects of the same language-learning cycle. In both aspects, there is close visual and tactile contact, with books becoming increasingly focused on the conventions of print. All of the most powerful strategies of mature reading are being established. (p. 61)

For their pretend reading, or **emergent storybook reading,** children typically select a favorite storybook, one that has been read to them many times. Children's storybook reading can be placed in any of five broad categories beginning with talking about the illustrations in a storybook (but not creating a story) to actually reading a storybook in conventional fashion. The five categories are presented in Table 2.1.

When young children play at reading, they rehearse the things a reader does, such as turning the pages, inspecting the pictures, thinking over the tone of the words, and pausing to savor or to return to particular moments. This is the foundation of successful reading behavior (Learning Media, 1991).

Emergent storybook reading is the evolving ability of a child to read storybooks, which progresses from simply telling a story suggested by the book's illustrations or having heard the book read aloud to reading the book conventionally.

TABLE 2.1 Emergent reading of storybooks

Category	Description
Attends to pictures but does not create a story	The child simply talks about the illustrations and does not attempt to make connections among the pictures so as to tell a story.
Uses pictures to create an oral story	Using the storybook's illustrations, the child creates a story. However, the child's expression and intonation are those of telling rather than reading a story.
Uses pictures to create a combined oral/reading story	Using the storybook's illustrations, the child retells a story. Portions of the retelling sound like oral storybook reading; however, other portions sound like an oral retelling of the story or are conversational.
Uses pictures to create a literary retelling	Using the storybook's illustrations, the child creates a literary rendition of a story. In wording, expression, and intonation, it sounds like the reading of a storybook. The reading may be verbatim but is not just memorized. The verbatim rendition is conceptual. The child uses knowledge of the specific events in the story to help recall the wording of the story (Sulzby, 1985).
Uses print to read	Ironically, the first subcategory here may be a refusal to read. As a child attempts to use print rather than pictures, the child may realize that she or he cannot decipher the print and therefore might say, "I don't know the words." In the second subcategory, the child pays attention to known aspects of print, such as a few known words or a repeated phrase.

Based on Classification Scheme for Children's Emergent Reading of Favorite Storybooks (simplified version) (pp. 137–138) by E. Sulzby (1992). In J. W. Irwin & M. A. Doyle (Eds.), *Reading/Writing Connections, Learning from Research*. Newark, DE: International Reading Association.

Encourage students to "read" to themselves, to you, and to each other, even though that reading may be a simple retelling of the story. By providing them with opportunities to interact with books in this way, you will be setting the scene for their construction of more advanced understandings about the reading process. You might provide ten minutes a day for reading time. Schedule it to follow your read-aloud segment so that students can choose to read or retell a book that you have just read. Students can read alone, to you, or to a classmate. Explain to them that they do not have to read like adults; they can read in their own way (Sulzby & Barnhart, 1992). You might also provide a read-aloud center where students can read to a doll or stuffed animal or read along with a taped or CD-ROM version of a story.

Observe children as they read to themselves (young children's "silent" reading is generally audible), to a stuffed animal, to a friend, or to you. Observing children's storybook reading will provide insight into their understanding of the reading process, which has implications for instruction. If children do not use storybook intonation, for example, they may not have a grasp of the language of books and so may need to be read to (Sulzby & Barnhart, 1992). Until they have

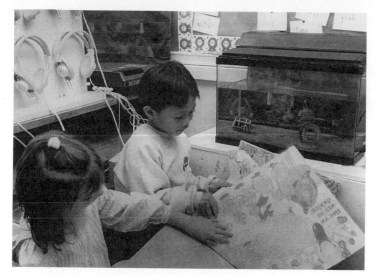

Students should be encouraged to read to each other, even though this rereading may be a simple retelling of the story.

a sense of literary language, children may have difficulty grasping the concept that the printed words on a page convey the story and can be read aloud.

USING SHARED BOOK EXPERIENCES

An excellent way to help students construct concepts of print (words are made up of letters, sentences are made up of words, reading goes from left to right and top to bottom, etc.) and other essential understandings is the **shared book experience.** Shared book experience is modeled on the bedtime story situation in which a parent or grandparent reads to a child, and, through observation and interaction, the child discovers the purpose of and satisfaction provided by books and begins to construct basic concepts of print (Holdaway, 1979). In order to make the print visible to a group, enlarged text or multiple copies are used. There are several ways of providing enlarged text. Holdaway (1979) suggested using a **big book,** an oversized book measuring approximately fifteen by nineteen inches, in which the text is large enough that students can follow the print as the teacher reads. Alternatives to a big book include using an opaque projector or an overhead projector and transparencies or carefully printing parts of the text on story paper or the chalkboard.

Before reading a big book, introduce the selection by discussing the title and cover illustration. Invite students to predict what the story might be about, build background and interest, and set a purpose for reading it. If it is a story that has already been shared with the class, the purpose can grow out of the original reading and discussion. Perhaps some details were not clear, and so children need to listen carefully to those parts. Or they may simply enjoy hearing a certain tale over and over again. The purpose also could lead to deeper involvement with the characters. Say, for example, that you have made a big book out of *Good as New*

Shared book experience, which is also known as shared reading, refers to the practice of reading repetitive stories, chants, poems, or songs, often from enlarged text, while the class follows along or joins in.

A **big book** is a book large enough that its words can be seen by all the members of the group or class.

Exemplary Teaching

Shared Reading with Big Books

Having seen the effectiveness of the traditional bedtime story, Don Holdaway (1979), a primary teacher, reading clinician, and consultant in Auckland, New Zealand, decided to duplicate this experience in a kindergarten classroom. Here is his account of trying out a big book—which he calls an "enlarged book"—for the first time:

> Now we bring out our first enlarged book— a version of *The Three Billy Goats Gruff*. We choose this partly because of the strongly emotional language of the repetitive section which may draw the children into prediction and participation even on the first reading. The children are delighted with the enormous book and many keep their eyes glued on it as we use a pointer to follow the story as we read. Sure enough, on the second occasion of the "Trip, trap!" and the "Who's that tripping over my bridge?" some of the children chime in, encouraged by the invitational cues we give off. They are delighted in the closing couplet, "Snip, snap, snout, This tale's told out," and want to say it for themselves. (p. 66)

The big book was a smashing success. After a period of experimentation and revision of the program, Holdaway concluded that the results seemed "more hopeful than we might at first have supposed" (p. 79). The shared experience apparently began a cycle of success in which the reading of high-quality literature led to more positive and enjoyable teaching, which led to a greater degree of attention and higher level of personal satisfaction among pupils, which, in turn, led to higher levels of achievement.

(Douglas, 1982), the story of a badly damaged teddy bear that was refurbished by its owner's grandfather. Students might imagine that they are the child who owns the bear. Have them read along with you and describe how they feel when K. C. cries for the bear. As the story progresses, ask them what they think when K. C. plays with the bear and treats it very roughly. What do they feel when the bear is just about ruined?

As you read, let your hand glide under the words so that students have a sense of going from left to right and also begin to realize that printed words have spoken equivalents. Help them see where words begin and end. Also discuss key happenings, and clarify confusing elements; have students revise or make new predictions. However, do not interrupt the flow of the reading. Focus should be on having students enjoy the experience. After you have shared a book, discuss it with the class, just as you would after reading a book orally to them.

SUCCESSIVE READINGS

One goal of shared reading is to involve the students more deeply in the reading. If the book that you have shared with students is one they would like to read again, conduct a second shared reading. During this second reading, encourage students to join in by reading refrains, or repeated phrases, sentences, or words that are readily predictable from context or illustrations. They can do this chorally as a group or as individual volunteers. In these subsequent shared readings, continue to point to each word or let your hand glide under the word as you read it

Adapting instruction for at-risk students

Shared reading works especially well with low-achieving children. After a shared reading (as compared to a traditional oral reading of a storybook), students in general had richer retellings and were more enthusiastic; however, average and below-average students benefit most (Coombs, 1987).

so that students can see that you are reading individual words. During a second reading of the book *Are You My Mother?* (Eastman, 1960), for instance, point out the sentence "Are you my mother?" Point to each word as you read it. Have volunteers read the sentence. Again, point to each word as the sentence is being read. Then read the story once more. Tell students that you are going to read the story, but they are going to help. As you come to "Are you my mother?" pause and have the class read the sentence in unison as you sweep your hand under the line. Schedule the book for additional readings with choral reading of the repeated sentence. From time to time, have individual volunteers read the line.

Once a big book or other repetitive selection has been shared, have students engage in follow-up activities. Some may choose to listen to a taped version of the book while reading a regular-size edition of the big book. A small group may want to read the big book once more, with one of their members assuming the role of teacher. Some may want to read to a partner, while still others may want to listen to a new story in the listening center or draw an illustration related to the big book. Some may want to look at Komori's (1983) *Animal Mothers*, which uses realistic paintings to show how animal mothers get their babies to travel with them. Viewing a filmstrip, videotape, or CD-ROM disk on animal mothers and their young may be another option. Later, the class might compose a group-experience story based on observations of how the class's mother gerbil cares for her young. Some students may want to dictate an individual story telling how their cat or dog cared for its young. Some students may want to compose their own stories, using drawings and **invented spellings**. Invented spellings reflect the evolving concept of how letter-sound relationships should be represented and include items like "I KN RT" for "I can write."

Periodically, introduce other repetitive selections. They need not be stories—poems, rhymes, songs, and even jump rope chants are suitable. Some of these selections may be in big books; others can be written on the chalkboard or on chart paper. As students' understanding of print develops, introduce additional concepts: Point out that words are composed of letters, talk about the sounds in words, discuss words that rhyme or begin with the same sound, and help students see that some words begin with the same letter and the same sound. Also discuss **print conventions,** such as punctuation marks, capital letters, and quotation marks. And, whenever introducing a new selection, point out the title and author's name.

OTHER SHARED READING ACTIVITIES

As part of the shared reading activities, make time for introducing new big books or other materials. Holdaway (1984) suggested the following schedule of activities for children who are growing into reading:

1. *Tune In.* A well-liked but brief song, poem, nursery rhyme, or similar piece is written on chart paper or on the chalkboard and read, sung, or dramatized by the teacher or by the class in unison. Alternatively, parts may be assigned.
2. *Old Favorite.* A favorite tale is presented in a big book or other format that is readable by the whole class.
3. *Learning about Language.* A skill is presented; it may be related to the old favorite and may have to do with the concept of word or sentence, alphabet knowledge, or letter-sound relationships. When reading Galdone's (1975) ver-

Invented spellings are the intuitive spellings that students create before learning or while learning the conventional writing system.

Print conventions are generally accepted ways of putting words on a page, such as arranging words from left to right and using capital letters and end punctuation.

Students who have been read to will pick up many concepts of print through observing the reading and interacting with the person reading. Parents or teachers may point out words on the page or talk about the letters that certain words begin with. Over time, children may notice how print functions, ask questions about words and letters, or try to match print with the words being read.

sion of *The Gingerbread Boy*, the class might discuss the fact that *couldn't*, *catch*, and *cow* all begin with the same sound, or they might learn *run* or *can* as sight words, words that are learned through memorizing rather than through sounding out. Children might also become involved in predicting words that the teacher has masked with tape or a large sticky note. This demonstrates the use of context clues. If the old favorite is *Brown Bear, Brown Bear, What Do You See?* (Martin, 1983), the skill could be a discussion of questions and question marks.

4. *New Story*. A new selection is presented just about every day. It might be Ivimey's (1987) *The Complete Story of the Three Blind Mice* or another one of his much-loved books.

5. *Independent Reading and Activity*. Students are given a choice of follow-up activities. A favorite for *Three Blind Mice* is listening to the musical version of the tale. The next day, the children might sing it themselves.

USING THE LANGUAGE EXPERIENCE APPROACH

Language experience is an approach to literacy teaching in which one or a group of students dictates a story, which is then used as a basis for reading and writing instruction.

Language experience stories can also be used to introduce the visual aspects of reading. They may be used instead of or in conjunction with big books and may be created by students working in groups or by individuals. As the name suggests, **language experience** is based on real-life experiences. For instance, the story in Figure 2.2 began with a class trip to a nearby apple orchard. When they returned to school, the students discussed the orchard and drew pictures to illustrate their trip. Pictures often result in more focused, coherent stories because they encapsulate the child's experience (Platt, 1978). The teacher (or an aide) discusses each child's picture, after which the child dictates a story about it. As the teacher writes the child's dictated story, the teacher tells the student what he or she is doing. Then the teacher reads the story back and asks if that is what the child wanted to say. The teacher invites the child to add to the story or make other changes. Once

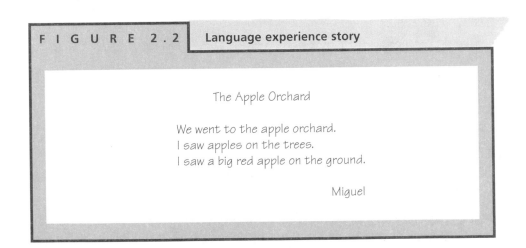

FIGURE 2.2 | Language experience story

The Apple Orchard

We went to the apple orchard.
I saw apples on the trees.
I saw a big red apple on the ground.

Miguel

any requested changes have been made, the teacher again reads the story. Then the teacher and the child read the story together. After this shared reading, the child is invited to read his or her story to the teacher. Aided by the drawing and the familiarity of the experience, children usually are able to read their stories.

Individual stories are gathered into books, which children are encouraged to take home and read to their parents. During the school year, students might create anywhere from one to a dozen books, depending on their interest in the activity and their emerging skills.

A NEW CONCEPT OF WRITING

Traditionally, writing was not taught until after students started reading. Often, it was equated with handwriting, copying, and spelling instruction. However, writing is not simply a matter of forming letters (Holdaway, 1979); it is a way of representing the world, progressing from apparently random scribbles to meaningful marks to increasingly more conventional letters and spellings. From their first day in school, children should be encouraged to write as best they can in whatever way they can, whether by drawings, letterlike forms, or invented spellings.

Literacy is constructed internally, not imposed from the outside. By observing everyday reading and writing, children form concepts about the nature and purposes of acts of literacy. Given their experiences with writing, they may construct the hypothesis that the first letter of someone's name stands for and belongs to that person, so that no one else may have that letter (Ferreiro, 1986). Later, when they see that other people's names begin with the same letter, they must revise this hypothesis. With additional encounters and reconstructions of their hypotheses, children gradually build a more conventional view of the writing system. The key to this process is continuing experience with print and lots of opportunities to write.

Regardless of where students are on the path to conventional writing, teachers should encourage them to write and draw, should accept and support their efforts, and should resist correcting "errors." Teachers should model the process, allowing students to see them writing on the chalkboard, chart paper, word processor, notepaper, and so on. Attempts at writing lead to discoveries about the system that help students gain essential insights into both writing and reading.

DEVELOPMENT OF SPELLING

When does writing start? At the age of 18 months, average toddlers will make marks on paper (Gibson & Levin, 1974). Apparently, the children enjoy the movement, but they also do it because of what they can create. When given an instrument that makes no mark, young writers soon cease the activity (S. Gibson & Yonas, 1968, cited in E. Gibson & Levin, 1974). Even the youngest writers like to see what they have written.

By age three, scribbling is no longer random or unorganized (Harste, Woodward, & Burke, 1984). Because it proceeds in a straight line across the page and may be composed of up-and-down or curved marks, it resembles genuine writing. In time, youngsters may create letterlike figures, may use a combination of numbers and letters, and may eventually use letters. Along the way, they discover the concept of sign (Clay, 1975)—that is, they arbitrarily use a graphic element to represent an idea or a word, a syllable, or a sound. For example, the child may use the letter *b* or *x* or a self-created letterlike form to represent the word *ball*.

The earliest spelling is prephonemic. At this stage, children realize that letters are used to create words but have not caught on to the alphabetic principle—that is, that letters represent sounds. At age four, Paul Bissex used strings of letters to cheer his mother up. The letters were a random selection and were designed to convey the messages "Welcome home" in one instance and "Cheer up" in another (Bissex, 1980).

The next stage of spelling is phonemic (also known as early letter-name), as children start putting the alphabetic principle to work. Single letters may at first represent whole words but later stand for syllables and then represent single sounds (Ferreiro, 1986). For instance, the letter *k* may be used to represent the word *car*. In later phases of this stage, a child may add the final consonant, spelling *car* as KR. Some consonant combination spellings may at first seem to have no connection to their sounds: *tr* is frequently spelled CH, and *dr* may be spelled JR. Try saying "train." Listen very carefully to the initial sound. The beginning sound is actually /ch/. Likewise, the *d* in *dr* combinations has a /j/ sound. The child is spelling what she or he hears (Read, 1971).

In time, the child begins representing vowel sounds and enters the letter-naming stage. In this stage, children continue to employ a strategy in which a letter is used to represent the sound heard in the letter's name, so *late* would be spelled LAT and *feet* would be spelled FET. This works for most consonants and long vowels but not for short ones, as the names of short vowels do not contain their pronunciations. To spell short vowels, children employ the "close to" tactic, in which they use the long-vowel name that is closest to the point in the mouth where the short vowel to be spelled is articulated. For instance, short *e* is formed very close to the point where long *a* is articulated, so the child spells short *e* with an A, as in BAD for *bed*. Based on the "close to" tactic, short *i* is spelled with an E, short *o* with an I, and short *u* with an O (Read, 1971).

As they are exposed to standard spellings in books and environmental print, children begin to notice that spelling incorporates certain conventions—that final *e* is used to mark long vowels, for instance. They enter the within-word pattern stage in which they begin to use visual or orthographic elements along with sound elements in their spelling (Henderson, 1990). Their spelling is no longer strictly guided by sound. Although their spelling may not always be accurate, they begin to use final *e* markers and double vowel letters to spell long vowel sounds. They might spell *mean* as MEEN or MENE. However, they begin to spell short vowels accurately. As children progress through this stage, their spelling becomes conventional, and ultimately they move into the stages of syllable juncture and derivational constancy, which are advanced stages of conventional spelling involving multisyllabic words (Henderson, 1990). See Table 2.2 for examples of the major stages of spelling. These stages of spelling are incorporated into the forms of emergent writing described below.

FORMS OF EMERGENT WRITING

Children's writing develops through seven forms, beginning with drawing and ending with conventional spelling. These forms include the spelling stages depicted

TABLE 2.2 Stages of spelling

Age	Stage	Example
18 months	Random scribbling	*cruo*
3 years	Wordlike scribbling	*m~*
4–5 years	Prephonemic writing	LWIƆ
4–6+ years	Phonemic spelling	WL
5–7+ years	Letter-name	WAL
6–7+ years	Within-word pattern	wale
8–10+ years	Syllable juncture	whaling
10–20+ years	Derivational constancy	aquatic

in Table 2.2 but go beyond spelling to include the writer's intentions. The major forms of emergent writing described in Table 2.3 are based on research completed with kindergarten students (Sulzby, Barnhart, & Hieshima, 1989).

At the beginning of the kindergarten year, many children are operating on a scribble level. Some continue to use that form throughout the year. However, even though some students cling to a scribble form of writing, the scribbles at the end of the year are more advanced than those created at the beginning of the year. How can one scribbled story be more advanced than another? Although, on the surface, two scribbled stories may seem very similar, they may have very different meanings for their creators. In children's writing, there may be more on the page than meets the eye. Sulzby (1989) cautions, "One can only judge the quality of the form of writing by comparing it with the rereading a child uses with it" (p. 51).

After students write stories in whatever form or forms they choose, they are asked to read them. Just as in emergent storybook readings, described in Table 2.1, students reread their pieces on a variety of levels of sophistication. A child asked to reread a scribble story may simply retell a story that apparently has no connection with the scribbles. Another child may read the scribble as though he or she is reading conventional writing. The child's voice may incorporate the intonation of a story. He or she may even point to the scribbles as they are read as though pointing to a line of words. When the child comes to the end of the scribbles, his or her rereading ceases. When asked to reread the scribbles, the child may use exactly the same words to retell the tale. In a sense, the student is reading the scribbles. Categories of rereading are presented in Table 2.4.

ENCOURAGING CHILDREN TO WRITE

Whether they are drawing, scribbling, copying, creating invented spellings, or entering into a transitional phase, children should be encouraged to write. The program should be informal but functional. The first prerequisite is that each

Through observation and discreet probing, find out where children are in their writing development. Some may be drawing or scribble writing; others may have advanced into invented or even conventional spelling. Also note how children approach the task of writing. Do they jump right in, or are they hesitant and unsure? Affirm children's efforts and encourage them, especially those who are timid or reluctant writers.

TABLE 2.3 Forms of emergent writing

Form	Description
Drawing	The drawing is not an illustration for a story but is the story itself. The child reads the drawing as though it were text.
Scribbling	The scribbling resembles a line of writing. It might have the appearance of a series of waves or, in a more advanced representation, may resemble a series of letterlike forms.
Letterlike forms	Letterlike forms resemble manuscript or cursive letters and are generally written as separate forms rather than the continuous forms seen in scribbling. They are not real letters, and care needs to be taken that poorly formed real letters are not placed in this category.
Prephonemic spelling	The child writes with real letters, but the letters are a random collection or a meaningless pattern, such as repeating the same letter. Although the letters are real, they do not represent sounds.
Copying	The child copies from print found in his or her environment: signs, labels, etc. One child copied from a crayon box but, when asked to read his piece, told a story that had nothing to do with crayons (Sulzby, 1989).
Invented spelling	Students make use of the alphabetic principle. The letters they write represent sounds. Initially, one letter may represent a whole word. Over time, there is a gradual movement to conventional spelling. See Table 2.2 for a chart of spelling stages, including the several stages of invented spelling.
Conventional spelling	Student's spelling is conventional.

Based on Appendix 2.1, Forms of Writing and Rereading, Example List (pp. 51–63) by E. Sulzby (1989). In J. M. Mason (Ed.), *Reading and Writing Connections*. Boston: Allyn & Bacon.

student should realize that she or he has something to say. Whatever a student produces should be accepted and valued.

The teacher's role should be an active one, modeling the writing process at every opportunity. When the teacher is writing a note to parents explaining a field trip, the children should be shown what the teacher is doing. They should see the teacher create signs for the room, draw up a list of supplies, complete a book order, and write messages on the board. Seeing real writing done for real purposes is especially important for students who may not have seen their parents do much writing.

Invitations to write should be extended to the children. The teacher might ask them to write about things they like to do. The teacher should model the process by writing a piece that tells what he or she likes to do. Students should then be encouraged to write as best they can or in any way they can. If they wish, they can

TABLE 2.4 Rereading from emergent writing

Category	Description
Null	The child refuses to read the story he or she has written, says that he or she cannot read it, or comments that nothing was written or the story does not say anything.
Labeling/describing	The child supplies labels or a description instead of reading. The child says "cat" or "This is a cat." A one-word response is a label; a sentence response is a description.
Dialogue	The child only responds if you ask questions, so the interchange takes on a question-answer format. The question-answer interchange may be initiated by the child.
Oral monologue	The child tells a story in the style of an oral retelling. It does not have the characteristics of the reading of a piece of writing.
Written monologue	The reading sounds as though the child is reading from a written piece. It has the sound and flow of oral reading of written text, but the child is not actually reading from the written piece.
Naming letters	The child names the letters that have been written.
Aspectual/strategic reading	The child is beginning to attend to the writing and may attempt to sound out some words and phrases while skipping others. The child may read the written piece while looking at the written words, but the written words may not completely match up with what the child is reading.
Conventional	The child uses the written words to read. The rendition may sound like written monologue, but the main difference is that the child is deciphering the written words while reading.

Based on Appendix 2.1, Forms of Writing and Rereading, Example List (pp. 51–63) by E. Sulzby (1989). In J. M. Mason (Ed.), *Reading and Writing Connections*. Boston: Allyn & Bacon.

draw pictures showing what they like to do, or they may both draw and write. The teacher should show samples of the various ways that children write—including scribbling, random letter strings, drawings, and invented spellings—and explain that each student is to write in her or his own way, the way a child might write.

During the year, the students should engage in several writing projects, such as letters or invitations to family members and friends, stories, accounts of personal experiences, and lists. After writing a piece, a child should read it to an adult, who might want to transcribe it on another sheet of paper if the original is not readable. Transcriptions should be kept with the written pieces in a writing folder, which becomes a file of the child's writing development. As Sulzby and Barnhart (1992) commented,

> Many people are still shocked at the ease with which children at kindergarten age (or younger) write, when we invite them and if we accept the forms of writing they prefer. From working with and observing hundreds of classrooms, we can say confidently that all kindergarteners reared in a literate culture like our own can and will write. (pp. 125–126)

Reinforce the concepts of print and print conventions whenever the opportunity presents itself. For instance, let students see you write on the board. Emphasize that you are writing from left to right. If you are writing information that students are giving you, tell them that you are writing their words. Explain that you are using a capital letter because you are starting a sentence and are putting down a period because you have finished the sentence.

REAL WRITING FOR REAL PURPOSES

Emphasis in a writing program for young children is on writing a variety of pieces for a variety of reasons. Young children adopt different strategies for different tasks. They might use invented spelling when compiling a list but use scribble writing for a lengthy tale (Martinez & Teale, 1987). Real-life activities have the effect of motivating them to use more sophisticated techniques.

Functional writing tasks have proven especially effective in facilitating students' development. This became apparent in the first year of the Kindergarten Emergent Literacy Program, an experimental program that included daily writing. When writing invitations for the class's Thanksgiving feast, many children, who until that time had used scribble writing, chose to use random strings of letters or even to attempt to spell words (Martinez & Teale, 1987). Other effective writing activities include making lists, writing names, and using routines.

Making Lists. One writing activity on which young children thrive is making lists. Clay (1975) called the motivation for this activity the inventory principle. Novice writers enjoy creating an inventory of letters or words that they can write. Suggested assignments include making lists of friends, family members, favorite foods, places visited, favorite toys, and so on.

Writing Names. One of the first words that children learn to spell is their name. Special attention should be given to this task, because once children learn their names, they frequently use the letters to spell other words. Thus each name becomes a source of known letters that can be used in various sequences and combinations (Temple, Nathan, Burris, & Temple, 1988).

Take full advantage of children's interest in their names. Put name tags on their cubbyholes, coat hooks, and/or shelf spaces. Ask the children to sign all their written work. When scheduling individuals for activities or assignments, write their names on the chalkboard so that they become used to seeing and reading their own names, as well as those of the other children.

In writing, form follows function. Children learn the functions of writing before they learn the forms. With their scribbles, they compose signs, invitations, and letters to grandparents (Parker & Morrow, 1994). Modeling is an important part of children's early writing attempts. In writing letters and notes, they imitate what they have seen parents, teachers, and older siblings do. Although much of children's writing is self-initiated and children may invent many of the forms they use, they respond to and seek out the support and guidance of adults.

Using Routines.   Whenever possible, use routines to demonstrate literacy lessons. The Kamehameha School in Honolulu, Hawaii, uses a device known as the morning message to impart literacy skills (Kawakami-Arakaki, Oshiro, & Farran, 1989). Written by the teacher, the morning message gives the date and important information about the day's activities. Messages in the beginning of the year are relatively simple, but they become increasingly complex to match the growth in children's skills. A September message might be "Today is Monday, September 12. We will go to the firehouse this morning." The teacher reads it aloud and encourages the students to read along with her. At this juncture, the teacher wants the children to see that writing is functional (it conveys important information), that one reads from left to right and top to bottom, and that written messages are made up of individual words and numbers. Later, longer messages are written, and more sophisticated skills—such as the concepts that words are made up of sounds and that certain sounds are represented by certain letters—are stressed.

Morning messages can be used to introduce or reinforce a variety of skills, such as capitalizing the names of the months, using end punctuation, and so on. Students can also be encouraged to add to the morning message. This assures them that what they have to say is important. These additions also help students and teacher get to know each other better, as the students' contributions might

Exemplary Teaching

Writing in Kindergarten

Using integrated units as a framework, Irmie Fallon's kindergarteners explored a variety of topics—ranches, hospitals, presidents, and seasons (Fallon & Allen, 1994). The explorations revolved around three basic questions: What do we know? What do we want to learn? How can we find out? The class's explorations involved field trips, discussions, being read to, and lots of student reading and writing. Students wrote on topics being explored but also had opportunities for self-selected writing. Through their writing, the children expanded and clarified concepts. One student, Mark, brought a woolly bear caterpillar to school and learned its features by writing a careful description of it. When another student, Brian, drew a spider with eight legs on each side of the creature, Fallon discussed the meanings of "on each side" and "altogether." When Kady wrote about Columbus taking part in a feast called Thanksgiving, Fallon created a timeline showing Columbus's voyages, the voyage of the *Mayflower,* and other key events.

The class embarked on a study of antelopes when one child, writing about Kansas's state song, wrote "where the deer and the cantaloupe play." As Fallon learned how the students constructed meaning from their experiences, she was better able to build on what they knew and could do. Having carefully observed her children and learned from them, she was better able to promote their learning.

In looking back over her twenty-two years as a kindergarten teacher, Fallon concluded that the foundation in her program was putting children at the center of what she did. Children flourished when someone really listened to what they said and wrote, when their contributions were valued, when the teacher inquired about their interests, concerns, and questions. Having children write on topics of their choosing as well as directed topics was also an important factor. Children's self-selected writings often proved to be a "window into children's interpretation of learning experiences" (p. 551).

include major family events such as the birth of siblings or the death of grandparents and other news of personal importance.

HELP WITH SPELLING

One question that arises in a program emphasizing invented spelling is what to do when children ask how to spell a word. The advice offered most often is to encourage them to spell it as best they can or to say the word very slowly and work out the spelling. You might ask, "How does the word start? What letter comes first? What letter comes next?" The idea is to have students develop their own sense of the spelling system. If you spell words for students, they will begin to rely on your help instead of constructing their own spellings. Keep in mind that students' invented spellings reflect their understanding of the spelling system. Words that they create belong to them in a way that words that are spelled for them do not (Wilde, 1995).

However, Henderson (1981) believed that children need information about spelling:

> Children bring a remarkable body of knowledge to their initial attempts at word formation. To augment that knowledge, they must exercise their ideas and test them against what is given. They must have an opportunity to make errors in word construction, and they must have access to standard spelling, not only in the eye but in the mind. Pedagogically the trick will be to keep their modes in balance—the disposition to construct in certain ways and the knowledge of "what is right." (p. 69)

Providing access to standard spelling could take the form of having picture dictionaries available; placing some frequently requested words on the board; posting word lists of animals, families, colors, foods, or other related words; labeling items; or creating a word wall (see Chapter 3). It could also mean providing assistance when students are unable to work out the spelling of a word and you believe that providing help will further their development. Occasionally, you might have students attempt to spell the word as best they can and then write the conventional spelling above their attempt, saying, "Here's how we usually spell _____. Look how close you came" (Ruddell & Ruddell, 1995, p. 103). Any help that you supply should take into account the child's understanding of the spelling system. If, for instance, the child spells *truck* with CH, you should say, "*Truck* sounds like it begins with a *ch* as in *Charles,* but it begins with a *t* as in *Tim* and an *r* as in *Raymond*" (Wilde, 1995).

Whatever you do, have a clear policy—one based on your beliefs about invented spelling. Be sure to explain your policy to both students and their parents. Figure 2.3 shows examples of a child's use of invented spelling in kindergarten and in first grade.

One reason for encouraging children to write before they can spell conventionally is that it gives them a reason to learn the real system, the "code":

> What we must avoid in school at all costs, with regard to both writing and reading, is any approach which denies children the possibility of *shaping their own meaning* from the very start. Conscientious efforts to give children plenty of practice, learning the code first, only serve to confuse, where they were intended to simplify, because the child is being required apparently, to learn the code for its own sake and not as a powerful mode of expression for his own thoughts, feelings and recollections. (D'Arcy, 1989, p. 23)

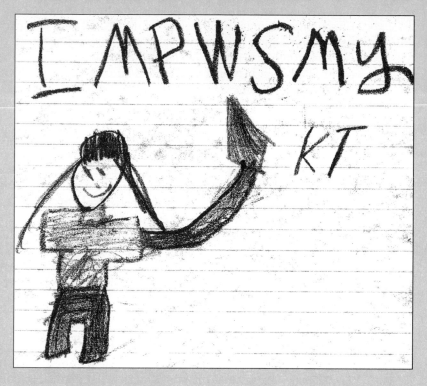

(a) Kindergarten

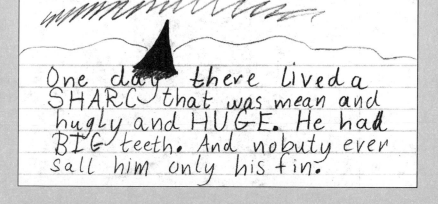

One day there lived a
SHARC that was mean and
hugly and HUGE. He had
BIG teeth. And nobuty ever
sall him only his fin.

(b) First Grade

From stories written by Anne Lincoln. Used by permission.

DICTATION IN THE WRITING PROGRAM

Although students should be encouraged to write as best they can, they may choose to dictate on occasion, such as when they are expressing heartfelt feelings or recounting events that touch them deeply. The content may be so intense that they cannot handle both it and the form. For example, one young student, who usually wrote on her own, chose to dictate when she told the story of how her mother had been involved in a serious auto accident. Both teacher-initiated and child-initiated writing and dictation are vital elements of a literacy program, as "they provide process as well as content for beginning reading" (Fields, Spangler, & Lee, 1991, p. 52).

Dictation is the process of recounting an experience orally and having someone else write down the words.

With the acceptance of invented spelling as a valid means of expression, dictation of experience stories has been deemphasized. However, research and practice suggest that children's dictated pieces are more fully developed than those they compose themselves. When content is essential, dictation may be the better approach.

Dictation helps children see the relationship between speaking and writing. They can see that if they speak too fast, the scribe has a difficult time keeping up. Over time, they learn to pace their dictation so that it matches the scribe's ability to record it. Of course, the scribe can also point out letters, words, and sentences as she or he writes so that the child is better able to see the relationship between written and spoken language. One thing that should be made clear is the role of dictation. The teacher does not want to create the impression that she or he is writing because the student cannot. The teacher should explain that dictating is another way of writing. In addition to being used to capture emotional stories that individuals have to tell, dictated writing can also be used to record a group experience (Sulzby, Teale, & Kamberelis, 1989).

PLANNED INSTRUCTION OF ESSENTIAL UNDERSTANDINGS

Setting the stage for developing reading and writing is important and arranging for many opportunities to read and write is vital, but explicit instruction should also be a key element in the literacy program. This is especially true when students are struggling. As Lesley Mandel Morrow (1994), an authority on emergent literacy, explains,

> Early in the emergent literacy and whole language movements, direct instruction was looked upon as the skill, drill, teach, test approach and had no place within whole language or emergent literacy classrooms. As we have spent a few years exploring these new ideas, we have come to realize that some of the old can blend and is needed along with the new. Direct instruction is important for most children. However, this type of instruction needs to be directed at the needs of individuals and to be a small part of the literacy program. . . . Without this direct instruction component, some children would miss learning many important skills. (p. 120)

Direct instruction should take place within the context of the kinds of reading and writing activities that are being explored in this chapter. As whole language advocate Constance Weaver (1994) explains,

> The teacher offers direct instruction, mostly within the context of authentic reading, writing, and learning experiences, when the learners' interest and motivation are high and/or when they demonstrate a definite need for instruction. (p. 95)

Two areas in which students are most likely to need direct instruction are phonological awareness (ability to detect separate sounds in words, rhyme, and beginning sounds) and the alphabetic principle (the system by which speech sounds are represented by letters). In fact, the major cause of difficulty in learning to read is a deficiency in these areas (Adams, 1990). Although being read to, participating in shared reading, and engaging in storybook reading and writing activities help students explore the purpose and nature of reading and writing, many students may still need instruction in these two critical areas. Knowledge of the alphabet can also be very helpful.

LEARNING THE LETTERS OF THE ALPHABET

Theoretically, it is not necessary to know the names of the letters of the alphabet in order to learn how the alphabetic system works. However, letter knowledge does facilitate instruction and gives an indication that the child has some memory for abstract visual symbols. It also facilitates long-term storage. Children who can name the letters of the alphabet with ease become better readers. Learning the names of the letters may be preparation for learning the sounds associated with the letters (Walsh, Price, & Gillingham, 1988). As noted earlier, children use their knowledge of letter names in their spelling. It is also essential that the child be able to distinguish one letter from another.

According to research by Durrell (1958), the ability to name letters is one of the best predictors of later success in reading. Since most children will probably begin school with some ability in this area, it is important for the teacher to build on that base. In addition to having a sense of how many letters students know, the teacher should also be aware of the level of that knowledge. Children's insight into letters develops with experience. For some, letters are simply objects that have a certain name and shape. They have not grasped that letters can represent sounds or even that they are used to spell words. As McGee and Richgels noted (1989), some children are focusing on the shapes of letters, others may be discovering that words are composed of letters, and some may be catching on to the alphabetic principle.

When should students be introduced to the letters of the alphabet? "As soon as the child is encouraged to write his name, his attention is being directed to letters. Often the first two or three letters that occur in his name become distinctive because of these efforts," comments Marie Clay (1991, pp. 266–267).

Teaching the Letters of the Alphabet.   Although it seems logical that students would learn letters by memorizing their shapes, that is not the way it happens. They learn to tell one letter from another and to identify particular letters by noting distinctive features such as whether lines are curved or slanted, open or closed (Gibson, Gibson, Pick, & Osser, 1962). To perceive distinctive features, students must be given many experiences comparing and contrasting letters. When introducing letters, teachers should present at least two at a time so that students can contrast them. It is also a good idea to present letters that have dissimilar appearances—s and b, for instance. Presenting similar letters such as b and d together can cause confusion. It is recommended, too, that upper- and lower-case forms of the letters be introduced at the same time, since students will see both in their reading.

Using names is a good way to introduce the alphabet. Discuss the fact that names are made up of letters. Write your name on the board, and talk about the letters in it. Explain that your first and last names begin with capital letters and that the other letters are lower-case. Write the names of some students, perhaps those that begin with the first three or four letters of the alphabet, and then move to other letters on succeeding days.

To emphasize a letter, ask students to raise their hands if their name has that letter—*m*, for example. Ask them to spell out their names; give assistance if they need it. Write the names on the board—*Manuel, Marcella,* and *Tom,* for example—and have students tell where the *m* is in each name.

Create signs for the class: "Writing Center," "In," "Out," and so on. Let students see you make the signs, and talk about the letters you used. Bring in familiar objects, such as cereal boxes, signs, and posters, and discuss the words printed on them and the letters that make up the words.

Obtain a computer or a typewriter, or both. Keyboards invite exploration of the alphabet. If you are using Dr. Peet's Talk/Writer (Hartley) or another word-processing program that has speech capability, the name of the letter will be pronounced when the child presses the key. Stamp printing sets and magnetic and felt letters also encourage working with the alphabet.

As with all learning activities, proceed from the concrete to the abstract. Letters by their very nature are abstract; when they are in the contexts of names, signs, and labels, they are more concrete than letters in isolation.

Display a model alphabet so that students can see how letters are formed. Try to provide each child with his or her own alphabet to refer to as needed. At this point, do not emphasize letter formation. Students who are overly conscious of forming their letters perfectly will have a difficult time moving beyond that task to writing.

Read to the class some of the many alphabet books that are available. *A to Zoo Subject Access to Children's Picture Books,* 2nd ed. (Lima & Lima, 1993) lists more than 200 alphabet books. Some of them are listed in the Children's Book List. Look for books that present the letters clearly. Overly ornate letters may be aesthetically pleasing, but they can be distracting and confusing. Many of these books show words containing the beginning sound that a particular letter frequently represents. Do not emphasize these letter-sound relationships, as they require advanced skill. Focus instead on the appearance of each letter and how it differs from a similarly formed letter—for example, how *y* is different from *t*. Point out that letters have two forms—capital and lower case. Avoid the words *little* and *big* so that children do not use size to determine whether a letter is upper or lower case. When possible, choose alphabet books that present both forms.

There are two major kinds of typefaces: serif and sans serif. A serif is a small line used to complete a stroke in a letter; sans serif type lacks these strokes. Serif type is more distinctive and probably easier to read than sans serif type. However, the *a*'s and *g*'s in sans serif type are similar to the *a*'s and *g*'s in manuscript writing and so may be easier for emergent readers to identify. At any rate, young children need to know that *a* and *g* may be formed in more than one way.

Children's Book List
Alphabet books

Aylesworth, J. *Old Black Fly.* New York: Holt (1991). Rhyming text follows a mischievous black fly through the alphabet as he has a very busy day landing where he should not be.

Ehlert, L. *Eating the Alphabet.* New York: Harcourt (1989). Drawings of foods beginning with letter being presented are labeled with their names in both upper- and lower-case letters.

Greenfield, E. *Aaron and Gayle's Alphabet Book.* New York: Black Butterfly Children's Books (1993). Alphabet letters are used as part of a key word within the context of a whole sentence.

Hoban, T. *A, B, See!* New York: Greenwillow (1982). Upper-case letters are accompanied by objects in silhouette that begin with the letter that is shown.

King-Smith, D. *Alphabeasts*. New York: Macmillan (1992). A poetic look is taken at unusual animals through the alphabet, from the anaconda to the zambia.

Mullins, P. *V for Vanishing: An Alphabet of Endangered Animals*. New York: HarperCollins (1994). Endangered and extinct animals from around the world are featured.

Musgrove, M. *Ashanti to Zulu*. New York: Dial (1976). This Caldecott winner gives information about African tribes as it presents the alphabet.

Scarry, R. *Richard Scarry's Find Your ABC*. New York: Random (1973). Each letter is illustrated with numerous objects and creatures whose names contain the letter. Names of the objects are placed nearby with the target letter printed in red, except for two letters, one capital and one lower case, that are printed in black. Readers are urged to find the black letters.

Shirley, G. C. *A Is for Animals*. New York: Simon & Schuster, Inc. (1991). Illustrations and information are provided about animals whose names begin with the target letter.

Wildsmith, B. *Brian Wildsmith's ABC*. New York: Watts (1963). Upper- and lower-case letters are illustrated with colorful drawings of things whose names begin with each letter.

Reinforcement Activities
Alphabet knowledge

- Have children create their own alphabet books.
- Help children create name cards. Explain that names begin with capital letters but that the other letters in a name are lower case.
- Make a big book of the alphabet song, and point to the letters and words as children sing along.
- If children are using classroom computers, teach the letters of the alphabet as you teach them keyboarding skills.
- Encourage students to write as best they can. This will foster learning the alphabet as they move from using pictures and letterlike forms to real letters to express themselves. Children's early writing and invented spelling tend to be written in capital letters, which are easier to make. Even those who know both forms tend to write in all capital letters (Bissex, 1980). At this early stage of development, refrain from correction since that could discourage students' output and exploration. As they approach the letter-name stage—or whenever you feel it is appropriate—guide them toward using both types of letters.
- As you write messages, announcements, or stories on the board, spell out the words so that students will hear the names of the letters in a very natural way.
- Sing songs such as "Bingo" and "Old MacDonald Had a Farm," which spell out words or use letters as part of their lyrics.

- Most important, provide an environment in which the child is surrounded by print. Encourage students to engage in reading and writing activities. These might include "reading" a wordless picture book, using a combination of drawings and letterlike figures to compose a story, creating some sort of list, using invented spelling to write a letter to a friend, exploring a computer keyboard, or listening to a taped account of a story. Interaction with print leads to knowledge of print. The ability to form letters improves without direct instruction (Hildreth, 1936).

BUILDING PHONOLOGICAL AWARENESS

For children, the sounds in words blur so that words seem like the continuation of a single sound. In their natural environment, children do not have to deal with individual sounds; however, the ability to segment words is absolutely crucial for literacy development. If children cannot hear the separate sounds in *hat* or the beginning sound of *ball,* they will not be able to read or write, except in a primitive way. They may learn to read a few words by sheer rote memory but will not be able to sound out words. Without the ability to hear separate sounds, they will not be able to understand, for example, that the letter *b* stands for the sound /b/ heard at the beginning of *ball.* They will not even be able to consider a beginning sound because they will not be able to abstract it from the word itself. These children will also have difficulty with rhyme because of their inability to abstract the ending sounds. They may be able to write a few letters, but their writing will not evolve beyond the early phonemic stage because they will be unable to isolate the sounds of words.

Savin (1972) stated, "In the present author's experience everyone who has failed to learn to read even the simplest prose by the end of first grade has been unable to analyze syllables into phonemes" (p. 321). **Phonemes** are individual speech sounds. The word *cake* has four letters but three phonemes: /k/, /ā/, /k/. Savin's assertion was echoed by Elkonin (1973), a Russian psychologist, who maintained that being able to analyze the sounds of words "is the most important prerequisite for the successful learning of reading and writing" (p. 571).

What makes detecting sounds in words so difficult? Two elements: metalinguistic awareness and coarticulation. Metalinguistic awareness requires students to reflect on language on an abstract level, to treat language as an object of thought. **Coarticulation** is a feature of language that makes listening and speaking easy but makes reading difficult. For instance, when saying the word *cat,* you do not say /k/, /a/, /t/; you coarticulate the phonemes: As you form the /k/, you also form the /a/, and as the /a/ is being formed, you coarticulate the final sound /t/. Because of coarticulation, *cat* is a blend of sounds, rather than three separate sounds. Coarticulation makes it easier to form and perceive words. However, because the sounds in the words are coarticulated, they seem to be one continuous sound and so are difficult for young children to ply apart (Liberman & Shankweiler, 1991).

Word Play.   One of the best ways to develop phonological awareness is to have fun with words. As students play and experiment with language, they become aware of it on a more abstract level. They begin to think of words as words and hear the sounds of language on an abstract level. In addition to playing games

Phoneme refers to the smallest unit of sound that distinguishes one word from another. *Pit* is different from *pat* because of the difference in the phonemes /i/ and /a/.

Coarticulation is the process of articulating a sound while still articulating the previous sound—for instance, saying /oy/ while still articulating /t/ in *toy.*

with words in the classroom, read books that have fun with words, especially those that call attention to the parts of words.

An excellent book for developing phonological awareness is *Jamberry* (Degan, 1983), in which both real and nonsense words are formed by adding *berry* to a variety of words. After reading the tale to students, have them create *berry* words. *Don't Forget the Bacon!* (Hutchins, 1976) is another good choice for developing phonological awareness. Afraid that he will forget an item on his shopping list (six farm eggs, a cake for tea, and a pound of pears), the child rehearses the list as he heads for the store. Unfortunately, as he rehearses it, he makes substitutions in some of the words so that "a cake for tea" becomes "a cake for me" and later "a rake for leaves." Read the story to students, and discuss how the boy kept changing the sounds. This will build their awareness of sounds in words. Also have them role-play the child rehearsing the shopping list so that they can see firsthand how the sounds in the words are changed (Griffith & Olson, 1992). Other books that play with sounds include most of the Dr. Seuss books and the sheep series by Shaw (including *Sheep in a Jeep, Sheep on a Ship,* and *Sheep in a Shop*).

Developing the Concept of Rhyme.   Since longer units are easier to perceive than individual speech sounds, a good place to begin to develop phonological awareness is through rhymes, which are the easiest of the phonological awareness tasks (Yopp, 1988). Read nursery rhymes and other rhyming tales to the students to help them develop the ability to detect rhyme. In a study conducted in Great Britain, children who knew nursery rhymes were better at detecting rhyme and also did better in early reading than those who had no such knowledge (Maclean, Bryant, & Bradley, 1987). At first, just read the nursery rhymes and rhyming tales so that the children enjoy the stories and the sounds. They may memorize some of the rhymes if they wish. Books that might be used to introduce and reinforce the concept of rhyme are listed in the Children's Book List.

Children's Book List
Rhyming books

Aylesworth, J. *One Crow, a Counting Rhyme.* Philadelphia: Lippincott (1988). The numbers 0 through 10 are presented through rhyming verses. The first series of eleven verses describes summer scenes. The second series depicts winter scenes.

Cameron, P. *"I Can't," Said the Ant.* New York: Coward (1961). With the help of an army of ants and some spiders, an ant helps repair a broken teapot amid the encouragement of the kitchen's inhabitants: " 'Push her up,' said the cup. 'You can,' said the pan. 'You must,' said the crust."

Carlstrom, N. W. *Jesse Bear, What Will You Wear?* New York: Macmillan (1986). Jesse wears not only clothes but sun, sand, flowers, food, sleep, and stars.

de Angeli, M. *Marguerite de Angeli's Book of Nursery and Mother Goose Rhymes.* New York: Doubleday (1953). This classic collection contains 376 traditional rhymes.

There is a reciprocal relationship between phonemic awareness and reading. Being able to detect phonemes helps the child learn to read. The act of reading fosters growth in phonological awareness. As you teach phonemic awareness, provide many opportunities, through shared reading and other activities, for students to apply what they are learning by reading and writing.

dePaola, T. *Tomie dePaola's Mother Goose*. New York: Putnam (1985). Traditional verses are accompanied by de Paola's lighthearted illustrations.

Hennessy, B. G. *Jake Baked the Cake*. New York: Viking (1990). To prepare for the wedding, Sally Price buys the rice, Mr. Fine paints a sign, and Jake bakes a magnificent cake.

Kirk, D. *Miss Spider's Tea Party*. New York: Scholastic (1994). When lonely Miss Spider tries to host a tea party, the other bugs refuse to come for fear of being eaten.

Lobel, A. *The Random House Book of Mother Goose*. New York: Random House (1986). More than 300 nursery rhymes are presented.

Martin, B. *Polar Bear, Polar Bear, What Do You Hear?* New York: Holt (1991). Zoo animals from polar bear to walrus make their distinctive sounds for each other, while children imitate sounds for the zoo keeper.

Marzollo, J. *Pretend You're a Cat*. New York: Dial (1990). Rhyming verses ask the reader to purr like a cat, scratch like a dog, leap like a squirrel, and so on.

Shaw, N. *Sheep Take a Hike*. Boston: Houghton Mifflin (1994). Having gotten lost on a chaotic hike in the great outdoors, the sheep find their way back by following the trail of wool they have left behind.

Wong, E. Y. *Eek! There's a Mouse in the House*. Boston: Houghton Mifflin (1992). After discovery of a mouse in the house, larger and larger animals are sent in after one another, with increasingly chaotic results.

Discuss any rhyming stories that you read to the children, thereby building a background of literacy. In time, discuss the concept of rhyme itself. Lead students to see that the last word in one line has the same sound as the last word in another line.

Listening to rhyming books on tape is one way of reinforcing the concept of rhyme.

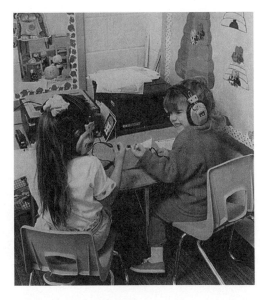

Reread some of the nursery rhymes aloud, emphasizing the rhyming words. Explain what rhyming words are, using examples such as *rake/cake, bell/well, ice/mice,* and so on. Have children point out the words that rhyme in a familiar poem.

Reinforcement Activities
The concept of rhyme

- Have students supply the final rhyming word of a couplet:

  There was an old lady who lived in a shoe.
  She had so many children she didn't know what to _____.

  I like to run.
  It's so much _____.

- Students can compose a rhyming pictionary in which they paste on each page illustrations of words that rhyme. A typical page might include pictures of a man, a can, a fan, and a pan. Pictures might come from old magazines or workbooks or can be drawn.

- Have students sort cards containing illustrations of objects whose names rhyme. Begin by providing a model card (*cat*) and having students arrange rhyming cards under it (*bat*, *rat*, *hat*). Provide students with cards that do not rhyme with *cat* as well as those that do. Later, have students sort two or three rhyming patterns at the same time. Discuss students' sorting.

- Sing traditional songs that have a strong rhyming element. After singing a song once, have students listen to a second singing to detect rhyming words. Also sing all of two rhyming lines except the last word, and let students say or sing the missing word. ● ● ● ●

Segmenting Words. After students have developed some sense of rhyme, introduce the concept of **segmenting,** or separating words into sounds. This can be done as you lead the class in reading a big book, an experience story, or the morning message. Choose three-phoneme words whose sounds are easily discriminated, and then elongate the words and discuss their sounds. For instance, after reading *Goldilocks and the Three Bears,* discuss the sounds of *h-o-t* and *s-a-t*.

As students try their hand at spelling, encourage them to stretch out words so they can hear the sounds. As you write on the board, say the separate sounds that correspond to the letters so that students can hear them. As you write "Bob has a new pet," say "B-o-b h-a-z uh n-oo p-e-t." After students have begun to catch on to the concept of sounds, say words slowly and ask them to tell how many sounds are in them.

If students experience difficulty learning to segment words, you might try a technique designed by Elkonin (1973), which Clay (1993b) used in her highly acclaimed Reading Recovery approach. Elkonin attempted to make the abstract skill of segmenting more concrete by using drawings and markers. The student is given a drawing of a short word, below which are blocks that correspond to the number of sounds in the word. Below a drawing of the word *sun,* for instance, there would be three blocks. A token is placed in the blocks to represent the three sounds in *sun.* To introduce the technique, carry out the steps outlined in Lesson 2.1.

Segmenting means dividing a word into its separate sounds—for example, *cat* is /k/ /a/ /t/.

Lesson 2.1
Elkonin phonemic segmentation technique

Step 1.

Explain the task, model it, and guide the child through it.

Step 2.

Give the child a drawing of the sun. Remind the child to say the word that names the picture and to stretch the word out so she or he can hear the separate sounds. If the child has difficulty noting the sounds, very carefully and deliberately pronounce the word. Emphasize each sound, but do not distort the word.

Step 3.

Have the child put a marker in each square while saying each sound. The child says /s/ and puts a marker in the first block, then says /u/ and puts a marker in the second block, and finally puts a marker in the third block while saying /n/.

Step 4.

Using the blocks tells the child how many separate sounds there are in a word. As the child becomes more proficient, eliminate the blocks and markers and have him or her simply tell how many sounds are in a word.

Once a child begins to catch on to the concept of segmenting, you might record a word's letters in the appropriate blocks. The child then puts markers on the letters that represent the segmented sounds. Elkonin (1973) did not do this, preferring the child to focus on the sounds rather than the spellings of words. According to Clay (1985), however, a student who can segment words and has learned the letters of the alphabet can deal with letters. Seeing the letters that spell the sounds conveys the concept that letters represent sounds.

Although phonemic segmentation might appear to be more applicable to a phonics approach to reading, Vellutino and Scanlon (1988) observed that it is actually required for whole language approaches as well. No matter how they are taught, all students must grasp the abstract concepts that words are composed of separate sounds and that individual letters and combinations are used to represent those sounds.

Continuants, consonant sounds that are articulated with a continuous stream of breath, are easiest to discriminate. Frequently occurring continuants include /s/, /f/, /h/, /j/, /m/, /r/, /l/, and /n/.

Perceiving Beginning Consonant Sounds. Students will have difficulty learning phonics if they are unable to perceive the sounds of beginning consonants, a skill that apparently is dependent on and also further develops the ability to segment. For example, if a child confuses the sound /p/ with the sound /d/, when he or she is taught the letter that represents /p/, the child may actually associate it with the sound /d/, or vice versa.

To introduce the concept of beginning sounds, read aloud alliterative stories or alphabet books such as *Nedobeck's Alphabet Book* (Nedobeck, 1981) and *All about Arthur (An Absolutely Absurd Ape)* (Carle, 1974). Some other alliterative books that might be used to reinforce the idea of beginning consonant sounds are listed in the Children's Book List. At first, simply read such a book as you would any other picture book, showing pictures and discussing content. Then lead students to see that many of the words begin with the same sound and let them read some selections along with you. Have them note the positions of their tongues as they read with you:

Little Leonard Lion climbs a
Ladder to mail a Love Letter to
Lori. (Nedobeck, 1981)

Also read the *L* page from Judith Gwyn Brown's (1976) *Alphabet Dreams*, shown in Figure 2.4.

FIGURE 2.4 **Pages from *Alphabet Dreams***

K My name is Kathy, and my husband's name is Ken. We live in a kettle, and we sell kites.

L My name is Lucy, and my husband's name is Lee. We live in a log, and we sell lamps.

From the book *Alphabet Dreams* by Judith Gwyn Brown, © 1976. Reprinted by permission of Prentice Hall/A Division of Simon & Schuster, Inc., Englewood Cliffs, NJ.

Bandes, H. *Sleepy River*. New York: Philomel (1993). A canoe ride at night-fall provides a Native American mother and child glimpses of the ducks, fire-flies, bats, and other wonders of nature.

Base, G. *Animalia*. New York: Harry N. Abrams (1987). Each letter is illustrated and accompanied by an alliterative phrase, such as "Lazy lions lounging in the local library."

Bayer, J. *A My Name Is Alice*. New York: Dial (1984). The well-known jump rope rhyme that is built on letters of the alphabet is illustrated with animals from all over the world.

Cole, J. *Six Sick Sheep*. New York: Morrow (1993). A collection of all kinds of tongue twisters—some only two or three words long, some that tell a story, and some featuring a theme.

Geisel, T. S. *Dr. Seuss's ABC*. New York: Beginner (1973). Letters of the alphabet are accompanied by an alliterative story and humorous illustrations.

Kellogg, S. *Aster Aardvark's Alphabet Adventures*. New York: Morrow (1987). A highly alliterative story accompanies each letter.

Knutson, K. *Ska-tat*. New York: Macmillan (1993). Children describe playing in the colorful, crunchy autumn leaves as the leaves fall to the ground.

Lobel, A. *Allison's Zinnia*. New York: Greenwillow (1990). Allison acquired an amaryllis for Beryl who bought a begonia for Crystal and so on through the alphabet. Accompanied by beautifully detailed, full-page illustrations for each letter.

Schwartz, A. *Busy Buzzing Bumblebees and Other Tongue Twisters*. New York: HarperCollins (1972). A fun collection of tongue twisters.

Steig, J. *Alpha Beta Chowder*. New York: HarperCollins (1992). An alliterative humorous verse for each letter of the alphabet is presented, including "The Enigmatic Egg," "Mishmash," and "Worrywart."

Stevenson, J. *Grandpa's Great City Tour*. New York: Greenwillow (1983). Letters in upper and lower case are accompanied by numerous unlabeled objects whose names begin with the sound commonly associated with the letter being presented.

Reinforcement Activities
The concept of beginning sounds

- Recite traditional alliterative pieces such as "Peter Piper picked a peck of pickled peppers" and have students attempt to repeat them. See *The Little Book of Big Tongue Twisters* by Foley Curtis (1977) for examples of alliterative pieces to accompany nearly every beginning sound. After reading each piece, give students examples of what is meant by "begin with the same sound," and then have them tell which words begin with the same sound.

- Say a word, and have students supply other words that begin with the same sound. Discuss students' names that begin with the same sound, such as Benjamin, Barbara, Billy.
- Play "I Spy" with students. Tell them that you spy something whose name begins like the word *boat*. Encourage them to say the names of objects in the classroom that begin like *boat*. If necessary, give added clues: It has covers; it can be read.
- In *There's a Wocket in My Pocket* (Geisel, 1974), nonsense names of imaginary monsters are created by changing the initial consonants of familiar words: a wasket in your basket, a zamp in the lamp, a yottle in the bottle. As you talk about the book, lead students to see how the names were made and help them form others: a zoot on my foot, a babinet in the cabinet.
- Using a troll doll or puppet, have it say that only people whose names begin like the name *Sandy* (or whatever name you choose) may cross the bridge. Supply names, and have students tell which persons would be allowed to cross (Stahl, 1990).
- Have students sort cards containing illustrations of objects whose names begin with the same sound (ball, boy, banana, baby). Sorts can be closed or open. In a closed sort, you provide a model (illustration of a ball). In an open sort, you provide the items (illustrations of /b/ words and /s/ words), and children decide how to sort them. Be sure to model sorting.
- Encourage students to stretch out the sounds of words, saying *soap* as "sss-ooo-ppp." This helps build awareness of separate sounds in words as well as perception of beginning sounds. It also helps students determine how to spell words.

Stretching out the sounds of words works best with continuants because they are articulated with a continuous stream of breath.

Phonemic awareness may be learned through interaction with print, through specific training in segmenting and other skills, or through some combination of the two. Watson (1984) commented:

> Although many pupils will learn the units of print incidentally, others, low in conceptual functioning, need deliberate teacher explanation of terms and daily instruction, e.g., through game or song, based on the various print units. The success of programs, such as those of Elkonin (1973) will depend on the effectiveness of the match between the greater structure they offer and the learning needs of the children. (p. 117)

Phonemic awareness is the consciousness of the sounds in words. It includes the ability to detect rhyme, separate the sounds in words, and detect consonant and vowel sounds.

Watson concluded that an underlying cognitive factor may be necessary for the development of phonemic awareness that is above and beyond what is required to develop listening and speaking skills. Thus students who are skilled users of language may not acquire phonemic awareness, even when working with print, without some sort of intervention. The Elkonin technique or other procedure could enhance the necessary underlying cognitive development.

THE ROLE OF THE SCHOOL IN FOSTERING LANGUAGE DEVELOPMENT

Although both home and school play essential roles in developing a child's language and literacy skills, they do so in somewhat different ways. At home, the child is the center of attention, and conversations are often one-on-one and gener-

One of the concepts that emergent readers have to learn is metalanguage, or the language used to talk about language. The word *word* is an example of metalanguage. Other examples include *letter, sentence, period, question mark, sound, line,* and *beginning of a word.* Young children have difficulty with these, as they do with terms like *same* and *different.* Durkin (1993) cites the example of the teacher who wrote *you* and *me* on the board and asked the class to tell how many words she had written. The response was "five," indicating that the students confused the terms *letters* and *words.*

ally involve topics of immediate concern to the child. This is an ideal environment for building basic language, but not for long-term growth in all intellectual areas. The coverage of topics, for instance, would probably be unbalanced and unsystematic (Wells, 1986). Some topics would be covered in depth, others would be barely mentioned, and some would not be explored at all. Formal schooling offers planned, systematic instruction in areas deemed to be essential. Schooling broadens the child's experiences, takes an in-depth look at essential topics, and prepares children to become aware of their learning and take responsibility for it (Wells, 1986).

Although the school is by necessity more formal and structured than the home, there should be continuity between home and school. The school should build on the language and literacy skills and understandings that children have learned at home. It should make use of the learning strategies that children are accustomed to using and the techniques employed by the best parents. As Wells (1986) states,

> As far as learning is concerned, therefore, entry into school should not be thought of as a beginning, but as a transition to a more broadly based community and to a wider range of opportunities for meaning making and mastery. *Every* child has competencies, and these provide a positive base from which to start. The teacher's responsibility is to discover what they are and to help each child extend and develop them. (pp. 68–69)

To ease the transition from home to school and to make full use of the knowledge and skills that the child brings to school, it is important that the school resemble a rich, warm home environment, using techniques employed by the parents in such homes. In his comparison of home and school conversations, Wells (1986) concluded that home conversations were far richer. At school, the teacher dominates conversations, saying approximately three times as much as the children do. Teachers ask more questions—often of a quizlike nature—make more requests, initiate conversations more often, and choose the topic to be talked about more frequently. Because the teacher dominates conversations and discussions, both the amount and complexity of students' contributions are drastically reduced. Syntax is less complex, vocabulary is more restricted, and utterances are briefer. Busy answering the teacher's many questions and requests, the students have limited opportunities to make a genuine contribution. Teachers are also only half as likely as parents to help children extend their statements (Wells, 1986).

To foster children's language development, try the following (Wells, 1986):

- Listen very carefully to what the student has to say. Try to see the world from the child's point of view. Do not run away with the topic. For instance, if a child mentions a trip to the zoo, find out what it was about the trip that intrigued her or him. Do not launch into a detailed description of your last trip to the zoo.
- Be open to what children want to talk about. Do not follow a preconceived plan for the direction you want the discussion to take. When discussing a story that you have read to the children, let them tell you what they liked best about it. Do not tell them what they should like best, and, of course, give them the freedom not to like it at all.
- Help students extend their responses by making encouraging comments.
- Provide students with opportunities to initiate conversations and ask questions.

- Although whole-class discussions are valuable, they do not allow for much interaction. As often as possible, arrange for small-group and one-on-one discussions.
- When you respond to students, use language that is on or slightly above their level.
- Students are active learners who are using what they know to try to make sense of their world. Use their comments and questions to help them construct meaning.

ISSUES IN EMERGENT LITERACY INSTRUCTION

Once students have a sense of story, understand the purpose and the basic concepts of print, can identify most of the letters of the alphabet, have a sense of rhyme, can segment the sounds in a word, and can perceive rhyme and detect beginning sounds in words, they are prepared for a higher level of instruction. Upcoming chapters contain suggestions for a more intensive and structured approach to reading that fosters children's growth in literacy areas such as phonics, sight words, and other word-attack skills. This section is devoted to a number of general issues in emergent literacy instruction.

USE OF COMMERCIAL MATERIALS

Most of the skills in an emergent literacy program can be taught using children's books, experience stories, children's writing, and environmental print. Kits and workbooks are not necessary, but they can help provide structure and additional practice if carefully selected and used judiciously.

For evaluating the quality of the kindergarten component of a basal series, the Adoption Guidelines Project of the Center for the Study of Reading (1990a) recommended the following:

Guideline 1. Before examining the specific content of kindergarten reading instruction in basal reading programs, discuss and agree upon the type of reading instruction that is most appropriate for your kindergarten classrooms. (p. 16)

Guideline 2. When examining the kindergarten levels of basal reading programs, evaluate the quantity and quality of instruction and practice opportunities for developing word awareness, phonemic awareness, knowledge of letter names, [and] print awareness. (p. 18)

Guideline 3. When examining kindergarten levels of basal reading programs, evaluate the quantity and quality of instruction and practice opportunities for oral language and listening experiences. (p. 19)

READING IN PRESCHOOL

The controversy just two decades ago was whether reading should be taught in kindergarten; now the debate concerns preschool. With more and more children attending day care and nursery schools, today's question is whether four-year-olds should be taught to read.

A prudent course would be to avoid formal instruction in literacy. Reading aloud regularly, developing oral language skills, and providing opportunities to write, draw, and explore will naturally develop emerging literacy. In a two-year program devised for four- and five-year-olds, Durkin (1970, 1974) found that the children did succeed in learning an encouraging number of letters, numbers, and words. However, the program apparently was not successful for all the participants. Overall, girls performed well, but only boys with high IQ scores were "consistently involved and interested in the program" (Durkin, 1970, p. 551).

For preschool instruction, Gibson (1989) suggested the hand-over principle in which teachers provide "experiences that children can learn from rather than explanations that they are asked to repeat or imitate" (p. 81). The hand-over principle involves the following kinds of informal interactions:

1. Teacher (or children) raises questions.
2. Teacher asks for and/or observes children's reasoning and/or hypotheses.
3. Teacher uses children's current views to guide them in designing subsequent teaching/learning experiences.

Through observation and interaction, the teacher determines why children read and write and what they understand about these activities. For instance, a child may believe that one reads pictures. Another may understand that reading consists of deciphering lines of print but not that the lines are composed of separate words. The teacher may provide opportunities for the first child to follow a line of print as she or he reads. Certain activities may help the second child see the relationship between printed and spoken words: carefully pointing out individual words as she or he reads a story from a big book, helping the child count the words in a sentence, or pausing before a predictable word and having the child read it. The basic principle is to see the task from the child's perspective and present opportunities to learn that will allow her or him to construct a revised understanding of the task.

McLane and McNamee (1990) suggested that preschoolers and kindergarteners learn literacy best when two conditions are met: when reading and writing are a natural part of classroom activities that have a purpose children can understand, and when children become part of a community of writers and readers.

> The learning of literacy is indeed a social process: children have a good chance of becoming writers and readers, and of becoming more sophisticated ones in time, if they use written language to communicate and interact with those they play and work with every day. (p. 116)

WORKING WITH PARENTS

Since today's emergent literacy practices are different from those parents experienced when they attended school and there was a readiness orientation, it is important that the emergent literacy program be explained to them. Trace the roots of reading and writing, and explain to parents the essential role that they have played and continue to play. Be sensitive to different styles of parenting. Some parents, not having been read to themselves, may not realize the value of reading aloud to their children or, because of limited skills, may not feel able to do it well.

Affirm what parents have done and encourage them to support their children's efforts as best they can. Also explain each element of the program. Pay special attention to invented spelling and process writing as these are areas that lend themselves to misunderstanding. Trace the development of children's writing from drawing and scribbling through invented spelling to conventional writing. Show examples of students' writing. Stress the benefits of early writing, and assure parents that invented spelling is transitory and will not harm their children's spelling.

MONITORING EMERGENT LITERACY

Emergent literacy can best be monitored through careful observation. As students read and write, try to get behind the product to the process. As a student is reading, try to determine what he or she is reading. Is the student reading the pictures? Has the student simply memorized the text? Is it some sort of combination? Ask yourself: What is the child attending to? Possibilities include pictures, overall memory of selection, memorized words or phrases, context, beginning letters, beginning letters and ending letters, all the letters in the word, or a combination of elements. Knowing where the student is, you can build on his or her knowledge and, through scaffolding, lift the student to a higher level. For instance, if the student is simply using picture clues, you can help him or her use highly predictable text along with pictures. A checklist for evaluating a child's use of early reading strategies is presented in Table 2.5.

Note the level of the student's writing. Does the student have a sense of what writing is? Is the student attempting to convey a message? Is the student using

In order to assess young children's writing, it is important to observe them during the writing process and to ask them to read the piece they have written. Surprisingly, children use different forms of writing for different tasks. When writing brief pieces or short words, kindergarteners tend to use invented spelling. When writing a long story, they may use scribbling. When children write as part of a group activity, the forms they use may be different from those used when they write during an individual interview (Sulzby, Barnhart, & Hieshima, 1989).

TABLE 2.5 Checklist for evaluating early reading strategies

Strategy	Never	Seldom	Often
1. Uses pictures exclusively to retell story.	____	____	____
2. Uses pictures and text to retell story.	____	____	____
3. Uses pictures to help with difficult words.	____	____	____
4. Uses memory of entire piece to read story.	____	____	____
5. Uses memory of repeated phrases.	____	____	____
6. Uses context to decipher words.	____	____	____
7. Uses initial consonants and context to decipher words.	____	____	____
8. Uses initial and final consonants and context to decipher words.	____	____	____
9. Uses all or most of each word's parts to decipher words.	____	____	____
10. Uses a variety of cues to decipher words.	____	____	____

FIGURE 2.5	Emergent literacy observation guide

Student's name: _____ Age: _____

Date: _____

Oral language	Below average	Average	Advanced
Uses a vocabulary appropriate for age level	1	2 3 4	5
Uses sentence structure appropriate for age level	1	2 3 4	5
Can make himself/herself understood	1	2 3 4	5
Listens attentively to directions and stories	1	2 3 4	5
Can retell a story in own words	1	2 3 4	5
Understands oral directions	1	2 3 4	5
Asks questions when doesn't understand something	1	2 3 4	5

Concepts about reading	Below average	Average	Advanced
Knows the parts of a book	1 2	3	4 5
Understands that the print is read	1 2	3	4 5
Can follow a line of print as it is being read	1 2	3	4 5
Can point to words as each is being read	1 2	3	4 5
Can name letters of the alphabet	1 2	3	4 5
Can perceive beginning sounds	1 2	3	4 5
Can detect rhyming words	1 2	3	4 5
Can tell how many sounds are in a word	1 2	3	4 5
Can discriminate between words that have a similar appearance	1 2	3	4 5
Recognizes environmental print signs and labels	1 2	3	4 5
Can read own name	1 2	3	4 5

Interest in reading and writing	Below average	Average	Advanced
Enjoys being read to	1	2 3 4	5
Browses among books in class	1	2 3 4	5
"Reads" picture books	1	2 3 4	5
Asks questions about words, sentences, or other elements in books	1	2 3 4	5

Writing	Below average	Average	Advanced
Shows interest in writing	1	2 3 4	5
Writes or draws stories or letters	1	2 3 4	5
Understands the purpose of writing	1	2 3 4	5
Writes to communicate with others	1	2 3 4	5

For the most part his/her writing is best described as being at the following level:

Unorganized scribbles	_____	(The scribbles have no perceptible pattern.)
Drawings	_____	(Drawing is the child's primary mode of written expression.)
Organized scribbles	_____	(The scribbles show a pattern. They may be linear.)
Letterlike figures	_____	(The characters aren't real letters, but have some of the features of letters.)
Prephonetic spelling	_____	(The child uses real letters, but the letters have no apparent relationship to the sounds of the words he or she is writing.)
Phonemic spelling	_____	(Consonant sounds are spelled; *kitten* may be spelled *KTN*.)
Letter name	_____	(Vowels are spelled with letter names; *RAN* for *rain*.)
Within-word pattern	_____	(Vowel markers are used; *RANE* for *rain*.)
Standard spelling	_____	

Work habits	Below average	Average	Advanced
Is able to work on own	1 2	3	4 5
Works at a task until it is finished	1 2	3	4 5
Works well with others	1 2	3	4 5
Is able to share materials	1 2	3	4 5
Is able to take turns	1 2	3	4 5

invented spelling? Use the checklists in the observation guide in Figure 2.5 to monitor writing, stages of storybook reading, oral language, concepts about reading, interest in reading and writing, and work habits. The observation guide is generic; use only those parts that fit in with your program.

Observation has also been referred to as kidwatching and has the dual purpose of understanding growth and documenting learning (Goodman, 1985). What is taught is not always what is learned. As Dahl (1992) noted, "We need to figure out how learners . . . are interpreting or make sense of reading and writing . . . what they think they are supposed to do as they read and write" (p. 50). This is best done from the child's, rather than the teacher's, perspective. Some sources of information include strategies that children use in reading and writing, the routines that students engage in every day, and the products of their efforts and the comments that they make about them (Dahl, 1992):

- *Strategies*. In addition to noting what strategies students use as they attempt to read a text, ask, What strategies do they use as they attempt to write a word? Do they elongate the sounds? Ask a teacher?
- *Routines*. How do students choose books? What do they do when they write? Do they typically use a book as a model? Do they use a drawing as a story starter?
- *Products*. What do the illustrations children have made of their reading look like? What do their written pieces look like? Are they scribble writing or using a combination of scribble writing and invented spelling? How are the products changing over time?
- *Comments*. What are children saying about their products? For instance, when Maurice tossed his piece of scribble writing into the wastebasket, his teacher asked him about it. Maurice replied, "My writing doesn't say anything." Maurice realized that he needed another form of writing in order to express meaning. His rejection of his scribble writing was a sign of development (Dahl, 1992). This is the kind of incident of which perceptive anecdotal records are made.

Observations should focus on what the child can do. For instance, the focus of the observation made about Maurice was that he has a new understanding of what is required to represent spoken words in writing.

Notes taken after a discussion has been completed or a reading or writing conference has been held can also offer valuable insights. If the notes are put on gummed labels or sticky notes, they can be pasted into a looseleaf notebook that contains separate pages for each child.

Since young children's literacy behavior changes rapidly, observations should be ongoing. However, progress should be checked on a more formal basis once a month. In addition to filling out checklists, keep anecdotal records. Note the emergence of significant behaviors, such as the appearance of finger pointing, word-by-word reading, and the use of invented spelling. Briefly describe the behavior and note the date. See Chapter 13 for more information on using anecdotal records.

CAP (CONCEPTS ABOUT PRINT)

Some emergent literacy assessment devices measure children's concept of what reading is, their familiarity with handling a book, and their metalinguistic knowledge, such as knowing what a sentence, word, and letter are. One of the best-known measures is CAP, or Concepts About Print (Clay, 1982). In a sense, it is an observation guide. The teacher reads a story to a child and asks a number of questions about it. As the child responds, the teacher's observations center on two aspects of behavior: "What is the child attending to and in what order?" (Clay, 1989, p. 269). By watching the child's actions and asking a series of questions, the teacher can discover where the student is in terms of emergent reading behavior.

The idea of CAP is to reveal the child's awareness of print conventions so that the teacher can plan a program accordingly and also track the child's progress. Kindergarten and first-grade students did vary in their performances on CAP (Day, Day, Spicole, & Griffin, 1981; Johns, 1980). The test results suggest the need for teachers to make sure students are taught the major concepts of print and the language of instruction (Johns, 1980). CAP has twenty-four items and takes only five to ten minutes to administer. Areas measured include knowing how to handle a book; how to read from left to right and top to bottom; the concepts of letter, word, first letter and last letter, upper- and lower-case letters, and punctuation. The test has two forms: *Sand* and *Stones*. The tests are equivalent and consist of a storybook and a series of questions. *Stones* was created after Clay discovered that *Sand* was inappropriate for students who were not familiar with the seashore.

Clay (1993a) also assembled a battery of reading and writing measures known as the Observation Survey, which can be used to assess emergent reading and early reading behaviors. In New Zealand, it is recommended that the Observation Survey be administered when a child reaches age 6 so that children who are struggling may be given Reading Recovery or other appropriate help. In the United States, an appropriate time would be the end of kindergarten or beginning of first grade. The Observation Survey includes a test of word recognition similar to the word-recognition subtest of the informal reading inventory (explained in Chapter 13), a writing sample, Writing Vocabulary, and Hearing and Writing Sounds in Words.

In the Writing Vocabulary task, a child is asked to write all the words he or she can think of, starting with his or her own name. Students are given a ten-minute time limit. If children are hesitant or stop before the ten minutes are up, they are given prompts with words that the teacher feels they may be able to write: "Can you write *cat*? Can you write *the*?" This assessment is easy to give and provides valuable information about a student's growing ability to write words; however, it is only useful for the first two years of school (Clay, 1993a). Some students may be reluctant to try writing words if they are not sure of their spellings. Urge these children to spell as best they can.

In the Hearing and Writing Sounds in Words task, students are asked to write a dictated sentence. Credit is given for each sound that the child is able to record.

INFORMAL ASSESSMENT MEASURES

Emergent literacy measures need not be purchased. Teachers can put together a measure that is geared to their own concept of reading and that meshes with their reading program. Although it can be a paper-and-pencil test to allow for group administration, an informal type of one-to-one assessment often works better. A sample informal assessment, which is administered individually, follows:

- *Letter knowledge.* Using an alphabet book that contains both upper- and lower-case letters, have students name ten of each.

- *Writing sample.* Ask the child to write his or her name as best he or she can. If the child can write his or her name, ask the child to write any other words that he or she knows. Ask the child to write a story as best he or she can. It may be done with letterlike forms or drawings. Note the level of the child's writing and the number of words that he or she can write, if any.
- *Print familiarity.* Give *Clifford the Small Red Puppy* (Bridwell, 1972), or a similar book, to the child. Discuss the book informally to find out how familiar the child is with print conventions. You might ask: "Have you ever seen this book? What do you think this book is about? How can you tell what the book is about? What do you do with a book? Show me how you would read a book." Point to a word and ask, "How many letters are in this word?" Point to a short line of print and ask, "How many words are in this line? Can you read any of the words?"
- *Assessing phonological awareness.* Because phonological awareness is such a critical skill, ways of assessing students' abilities to detect rhyme and to match beginning consonant sounds are described below.

Rhyme. To assess the ability to detect rhyme, the easiest of phonological awareness tasks, draw or cut up pictures of objects whose names rhyme: boat, goat, house, mouse, cake, snake, bee, tree, car, star, moon, spoon. Mix up seven pairs of rhyming pictures. Explain to the student that some words rhyme: *book* and *look* rhyme because they both have an *ook* sound, and *ball* and *tall* rhyme because they both have an *all* sound. Then tell the student that each card on the table has a rhyming partner. Discuss each card with the student to make sure she or he knows the name of each pictured object; then show the student how to match up a pair. Picking up the card containing an illustration of a boat, tell the student that you will be looking for a word that rhymes with *boat*, so you will be looking for a word that has an *oat* sound. Go through all the cards until the rhyming partner is found. Then give the student a picture of a star, and have her or him search for a picture whose name rhymes with *star*. Give guidance as needed. Once the student has grasped the concept, have her or him match up the remaining pairs. An adequate performance would be matching up at least four out of five pairs.

If students do not achieve an adequate performance, try dynamic testing. Using Vygotsky's concept of zone of proximal development, teach the child the concept of rhyming (using the suggestions made earlier in this chapter). Note whether the student was able to grasp the concept of rhyming, and, if so, how much instruction was required.

Beginning Consonant Sounds. Using procedures similar to those described above for rhyming, assess students' ability to match beginning sounds. Display, in mixed-up fashion, seven pairs of cards containing pictures of items whose names begin with the same sound: dog, deer, cat, cow, saw, sun, moon, man, fish, fork, hammer, hat, ring, rabbit. Explain to the student being tested that some words begin with the same sound. Tell him or her that *soup* and *soap* begin with the same sound, /s/. Also, *nail* and *net* begin with the same sound, /n/. Tell the student that he or she will be matching pictures whose names begin with the same sound. Pick up the picture of a dog and say that you want to find a picture whose name begins like *dog*. Note that *deer* and *dog* begin the same way. Give the student the picture of a cat. Ask him or her to name the picture. Then explain that he or she should find the picture whose name begins like *cat*. Give help as needed. Then have the student match up the remaining five pairs. A performance of four out of five is adequate.

OTHER MEASURES OF EMERGENT LITERACY

Measures of emergent literacy are typically included in the teacher's manual of a basal series or as a separate item. One advantage of basal criterion-referenced measures is that they are geared to the program for which they have been constructed. They are also generally accompanied by suggestions for working with students who do poorly on them.

USING THE ASSESSMENT RESULTS

The results of an emergent literacy assessment should help you plan instruction. Generally, an acceptable standard for letter knowledge and phonological awareness is 80 percent. Students falling below that level require additional help. Those who are lacking in print familiarity need more experience with concepts with which they had difficulty. Writing samples are also indicators of emergent literacy concepts. Based on the samples, note where children are on the path to literacy and, according to their level of development, what experiences will be most beneficial.

As indicated earlier, not every ability important to reading can be measured formally or informally. Learning to read requires hard work, perseverance, and a certain degree of maturity. It also demands reasonably good health, sufficient social skills to allow one to work with others, and adequate language skills so that the teacher's instructions and the material to be read can be understood. These areas are best assessed through teacher observation, which is just as good a predictor as traditional readiness assessments, intelligence tests, or measures of perceptual-motor development (Heilman, Blair, & Rupley, 1982). Ample opportunity must be allowed for the observation, and the behavior to be observed should be expressed in concrete terms (Thorndike & Hagen, 1984).

SUMMARY

1. The concept of readiness was devised to protect children from experiencing excessive difficulty in learning to read when reading is introduced before they are ready. However, it is now recognized that all children have acquired some literacy skills and concepts before entering school. The concept of readiness has given way to that of emergent literacy, which attempts to capitalize on the literacy learnings that the child brings to school. To foster literacy, the teacher's attitude should show that he or she believes young children are readers and writers, and the teacher should immerse the class in literacy activities.

2. By reading selected books to children, the teacher builds knowledge of story structure and story language, vocabulary, and background of experience. Students who are not read to at home have a special need in this area.

3. To make full use of the knowledge and skills that the child brings to school, it is important to make the school more like a rich, warm home environment. To build language, the school should use techniques employed by the parents in such home environments. Such techniques make the child an active partner in conversations and discussions.

4. Through shared book reading in the form of big books or other enlarged texts, children can be introduced to basic concepts of print and other emergent literacy skills. Repetitive materials work especially well. The language experience story, in which the child dictates a story and the teacher writes it down, is also a valuable instructional tool for fostering emergent literacy.

5. Over the past few years, the concept of writing has changed dramatically, with children being encouraged to write even before they can read. Once primarily a matter of copying and learning letter formation, writing in kindergarten is now seen as a valid means of expression. Children are invited to write and spell as best they can, whether that entails drawing, scribbling, creating letterlike forms, using real letters and invented spellings, or writing in the conventional manner.

6. Progress in literacy is closely tied to knowledge of the alphabet and phonological awareness, including rhyming and perception of beginning sounds. These abilities may be improved through reading alphabet books and other natural materials as well as through direct instruction.

7. Many of the skills and understandings available in commercial material can be taught through alphabet books, songs, rhymes, and games. However, commercial materials, if carefully selected and used with discretion, can play a part in the program.

8. Because the concept of emergent literacy may be unfamiliar to many parents, it is important that they be given information about this topic.

9. Reading instruction in kindergarten, although controversial just a few years ago, is now widespread. However, the teaching of reading in preschool has become an issue. A prudent course would be to provide informal opportunities for students to explore reading and writing.

10. A number of formal and informal measures assess emergent literacy. Observation and anecdotal records are growing in popularity.

CLASSROOM APPLICATIONS

1. Examine stories written by a kindergarten class. What are some characteristics of children's writing at this age? How do the pieces vary?

2. Read Jim Trelease's (1989) best-selling *The New Read-Aloud Handbook* or a similar book on reading aloud. Start a bibliography of books that would be appropriate to read aloud to the children you now teach or plan to teach. Remember that students of all ages like to be read to.

3. Search out alphabet books, rhyming tales, song books, and other materials that you might use to enhance alphabet knowledge, rhyming, or perception of beginning sounds. Keep an annotated bibliography of these materials.

FIELD APPLICATIONS

1. Observe a kindergarten class. How does the teacher foster literacy? How do the children react to the activities?

2. Read a book to a kindergarten class or preschool child. Follow the procedures outlined in this chapter. Note how the children react to the story.

3. Draw up a plan for introducing a big book or other enlarged text. State your objectives, describe the class, note the material you will be using, and explain how you might introduce it. Tell what language skills you will present, and describe a follow-up activity. Teach the lesson, and note the class's reaction.

4. Using the procedures described in this chapter, plan a lesson teaching alphabet letters, rhyming, or beginning sounds. Teach the lesson, and rate its effectiveness.

c h a p t e r 3

Teaching Phonics

Agree

For each of the following statements, put a check under "Agree" or "Disagree" to show how you feel. Discuss your responses with classmates before you read the chapter.

Disagree

1. Before they start to read, students should be taught all of the consonant letters and their sounds.

2. Consonants should be taught before vowels.

3. Phonics rules have so many exceptions that they are not worth teaching.

4. The phonics students learn should be related to stories that they are about to read.

5. Phonics rules are hard to learn because English is so irregular.

6. The natural way to decode a word is sound by sound or letter by letter.

7. Phonics workbooks are effective for reinforcing phonics.

8. Phonics is a tool, a means to an end.

Using What You Know

The writing system for the English language is alphabetic. Because a series of twenty-six letters has been created to represent the speech sounds of the language, our thoughts and ideas can be written down. To become literate, we must learn the relationship between letters and speech sounds. Chapters 1 and 2 presented techniques for teaching the nature and purpose of writing and reading, concepts of print, the alphabet, and awareness of speech sounds. These techniques form a foundation for learning phonics, which is the relationship between spelling and speech sounds as applied to reading. This chapter will be more meaningful if you first reflect on what you already know about phonics.

Think about how you use phonics to sound out strange names and other unfamiliar words. Think about how you might teach phonics, and ask yourself what role phonics should play in a reading program. What are some approaches to teaching phonics? What are the elements of phonics? What are the consonant elements? What are the vowel elements?

RATIONALE AND APPROACHES FOR PHONICS INSTRUCTION

Phonics is the study of speech sounds related to reading.

How important is **phonics**? At the conclusion of a landmark study commissioned by Congress, Adams (1990) stated:

> In summary, deep and thorough knowledge of letters, spelling patterns, and words, and of the phonological translations of all three, are of inescapable importance to both skillful reading and its acquisition. By extension, instruction designed to develop children's sensitivity to spellings and their relations to pronunciations should be of paramount importance in the development of reading skill. (p. 416)

Summarizing the same report, Stahl, Osborne, and Lehr (1990) added:

> Insufficient familiarity with the spellings and spelling-to-sound correspondences of frequent words and syllables may be the single most common source of reading difficulties. (p. 115)

Decoding literally means to "break the code." The code is printed English and the sounds that letters represent. However, as Gough, Juel, and Griffith (1992) pointed out, codes are arbitrary (for instance, using 007 to represent a particular secret agent), while ciphers are systematic. In this sense, the alphabetic system of representing sounds is more like a cipher than a code.

These are strong words, but they are buttressed by extensive research and duplicate the conclusions based on earlier reviews of research, which also indicate that children who are taught through an approach based on **decoding** do better than those who are not (Anderson, Hiebert, Scott, & Wilkinson, 1985; Chall, 1967, 1983a; Dykstra, 1974). Although these scholarly reports argue the importance of phonics, they do not state specifically how it should be taught, except in very general terms. Adams (1990) concluded: "The best way to build children's visual vocabulary is to have them read meaningful words in meaningful contexts" (p. 156).

The key word is *contexts*. Phonics is a means to an end and not an end in itself. The purpose of teaching phonics is to enable students to decode words. The skills should be presented in the context of their use. For instance, if students are going to read a story about a duck in which the words *quack, quick,* and *quiet* appear, the **correspondence** (letter-sound relationship) by which the letters *qu* represent the sounds /kw/ should be introduced. Students would immediately apply this phonics element and so would see the purpose and value of phonics; in this instance, phonics enables them to read words that may have posed problems for them. Adams (1990) commented further:

> The goal of teaching phonics is to develop students' ability to read connected text independently. For students, however, the strongest functional connection between these two skills may run in the reverse direction. It is only the nature of reading that can make the content of a phonic lesson seem sensible; it is only the prospect of reading that can make them seem worthwhile. (p. 272)

A **correspondence** is a letter-sound relationship, for example, *s* = /s/.

BASIC PRINCIPLES OF PHONICS INSTRUCTION

Phonics instruction is of no value unless it fulfills some specific conditions. First, it must teach skills necessary for decoding words. Being able to read the short *a* in *hat* is an important skill, but knowing whether the *a* is long or short is not important; students can guess that the *a* is short without being able to read the word. Noting so-called silent letters is another useless skill. Knowing that the *k* in *knight* is silent does not ensure that a student can read the word.

Second, the skill should be one that students do not already know. One second-grader who was reading a fourth-grade book was put through a second-grade phonics workbook to make sure she had the necessary skills. If students can read material on a third-grade level or above, they obviously have just about all the phonics skills they will ever need.

Finally, the skills being taught should be related to reading tasks in which students are currently engaged or will soon be engaged. For instance, the time to teach that *ee* = /ē/ in words such as *jeep* and *sheep* is when students are about to read a book like *Sheep in a Jeep* (Shaw, 1986). All too often, they are taught skills far in advance of the time they will use them, or well after the relevant selection has been read, with no opportunity to apply the skills within a reasonable amount of time. This is ineffective instruction. Research indicates that children do not use or internalize the information unless the skills they have been taught are applicable in their day-to-day reading (Adams, 1990).

In summary, phonics instruction must be functional, useful, and contextual to be of value. It also should be planned and systematic.

Rather than teaching about silent letters, it is better to consider the *kn* in *knight* and *know* as another way to spell /n/.

When readers miss a word here or there, teachers may get the impression that they do not know their phonics and so may review phonics from the beginning. Students become bored when taught skills they already know. A better approach is to observe students carefully as they read or to give them a test, such as the word list tests of the informal reading inventory presented in Chapter 13, to see what they know and where they might need help.

APPROACHES TO TEACHING PHONICS

There are two main approaches to teaching phonics: analytic and synthetic. In the **analytic approach,** which is also known as implicit phonics, consonants are generally not isolated but are taught within the context of a whole word. For example, the sound /b/ would be referred to as the one heard in the beginning of *ball* and *boy*. The sound /b/ is not pronounced in isolation because that would distort

The **analytic approach** involves studying sounds within the context of the whole word; for example, /w/ is referred to as "the sound heard at the beginning of *wagon.*"

The purpose of using phonics is to enable students to decode words that are in their listening vocabularies but that they fail to recognize in print.

The **synthetic approach** involves saying a word sound by sound and then synthesizing the sounds into words.

In the first edition of this book, I recommended that an analytic approach be used to teach phonics. However, after taking another look at the research and working with underachieving readers who found it next to impossible to abstract sounds from words but who did better with a combined analytic and synthetic approach, I decided to recommend this combined approach. Although it is true that consonant sounds spoken in isolation are distorted, it is also true that some students do better when the target sound, albeit somewhat distorted, is presented explicitly.

it to "buh." Although somewhat roundabout, the analytic approach does not distort the sound /b/.

In the synthetic approach, which is sometimes called explicit phonics, words are decoded sound by sound, and both consonant and vowel sounds are pronounced in isolation. A child decoding *cat* would say, "kuh-ah-tuh." This approach is very direct, but it distorts consonant sounds, which cannot be pronounced accurately without a vowel. However, Ehri (1991) maintained that artificial procedures, such as saying the sound represented by each letter in a word, may be necessary to help beginning readers decipher words. As Groff (1986) noted:

> For over 40 years linguists have protested that isolating speech sounds was improper and contrary to the productive development of children's word recognition skills (Bloomfield, 1942). . . . Linguists who have opposed the teaching of explicit phonics apparently have failed to understand the difficulty that young children have in identifying and reproducing (segmenting) separate speech sounds when these phonemes are heard only within words. Telling children to listen to the first sound in *fed*, for example, and to say another word that begins with this sound (implicit phonics), does not teach children to segment speech sounds. Instead, this direction presupposes the child already knows what it intends to teach. Explicit phonics instruction makes no such presumption. (p. 922)

Most basal reading programs use an analytic approach. However, this book recommends a combination of the analytic and synthetic approaches. Novice readers need to have the target sound highlighted by hearing it in isolation, which is what the synthetic approach does. And they need to hear it in the context of a real word, which is what the analytic approach does. Actually, the most effective method for teaching students to decipher words seems to be a pattern, or word-building, technique that presents frequently appearing letter combinations, such as *-at, -an, -oat, -ake*. Experience and research indicate that it is easier to learn patterns than it is to learn individual letter-sound relationships, as in *t* = /t/ or *a* =

/a/ (Goswami & Bryant, 1990; Gunning, 1995). This approach is described more fully later in the chapter.

STAGES IN DECODING

LOGOGRAPHIC STAGE

Young children surprise their elders by reading a McDonald's sign, soda can and milk carton labels, and the names of cereals. However, for the most part, these children are not translating letters into sounds as more mature readers would do; instead, they are associating "nonphonemic visual characteristics" with spoken words (Ehri, 1994). For instance, a child remembers the word *McDonald's* by associating it with the golden arches, *Pepsi* is associated with its logograph, and *snake* is remembered because the letter *s* curls around like a snake. At times, teachers take advantage of the nonphonemic characteristics of words. They tell students that the word *tall* might be remembered because it has three tall letters and that *camel* is easy to recall because the *m* in the middle of the word has two humps.

In the logographic stage, students learn a word by selective association, by selecting some nonphonemic feature that distinguishes it from other words (Gough, Juel, & Griffith, 1992). For the word *elephant,* it could be the length of the word; or in the word *look,* it could be the two *o*'s that are like eyes. The problem with selective association is that students run out of distinctive clues, and the clues that they use do not help them decode new words. As students become aware of individual sounds in words and the fact that letters represent sounds, they move into the second stage of reading, the alphabetic stage (Byrne, 1992).

ALPHABETIC STAGE

In the alphabetic stage, learners use letter-sound relationships to read words. At first, they might just use a letter or two. They might use only the first letter of a word and combine the sound of that letter with context. For instance, in the sentence "The cat meowed," students may only process the initial *m* and then use context and their experience with cats to guess that the word is *meowed.* Or they may use the first and last letter to decode the word *cat* in "I lost my cat"; so they read the word *cat* as opposed to *cap* or *car.* As students gain in skill, they begin processing all the letters in words.

ORTHOGRAPHIC STAGE

In the orthographic phase, students process longer and more sophisticated units. For instance, instead of processing *hen* as *h-e-n,* they might divide it into two units: *h + en.* They process *light* as *l + ight* and make use of such elements as a final *e* (as in *cape*) to help them determine the pronunciation of a word.

As students process the same words over and over again, connections are made, and they do not have to read *cat* as /k/ /a/ /t/, or even /k/ /at/. Rather, the printed representation of the word as a whole elicits its spoken equivalent. The printed representation becomes bonded with the spoken equivalent (Perfetti, 1992). Gough, Juel, and Griffith (1992) explained the process somewhat differently. They believe that just about all the letters in a word are analyzed. Through practice, access speed increases so that even though words are analyzed element by element, this is done so rapidly as to be almost instantaneous. Regardless of how the process is explained, the end result is the same. In time, nearly all the words expert readers encounter in print are read as "sight" words. They are recognized virtually instantaneously. What makes the instantaneous recognition possible are the connections that have been created between each word's spelling or phonics elements and its pronunciation.

This theory of the stages of reading has a very important implication for the teaching of reading. It posits that nearly all the words we acquire are learned through phonics. Therefore, words to be learned, except for a few highly irregular ones, such as *of* or *one,* and perhaps a few learned in the very beginning, should be taught through a phonics approach, rather than one based on visual memory.

Most words that have been classified as sight words are at least partly predictable. For instance, the first and last letters of *was* are regular, as are the first and last letters of *been.* In fact, except for *of,* it is hard to find any word that does not have some degree of spelling-sound predictability. In teaching words, take advantage of that regularity. It will make the words easier to learn and to recognize. And establishing links between letters and sounds helps fix words in memory so that they are eventually recognized instantaneously, or at sight.

PHONICS ELEMENTS

When infrequent spellings are included, there are more than three hundred spellings of the forty-plus sounds of English. Many of these infrequent spellings occur in words borrowed from other languages, such as the spelling of the long *a* sound.

The content of phonics is fairly substantial. Depending on the dialect, English has forty or more sounds; however, many of them, especially vowels, may be spelled in more than one way. As a result, children have to learn more than one hundred spellings. The number would be even greater if relatively infrequent spellings were included, such as the *eigh* spelling of /ā/ in *neighbor* or the *o* spelling of /i/ in *women.*

CONSONANTS

Although vowels could be introduced first in a reading program, it is recommended that consonants be presented initially, as their sounds have fewer spelling options. The consonant sound /b/, for example, is spelled *b* most of the time. In addition, initial letters, which are usually consonants, yield better clues to the pronunciation of a word than do medial or final letters.

When teaching initial consonants, it is best to first present consonants that are easiest to say and that appear with the highest frequency. The sounds /s/, /m/, and /r/ are recommended for early presentation because they are easy to distinguish and are among the most frequently occurring sounds in the English language. Table 3.1 lists the twenty-five consonant sounds and their major spellings. Note that many have just one major spelling.

TABLE 3.1   Consonant spellings

Sound	Initial	Final	Model Word
/b/	*b*arn	ca*b*, ro*b*e	ball
/d/	*d*eer	ba*d*	dog
/f/	*f*un, *ph*oto	laug*h*	fish
/g/	*g*ate, *gh*ost, *gu*ide	ra*g*	goat
/h/	*h*ouse, *wh*o		hat
/hw/	*wh*ale		whale
/j/	*j*ug, *g*ym, sol*di*er	a*ge*, ju*dge*	jar
/k/	*c*an, *k*ite, *qu*ick, *ch*aos	ba*ck*, a*che*	cat, key
/l/	*l*ion	mai*l*	leaf
/m/	*m*e	hi*m*, co*mb*, autu*mn*	man
/n/	*n*ow, *kn*ow, *gn*u, *pn*eumonia	pa*n*	nail
/p/	*p*ot	to*p*	pen
/r/	*r*ide, *wr*ite		ring
/s/	*s*ight, *c*ity	bu*s*, mi*ss*, fa*ce*	sun
/t/	*t*ime	ra*t*, jump*ed*	table
/v/	*v*ase	lo*ve*	vest
/w/	*w*e, *wh*eel		wagon
/y/	*y*acht, on*i*on		yo-yo
/z/	*z*ipper	ha*s*, bu*zz*	zebra
/ch/	*ch*ip, *c*ello, ques*ti*on	ma*tch*	chair
/sh/	*sh*ip, *s*ure, *ch*ef, ac*ti*on	pu*sh*, spe*ci*al, mi*ssi*on	sheep
/th/	*th*in	brea*th*	thumb
/th/	*th*is	brea*the*	the
/zh/	a*z*ure, ver*si*on	bei*ge*, gara*ge*	garage
/ŋ/		si*ng*	ring

INITIAL CONSONANTS

Students might pick up some knowledge of initial consonants through shared reading and through writing activities, but letter-sound relationships should also be taught formally to make sure that students have learned these important elements, to clarify any misconceptions that may have arisen, and to provide addi-

Auditory perception is the ability to perceive a speech sound such as /s/ or /i/ or to note a common speech sound in two or more words.

tional reinforcement. A phonics lesson starts with **auditory perception** to make sure students can perceive the sound of the element and proceeds to the visual level, where the children integrate sound and letter knowledge. A four-step lesson for teaching initial consonants is detailed below. It assumes that the students can segment a word into its separate sounds, have a concept of beginning sounds, and realize that sounds are represented by letters. These are skills that were explained in Chapter 2. The lesson is synthetic and analytic, so the consonant sound is presented both in isolation and in the context of a whole word.

Lesson 3.1
Analytic-synthetic introduction of initial consonant correspondence

Step 1. Auditory perception

Teach the letter-sound relationship in the initial position of words. In teaching the correspondence (letter-sound relationship) *m* = /m/, hold up items or pictures whose names begin with /m/ and have the class name them; use, for example, a mop, a map, a picture of a man, and a picture of the moon. Ask the students to name all the items. Repeat the names, emphasizing the beginning sound. Ask what is the same about the words *mop, map, man,* and *moon*. Lead students to see that all the words begin in the same way. Ask them to supply other words that begin like *mop, map, man,* and *moon*. Give hints, if necessary—an animal that can climb trees (*monkey*), something that we drink (*milk*).

Step 2. Letter-sound integration

Have students name the items once more. Write the four words on the board, and ask what is the same about the way *mop, map, man,* and *moon* are written. Lead students to see that the words all begin with the letter *m* and that the letter *m* stands for the sound /m/ heard at the beginning of *moon*. At this point, *moon* becomes a model word. This is a simple word that can be depicted and that contains the target letter and sound. When referring to the sound represented by *m*, say that it is /m/, the sound heard at the beginning of *moon*, so that students can hear the sound both in isolation and in the context of a word.

Although consonants are distorted when pronounced in isolation, students can more readily perceive a sound when it is pronounced alone than when it is spoken as part of a word. This is especially true of students who are still learning to detect separate sounds in words. However, continuants such as /m/, /f/, and /s/ are less distorted because they are articulated with a continuous stream of breath.

Adapting instruction for Spanish-speaking students
Native speakers of Spanish may have difficulty perceiving /b/, /v/, /k/, /j/, /z/, /sh/, /th/, and /ch/. You may need to spend additional time developing students' perception of these sounds.

Step 3. Guided practice

Provide immediate practice. Help students read food labels that contain /m/ words: *milk, mayonnaise, margarine*. Read a story together about monkeys or masks, or sing a song or read a rhyme that has a generous share of /m/ words. Try to choose some items in which students integrate knowledge of the correspondence with context. Compose sentences such as "I will drink a glass of milk" and "At the zoo we saw a monkey," and write them on the chalkboard. Read each sentence, stopping at the word beginning with /m/. Have students use context and their knowledge of the correspondence *m* = /m/ to predict the word.

Step 4. Application

On their own, have students read selections that contain /m/ words.

Using Children's Books to Teach Initial Consonants. A good children's book can be a powerful medium for presenting phonics. To teach an initial consonant, choose a page from an alphabet book that presents a number of words containing the target consonant. For example, if you are using *Nedobeck's Alphabet Book* (Nedobeck, 1981), read the *S* page: "Sidney Sparrow Soars through a Sunlit Sky." Discuss the fact that many of the words begin in the same way. Read the page again, pointing to each *s* word as you do so. Lead students to see that *s* spells the sounds heard at the beginning of *Sidney, sparrow, soars, sunlit,* and *sky.* Also read and discuss the *S* page from Carle's (1974) *All About Arthur:* "South of Seattle he met a silly seal Sally suffering from the sun. She had a scorched stomach."

Use a model word to demonstrate /s/. Choose a word that is easily depicted as the model word (refer to Table 3.1 for suggestions); for *s,* a good choice would be *sun.* When you talk about the sound /s/, refer to it as /s/, the sound heard at the beginning of *sun.* Draw or obtain a picture of the sun. In the upper left-hand corner, write *S s* in manuscript form. Underneath the picture, write *sun.* Place the illustration in a prominent place for future reference.

Once students have a solid grasp of the idea that *s* represents /s/, the sound heard at the beginning of *sun,* provide activities that will help them to use this knowledge to decode words. Using a book such as *Helen Oxenbury's ABC of Things* (Oxenbury, 1971), have them try to read the words on the *S* page. The words on the left page—*sea, seal, sun*—are illustrated by the drawings on the facing page. Discuss the drawings of those three words. Then tell students that they will be reading the three *s* words and that each one names something shown in the picture. Cover up the *s* of *sea* and say, "This part of the word says /ē/. Now let's add *s.* What does the word say?" Discuss the remaining two words in the same way. Then have the students read all three words. Present other consonants in the same manner.

After children have learned a half-dozen consonants or so, present contextual sentences or stories in which they can use the content of the piece and their emerging knowledge of letter sounds; books such as *Easy as Pie* (Folsom & Folsom, 1986) are good (see Figure 3.1). Common similes, except for the last word, are shown on the right-hand page, as is the letter of the missing word. The answer appears when the child turns the page. For instance, the *S* page contains the letter *S* and the words "Deep as the." Read the first part of the simile aloud, and tell the students that the last word begins with the letter *s.* Ask students to guess what they think the word is. Remind them that the word must begin with /s/, the sound heard at the beginning of *sun.* Write their responses on the board. If any word supplied does not begin with /s/, discuss why this could not be the right answer. Turn the page to uncover the word that completes the riddle, and let students read the answer. Discuss why the answer is correct. Emphasize that it makes sense in the phrase and begins with /s/, the same sound heard at the beginning of *sun.*

Using context to verify the results of decoding a word is known as cross checking. For instance, if a student decoded an unfamiliar word beginning with *b* as *barked,* he or she could cross-check by seeing whether the word makes sense in the sentence in which it appears.

FIGURE 3.1   *S* pages from *Easy as Pie*

Deep as the Sea

From *Easy as Pie* by Marcia Folsom and Michael Folsom, 1986, Boston: Houghton Mifflin. Copyright © 1986 by Marcia Folsom and Michael Folsom. Reprinted by permission of Marcia Folsom.

Another book that combines context and knowledge of beginning consonant correspondence is *The Alphabet Tale* by Jan Garten (1964) (see Figure 3.2). Shown on the *S* page is a large red *S*, a seal's tail, and a riddle:

> He balances balls and swims a great deal.
> This tail is the tail of the flippered _____.

The next page shows the rest of the seal and the word *seal*.

When using alphabet books, be on the lookout for confusing presentations. Often the books use consonant clusters, in which the initial consonant is followed directly by one or more other consonants, rather than a vowel. In *Nedobeck's Alphabet Book* (Nedobeck, 1981), for instance, *sparrow* and *sky* are presented together with *Sidney, soars,* and *sunlit.* All five of these *s* words do begin with /s/,

He balances balls and swims a great deal.
This tail is the tail of the flippered ____

Seal

From *The Alphabet Tale* by J. Garten (1964). New York: Random House. © 1964 by Jan Garten and Muriel Batherman. Reprinted by permission of Jan Garten and Muriel Batherman.

but it is harder to perceive the sound when it is part of a consonant cluster. In addition, two or three sounds may sometimes be included in the presentation of one letter. In one book, the words *tiger, thin,* and *the* are used to demonstrate the sound usually represented by the letter *t*. However, *th* in *thin* represents a different sound than that heard at the beginning of *tiger,* and *th* in *the* represents the voiced counterpart of *th* in *thin*.

A number of alphabet books are published in paperback form, and so are relatively inexpensive.

Despite their shortcomings, alphabet books provide excellent reinforcement for beginning consonants. Listed in the Children's Book List are some titles that might be used.

Children's Book List
Recommended alphabet books for reinforcing initial consonants

Calmenson, S. *It Begins with an A*. New York: Hyperion (1993). Rhyming riddles challenge the reader to guess objects whose names begin with letters *A* to *Z*.

Cohen, N. *From Apple to Zipper*. New York: Macmillan (1993). Rhyming text, with illustrations forming the letters they represent, is included.

Demi. *Demi's Find the Animal ABC*. New York: Grosset & Dunlap (1985). The reading of a patterned sentence ("Can you find this_____?") is combined with use of words starting with the letter being presented. Students are asked to find the match for the key picture from among dozens of illustrations.

Downie, J. *Alphabet Puzzle*. New York: Lothrop (1988). Half the letters shown are involved in a guessing game. For instance, the letters *k* and *l* are on facing pages. The *k* page says, "K, k is for kite." However, the *l* page has a cutout square that shows a kite in a tree and is accompanied by the sentence "L, l is for ?" The answer appears on the next page.

Eichenberg, F. *Ape in a Cape*. San Diego, CA: Harcourt (1952). Humorous rhyming phrases label drawings showing a creature or object whose name begins with the letter being presented: "Goat in a boat." Use of rhyme allows contrast of the letter-sound being presented with another beginning letter-sound.

Geisel, T. S. *Dr. Seuss's ABC*. New York: Beginner (1963). Letter-sound correspondences are presented in typical Dr. Seuss fashion.

Hoban, T. *A, B, See!* New York: Greenwillow (1982). Upper-case letters are accompanied by objects in silhouette that begin with the letter that is shown.

MacDonald, S. *Alphabetics*. New York: Bradbury (1986). Letters are used to form objects whose names begin with them. For example, *t* is used to create a tree.

Oxenbury, H. *Helen Oxenbury's ABC of Things*. New York: Delacorte (1971). Both upper- and lower-case letters in easy-to-recognize forms are illustrated with creatures and objects that begin with them. The *B* page shows a baker holding a baby while a badger and a bear cling to him and a bird is perched on his hat. The names of the objects are given.

Watson, C. *Applebet: An ABC*. New York: Farrar, Straus and Giroux (1982). Readers follow an apple through the alphabet from the time it is picked from a tree. The special feature of this book is that it covers sounds for hard and soft *c* and *g*, and the digraphs *ch*, *sh*, *th*, and *wh*. The letters *qu* are presented as a unit, which is the way they appear in almost all words.

After an alphabet book has been discussed, place it in the class library so that students may "read" it. Encourage children to check out books for home use.

Also have students create their own alphabet books. After a letter-sound relationship has been presented, direct students to create a page showing the upper- and lower-case forms of the letter along with a key word and an illustration of the word. As students learn to read words beginning with the letter and sound, they may add them to the page.

Be sure to make use of students' emerging knowledge of letter-sound relationships when reading big books. After reading Paul Galdone's (1975) *The Gingerbread Boy,* for instance, turn to the page on which the gingerbread boy meets the cow. Read the words *cow, can,* and *catch.* Discuss how the words sound alike and begin with the letter *c.* Encourage the use of context. Reread the story, stopping when you come to a word that begins with *c.* Encourage students to read the word. Using *cow* as a key word, remind students that the word should begin with /k/ as in *cow.* Also remind them of the context of the sentence to help them learn to integrate letter-sound relationships with context. To further reinforce the *c* = /k/ correspondence, have students draw a picture of something they can do and write a short piece about it. Individual stories could be the basis for a group story or booklet that tells about the talents and abilities of all class members.

Reinforcement Activities
Consonant letter-sound relationships

- Have students encounter initial consonants they know in books.
- Creating experience stories affords students the opportunity to meet phonics elements in print. While reading the story with an individual or group, the teacher can call attention to any consonants that have already been introduced. The teacher might pause before a word that begins with a known consonant and have a student attempt to read it.
- If possible, all of the language arts should be integrated. Handwriting may be used to reinforce initial consonants. After the letter-sound relationship *s* = /s/ has been introduced, teach students how to form the letter. Students may also use their growing knowledge of letter-sound relationships to write short pieces. See Chapter 11 for suggestions on introducing a writing program.
- Play the game "Going to Paris" (Brewster, 1952). Players recite this:

  I'm going to Paris.
  I'm going to pack my bag with _____.

  The first player says an object whose name begins with the first letter of the alphabet or the letter-sound relationship being studied. Subsequent players then say the names of all the objects mentioned by previous players and identify an object whose name begins with the next letter of the alphabet.
- Play the game "Alphabet It." In this counting-out game, one child recites the letters of the alphabet. As the child says each letter, she or he points to the other members of the class whose name begins with the letter being recited. Each child pointed to removes himself or herself from the game. The alphabet is recited until just one child is left. That child is it for the next round or next game.
- Use software that helps students discover letter-sound relationships: *Dr. Peet's Talk/Writer* (Hartley) or *Special Writer Coach* (Tom Snyder). These word-processing programs will say words that have been typed in. You

Adapting instruction for ESL students

Since experience stories are based on students' experiences and their language, they are generally easier for students to read than text in books. Keeping such stories short also makes them easier to read. Experience stories work especially well with students who have just begun to speak English.

might give students a list of three words that begin with *s* to type in, and have them listen to hear what sound the letter *s* makes. However, it is not necessary to give students assignments. Just introduce them to *Dr. Peet's Talk/Writer* or *Special Writer Coach,* and let nature take its course. As they explore the program, they will make valuable discoveries about letter-sound relationships. Each program also can be used as a kind of sound dictionary. When students want to find out what a word says, all they have to do is type it in and the speech synthesizer will say it. A small number of words are distorted by the synthesizer, so students may have to make some minor adjustments in pronunciation. If the word does not make sense, even after adjustments, the student should ask for a teacher's help.

- Use the CD-ROM software entitled *The Big Bug Alphabet* (Spectrum, HoloByte, 1994). The viewer joins Buzzy the Bug in a trip through the circus that illustrates consonant correspondences.

- As a review of initial consonant spelling-sound relationships, read the following jump-rope chant with students. Help students extend the chant through all the letters of the alphabet. Adapt the chant for boys by substituting "wife's" for "husband's."

> *A*—my name is *A*lice,
> My husband's name is *A*ndy,
> We live in *A*labama,
> And we sell apples. . . .

A good source of jump-rope chants and other rhymes is *A Rocket in My Pocket* (Withers, 1948), which is available in paperback.

- Consonant rhymes can also be used to reinforce initial consonant sounds. Do a shared reading of the rhyme first. Stress the target consonant letter-sound relationship. After an initial reading, encourage the class to read the words beginning with the target letter. The first rhyme below is a ball-bouncing piece from Australia (Turner, 1972); the second is a traditional rhyme called "Cakes and Custard."

> Ball, ball, bouncing
> Bingo in the bath
> Bunny's eating lettuce
> Up the garden path
> Mouse's in the garden
> Geese rather lame
> So ball, ball bouncing
> Let us have a game.

> When Jack's a good boy,
> He shall have cakes and custard;
> But when he does nothing but cry,
> He shall have nothing but mustard.

FINAL CONSONANTS

Final consonants are handled in much the same way as initial consonants. Relate them to their initial counterparts. And do not neglect them. According to a classic research study by Gibson (1966), final consonants are a significant aid in the decoding of printed words.

CONSONANT DIGRAPHS

If you look at the consonant chart in Table 3.1, you will notice that some of the sounds are spelled with two letters. The sound /f/, for example, is usually spelled with *f* as in *fox* but may also be spelled with *ph* or *gh* as in *photograph*. When two letters are used to spell a single sound, these double letters are known as **digraphs** (*di*, "two"; *graphs*, "written symbols").

Since they represent only one sound, digraph correspondences should not be any harder to learn than single-consonant correspondences. However, students do have to get used to grouping the letters of a digraph and must also realize that each letter does not represent a separate sound. The most frequently occurring digraphs are *sh* (shop), *ch* (child), *-ng* (sing), *wh* (whip), *th* (thumb), and *th* (that). Common digraphs are listed in Table 3.2.

A **digraph** is two letters that represent one sound, such as *ph* for /f/ in *photo*.

CONSONANT CLUSTERS

Like digraphs, **clusters**, or *blends* as they are sometimes called, are also composed of more than one letter. However, they represent two sounds, as in *drop* or *green*, or, in some instances, three sounds, as in *string* or *strange*. Common clusters are presented in Table 3.3. Clusters are more difficult to decode than single-consonant correspondences or digraph correspondences. Students who know all the single-consonant and digraph correspondences may still have difficulty with clusters (Gunning, 1988b). Clusters, therefore, must be taught with care and with much reinforcement. You cannot assume that because a child knows *d* = /d/ and

A **cluster** is composed of two or more letters that represent two or more sounds, such as *br* in *broom*. Clusters are sometimes called *blends*. Technically, however, the sounds are clustered rather than blended together. When you say *broom,* you can detect a separate /b/ and a separate /r/. Perhaps because it is difficult to hear the separate sounds in a cluster, this element poses a special difficulty for many children.

When students misread a cluster—reading *fog* for *frog*, for instance—ask questions that lead them to see that they need to process two initial sounds rather than just one: What letter does the word *fog* begin with? What two letters does the word in the sentence begin with? What sound does *f* stand for? What sound does *r* stand for? What sounds do *f* and *r* make when said together? How would you say the word in the story?

TABLE 3.2 Common consonant digraphs

Correspondence	Examples
ch = /ch/	chair, church
ck = /k/	tack, pick
gh = /f/	rough, tough
kn = /n/	knot, knob
ng = /ŋ/	thing, sing
ph = /f/	phone, photograph
sc = /s/	scissors, scientist
sh = /sh/	shoe, shop
(*s*)*si* = /sh/	mission
th = /th/	there, them
th = /th/	thumb, thunder
ti = /sh/	station, action
wh = /w/	wheel, where
wr = /r/	wrench, wrestle

TABLE 3.3 Common consonant clusters

Initial Clusters

With *l*	Example Words	With *r*	Example Words	With *s*	Example Words	Other	Example Words
bl	blanket, black	*br*	broom, bread	*sc*	score, scale	*tw*	twelve, twin
cl	clock, clothes	*cr*	crow, crash	*sch*	school, schedule	*qu*	queen, quick
fl	flag, fly	*dr*	dress, drink	*scr*	scream, scrub		
gl	glove, glue	*fr*	frog, from	*sk*	sky, skin		
pl	plum, place	*gr*	green, ground	*sl*	sled, sleep		
sl	slide, slow	*pr*	prince, prepare	*sm*	smoke, smile		
				sn	snake, sneakers		
				sp	spider, spot		
				st	star, stop		
				sw	sweater, swim		

Final Clusters

With *l*	Example Words	With *n*	Example Words	Other	Example Words
ld	field, old	*nce*	prince, chance	*ct*	fact, effect
lf	wolf, self	*nch*	lunch, bunch	*mp*	jump, camp
lk	milk, silk	*nd*	hand, wind	*sp*	wasp, grasp
lm	film	*nk*	tank, wink	*st*	nest, best
lp	help	*nt*	tent, sent		
lt	salt, belt				
lve	twelve, solve				

r = /r/, she or he will be able to handle *dr* = /dr/. Such clusters need to be taught as new elements. Many of the same activities that are used to reinforce single-consonant correspondences can be used.

TROUBLESOME CORRESPONDENCES AND UNNEEDED LETTERS

Although consonant correspondences are generally easier to learn than vowels, some consonant letters pose special problems. One of these letters is *x,* which is a reverse digraph, except when it represents /z/ as in *xylophone.* It may represent either /ks/, as in *tax,* or /gz/, as in *example.* Actually, *x* and *q* are unnecessary letters. Neither represents a sound that could not be represented by another letter or group of letters.

The most difficult consonant letters are *c* and *g.* Both regularly represent two sounds: The letter *c* stands for /k/ and /s/, as in *cake* and *city;* the letter *g* represents /g/ and /j/, as in *go* and *giant.* The letter *c* represents /k/ far more often than it stands for /s/ (Gunning, 1975), and this is the sound students usually attach to it (Venezky,

1965); the letter *g* more often represents /g/. In teaching the consonant letters *c* and *g*, the more frequent sounds (*c* = /k/, *g* = /g/) should be presented first. The other sound represented by each letter (*c* = /s/, *g* = /j/) should be taught sometime later. At that point, it would also be helpful to teach the following generalizations:

- The letter *c* usually stands for /k/ when it is followed by *a*, *o*, or *u*, as in *cab*, *cob*, or *cub*.
- The letter *c* usually stands for /s/ when followed by *e*, *i*, or *y*, as in *cereal*, *circle*, or *cycle*.
- The letter *g* usually stands for /g/ when followed by *a*, *o*, or *u*, as in *gave*, *go*, or *gum*.
- The letter *g* usually stands for /j/ when followed by *e*, *i*, or *y*, as in *gem*, *giant*, or *gym*. (There are a number of exceptions: *geese*, *get*, *girl*, *give*.)

The *g* generalizations help explain the *gu* spelling of /g/ as in *guide* and *guilt*. Without the *u* following the *g*, there would be a tendency to pronounce those words with the /j/ sound (Venezky, 1965). Determining the sound of *c* and *g* at the end of a word is relatively easy. If a word ends in *e*, *c* represents /s/ and *g* stands for /j/ (*lace*, *page*). The letter *e* serves as a marker to indicate that *c* and *g* use their soft sounds.

When teaching the *c* and *g* generalizations, do it inductively. For instance, list examples of the *c* spelling of /k/ in one column and of /s/ in another. Have students read each word in the first column and note the sound that *c* represents and the vowel letter that follows *c*. Do the same with the second column. Then help students draw up generalizations based on their observations.

There is no conclusive evidence that generalizations help; however, building awareness of them may assist some students, especially poorer readers. Better students are more likely than poorer students to construct phonics generalizations intuitively (Harris & Sipay, 1990). Spending a lot of time teaching generalizations and having students invest a great deal of energy memorizing them is not advised. A better procedure would be to have students spend the bulk of their time applying their knowledge by reading selections with words in them that embody the generalizations. Ironically, some students apply generalizations without being able to state them, while other students can state generalizations but do not apply them (Gunning, 1988a).

Even when not taught phonics systematically, many students infer phonics generalizations. After reading a number of words like *cat*, *ran*, *nap*, and *hat*, they come to the conclusion that the letter *a* followed by a consonant has an /a/ sound. However, some children will fail to generalize and will need direct, systematic instruction.

Variability Strategy. An alternative to presenting the *c* and *g* generalizations is to teach students to be prepared to deal with the variability of the spelling of certain sounds. Students need to learn that, in English, letters can often stand for more than one sound. After learning the two sounds for *c* and *g*, students should be taught to use the following variability strategy when they are unsure how to read a word that begins with *c* or *g*.

Student Strategy
Applying the variability strategy to consonant correspondences

1. Try the main pronunciation—the one the letter usually stands for.
2. If the main pronunciation gives a word that is not a real one or does not make sense in the sentence, try the other pronunciation.

3. If I still get a word that is not a real word or does not make sense in the sentence, ask for help.

Students need to see that the aim of phonics is to help them construct meaning from print. If they use phonics to decipher a word but end up with a non-word, then they should try again. Even when they construct a real word, they should cross-check it by seeing if it makes sense in the sentence they are reading.

Just as you post a chart to remind students of correct letter formation, display a chart showing all the major consonant correspondences and a key word for each. Students experiencing difficulty sounding out a word can refer to the chart. A child feeling puzzled when he pronounces *cider* as "kidder" could look at the chart and note that *c* has two pronunciations: /k/ as in *cat* and /s/ as in *circle*. Since the /k/ pronunciation did not produce a word that made sense, the child would try the /s/ pronunciation. Table 3.1 could be used as a basis for constructing a consonant chart; a sample of such a chart is shown in Figure 3.3. Drawings, photos, or pictures might be used to illustrate each of the sounds. As new correspondences are learned, they could be added to the chart. The chart could also be used as a spelling aid.

The variability strategy is a simpler procedure than the application of rules. Rather than trying to remember a rule, all the student has to do is try the major pronunciation, and, if that pronunciation does not work out, try another.

VOWELS

English has about sixteen vowel sounds. (The number varies somewhat because some dialects have more than others.) Each vowel sound has a variety of spellings. For example, /ā/, which is commonly referred to as long *a,* is usually spelled *a_e,* as in *late; a* at the end of a syllable, as in *favor;* or *ai* or *ay,* as in *train* and *tray.* We can say then that the vowel sound /ā/ has four main spellings, two of which are closely related: *ay* appears in final position, and *ai* is found in initial and medial positions; so these two spellings work together.

Short vowels are the vowel sounds heard in *cat, pet, sit, hot,* and *cut.*

Long vowels are the vowel sounds heard in *cake, sleep, pie, boat,* and *use.*

Collections for Young Scholars (Open Court, 1995) is one of the few reading programs that presents long vowels first. The rationale for teaching long vowels first is that they are easier to perceive. To take advantage of this characteristic, introduce a few easy long-vowel patterns, such as *-ē: he, me, we, she; -ēē: bee, see, tree;* and *-ō: go, no, so.* Once these easy patterns have been presented, introduce short-vowel patterns.

All the other vowel sounds are similar to /ā/ in having two to four major spellings. Considering correspondences in this way makes vowel spellings seem fairly regular. It is true that /ā/ and other vowel sounds can each be spelled in a dozen or more ways, but many of these spellings are oddities. For instance, the *Random House Dictionary* (Flexner & Hauck, 1994) lists nineteen spellings of /ā/: *ate,* G*ael,* champ*a*gne, r*ai*n, arr*aig*n, g*ao*l, g*au*ge, r*ay,* expos*é,* su*e*de, st*ea*k, matin*ee, eh,* v*ei*l, f*eig*n, Mars*eilles,* dem*e*sne, ber*et,* and ob*ey.* Note that many of these are in words borrowed from other languages.

A chart of vowels and their major spellings is presented in Table 3.4. Note that the chart lists twenty-one vowel sounds and includes *r* vowels. When *r* follows a vowel, it often affects the quality of the vowel.

SCOPE AND SEQUENCE

A well-planned program of instruction would include all the vowels in Table 3.4 and their major spellings, but they would be taught over a period of two or three years. In general, **short vowels** are taught first because they have fewer spellings. However, a case could be made for teaching **long vowels** first. Some long vowels, especially those that are spelled with the final letter in two-letter words (*he, we, so, go*) are very easy to learn.

Table 3.5 is a four-level phonics scope-and-sequence chart that contains both consonants and vowels. The preparatory level includes the skills and understand-

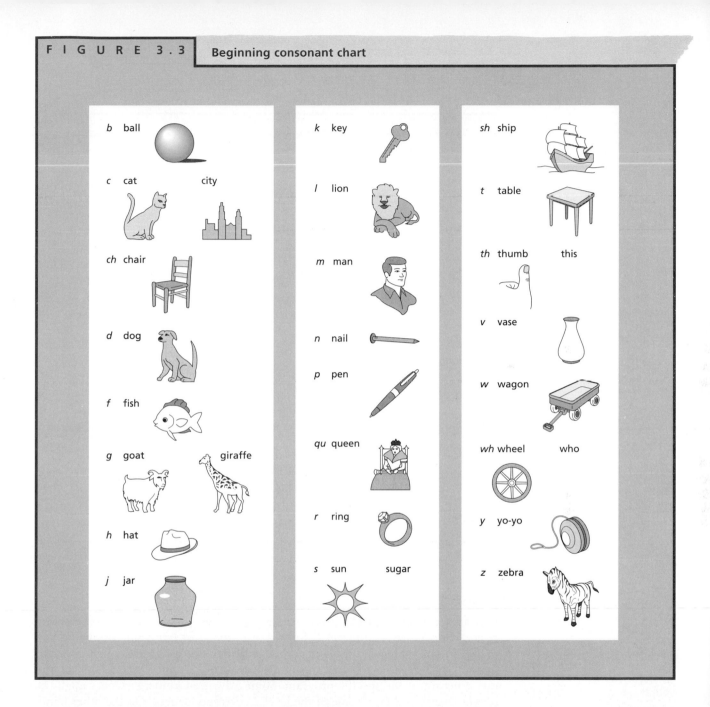

ings that would generally be covered in kindergarten or the beginning of grade 1. Level 1 includes correspondences typically taught in grade 1. Level 2 encompasses second-grade correspondences, and level 3 presents advanced correspondences and those that have limited usefulness and would be presented in grade 3 or

TABLE 3.4 Vowel spellings

	Vowel Sound	Major Spellings	Model Word
Short Vowels	/a/	rag, happen, have	cat
	/e/	get, letter, thread	bed
	/i/	wig, middle, event	fish
	/o/	fox, problem, father	mop
	/u/	bus	cup
Long Vowels	/ā/	name, favor, say, sail	rake
	/ē/	he, even, eat, seed, bean, key, these, either, funny, serious	wheel
	/ī/	hide, tiny, high, lie, sky	nine
	/ō/	vote, open, coat, bowl, old, though	nose
	/ū/	use, human	cube
Other Vowels	/aw/	daughter, law, walk, off, bought	saw
	/oi/	noise, toy	boy
	/o͝o/	wood, should, push	foot
	/o͞o/	soon, new, prove, group, two, fruit, truth	school
	/ow/	tower, south	cow
	/ə/	above, operation, similar, opinion, suppose	banana
r Vowels	/ar/	far, large, heart	car
	/air/	hair, care, where, stair, bear	chair
	/i(ə)r/	dear, steer, here	deer
	/ər/	her, sir, fur, earth	bird
	/or/	horse, door, tour, more	four

As you can see from Table 3.4, short-vowel words have fewer spellings than long-vowel, other-vowel, or *r*-vowel words. There are also a greater number of short-vowel words.

Adapting instruction for ESL students

Both Chinese- and Spanish-speaking children have difficulty with /ē/. When working with these children, start with the /ō/ words.

Schwa is the unaccented vowel sound heard at the end of *sofa* and is the most frequently occurring vowel sound.

beyond. Correspondences within each level are listed in order of approximate frequency of occurrence. In level 1, for instance, the most frequently occurring and easiest-to-discriminate consonants are listed first. The levels are rough approximations and must be adjusted to suit the needs and abilities of the students and the structure of the specific program. Some advanced kindergarteners might be taught level 1 and even some of the level 2 correspondences. On the other hand, a fourth-grader with a disability may have difficulty with short vowels and would need to work in level 1.

Omitted from Table 3.5 are some correspondences that rarely occur (for example, *ge* or *z* = /zh/ in *beige* or *azure*). Because these elements are encountered infrequently, words containing them are best taught as sight words. Also omitted from Table 3.5 is **schwa**, /ə/, the most frequently occurring vowel sound, often

TABLE 3.5 Scope-and-sequence chart for phonics

Level	Categories	Correspondence	Model Word	Correspondence	Model Word
Preparatory	Letter names, phonemic awareness, rhyming, segmentation, perception of initial consonants				
1	High-frequency initial consonants	*s* = /s/	sea	*r* = /r/	rug
		f = /f/	fish	*l* = /l/	lamp
		m = /m/	men	*b* = /b/	boy
		t = /t/	toy	*c* = /k/	can
		d = /d/	dog	*p* = /p/	pot
	Lower-frequency initial consonants and *x*	*n* = /n/	nine	*c* = /s/	city
		g = /g/	game	*g* = /j/	gym
		v = /v/	vase	*y* = /y/	yo-yo
		j = /j/	jacket	*z* = /z/	zebra
		h = /h/	hit	*x* = /ks/	box
		w = /w/	wagon	*x* = /gs/	example
		k – /k/	kite		
	High-frequency initial consonant digraphs	*ch* = /ch/	church	*th* = /th/	thumb
		sh = /sh/	ship	*wh* = /wh/	wheel
		th = /th/	this		
	Long vowels: word-ending single-letter vowels and digraphs	*e* = /ē/	he, me	*ee* = /ē/	bee, see
		o = /ō/	no, so	*ea* = /ē/	sea, tea
	Short vowels	*i* = /i/	fish	*u* = /u/	pup
		e = /e/	net	*o* = /o/	pot
		a = /a/	hat		
2	Initial consonant clusters	*st* = /st/	stop	*fr* = /fr/	free
		pl = /pl/	play	*fl* = /fl/	flood
		pr = /pr/	print	*str* = /str/	street
		gr = /gr/	green	*cr* = /kr/	cry
		tr = /tr/	tree	*sm* = /sm/	small
		cl = /kl/	clean	*sp* = /sp/	speak
		br = /br/	bring	*bl* = /bl/	blur
		dr = /dr/	drive		
	Final consonant clusters	*ld* = /ld/	cold	*mp* = /mp/	lamp
		lf = /lf/	shelf	*nd* = /nd/	hand
		sk = /sk/	mask	*nt* – /nt/	ant
		st = /st/	best	*nk* = /ŋk/	think

(continued)

TABLE 3.5 *(continued)*

Level	Categories	Correspondence	Model Word	Correspondence	Model Word
2	Less frequent digraphs and other consonant elements	*ck* = /k/	lock		
		dge = /j/	bridge		
	Long vowels: final *e* marker	*a-e* = /ā/	save	*e-e* = /ē/	these
		i-e = /ī/	five	*u-e* = /ū/	use
		o-e = /ō/	hope		
	Digraphs and trigraphs	*ee* = /ē/	green	*ow* = /ō/	show
		ai/ay = /ā/	aim, play	*igh* = /ī/	light
		oa = /ō/	boat	*ea* = /e/	bread
		ea = /ē/	bean		
	Other vowels	*ou/ow* = /ow/	out, owl	*oo* = /o͝o/	book
		oi/oy = /oi/	oil, toy	*oo* = /o͞o/	tool
		au/aw = /aw/	author, paw		
	r vowels	*ar* = /ar/	car	*are* = /air/	care
		er = /ər/	her	*air* = /air/	hair
		ir = /ər/	sir	*ear* = /i(ə)r/	fear
		ur = /ər/	burn	*eer* = /i(ə)r/	steer
		or = /or/	for		
3	Consonants	*ti* = /sh/	action		
		ssi = /sh/	mission		
		t, ti = /ch/	future, question		
	Consonant digraphs	*ch* = /k/	choir	*kn* = /n/	knee
		ch = /sh/	chef	*wr* = /r/	wrap
		gh = /g/	ghost	*ph* = /f/	photo
	Vowels	*y* = /ē/	city	*o* = /aw/	off
		y = /ī/	why	*al* = /aw/	ball
		y = /i/	gym	*ew* = /ū/	few
		a = /o/	father		
		e = /i/	remain		

heard in unaccented syllables. It may be spelled with any vowel letter and is the sound heard in so*fa*, sil*e*nt, d*i*vide, c*o*nnect, and circ*u*s. To make the situation even more complex, many unaccented syllables do not contain a schwa. Knowledge of schwa is not much help in decoding words, since identifying it entails being able to tell which syllable is accented. However, schwa should be learned when the dictionary pronunciation key is presented.

TEACHING VOWEL CORRESPONDENCES

Vowels are taught in the same way as consonants. The main difference is that vowels can be spoken in isolation without distortion, so teaching vowels synthetically should not be confusing to students. Lesson 3.2 outlines how short *i* might be taught.

Lesson 3.2
Vowel correspondence

Step 1. Auditory perception

Hold up a ring, a stick, the numeral 6, and a picture of a fish. Name each object, and have children listen to see if they can tell which sound can be heard in all of the names. As you say each name, emphasize the vowel sound. Then say the vowel sound in isolation. Lead students to see that the words all have the sound /i/.

Vowels can be taught in isolation or as part of patterns. In this lesson, they are taught in isolation. Teaching vowels in isolation is helpful for children who are still learning to detect individual sounds in words.

Step 2. Letter-sound integration

Write the words *ring, stick, six,* and *fish* on the board, saying each word as you do so. Ask students if they can see what is the same about the words. Show them that all four words have an *i,* which stands for the sound /i/ as pronounced in *fish.* Have students read the words. Discuss other words that have the sound /i/. Have students read the words chorally and individually.

Step 3. Guided practice

Share-read a story that contains a number of short *i* words. Pause before the short *i* words and invite students to read them. Also share songs, rhymes, announcements, and signs that contain short *i* words.

Step 4. Application

Have students read selections or create experience stories that contain short *i*.

As students begin to learn decoding strategies that combine context and knowledge of letter-sound correspondences, it is important that they have opportunities to apply them to whole selections. If they read materials that contain elements they have been taught, they will learn the elements better and also be better at applying them to new words (Juel & Rope-Schneider, 1985). Students who have been introduced to short *u* correspondences might read *Bugs* (McKissack & McKissack, 1988) and *Joshua James Likes Trucks* (Petrie, 1983), both of which are very easy to read; a somewhat more challenging text is *Buzz Said the Bee* (Lewison, 1992). Other children's books that might be used to reinforce vowel letter-sound relationships are listed in the Children's Book List.

Children's Book List
Children's books that reinforce vowel patterns

Short-Vowel Patterns

Short a

Antee, N. (1985). *The good bad cat.* Grand Haven, MI: School Zone.

Carle, E. (1987). *Have you seen my cat?* New York: Scholastic.

Hawkins, C., & Hawkins, J. (1983). *Pat the cat.* New York: Putnam.

Moncure, J. B. (1981). *Word Bird makes words with cat.* Elgin, IL: Child's World.

Wildsmith, B. (1982). *Cat on the mat.* New York: Oxford.

Ziefert, H. (1988). *Cat games.* New York: Puffin.

Short e

Gregorich, B. (1984). *Nine men chase a hen.* Grand Haven, MI: School Zone.

Hawkins, C., & Hawkins, J. (1985). *Jen the hen.* New York: Putnam.

Snow, P. (1984). *A pet for Pat.* Chicago: Children's Press.

Short i

Greydanus, R. (1988). *Let's get a pet.* Mahwah, NJ: Troll.

Moncure, J. (1984). *Word Bird makes words with pig.* Elgin, IL: Child's World.

Wang, M. L. (1989). *The ant and the dove.* Chicago: Children's Press.

Short o

McKissack, P. C. (1983). *Who is who?* Chicago: Children's Press.

Moncure, J. B. (1981). *No! no! Word Bird.* Elgin, IL: Child's World.

Short u

Gregorich, B. (1984). *The gum on the drum.* Grand Haven, MI: School Zone.

Lewison, W. C. (1992). *Buzz said the bee.* New York: Scholastic.

McKissack, P., & McKissack, F. (1988). *Bugs!* Chicago: Children's Press.

Petrie, C. (1983). *Joshua James likes trucks.* Chicago: Children's Press.

Ziefert, H. (1987). *Nicky upstairs and down.* New York: Puffin.

Review of short vowels

Boegehold, B. D. (1990). *You are much too small.* New York: Bantam.

Kraus, R. (1971). *Leo, the late bloomer.* New York: Simon & Schuster.

Long-Vowel Patterns

Long a

Neasi, B. J. (1984). *Just like me.* Chicago: Children's Press.

Oppenheim, J. (1990). *Wake up, baby!* New York: Bantam.

Raffi. (1987). *Shake my sillies out.* New York: Crown.

Robart, R. (1986). *The cake that Mack ate.* Toronto: Kids Can Press.

Stadler, J. (1984). *Hooray for Snail!* New York: Harper.

Long e

Bonsall, C. (1974). *And I mean it, Stanley.* New York: Harper.

Pigeen, S. (1985). *Eat your peas, Louise.* Chicago: Children's Press.

Shaw, N. (1986). *Sheep in a jeep.* Boston: Houghton Mifflin.

Ziefert, H. (1988). *Dark night, sleepy night.* New York: Puffin.

Ziefert, H. (1990). *Follow me!* New York: Puffin.

Long i

Gelman, R. G. (1977). *More spaghetti I say.* New York: Scholastic.

Hoff, S. (1988). *Mrs. Brice's mice.* New York: Harper.

Ziefert, H. (1984). *Sleepy dog.* New York: Random House.

Ziefert, H. (1987a). *Jason's bus ride.* New York: Random House.

Ziefert, H. (1987b). *A new house for Mole and Mouse.* New York: Puffin.

Long o

Hamsa, B. (1985). *Animal babies.* Chicago: Children's Press.

Oppenheim, J. (1992). *The show-and-tell frog.* New York: Bantam.

Schade, S. (1992). *Toad on the road.* New York: Random House.

Review of long vowels

Matthias, C. (1983). *I love cats.* Chicago: Children's Press.

Parish, P. (1974). *Dinosaur time.* New York: Harper.

Phillips, J. (1986). *My new boy.* New York: Random House.

Ziefert, H. (1985). *A dozen dogs.* New York: Random House.

r and Other Vowel Patterns

r vowels

Hooks, W. H. (1992). *Feed me!* New York: Bantam.

Penner, R. (1991). *Dinosaur babies.* New York: Random House.

Wynne, P. (1986). *Hungry, hungry sharks.* New York: Random House.

/aw/ vowels

Oppenheim, J. (1991). *The donkey's tale.* New York: Bantam.

Oppenheim, J. (1993). *"Uh-oh!" said the crow.* New York: Bantam.

/o͞o/ vowels

Blocksma, M. (1992). *Yoo hoo, Moon!* New York: Bantam.

Brenner, B. (1990). *Moon boy.* New York: Bantam.

Wiseman, B. (1959). *Morris the moose.* New York: Harper.

/ōo/ vowels
Platt, K. (1965). *Big Max*. New York: Harper.

/ow/ vowels
Lobel, A. (1975). *Owl at home*. New York: Harper.
Oppenheim, J. (1989). *"Not now!" said the cow*. New York: Bantam.
Siracusa, C. (1991). *Bingo, the best dog in the world*. New York: Harper Collins.

/oy/ vowels
Marshall, J. (1990). *Fox be nimble*. New York: Puffin.

Review of r and other vowels
Brenner, B. (1989). *Annie's pet*. New York: Bantam.
Hopkins, L. B. (1986). *Surprises*. New York: Harper.
Marshall, E. (1985). *Fox on wheels*. New York: Dutton.
Milton, J. (1985). *Dinosaur days*. New York: Random House.
Rylant, C. (1987). *Henry and Mudge: The first book*. New York: Bradbury.
Stambler, J. (1988). *Cat at bat*. New York: Dutton.

Adapted from *Books for Beginning Readers* by Thomas Gunning. Copyright 1996 by Thomas G. Gunning. Used by permission of Galvin Publications.

TEACHING THE WORD-BUILDING APPROACH

The **onset** is the initial part of a word, the part that precedes a vowel. The onset could be a single consonant (*c* + *at*), a digraph (*sh* + *eep*), or a cluster (*tr* + *ip*). A word that begins with a vowel such as *owl* or *and* does not have an onset. The **rime** is the part of a word that rhymes. A linguistic term, it refers to *ook* in *look* or *ow* in *cow*.

One way to keep phonics functional—that is, to teach elements when they are needed and to make sure they are applied—is to analyze a text that students are about to read and note which phonics elements students will need to know in order to read the text. For instance, if the selection is about trains, you might present or review the *-ain* pattern.

One convenient, economical way of introducing vowels is in patterns: for example, *-at* in *hat, pat,* and *cat,* or *-et* in *bet, wet,* and *set*. Patterns are easy to learn and are meaningful, since they are composed of whole words.

Recent research suggests that the components of a pattern, its **onset** and **rime,** are natural units of language and so are easier for youngsters to perceive and grasp (Adams, 1990; Goswami & Bryant, 1990; Treiman, 1992). The onset is the consonant or consonant cluster preceding the rime: *b-, st-, scr-*. The rime is the pattern's vowel and any consonants that follow it: *-o, -at, -op, -ean*. Rimes are also known as phonograms, word families, or graphemic bases. A list of common rimes is contained in Table 3.6.

Commenting on the advisability of presenting rimes and patterns, Goswami and Bryant (1990) stated:

> English is a capricious orthography in general, but is much less predictable at the level of the single letter than of groups of letters. Thus a word like "light" cannot be easily read letter-by-letter, because the individual letters represent sounds which do not add up to the word "light." But it is quite possible that a child could come to read this word by learning that there is a group of written words which end in the letters "-ight," and which always end in the same rhyming sound. (pp. 26–27)

Patterns can be presented in a number of ways. A word-building approach helps children note the onset and the rime in each word (Gunning, 1995). Students are presented with a rime and then add onsets to create words. Lesson 3.3 describes how the rime *-et* might be presented.

TABLE 3.6 Common rimes

	Vowel Sound	Rimes
Short Vowels	/a/	-ab, -ack, -ad, -ag, -am, -amp, -an, -and, -ang, -ank, -ap, -ask, -at
	/e/	-ed, -ell, -en, -end, -ent, -est, -et
	/i/	-id, -ig, -ill, -im, -in, -ing, -ink, -ip, -it
	/o/	-ob, -ock, -od, -og, -op, -ot
	/u/	-ub, -uck, -uff, -ug, -um, -ump, -un, -ung, -unk, -ut
Long Vowels	/ā/	-ace, -ade, -ake, -ale, -ame, -ane, -ate, -aid, -ail, -ain, -ay
	/ē/	-eak, -eal, -eam, -eat, -eed, -eep, -eet
	/ī/	-ice, -ide, -ime, -ine, -ive, -ind, -y
	/ō/	-oke, -one, -ope, -old, -ow
Other Vowels	/aw/	-all, -aw, -ought
	/oi/	-oil, -oy
	/o͝o/	-ook
	/o͞o/	-ew, -oot
	/ow/	-out, -ow
r Vowels	/air/	-air, -are, -ear
	/ar/	-ar, -ark, -arm, -art
	/i(ə)r/	-ear, -eer
	/or/	-ore, -orn

Lesson 3.3
Word-building pattern

Step 1. Building words by adding onsets

To introduce the *-et* pattern, write *et* on the board and ask the class what letter would have to be added to *et* to make the word *pet*. (This reviews initial consonants and helps students see how words are formed.) As you add *p* to *et*, carefully enunciate the /p/ and the /et/ and then the whole word. Have several volunteers read the word. Then write *et* underneath *pet*, and ask the class what letter should be added to *et* to make the word *wet*. As you add *w* to *et*, carefully enunciate /w/ and /et/ and then the whole word. Have the word *wet* read by volunteers. The word *pet* is then read, and the two words are contrasted. Ask students how the two are different. Other *-et* words are formed in the same way. After the *-et* words have been formed, have students tell what is the same about all the words. Have students note that all the words end in the letters *e* and *t*, which make the sounds heard in *et*. Then have them tell which letter makes the /e/ sound and which makes the /t/, or ending, sound in *et*. Calling attention to the individual sounds in *et* will help students discriminate between the -*et* pattern and other short *e* patterns. It should also help students improve perception of individual sounds in words and so help improve their reading and spelling.

Onsets and rimes are believed to be the natural units of words. When words are analyzed or broken up, the tendency is to divide them as onsets and rimes.

Step 2. Building words by adding rimes to onsets

To make sure that students have a thorough grasp of both key parts of the word—the onset and the rime—present the onset and have students supply the rime. Write *p* on the board, and have students tell what sound it stands for. Then ask them to tell what should be added to *p* to make the word *pet*. After adding -*et* to *p*, say the word in parts—/p/ /e/ /t/—and then as a whole. Pointing to *p*, say the sound /p/. Pointing to *e* and *t*, say /e/ and then /t/. Running your hand under the whole word, say "pet." Show *wet, get, let, jet,* and *net* being formed in the same way. After all words have been formed, have students read them.

Step 3. Providing mixed practice

Realizing that they are learning words that all end in the same way, students may focus on the initial letter and fail to take careful note of the rest of the word, the rime. After presenting a pattern, mix in words from previously presented patterns and have students read these. For example, after presenting the -*et* pattern, you might have students read the following words: *wet, when, pet, pen, net, Ned* (assuming that -*en* and -*ed* have been previously taught). This gives students practice in processing all the letters in the words and also reviews patterns that have already been introduced.

Step 4. Creating a model word

Create a model word. This should be a word that is easy and can be depicted. Construct a chart on which model words are printed and depicted with a photo or illustration. (A sample model words chart for short-vowel patterns is presented in Figure 3.4.) For the -*et* pattern, the word *net* might be used. Students can use the chart to help them decipher difficult words that incorporate patterns that have already been taught. Place the chart where all can see it. Explain to students that if they come across a word that ends in *et* and forget how to say it, they can use their model words chart to help them figure it out. Explain that the model word *net* has a picture that shows the word. In case they forget how to say the model word, the picture will help them.

Step 5. Guided practice

Under the teacher's direction, the class might read sentences or rhymes about a pet that got wet and was caught in a net, or they might create group or individual experience stories about pets they have or wish they had.

Step 6. Application

Students read stories and/or create pieces using -*et* words. Two very easy books that might be used to reinforce the -*et* pattern are *Let's Get a Pet* (Greydanus, 1988) and *A Pet for Pat* (Snow, 1984).

For a fuller discussion of word building, see T. Gunning, "Word building: A strategic approach to the teaching of phonics," in *The Reading Teacher, 48,* pp. 484–488.

Step 7. Extension

Students learn other short -*e* patterns: -*en*, -*ep*, -*ell*, and so on.

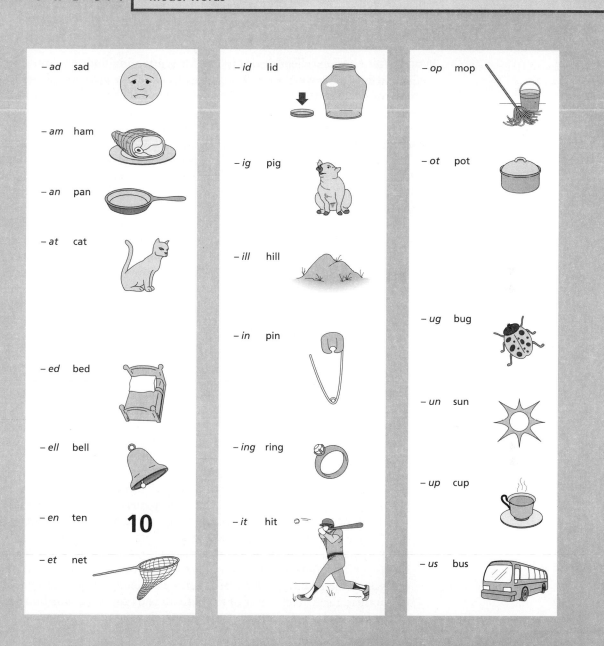

– ad   sad

– am   ham

– an   pan

– at   cat

– ed   bed

– ell   bell

– en   ten   **10**

– et   net

– id   lid

– ig   pig

– ill   hill

– in   pin

– ing   ring

– it   hit

– op   mop

– ot   pot

– ug   bug

– un   sun

– up   cup

– us   bus

From *Word Building, Book A* by T. Gunning (1994). New York, NY: Phoenix Learning Resources.

A children's book that might be used to introduce the concept of building words is dePaola's (1973) *Andy: That's My Name,* in which Andy watches as older kids use his name to construct a number of words: *and, sand, handy, sandy,* and so on.

Word Wall. An excellent device to use for reinforcing both patterns and high-frequency words is a word wall. Words are placed on the wall in alphabetic order. About five new words are added each week (Cunningham & Allington, 1994), drawn from basals, trade books, experience stories, and real-world materials that students are reading. These are high-frequency words that students are sure to meet many times in their reading and writing.

Because the words are on the wall, they can be used as a kind of dictionary. If students want to know how to spell *there* or *ball,* they can find it on the wall. On the wall, the words are readily available for quick review. Troublesome words can be reviewed on a daily basis.

After a pattern has been introduced, place the pattern words on the wall. However, place them on a separate part of the wall and arrange them alphabetically by pattern. The *-ab* pattern would be placed first, followed by the *-ack, -ad* patterns, and so on. The first word in each pattern should be the model word, accompanied by an illustration so that students can refer to the illustration if they forget how to read the model word. When students have difficulty with a pattern word and are unable to use a pronounceable word part to unlock the word's pronunciation, refer them to the word wall. Help them read the model word, and then use an analogy strategy to help them read the word they had difficulty with.

Review the pattern words periodically, using the following or similar activities:

- Find as many animal names, color names, and number names as you can.
- Pantomime an action (sit, run) or use gestures to indicate an object or other item (pan, hat, cat, pen), and have students write the appropriate pattern word and then hold it up so that you can quickly check everyone's response. Have a volunteer read the word and point to it on the word wall. Before pantomiming the word, tell students what the model word of the pattern is—for example, *cat* or *pan.* To make the task a bit more challenging and to get students to analyze the ending letters of patterns, tell students that the word will be in one of two patterns—for example, the *-at* or the *-an* pattern.
- Try "The Secret Word" (Cunningham & Allington, 1994). Select a word from a pattern, and jot it down on a sheet of paper, but do not reveal its identity. Have students number a paper from 1 to 5. Give a series of five clues as to the identity of the word. After each clue, students should write down their guess. The object of the activity is to guess the word on the basis of the fewest clues. The clues might be as follows:

1. The secret word is in the *-at* pattern.
2. It has three letters.
3. It is an animal.
4. It can fly.
5. Into the cave flew the _____.

After supplying the five clues, show the secret word (*bat*) and discuss students' responses. See who guessed the secret word first.

Making Words.   "Making Words" is a hands-on manipulative activity in which students put letters together to create words. It provides excellent reinforcement for word building with patterns. Students assemble approximately a dozen words, beginning with two-letter words and extending to five-letter or even longer ones (Cunningham & Cunningham, 1992). The last word that the students assemble contains all the letters they were given. For example, students are given the letters *a*, *d*, *n*, *s*, and *t* and are asked to do the following:

- Use two letters to make *at*.
- Add a letter to make *sat*.
- Take away a letter to make *at*.
- Change a letter to make *an*.
- Add a letter to make *Dan*.
- Change a letter to make *tan*.
- Take away a letter to make *an*.
- Add a letter to make *and*.
- Add a letter to make *sand*.
- Now break up your word and see what word you can make with all the letters (*stand*).

Lesson 3.4
A Making Words lesson

Step 1. Distribute the letters. You may have one child distribute an *a* to each student, a second child distribute a *t*, and so on. Lower-case letters are written on one side of the card, and upper-case on the other. The upper-case letters are used for the spelling of names.

Step 2. Give the directions for each word: "Use two letters to make *at*."

Step 3. Have a volunteer assemble the correct response, the word *at*, on the chalkboard ledge (or pocket chart or letter holder). Have the volunteer read the word. Students should check and correct their responses.

Step 4. Give the directions for the next word. Use the word in a sentence so that students hear it in context. If you have students who are struggling with phonological awareness and letter-sound relationships, slowly articulate each of the target words and encourage them to stretch out the sounds as they spell them with their letters. If a target word is a proper name, make note of that.

Step 5. On the chalkboard ledge, line up in order enlarged versions of the words the students were asked to make. Have volunteers read each of the words. Also have volunteers help sort the words according to patterns or beginning or ending sounds. For instance, holding up the word *at*, the teacher might ask a student to come up to the ledge and find the words that rhyme with *at*.

To plan a Making Words lesson, decide which patterns you wish to reinforce and how many letters you wish students to assemble. The letters chosen must form the word, so you may want to select the final word right after you have chosen the pattern. As students grow more adept, they can be given more challenging patterns and asked to make longer words using a greater variety of patterns. You might also include two or more vowels so that students become involved in vowel substitution.

WHOLE-PART-WHOLE APPROACH

Many of the phonics lessons presented have proceeded from the part to the whole. The correspondence or pattern has been presented and then it has been applied within the context of a whole story. However, some practitioners prefer starting with the whole, then breaking it into parts, and finally working back to the whole (Trachtenburg, 1990). Any of the lessons presented can be adapted to start with the whole. For instance, if you were presenting the -*eep* pattern, you might begin by share-reading with the class a big book version of *Sheep in a Jeep* (Shaw, 1986). After reading the text and discussing it, point out the -*eep* words. Read the sentences in which the -*eep* words appear. Then proceed to build words using -*eep* as the base just as you would in a word-building lesson.

Because of the natural presence of repeated elements, traditional rhymes also lend themselves to a whole-part-whole approach. They also acquaint children with a portion of their literary heritage, help them remember the elements, and put some fun into an area that is usually not very exciting. Here is how short *o* pattern words might be introduced in whole-part-whole fashion. Write the following rhyme or a similar one on story paper:

> Davy Dumpling
> Boil him in the pot;
> Sugar him and butter him,
> And eat him while he's hot.

Before reading the rhyme with the class, ask students if they can guess what Davy Dumpling is. After reading the rhyme, discuss what a dumpling is. Read the rhyme a second time, while students read along with you. Then ask students which words rhyme. When they have located *pot* and *hot,* write those words on the chalkboard. Ask students how the two words look the same. Note that they both end with *o-t.* Ask students to supply other words that rhyme with *pot* and *hot.* List the words on the board, spelling each one aloud as you write it. Have volunteers read the list of words. Then read "Davy Dumpling" again. Pause before *pot* and *hot,* and have students read those words. Apply knowledge of the -*ot* pattern by reading other rhymes, songs, or stories. Pause before -*ot* words, and have students attempt to read them.

Extend knowledge of short *o* by reading other *o* patterns: -*op,* -*ob,* and so on. After covering several short *o* patterns, lead students to see that *o,* when followed by a final consonant or two or more consonants, usually has its short sound. As you read aloud other pieces, provide students with opportunities to apply their knowledge of short *o* by having them attempt to read any short *o* words contained in the selections. As a final step, students can read on their own books that contain the pattern presented.

Adapting instruction for special needs students
All too often special needs students have been given too much instruction in phonics. What they frequently need are many opportunities to practice their skills by reading easy books. A little instruction in phonics should be followed by a lot of application.

TEACHING VOWEL GENERALIZATIONS

"When two vowels go walking, the first one does the talking." Recited by millions of students, this generalization is one of the best known of the vowel rules. It refers to the tendency for the first letter in a digraph to represent the long sound typically associated with that letter: For example, *ea* in *team* represents long *e*, and *ai* in *paid* represents long *a*. Although heavily criticized because, as expressed, it only applies about 50 percent of the time, it can be helpful (Gunning, 1975). About one word out of every five has a double vowel, or digraph; however, the generalization does not apply equally to each situation. For some spellings—*ee*, for example—it applies nearly 100 percent of the time. The letters *ea*, however, represent at least four different sounds (*bean*, *bread*, *earth*, and *steak*). Moreover, the generalization does not apply to such vowel-letter combinations as *au*, *aw*, *oi*, *oy*, and *ou*.

This generalization about digraphs should not be taught as a blanket rule because it has too many exceptions. Instead, it should be broken down into a series of mini-generalizations in which the most useful and most consistent correspondences are emphasized. These mini-generalizations include the following:

- *Instances where the double vowels usually represent a long sound.* The letters *ai* and *ay* usually represent long *a*, as in *way* and *wait*. The letters *ee* usually represent long *e*, as in *see* and *feet*. The letters *ey* usually represent long *e*, as in *key*. The letters *oa* usually represent long *o*, as in *boat* and *toad*.
- *Instances where the double vowels regularly represent a long sound or another sound.* Except when followed by *r*, the letters *ea* usually stand for long *e* (*bean*) or short *e* (*bread*). The letters *ie* usually stand for long *e* (*piece*) or long *i* (*tie*). The letters *ow* usually stand for a long *o* sound (*snow*) or an /ow/ sound (*cow*).

The mini-generalizations could also be taught as patterns, such as *seat*, *heat*, *neat*, and *beat* or *boat*, *goat*, and *float*. Whichever way they are taught, the emphasis should be on providing ample opportunities to meet the double vowels in print. Providing exposure is the key to learning phonics. Generalizations and patterns draw attention to regularities in English spelling, but actually meeting the elements in print is the way students' decoding skills become automatic; then they can direct fuller attention to comprehension.

A number of additional vowel combinations are not used to spell long vowels:

au or *aw* = /aw/	*fault*, *saw*
oi or *oy* = /oy/	*toil*, *toy*
oo = /ōō/	*moon*
oo = /o͝o/	*book*
ou or *ow* = /ow/	*pout*, *power*

These combinations can be presented inductively as correspondences in the way that short *i* was presented in Lesson 3.2, or they can be introduced in patterns. As new correspondences are taught, they should be added to the vowel chart (see Table 3.4).

The digraphs *au/aw*, *oi/oy*, and *ou/ow* are said to be in complementary distribution (Venezky, 1965): *au*, *oi*, and *ou* do not appear in final position, but *aw*, *oy*, and *ow* do.

The sounds /oi/ and /ow/ are also known as diphthongs. Diphthongs, which are sometimes called glides, are single sounds that are formed by combining two sounds. Technically speaking, long *i* (*ice*) and long *u* (*use*) are also diphthongs since both are formed by blending vowel sounds. However, in reading instruction, the term *diphthong* is generally restricted to /oi/ and /ow/.

One of the few generalizations that students seem to make use of in their reading is the final e generalization. When asked how they figured out hard words that appeared in lists and in stories, a number of second-graders reported that the e at the end of a word indicates that the vowel is long (Gunning, 1988a). When they reach the orthographic stage of reading, students automatically make use of final e as part of a larger pattern: -age, -ate, -ive.

Most vowel rules are not worth teaching because they have limited utility, have too many exceptions, or are too difficult to apply. However, the following generalizations are highly useful (Gunning, 1975, 1988b):

- *Closed syllable generalization.* A vowel is short when followed by a consonant: *wet, butter.* This is known as the closed syllable rule because it applies when a consonant "closes," or ends, a word or syllable.
- *Open syllable generalization.* A vowel is usually long when it is found at the end of a word or syllable: *so, moment.* This generalization is known as the open syllable rule because the word or syllable ends with a vowel and so is not closed by a consonant.
- *Final e generalization.* A vowel is usually long when it is followed by a consonant and a final *e: pine, note.*

Vowel generalizations should be taught inductively. After experiencing many words that end in *e* preceded by a consonant, for example, students should conclude that words ending in a consonant plus *e* often have long vowels.

The real payoff from learning generalizations comes when students group elements within a word in such a way that they automatically map out the correct pronunciation most of the time. For example, when processing the words *vocal, token,* and *hotel* so that the first syllable is noted as being open, students are able to decode the words quickly and accurately. This is a result of many hours of actual reading. However, it is also a process that can be taught (Glass, 1976).

The best way to learn generalizations is to have plenty of practice reading open and closed syllable words, final e words, and other words covered by generalizations. The aim is to have recognition of the words become automatic.

Although highly useful, none of the vowel generalizations applies 100 percent of the time. After students have had plenty of opportunities to master and practice using the main correspondence for a particular element—*ea* = /ē/, for instance—they should be introduced to the variability principle. They have to learn that digraphs and single vowels can represent a variety of sounds. If they try one pronunciation and it is not a real word or does not make sense in context, then they must try another. A child who read "heevy" for *heavy* would have to try another pronunciation, because *heevy* is not a real word. A child who read "deed" for *dead* would then check if that pronunciation fits the context of the sentence in which the word was used. Although *deed* is a real word, it does not make sense in the sentence "Jill's cat was dead"; so the student would try another pronunciation. This strategy needs to be taught explicitly, and students must have plenty of opportunity for practice. To sound out a word, they should be taught the general steps outlined in the Student Strategy below.

Since there is no way to predict on the basis of spelling whether *ow* will represent /ow/ (*cow*) or /ō/ (*snow*), you need to teach children to check whether the sounds they construct create a real word. If not, have them try the other major pronunciation of *ow.* Model this process for your students.

Student Strategy
Applying the variability strategy to vowel correspondences

1. Sound out the word as best you can.
2. After sounding out the word, ask yourself, "Is this a real word?" If not, try sounding out the word again. (Applying the variability principle to a word containing *ea*, a student would try the long-vowel pronunciation first. If that did not work out, he or she would try the short-vowel pronunciation. If there is a chart of spellings available, students can use it as a source of other pronunciations.)

3. Read the word in the sentence. Ask yourself, "Does this word make sense in the sentence?" If not, try sounding it out again.
4. If you still cannot sound out a word so that it makes sense in the sentence, try context, skip it, or get help.

USING AN INTEGRATED APPROACH

Although phonics, context clues, and vocabulary are treated as separate topics in this book, students make use of all three when they face an unknown word. In fact, they make use of their total language system.

As K. Goodman (1974, 1984) observed, children use three cueing systems: syntactic, semantic, and graphophonic (phonics). For instance, if the word *bike* were unknown and encountered in the sentence "I rode my new bike to school," the reader would use her or his knowledge of the way language is constructed to predict that the unknown word is a noun. The reader would know this intuitively through experience with language, although she or he might not know the label *noun*. Semantic knowledge—knowledge of the meaning system of language—and awareness of what kinds of objects a young person might ride would also help the reader predict what the unknown word is. Seeing that the word begins with a *b*, the reader can predict that the word is *bike*. Because of the strength of syntactic and semantic cues, only minimal use of graphophonic cues is made. The reader may even be able to get by without using phonics at all.

Adams (1990, 1994) supplied a somewhat different explanation of the process of decoding words. In her model, four processors are at work: orthographic, phonological, meaning, and context. The orthographic processor is responsible for perceiving the sequences of letters in text. The phonological processor is responsible for mapping the letters into their spoken equivalents. The meaning processor contains one's knowledge of word meanings, and the context processor is in charge of constructing a continuing understanding of the text (Stahl, Osborne, & Lehr, 1990, p. 21). The processors work simultaneously and both receive information and send it to the other processors; however, the orthographic and phonological processors are always essential participants. Context might speed and/or assist the interpretation of orthographic and phonological information but does not take its place. When information from one processor is weak, another may be called upon to give assistance. For instance, when a word like *lead* is encountered, the context processor provides extra help to the meaning and phonological processors in assigning the correct meaning and pronunciation.

Although Goodman's model differs significantly from that of Adams, both have similar implications. Phonics instruction must be viewed as being part of a larger language process. Phonics is easier to apply when context clues are used, and, in turn, it makes those clues easier to use. Students who are adept decoders will be able to recognize more words and so will have more context to use. Moreover, greater knowledge of the world, larger vocabularies, and better command of language increase students' ability to use phonics. A student who has a rich vocabulary has a better chance that the word he or she is decoding will be recognized by his or her meaning processor. Even if the word is not known, the student will have a better chance of deriving its meaning from context if most of

Exemplary Teaching

Singing Initial Consonants

Don Holdaway (1979), a leading figure in holistic approaches to teaching literacy, recounted how he uses songs, children's names, and big books to introduce initial consonants:

> One day we discover Bill Martin's version of the old song "K-K-K-Katy" in *Sounds of a Pow Wow.* We soon locate other children in the classroom with K-K-K-names—Karen, Ken. . . . The interest is compulsive and irresistible, so we end up with many versions including "T-T-T-Teacher" and "M-M-M-Mummy." In establishing letter-sound associations, we decide to stay with three or four letters that are highly contrastive in sound, in feel in the mouth, and look in the mirror. We choose *M, S, F* and of course are stuck with *K,* but we encourage each child to develop an interest in the letter-sound association of his or her own initial. (pp. 116–117)

Later, Holdaway used poems and books to reinforce the correspondences that he had introduced. In a big book story, all the letters except the initial one in words beginning with *f, s,* and *m* are blacked out. Using their sense of the story and knowledge of the initial consonant, students guess what the missing words are.

Good evidence for the integration of phonics and context clues comes from reading sentences that contain a word whose pronunciation depends upon its meaning. Good readers can read the following sentences without difficulty: "The does have no antlers, but the bull does"; "He wound the bandage around the wound" (McCracken, 1991, p. 91).

the other words in the passage are known, and if his or her background knowledge of the concepts in the passage is adequate.

To be most effective, therefore, phonics instruction should be presented in context and practiced and applied through extensive reading, which enables students to connect phonics instruction with its functioning as part of a total language system. Extensive reading also provides practice of phonics skills so that students' decoding becomes so effortless and automatic that they can devote full attention to comprehension, which is what reading is all about.

PHONICS AND SPELLING

One way to learn letter-sound relationships is through spelling. Years ago, Maria Montessori (1964) devised a method for teaching poor children to read through spelling, and spelling-tracing techniques have long been used to teach children who have severe difficulties in learning to read (Fernald, 1943; Gillingham & Stillman, 1960). More recently, Freppon and Dahl (1991) observed how a whole language teacher used spelling to acquaint students with the letter-sound system. This teacher drew out the sounds of a word that a child was trying to spell and asked, "What do you hear?" The teacher also modeled the process:

> "I want to write about dinosaurs, di-no-saurs, di-no, I hear a *D,* that starts *dinosaurs.*" As she writes the letter *D* on her own paper, she adds as an aside, "Yes, *D* like in *dinosaurs* and like in *David* in our class." (p. 204)

Recent research suggests that children who are encouraged to write early and allowed to spell as best they can develop insights that carry over into their ability to read words (Burns & Richgels, 1989). As noted in Chapter 2, children pass through stages of spelling. The stages are marked by increasingly sophisticated concepts of the relationship between spelling and sound. For instance, in the phonemic stage, students focus on one or two consonant sounds and fail to represent vowels in their spellings. In the letter-name stage, students represent vowels but are focused on the individual sounds in a word. In the within-word pattern stage, they begin to consider visual patterns such as vowel digraphs and the *e* marker. By noting which stage children are in, you can gain insight into the processes they are using to read words and gear instruction in word recognition accordingly. For instance, if children are in the phonemic phase, work on initial consonants. Later, as they begin to use vowels and move into the within-word pattern stage, work on short-vowel patterns and then long-vowel patterns, followed by other-vowel and *r*-vowel patterns.

One activity that is especially useful is sorting (Bear, 1995). Sorting forces children to analyze the elements in a word and select critical features as they place the words in piles. Through sorting, students construct an understanding of the spelling system, and they also enjoy this active, hands-on, nonthreatening activity.

Students should sort only elements and words that they know. This allows them to construct basic understandings of the spelling system. Although they may be able to read *cat*, *hat*, and *bat*, they may not realize that the words all rhyme or

Saying a word out loud and encouraging students to think of the sounds they hear helps students spell words and builds their knowledge of phonics.

that they follow a CVC (consonant-vowel-consonant) pattern. Sorting helps them come to these understandings.

Students' sorting activities are determined by their stage of spelling development. Students in the phonemic stage might sort pictures and, later, words according to their beginning sounds. In the letter-name phase, they might sort pictures and words according to short-vowel patterns. In the within-word pattern stage, students sort words according to whether they are long or short, follow an *e* marker, or have a double-vowel pattern, and then according to the specific long-vowel or other vowel pattern they illustrate. Words can also be sorted according to initial digraphs or consonant clusters or any other element that students need to study. The within-word stage encompasses all single-syllable elements.

Here is how students in the phonemic stage might be taught to sort initial consonant sounds. The lesson is adapted from Bear (1995).

Lesson 3.5
Sorting beginning consonant sounds

Step 1. Set up the sort

Set up two columns. At the top of each column, place an illustration of the sound to be sorted and its name. If you plan to have students sort /s/ and /r/ words, use an illustration of the sun and an illustration of a ring. Place the words *sun* and *ring* under their illustrations.

Step 2. Explain sorting

Tell students that you will be giving them cards that have pictures on them. Explain that they will be placing the cards under the picture of the sun if the words begin with /s/, the sound heard at the beginning of *sun*, or under the picture of the ring if the words begin with /r/, the sound heard at the beginning of *ring*.

Step 3. Model the sorting procedure

Shuffle the cards. Tell the students, "Say the name of the picture. Listen carefully to see if the name of the picture begins like /s/ as in *sun* or /r/ as in *ring*." Model the process with two or three cards: "This is a picture of a saw. Saw has an /s/ sound and begins like *sun*, so I will put it under *sun*. *Sun* and *saw* both begin with /s/."

Step 4. Children sort the cards

Distribute cards. Have students take turns placing a card in the /s/ column. Then have students take turns placing cards in the /r/ column. When students place their cards, have them say the picture's name and the sound it begins with. Correct errors quickly and simply. For instance, if a student puts a picture of a rat in the /s/ column, say, "*Rat* begins with /r/ and goes under *ring*" or ask why *rat* was put there and discuss its correct placement.

Step 5. Application

Have students find objects or pictures of objects whose names begin with /s/ or /r/. Proceed to other initial consonants, or sort known words that begin with /s/ or /r/.

A simple way of sorting is to place a target word or illustration in the center of a table and then distribute cards, some of which contain the target element. Have students read or name the target element, and then have them take turns placing cards containing the target element. As students place cards, they should read the words or name the illustrations on them (Temple, Nathan, Temple, & Burris, 1993).

Sorts can be open or closed. In a closed sort, the teacher provides the basis for sorting the cards, as in Lesson 3.4. In an open sort, students decide the basis for sorting the cards.

Although invented spellings and spelling instruction can help children gain insights into alphabetic principles, a systematic program of teaching phonics is still necessary. Neither invented spellings nor regular spelling instruction provides all the skills necessary to decode printed words. Spelling is best seen as a useful adjunct to phonics instruction, especially in the beginning stages of reading, rather than as a major method of teaching students to crack the code.

STRATEGY INSTRUCTION

The ultimate value of phonics instruction is whether it provides students with the keys for unlocking the pronunciations of unknown words encountered in print. For instance, a child who has studied both the *-at* and the *-et* patterns but has difficulty with the words *flat* and *yet* needs strategies for decoding those words. In addition to context, there are two powerful decoding strategies that the student might use: pronounceable word part and analogy (Gunning, 1995).

To apply the pronounceable word part strategy, the student seeks out familiar parts of the word. You might prompt the student by pointing to *yet* and asking, "Is there any part of the word that you can say?" If the student fails to see a pronounceable word part, cover up all but that part of the word (*et*) and ask the student if she or he can read it. Once the student reads the pronounceable part, she or he adds the onset (*y*) and says the word *yet*. (This assumes that the student knows the *y* = /y/ correspondence.) In most instances, the student will be able to say the pronounceable word part and use it to decode the whole word.

If a student is unable to use the pronounceable word part strategy, try the analogy strategy. With the analogy strategy, the student compares an unknown word to a known one. For instance, the student might compare the unknown word *yet* to the known word *pet*. The teacher prompts the strategy by asking, "Is the word like any word that you know?" If the student is unable to respond, the teacher writes the model word *net*, has the student read it, and then compares *yet* to *net*. Or the teacher might refer the child to a model words chart.

When students reconstruct a word using the pronounceable word part or analogy strategy, they must always make sure that the word they have constructed is a real word. They must also make sure it fits the context of the sentence. The pronounceable word part strategy should be tried before the analogy strategy because it is easier to apply and is more direct. Although students may have to be prompted to use the strategies, ultimately they should apply the strategies on their own.

INCORPORATING PHONICS STRATEGIES WITH CONTEXT

Pronounceable word part and analogy strategies should be integrated with the use of context clues. Most programs advocate using context clues first and then resorting to phonics strategies if the context clues do not work. This book recommends flexible use of the strategies. There are some situations in which context simply does not work. There are others in which neither pronounceable word part nor analogy will work. For instance, the pronounceable word part and analogy strategies would not work with *have* in the following sentence, but context clues probably would: "I have three pets." However, in the sentence "I like trains," context probably would not be of much help in decoding the word *trains*, but the pronounceable word part or analogy strategy would be if the student knows the *-ain* pattern or the word *rain*.

Student Strategy
Word recognition

To cue the use of word recognition strategies, the teacher (or the student prompting himself or herself) should ask one or more of the following questions when a student encounters an unknown word in print:

1. Is there any part of this word that you (I) can say?
2. Is this word like any word you (I) know?
3. What word would make sense here?

BUILDING INDEPENDENCE

Adapting instruction for at-risk students

At-risk readers may need additional guidance and prompting in order to apply strategies.

When a student has difficulty with a printed word, you may be tempted to supply the word or give some unhelpful admonition, such as "You know that word. We had it yesterday." Size up the word. Think of the skills the student has, the nature of the word, and the context in which it appears. Then ask the question (from the Student Strategy) that will prompt the use of the cue that seems most likely to work. (Of course, if you feel the child has no chance of working out the word, simply supply it.) Helping students apply decoding strategies provides them with a powerful tool that empowers them as readers. Encouraging them to work out words also affirms your faith in them and builds their confidence as readers.

If a student is reading orally in a group situation, do not allow another student to correct her or him. This robs the student of her or his academic self-concept and also of the opportunity to apply strategies. If a student misreads a word and does not notice the error, do not immediately supply a correction or even stop the reading. Let the student continue to the end of the sentence or paragraph; there is a good chance that she or he will notice the misreading and correct it. If the student does correct the misreading, make sure that you affirm this behavior: "I like the way you went back and corrected your misreading. You must have seen that the word _____ didn't make sense in the sentence."

If the student does not self-correct a misreading, you have two choices. If the error is a minor one, such as *this* for *that* or *the* for *these,* which does not change the meaning of the sentence, ignore it. If the misreading does not fit the sense of the sentence, use a prompt that will help the student correct the misreading:

- If the misreading does not make sense, ask, "Does _____ make sense in that sentence?"
- If the misreading is not a real word, ask, "Does that sound right?"
- If the misreading makes sense but does not fit phonically, say, "*Dog* makes sense in the sentence but the word in the sentence begins with a *c.* What letter does *dog* begin with? What letter does the word in the story begin with?" (Clay, 1993b). (Prompt for a pronounceable word part or analogy, if you think the student can work out the pronunciation of the word).

Reinforcement Activities
Phonics

- "Hinky Pinks," which is also known as "Stinky Pinky," can be used to reinforce both rhyming and a phonics element (initial or final consonants, consonant clusters, or word patterns). One person gives a definition, to which the partner responds with a two-word rhyme. For instance, the response to the definition "brown truck" is "tan van." To make the task somewhat easier, the teacher might supply the rime part of the word and have students add the consonant or cluster. Listed below are some examples. Others can be found in *Playing with Words* (Golick, 1987).

  Large hog: _____ ig _____ig

  Unhappy boy: _____ ad _____ad

  Place for old pieces of cloth: _____ ag _____ag

  Plane in the rain: _____ et _____et

  Bright place to sleep: _____ ed _____ed

- Have students create secret messages by substituting onsets in familiar words and then putting the newly formed words together to create a secret message (QuanSing, 1995). Besides being motivational, secret messages help students focus on the onsets and rimes of words and also foster sentence comprehension. Once students become familiar with the procedure, you can invite them to create secret messages as an individual or cooperative learning activity. Here is a sample secret message. (To make the exercise more challenging, you might put the words in random order.)

  Take *H* from *He* and put in *W*. ___We___

  Take *l* from *lot* and put in *g*. ___got___

  Take *p* from *pen* and put in *t*. ___ten___

  Take *st* from *stew* and put in *n*. ___new___

  Take *l* from *looks* and put in *b*. ___books___

  Secret message: ___We___ ___got___ ___ten___ ___new___ ___books___ .

- Encourage students to create mnemonic letters that incorporate a drawing suggesting the sound each letter usually represents. For example, the circle in the letter *d* might be drawn to look like a doughnut. Students might want to work in small groups on this project.
- In the morning message, use words that begin with the phonics elements taught recently.
- Integrate phonics with other subject areas. After *c* = /k/ has been introduced, you might read about cows or corn, or the class might follow a printed recipe for carrot cake.
- Have students create a consonant chart and a vowel chart and add new elements as they are being taught. The charts should contain a drawing of a key word, the key word spelled out, and other spellings of the sound being studied. The entry for *f* might show an *f*, a drawing of a fish, and the key word *fish*. Later, when the *ph* spelling of /f/ is studied, this additional element would be added to the chart.
- Students can create dictionaries that contain new phonics elements. After *ch* has been introduced, have them make a *ch* page and list *ch* words they know.
- Display real-world materials that contain the phonics element you are working on. If working on *ch*, for example, bring in a box of Cheerios, chocolate chip cookies, and a menu that features cheeseburgers or chicken. Help students read the items, and encourage them to bring in some of their own.

SUMMARY

1. Phonics is a means to an end and should be related to reading tasks that students are about to perform. The ultimate goal is to enable students to become independent readers, and functional practice and extensive reading are recommended to help them reach that goal. Alphabet books, alliterative texts, nursery rhymes, jump-rope chants, games, and easy books can be used to provide practice.

2. The two main approaches to teaching phonics are analytic (whole word) and synthetic (sound by sound). This book recommends combining the approaches. Phonics can also be taught through a pattern, or word-building, approach.

3. Consonants are generally taught before vowels because their sounds have fewer spellings and because they are more useful in helping students sound out unfamiliar words.

4. Consonant elements to be taught include single consonants, digraphs, and clusters. Vowel elements include short and long vowel correspondences, other vowels, *r* vowels, and schwa. Some consonant and vowel generalizations may be useful to students.

5. Along with phonics, students should use semantic and syntactic clues and their general knowledge to decode words. According to Goodman's theory, context clues may reduce or even eliminate the need for graphophonic cues. According to Adams's theory, four processors operating simultaneously are used to decode words: orthographic, phonological, meaning, and context. Information from the other processors assists, and may speed up, but does not eliminate the operation of the phonological and orthographic processors. On the contrary, students who excel at using phonics also tend to make superior use of context clues. Along with context clues, students should be taught how to use two powerful word identification strategies: pronounceable word part and analogy.

6. Spelling may assist the learning of phonics. As children invent spellings, they make important discoveries about their language's writing system. Invented spellings can also give the teacher insight into a child's grasp of the reading system. However, spelling is seen as providing only supplementary information about phonics.

CLASSROOM APPLICATIONS

1. Read over the pronunciation key of a dictionary. Notice the spellings given for the consonant sounds and the vowel sounds. Check each of the sounds. Are there any that are not in your dialect? The following vowel sounds have at least two pronunciations: *dog* (dawg or dog), *roof* (rōof or roŏf), *route* (rōot or rowt). How do you pronounce them?

2. Locate five children's books that might be used to reinforce phonics skills. Note the level of decoding skill needed to read each book and the main phonics patterns that the book reinforces.

3. Examine the phonics component of a basal series. Is its approach to teaching phonics analytic or synthetic? Are the lessons and activities functional and contextual? Are elements introduced and/or reviewed before or after the selection in which they are used? Which phonics generalizations are taught? What is your overall evaluation of the phonics program in this series?

FIELD APPLICATIONS

1. Using the word-building approach described in this chapter, plan a lesson in which a phonics element is introduced. State your objectives, and describe each of the steps of the lesson. List the titles of children's books or other materials that might be used to reinforce or apply the element taught. Teach the lesson and evaluate its effectiveness.

2. Working with a small group of elementary students, note which strategies they use when they encounter difficult words. Providing the necessary instruction and prompts, encourage them to use the pronounceable word part, analogy, and context strategies.

① The use of the dictionary will be helpful in decoding words.

② Phonics is a tool a means to an end

③ consonants should be taught first. not vowels.

④ pronounceable word part and analogy.

Sight Words; Syllabic, Morphemic, and Contextual Analyses; and Dictionary Usage

ANTICIPATION GUIDE

Agree

For each of the following statements, put a check under "Agree" or "Disagree" to show how you feel. Discuss your responses with classmates before you read the chapter.

Disagree

1. Memorizing is an inefficient way to learn new words. ✓

2. The best way to learn words so that you recognize them immediately is by studying flash cards. ✓

3. Syllabication is not necessary until students are reading on a third-grade level. ✓

4. Syllabication is not a very useful skill because you have to know how to decode a word before you can put it into syllables. ✓

5. Context is the most frequently used word attack skill. ✓

6. Using context is the easiest way to get the meaning of an unfamiliar word. ✓

7. The best way to learn about roots, prefixes, and suffixes is to have a lot of experience with these word parts. ✓

8. Using the dictionary as a strategy to get the meanings of unfamilar words is a tiresome chore. ✓

Using What You Know

Chapter 3 explained how to teach phonics, which is one technique for deciphering or decoding words. This chapter complements that material, exploring five additional word recognition skills. Before reading it, probe your knowledge of the topic.

What strategies do you use when you encounter an unfamiliar word? How useful are they? What difficulties, if any, do you have applying them? Were they taught to you in school? If not, where did you learn them? How would you go about teaching them?

WORD RECOGNITION STRATEGIES FOR NOVICE AND ADVANCED READERS

Imagine yourself as a first-grade teacher. Your students are experiencing difficulty with the italicized words in the sentences below. What strategies or word recognition techniques would you teach to help them decode the words?

1. The boys and girls ran to the *van*.
2. My flat tire needed *air*.
3. You can have *one*.

For sentence 1, phonics is probably the students' best bet. The word *van* is easy to decode. It has just three letters, and its pronunciation is easy to predict. Note, too, that the students had no difficulty in the same sentence with *ran*, which differs from *van* by only one consonant.

For sentence 2, phonics is not a good choice, as *air* would be difficult to decode. However, the sense of the sentence gives excellent clues to the meaning of the word, and students have a good chance of surmising what the word is.

The word in sentence 3 is a puzzler. It is not decodable: *one* is pronounced /wun/, so the only letter that can readily be decoded into a sound is the *n*. Furthermore, context is rather impoverished, as almost any noun could be substituted for *one*. Words whose pronunciation cannot be predicted from their spellings are best memorized or learned as sight words.

For novice readers, the three major decoding strategies are phonics, sight vocabulary, and context. As they grow in skill, the words they meet become more complex. Syllabication, which involves breaking down multisyllabic words; morphemic analysis, which consists of working with prefixes, suffixes, and root words; and using the dictionary are added to the students' repertoire of word recognition strategies.

SIGHT WORDS

Although the easiest way for most beginning readers to learn words is memorizing them, this is not a generative approach; students simply learn specific words. When taught new words through phonics, students learn the words and also learn letter-sound relationships, which provide a means for learning other new words.

A **sight word** is one that is recognized immediately. However, the term also refers to words that occur with high frequency and words that are learned through visual memorization.

Automaticity means performing tasks without attention or conscious effort.

For most children, the easiest way to learn to read is simply to memorize words (Richek, 1977–1978). Then it is not necessary to learn which letters represent which sounds or to match letters with sounds, both of which are complex undertakings. As noted in Chapter 3, novice readers in the logographic stage use visual clues to learn words. For instance, they may use the length of a word as a memory aid: The word *elephant* is easy to learn because it is especially long. Students may use one or more letters and associate them with the word: They may remember that *dog* begins with the letter *d*, without translating *d* into its spoken equivalent. The problem with learning words through visual clues is that the student soon runs out of distinctive clues. Besides, such clues are arbitrary and are, therefore, difficult to remember.

The sight approach is still a necessary strategy, however, for three reasons. First, a number of words simply cannot be sounded out or are difficult to sound out: for example, *of, once, are,* and, to a lesser extent, *were, some,* and *where.* Note that these are all common words. Ironically, those that appear most frequently tend to have the most irregular spellings, mainly because they are some of the oldest words in the language. Over the years, English evolved so that, in many instances, spellings do not do a very good job of representing pronunciations.

Some words are taught as **sight words** because, although they are regularly spelled, they incorporate advanced letter-sound relationships: for example, *house, green, rain, grow,* and *found.* If these are introduced early, before students have the chance to learn the phonics correspondences they need to decode them, it is possible to create stories that use a greater variety of words and that are more interesting. Sight words are also known as high-frequency words.

The word *sight* in *sight words* has a double meaning: It implies words that are to be memorized through sight, and it also refers to the immediate recognition of words—taking in a word at sight and not having to decode it. Fry (1977a) coined the phrase *instant words* for his lists of sight words. The idea behind the instant recognition of words is that the human mind has only so much mental-processing ability and time. Students can get so caught up trying to sound out a word that they lose the memory of what they are attempting to read. They need **automaticity,** the ability to process words effortlessly and automatically (Laberge & Samuels, 1974). Students who are able to recognize words instantly have ample attention and mental energy left to comprehend what they are reading. Ultimately, because of lots of practice, most of the words that skilled readers meet in print are processed as sight words. Only when they meet strange names or unfamiliar words do they resort to decoding words.

SOURCES OF SIGHT WORDS

The list of high-frequency sight words in Table 4.1 gives two hundred words in order of their frequency of appearance. The list is drawn from a compilation of words that appear in schoolbooks and other materials that students in grades 3 through 9 are likely to read (Carroll, Davis, & Richman, 1971). These two hundred words would make up about 60 percent of the words in continuous text. For

TABLE 4.1 High-frequency sight words

the	not	out	its	know	come	tell	left
of	or	then	who	get	work	men	end
and	by	them	now	through	must	say	along
a	one	she	people	back	part	small	while
to	had	many	my	much	because	every	sound
in	but	some	made	good	does	found	house
is	what	so	over	before	even	still	might
you	all	these	did	go	place	big	next
that	were	would	down	man	old	between	below
it	when	other	way	our	well	name	saw
he	we	into	only	write	such	should	something
for	there	has	may	used	here	home	thought
was	can	more	find	me	take	give	both
on	an	two	use	day	why	air	few
are	your	her	water	too	things	line	those
as	which	like	little	any	great	mother	school
with	their	him	long	same	help	set	show
his	said	time	very	right	put	world	always
they	if	see	after	look	years	own	large
at	will	no	word	think	different	under	often
be	do	could	call	also	number	last	together
this	each	make	just	around	away	read	asked
from	about	than	new	another	again	never	went
I	how	first	where	came	off	am	boy
have	up	been	most	three	went	us	earth

Adapted from *The American Heritage Word Frequency Book* by J. B. Carroll, P. Davis, & P. Richman, 1971, New York: American Heritage.

example, the most frequently occurring word *the* would appear about 2 percent of the time.

Two factors should be considered when deciding which **high-frequency words** should be taught first: utility and ease of learning. The biggest payoff for students will be learning those words that occur most frequently. Students are almost sure to run into the words *the, of, and, a, to, in, is, you, that,* and *it* in almost anything they read. They are the ten words that occur with the highest frequency and account for more than 20 percent of the words that children will see in continuous text. When considering ease of learning, note that nouns and words with distinctive shapes are easiest to learn. Ultimately, the most useful sight words are those that students will actually find in their reading. Culyer (1982) suggested

High-frequency words are words such as *the, of, at,* and *them* that appear in printed material with a high rate of occurrence.

that schools or school districts prepare their own lists based on the basal readers that their beginning readers will most likely use.

TEACHING HIGH-FREQUENCY WORDS

Many students will pick up a number of sight words through reading signs and other print to which they are exposed in the class and through shared reading of big books and other materials. Eeds (1985) noted that the sight word *said* occurs thirty-seven times in Bodecker's (1974) *Let's Marry, Said the Cherry*. Through shared reading in a big book format, students can read the following rhythmic lines:

"Why me?" said the pea.
"'Cause you're sweet," said the beet. (p. 34)

It is hard to imagine a more enjoyable way to learn or practice sight words. However, direct teaching is also helpful and, in many instances, necessary.

When teaching sight words, limit the number being taught to three or four. Choose words that students will soon be meeting in print. If they are about to read Dr. Seuss's *The Cat in the Hat Comes Back* (Geisel, 1961), you might present *this, off, done,* and *know,* irregular words that figure prominently in the story. Select words that are different in appearance. Presenting *put* and *but* or *where, when,* and *were* together is asking for trouble, as students are almost sure to confuse them.

Also, be certain that the words are presented both in isolation and in context. When words are taught in isolation, students tend to note the way they are formed (Samuels, 1967; Singer, Samuels, & Spiroff, 1973–1974). When words are presented in context, students pay more attention to meanings and the way they are used. Teaching articles, prepositions, and conjunctions in context is especially important, since the best way to understand function words is to see how they are actually used. Although this takes more time, students may learn additional skills that prepare them for contextual reading (Ceprano, 1981).

Showing sight words in isolation and in context helps students learn both their meanings and their pronunciations. However, if the students already know the meanings, spend most of the time teaching the words' distinctive features, including spellings, and noting pronounceable word parts. Knowing how to spell and/or sound out a word partially or fully helps students learn and remember new words (Ehri, 1991), but time spent discussing known definitions may be wasted (Kibby, 1989).

Although novice readers who lack a knowledge of phonics may learn a few words by memorizing them, research suggests that knowledge of letter-sound relationships is a necessary but not sufficient condition for learning irregular or exception words (Gough & Walsh, 1991). In other words, students who do not have some basic knowledge of phonics will have difficulty learning a list of sight words. They will not be able to use their knowledge of letter-sound relationships to learn and remember sight words. However, having a grasp of basic phonics does not ensure that students will learn irregular or exception words. Instruction and practice in the recognition and reading of exception words is necessary. As Gough and Walsh (1991) comment,

There is some disagreement about how expert readers recognize words. Ehri (1994) theorizes that words are recognized holistically because the letters and pronunciation have become bonded or amalgamated through repeated encounters, providing a sight access route, which leads instantaneously from a word's graphic representation to its pronunciation and meaning. Gough and Hillinger (1980) believe that even expert readers process words phonologically, but the processing is so rapid that recognition appears to be instantaneous.

We conclude, then, that the cipher is the basis of reading ability in English. It is not one of two equivalent mechanisms for word recognition, two equal partners in the practice of reading. The cipher is the basic mechanism, the senior partner. To be sure, it is not enough; it must have help. By itself, the cipher will fail to recognize many (perhaps a majority) of the words in English. So further information, word-specific information, must also be acquired. But that information must be added to the cipher, and the cipher supports the whole endeavor. (p. 208)

As was noted in Chapter 3, average students can only learn about forty words logographically, or at sight. To learn more sight words, they must have some knowledge of letter-sound relationships. However, if students are learning exception words such as *know* or *sure*, they also need to be taught specific features of these words.

When teaching high-frequency words, take full advantage of phonic regularities, such as initial and final consonant correspondences. Also seek out commonalities of words. For instance, when teaching *at* as a high-frequency word, also teach *that* and show how the two are related; have students note that *that* contains the pronounceable word part *at*. However, high-frequency words should not be used as a vehicle for teaching word patterns and individual correspondences. Rather, phonics is used as a device for teaching high-frequency words. The difference is subtle but crucial. The focus should be on fostering fast recognition of high-frequency words to promote fluency or speed and ease of reading. You do not want students getting bogged down in sounding out words. You want them reading as smoothly and as naturally as possible. When presenting high-frequency words, emphasize activities that reflect this purpose. Use phonics to help students accurately decode words—accuracy must come first. As Samuels (1994) notes, accuracy precedes automaticity, or rapid recognition. Use of knowledge of patterns and individual correspondences facilitates accurate recognition. Once accuracy has been achieved, stress rapid recognition rather than sounding out. Use the steps listed in Lesson 4.1 as a framework for presenting sight words.

K. Goodman (1976) theorized that readers make minimal use of orthographic information but use context to help them predict what a word might be. An expert reader is able to recognize words more rapidly by making better use of context. This book takes the position that there is an interaction of four processors, which, working in parallel, process graphic, phonemic, word meaning, and contextual information (Adams, 1994).

As noted in Chapter 3, there are actually few words in which phonics cannot be used at least partially. These include such irregular words as *one, once, of,* and *aisle*.

Lesson 4.1
Sight words

Step 1. Develop understanding of the words

This step is only necessary if students do not have an adequate understanding of the words being presented. Since most sight words are among the most common in the language, they will be in the listening vocabularies of the majority of students.

Step 2. Present printed words in isolation

Write each word to be learned on the chalkboard, or present each one on a large card. Although students may not be able to read the words, they may know parts of them. Build on any part they know. This will make the task of learning the word easier, as students will only be faced with learning a portion of the word rather than the whole word; it also helps them connect new knowledge with old knowledge. If students know only initial consonant correspondences, then build on that knowledge: Emphasize the *y* = /y/ in *you* and the *f* = /f/ in *for.* If they know initial and final consonants, talk about the *c* = /k/ and *n* = /n/ in *can.* If they know word patterns, then make use of those: Help them use their knowledge of *-at* to read *that* and their knowledge of *-op* to read *stop.* Present these elements as ways of perceiving and remembering sight words, but do not turn the sight word lesson into a phonics lesson. For words that are highly irregular, such as *of, one,* and *once,* simply stress their spellings. Do not atttempt to discuss any phonics elements.

After all the words have been introduced, have students read them chorally and individually. Distribute cards containing the words so that each student has a set. If long cards are used, the reverse side might contain the word used in a sentence.

Step 3. Present printed words in context

On the chalkboard, story paper, or overhead transparency, present the sight words in context. Underline the target words so that they stand out. Take care to use each word in the same sense in which students will most likely see it. For instance, if the sight word *drink* is going to be a verb in an upcoming story, show it as a verb. In composing sample sentences, except for the target sight words, use words already taught so that students can concentrate their efforts on the new ones. Actually, using sight words that have already been taught is a good way to review. Read the sentences to the students, and then have them read in unison as you sweep your hand under the words. Later, individual volunteers can read the sentences.

Step 4. Practice

Provide ample practice for sight words. Practice could be in the form of maze worksheets on which students choose from three words the one that correctly completes the sentence:

```
          take
I am new years old.
          five
```

Or it could be a brief story, a game, or a piece of computer software such as *Richard Scarry's Busytown* (Paramount Interactive) in which a few high-frequency words are featured.

Step 5. Application

Have students create experience stories or read easy stories that contain target sight words. Experience stories naturally contain a high proportion of sight words. Easy readers also provide an opportunity for students to meet sight words in context. In one study, students who read easy books learned more sight words than those who used a basal series (Bridge, Winograd, & Haley, 1983). They also expressed more positive feelings about reading, and, since their books were written about a variety of topics, they had an opportunity to learn more about their world.

 Easy readers provide the best reinforcement for high-frequency words.

ACHIEVING AUTOMATICITY

As noted earlier, two factors are involved in rapid recognition of words: accuracy and automaticity (Samuels, 1994). In order to reach an effective level of accuracy, students must actively process words. They must pay attention as they scan the words. Students need varying amounts of time to reach a high level of accuracy. Once they have reached an acceptable level of accuracy, they seem to gain automaticity at similar rates (Samuels, 1994). Children who seem to take longer to become fluent readers may not have achieved accuracy.

Automaticity means that students do not have to devote attention to the task. As they decode words, students can be thinking about the meaning of what they are reading because they have read the words so often that their active attention is not required. When learning a new skill, such as driving a car with a manual transmission, you have to pay active attention to actions such as shifting gears and coordinating the use of the clutch and the brake. In time, these skills become so practiced that they no longer require your active attention. Instead, you can devote your attention to a conversation with a passenger or watching the road. "The critical test of automaticity is that the task, which at the beginning stage of learning could only be performed by itself, can now be performed along with one or more other tasks" (Samuels, 1994, p. 819).

What are some indicators of automaticity? If a student can read orally with reasonably good expression or can read silently with reasonably good comprehension, he or she is using automatic decoding processes. To foster automaticity in reading, give students easier texts or have them read the same texts several times. Also, you might provide students with more opportunities for application. As Samuels (1994) explains,

> In human activities that require high levels of proficiency, a considerable amount of time must be spent in practicing the skills leading to mastery. Only by spending

a great deal of time reading will students develop beyond the level of mere accuracy. Practice may be on important subskills in reading, but it must also include time spent on reading easy, meaningful material. (p. 834)

USING CHILDREN'S BOOKS TO BUILD SIGHT VOCABULARY

Several types of children's books can be used to build sight vocabulary, including predictable books, caption books, and label books. Predictable books are those that follow a set pattern, making it easy for the child to predict what the sentences are going to say. Caption books feature a single sentence per page that describes or relates to the illustration in much the same way that a caption goes with a photo. Label books, as their name suggests, depict a number of objects, actions, or people and provide printed labels for them. These kinds of books may be read over and over again. Repetition does wonders for fluency, but the rereadings have to be genuine. They cannot just be an excuse for memorizing sight words. As Henderson (1981) cautioned,

> It is important to conceptualize and to direct such rereadings as in fact *rereadings,* not as conditioning exercises for memorizing words. This distinction is critical. Reading does not emerge from sight vocabulary. Quite the other way around, vocabulary emerges from reading. This tenet holds, moreover, not only at this tender stage but throughout life. (p. 91)

There are literally thousands of children's books that can be used to foster instant recognition of words. However, it is important that the books be on the right level. Students should know most of the words, so that their focus is on moving just introduced or barely known words to the category of words that are well known and rapidly recognized. Although it is helpful for students to build fluency by rereading the same book or story, it is also important that they read many different books to see the same words in a variety of contexts.

However, it is not enough to just read the books. Many predictable books are, in fact, so predictable that students are actually "reading" the pictures; in a pattern book, students may simply have memorized the pattern and so are not actually processing the words. Therefore, it is important to follow the procedure outlined by Bridge, Winograd, and Haley (1983) in Lesson 4.2.

Lesson 4.2
Using predictable books to build sight vocabulary

Step 1. Select a book that students will enjoy and that contains words that you want to reinforce. Obtain a big book version so that students can follow along as you read.

Step 2. Preview the text, read it to students, and discuss it. Point to each word as you read it.

Step 3. Reread the text. Invite students to read the repeated portions or other easy parts.

Step 4. After several rereadings, copy the text onto chart paper or cover the illustrations in the big book. With the pictures eliminated, students can concentrate on reading the words. Have students read the pictureless version, with your help.

Step 5. Duplicate the story, and cut the duplicated versions into sentence strips. Have students match the individual sentence strips to those in the chart version. Also have students reassemble the story, sentence by sentence. Sentences can be cut up into individual words as well. Have students match the individual words with those in the chart story. Also have students reconstruct individual sentences by putting the cut-out words in the right order.

Some books of opposites and picture dictionary books that might be used to reinforce sight words are listed in the first Children's Book List. The second Children's Book List presents additional children's books that can be used to present or reinforce sight words. All of the books listed are brief and well illustrated. They increase in difficulty from those that require a minimum of reading to those that contain four or five lines of text on a page. The books are classified according to approximate level of difficulty into three categories: Easy 1, Easy 2, and Easy 3. This classification is an adaptation of a system devised in New Zealand (Weaver, 1992). Key factors in estimating difficulty are length of the book, total number of words in the book, words per page, number of illustrations, and helpfulness of illustrations. In some books, an illustration will depict the text completely. In others, the illustration is simply an attractive addition.

Children's Book List
Books reinforcing sight words

Hoban, T. *Push. Pull. Empty. Full.* New York: Macmillan. (1972).

Hoban, T. *Over, Under and Through.* New York: Macmillan. (1973).

Kaufman, J. *Words.* Racine, WI: Golden. (1968).

Maestro, B., & G. Maestro. *Busy Day: A Book of Action Words.* New York: Crown. (1978).

Matthias, C. *Over-Under.* Chicago: Children's Press. (1984).

McLenighan, V. *Stop-Go, Fast-Slow.* Chicago: Children's Press. (1982).

Scarry, R. *Richard Scarry's Best Word Book Ever.* Racine, WI: Golden. (1963).

Children's Book List
Books containing high-frequency words

Easy 1
Pictures illustrate all or most of the text. There is usually just one line of print per page. Vocabulary is easy. Words and phrases are usually repeated.

Carle, E. *Do You Want to Be My Friend?* New York: Harper. (1971).

Carle, E. *Have You Seen My Cat?* New York: Scholastic. (1987).

Petrie, C. *Joshua James Likes Trucks.* Chicago: Children's Press. (1982).

Maris, R. *My Book.* Chicago: Children's Press. (1983).

Pomerantz, C. *Where's the Bear?* New York: Greenwillow. (1984).

Tafuri, N. *Have You Seen My Duckling?* New York: Greenwillow. (1984).

Wildsmith, B. *All Fall Down.* New York: Oxford. (1983).

Wildsmith, B. *Cat on the Mat.* New York: Oxford. (1983).

Wildsmith, B. *What a Tail!* New York: Oxford. (1986).

Easy 2
Pictures illustrate the text but not as fully as in Easy 1. Lines of print per page vary from 1 to 3 or 4.

Gordon, S. *What a Dog!* Mahwah, NJ: Troll. (1980).

Hutchins, P. *Good-Night, Owl.* New York: MacMillan. (1972).

Jenssen, P. *The Mess.* Chicago: Children's Press. (1990).

Kraus, R. *Whose Mouse Are You?* New York: Macmillan. (1970).

Matthias, C. *I Love Cats.* Chicago: Children's Press. (1983).

McKissack, P. C. *Who Is Who?* Chicago: Children's Press. (1983).

Raffi. *One Light, One Sun.* New York: Crown. (1988).

Ziefert, H. *A Dozen Dogs.* New York: Random House. (1985).

Ziefert, H. *A New House for Mole and Mouse.* New York: Puffin. (1987).

Ziefert, H. *Nicky Upstairs and Down.* New York: Puffin. (1987).

Easy 3
Pictures complement but do not fully illustrate the text. Text may be 3 to 6 lines long. Vocabulary is more varied.

Blocksma, M. *Yoo Hoo, Moon!* New York: Bantam. (1992).

Bonsall, C. *And I Mean It, Stanley.* New York: Harper. (1974).

Brown, M. W. *Where Have You Been?* New York: Scholastic. (1952).

Cebulash, M. *Willie's Wonderful Pet.* New York: Scholastic. (1972).

Gelman, R. G. *More Spaghetti, I Say.* New York: Scholastic. (1977).

Hoff, S. *Mrs. Brice's Mice.* New York: Harper. (1988).

Oppenhein, J. *"Not Now!" Said the Cow.* New York: Bantam. (1989).

Phillips, J. *My New Boy.* New York: Random House. (1986).

Robart, R. *The Cake That Mack Ate.* Toronto: Kids Can Press. (1986).

In addition to the children's books presented in the Children's Book Lists, there are several series of books designed to reinforce sight words. These include the following:

Reading Corners. San Diego, CA: Dominie Press. This series reinforces a number of basic patterns: I like_____; I have_____; I do_____. Consisting of just eight to twelve pages of text, these books are very easy.

Read More Books. San Diego, CA: Dominie Press. This series reinforces a number of basic sentence patterns. The text is brief and explicitly illustrated with color photos and so is very easy to read.

Seedlings. Columbus, OH: Seedling Publications. This series features sixteen-page booklets in which each page contains one line of text accompanied by an illustration. Vocabulary is varied.

Sometimes students have so much difficulty learning sight words, especially words such as *were* and *where* that are easily confused, that you have to resort to a technique that Cunningham (1980) called a drastic strategy. Lesson 4.3 shows how it is applied. In addition to being taught through this technique, poor readers may require even more practice, as they can fall behind rapidly. Good readers apparently learn four times as many new words as poor readers (Adams & Higgins, 1985).

Lesson 4.3
A drastic strategy

Step 1. Write the sight word on cards, and distribute one to each child.

Step 2. Tell a story in which the word is used several times. Students hold up their cards every time they hear the word.

Step 3. Students make up their own stories using the word. As one student reads his or her story, the others hold up their cards when they hear the target word.

Step 4. The word is cut into separate letters. Students reassemble the letters to form the word.

Step 5. The word is written on the board. Students memorize the word and spell it from memory three times.

Step 6. The word is put into story context.

Exemplary Teaching

Building a Sight Vocabulary

Reading was not much fun for Wendy. Although Wendy was a second-grader, she had a very limited sight vocabulary and struggled with the easiest of texts. Her teacher obtained a series of big books that recounted a number of classic folktales. Wendy followed along as her teacher read *The Gingerbread Man,* sweeping her hand under the print as she read the words. After two such shared readings, Wendy was invited to read the refrain each time it appeared. At first she hesitated, but soon she was carried away by the rhythm of the tale. By the time the teacher reached the end of the story, Wendy was reading with gusto, "I'm the gingerbread man! Catch me if you can!" For the first time, Wendy was experiencing the pleasure of fluent, expressive reading. Captivated by the simple repetitive tale, she reread it and the other tales countless times. As her store of sight words increased, she became a confident, eager reader.

Reinforcement Activities
Building a sight vocabulary

The difficulty of the suggested activities can be regulated by the level of high-frequency words introduced and the number introduced at one time. For instance, when planning to have students assemble words into sentences, start with a few easy sight words and then gradually increase the number, making sure that the activity retains sufficient challenge. If the activity is too easy, it will be boring and have no instructional benefit.

A useful device for reinforcing sight vocabulary is the card reader. Containing a strip of magnetic tape on the bottom and a surface for writing on the top, the cards can have a word or phrase recorded on the tape and also written on the upper portion of the card. As the card passes through the reader, its taped message is read. Students can both hear and see the sight word or sight word phrase and so may practice on their own.

- Have students use their sight word cards to create sentences.
- Encourage students to create stories about sight words or draw pictures illustrating them.
- Categorize sight words into color words, words that tell how many, and so on. After demonstrating the technique, encourage students to create their own categories. Of course, not all words can be categorized.
- Encourage students to quiz each other on sight words.
- Promote fluent reading by encouraging students to spend substantial amounts of time reading materials that are well within their grasp. Like any other complex behavior, reading requires substantial practice before it becomes automatic and seemingly effortless. If students persist in reading in a labored, halting fashion, the material is probably too difficult. Try material that is easy, and gradually move up to more difficult selections.
- Play sight-word Bingo and Concentration. However, be sure students also have the opportunity to meet the words in context.
- As you gradually introduce added phonics skills, include sight words as part of your instruction. For instance, when teaching the consonant cluster *bl*, use the sight words *black* and *blue* as examples. When studying short *a*, present the sight words *am, an*, and *at*. Being able to relate the printed versions of these words with their sounds gives students another way to process them, which aids memory and speed of processing.

INTEGRATION OF SIGHT WORDS WITH OTHER WORD RECOGNITION SKILLS

For the sake of clarity, sight words have been presented as a separate section. However, as a practical matter, they are taught with phonics. Analytic phonics programs typically start out by teaching initial consonant correspondences and a dozen or so sight words so that students can read some simple selections. Synthetic phonics programs generally present initial and final consonants, at least one short vowel, and a small number of sight words before students start reading brief selections. Literature-based programs teach high-frequency words by presenting them in pattern or predictable books that gradually increase in difficulty. Context is also integrated with both phonics and sight words.

SYLLABICATION

Fortunately, many of the most frequently used words in English have just one syllable. The Harris-Jacobson list of words (Harris & Jacobson, 1982) that appears in at least four out of eight basal readers has no multisyllabic words on the preprimer level. On the primer level, however, 15 percent are polysyllabic, and many are compounds; on the first-grade level, the figure rises to more than 25 percent. By second grade, more than 30 percent are multisyllabic; by sixth grade, the figure is more than 80 percent. The implications are clear. Students have to know early on how to deal with multisyllabic words. That need grows rapidly as students progress to higher levels. **Syllabication,** or structural analysis, may be introduced informally in the latter half of grade 1 and should be taught formally in grade 2 and beyond. The two approaches to teaching syllabication are generalization and pattern.

GENERALIZATION APPROACH TO TEACHING SYLLABICATION

In the generalization approach, students learn general rules for dividing words into syllables. The generalizations listed below seem to be particularly useful (Gunning, 1988b). These should be presented in the following order, which reflects both their frequency of occurrence and approximate order of difficulty:

1. *Easy affixes: -ing, -er, -ly.* Most prefixes and suffixes form separate syllables: *un-safe, re-build, help-ful, quick-ly.* Except for *s* as a plural marker, **affixes** generally are composed of a vowel and consonant(s). Thus they are syllables in themselves: *play-ing, re-play.*

2. *Compound words.* The words that make up a compound word usually form separate syllables: *sun-set, night-fall.*

3. *Two consonants between two vowels.* When two consonants appear between two vowels, the word generally divides between them: *win-ter, con-cept.* The place of division is often an indication of the pronunciation of the vowel. The *i* in *winter,* the *o* in the first syllable of *concept,* and the *e* in the second syllable of *concept* are short. Note that all three vowels are in closed syllables—that is, syllables that end in consonants: *win, con, cept.* Closed syllables often contain a short vowel. (The *e* in *winter* is not short because it is followed by *r.*) Note, too, that digraphs are not split: *broth-er, with-er.*

4. *One consonant between two vowels.* When one consonant appears between two vowels, it often becomes a part of the syllable on the right: *ma-jor, e-vil.* When the single consonant moves to the right, the syllable to the left is said to be open because it ends in a vowel. If a syllable ends in a vowel, the vowel is generally long. In a number of exceptions, however, the consonant becomes a part of the syllable on the left: *sev-en, Lat-in.*

5. *Final le.* The letters *le* at the end of a word usually are combined with a preceding consonant to create a separate syllable: *cra-dle, ma-ple.*

It is important to keep in mind that syllabication is designed to help students decode an unfamiliar word by separating it into its syllabic parts and then recombining the parts into a whole. It is not necessary for students to divide the word exactly right, which is a highly technical process. All that matters is whether students are able to arrive at the approximate pronunciation.

As with other skills and strategies that involve sounds in words, instruction in syllabication begins on an auditory level. Students must be able to hear the syllables before they can be expected to break a word into syllabic parts and

Syllabication is the division of words into syllables. In reading, words are broken down into syllables phonemically, or according to their sounds, rather than orthographically, or according to the rules governing end-of-line word division: *gen-(e)-rous* and *butt-er* rather than *gen-er-ous* and *but-ter.*

An **affix** is a morphemic element added to the beginning or ending of a word or root, as in *prepayment,* in order to alter the meaning of the word or change its function. Both prefixes and suffixes are affixes.

Putting words in syllables can be a challenging task because it is sometimes difficult to tell where one syllable ends and another begins. Even the experts disagree; if you look up the word *vocational,* for instance, you will see that Merriam-Webster dictionaries syllabicate it in one way and Thorndike-Barnhart dictionaries in another.

When students decode multi-syllabic words, do not insist upon exact syllable division. All that should be expected is that the student break multisyllabic words into smaller units so that she or he can pronounce each one and then put the units back together again to form a whole word.

reconstruct it. Lesson 4.4 presents the steps in teaching syllabication using the generalization approach.

Lesson 4.4
Syllabication using the generalization approach

Step 1. Auditory perception of syllables

Explain to students that words have parts called *syllables*. Say a group of words, and clap for each syllable: *be-cause, chil-dren, help-er, pic-ture*. Once students catch on to the idea, have them join in.

Step 2. Perception of printed syllables

Present one- and two-syllable words that contrast with each other so that students get a sense of printed syllables:

a	*fast*	*be*	*win*	*some*
ago	*faster*	*being*	*window*	*sometime*

Have students read the one-syllable word and then the two-syllable word with which it contrasts. Emphasize that the top word has one syllable and the bottom word has two syllables.

Step 3. Perception of syllable generalization

Once students have a sense of what syllables are, present words that illustrate a syllable generalization. The following words illustrate the affix *-ing* generalization:

do	*call*	*play*	*see*	*sing*
doing	*calling*	*playing*	*seeing*	*singing*

Have students read the words and contrast them. Lead them to see that the words on the top have one syllable and those on the bottom have two. Read each word on the bottom, and encourage the class to clap as they hear the separate syllables in each one. Lead students to see that *-ing* at the end of a word forms a separate syllable. In ensuing lessons, cover other affixes and broaden the generalization.

Step 4. Guided practice

Have the class read rhymes, poems, signs, and short pieces and sing songs that contain words incorporating the generalization that has been taught. Have students complete reinforcement exercises in which they use both context and syllabication clues to choose the word that correctly completes a sentence, for example:

Did you (*call, calling*) me up?
I hear a bird (*sing, singing*).
I cannot (*see, seeing*) you from here.
We are (*play, playing*) a new game.
Are you (*do, doing*) your work?

Provide assistance and additional feedback if students experience difficulty using the syllabication generalization.

Step 5. Application

Have students read stories and articles that contain multisyllabic words. Encourage them to apply the generalization(s) they have learned.

PATTERN APPROACH TO TEACHING SYLLABICATION

Knowing syllabic generalizations is one thing; applying them is quite another. Research (Gunning, 1988a) and experience suggest that many students apparently do not apply syllabic generalizations. When faced with unfamiliar, multisyllabic words, they attempt to search out pronounceable elements or simply skip the words. These students might fare better with an approach that presents syllables in patterns (Cunningham, 1978).

In a pattern approach, students examine a number of words that contain a syllable that has a high frequency. For example, dozens of words that begin with a consonant and are followed by a long *o* could be presented in pattern form. The advantage of this approach is that students learn to recognize pronounceable units in words and also to apply the open-syllable generalization in a specific situation. The pattern could be introduced with a one-syllable word contrasted with multisyllabic words to make it easier for students to grasp, for example:

so
soda
total
local
vocal
motel
hotel
notice

The steps to follow in teaching a syllabication lesson using the pattern approach are presented in Lesson 4.5.

Lesson 4.5
Syllabication using the pattern approach

Step 1. Introducing the pattern

Write the word *go* on the board, and have students read it. Then write *ago* under it, and have students read it. Contrast *go* and *ago* by pointing to the sound that each syllable makes. To help students perceive the separate syllables in *ago*, write them in contrasting colors or underline them. Then have students read *ago*. Present the words *away, alone, awake*, and *asleep* in the same way. As students read the separate syllables in each word, point to each one. Note similarities among the words.

Step 2. Formulating a generalization

Lead students to see that *a* at the beginning of a word often has the schwa sound /uh/. Since schwa, according to most systems of categorizing speech sounds, occurs only in multisyllabic words, provide students with a multisyllabic model word for the *a* spelling of schwa. Tell students that *ago* is the model word for this pattern. If they forget the pattern or have difficulty with a schwa *a*, they can use the model word to help them. If you have a model words chart, add *ago* to it. If you do not have a model words chart, you may wish to start one.

Step 3. Guided practice

For guided practice, have students read a second set of schwa *a* words: *around, along, alive, across, about*. Also have students complete exercises similar to the following:

> Make words by putting together two of the three syllables in each row. Write the words on the lines.
>
> | sleep | a | read | _____ |
> | a | go | play | _____ |
> | head | a | next | _____ |
> | over | a | round | _____ |
> | a | long | lamp | _____ |

> Underline the word that fits the sense of the sentence better.
>
> Toads and frogs look (*alike, away*).
>
> Do you know how to tell them (*alive, apart*)?
>
> Toads like to live in gardens that are (*alive, alone*) with bugs.
>
> Toads eat an (*amazing, awakening*) number of bugs.
>
> A toad can flick its tongue so fast that a bug would have a hard time getting (*awake, away*). (Gunning, 1994)

Step 4. Application

Have students read selections—stories, informational pieces, and/or real-world materials—that contain schwa *a* words.

In approximate order of difficulty, the numerous multisyllabic patterns are:

- Easy affixes: *play-ing, quick-ly*
- Compound words: *base-ball, any-one*
- Closed-syllable words: *rab-bit, let-ter*
- Open-syllable words: *ba-by, ti-ny*
- *e* marker words: *es-cape, do-nate*
- Vowel digraph words: *a-gree, sea-son*
- Other patterns: *cir-cle, sir-loin*

Whether you teach using generalizations, patterns, or, as this book recommends, a combination of approaches, students must have a plan of attack or strategy when facing an unfamiliar multisyllabic word. Students can use the steps in the following Student Strategy on their own.

Student Strategy
Attacking multisyllabic words

1. See whether the word has any prefixes or suffixes. If so, pronounce the prefix, then the suffix, and then the remaining part of the word. If the word has no prefix or suffix, start with the beginning of the word and divide it into syllables. Say each syllable.
2. Put the syllables together. If the word is not a real word, try other pronunciations until you get a real word.
3. See if the word makes sense in the sentence in which it appears. If it does not, try other pronunciations.
4. If nothing works, use a dictionary or ask the teacher.

USING THE PRONOUNCEABLE WORD PART AND ANALOGY STRATEGIES

The pronounceable word part and analogy strategies recommended in Chapter 3 may also be used to decode multisyllabic words. For instance, if students are having difficulty with the word *silver,* they might look for a pronounceable word part such as "il" and add /s/ to make "sil." They would then say "er," add /v/ to make "ver" and reconstruct the whole word. In many instances, saying a part of the word—the "sil" in *silver,* for example—is enough of a clue to enable students to say the whole word. If the pronounceable word part strategy does not work, they may use an analogy or compare/contrast strategy, as advocated in the Benchmark Program. Students using the Benchmark Program employ common words to help them sound out the syllables in a multisyllabic word that is in their listening but not their reading vocabulary. For instance, faced with the word *envelope,* the student works it out by making a series of comparisons. The first syllable is *en,* as in *ten;* the second is *vel,* which is similar to *tell;* and the third has the sound of *ope,* as in *hope.* Putting them all together, and making a slight adjustment in the pronunciation of *vel,* the student synthesizes the word *envelope* (Anderson & Au, 1991; Gaskins, Gaskins, & Gaskins, 1991).

As students read increasingly complex materials and meet a higher proportion of polysyllabic words, their ability to perceive the visual forms of syllables should develop naturally. As with phonics skills, the best way to practice dealing with polysyllabic words is through a combination of instruction and wide reading.

Adapting instruction for students with difficulty reading

The Benchmark Program is one of the country's best-known programs for students who are having serious difficulty learning to read. However, many of the principles used to teach students in the program may also be used in regular classrooms. The program consists of lessons housed in three large notebooks and is available from Benchmark School, 2107 N. Providence Road, Media, PA 19063.

MORPHEMIC ANALYSIS

One of the most powerful word-attack skills is **morphemic analysis**—but it is also one of the most neglected (O'Rourke, 1974). Henry (1990) found that elementary school students knew very little about morphemic elements. Henry also

Morphemic analysis is the examination of a word in order to locate and derive the meanings of the morphemes.

found that both regular elementary school children and children classified as learning disabled showed significant gains after instruction in morphemic analysis. Based on their research, White, Power, and White (1989) estimated that average fourth-graders double their ability to use morphemic analysis after just ten hours of instruction.

Morphemic analysis is the ability to determine a word's meaning through examination of its prefix, root, and/or suffix. A **morpheme** is the smallest unit of meaning. It may be a word, a prefix, a suffix, or a root. The word *believe* has a single morpheme; however, *unbelievable* has three: *un-believe-able*. *Telegraph* has two morphemes: *tele-graph*. Whereas structural analysis involves chunks of sounds, morphemic analysis is concerned with chunks of meaning.

Talk of prefixes, suffixes, root words, and compounds may conjure up images of memorizing lists of word elements; however, learning morphemes is a constructive, generative process. Children demonstrate the ability to construct morphemes as early as age 2 (Brown, 1973). The process continues into elementary school, where they refine their knowledge of past tense and third-person plural. Evidence that morphemic knowledge is constructive rather than imitative comes from the "mistakes" of young speakers—for instance, "We bringed our lunch to the zoo." The process is not simply a question of parroting what adults say because no adult would say "bringed." Rather, having heard *-ed* added to other words to indicate past tense, the child constructs a rule wherein *-ed* is added to all verbs, including *bring,* as a past tense marker. Later, the child refines the process and says *brought* instead of *bringed.*

Morphemic analysis as a word-attack skill should build on this constructive element. Instruction must be generative and conceptual rather than mechanical and isolated. For example, students can use their knowledge of the familiar word *microscope* to figure out what *micro* means and to apply that knowledge to *microsecond, microwave, micrometer,* and *microbe.* By considering known words, they can generate a concept of *micro* and apply it to unknown words, which, in turn, enriches that concept (Dale & O'Rourke, 1971). The key to teaching morphemic analysis is to help students note prefixes, suffixes, and roots and discover their meanings. It is also essential that elements with a high transfer value be taught and that students be trained in transferring knowledge (Dale & O'Rourke, 1971).

COMPOUND WORDS

One way of generating or creating new words is to put two words together. In this way, the English language has been enriched with thousands of **compound words** and is growing richer by the day. For novice readers, however, compounds often pose a problem. For example, even though students might have no difficulty reading *out* and *doors* when they see the words separately, they may give up when they come to *outdoors* because it looks long and difficult. Reassure them that they can read most compounds if they break them down into their component parts. Except for words like *necklace,* components generally retain their single-word pronunciations.

Help students see that the separate words in a compound often give a clue to the long word's meaning, so that *sunburn* is a *burn* from the *sun* and a *birdhouse* is a *house* where a *bird* lives. There are exceptions, of course, such as *shortstop*

A **morpheme** is the smallest unit of meaning. The word *nervously* has three morphemes: *nerv(e)-ous-ly.*

Adapting instruction for learning-disabled students
Learning-disabled students' knowledge of morphemic elements is especially poor. However, given systematic instruction, they make encouraging gains (Henry, 1990).

Compound words actually come in three forms: solid, hyphenated, or open. That is, the compound may be written as one word (*sunup*), as a hyphenated word (*good-by*), or as two words (*home run*). Most compounds provide clues to the word's meaning; examples are *backdoor, fireplace, sundown,* and *sidewalk.* But some, such as *breakfast, otherwise,* and *shortstop,* do not.

and *hangup*. The Children's Book List provides titles of some books that reinforce the concept of compound words.

Children's Book List
Books that reinforce compound words

Berenstain, S., & Berenstain, J. *Inside, Outside, Upside Down*. New York: Random House (1969).

Freeman, P. *A Rainbow of My Own*. New York: Viking (1986).

Heller, R. *Merry-Go-Round*. New York: Grosset & Dunlap (1990).

Kessler, L. *Old Turtle's Riddle and Joke Book*. New York: Greenwillow (1986).

Moncure, J. *The Biggest Snowfall*. Chicago: Children's Press (1988).

Rice, E. *Goodnight, Goodnight*. New York: Greenwillow (1980).

PREFIXES

In general, **prefixes** are easier to learn than suffixes (Dale & O'Rourke, 1964, cited in O'Rourke, 1974). According to Graves and Hammond (1980), there are relatively few prefixes, and they tend to have constant, concrete meanings and relatively consistent spellings. When learning prefixes and other morphemic elements, students should have the opportunity to observe each one in a number of words so that they have a solid basis for constructing an understanding of the element. Lesson 4.6 describes how the prefix *pre-* might be taught.

> A **prefix** is an affix placed at the beginning of a word or root in order to form a new word—for example, *prepay*.

Lesson 4.6
Prefixes

Step 1. Construct the meaning of the prefix

Place the following words on the board:

> *pregame*   *prepay*   *preview*   *pretest*   *predawn*

Discuss the meanings of these words and the places where students may have seen them. Note in particular how *pre-* changes the meaning of the word it precedes. Encourage students to construct a definition of *pre-*. Lead students to see that *pre-* is a prefix. Discuss, too, the purpose and value of knowing prefixes. Explain to students how knowing the meanings of prefixes will help them figure out unknown words. Show them how you would syllabicate words that contain prefixes, and how you would use knowledge of prefixes to sound out the words and determine their meanings.

> Prefixes are most useful when they contribute to the meaning of a word and can be added to other words. Thus, the prefix *un-* is both productive and easy to detect (*unafraid, unable, unhappy*), but the prefix *con-* in *condition* is unproductive and difficult to detect (McArthur, 1992). In your teaching, stress productive affixes, which is what this book emphasizes.

Step 2. Guided practice

Have students complete practice exercises similar to the following:

> Fill in the blanks with these words containing prefixes—*preview, pregame, prepay, predawn, pretest*.

To make sure they had enough money to buy the food, the party's planners asked everyone to _____.

The _____ show starts thirty minutes before the kickoff.

The _____ of the movie made it seem more exciting than it really was.

Everyone got low marks on the spelling _____ because they had not been taught the words yet.

In the _____ quiet, only the far-off barking of a dog could be heard.

Step 3. Application

Have students read selections that contain the prefix *pre-*, and note its use in real-world materials.

Step 4. Extension

Present the prefix *post-*, and contrast it with *pre-*. Since *post-* is an opposite, this will help clarify the meaning of *pre-*.

SCOPE-AND-SEQUENCE CHART

The most frequently occurring prefixes include *un-, re-, ir-, il-, dis-, en-, em-, non-, in-, im-* (meaning "into"), *over-, mis-, sub-, pre-, inter-, fore-, de-, trans-, super-, semi-, anti-, mid-,* and *under-* (White, Sowell, & Yanagihara, 1989).

Some prefixes appear in reading materials as early as grade 2; however, since they do not become an important element until grade 3, this seems to be the appropriate level at which to initiate instruction. A scope-and-sequence chart based on an analysis of words in the Harris-Jacobson list (Harris & Jacobson, 1982) is presented in Table 4.2. At each level, elements from earlier grades should be reviewed.

TABLE 4.2   Scope-and-sequence chart for common prefixes

Grade	Prefix	Meaning	Example	Grade	Prefix	Meaning	Example
3	*un-*	not	unhappy	6	*ex-*	out, out of	exhaust
	un-	opposite	undo		*ex-*	former	explayer
	under-	under	underground		*inter-*	between	international
					mis-	not	misunderstanding
4	*dis-*	not	dishonest		*mis-*	bad	misfortune
	dis-	opposite	disappear	7	*en-*	forms verb	enrage
	re-	again	reappear		*ir-*	not	irresponsible
	re-	back	replace		*trans-*	across	transatlantic
5	*im-*	not	impossible	8	*anti*	against	antiwar
	in-	not	invisible		*pro-*	in favor of	prowar
	pre-	before	pregame		*sub-*	under	submarine
	sub-	under	submarine		*super-*	above	supersonic

SUFFIXES

The two kinds of **suffixes** are derivational and inflectional. **Derivational suffixes** change the part of speech of a word or change the function of a word in some way. Common derivational suffixes are presented in Table 4.3. Some of these suffixes form adjectives: *-al* (music*al*), *-less* (help*less*), *-ous* (joy*ous*). Others form nouns: *-ance* (resist*ance*), *-ence* (occurr*ence*), *-ness* (happi*ness*). Still others change the function of a noun so that it indicates a person rather than a thing: *-er* (farm*er*), *-ist* (art*ist*). You may want to emphasize the following suffixes because they occur with the highest frequency: *-er, -(t)ion, -able, -al, -y,* and *-ness* (White, Sowell, & Yanagihara, 1989).

Inflectional suffixes mark grammatical items and include plural *-s* (boy*s*), third-person singular *-s* (he help*s*), present participle *-ing* (hopp*ing*), past tense *-ed* (hopp*ed*), past participle *-en* (chos*en*), comparisons *-er* and *-est* (tall*er*, tall*est*), and the adverbial *-ly* (quick*ly*). Inflectional suffixes appear early. In fact, *-s, -ed,* and *-ing* occur in the easiest materials and are taught in grade 1; *-er, -est, -ly* are introduced in most basals by grade 2 (Harris & Jacobson, 1982). For the most part, students are already using inflectional suffixes widely in their oral language by the time they meet them in their reading. They simply have to become used to translating the letters into sounds. If they are reading for meaning and using syntactic as well as semantic cues, translating the letters into sounds should happen almost automatically. For example, children's grammatical sense will tell them that a /z/ sound is used in the italicized word in the following sentence: The two *boys* were fighting. Also, it is not necessary to teach students that *s* represents /z/ at the end of some words: *friends, cars,* and so on. The sound is automatically translated. In the same way, students automatically pronounce the *-ed* correctly in the following words, even though three different pronunciations are represented: *called, planted,* and *jumped.* Exercises designed to have children identify which pronunciation each *-ed* represents—/d/, /id/, or /t/—are time wasters.

Suffixes are taught in the same way as prefixes. As can be seen from Tables 4.2 and 4.3, the definitions of prefixes and suffixes are sometimes vague. Although only one or two definitions are given in the tables, in reality, some affixes have four or five. To give students a sense of the meaning of each affix, provide experience with several examples. Experience is a better teacher than mere definition.

ROOT WORDS

As students move through the grades, knowledge of morphemic elements becomes more important for handling increasingly complex reading material. As the reading becomes more abstract and therefore more difficult in every subject area, the number of words made up of **roots** and affixes becomes greater. Science, for instance, often uses Greek and Latin words and compounds (O'Rourke, 1974).

As with prefixes and suffixes, roots that should be taught are those that appear with high frequency, transfer to other words, and are on the appropriate level of difficulty. For example, the root *cil* (coun*cil*) meaning "call" should probably not be taught because it is difficult to distinguish in a word. Roots such as *graph* (auto*graph*), *cred* (in*cred*ible), and *phon* (tele*phon*e) are easy to spot and appear

A **suffix** is an affix added to the end of a word or root in order to form a new word—for example, help*less*.

A **derivational suffix** produces new words by forming derived words or words whose meanings have been added to—for example, happi*ness*, penni*less*. An **inflectional suffix** changes a word by adding an inflected ending such as *-s* or *-ed* that shows number or tense—for example, girl*s*, help*ed*.

Although more complex than prefixes, suffixes, especially those that appear with high frequency, are worth teaching because they do help students add words to their meaning vocabularies. The most frequently occurring derivational suffixes include *-er, -tion (-ion), -ible (-able), -al (-ial), -y, -ness, -ity (-ty), -ment, -ic, -ous (-ious), -en, -ive, -ful,* and *-less* (White, Sowell, & Yanagihara, 1989).

The **root** of a word is the part of the word that is left after all the affixes have been removed. A root is also defined as the source of present-day words; for example, the Latin verb *decidere* is the root of the English verb *decide* (McArthur, 1992). The language of morphemic analysis can be confusing. The words *base, combining form, root,* and *stem* are sometimes used interchangeably but actually have different meanings. To keep matters simple, this book uses the word *root* (McArthur, 1992).

TABLE 4.3 Scope-and-sequence chart for common derivational suffixes

Grade	Suffix	Meaning	Example
2	*-en*	made of	wooden
	-er	one who	painter
	-or	one who	actor
3	*-able*	is; can be	comfortable
	-ible	is; can be	visible
	-ful	full of; having	joyful
	-ness	having	sadness
	-(t)ion	act of	construction
	-y	being; having	dirty
4	*-al*	having	magical
	-ance	state of	allowance
	-ence	state of; quality of	patience
	-ify	make	magnify
	-less	without	fearless
	-ment	state of	advertisement
	-ous	having	curious
5	*-ian*	one who is in a certain field	musician
	-ic	of; having	gigantic
	-ish	having the quality of	foolish
	-ive	being	creative
6	*-ian*	one who	guardian
	-ist	a person who	scientist
	-ity	state of	reality
	-ize	make	apologize
7	*-ar*	forms adjectives	muscular
	-age	forms nouns	postage
	-ess	female	hostess
8	*-ary*	forms adjectives	budgetary
	-ette	small	dinette
	-some	forms adjectives	troublesome

in words likely to be read by elementary school students. Roots that are good candidates for inclusion in an elementary school program are shown in Table 4.4. The sequence is based on O'Rourke's research (1974) and an analysis of the roots found at various levels in the Harris-Jacobson list (Harris & Jacobson, 1982).

TABLE 4.4 Scope-and-sequence chart for common roots

Grade	Root	Meaning	Example
3	*graph*	writing	autograph
	tele	distance	telescope
4	*port*	carry	import
	saur	lizard	dinosaur
	phon	sound	telephone
	vid, vis	see	visible
5	*astro*	star	astronaut
	cred	believe	incredible
	duct	lead	conductor
	tri	three	triangle
6	*aud*	hearing	auditorium
	auto	self	autobiography
	bi	two	bicycle
	ology	study of	geology
	scrib, script	writing	inscription
	therm	heat	thermometer
7	*mid*	middle	midday
	ped	foot	pedestrian
	chrono	time	chronometer
	dict	say	dictate
	hemi	half	hemisphere
	manu	hand	manuscript
8	*bio*	life	biology
	geo	earth	geology
	micro	small	microscope
	mono	one	monotone
	semi	half, part	semisweet
	some	group	foursome

Included among the list of roots in Table 4.4 are combining forms. A combining form is a root designed to combine with another combining form (*tri+pod*) or a word (*tri+angle*). As combining forms usually appear first or last in a word, they are often listed with prefixes or suffixes and sometimes with roots. Combining forms differ from affixes because two combining forms can be put together to make a word, but two affixes cannot. Although technically speaking, combining forms are not roots, they are included with the roots because that is where they are presented in most textbooks (McArthur, 1992).

TEACHING ROOT WORDS

Teach root words inductively, and take advantage of every opportunity to develop students' knowledge of them. For example, if students wonder what a thermal wind is, discuss known words such as *thermos*, *thermostat*, and *thermometer*. Lead them to see that in all three words, *therm* has to do with heat; thus, thermal winds are warm winds. Henry (1990) found that it is also helpful if students are taught the origin of morphemic elements. For instance, elements derived from Greek can be grouped for study: *hemi, auto, bio, tele, poly, gon, ology,* and *scope.*

If students read about dinosaurs, use the opportunity to introduce *tri, saurus, pod, ornitho,* and other roots. This often helps students use the name to identify the distinguishing characteristics of the creature. For example, *triceratops* uses three word parts to describe a dinosaur that has three horns, two of which are over the eyes: *tri,* "three"; *cerat,* "horn"; and *ops,* "eyes." Two of the parts also transfer to a number of other words: *tri* to *triangle, tripod,* etc., and *op* to *optical, optician,* etc.

Scope-and-sequence charts for affixes and roots have been provided to give you a sense of when certain ones are usually presented. The real determinants, however, are the needs of the students and the demands of their reading tasks. For example, before they read the supplementary text *Pesticides* (Duggleby, 1990), you might discuss the words *pesticide, insecticide, herbicide,* and *fungicide.* This would be an opportune time to present a morphemic analysis lesson showing how the four words are related and to help the class discover what *-cide* means. Relating instruction to the needs of students and the demands of the text in this way keeps your teaching functional and contextual. Best of all, students see the connection between skills and their use in real reading.

Reinforcement Activities
Morphemic analysis

- Provide students with several long words composed of a number of morphemic units, for example:

enrollment	*improperly*	*transoceanic*	*unimaginable*
disagreeable	*prehistoric*	*photographer*	*disagreeable*
misjudgment	*irregularly*	*unfavorable*	*autobiographical*
uncomfortable	*disallowable*	*unpresidential*	*oceanographer*

Have them determine the morphemic boundaries and try to figure out what the words mean based on analysis of the units. Good sources of other words to analyze are the readers and texts that students are encountering in class.

- Ask students to create webs of roots and affixes in which the element is displayed in several words (Tompkins & Yaden, 1986). A web of the root *loc* might look like Figure 4.1.

- Students can incorporate roots and affixes into their everyday lives by constructing personal reactions. In a list like the following, have them underline the prefix *pro-* or *anti-* to show that they are for or against each item:

pro-	*anti-*	*spinach*
pro-	*anti-*	*baseball*
pro-	*anti-*	*spiders*

FIGURE 4.1 | Web of the root *loc*

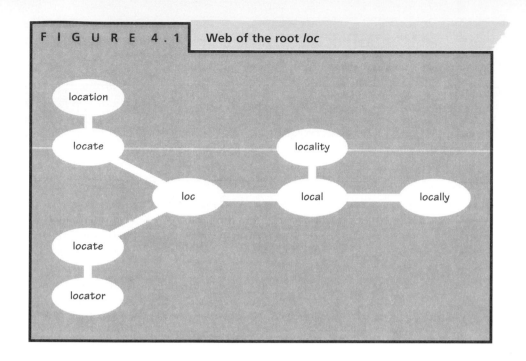

pro-	anti-	ice cream
pro-	anti-	rock music
pro-	anti-	snakes
pro-	anti-	chores
pro-	anti-	homework
pro-	anti-	pizza
pro-	anti-	bubble gum

- To help students discover the underlying meanings and functions of affixes, have them sort words containing affixes in a variety of ways—according to whether the affix forms a noun (*narration*), an adjective (*natural*), or a verb (*terrify*)—and sort prefixes that indicate number (*mono-*, *bi-*, *tri-*), negation (*il-*, *im-*, *in-*, *un-*, *ir-*), size (*micro-*, *macro-*, *mega-*), etc.

- Using root words, prefixes, and suffixes, let students create words that label a new creature, invention, or discovery. For example, a *quintocycle* would be a cycle with five wheels. A *monovideopod* would be a single walking eye.

- Ask students to bring in examples of roots and affixes from periodicals, children's books, textbooks, signs, and labels, or from spoken language. For example, a child who has recently been on an airplane may have noted the word *preboard*. Let the class determine the word's root and/or affix and discuss the word's meaning.

CONTEXTUAL ANALYSIS

Even with context clues as rich as they are in this excerpt from *Charlotte's Web,* some students still may not pick up the meaning of *salutations.* After the story has been read, it would be a good idea to write *salutations* and other words that have rich context clues on the board and ask the class what the words mean. This would give you a rough idea of how well students are using context. Discussing the words and the context in which they appear reinforces the meanings of the words and the use of context clues.

Contextual analysis refers to an attempt to derive the meaning of a word by examining the context in which the unknown word appears.

Imagine that you are a fourth-grader who has never seen or heard the word *salutations.* What does the following passage indicate about its meaning?

> "Salutations!" repeated the voice.
>
> "What are *they,* and where are *you*?" screamed Wilbur. "Please, *please,* tell me where you are. And what are salutations?"
>
> "Salutations are greetings," said the voice. "When I say 'salutations' it's just my fancy way of saying hello or good morning." (White, 1952, p. 35)

Not only does E. B. White define the word *salutations* in context in *Charlotte's Web,* he also implies that its use is somewhat pompous. Of course, not all difficult words are explained with such care; in fact, in many instances, **contextual analysis** is not at all helpful (Schatz & Baldwin, 1986). Context determines the particular meaning of a word, but it may not reveal it (Deighton, 1959).

An informal survey of difficult words in children's periodicals, textbooks, and trade books indicates that definitions or usable context clues are supplied about one-third of the time (Gunning, 1990). However, it is estimated that the average reader is able to use context successfully only between 5 and 20 percent of the time (Jenkins, Matlock, & Slocum, 1989; Nagy, Anderson, & Herman, 1987). Even when context clues are fairly obvious, students may fail to take advantage of them. Fortunately, children do become more proficient at using context clues as they progress through the grades. They also do significantly better with practice. Simply directing students to use context to get the meaning of an unfamiliar word is not effective. The directive has to be accompanied by practice and feedback to let them know if their contextual guesses are correct (Carnine, Kameenui, & Coyle, 1984).

PROCESSING CONTEXT CLUES

Instruction in the use of context clues should make explicit the thinking processes involved. Sternberg and Powell (1983) postulated a three-step cognitive process in using context clues:

1. *Selective encoding.* Students separate relevant from irrelevant information, choosing only information that will help them construct a meaning for an unfamiliar word.
2. *Selective combination.* Students combine clues into a tentative definition.
3. *Selective comparison.* Students use their background of experience to help figure out the meaning of a word.

Here is how the three steps would be put to use to figure out the meaning of *brigantine* in this passage from Speare's (1958) *The Witch of Blackbird Pond:*

> On a morning in mid-April, 1687, the brigantine *Dolphin* left the open sea, sailed briskly across the Sound to the wide mouth of the Connecticut River and into Saybrook Harbor. Kit Tyler had been on the forecastle deck since daybreak, standing close to the rail, staring hungrily at the first sight of land for five weeks. (p. 5)

1. *Selective encoding.* What information in the sentence containing the unknown word will help me figure out what this word means? Is there any information in earlier sentences that will help? Is there any information in later sentences that will help?

Helpful clues include information about leaving the open sea, sailing, standing on a deck, and seeing land for the first time in five weeks. The facts that it was a morning in mid-April and Kit had been waiting since daybreak are not relevant clues.

2. *Selective combination.* When I think about all the information given about this unknown word, what does the word seem to mean?

When readers put all relevant clues together, they will see that *brigantine* is some kind of ship or boat. Because the passage states that the ship had been on the open sea and that it had a deck with a rail, readers might also infer that the ship was large.

3. *Selective comparison.* What do I know that will help me figure out the meaning of this word?

Using past experience, readers might realize that in the 1600s there were no engine-driven ships, so a brigantine is probably powered by sails. Once readers have used context to construct a tentative meaning for the unknown word, they should try substituting the tentative meaning for the word. If the meaning does not fit the sense of the sentence, they should revise their substitution, use the dictionary, or get help.

TYPES OF CONTEXT CLUES

Listed in the following paragraphs in approximate order of difficulty are eight main types of **context clues.** They have been drawn from a variety of materials that elementary school students might read.

1. *Explicit explanation or definition.* The easiest clue to use is a definition in context. For instance, the following passage from *The Wright Brothers at Kitty Hawk* (Sobol, 1961) gives a detailed, conceptual explanation of warping:

> "Why the wings are twisting!" exclaimed Bill Tate.
>
> "We call it *warping*," said Orville. "See the wings on the side? Their ends are turned upward and forward."
>
> "And the wings on the left side are pulled downwards and rearward," said Bill Tate.
>
> Orville let go of the rope. "Now, in front—"
>
> "Hold on," said Bill Tate. "I'm not sure I understand what I saw."
>
> "The warping is our idea for keeping the glider level," said Orville. Carefully he explained how it changed the way the wind pushed against the wings. (p. 24)

Explicit definitions are usually more concise, as in this excerpt from *A Book about Planets and Stars* (Reigot, 1988): "The only water we know of on Venus is in the form of water vapor. (Water vapor is a gas, which you cannot see.)" (p. 26).

2. *Appositives.* Definitions are sometimes supplied in the form of appositives immediately after the difficult word: "Mars has two satellites—tiny moons that revolve around it" (Reigot, 1988, p. 24).

Context clues are bits of information in the surrounding text that might be used to derive the meaning of an unknown word. Context clues include appositives, restatement of the word's meaning, comparative or contrasting statements, and other items that might provide clues to the word's meaning.

3. *Synonyms*. Finding a synonym sometimes takes some searching. It often appears in a sentence after the one that used the target word. In the following passage from *Little House on the Prairie* (Wilder, 1941), the synonym for *ague* is given in a preceding sentence:

> Next day she had a little chill and a little fever. Ma blamed the watermelon. But next she had a chill and a little fever. So they did not know what could have caused their fever 'n' ague. (p. 198)

4. *Function indicators*. Sometimes context provides clues to meaning because it gives the purpose or function of the difficult word (Sternberg, 1987). In the following sentence, the reader gets an excellent clue to the meaning of *derrick* in a sentence that indicates what a derrick does: "The derrick lifted the glider into the sky" (Sobol, 1961, p. 27).

5. *Examples*. The examples in the following passage would give the reader a concrete understanding of *athletic*:

> "My parents were very athletic," the President said. "My dad played on the baseball team in college, and he was a wonderful golfer. My mother was a very good tennis player, and she was fast!" (Hacker & Kaufman, 1990, p. 44)

6. *Comparison-contrast*. By contrasting the unknown word *opponents* with the known word *teammates* in the following passage, readers can gain an understanding of the unknown word: "You should always know where on the field your teammates and opponents are" (Rolfer, 1990, p. 46). Students must be able to reason that the word *opponents* is the opposite of *teammates*, however.

7. *Classification*. By noting similarities in items, some of which are known, readers can guess what an unknown word means. In the following sentence, they know from the word *town* and the earlier mention of *Canada* that places are being talked about; based on this conclusion, they can infer that *province*, the unknown word, is also a place: "Gordie was born on March 31, 1928, in the town of Floral, in the province of Saskatchewan" (Neff, 1990, p. 48). Since the sentence says that the town is in the province, they could infer that a province is larger than a town.

8. *Experience*. A main clue to the meaning of an unfamiliar word is students' background of experience. In the following passage, readers can use their own experience of being cut or injured together with imagining what it might be like to undergo the experience that is described; this will enable them to make an informed guess as to what the unfamiliar word *excruciating* means: "Suddenly, the hedge clippers caught a branch, and my left middle finger was pulled into the blades. I felt an excruciating pain. The tip of my finger was hanging by a thread" (Rolfer, 1990, p. 52).

PRESENTING CONTEXT CLUES

Use of context should permeate the reading program from its very beginning. When emerging readers use phonics skills to try to decode words that are in their listening but not in their reading vocabulary, they should use context as well, both as an aid to sounding out and as a check to make sure they have decoded the words correctly. From the very beginning, novice readers must be seekers of meaning. Although one hopes that over the years the use of context will become automatic, context clues should be taught explicitly. Using a direct teaching model, the teacher should explain what the clues are, why it is important to use context, and how they can be applied. Modeling use of clues, guided practice, and application are important elements in the process. Lesson 4.7 describes how context clues might be presented.

Lesson 4.7
Context clues

Step 1. Explain context

Demonstrate the usefulness of context clues. Select five or six difficult words from a book the class is reading and show how context could be used to derive their meanings.

Step 2. Demonstrate Sternberg and Powell's (1983) three-step process

This can be done by asking the following questions:

> What information in the selection will help me figure out what the unknown word means? (selective encoding)

> When I put together all the information about the unknown word, what does the word seem to mean? (selective combination)

> What do I know that will help me figure out the meaning of this word? (selective comparison)

Step 3. Try out the tentative meaning of the unknown word

Show students how they should try out the tentative meaning of the unknown word by substituting the meaning for the word and reading the sentence to see if the substitution fits. Explain that if the tentative meaning does not fit the sense of the sentence, they should revise it.

Step 4. Model the process

Model the process of using context with a variety of words. Explain the thinking processes that you go through as you attempt to figure out their meanings and then try out these tentative meanings. Show, for example, how you might use examples as clues, use a comparison, search out synonyms, look for appositives, use your background of experience, or try a combination of strategies. Show, too, how you would use context and experience to construct a tentative meaning for the unknown word and then try out the meaning by substituting it in the sentence.

Step 5. Guided practice

Have students use context clues to figure out unfamiliar words in selected passages that provide substantial clues. Do one or two cooperatively. Then have students try their hand. Discuss the meanings of the unfamiliar words and the types of clues they used.

Although there are a large number of different kinds of context clues, this chapter highlights those that seem to occur most frequently and are easiest to use. While you should discuss the different types of context clues, students do not need to be able to identify the specific type of context clue provided. It is more important that they direct their efforts toward figuring out the meaning of the unknown words.

As your class studies context clues, encourage students to be alert to especially good ones that they encounter in their outside reading and to bring these into class. Perhaps you could set aside a few minutes each day for a discussion of context clues, with one student reading the clue he or she discovered and the rest of the class attempting to use it to derive the meaning of the word.

Context clues can and should be used to complement phonics strategies and help students predict the pronunciations of words that are in the students' listening vocabularies but not in their reading vocabularies. However, context clues in this section are designed to help students derive the meanings of unknown words, words that are not in the students' listening vocabularies.

Assembling cut-up sentences is an excellent way to reinforce sight word reading, phonics, and context.

Step 6. Application

Encourage students to try using context clues in selections that they read. After the reading, talk over the meanings that they derived and the strategies they used. Ask how they went about determining what the unknown word meant, what clues they used, and how they decided on their definition of the unknown word.

SUBSEQUENT LESSONS IN THE USE OF CONTEXT CLUES

As with other essential strategies, the use of context clues should be reviewed periodically. Whenever a selection is discussed, talk over passages that contain especially effective context clues so as to remind students to use them and also to refine students' usage of them.

In a series of lessons, present other major context clues, emphasizing the thinking processes involved in using each one. After introducing all the types of clues appropriate for students' level, review them and have students complete exercises in which they identify the types. Draw sample sentences from children's periodicals, trade books, and content area texts so that students can see that the skills have relevance and that context clues will help them analyze words.

Most importantly, encourage students to get in the habit of using context to figure out the meanings of unfamiliar words. Instead of merely suggesting that they use clues, model the process from time to time to remind them about it. Also, encourage them to use the dictionary as a means of checking definitions derived by using context clues.

SUPPLYING CORRECTIVE FEEDBACK

Corrective feedback refers to information that is provided to a student who has failed to give a correct response and is designed to help the student respond correctly.

A student is reading and is suddenly stopped cold by an unknown word. What should the teacher do? Some theorists would say to do nothing—let the child work out the word or skip it. They feel that providing **corrective feedback,** because it focuses on the word level, might interfere with comprehension (Goodman, 1973, cited in McCoy & Pany, 1986). Research suggests, however, that correcting errors of word recognition is more beneficial than ignoring them (McCoy & Pany, 1986). In fact, the best procedure might be somewhere in between not supplying any help and immediately telling the child the word. However, if the error is not substantive and makes no change in the meaning of the sentence—the student says "this" for "that," for example—it might be best to ignore it.

Sometimes an error is substantive and disturbs the sense of the sentence, but it is obvious that the child will not be able to work out the word using phonics, context, morphemic analysis, or syllabication, either because of the nature of the word and the context or because the child lacks adequate skill. In such a case, it is best to supply the word immediately so that the student can get on with the reading. If there is a chance that the child can use strategies to decode the word, pause briefly—about five seconds or so—to provide an opportunity for the child to work out the word (Harris & Sipay, 1990). If the child fails to work out the word but might be able to with a little help, try a **corrective cues hierarchy** (McCoy & Pany, 1986). Most authorities in the field suggest using context first and then phonics or structural analysis if context does not work. However, sometimes context is not helpful, but the word is decodable; thus you may want to suggest that the student seek a pronounceable word part or use some other decoding strategy.

A **corrective cues hierarchy** is a series of corrective feedback statements arranged in order of utility and ease of application.

Ideally, as students are taught how to use word recognition strategies, they should also be taught when to apply them so that they can make the choice as to whether to try context, phonics, syllabic analysis, or morphemic analysis first. So, in a very real sense, the corrective cues hierarchy depends upon the nature of the word to be identified, the student's background, and the student's ability to apply strategies.

APPLYING A CORRECTIVE CUES HIERARCHY

The following corrective cues hierarchy is adapted from McCoy and Pany (1986):

- *Strategy 1.* Most programs advocate the use of context first when a student encounters an unknown word. Context should be used first if the difficult word does not lend itself to a decoding strategy or if the student's decoding skills are not advanced enough. However, seeking out a pronounceable word part and using it to reconstruct a word is often the simplest, most direct strategy and, in most instances, should be attempted first. When encountering an unknown word, the student should ask, "Is there any part of this word that I can say?" If that does not work, the student should try an analogy strategy, asking, "Is this word like any word I know?" If the word is a multisyllabic one, the student should reconstruct the word part by part. Once the word has been reconstructed, the student should verify the reconstruction by checking whether the word is real and fits the context of the sentence.
- *Strategy 2.* If the student is unable to use the pronounceable word part or analogy strategy to work out the difficult word rapidly, encourage the use of context. The student should determine what information in the sentence containing the unknown word—and additional sentences, if necessary—

Some difficult words lend themselves to the use of context clues. Others are more amenable to morphemic analysis or the use of pronounceable word parts or analogy. This corrective cues hierarchy is generic and should be adapted to fit the needs of your students and the type of word being processed. In general, it is best to use the cue that is the easiest and fastest to use and has the greatest chance of being successful.

helps him or her to figure out the word. The student should think about all the information given and about what he or she knows that might help in determining the meaning of the word. The student should then check to make sure that a real word has been constructed and that the word fits the context of the sentence.

- *Strategy 3.* If the meaning of the word is unknown and context does not help, then the student should use morphemic analysis. The student should look for parts of the word whose meaning he or she knows and use those to construct the meaning of the word. The student should then reread the sentence, substituting the constructed word to see whether it fits the sense of the sentence.

Although the strategies are presented here in consecutive order, they may be applied in tandem. For instance, a student may use both morphemic analysis and context to derive the meaning of a word or may use context and pronounceable word parts or phonics and syllabication to reconstruct the pronunciation of a word.

USING PROMPTS

When students are having difficulty with a word, use a prompt to encourage the use of decoding strategies. Listed below are suggested prompting questions that you might ask students in order to cue the use of a particular strategy. Some of the prompts have been adapted from the highly successful early intervention program *Reading Recovery.*

- *Pronounceable word part.* Is there any part of the word that you can say?
- *Analogy.* Is the word like any that you know?
- *Context.* What would make sense here? What would fit? Say "blank" for the word, and read to the end of the sentence. Then ask yourself, "What word would make sense here?"

Exemplary Teaching

Fostering Self-Correction

When Nora made mistakes in her reading, John Holt (1983) restrained himself from correcting them. He reasoned that no one likes to be corrected, and, besides, constant correction can undermine self-confidence, making children afraid to make educated guesses, afraid to trust their own judgment, and over-reliant on the teacher for the correct answer. But there was still another, more compelling reason for not correcting Nora's errors:

Left alone, not hurried, not pressured, not made anxious, she was able to find and correct most of them herself. It was most interesting to note how she did this. When she

made a mistake, she rarely noticed it at first. But as she read on, I could feel growing in her an uneasy sense that something had gone wrong, that something she had said didn't make sense, didn't fit with other things that she was saying. . . . At first she tried to ignore this feeling. . . . But this awareness of something not quite right would not let her alone. . . . Finally, after fidgeting and squirming, she would turn the page back in an irritated way and try to find what she had done wrong. Most of the time, she was able to find her mistake and correct it. . . . Like most young children she had a strong desire to see things fit together, make sense, come out right. (p. 146)

- *Syllabic analysis.* How would you say the first syllable? The second syllable? The next syllable? What does the word seem to be?
- *Morphemic analysis.* Is there any part of the word that you know?

DICTIONARY USAGE

Context, especially when combined with phonics and morphemic and structural analysis, is a powerful word-attack strategy, but some words defy even these four skills. When all else fails, it is time for the student to consult the world's greatest expert on words, the dictionary. Although students might not use a real dictionary in first and second grades, preparation begins early. In first grade and, in some cases, kindergarten, students compile word books and picture dictionaries that convey the concept. They also learn alphabetical order, a prerequisite skill for locating words, and phonics, which is necessary for using the pronunciation key.

USING PREDICTIONARIES

Most students are not able to use dictionaries until the third grade. However, **predictionaries,** which can be used by first- and second-graders, have been compiled by several publishers. Predictionaries are books in which limited numbers of words are defined through illustrations. A more advanced predictionary, which is usually called the first dictionary, uses sentences and pictures to define words but does not supply syllabications or pronunciation. Predictionaries are available on CD-ROM (see Table 14.4); the advantage of this format is that the selected words are pronounced orally and their definitions spoken. Predictionaries are a useful tool but must be used with care. Since they can include only a limited number of words, students may find that many they want to look up are not there. Locating entry words may also be fairly time-consuming.

A **predictionary** is an easy dictionary that has fewer entries and simpler definitions than a regular dictionary and does not contain a pronunciation key.

USING DICTIONARIES

By third grade, students with average reading achievement are ready to use real dictionaries. They should, of course, use beginning dictionaries that are simplified so that the definitions are readable. Using a dictionary is a complex task. Care must be taken that students do not feel defeated by it. Landau (1984) cautioned:

> The skills required to use a dictionary are often taken for granted by adults; teachers, however, know very well that they must be taught and are not easily mastered by everyone. One's grasp of the alphabet must be secure, and more, one must grasp conceptually the sequential way in which alphabetizing is done. Even if the child can perform the operation of finding the word he seeks, if it is a great chore filled with false starts, he is likely to give up the battle. (p. 14)

To keep students from believing that looking up words is a great chore, teachers must provide them with systematic instruction in the process and tasks that are well within their grasp. For reading, students must have three major skills:

An important element of dictionary instruction is demonstrating to pupils that the dictionary is a valued tool. Model the use of the dictionary by letting students see how you use the dictionary to look up an unfamiliar word, check the spelling or pronunciation of a word, or get information on a question of style in its style guide.

locating the target word, finding the proper definition, and learning the pronunciation. For writing, determining correct spelling and usage is also important.

LOCATING THE WORDS TO BE LOOKED UP

The first thing that students must realize is that words are arranged in alphabetical order—*a* to *z*—by first letter and then by second letter, and, if necessary, by third letter, and so on. To provide practice with the concept that it is necessary to go beyond the first letter to find words, have children look up some *z* words—*zebra, zip,* and *zoo*—so that they can see that it is necessary to apply alphabetical order to the second and third letters to find those words. Once students understand how to use the second and third letters for alphabetizing, have them locate words that require alphabetizing by the fourth letter. These might include words such as *visor, volt, vise, vein,* and *vassal.*

From the beginning, train students to use guide words so that they do not adopt the time-wasting habit of simply thumbing through the *s*'s or the *w*'s page by page until they find the appropriate location. Explain the function of guide words, and show students where they appear. Write a pair of guide words and a list of other words on the board and ask students which words from the list would appear on that page of the dictionary. For the guide words *stun* and *subside,* for example, have students indicate which of the following would appear on the page: *study, suburb, style, sturgeon, subtract, subject, stunt, student.*

Explain that not all letters encompass the same number of words; for example, *c* words take up many more pages than *x, y,* and *z* words put together. Describe how the dictionary can be divided in such a way that each of the following groups of letters covers approximately one-fourth of all the words: *a–d, e–l, m–r,* and *s–z.*

Students should practice finding the approximate location of the following words: *bell, potash, habit, expense, square, lancet, pearl, dome,* and *ruff.* Finally, show them how to use the thumb index, if the dictionary has one.

Even after they have mastered alphabetical order, students may be confused as they search for some entry words. Entry words often exclude inflected forms. A student looking up *rallies* or *exporter,* for example, will have to look under *rally* or *export.*

Other possible points of confusion include the following:

- Initials are listed in alphabetical order as they appear: *CIA* is followed by *cicada.*
- Abbreviations are listed in alphabetical order by letters used in the abbreviation, not by the word written out: The abbreviation *km* apears right before *knack.*
- Numerals are written as words: *seven.*
- Compounds, whether joined or appearing as separate words, appear according to the first word: *headquarters, home run.*
- In some dictionaries, *Mc-* is treated as though it is written *Mac.* In others, *Mc-* words are arranged in strictly alphabetical fashion.
- Contractions are placed in strict alphabetical order: *Isn't* appears before *isobar.*
- In many dictionaries, prefixes and suffixes such as *re-* and *-ness* are listed as main entries and defined.

For practice, have students locate the following or similar words or affixes:

McKinley	pre-	passenger	pigeon	kg
helpless	automobile	doubted	-ful	gullies
NFL	shelved	chapped	FBI	re-

LOCATING AND UNDERSTANDING MEANINGS

Definitions are not the only way words are explained. Many dictionaries also include synonyms, illustrations, and phrases or sentences in which the word is used. Some give a word history for selected words and explain how words that are synonyms differ in meaning. For instance, *Webster's New World Dictionary* supplies a definition for *kiosk,* gives a history of the term, and includes a photo of a kiosk. For the word *model,* it presents a brief explanatory paragraph that contrasts *model* and *pattern.*

Demonstrate the various ways a dictionary explains words. Direct students to look up words that are accompanied by illustrations. Discuss the definition, illustration, synonym, and example, if given, for each one. Words likely to have illustrations include the following (this will vary from dictionary to dictionary): *manatee, lattice, isobar, ibex, hoe, heart,* and *funnel.* Choose examples that are at the appropriate level for your students and that would be helpful for them to know.

Once students have a good grasp of how to locate words and how to use the several kinds of defining and explanatory information, have them look up words. Choose words that students have a genuine need to know, such as hard words from a content area text or children's book that they are reading. In the beginning, stress words that have just one or two meanings, like *edifice, egret,* or *cellist.*

As students grow in skill in using the dictionary, tell them that some words may have many meanings. Have them look up the following words and count the

Illustrations in dictionaries and glossaries supplement verbal definitions.

number of meanings given: *ace, bit, bowl, comb,* and *free*. Emphasize that context can help them choose the correct meaning for a word that has several definitions. They should practice finding the correct meaning for each of several words that have just two or three distinct meanings:

Because I moved the camera, the photo was a bit *fuzzy.*

The blanket was warm and *fuzzy.*

The explorers packed up their *gear* and left.

The sailors put on their foul weather *gear.*

HOMOGRAPHS

Homographs are not just words that have different meanings. Although they are spelled the same, homographs are really separate words with distinct meanings: for example, *troll* (mythical creature) and *troll* (method of fishing). They may even have different pronunciations: *bass* = /bas/ (fish) and *bass* = /bās/ (low pitch of voice). Homographs may also have different origins: *boss* (person in charge, from the Dutch word *baas*) and *boss* (ornament on a flat surface, from the French word *boce*). Have students note how homographs are handled in their dictionaries. Usually, they are listed as separate entries and numbered, as in Figure 4.2.

For practice, students can use context to help them determine which definition is correct in sentences like the following:

The doctor gave me medicine for my *sty.*

The king signed the paper and put his *seal* on it.

We landed on a small sandy *key.*

DETERMINING PART OF SPEECH

After students have become familiar with basic parts of speech, explain that some words, such as *hush* and *notice,* have both a noun and a verb form. In sentences

---

F I G U R E 4 . 2 **Homographs in a dictionary**

> **bay**[1] (bā), a part of a sea or lake extending into the land. A bay is usually smaller than a gulf and larger than a cove. *noun.*
> **bay**[2] (bā), **1** a long, deep barking, especially by a large dog: *We heard the distant bay of the hounds.* **2** to bark with long, deep sounds: *Dogs sometimes bay at the moon.* 1 *noun,* 2 *verb.*
> **bay**[3] (bā), **1** reddish-brown. **2** a reddish-brown horse with black mane and tail. 1 *adjective,* 2 *noun.*

Scott, Foresman Beginning Dictionary (p. 51) by E. L. Thorndike & C. L. Barnhart, 1988, Glenview, IL: Scott, Foresman and Company. Copyright © 1988 by Scott, Foresman and Company. Reprinted by permission of Scott, Foresman and Company.

similar to the following, ask them to indicate whether the italicized words are used as nouns or verbs and to select the correct definition for each:

A *hush* fell over the crowd.

Hush! You are yelling!

Did you read the *notice* about basketball practice?

I didn't even *notice* your new sneakers.

CONSTRUCTING THE CORRECT PRONUNCIATION

While reading a historical selection, one young girl pronounced the word *plagues* as /plā-jiz/. From context, she had a sense of what the word meant and so mispronouncing it did not interfere with her comprehension. Students do not have to be able to pronounce a word accurately to understand its meaning. Most of us have had the experience of discovering that for years we have been mispronouncing a word we see in print. Even so, being aware of the correct pronunciation means that students can make connections between the word they see in print and the word when spoken. For example, if they have read the word *quiche* but have no idea how to pronounce it, they will not recognize it as being the same word they saw in print when they hear it spoken. Not knowing how to pronounce a word also means that they will not be able to use it in speech. On the other hand, knowing how to pronounce a word is another aid to remembering it.

After students have acquired some skill in locating words and deriving appropriate meanings, introduce the concept of phonetic respellings. Display and discuss the pronunciation key contained in the dictionary your class is using. To avoid confusion, have all students use the same dictionary series, if possible, because different publishers use different keys. Help students discover what they already know about the key. Almost all the phonemic respellings of consonants will be familiar, except for, perhaps, *ng* in words like *sung,* which is signified by /ŋ/ in some systems. Short vowels, indicated by a, e, i, o (sometimes symbolized as /ä/), and u, will also be familiar. Inform the students that long vowels are indicated by a symbol known as a macron, as in /gāt/. Explain that the macron is a diacritical mark and that such marks are used to show pronunciation.

Show how diacritical marks are used to indicate the pronunciation of *r* vowels. Note that different dictionaries use different systems. Listed below are the Thorndike-Barnhart and Merriam-Webster markings for *r* vowels.

Word	*Thorndike-Barnhart*	*Merriam-Webster*
fair	/er/ or /ar/	/a(ə)r, /e(ə)r/
star	/är/	/är/
her	/ėr/ or /ar/	/ər/
more	/ôr/	/ō(ə)r/, /ȯ(ə)r/

Other symbols that may have to be explained to students are the pronunciations of short and long double *o*, schwa, the vowel sounds heard in *paw, toy,* and *out,* and short *o* (in Merriam-Webster).

Word	Thorndike-Barnhart	Merriam-Webster
book	/u̇/	/u̇/
soon	/ü/	/ü/
above	/ə/	/ə/
paw	/ô/	/ȯ/
toy	/oi/	/ȯi/
out	/ou/	/au̇/
hot	/o/	/ä/

After providing an overview of the pronunciation key, concentrate on its segments so that students acquire a working knowledge of the system. In order of difficulty, these segments might include consonants and short vowels, long vowels, *r* vowels, short and long double *o*, other vowels, and schwa. After introducing each segment, have students read words using the elements discussed. Encourage the active use of the pronunciation key. Practice words for the consonants and short vowels segment might include the following:

kat	jim	haz
ges	gilt	lik
bak	klas	gruj

Although the words are completely phonemic, students will find that they take longer to read. Reading the regular spellings has become automatic. Reading phonemically spelled words takes conscious effort.

Accent. Once students have mastered phonemic respelling, introduce the concept of accent. One way to do this would be to say a series of words whose meaning changes according to whether the first or second syllable is accented. As you say the words, stress the accented syllable. Have students listen to hear which syllable is said with more stress:

record	ri kôrd′	rek′ ərd
present	prez′ ənt	pri zent′
desert	dez′ ərt	di zert′
minute	mī no͞ot′	min′ it
object	ob′ jikt	əb jekt′

After the class decides which syllable is stressed, write the words on the board and put in the accent marks while explaining what they mean. Discuss how the change in stress changes the pronunciation, meaning, or use of each word. To provide guided practice, select unknown words from materials students are about to read and have students reconstruct their pronunciation. Discuss these reconstructions, and provide ample opportunity for independent application. Later, introduce the concept of secondary stress.

Dialects and Variant Pronunciations. As students grow in their ability to use the dictionary, discuss **dialects** and variant pronunciations. Explain that people in various parts of the country have different pronunciations because of the regional or cultural dialect that they speak. Encourage respect for dialects, and show children how to select the pronunciation appropriate for the regional dialect that they

A **dialect** is a form of a language that differs from other forms of the same language in pronunciation, vocabulary, or grammar. In English, the differences are not so great that speakers of one dialect cannot understand speakers of another. Dialects vary by region, class, occupation, and age.

speak. For instance, looking up the word *route*, students see that it has two pronunciations: /r$\overline{oo}$t/, /rout/. Neither pronunciation is preferred; the appropriate pronunciation is the one that the student and the other members of her or his speech community use. Of course, not all possible pronunciations are listed in the dictionary; just because a certain pronunciation is not listed does not mean that it is not acceptable.

THE DICTIONARY AS A TOOL

Many school dictionaries include generous instructions for use, along with practice exercises. Use these selectively. Avoid isolated drill on dictionary skills. Concentrate on building dictionary skills through functional use—that is, show students how to use the dictionary, and encourage them to incorporate it as a tool for understanding language. For instance, when they have questions about word meaning, pronunciation, spelling, or usage, encourage them to seek help in the dictionary.

One word of caution is in order: For word recognition, the dictionary should generally be used as a last resort. Looking up a word while reading a story interrupts the flow of the story and disturbs comprehension. Students should try context, phonics, and morphemic or syllabic analysis before going to the dictionary. Moreover, unless the word is crucial to understanding the story, they should wait until they have read the selection to look up the word. The dictionary is also a good check on definitions derived from context clues. After reading a story in which they used context clues, students should check their educated guesses against the dictionary's definitions.

Above all, do not make dictionary use so tiresome that students acquire genuine dislike of this most indispensable of reference tools. Looking up all one's vocabulary words is just the type of assignment that gives the dictionary a bad name. Also make sure that tasks that students are required to do are not too complex for them. For the novice, looking up words like *key* and *foul*, which have numerous definitions, could be daunting. Asking students to use new words in sentences after looking them up is also difficult. It often takes a number of experiences with a word before a child acquires enough feeling for it to use it in a sentence.

Adapting instruction for students with limited reading skills

If possible, acquire a CD-ROM or other electronic dictionary. The advantages of an electronic dictionary are that it locates the word faster, pronounces the word, and is motivational. A CD-ROM dictionary may also read the word's definition. This is helpful for children whose reading skills are limited.

Reinforcement Activities
Dictionary usage

- An excellent game for acquainting students with the creation of definitions for words is "Fictionary Dictionary," which is designed to be played by four to six children, although more may be included. From a bank of difficult or obscure words whose definitions and pronunciations are noted, the moderator chooses one word which is read to the group and spelled for them, but not defined. (The moderator may also simply select a difficult word from the dictionary.) The students write fictitious definitions for the word on slips of paper identical to the one held by the moderator. The moderator collects the slips, includes the one with the correct definition written on it, shuffles the slips, and reads them aloud. Taking turns, each player is asked to tell which definition is the correct one. The round ends when the correct definition is identified. Players receive one point if the definition they wrote was selected as the correct one and two points for guessing the correct definition. After the first round, the player to the right of the moderator takes over. The game is over when each child has had a turn to be the moderator. The player with the most points wins.

- Have students find out how the following words should be pronounced: *psalm, ptomaine, crepes, depot,* and *czar.*

- Have students use the dictionary to find out what the following sports are and tell which one(s) they might enjoy: *quoits, cricket, boccie, curling, biathlon, rugby,* and *billiards.*

- Ask students to determine from whose names the following words were created: *Braille, xylophone, boycott, silhouette,* and *gardenia.*

- Have students use the dictionary to determine which of the following are animals:

oryx	*peccary*	*marten*
okapi	*parka*	*manatee*
ocarina	*parabola*	*marmoset*
oboe	*pagoda*	*marquee*

- To give students guided practice in looking up words, have them answer questions similar to the following:

Are all *nocturnal* animals dangerous?

Would a *yurt* taste good?

Would a *filigree* make a good pet?

Have you ever been *reticent?*

Could you use the word *bayou* to say goodbye to a friend?

THE NEED FOR AN INTEGRATED APPROACH

The six major word-attack skills are phonics (which was the subject of Chapter 3,) sight words, context clues, morphemic analysis, syllabication, and dictionary use. Each was presented separately; however, in actual practice, they are applied in integrated fashion. Context is used to act as a check on the results of the student's attempt to use one of the other strategies. If a word the student has reconstructed does not make sense or if the definition selected by the dictionary does not quite fit the sense of the passage, this is a signal for the student to try again.

Context can also speed the process of using the other word-attack skills. For instance, if context has given the student a sense of what an upcoming word will probably be, decoding the word will be faster and easier. Phonics and syllabication also go hand in hand. A student puts a word into syllables so that it becomes easier to sound out. When used in integrated fashion, word-attack skills make reading more efficient and more meaningful.

The use of the Dictionary.
Was unaware' skills.

SUMMARY

of the various skills.

1. In addition to phonics, the five major word recognition skills are sight words, context, syllabication, morphemic analysis, and dictionary use. They should be used in integrated fashion to help the reader construct meaning.

2. Sight words are frequently appearing words that cannot be sounded out or that require advanced decoding skills. They are learned through memorization and frequent use and are expected to be recognized instantly. If possible, phonics should be used to supply additional memory pegs for storing and retrieving sight words.

3. In syllabication, words are broken up into parts primarily based on sound patterns. Syllabication may be taught through generalizations, patterns, usage, or some combination of the three.

4. Morphemic analysis deals with meaningful word parts: roots, prefixes, suffixes, and compound words. Although a high proportion of words contain roots and affixes, this skill is generally underused.

5. Context is one of the most useful word recognition skills. Approximately one difficult word out of every three lends itself to use of context clues, but students are able to use context successfully only 5 to 20 percent of the time. Deriving meaning from context involves the use of three strategies: selective encoding, selective combination, and selective comparison. Once derived, a tentative meaning should be substituted for the unknown word to see if it fits the sense of the sentence.

6. Dictionary use involves locating the words being looked up, obtaining appropriate definitions, and deriving the correct pronunciations. The dictionary should be used when all other word recognition skills fail or as a check on the successful use of these strategies.

7. Phonics, syllabication, morphemic analysis, contextual analysis, and dictionary skills should be taught functionally and used in integrated fashion. Often, two or three of these strategies are used at the same time.

CLASSROOM APPLICATIONS

1. Compare three school dictionaries. What are their major differences? What are their strengths and weaknesses? Which one would you select for classroom use?

2. Investigate a CD-ROM dictionary. In what ways might such a dictionary be superior to a print dictionary? What might be some disadvantages of a CD-ROM dictionary?

3. Obtain a children's book that might be used to reinforce one or more of the word recognition skills. Examine one chapter of the book. Check to see what major word recognition skills children would have to know to read and understand that chapter. Make a list of these skills.

FIELD APPLICATIONS

1. Find out what strategies elementary school students use when they encounter an unfamiliar word. Interview an elementary school student by asking such questions as "What do you do when you come across a hard word in your reading? How do you try to figure it out? What do you do if you can't sound it out?"

2. Create a game that is fun to play and reinforces one of the word recognition skills. Test it out with students.

3. Plan a word recognition lesson in which you teach four sight words, a morphemic element, a syllabic generalization or pattern, or a dictionary skill. If possible, teach the lesson.

c h a p t e r 5

Building Vocabulary

Agree

For each of the following statements, put a check under "Agree" or "Disagree" to show how you feel. Discuss your responses with classmates before you read the chapter.

Disagree

1. Vocabulary words should be taught only when students have a need to learn them.

2. All or most of the difficult words in a selection should be taught before the selection is read.

3. Learning the meaning of a technical word, such as *laser,* is easier than learning an abstract word, such as *truth* or *justice.*

4. Building vocabulary leads to improved comprehension.

5. It is important to show how new words are related to each other and to known words.

6. The best way to build vocabulary is to study a set number of words each week.

7. Experience helps build vocabulary.

8. More time should be spent helping students remember words that they have already learned.

Using What You Know

Chapters 3 and 4 explained techniques for teaching children how to recognize unfamiliar words. This chapter is also concerned with learning words as it explores techniques for developing vocabulary. In preparation for reading this chapter, explore your knowledge of this topic.

How many words would you estimate are in your vocabulary? Where and how did you learn them? Have you ever read a book or taken a course designed to increase your vocabulary? If so, how well did the book or the course work? How would you go about teaching vocabulary to an elementary school class?

THE NEED FOR VOCABULARY INSTRUCTION

The latter part of this century has been witness to an explosion of knowledge; it is estimated that human knowledge doubles every ten years. Accompanying that explosion are new words to label new discoveries and concepts. The most up-to-date unabridged dictionary, *The Random House Dictionary of the English Language,* 2nd rev. ed. (Flexner & Hauck, 1994), which contains 2,500 pages and more than 315,000 entries, is a silent tribute to the richness of our language. The editors added *fax, golden parachute, hairweaving, cellular phone, telemarketing, video text,* and more than 50,000 other new entries to those in the first edition, providing clear evidence that the English language is alive and thriving.

Even the largest dictionaries, however, contain only a small proportion of the words in the language, with many technical terms never making it into a general lexicon. When these terms are included in the count, the English language has approximately five million words (Landau, 1984).

This rich store of words allows us to transmit knowledge with precision and imagination. The abundance of new words also poses a challenge to students, who, to be fully literate, must acquire a larger vocabulary than any preceding generation. Nagy and Anderson (1984) estimated that there are 110,000 words in printed school English when homographs and important people's names are included. Many of these words are relatively rare, however; approximately one-half would occur only once in a billion words of running text. Even so, students have a good chance of encountering some 55,000 words in their school-related reading.

The average child begins first grade with a store of approximately 5,000 to 6,000 words (Chall, 1987). During twelve years of schooling, it is estimated that another 36,000 are learned. That is an amazing accomplishment, but it is

Estimates of the number of words known by the average first-grader vary widely from 2,500 to 24,000. However, 5,000 to 6,000 seems a reasonable figure.

still short of the 55,000 words contained in printed school English. Even greater gains are required to keep up with the accelerated coinage of new words. Understanding one's world means knowing more words than ever before.

 ## STAGES OF WORD KNOWLEDGE

It is difficult to say when a word is learned. Some concrete words may be learned instantaneously; others may be learned slowly, after repeated encounters. In time, words take on greater depth of meaning as they conjure up more associations.

Knowing a word's meaning is not an either/or proposition. Dale and O'Rourke (1971) posited four stages in word knowledge:

1. I never saw it before.
2. I've heard of it, but I don't know what it means.
3. I recognize it in context—it has something to do with . . .
4. I know it. (p. 3)

Graves (1987) expanded these stages in learning words to six tasks:

Task 1: Learning to read known words. Learning to read known words involves sounding out words that students understand but do not recognize in print. It includes learning a sight vocabulary and using phonics and syllabication to sound out words.

Task 2: Learning new meanings for known words. Even a cursory examination of a dictionary reveals that most words have more than one meaning. A large part of expanding a student's vocabulary is adding new shades of meaning to words partly known.

Task 3: Learning new words that represent known concepts. Since the concept is already known, this really is little more than learning a new label.

Task 4: Learning new words that represent new concepts. As Graves (1987) observed, "Learning new words that represent new concepts is the most difficult word-learning task students face" (p. 169).

 Task 5: Clarifying and enriching the meanings of known words. Although this task is accomplished when students meet known words in diverse contexts, Graves felt that more systematic, more direct involvement is called for. Teachers have to help students forge connections among known words and provide a variety of enrichment exercises to ensure greater depth of understanding.

Task 6: Moving words from receptive to expressive vocabulary. It is necessary to teach words in such a way that they appear in students' speaking and writing vocabularies. The ultimate test is whether students actually use newly learned words correctly.

As can be seen from the the six tasks just described, even when a word is known, it is often a question of degree. The person who uses a fax machine on a daily basis has a better knowledge of the word *fax* than does one who has simply seen the machines advertised on television. Instruction needs to be devoted to refining as well as to introducing vocabulary and concepts.

SEVEN PRINCIPLES OF DEVELOPING VOCABULARY

Developing vocabulary is not simply a matter of listing ten or twenty words and their definitions on the board each Monday morning and administering a vocabulary quiz every Friday. In a sense, it is a part of living. Children learn their initial 5,000 to 6,000 words by interacting with parents and peers, gradually learning labels for the people, objects, and ideas in their environment. As children grow and have additional experiences, their vocabularies continue to develop. They learn *pitcher, batter, shortstop,* and *home run* by playing or watching softball or baseball. They learn *gear shift, brake cable, kick stand,* and *reflector* when they begin riding a bicycle.

BUILDING EXPERIENTIAL BACKGROUND

The first and most effective step that a teacher can take to build vocabulary is to provide students with a variety of rich experiences. These experiences might involve taking children to an apple orchard, supermarket, zoo, museum, or office. Working on projects, conducting experiments, handling artifacts, and other hands-on activities also build a background of experience.

Not all activities can be direct. Viewing films, videotapes, filmstrips, and special TV shows helps build experience, as do discussing, listening, and reading. The key is to make the activity as concrete as possible.

TALKING OVER EXPERIENCES

Although experiences form the foundation of vocabulary, they are not enough; labels or series of labels must be attached to them. A presurvey and postsurvey of visitors to a large zoo found that people did not know much more about the animals after leaving the park than they did before they arrived. Apparently, simply looking at the animals was not enough; visitors needed words to define their experiences. This is the especially true for young children.

LEARNING CONCEPTS VERSUS LEARNING LABELS

For maximum benefit, it is important that experiences be discussed. It is also important to distinguish between learning labels and building **concepts.** For example, the words *petrol* and *lorry* would probably be unfamiliar to American students preparing to read a story set in England. The students would readily understand them if the teacher explained that to the British *petrol* means "gasoline" and *lorry* means "truck." Since the concepts of gasoline and truck are already known, it would simply be a matter of learning two new labels. If the word *fossil* appeared in the selection, however, and the students had no idea what a fossil was, the concept would have to be developed. To provide a concrete experience, the teacher might borrow a fossil from the science department and show it to the class while explaining what it is and relating it to the children's experiences. Building the concept of a fossil would take quite a bit more teaching than would learning the labels *petrol* and *lorry.*

Over time, our expanding background of experience allows us to attach richer meaning to words. For example, *love, truth, justice,* and *freedom* mean more to

A **concept** is a general idea, an abstraction derived from particular experiences with a phenomenon. Concepts, especially complex ones such as truth and freedom, develop slowly over a period of years. In our rush to cover content, we may not take the necessary time to develop concepts thoroughly; thus students may simply learn empty labels for complex concepts such as democracy and gravity.

us at age 20 than they did at age 10, and even more as we approach 30 or 40. In many instances, when dealing with abstract terms, students know the forms of words but not the concepts behind them. A child may have heard and seen the word *independence* many times but have no real idea of what it means. The child may not even realize that as she or he grows and develops, her or his own independence is gradually being gained. The student must learn the concept behind the label; otherwise, the word will be literally meaningless.

RELATING VOCABULARY TO BACKGROUND

The second principle of vocabulary development is relating vocabulary to students' background. It is essential to relate new words to experiences that students may have had. To teach the word *compliment*, the teacher might mention some nice things that were said or done that were complimentary. Working in pairs, students might compose compliments for each other.

Gipe (1980) devised a background-relating technique in which students are asked to respond to new words that require some sort of personal judgment or observation. For example, after studying the word *beacon*, students might be asked, "Where have you seen a beacon that is a warning sign?" (p. 400). In a similar vein, Beck and McKeown (1983) asked students to "Tell about someone you might want to *eavesdrop* on," or "Describe the most *melodious* sound you can think of" (p. 624). Carr (1985) required students to note a personal clue for each new word. It could be an experience, object, or person. One student associated a local creek with *murky;* another related *numbed* to how one's hands feel when shoveling snow.

BUILDING RELATIONSHIPS

When applying the third principle of developing vocabulary relationships, show how new words are related to each other. For example, students may be about to read a selection on autobiographies and biographies that includes the unfamiliar words *accomplishment, obstacles,* and *nonfiction,* as well as *autobiography* and *biography.* Instead of simply presenting these words separately, demonstrate how they are related to each other. That is, autobiography and biography are two similar types of nonfiction, and they often describe the subject's accomplishments and some of the obstacles that he or she had to overcome.

Other techniques for establishing relationships include noting synonyms and opposites, classifying words, and completing graphic organizers. These techniques are covered later in this chapter.

DEVELOPING DEPTH OF MEANING

The fourth vocabulary-building principle is developing depth of meaning. The most frequent method of teaching new words is to define them. Definitions, however, may provide only a superficial level of knowledge (Nagy, 1988). They may be adequate when new labels are being learned for familiar concepts, but they are not sufficient for new concepts. Definitions also may fail to indicate how a word should be used. The following sentences were created by students who had only definitional knowledge. Obviously, they had some understanding of the words, but it was inadequate.

The *vague* windshield needed cleaning.

At noon we *receded* to camp for lunch.

Words may have subtle shades of meanings that dictionary definitions may not quite capture. Most students have difficulty composing sentences using new words when their knowledge of the words is based solely on definitions (McKeown, 1993). Placing words in context (Gipe, 1980) seems to work better, as it illustrates use of words and thereby helps to define them. However, both the definition and the context should reflect the way the word is used in the selection the students are about to read.

Obviously, word knowledge is a necessary part of comprehension. Ideas couched in unfamiliar terms will not be understood. However, preteaching difficult vocabulary has not always resulted in improved comprehension. In their review of the research on teaching vocabulary, Stahl and Fairbanks (1986) found that methods that provided only definitional information about each word to be learned did not produce a significant effect on comprehension; nor did methods that gave only one or two exposures to meaningful information about each word. For vocabulary instruction to have an impact on comprehension, students must acquire knowledge of new words that is both accurate and enriched (Beck, McKeown, & Omanson, 1987). Experiencing a newly learned word in several contexts broadens and deepens understanding of it. For instance, the contexts *persistent detective, persistent salesperson, persistent pain,* and *persistent rain* provide a more expanded sense of the word *persistent* than might be conveyed by a dictionary or glossary definition.

One way of developing depth of meaning for abstract terms is through simulation. When children are about to encounter abstract concepts such as *democracy* and *republic,* have them form groups, each of which sets up a governing structure for a mythical country; then have the students in each group describe their form of government to the rest of the class. Note on the chalkboard the main features of each type and compare them. Then introduce *democracy* and *republic.* Ask students to again discuss the types of government they set up; also discuss what type of government the United States has. Many will undoubtedly be surprised to learn that they live in a republic. Although they probably have heard the word, some will begin to understand this conceptually complex term for the first time.

PRESENTING SEVERAL EXPOSURES

Frequency of exposure is the fifth principle of vocabulary building. Beck, McKeown, and Omanson (1987) suggested that students meet new words at least ten times; however, Stahl and Fairbanks (1986) found that as few as two exposures were effective. It also helps if words appear in different contexts so that students experience their shades of meaning. Frequent exposure or repetition of vocabulary is essential to comprehension because of limitations of attention and memory. Fifth-graders reading a selection about the brain that uses the new words

Although students may only derive a vague idea of a word's meaning after a single exposure, additional incidental exposures help clarify the meaning. Over a period of time, many words are acquired in this way. Although some kinds of vocabulary instruction do not have an immediate, measurable impact on comprehension, they should enhance comprehension in the long run.

lobe and *hemisphere* may not recall the words if the teacher has discussed them only once. Although the students may have understood the meanings of the words at the time of the original discussion, when they meet them in print they are vague about their definitions and must try to recall what they mean. Because they give so much attention to trying to remember the meanings of the new words, they lose the gist of the fairly complex passage. Preteaching the vocabulary did not improve their comprehension because their reading was interrupted when they failed to recall the words' meanings immediately or their knowledge of the words was too vague.

Even if the students do recognize the words, their recognition might be slower because they have only seen the words once before. Slowness in accessing the meanings of words from one's mental dictionary can hinder comprehension (Samuels, 1994). This discouraging situation does have a positive side. Although limited exposure may not help immediate comprehension, the long-term payoff is that students should gain some knowledge of words even from just a single, brief encounter. Perhaps it is enough to move the word from the I-never-saw-it stage to the I've-heard-of-it plateau. Added encounters may bring added knowledge until the word moves to the I-know-it stage.

> When you feel concerned about comprehension, choose a few key terms for intensive teaching before students read the piece. The words should be taught so well that children do not have to pause when they encounter them.

> Vocabulary knowledge is the most important predictor of reading comprehension (Davis, 1968; Thorndike, 1973).

CREATING AN INTEREST IN WORDS

Generating interest in words can have a significant impact upon vocabulary development. In their experimental program, Beck and McKeown (1983) awarded the title of "Word Wizard" to any student who noted an example of a taught word outside of class and reported it to the group. Children virtually swamped their teachers with instances of seeing, hearing, or using the words as they worked toward gaining points on the Word Wizard Chart. On some days, every child in the class came in with a Word Wizard contribution. Teachers also reported that the children would occasionally cause a minor disruption—for example, at an assembly when a speaker used one of the taught words and the entire class buzzed with recognition (p. 625).

PROMOTING TRANSFER

The seventh and last principle of vocabulary development is promoting transfer. Teaching vocabulary thoroughly enough to make a difference takes time. If carefully taught, only about 400 words a year can be introduced (Beck, McKeown, & Omanson, 1987). However, students have to learn thousands of words, so teachers also have to show them how to use such tools of vocabulary acquisition as context clues, morphemic analysis, and dictionary skills. Vocabulary instruction must move beyond the teaching of words directly as a primary activity. Because students derive the meanings of many words incidentally, without instruction, another possible role of instruction is to enhance the strategies readers use when they do learn words incidentally. Directly teaching such strategies holds the promise of helping children become better independent word learners (Kameenui, Dixon, & Carnine, 1987).

TECHNIQUES FOR TEACHING WORDS

Dozens of techniques are available for introducing and reinforcing new vocabulary. Those discussed here follow all or some of the seven principles presented above.

GRAPHIC ORGANIZERS

Graphic organizers are semantic maps, pictorial maps, webs, and other devices that allow students to view and construct relationships among words. Because they are visual displays, they allow students to picture and remember word relationships.

A **graphic organizer** is a diagram used to show the interrelationship among certain words or ideas.

SEMANTIC MAPS

Suppose that your students are about to read an informational piece on snakes that introduces a number of new concepts and words. For example, it states that snakes are reptiles, a concept that you believe will be new to the class. You have scheduled an article about alligators and crocodiles for future reading. Wouldn't it be efficient if you could clarify students' concept of snakes and also prepare them to relate it to the upcoming article? There is a device for getting a sense of what your students know about snakes, helping them organize their knowledge, and preparing them for related concepts: semantic mapping, or, simply, mapping.

A **semantic map** is a device for organizing information graphically according to categories. It can be used for concepts, vocabulary, topics, and background. It also may be used as a study device to track the plot and character development of a story or as a prewriting exercise. Mapping may be presented in a variety of ways but is generally introduced through use of the following steps (Heimlich & Pittelman, 1986; Johnson & Pearson, 1984):

A **semantic map** is a graphic organizer that uses lines and circles to organize information according to categories.

1. Introduce the concept, term, or topic to be mapped. Write the key word for it on the chalkboard, overhead transparency, or chart paper.
2. Brainstorm. Ask students to tell what other words come to mind when they think of the key word. Encourage them to volunteer as many words as they can. This may be done orally, or students may write their lists and share them.
3. Group the words by category, discussing why certain words go together. If the new words that you plan to teach are not suggested, present them and discuss them. Encourage students to supply category names.
4. Create the class map, putting it on a large sheet of paper so that the class can refer to it and add to it.
5. Once the map has been finished, discuss it. Encourage students to add items to already established categories or to suggest new categories.
6. Extend the map. As students discover, through further reading, additional new words related to the topic or key word, add these to the chart.

Lesson 5.1 shows, in abbreviated form, how a map on snakes was produced by a class of third-graders.

Semantic maps help students develop
conceptual knowledge of words.

Lesson 5.1
Semantic mapping

Step 1. The teacher writes the word *snakes* on the board and asks the class to tell what words come to mind when they think of snakes.

Step 2. Students suggest the following words, which are written on the chalkboard: *poisonous, rattlesnakes, nonpoisonous, garter snakes, sneaky, king snakes, dangerous, frightening, deserts, rocky places,* and *forests.* No one mentions *reptiles,* which is a key word in the article students are about to read. The teacher says that he would like to add that word and asks students if they know what a reptile is. One student says reptiles are cold-blooded. This word is also added to the list.

Step 3. Words are grouped, and category names are elicited. Students have difficulty with the task, so the teacher helps. He points to the words *forests* and *deserts* and asks what these tell about snakes. The class decides that they tell where snakes live. The teacher then asks the class to find another word that tells where snakes live. Other words are categorized in this same way, and category labels are composed. The map in Figure 5.1 is created.

Step 4. Students discuss the map. Two of them think of other kinds of snakes—water moccasins and boa constrictors—which are added. During the discussion, the teacher clarifies concepts that seem fuzzy and clears up misconceptions. One student, for instance, thinks that all snakes are poisonous.

Step 5. Students read to find out more information about snakes. They refer to the map, which is displayed in the front of the room, to help them with vocabulary and concepts. After reading and discussing the selection, students

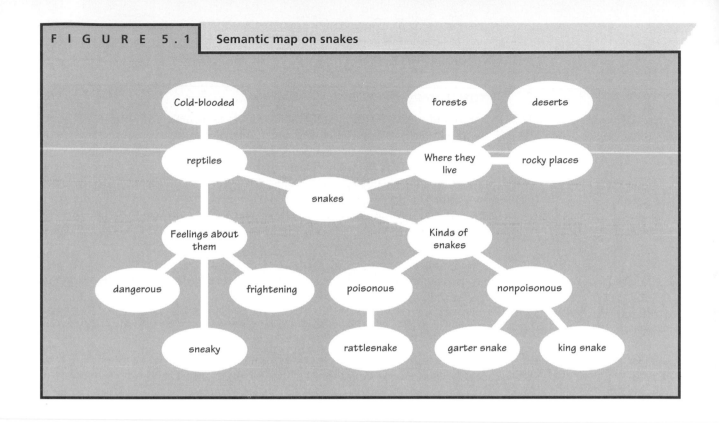

are invited to add words or concepts they learned. The following are added: *dry, smooth skin, scales, vertebrae,* and *flexible jaws.*

Step 6. A few weeks later, the class reads a selection about helpful snakes. The map is reviewed before reading the story and then expanded to include new concepts and vocabulary.

After students have grasped the idea of mapping, they can take a greater share of responsibility for creating maps. The sequence listed below gradually gives children ownership of the technique (Johnson & Pearson, 1984).

1. Students cooperatively create a map under the teacher's direction.
2. Students begin assuming some responsibility for creating maps. After a series of items has been grouped, they might suggest a category name.
3. Students are given partially completed maps and asked to finish them. They can work in groups or individually.
4. The teacher supplies the class with a list of vocabulary words. Working in groups, students use the list to create maps.
5. Working in groups or individually, students create their own maps.

Actively involving students aids both their understanding of the concepts and their retention. In one project in which maps were used to help portray complex concepts, students failed to show much improvement. Analysis revealed that the instructors were doing much of the map making. Having minimal involvement in the process, students received minimal benefit (Santa, 1989). Berkowitz (1986) reported similar findings.

PICTORIAL MAPS AND WEBS

A **pictorial map** uses drawings, with or without labels, to show interrelationships among words or concepts.

A **web** is another name for a semantic map, especially a simplified one.

Pictorial and mixed pictorial-verbal maps work as well as, and sometimes better than, purely verbal maps. A **pictorial map,** which is a map that uses pictures along with words, is shown in Figure 5.2.

For some words or concepts, teachers may want to use a more directed approach to constructing semantic maps. After introducing the topic of the planet Mars, the teacher might discuss the characteristics in a **web,** which is a simplified map. A web does not have a hierarchical organization, and it is especially useful for displaying concrete concepts (Marzano & Marzano, 1988). A web is displayed in Figure 5.3.

Computer technology can be used to help create graphic organizers. An ingenious piece of software known as *The Semantic Mapper* (Teacher Support Software) can be used in grade 3 and beyond to help create maps.

SEMANTIC FEATURE ANALYSIS

A **semantic feature analysis** is a graphic organizer that uses a grid to compare a category of words or other items on a number of characteristics.

Semantic feature analysis uses a grid to compare words that fall in a single category. For example, it could be used to compare different mammals, means of transportation, tools, sports, and so on. In constructing a semantic feature analysis, complete the steps outlined in Lesson 5.2, which are adapted from Johnson and Pearson (1984).

Lesson 5.2
Semantic feature analysis

Step 1. Announce the topic, and ask students to give examples. In preparation for reading a story about boats, ask students to name different kinds of boats.

Step 2. List the boats in the grid's left-hand column.

Step 3. Ask students to suggest characteristics or features that boats have. List these in a row above the grid.

Step 4. Look over the grid to see if it is complete. Have students add other boats or their qualities. At this point, you might suggest additional kinds of boats or added features of boats.

Step 5. Complete the grid with the class. Put a plus or minus in each square to indicate whether a particular kind of boat usually has the quality or characteristic being considered. If unsure, put a question mark in the square. Encourage students to discuss items about which they may have a question—for example, whether hydrofoils sail above or through the water. As students become proficient with grids, they may complete them independently.

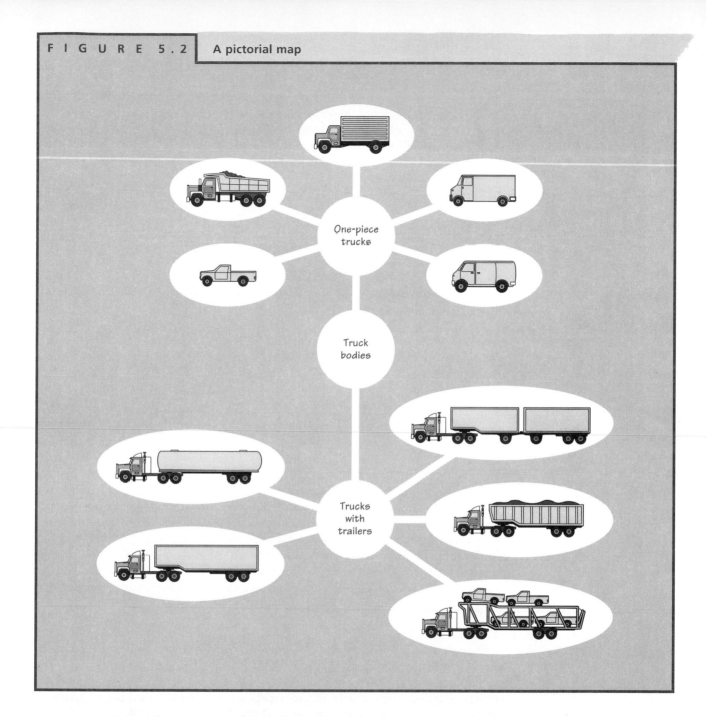

One-piece
trucks

Truck
bodies

Trucks
with
trailers

Step 6. Discuss the grid. Help students get an overview of how boats are alike, as well as how specific types differ.

Step 7. Extend the grid. As students acquire more information, they may want to add other kinds of boats and characteristics.

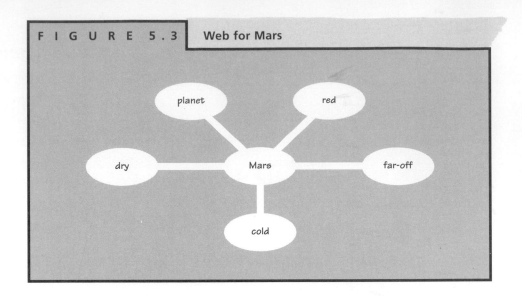

FIGURE 5.3   Web for Mars

planet

red

dry

Mars

far-off

cold

Eventually, students should compose their own grids. Through actively creating categories of qualities and comparing items on the basis of a number of features, students sharpen their sense of the meaning of each word and establish relationships among them. A sample of a completed grid is shown in Figure 5.4.

VENN DIAGRAM

A **Venn diagram** is a graphic organizer that uses overlapping circles to show relationships between two words or other items. The Venn diagram was originally used in math to show relationships among sets.

Somewhat similar in intent to the semantic feature analysis grid is the **Venn diagram** (Nagy, 1988), in which two concepts or subjects are compared. The main characteristics of each are placed in overlapping circles. Those traits that are shared are entered in the overlapping area and individual traits are entered in the portions that do not overlap. In discussing crocodiles and alligators, the teacher might encourage students to list the major characteristics of each, noting which belong only to the alligator and which belong only to the crocodile. A Venn diagram like that in Figure 5.5 could then be constructed. After they grasp the concept, students should be encouraged to construct their own diagrams. Because this activity requires active comparing and contrasting, it aids both understanding and memory.

DRAMATIZING

Pantomiming *amble, saunter, scamper, dash,* and other movement words gives students a concrete sense of their meanings and also helps them feel their distinctive connotations. In addition, it adds interest to vocabulary study.

Although direct experience is the best teacher of vocabulary, it is not possible to provide it for all the words that have to be learned. Dramatization can be a reasonable substitute. Putting words in the context of simple skits adds interest and reality. It also "helps clarify the meanings of words by indicating experiences associated with them" (Duffelmeyer & Duffelmeyer, 1979, p. 142).

Dramatizations can be excerpted from a book or created by teachers or students. They need not be elaborate; a simple skit will do in most instances. Here is one dramatizing the word *irate*.

Student 1: Hey, Brian, what's wrong? You seem really mad.

FIGURE 5.4   Semantic feature analysis

BOATS	On water	Under water	Above water	Paddles, oars	Sails	Engines
Canoe	+	−	−	+	−	−
Rowboat	+	−	−	+	−	−
Motorboat	+	−	−	?	−	+
Sailboat	+	−	−	?	+	?
Submarine	−	+	−	−	−	+
Hydrofoil	−	−	+	−	−	+
Hovercraft	−	−	+	−	−	+

Student 2: Someone's eaten my lunch. They must have known my dad packed my favorite sandwich, peanut butter and banana with raisins. I'm boiling inside. I'm really irate.

Student 1: I'd be irate, too, if someone took my lunch. But before you blow your lid, calm down. Maybe you misplaced it. Say, isn't that your dad coming down the hall? And what's that in his hand? It looks like a lunch bag.

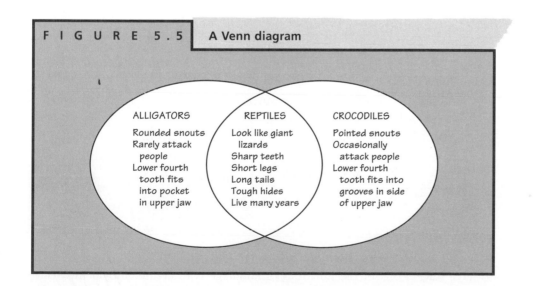

FIGURE 5.5   A Venn diagram

ALLIGATORS

Rounded snouts
Rarely attack
  people
Lower fourth
  tooth fits
  into pocket
  in upper jaw

REPTILES

Look like giant
  lizards
Sharp teeth
Short legs
Long tails
Tough hides
Live many years

CROCODILES

Pointed snouts
Occasionally
  attack people
Lower fourth
  tooth fits into
  grooves in side
  of upper jaw

Another way of dramatizing words is to use a hinting strategy (Jiganti & Tindall, 1986). After a series of new words has been introduced and discussed, the teacher distributes to individuals or pairs of students cards on each of which is one of the new words. Each student or pair creates a series of sentences that contain hints to the identity of the target word. Hints for *exaggerate* can be found in the following paragraph:

> I like being around Fred, but he tends to stretch the truth a little. The other day he caught a fairly large fish. But to hear him tell it, it sounded like a whale. When Fred catches five fish, he pretends that he really caught twenty. And when it's a little chilly, Fred says it's the coldest day of the year. I like Fred, but I wish he'd stick a little closer to the facts.

The new words are written on the chalkboard. Students read their hints, and the class then tries to figure out which of the new words they describe.

EXPLORING WORD HISTORIES

Find the origins of *boycott, pasteurized,* and *iridescent.* How would knowing the origins help your students better understand these words?

Knowing the histories of words helps students in three ways: It sheds light on their meanings and helps students remember them better and longer; it "can function as a memory device by providing additional context" (Dale & O'Rourke, 1971, p. 70); and it can spark an interest in words.

Large numbers of words and expressions are drawn from Greek and Roman mythology. Four months of the year—January, March, May, and June—are named for Roman gods and goddesses, and the other eight are named for Roman rulers or special occasions or are derived from Latin words. Read Greek and Roman myths to students, or, if they are able, have them read some on their own. As a follow-up, discuss words that have been derived from them. After reading about one of Hercules' adventures, discuss what a herculean task might be. After reading about Mars, the god of war, ask what martial music is. Discuss, too, expressions that are drawn from Greek and Roman mythology: *Achilles heel, Midas touch, Gordian knot, Pandora's box, martial law,* and *laconic reply.* The books in the Children's Book List provide word histories.

Children's Book List
Word histories

Sarnoff, J., & Ruffins, R. *Words: A Book About the Origins of Everyday Words and Phrases.* New York: Scribner's (1981).

Steckler, A. *101 Words and How They Began.* New York: Doubleday (1979).

Terban, M. *Guppies in Tuxedos: Funny Eponyms.* New York: Clarion (1988).

Terban, M. *Superdupers: Really Funny Real Words.* New York: Clarion (1989).

ENJOYING WORDS

In school, words are used to instruct, correct, and direct. They should also be used to have fun, as one of the functions of language is to create enjoyment. Recite appropriate puns, limericks, and jokes to the children, and encourage them to share their favorites. Include word play collections, such as those listed in the Children's Book List, in the classroom library.

Children's Book List
Word play

Bernstein, J. E., & Cohen, P. *Grand-Slam Riddles*. New York: Whitman (1988). Baseball riddles are presented.

Burns, D. L. *Snakes Alive!* Minneapolis: Lerner (1988). A variety of clever snake riddles is included.

Cerf, B. *Bennett Cerf's Book of Riddles*. New York: Beginner (1960). This collection features a variety of easy to read riddles.

Clark, E. C. *I Never Saw a Purple Cow and Other Nonsense Rhymes*. Boston: Little, Brown (1991). The collector has illustrated her collection of more than 120 nonsense rhymes about animals.

Cole, J. *Anna Banana: 101 Jump-Rope Rhymes*. New York: Morrow (1989). A collection of jump-rope rhymes are arranged according to the kind of jumping that accompanies each rhyme.

Corbett, P. *The Playtime Treasury*. New York: Doubleday (1990). An illustrated collection of games, rhymes, and songs involving guessing, choosing, pretending, counting, clapping, and acting.

Defty, J. *Creative Fingerplays and Action Rhymes*. Phoenix, AZ: Oryx Press (1992). An index of many fingerplays and action rhymes is included with a guide.

Heller, R. *A Cache of Jewels and Other Collective Nouns*. New York: Grosset & Dunlap (1991). Rhyming text and illustrations introduce a variety of collective nouns, such as a "drift of swans" and a "clutch of eggs." See also *Many Luscious Lollipops* (adjectives) and *Up, Up, and Away* (adverbs).

Kitchen, B. *Gorilla/Chinchilla and Other Animal Rhymes*. New York: Dial (1990). Rhymed text describes a variety of animals whose names rhyme but who have very different habits and appearance.

Lear, E. *The Owl and the Pussycat*. New York: Putnam (1991). After a courtship voyage of a year and a day, Owl and Pussy finally buy a ring from Piggy and are blissfully married; set in the Caribbean with beautifully detailed illustrations.

Meddaugh, S. *Martha Speaks*. Boston: Houghton Mifflin (1992). Problems arise when Martha, the family dog, learns to speak after eating alphabet soup.

Rattigan, J. *Truman's Aunt Farm*. Boston: Houghton Mifflin (1994). When Truman sends in the coupon for an ant farm, a birthday present from his Aunt Fran, he gets more than he bargains for when aunts instead of ants show up.

Rosenbloom, J. *The World's Best Sports Riddles and Jokes*. New York: Sterling (1988). This collection features riddles and jokes from the world of sports.

CROSSWORD PUZZLES

Crossword puzzles are excellent for reinforcing students' vocabulary. When creating them, also use previously introduced words. Puzzles are more valuable if they revolve around a theme—such as farm implements, the parts of the eye, or words that describe moods, for example. For younger readers, start out with limited puzzles that have only five to ten words and expand them as students gain in proficiency. *Crossword Magic* (L & S Computerware) or a similar piece of software can be used to create crossword puzzle grids. All you have to do is supply the words and definitions. Crossword puzzles and word games frequently appear in the following periodicals: *Chickadee Magazine, Child Life, Children's Digest, Cobblestone, Cricket, Highlights for Children, Humpty Dumpty's Magazine, Lady Bug, My Friend, National Geographic World, Ranger Rick, Sports Illustrated for Kids,* and *Wee Wisdom.*

RIDDLES

Riddles are inherently interesting to youngsters, and they provide an enjoyable context for developing vocabulary. They can be used to expand knowledge of homonyms, multiple meanings, figurative versus literal language, and intonation as a determiner of word meaning (Tyson & Mountain, 1982). Homonyms can be presented through riddles such as the following:

> Why is Sunday the strongest day?
> Because the other days are weak days. (p. 171)

Multiple meanings might be reinforced through riddles of the following type:

> Why couldn't anyone play cards on the boat?
> Because the captain was standing on the deck. (p. 171)

Riddles containing figurative language can be used to provide practice with common figures of speech:

> Why were the mice afraid to be out in the storm?
> Because it was raining cats and dogs. (p. 172)

Some of the riddle books listed earlier in the chapter might be used to implement these suggestions. Also, plan activities in which riddles and puzzles are not tied to a lesson, so that students can use them just for the fun of it.

Because they are distinctive, long words are often easier to remember than short ones.

Build students' skill in using dictionary phonetic respellings to get the correct pronunciations of unknown words. Mastering this complex skill requires both direct instruction and many opportunities for application.

DISCOVERING SESQUIPEDALIAN WORDS

Students enjoy the challenge of sesquipedalian words (Dale & O'Rourke, 1971). Composed of the Latin form *sesqui* ("one and one-half") and *ped* ("foot"), *sesquipedalian* means "foot and a half," or very long words. Long or obviously difficult words tend to be easier to learn than short ones because they are distinctive. Given the prestige and pride involved in learning them, students are also willing to put in more effort. Learning long, difficult words does not help comprehension more than learning short difficult ones, but it does boost self-esteem and create an interest in words.

Set up a sesquipedalian bulletin board. Encourage students to contribute to it. They can write the words on three-by-five cards, which can then be placed on the sesquipedalian bulletin board. Other students should be encouraged to read each word and see if they can use context to determine its meaning. Then they can use the dictionary to check whether their guess is correct and learn how to pronounce the word. The ultimate aim is to have students become lifetime collectors of long and interesting words.

As students use pronunciation guides, discuss the fact that many words have more than one acceptable pronunciation and that how a word is pronounced may depend on one's dialect.

LABELING

Labeling provides greater depth of meaning to words by offering at least second-hand experience and, in some instances, helps illustrate relationships. The parts of plants, the human body, an airplane, and many other items lend themselves to labeling. For instance, when students are about to read a true-life adventure about a pilot whose life was endangered when the flaps and ailerons froze, present a labeled diagram showing these and other airplane parts, such as *fuselage*, *landing gear*, *aileron*, *stabilator*, *fin*, *rudder*, and *trim tab*. A sample of such a labeled drawing is presented in Figure 5.6. Discuss each part and its function. Relate the parts to each other and show how they work together to make the plane fly. Ask students to picture the parts in operation during takeoff, level flight, turns, and landing. After the story has been read, give them drawings of a plane. Have them label the parts. Better yet, let them label their own drawings of a plane.

Labeling helps students visualize words. Information may be represented in words or images (Paivio, 1971, 1986; Sadowski & Paivio, 1994), and if it can be coded into both, memory is enhanced. In addition, nonverbal memories are more powerful than verbal ones. Therefore, labeling and other techniques that involve the use of the visual imaging system have a double payoff: They clarify meaning and strengthen memory.

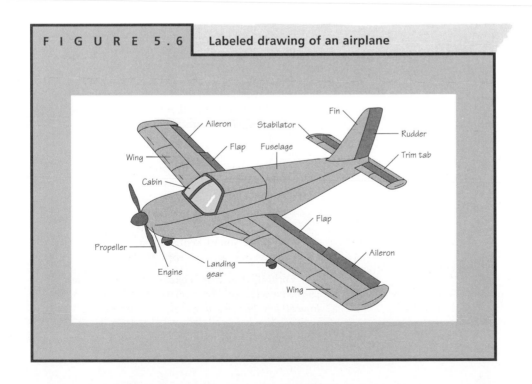

FIGURE 5.6 Labeled drawing of an airplane

FEATURE COMPARISON

Through questions that contain two newly learned words, students can compare major meanings (Beck & McKeown, 1983). For example, ask such questions as "Could a virtuoso be a rival?" and "Could a philanthropist be a miser?" (p. 624). Answering correctly is not the crucial point of this kind of activity. What is important is that students have the opportunity to discuss their responses so as to clarify their reasoning processes and their grasp of the meanings of the words.

USING WORD-BUILDING REFERENCE BOOKS

Dictionaries give definitions, illustrative sentences, and sometimes drawings of words. However, this often is not enough, especially for words that apply to concepts that are unknown or vague. For example, a dictionary definition of *laser* is not sufficient for a student who is reading a selection that assumes knowledge of both the operation and uses of lasers. A good source for conceptual information is an encyclopedia. The entry on lasers explains how they work, what their major uses are, and how they were invented. Encourage the use of the encyclopedia so

Exemplary Teaching

How to Create an Interest in Words

In his first year at an elementary school in Harlem, sixth-grade teacher Herbert Kohl (1967) was having a difficult time reaching his students until a boy named Ralph called a boy named Alvin "psyches." The following interchange ensued:

> "Ralph, what does *psyches* mean?"
> An embarrassed silence.
> "Do you know how to spell it?"
> Alvin volunteered. "S-i-k-e-s."
> "Where do you think the word came from? Why did everybody laugh when you said it, Ralph?"
> "You know, Mr. Kohl, it means, like crazy or something."
> "Why? How do words get to mean what they do?"
> Samuel looked up at me and said: "Mr. Kohl, now you're asking questions like Alvin. There aren't any answers. You know that."

> "But there are. Sometimes by asking Alvin's kind of questions you discover the most unexpected things. Look." I wrote *psyche,* then *cupid,* on the blackboard.
> "That's how *psyche* is spelled. It looks strange in English, but the word doesn't come from English. It's Greek. There's a letter in the Greek alphabet that comes out *psi* in English. This is the way *psyche* looks in Greek."
> Some of the children spontaneously took out their notebooks and copied the Greek.
> "The word *psyche* has a long history. *Psyche* means mind or soul for the Greeks, but it was also the name of a lovely woman who had the misfortune to fall in love with Cupid, the son of Venus, the jealous Greek goddess of love. . . . "(pp. 23–24)

Enthralled by Kohl's explanation, the students learned a series of words related to *psyche*—*psychological, psychic, psychotic,* and *psychosomatic*—with relative ease and demanded to learn more. The class became "word-hungry."

that eventually students refer to it or other suitable references independently to clarify difficult words.

USING TECHNOLOGY

A piece of software specifically designed to provide reinforcement for vocabulary is *Word Attack Three!* (Davidson). Designed for grades 4 through 12, it presents definitions and illustrative sentences for words on nine levels. Five activities, including a game, provide practice. *Word Attack Three!* features a system that allows the teacher to add words.

Because of its speech capability, much CD-ROM software also has the potential for use in developing vocabulary, sometimes in imaginative ways. For example, *The New Kid on the Block* (Broderbund) presents poems by Jack Prelutsky. Viewers hear the poems read aloud as text is displayed on the screen with accompanying animation. When words or phrases are clicked on, they are dramatized: For example, if a student clicks on the word *sonata,* one is played.

Videodiscs, a technology that is becoming more prominent in education, can also be used to build vocabulary. Although videodiscs perform the same function as videotapes, any of a videodisc's 54,000 frames can be accessed instantly. For instance, on a videodisc entitled *Brazil* (BFA), in which twenty vocabulary words are presented, the words are defined and used in sentences. However, by using a bar code reader or remote control, each of the words can be pronounced and every sentence in which the words appear can be accessed instantaneously. If a student wishes, she or he can access the pronunciation, meaning, or usage of a word at any point in the presentation.

PREDICTING VOCABULARY WORDS

The main purpose of studying vocabulary words before reading a selection is to improve comprehension. Two techniques that relate new vocabulary to the selection to be read are the predict-o-gram, which works only with fictional pieces, and possible sentences, which works best with informational text.

PREDICT-O-GRAM

In a predict-o-gram, students organize vocabulary in terms of the story grammar of a selection (Blachowicz, 1977). Students predict which words would be used to describe the setting, the characters, the story problem, the plot, or the resolution. Here's how the technique works: First, the teacher selects key words from the story. The words are written on the board and discussed to make sure students have some grasp of the meanings of the words. Students are then asked to predict which words the author would use to tell about the main parts of a story: the setting, the characters, the story problem, the plot, the resolution. The teacher asks the class to predict which words might fit in each part of the story grammar: "Which words tell about the setting? Which tell about the characters?" and so on. Once all the words have been placed, students might predict what the story is about. A completed predict-o-gram based on *Make Way for Ducklings* (McCloskey, 1941) is presented in Figure 5.7.

Setting	Characters	Story Problem	Plot	Resolution
Boston	Mr. and Mrs. Mallard	nest	hatched	Michael
Public Garden	Michael	pond	responsibility	police
Charles River		island	trip	
		ducklings		
		eggs		

The predict-o-gram forces students to think about new vocabulary words in terms of a story that is to be read. It also helps students relate the words to each other. After the story has been read, students should discuss their predictions in terms of the actual content and structure of the story. They should also revise their predict-o-grams, which provides them with additional experience with the new words.

POSSIBLE SENTENCES

Possible sentences is a technique by which students use new vocabulary words to predict sentences that might appear in the selection to be read. Possible sentences has five steps (Moore & Moore, 1986):

1. *List key vocabulary.* The teacher analyzes the selection to be read and selects two or three concepts that are the most important. Vocabulary words from the selection that are essential to understanding those concepts are chosen. These words are listed on the board, pronounced by the teacher, and briefly discussed with the class.

2. *Elicit sentences.* Students use the words listed to compose sentences. They must use at least two words in each sentence and create sentences they feel might occur in the selection. It is suggested that the teacher model the creation of a sample sentence and the thinking processes involved. Students' sentences are written on the board even if not correct. Words may be used more than once. This step ends when all the words have been used in sentences or after a specified time.

3. *Read to verify sentences.* Students read the text to verify the accuracy of their possible sentences.

4. *Evaluate sentences.* After reading the selection, students evaluate their sentences. They discuss each sentence in terms of whether or not it could appear in the selection. Sentences are modified as needed.

5. *Create new sentences.* Students use the words to create new sentences. These sentences are also discussed and checked for accuracy of usage.

The value of possible sentences is that, in addition to being motivational, it helps students use informational text to refine their knowledge of new words.

Because students write the words, it also helps them put new words into their active vocabularies. Putting new words in sentences is difficult, so the teacher should provide whatever guidance is necessary.

WIDE READING

The most productive method for building vocabulary—wide reading—requires no special planning or extra effort (Nagy & Herman, 1987). Research (Herman, Anderson, Pearson, & Nagy, 1987) indicates that average students have between a one in twenty and a one in five chance of learning an unfamiliar word they meet in context. Those who read for 25 minutes a day at the rate of 200 words per minute 200 days of the year will encounter a million words (Nagy & Herman, 1987). About 15,000 to 30,000 of these words will be unfamiliar. Given just a one-in-twenty chance of learning an unfamiliar word from context, students should pick up between 750 and 1,500 new words. Of course, if they read more, they have even greater opportunity for vocabulary growth. If they read 2 million rather than 1 million words a year, they theoretically would double the number of new words they learn.

Although this remarkable growth takes place naturally, the right kind of intervention should accelerate vocabulary acquisition. Low-income students in grades 2 through 7 experienced greater gains in reading vocabulary and comprehension when they had a variety of challenging materials (Chall et al., 1982). Materials below their reading levels contain few unknown words and so there are fewer to learn. However, if reading contains too many hard words, students are unable to use context and regress to a more primitive mode of word attack, such as sounding out; comprehension also drops. The best reading material for building vocabulary would have some challenging words, but not too many. As a rule

Adapting instruction for at-risk students

Ironically, many students who would benefit most from wide reading seldom read for pleasure. Reading less, they fall further behind their peers. One way for at-risk youngsters to catch up and move ahead is to read on their own.

 The best way to develop vocabulary is through wide reading.

of thumb, no more than four or five out of a hundred should be unfamiliar. Almost any challenging book will develop vocabulary. All other things being equal, however, choose materials for your classroom library that provide assistance with hard words. Many of today's informational books for young people contain glossaries or phonetic spellings of difficult words and provide definitions in context. Some also contain labeled diagrams of technical terms.

In addition to encouraging wide reading of varied materials, teachers can also provide students with strategies for using context clues, morphemic analysis, and the dictionary to decipher unknown words. Sternberg (1987) found that average adults trained to use context clues were able to decipher seven times as many words as those who spent the same amount of time memorizing words and definitions. If elementary school students are taught to use such clues with greater efficiency, it should boost their vocabulary development as well.

READING TO STUDENTS

There are other methods for learning vocabulary besides direct instruction and wide reading. Reading to students is a significant source of new vocabulary (Elley, 1989). Seven-year-olds learned three out of twenty words just by listening to them read in a story. When the teacher explained them, the students learned as many as eight out of twenty. Older students also benefit from having stories read aloud to them. Sixth-graders showed a significant gain in vocabulary after having selections from a seventh-grade anthology read to them (Stahl, Richek, & Vandeiver, 1991).

Some books are better than others for developing vocabulary. The frequency with which a new word appears in the text, the number of illustrations of the word, and the helpfulness of the context in which the word appears are factors that promote the learning of a new word (Elley, 1989). Retelling the story in which the word appears also seems to foster vocabulary growth. Words are used with more precision and in more elaborated fashion during students' second and third retellings (Leung, 1992).

To be more effective at building vocabulary, the story being read to students should be within their listening comprehension. If the words are too abstract for the students' level, gains may be minimal. In one study in which a fairly difficult text was read to students aged 8 to 10, only the best readers made significant gains (Nicholson & Whyte, 1992). An inspection of the target words in the text suggested that they may have been too far above the level of the average and below-average readers. The study also suggested that while bright students might pick up words from a single reading, average and below-average students may require multiple encounters with the words.

A **planned program** is one in which a certain amount of time is set aside each week for vocabulary instruction. Words to be studied may be preselected from materials students are about to read or may be words they need to understand content area concepts. The key to an effective planned program is to focus on words that students are meeting in and out of school and to make sure that students encounter these words in real contexts. The danger in a planned program is that words will be arbitrarily chosen and therefore will not relate to students' needs.

A PLANNED PROGRAM

Although young people apparently learn an amazing number of words incidentally, a **planned program** of vocabulary development is highly advisable. Research from as far back as the 1930s (Gray & Holmes, 1938, cited in Curtis, 1987) suggested that direct teaching is more effective than a program that relies solely on

incidental learning. A more recent review of a number of research studies confirmed these results (Petty, Herold, & Stoll, 1968).

Based on their extensive investigations, Beck, McKeown, and Omanson (1987) opted for a program that includes both direct teaching and incidental learning of words and also differentiates among words. Words especially important to the curriculum are given "rich instruction." These words are chosen from basals, content area texts, or trade books that are to be read by students and are selected on the basis of their importance in understanding the text, frequency of appearance in students' reading, and general usefulness. Rich instruction goes beyond simple definition to include discussion, application, and further activities. Words selected for rich instruction might be presented ten times or more. Less important words are simply defined and used in context. This process introduces words that become more familiar as students meet them in new contexts. Any remaining new words are left to incidental learning. Perhaps the most important feature of this program is that words are taught within the context of reading, as opposed to being presented in isolated lists.

Another important component of a planned vocabulary program is motivation. Students will try harder and presumably do better if they encounter intriguing words in interesting stories and if they can relate learning vocabulary to their personal lives. As Sternberg (1987) commented, "In most of one's life, one learns because one wants to or because one truly has to, or both" (p. 96).

Incidental learning occurs when vocabulary words are studied as they are encountered in the natural course of reading and writing. A balanced vocabulary development program is both incidental and planned.

A BALANCED BLEND

Vocabulary instruction should be a balanced blend of the planned and the incidental. The incidental approach capitalizes on students' immediate need to know words. It gives the program spontaneity and vitality. A planned approach ensures that vocabulary instruction is given the attention it deserves. Important words and techniques for learning words are taught systematically and in depth. Combining these two types of approaches should provide the best possible program.

Based on her thoughtful review of the research, M. R. Ruddell (1994) recommends abandoning the controversy surrounding direct instruction as opposed to other approaches:

> Interesting also is that this analysis creates no dichotomy between vocabulary instruction and other instructional approaches; rather, each appears to benefit various aspects of the comprehension process. It may be it is time for a rapprochement, time for us to abandon the "which is best" research efforts and to look more closely at how each approach contributes to students' overall vocabulary development. (p. 438)

REMEMBERING VOCABULARY

Most of this chapter has been devoted to a discussion of teaching new words. But learning the words is only part of the task—students must also remember them.

Organizing new words to show relationships helps students remember them. So does elaboration (Bradshaw & Anderson, 1982). Elaborating on, or expanding, sentences in which vocabulary words are used should aid students' recall. Consider the sentence "The Tigers were defeated ten to one." If you elaborate on *defeated* by asking why the Tigers were defeated by such a lopsided score, how they felt about being defeated, and how many times they have been defeated, the word becomes more vivid and will be remembered better.

KEY WORD APPROACH

The **key word approach** is a strategy in which students create images to help them associate a meaning with a new word.

Images can also be used to improve memory. In the **key word approach,** students create an image to form a link between the word they are learning and its meaning. The key word portrays the meaning of the word being learned and also incorporates a portion of it. For instance, for the word *educator,* the student might imagine a teacher named Ed. *Educator* begins with *ed-* and Ed is a teacher, so Ed portrays the meaning of *educator.* The student can make the image as vivid as possible. He or she may picture Ed wearing a bow tie and thick glasses pointing to math examples on a blackboard. Thus, when the student sees the word *educator,* he or she uses the word *Ed* to conjure up the image and is led to the meaning of the new word.

Although used originally to teach students foreign words, the key word approach has been successful in helping both older and younger students retain associations between English words and their definitions (Pressley, Levin, & McDaniel, 1987). Since it involves creating an image of words' meanings, it also fosters a deeper understanding of words. Older students are encouraged to create their own key words and images. It is not necessary that the key words be whole words, since some vocabulary words do not lend themselves to this. The key words can show just the beginning letters—for instance, the key word for *pelican* might be *pet;* a person with a pet pelican might be pictured. Children aged 10 and younger may need to have the teacher create an image for them. The technique works even if the teacher constructs the interactive image (Pressley, Levin, & Miller, 1981). Lesson 5.3 describes how the key word approach might be used to present the words *antique, fortune,* and *messenger* to a fourth-grade class.

Lesson 5.3
Key word approach

Step 1. Introducing the technique

If this is the first time the class has used the key word approach, the teacher explains that the class will be using a new way to learn vocabulary words. She tells the students that this method of learning words has been used with boys and girls their age, as well as with high school and college students and adults, and that it helped all these people remember new words longer.

Step 2. Demonstrating the technique

The teacher writes the word *tarpaulin* on the board and explains that it means a large piece of waterproof cloth. She tells the class that she is going to form a word and create a picture in her mind that will help her remember the word *tarpaulin* and its meaning. Then she explains that from the word *tarpaulin* she is going to form a word she already knows: *tar.* She says she is going to make a picture of the meaning of the word *tarpaulin* and put it together with the meaning of the word *tar;* she draws a giant mound of tar being covered by a tarpaulin because rain is beginning to fall. The teacher tells the class that when she sees the word *tarpaulin* in the future, she will think of the key word *tar* and use it to bring to mind the meaning of the word *tarpaulin* by recalling the picture.

Step 3. Presenting words and images

The teacher then presents the words *antique, fortune,* and *messenger.* She helps the class select *ant* as the key word for *antique.* In the interactive image, the ant could be seen rocking back and forth in an antique chair. For *fortune,* the key word is *fort;* the interactive image shows a fortune in gold and diamonds stored in a fort. The key word for *messenger* is *mess.* In the interactive image, a messenger delivers a package to a house that is a mess because it is full of packages that have not been put away.

Step 4. Guided application

The students then try out the technique themselves. The teacher says the vocabulary word *antique* and asks the class what the key word is. Repeating *ant,* the teacher asks the students to tell what picture they have formed and to tell what *antique* means. After the teacher has gone over the three words and is sure that the students have mastered the technique, she simply says each vocabulary word and directs the students to say the key word to themselves, call up the picture, and then the definition. Gradually, the teacher leads the students to the point at which they are able to use the technique independently.

Try the key word approach with several technical words that you have to learn. How well did the technique work?

Besides being a research-based method for learning vocabulary, the key word approach is fun to use. Students enjoy choosing key words and creating images. They will also be surprised at how well the technique works. Eventually, students should adapt the key word technique and use it on their own as an independent study technique. To help them get to this point, actively use the key word approach for several months, gradually leading students to a point where they can use it on their own. Since students are most likely to use a strategy when they see its value, have students compare their achievement on vocabulary tasks undertaken before and after the key word technique is used.

TEACHING SPECIAL FEATURES OF WORDS

Many words have special characteristics that have to be learned if the words are to be understood fully. Among such important features are homophones, homographs, figurative language, multiple meanings, connotation and denotation.

HOMOPHONES

The combining form *phon* means "sound," so **homophones** are words that have the same sound but differ in meaning. They may or may not have the same spelling: *be, bee; him, hymn.* To convey the concept of homophones, you might have students translate sentences that have been written in homophones: "Aye gnu Gym wood bee hear" or "Dew ewe no hymn?"

Homophones are words that are pronounced the same but differ in spelling and meaning and often have different origins as well: for example, *cheap* and *cheep* or *knew, gnu,* and *new.* In reality, homophones are more of a problem for spelling than for reading because context usually clarifies their meaning. In some instances, however, it is important to note spelling to interpret the meaning of a sentence correctly—for example:

He complements his wife.

The shed is dun.

She was last seen hanging onto a buoy.

To avoid being tackled, you must feint.

To build awareness of homophones, discuss riddles. Write a riddle on the chalkboard, and have students identify the homophone—for example, "What is black and white and read all over?" (the newspaper). Additional riddles may be found in the books listed on p. 177. Students might also enjoy reading Fred Gwynne's books on homophones, such as *The King Who Rained* (1970), *Chocolate Moose for Dinner* (1988a), and *A Little Pigeon Toad* (1988b), or one of Peggy Parrish's *Amelia Bedelia* books.

HOMOGRAPHS

Since *graph* is a combining form meaning "written element," **homographs** are two or more words that have the same spelling but different meanings and different origins. Homographs may have the same or different pronunciations.

Homographs are words that have the same spelling but different meanings and possibly different pronunciations—for example, *palm* (part of the hand or a tree) and *bat* (a club or a mammal). They make spelling easier but reading more difficult. For instance, on seeing the word *page,* the reader must use context to decide whether the word means "a piece of paper" or "someone who attends a knight or runs errands for lawmakers." Homographs may share a single pronunciation or have different pronunciations. Homographs such as the following, which have two distinct pronunciations, can be particularly troublesome for students: *bass, bow, desert, dove, lead, minute, sewer,* and *sow.*

As students learn that a word may have two, three, or even more entirely separate meanings, stress the importance of matching meaning with context. Students might also need to learn an entirely new meaning, and perhaps a pronunciation, for a word that looks familiar. Reading the sentence "The neighbors had a terrible row," students will see that neither of the familiar meanings "paddle a boat" or "in a line" fits this sense of *row.* They must learn from context, a dictionary, or another source that the word's third meaning is "a noisy fight or quarrel." They will also need to learn that *row* in this context is pronounced /rau/.

Students will require extra help and reinforcement when learning homographs. Research indicates that learning a new meaning for an old word is more difficult than learning a new meaning for a new word (Tetewsky & Sternberg, 1986). Apparently, past learning interferes with new learning. It might be helpful to trace the etymology of some homographs. For example, the word *page* meaning "paper" comes from the Latin word *pagina,* "a sheet of writing." The word *page* meaning "someone who attends a knight" is derived from the Italian word *paggio,* which in turn comes from the Greek word *paidon* for "boy" (Davies, 1986). Also, students might keep a dictionary of homographs they find in their reading, adding new meanings as they come across them. For example, reading the sentence "It was a beautiful bay horse," students might add for the word *bay* the meaning "reddish-brown" to "a body of water" and "make a barking sound."

FIGURATIVE LANGUAGE

If taken literally, **idiomatic expressions** and figures of speech such as "catch her eye," "lose heart," and "save face" can be gruesomely frightening. However, language is replete with phrases in which words take on new meaning that is no longer literal. Sometimes idiomatic expressions are not counted as difficult because they consist of easy words; in "catch her eye," for example, all the words are on a first-grade level (Harris & Jacobson, 1982). However, this expression is probably unfamiliar to many first-graders. Because idiomatic phrases hinder comprehension in much the same way as difficult vocabulary words do, they should be discussed before students read a selection in which they appear, especially if they might obscure the meaning of the reading.

Young students tend to interpret language literally and may have difficulty with figurative language. This is especially true for children who have a profound hearing loss and those whose native language is not English. It is important to make them aware that language is not always to be taken literally. As they grow in their ability to handle figurative expressions, they should be led to appreciate phrases that are especially apt and colorful. The *Amelia Bedelia* books, in which Amelia takes language very literally, can serve as a good introduction. Children might also keep a dictionary of idiomatic and figurative expressions. Some books of idioms are listed in the Children's Book List.

An **idiomatic expression** is one that is peculiar to a language and cannot be understood from the meanings of the individual words making up the expression.

Elementary school pupils may not realize that figures of speech can be found in the dictionary, usually under the key word in the phrase. For instance, the expressions "big heart," "take to heart," and "with all one's heart" can be found under *heart.*

Children's Book List
Figurative language

Cox, J. *Put Your Foot in Your Mouth and Other Silly Sayings.* New York: Random House (1980).

Terban, M. *In a Pickle and Other Funny Idioms.* Boston: Clarion (1983).

Terban, M. *Mad as a Wet Hen!* Boston: Clarion (1987).

MULTIPLE MEANINGS

One study found that 72 percent of the words that frequently appear in elementary school materials have more than one meaning (Johnson, Moe, & Baumann, 1983). When teaching new meanings for old words, stress the fact that words may have a number of different meanings and that the context is the final determinant of meaning. Some words with apparently multiple meanings

When learning words with multiple meanings, students learn concrete and functional meanings first (The dog *barked* at me) followed by more abstract meanings (The coach *barked out* instructions for the team (Asch & Nerlove, 1967).

Exemplary Teaching

Developing Vocabulary and Confidence

Borrowing from Sylvia Ashton-Warner, Mrs. Warren, a resource room teacher at P. S. 94 in Bronx, New York, invites her remedial readers to choose each day a word that they would like to learn. A second-grader chose *discrimination;* a third-grader asked to learn *suede;* a sixth-grader studied *customary.* The words chosen were as varied as the children.

Warren's students are operating well below grade level. Having a history of failure, they feel discouraged, frustrated, and incompetent. Learning long words builds their confidence and their self-esteem. As they learn words such as *discombobulate, spectacular,* and *advise,* they begin to see themselves as competent learners.

As Warren explains, "You have to prove to these children that they can learn. Telling them is not enough. You have to get them to be successful at something. The words convince them they're smart." Learning new words also builds an interest that snowballs. "If you can get children to love words, for whatever reason, you've got it made," Warren comments (Rimer, 1990, p. B5).

The students draw their words from many sources. Some come from their reading, others from discussions or television. A favorite source is a 365 new-words-a-year calendar. Students record their words on three-by-five index cards and keep them in a file box. The growing number of cards becomes a testament to their success in building their vocabularies and their overall competence as learners.

are actually homographs. For instance, *bark* means "a noise made by a dog," "the covering of a tree," and "a type of sailing ship." These are really three different words and have separate dictionary entries. Other examples for which there are diverse meanings associated with one word are *elevator* ("platform that moves people up and down," "place for storing grain," "part of airplane") and *magazine* ("periodical" and "building where arms and/or ammunition are stored"). Provide exercises that highlight the new meaning of an old word by asking questions specific to a definition: "What does a plane's elevator do? Why would a fort have a magazine?"

CONNOTATIONS

The **connotation** of a word is its implied, suggested, or associated meaning or meanings. The **denotation** of a word is its explicit meaning.

It is important to introduce the concept of **connotations** and **denotations** of words. Comparing words and noting connotations helps students to detect subtle shades of meaning (Dale & O'Rourke, 1971). For example, in comparing the synonyms *slender, skinny, lanky,* and *scrawny,* students find that although all refer to being thin, they are not interchangeable. *Scrawny* and *skinny* convey less favorable meanings than do *slender* and *lanky.* Provide students with opportunities to discriminate between synonyms, such as which word in the following pairs sounds better: *chuckle/guffaw; gossip/chat; request/demand.* Have students tell which word in each of the following pairs sounds worse: *scribbled/wrote; sip/slurp; muttered/said.* Encourage students to find words in their reading that have favorable and unfavorable connotations and discuss them.

SUMMARY

1. Average first-graders know between 5,000 and 6,000 words and learn about 3,000 new ones each year. By the end of high school, students generally know more than 40,000 words. However, printed English encountered in school-related reading contains about 55,000 different words.
2. Having rich experiences and talking about them are important factors in learning new words. Also important are relating vocabulary to background, building relationships, developing depth of meaning, presenting numerous exposures, creating an interest in words, and promoting transfer.
3. A variety of graphic devices can be used to help students learn words, including semantic and pictorial maps and webs, semantic feature analysis, and Venn diagrams. Other reinforcement activities include dramatizing; studying word histories; playing word games; discovering long words; labeling; using references; making comparisons; using software; predicting through the use of predict-o-grams or possible sentences; reading aloud; and, one of the most important, wide reading by students.
4. Although students learn many words incidentally, a planned program of vocabulary development is also advisable. Words chosen for intensive instruction should be key words that will be encountered again and again.
5. Techniques that help students remember new words include organizing the words to show relationships, elaboration, and the key word approach in which a key word is linked to the new word through an interactive image.
6. Special features that add to a fuller understanding of words include homophones, homographs, figurative language, multiple meanings, and connotations.

CLASSROOM APPLICATIONS

1. Try using graphic devices, such as semantic feature analysis, a Venn diagram, or a semantic map, to organize words that you are studying or in which you are interested. Which of these devices works best for you? Why?
2. Plan a program of vocabulary development. Include a description of the class, your objectives, the source of words, and the activities that you will use to reinforce words. Also tell how you will evaluate the program.

FIELD APPLICATIONS

1. Choose five to eight words from a chapter in a children's book. Then, using the steps detailed in this chapter, create a vocabulary lesson. Teach the lesson to a group of students, and critique it. What worked well? What might be changed?
2. Using procedures explained in this chapter, create a semantic map with an elementary school class. Evaluate the map's effectiveness. In what ways did it help students? Did the activity engage their attention?
3. Try one of the other vocabulary reinforcement devices with an elementary school class and evaluate its effectiveness. Compare your experience with those of your classmates. Based on these experiences, what devices seemed to work best?

Comprehension:
Theory and Strategies

ANTICIPATION GUIDE

For each of the following statements related to the chapter you are about to read, put a check under "Agree" or "Disagree" to show how you feel. Discuss your responses with classmates before you read the chapter.

Agree   **Disagree**

1. Reading comprehension is understanding the author's meaning.

2. The more one knows about a topic the better one will understand something that one reads about it.

3. Readers do not really start making inferences until about the third grade.

4. Knowledge of words is the most important ingredient in comprehension.

5. As students read, they should be aware of whether they are comprehending.

6. Before learning to draw inferences, the reader must master comprehension of literal details.

7. In comprehension instruction, the teacher should focus on the processes students use rather than on whether they obtain the right answers.

Using What You Know

In a sense, all the previous chapters have provided a foundation for this one, which is about comprehension. This chapter begins with a discussion of the nature of comprehension and goes on to describe the strategies used to obtain meaning from reading, with suggestions for teaching them. Comprehension is very much a matter of bringing your knowledge to the task. What do you know about comprehension? What strategies do you use as you try to understand what you read? What do you do when your comprehension goes astray? What tips for comprehension might you share with a younger reader?

THE PROCESS OF COMPREHENDING

Comprehension is the main purpose of reading. In fact, without it, there is no reading, since reading is the process of constructing meaning from print. Comprehension is a constructive, interactive process involving three factors—the reader, the text, and the context in which the text is read. For comprehension to improve, the interaction among all three factors must be taken into consideration.

SCHEMA THEORY

To gain some insight into the process of comprehension, read the following paragraph, which has been divided into a series of sentences. Stop after reading each sentence and ask yourself: "What did the sentence say? How did I go about comprehending it? What does this paragraph seem to be about?"

> A hoatzin has a clever way of escaping from its enemies.
>
> It generally builds its home in a branch that extends over a swamp or stream.
>
> If an enemy approaches, the hoatzin plunges into the water below.
>
> Once the coast is clear, it uses its fingerlike claws to climb back up the tree.
>
> Hoatzin are born with claws on their wings but lose the claws as they get older.

To make sense of the selection, you would have to rely heavily on the knowledge you bring to the text. One definition of comprehension is that it is the process of building a connection between what we know and what we do not know, or the new and the old (Searfoss & Readence, 1994).

It is currently theorized that our knowledge is packaged into units known as schemata. A **schema** is the organized knowledge that one has about people, places, things, and events (Rumelhart, 1984). A schema may be very broad and general (for example, a schema for animals) or it may be fairly narrow (for example, a schema for Siamese cats).

Schema (pl. *schemata*) is a unit of organized knowledge.

In R. Anderson's (1984) view, comprehension primarily involves activating or constructing a schema that accounts for the elements in a text, similar to constructing an outline of a script. For example, a script outline for buying and selling includes the following categories, which are known as slots: BUYER, SELLER, MERCHANDISE, MONEY, and BARGAINING (Rumelhart, 1980). Comprehending a story involves filling these slots with particular examples or instances. As a student reads about a character in a story who is purchasing a bicycle, her or his BUYER schema is activated. The student fills in the BUYER and SELLER slots with the characters' names. The bicycle is placed in the MERCHANDISE slot. The story says that the buyer got a good deal, so that is placed in the BARGAINING slot. The story may not say how the character paid for the bike—cash, check, charge card, or an IOU—but the reader may infer that it was with cash because in her or his BUYER schema goods are purchased with cash. A schema thus provides a framework for comprehending a story and making inferences that flesh it out. A schema also aids retention, as students use it to organize their reconstruction of the events.

In constructing the meaning of the selection on the hoatzin, you used various processes to activate the appropriate schema and fill the slots. In reading the first sentence, assuming that you did not know what a hoatzin is, you may have made a reasoned prediction that it was some kind of animal. The information in the first sentence was probably enough to activate your ANIMAL-SURVIVAL-FROM-ENEMIES schema. The slots might include TYPE OF ANIMAL, ENEMIES, ABILITY TO FLEE, and ABILITY TO FIGHT; guided by your schema, you may have been on the lookout for information to fill them. Integrating or summarizing the first three sentences made it possible for you to place "plunges into the water" into the ABILITY TO FLEE slot. You also did quite a bit of inferencing. When you read about the wings in the last sentence, you probably inferred that the hoatzin is a bird, even though it dives into the water. Thus you were able to fill in the TYPE OF ANIMAL slot. You probably also inferred that the hoatzin's enemies could not reach it in the water. You may have inferred, too, that the creature is not fierce, since it seems to prefer fleeing to fighting. These inferences enabled you to fill in the ENEMIES and ABILITY TO FIGHT slots. As you can probably see, comprehending the selection about the hoatzin was not so much a question of getting meaning from the text as it was bringing meaning to it or constructing meaning by transacting with the text.

Although activating schemata is essential in reading, reading is more complex than simply filling slots. As they transact with text, proficient, active readers are constantly relating what they are reading to other experiences they have had, other information in the text they have read, and texts previously read. Their interest in the text plays a powerful role in the web of linkages that they construct (Hartman, 1994). A student captivated by the idea that a bird has claws on its wings might relate this text to passages that he or she has read or a TV show about unusual animals.

MENTAL MODELS

Comprehension also can be thought of as the construction of **mental models**. Schema theory provides a good description of what happens when the reader deals with objects or events for which she or he has a schema. But what happens when the reader is dealing with novel objects or events? Mental model construction

Mental models can be images or nonperceptual information such as goals and causal relationships. The mental model theory views comprehension as a process "of building and maintaining a model of situations and events described in text" (McNamara, Miller, & Bransford, 1991, p. 491). While schema theory describes how familiar situations and events are understood, mental model theory describes how new situations and events are comprehended.

is a more inclusive theory of comprehension because it can handle both schema-based and novel activities (McNamara, Miller, & Bransford, 1991). Actually, activating schemata is part of a mental model. Even when reading a science fiction novel or a how-to article, the reader brings some background knowledge to the situation. As McCormick (1992) noted,

> Mental model theories have added to our understanding by providing data on how readers operate on their schemata and explanations of how they are able to understand new information inconsistent with schemata already intact. (p. 55)

A mental model is constructed most often when a student is reading fiction. Keying in on the apparent main character, the reader creates a mental model of the circumstances in which the character finds himself or herself. As the situation changes, the mental model is reconstructed or updated to reflect the new circumstances, but items important to the main character are kept in the foreground. In one experiment, subjects were given two versions of a story: one in which the main character put a flower in the buttonhole of his coat, and a second in which he placed the flower in a vase. When asked questions about the story, the subjects who read the first version were faster at recognizing that there had been a flower. That is, the flower was apparently in the foreground of their mental model because it had retained its association with the main character (McNamara, Miller & Bransford, 1991).

The two kinds of mental models are working and passage. A working mental model constructs the present events in the story, and a passage mental model constructs an awareness of the whole story by building links between events. Often these are cause/effect connections. McNamara, Miller, and Bransford (1991) supplied the following example:

> In a story about a father's and son's journey to town to sell a donkey, the proposition expressing the idea of taking the donkey to town would be connected to the proposition expressing their movement over a bridge. If the characters were not going to town, then they would have not gone over the bridge; the goal of going to town "caused them to go over the bridge." (p. 507)

Constructing links, especially causal ones, is important, as the events in a story are most readily remembered when such connections have been constructed.

PROPOSITIONAL THEORY

A third explanation of comprehension is propositional theory. A propositional model of comprehension emphasizes the structure of text in terms of a series of propositions. A **proposition** is a statement of information. *Janice hit the ball* is a proposition; *Janice hit the red ball* is two propositions, containing two pieces of information: *Janice hit the ball* and *The ball is red* (Kintsch, 1994).

As students read, text is transformed into propositions. However, in the process, propositions are combined, deleted, and integrated so that a **macrostructure** is formed. The macrostructure is a running summary of the text. The propositions are organized according to their relative importance in a hierarchy. A general statement would be toward the top of the hierarchy; propositions toward the top of the hierarchy are generally better remembered than those lower in the

A **proposition** is the smallest unit of text that can be proven false. The two kinds of propositions are predicates and arguments. Predicates represent the relationships among objects, whereas arguments represent the objects themselves. In the sentence "Janice hit the ball," *hit* is the predicate or relationship between Janice and the ball; Janice and the ball are the arguments or objects of the relationship. Adding modifiers increases the number of propositions. In the sentence "Janice hit the big, red ball," two propositions have been added: big and red (Weaver & Kintsch, 1991).

Macrostructure is the global meaning or topic and general organization of a piece of writing.

hierarchy. A reader who is able to detect the main idea of a text and its supporting details will better understand and retain information in the text than a reader who fails to use the text's organization. Likewise, a reader who has a good sense of story structure can use the structure of a story as a framework for understanding and remembering it (Gordon, 1989b). Even though text is emphasized in a propositional theory of comprehension, the reader's role is still important. The macrostructure is formed "not only on the basis of what the author intended as important but also in terms of the reader's own goals, knowledge, and interests" (Williams, 1986b, p. 76).

Schema theory and mental models emphasize the role of the reader. Propositional theory stresses the importance of the text. Both aspects and their interactions are obviously important. In order to process propositions, a reader needs general background knowledge and schemata as well as a schema for text structure. In experiments conducted by Van Dijk and Kintsch (1985), expert readers were better able to summarize a story that was written according to a familiar story schema than they were to summarize a Native American tale written according to an unfamiliar schema. In summarizing both stories, however, the expert readers made use of macrostructure to help them retrieve the details of the stories.

Ultimately, propositional theory fits in with schema theory, since well-structured text works better for activating schema. For instance, cause/effect organization results in better comprehension than does a simple listing of details because the cause/effect structure provides the reader with "additional schemata to help them understand and remember the information" (Pearson & Camperell, 1994, p. 460).

Applying propositional theory, McKeown, Beck, Sinatra, and Loxterman (1992) rewrote an American history text used by fifth-graders to make it more coherent. The revised text was designed to highlight important information and relationships. As predicted, students' comprehension increased. However, the students still complained about the difficulty of the material. Closer examination revealed that the text made too many assumptions about the students' **prior knowledge.** When the researchers built on students' prior knowledge *and* provided the students with a more coherent text, comprehension increased significantly. These students did better than others who were provided with additional background knowledge but were given the unrevised text. Apparently, having enhanced background knowledge is not sufficient to override the obstacle posed by poorly organized text. In reading, both text factors and reader factors interact. A coherent text enables students to make use of background knowledge and to construct meaning.

Readers can encode information as a mental model or a set of propositions. Propositional encoding is preferred when retaining the structure of the text is important or when dealing with abstract information. Mental model encoding works better with concrete information that is not in the reader's schemata.

According to a propositional theory of reading, readers construct a main idea or macrostructure as they process text. Comprehension, organization, and retrieval of information from text is based on the formation of this macrostructure.

Prior knowledge is the background information that a reader brings to the text.

COMPREHENSION STRATEGIES

According to all three models of comprehension, the reader plays a very active role in constructing an understanding of text. One way the active reader constructs meaning is by using **strategies.** Comprehension strategies include preparing, organizing, elaborating, rehearsing, and monitoring. There are also affective

A **strategy** is a deliberate, planned activity or procedure designed to achieve a certain goal. It includes how a person thinks and acts when planning, executing, and evaluating performance on a task and its outcomes (Lenz, Clark, Deschler, & Schumaker, 1988).

strategies (Weinstein & Mayer, 1986), in which motivation and interest play a role in the construction of meaning.

Preparational strategies are processes that readers use, such as surveying a text and predicting what it will be about, to prepare themselves to construct meaning. Using organizational strategies, readers construct relationships among ideas in the text, specifically between the main idea and supporting details. Paraphrasing, summarizing, clustering related words, noting and using the structure of a text, and creating semantic maps are also ways of organizing.

Elaborating involves building associations between information being read and prior knowledge, or integrating them by manipulating or transforming information. Elaboration strategies include drawing inferences, creating analogies, visualizing, and evaluating, or reading critically. (Evaluating is discussed in Chapter 7.)

Rehearsing involves taking basic steps to remember material. Outlining, taking notes, underlining, testing oneself, and rereading are rehearsal strategies. Elaborating or organizing and rehearsing are often used in combination to learn complex material.

Monitoring consists of being aware of one's comprehension and regulating it. Monitoring strategies include setting goals for reading, adjusting reading speed to difficulty of material, checking comprehension, and taking corrective steps when comprehension fails. (Some preparational strategies are actually a special set of monitoring strategies that are employed prior to reading.)

Traditionally, comprehension strategies are organized according to their time of occurrence in the reading process: before, during, or after. In this book, strategies are presented according to the cognitive or affective processes involved.

PREPARATIONAL STRATEGIES

Preparational strategies include activating prior knowledge about a topic before reading and predicting what a piece is about or what will happen in a story. Setting purposes and goals and previewing are also in this category.

Preparational strategies can also be applied during reading. A reader may complete a section and then activate prior knowledge and make predictions for the upcoming selection.

ACTIVATING PRIOR KNOWLEDGE

Typically, the teacher activates students' prior knowledge in a prereading discussion. The teacher should model the process: In preparation for reading an article about computers, the teacher should show the class how she asks herself what she already knows about the subject and then decides what she would like to find out. Before students read a selection, the teacher should ask them what they know about the topic and what they would like to find out. In time, students should be led to activate prior knowledge on their own, since much of their reading will be done without benefit of preparatory discussion or teacher assistance.

SETTING PURPOSE AND GOALS

Although the teacher often sets the purpose for reading a piece by giving students a question to answer, students must be able to set their own purpose. This could fit in with activating prior knowledge. As readers activate knowledge about computers, they may wonder how the machines work, which could be a purpose for reading. Readers also have to decide their overall goal for reading—for pleasure, to gain information, or to study for a test—as each goal requires a different style of reading. Again, these are processes that the teacher should model and discuss. However, students should gradually take responsibility for setting purposes and goals.

PREDICTING

A strategy that helps readers set a purpose for reading is predicting. Powerful, but remarkably easy to use, it activates readers' schemata, since predictions are made on the basis of prior knowledge. Predicting also gives readers a purpose for reading and turns reading into an active search to see whether a prediction is correct. This strategy can and should be taught even before children can read on their own. Before reading a storybook aloud, the teacher should read its title, show the students one or more illustrations, and have them predict what they think the story might be about or what they think will happen. Consensus is not necessary. Each student should feel free to make her or his own prediction. However, the teacher might ask students to justify their predictions; for example, for a prediction for Zion's (1956) *Harry the Dirty Dog*, the teacher might ask, "What makes you think that Harry will be given a bath?"

For setting up predictions, Nessel (1987) suggested two questions that could be asked at the beginning or at crucial points in the story:

1. What do you think will happen? (e.g., What do you think X will do? How do you think this problem will be resolved?)
2. Why do you think so? What have you experienced and what did you read in the story that leads you to make that prediction? (p. 604)

The first question elicits the prediction; the second asks students to explain it to ensure that it is thoughtful and plausible. Students also must learn to be flexible so that they can alter a prediction if it proves to be off the mark.

In addition to teaching students what kinds of questions to ask, the teacher should show them the best sources of predictions: title, illustrations, introductory note, and first paragraph. Gradually, they can create their own predictions as they read. Predicting becomes an excellent device for enhancing comprehension when students are reading independently—ideally, it will become automatic. Predicting should also be a lifelong strategy. As they move into higher grades, students should use predicting as part of a study technique as well as for other sustained reading.

Part of being an effective user of strategies is knowing when and where to use a particular strategy. Making predictions requires prior knowledge. Students beginning to read about a topic for which they have little background information will have difficulty making reasonable predictions and so should use another strategy.

PREVIEWING

In previewing, also known as surveying, students read the title, headings, introduction, and summary for a selection and look at illustrations to get an overview of the selection. This preview orients them to the piece so that they have some sense of what it will be about. It can function as a kind of blueprint for constructing a mental model of the text and also activates readers' schemata. As readers preview, they ask themselves what they know about the subject. Previewing is often used with predicting: Information gathered from previewing can be used to make predictions.

ORGANIZATIONAL STRATEGIES

Organizational strategies are at the heart of constructing meaning. In contrast to preparational strategies, they are employed during reading as well as after reading.

As students read, they form a macrostructure or mental model. Organizational strategies involve selecting important details and building relationships among them. For reading, this entails identifying the main idea of a passage and its supporting details and summarizing.

COMPREHENDING THE MAIN IDEA

Deriving the **main idea** is at the core of constructing meaning from text, as it provides a framework for organizing, understanding, and remembering the essential details. Without it, students wander aimlessly among details. Being able to identify or compose main ideas is essential for summarizing, note taking, and outlining. (Although suggestions for teaching comprehension of main ideas and important details are presented separately in this chapter for the sake of clarity, these should be taught together.)

The **main idea** is the overall meaning, or gist, of a passage. It is what the passage is all about, a summary statement of its meaning

One instructional problem is defining the term *main idea*, which has been defined in a variety of ways (Cunningham & Moore, 1986). In this book, *main idea* will be defined as a summary statement that includes the other details in a paragraph or longer piece; it is what all the sentences are about.

Despite the importance of main ideas, little is known about how elementary school children generate them. Older, more adept readers construct main ideas as they read. For many, it is an automatic process, especially if the text is about familiar topics (Afflerbach, 1990). These readers use a process known as crunching, which means that they reduce the text to a few essential bits or kernels of information (Afflerbach & Johnston, 1986).

When not constructing main ideas automatically, adept readers tend to use an initial hypothesis strategy. Cues such as title, heading, and first sentence activate their schemata, or knowledge structures, and allow such readers to create a hypothesis about the main idea. By reading further, they test the hypothesis and confirm or modify it. For unfamiliar text, adept readers most often use a draft-and-revision strategy to construct main ideas. This is essentially a two-part procedure. After reading a piece, these readers draft and store in memory a tentative main idea statement; after rereading portions of the piece, they return to the statement to revise it. Listing is another approach that is used frequently with unfamiliar material. Readers search for important or related words or ideas and use them as the basis for composing main ideas. This approach requires readers to note relationships among words and ideas as they read.

Basically, then, adept readers tend to use either a whole-part strategy, in which they draft or hypothesize the whole and confirm it by reading the parts, or a part-whole strategy, in which they note important parts, construct relationships among them, and compose a main idea statement. The whole-part strategy fits best with a schema theory of comprehension; the part-whole strategy exemplifies the construction of a mental model or macrostructure.

Because of its complexity and importance, main idea comprehension has to be taught step by step. Instruction should include presenting underlying processes, one of which is classifying.

Classifying.   Determining the main idea is partly a classification skill. The main idea statement is a category label for all or most of the details in the piece. The best way to convey the concept of a main idea and to provide instruction in its underlying cognitive process is to have students classify a series of objects or words (Baumann, 1986; Gunning, 1977; Johnson & Kress, 1965; Williams, 1986b).

To demonstrate classifying, bring in a variety of objects and indicate how they might be sorted. For example, display an apple, orange, pear, banana, and book, and ask students to tell which go together. Discuss why the book does not belong. Put the objects in a box. Tell students you want to label the box so that you know what is in it and ask them what word you might use. Students can name other objects that might be put in the box, with a discussion of why they belong there. Follow a similar procedure with tools, toys, and other objects.

Once students have grasped the idea of classifying objects, have them classify words. First, give them lists of words that include labels. Model how you would go about choosing the category label. Tell students that you are looking for a word that tells about all the others. Read a series of related words that have been written on the board: *cats, fish, pets, dogs*. Model how you would choose *pets* as the label because it describes the other three words. After working through several sample series of words, have students complete exercises similar to the following (which includes words that are easy enough for first-graders):

ball	toys	blocks	doll
oak	trees	maple	pine
fruit	apple	peach	banana

To vary the activity, include an item in the series that does not belong (*train, bus, car, ball*) and have students identify it. Also, list a series of related items (*three, nine, four, two*) and let students supply a category label.

After students are able to categorize words with ease, have them categorize groups of sentences by identifying the one that tells about all the others. Call this the main idea sentence. To construct exercises of this type, locate brief paragraphs that have an explicitly stated main idea. Write the sentences in list form, and have students point out which sentence tells about all the others. Groups of sentences similar to the following can be used:

Car door locks were frozen.

Small children refused to venture from their warm homes.

It was the coldest day that anyone could remember.

The temperature was twenty below zero.

The lake was frozen solid. (Gunning, 1977, p. 9)

Model the process of choosing the most inclusive sentence, thinking aloud as you choose it. Let students see that the process involves checking each sentence to determine which one includes all the others and then examining the other sentences to make sure that each one can be included under the main sentence. Then have students complete a series of similar exercises under your guidance.

Recognizing Topic Sentences.

Once students have a sense of what a main idea is, begin working with brief paragraphs that contain an explicitly stated main idea, a sentence that tells about all the others. Explain that the main idea sentence is called a *topic sentence* because it contains the topic of the paragraph. It is often the first sentence of a paragraph, but may be last or in the middle. Move the topic sentence in a sample paragraph around to show students how it could make sense in a number of positions. Also point out how the details in a paragraph support the main idea.

Provide students with guided practice in locating topic sentences and supporting details in paragraphs. Locating supporting details is like proving a problem in math: If the details do not support the sentence chosen as the topic sentence, the student has probably not located the real topic sentence. Take practice paragraphs from children's periodicals, books, and textbooks. At first, select paragraphs in which the main idea sentence comes first, as this is the easiest organizational pattern to understand. Students have more difficulty with paragraphs in which the topic sentence occurs last (Kimmel & MacGinitie, 1984). Also choose paragraphs that are interesting and well written. Students will then enjoy the activity more and will pick up incidental information. Using real books and periodicals also demonstrates that this is a practical activity, one students can use in their everyday reading. It also makes the practice more realistic because students will be working with the kinds of material they actually read rather than with paragraphs contrived for teaching the main idea. The following is an example of a paragraph that might be used:

> An Old English sheepdog's hearing is better than yours in three ways. A dog can hear higher tones, detect fainter sounds, and locate the source of a sound more accurately. If a high-pitched sound goes over 20,000 cycles a second, humans can't hear it. Dogs can, and that's why they can hear a "silent" dog whistle. (Sanford & Green, 1989b, p. 15)

Presenting paragraphs that contain topic sentences makes sense in the beginning stages of instruction as it simplifies identifying the main idea, but you must emphasize that not all paragraphs contain topic sentences. In fact, most do not. Baumann and Serra (1984) found that only 44 percent of the paragraphs in elementary social studies textbooks had explicitly stated main ideas, and only 27 percent of the main ideas occurred in the opening sentence.

Even when the main idea is explicitly stated and is in the opening sentence, readers must still infer that the first sentence tells what the rest of the paragraph is about. Young readers and poor readers tend to select the first sentence as the topic sentence almost automatically (Gold & Fleisher, 1986). To prevent this, ask them to check by specifying the supporting details in this paragraph, and whether all the other sentences support the first one (Duffelmeyer, 1985). If that is the case, the first sentence is the topic sentence. If not, the students should search for a sentence that does serve that function.

Student Strategy
Constructing the main idea

Constructing the main idea for paragraphs that do not have an explicitly stated one can be difficult. In one study, students improved by 95 percent when the main idea was contained in the first sentence as opposed to being implied

Although well-formed paragraphs might be used for initial instruction in construction of main ideas, students should eventually apply their strategies to informational trade books and texts. In general, authors do not begin each paragraph with a main idea. Often the main idea is implied; some paragraphs simply provide an introduction or additional information and lack a clear-cut main idea.

(Gold & Fleisher, 1986). Students might use the following steps to construct a main idea:

1. Use the heading, title, or first sentence to create a hypothesis as to what the main idea is.
2. Read each sentence and note whether it supports the hypothesis. If not, revise the hypothesis.
3. If you can't create a hypothesis as to what the main idea is, infer what all or most of the sentences have in common.
4. Create a statement that expresses the hypothesis or indicates what all the sentences are about.

Comprehension instruction requires scaffolding. When helping students learn strategies, teachers provide examples, modeling, explicit instruction, prompts, and discussions (Dole, Duffy, Roehler, & Pearson, 1991). In time, the scaffolding is reduced, and students apply the strategies independently.

After students have constructed a hypothesis about the overall meaning of a selection, it is important that they continue to monitor as they read to make sure that the sense of the passage supports their hypothesis as to what the main idea is and that they revise their main idea statement as necessary (Afflerbach, 1990). To monitor the main idea of the passage, students might simply ask themselves from time to time, "What is this passage mainly about?" If the details in the selection fail to support the hypothesis, then the hypothesis needs to be revised.

If students fail to construct a main idea during their first pass through the text, teach them how to use the list strategy that expert readers employ. Show them how to skim through the passage and note related words, ideas, or concepts. Have them create a main idea statement that tells what all the sentences are about. As an alternative, show students how to use the draft-and-revise strategy. That is, they use their initial reading to construct a main idea statement and then check the validity of their statement by rereading the passage.

One problem that students have in recognizing or generating main ideas is a tendency to focus on a narrow detail of a single sentence instead of on a broad statement that includes all the essential information in a paragraph (Williams, 1986a). As students work with paragraphs, use a series of prompts to help them identify what the paragraph is about. Start off by asking them what the general topic of the paragraph is, and then ask them to identify the specific topic and check whether all the details support it. For instance, using the following simple paragraph about robots, you might ask, "What is the general topic of the paragraph? What is the specific topic? What does the paragraph tell us about robots?"

> Robots help us in many ways. Robots work in factories. They help put cars and TVs together. In some offices, robots deliver the mail. And in some hospitals, robots bring food to sick people. A new kind of robot can mow lawns. And some day there may even be robots that can take out the trash and take the dog for a walk.

If students provide the correct specific topic, ask them to verify their response. The class should go over each sentence to determine whether it tells how robots help out. If, on the other hand, students supply details rather than a statement of the specific topic, the class would examine each detail and decide what each had in common.

Lesson 6.1
Determining the main idea and its supporting details

Step 1. Introducing the strategy

Explain what main ideas and supporting details are and why it is important to locate and understand them in reading. Give a clear definition of what a main idea is—it tells what the paragraph or section is all about. Provide examples of main ideas.

Step 2. Modeling the process

Show how you would go about determining a main idea and its supporting details. Starting off with well-constructed paragraphs, demonstrate the hypothesis strategy, since this is the strategy most frequently used by adept readers. Show students how you would use a title, heading, graphic clues, and the apparent topic sentence to predict the main idea. Then confirm or revise your hypothesis as you read and see whether the details support your hypothesized main idea. (Even if the main idea is directly stated, it is still necessary to use a hypothesis or other strategy because readers cannot be sure that the sentence is indeed a topic sentence until they read the rest of the paragraph.) For some implied main-idea paragraphs that have no titles or headings that could be clues to the main idea, you may have to use the listing strategy. Note the details in such a paragraph and then construct a main idea statement after seeing how the details are related or what they have in common. Listing is best taught after students have a firm grasp of the hypothesis-confirmation and draft-revision strategies. Model the process with a variety of paragraphs.

Step 3. Guided practice

Have students derive main ideas from brief, well-constructed paragraphs. If possible, choose paragraphs that cover familiar topics, as it is easier to construct main ideas when the content and vocabulary are known. Students face a double burden when they must grapple with difficult concepts and vocabulary while trying to construct a main idea. Although shorter paragraphs should be used in the beginning stages, have students gradually apply this skill to longer pieces, such as selections from content area textbooks.

Step 4. Independent practice and application

Have students derive main ideas and supporting details in children's books, textbooks, periodicals, and other materials that they read on their own. From well-written, well-organized science or social studies textbooks or children's books, choose sections that convey an overall main idea or theme and develop it in several paragraphs. At first, choose pieces that have an explicitly stated main idea. Show students how you would use a hypothesis strategy to derive the main idea. Using a section similar to that illustrated in Figure 6.1, demonstrate how you would use the heading "Life in the Desert," the photos, and the first paragraph to guess what the main idea of the section is. Explain that the main idea seems to be stated in the last sentence of the first paragraph: "How do plants and animals live in such a dry climate?"

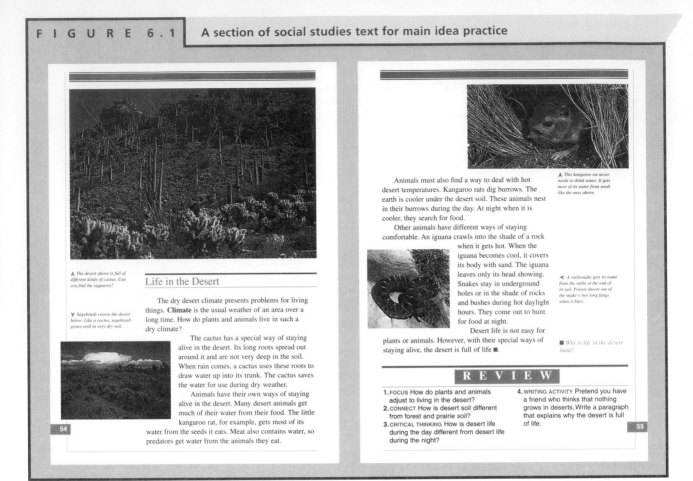

▲ *The desert above is full of different kinds of cactus. Can you find the saguaros?*

Life in the Desert

The dry desert climate presents problems for living things. **Climate** is the usual weather of an area over a long time. How do plants and animals live in such a dry climate?

The cactus has a special way of staying alive in the desert. Its long roots spread out around it and are not very deep in the soil. When rain comes, a cactus uses these roots to draw water up into its trunk. The cactus saves the water for use during dry weather.

Animals have their own ways of staying alive in the desert. Many desert animals get much of their water from their food. The little kangaroo rat, for example, gets most of its water from the seeds it eats. Meat also contains water, so predators get water from the animals they eat.

▼ *Sagebrush covers the desert below. Like a cactus, sagebrush grows well in very dry soil.*

Animals must also find a way to deal with hot desert temperatures. Kangaroo rats dig burrows. The earth is cooler under the desert soil. These animals nest in their burrows during the day. At night when it is cooler, they search for food.

Other animals have different ways of staying comfortable. An iguana crawls into the shade of a rock when it gets hot. When the iguana becomes cool, it covers its body with sand. The iguana leaves only its head showing. Snakes stay in underground holes or in the shade of rocks and bushes during hot daylight hours. They come out to hunt for food at night.

Desert life is not easy for plants or animals. However, with their special ways of staying alive, the desert is full of life ■.

▲ *This kangaroo rat never needs to drink water. It gets most of its water from seeds like the ones above.*

◄ *A rattlesnake gets its name from the rattle at the end of its tail. Poison shoots out of the snake's two long fangs when it bites.*

■ *Why is life in the desert hard?*

R E V I E W

1. **FOCUS** How do plants and animals adjust to living in the desert?
2. **CONNECT** How is desert soil different from forest and prairie soil?
3. **CRITICAL THINKING** How is desert life during the day different from desert life during the night?
4. **WRITING ACTIVITY** Pretend you have a friend who thinks that nothing grows in deserts. Write a paragraph that explains why the desert is full of life.

54 / 55

From *Houghton Mifflin Social Studies: From Sea to Shining Sea* (pp. 53–54) by B. J. Armento, G. B. Nash, C. L. Salter & K. K. Wixson, 1991, Boston: Houghton Mifflin. Photos in text courtesy of Milton Rand/Tom Stack & Associates, Stephen Kraseman/Photo Researchers, John Cancalosi/Tom Stack & Associates, and Bob McKeever/ Tom Stack & Associates. Copyright © 1991 by Houghton Mifflin Company. Reprinted by permission of Houghton Mifflin Company.

Noting main ideas in longer sections is the ultimate payoff. This is the level of activity that helps students better understand and remember information. Fortunately, most content area textbooks make plentiful use of heads and subheads, which announce main ideas or can be used to construct them.

Extending the Ability to Construct the Main Idea.   Take advantage of discussions of selections that students have read and other naturally occurring opportunities to apply and extend the skill of constructing main ideas. Note how important details are related to the main idea of a selection. Also apply the concept to writing. Have students create and develop topic sentences on nonfiction subjects of their own choosing.

Graphic displays can help students identify the topic sentence and its supporting details. Use a simplified semantic map, which is sometimes called a *spider web* when the supporting details are equal, as shown in Figure 6.2. Use a linear display like that in Figure 6.3 when the piece has a sequential order; that is, the ideas are listed in order of importance.

Main idea instruction is more appropriate for nonfiction than for fiction. Fiction has a theme rather than a main idea. Identifying a theme can be subtler and more complex than noting a main idea. Most children's fiction also has a central problem that gives coherence to the story (Moldofsky, 1983).

Reinforcement Activities
Main idea construction

- Cut out newspaper headlines and titles of articles, and have students match them with the articles.
- Have students classify lists of items.
- When discussing selections that students have read, include questions that require them to identify and/or construct a main idea.

DETERMINING THE RELATIVE IMPORTANCE OF INFORMATION

The ability to determine what is important in a selection is a key factor in comprehension as it keeps readers from drowning in a sea of details or having to cull out trivial information. Determining main ideas and the relative importance of information should be taught together. Determination of what is important in a selection is often dependent on the derivation of the main idea. Once they know the main idea, readers are in a better position to identify the relative importance

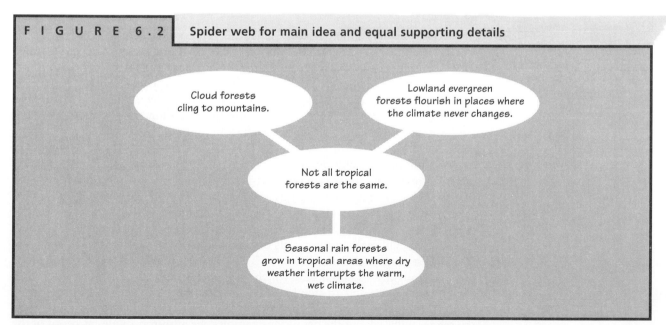

FIGURE 6.2   **Spider web for main idea and equal supporting details**

Cloud forests cling to mountains.

Lowland evergreen forests flourish in places where the climate never changes.

Not all tropical forests are the same.

Seasonal rain forests grow in tropical areas where dry weather interrupts the warm, wet climate.

Adapted from *Our Endangered Planet: Tropical Rain Forests,* by C. F. Mutel and M. M. Rodgers, 1991, Minneapolis: Lerner.

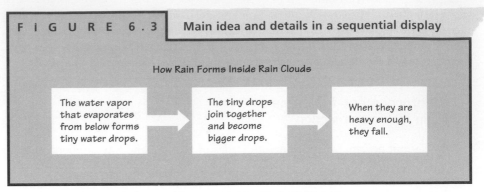

FIGURE 6.3 Main idea and details in a sequential display

How Rain Forms Inside Rain Clouds

The water vapor that evaporates from below forms tiny water drops. → The tiny drops join together and become bigger drops. → When they are heavy enough, they fall.

Text from *Weather Words*, by G. Gibbons, 1990, New York: Holiday House.

of information and to construct a mental model of the text. For instance, once they know that the main idea of an article is how to use a video camera, they can assume that the steps in the process will be the important details. Readers have to ask themselves which details support or explain a selection's main idea or, if the article is especially rich in details, which are the most important. If an article cites twenty capabilities of lasers, readers might decide which five are most essential.

Adept readers will use textual clues to help determine which details are most important. A carefully written text might state which details are essential. Or the reader might note those details that are discussed first and given the most print. Minor details might be signaled by words such as *also,* as in the sentence "Laser readers are also used to check out books in many libraries and to check times in many competitive sports."

Expert readers also use text structure, relational terms, and repetition of words or concepts to determine importance. Relational terms and expressions such as *most important of all* and *three main causes* help readers determine important ideas. A repeated word or concept is an especially useful clue. The structure of the piece also gives clues as to which details are most essential (Afflerbach & Johnston, 1986). With a problem/solution organization, an adept reader will seek out the problem and solution and ignore or strip away extraneous descriptions or examples.

In addition to using textual clues, readers can use their schemata or background knowledge to determine what is important. A child who raises tropical fish would seek out certain kinds of information when reading about a new species, such as a description of the species, its habits, and where it is found. The purpose for reading is also a factor. A child who is contemplating buying a new tropical fish will realize that details on cost and care are significant.

Expert readers also use their beliefs about the author's intention to determine which details are essential and which are not (Afflerbach & Johnston, 1986). Expert readers are able to step back from the text and consider the author's purpose. If, for instance, the author is trying to establish that a certain point is true, the reader will seek out the details or examples the author provides as proof of the contention. Lesson 6.2 includes some steps that might be used to help students determine important information.

Lesson 6.2
Determining important details

Step 1. Introduction of strategy

Explain what is meant by "important details" and why being able to identify them is an essential skill. Display and discuss several short selections that contain both important and unimportant information, and help students discriminate between the two.

Step 2. Model the process

Determine important information in a sample paragraph. Show how you would use contextual clues: topic sentence, placement of ideas, and graphic aids. In another session, demonstrate how you might use knowledge of the topic or your purpose for reading.

Step 3. Guided practice

Provide guidance as students determine important information in a selection. Start with well-structured texts that supply plenty of clues and gradually work up to selections from their basal readers, content area textbooks, library books, or periodicals. Ask students to justify their choice of important details, since this skill is somewhat subjective.

Step 4. Application

Have students note important ideas in materials that they read independently. The more experience students have with varied reading materials and the broader and deeper their knowledge base, the better prepared they will be to determine the relative importance of information. Set purposes that lead students to grasp essential information. Ask questions that focus on important information. By asking such questions, you will be modeling the kinds of questions that students should be asking themselves before they read and as they read.

Reinforcement Activities
Determining importance of information

- Have students predict the important ideas in a selection they are about to read.
- After they have read a selection, ask students to tell which ideas are most important.
- Encourage students to write newspaper stories in which the most important information is provided in the first paragraph.

ORGANIZING DETAILS

Sequencing.   Because some details have to be comprehended and then remembered in a certain order, readers must organize them sequentially. These include historical or biographical events, steps in a process, and directions. Because the extra step of noting the sequence is involved, organizing sequential details often poses special problems, especially for younger readers. To introduce sequence, have students tell about some simple sequential activities in which they engage, such as washing dishes, making cookies, or assembling a puzzle. Discuss the order of the activities, and place them on the chalkboard using cue words such as *first, second, next, then, before, last,* and *after.*

Place lists of other events on the chalkboard, and ask students to put them in order. Start with a series of three or four events for younger students and work up to six or seven items for more advanced readers. Encourage students to use their sense of the situation or the process to put the events in order. Show how cue words help indicate sequence.

After students have become adept at this activity, let them apply their skill to stories and articles. To help them become aware of the sequence of a story, have them map out the main events, showing how the story progresses to its climax and the resolution of a problem. Help students create causal links between events in a story, as this aids retention (McNamara, Miller, & Bransford, 1991). Two literary techniques that might make a story more appealing but cause the sequence to be more difficult to comprehend are flashback and *in medias res*. When a flashback occurs in a story, point it out and discuss why the author used it. Encourage students to try this technique in their writing. Also point out occurrences of *in medias res* and talk about why an author would want to start a story in the "middle of things."

For biographies and historical accounts, show students how to use dates to keep events in order. Encourage students to create a time line to help keep track of a sequence of events. As students read about the steps in a process (e.g., a caterpillar becoming a butterfly or a bill becoming a law), have them note the sequence. Show them how they might use a graphic organizer to display a process or chain of events. Figure 6.4 presents a chain map showing how radar works.

Following Directions.   Following directions is a natural outgrowth of sequencing. As students read directions, remind them to make use of cue words such as *first, next,* and *last.* Also introduce words such as *list, match,* and *underline,* which are frequently found in directions and with which young children often

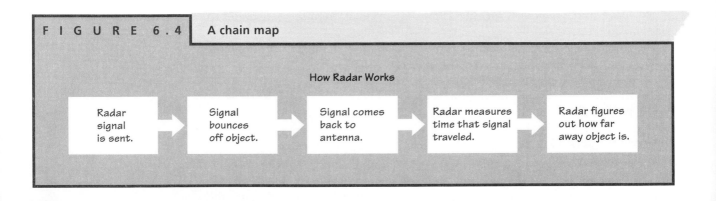

FIGURE 6.4   A chain map

How Radar Works

Radar signal is sent. → Signal bounces off object. → Signal comes back to antenna. → Radar measures time that signal traveled. → Radar figures out how far away object is.

Students should be taught strategies for reading to follow directions.

have difficulty (Boehm, 1971). Students can create mental models of directions by visually depicting the process, using an accompanying diagram or other illustration, or describing the steps. If possible, have students carry out the procedures outlined in the directions.

After techniques for understanding directions have been taught, students should be made responsible for reading and following directions. They should read the directions once to get an overview, and then a second time to find out exactly what they are to do. Encourage them to study any samples that are given; however, these samples should be examined after the directions are read, not before. Some students skip the directions and look only at the sample, and some do not even bother looking at the sample. They simply plunge ahead or ask the teacher what to do. If students ask what they are supposed to do, tell them to read the directions carefully. If they still fail to understand, have them tell you what they think they are to do, and then redirect their thinking as necessary.

Use printed directions for some classroom routines—for example, how to operate the computer or the tape recorder. Also use directions that accompany real-world materials. Students might follow sets of printed directions for assembling a simple toy or a piece of furniture. Have them note how studying the illustration is an important part of following the directions.

Use writing to support reading. Encourage students to write a series of directions for a favorite game or other activity. Have students work in pairs; the partners can check the clarity of each other's directions by trying them out and seeing if they can follow them.

Student Strategy
Following directions

Students can use these steps to follow directions:

1. Read the directions to get an overview.
2. Look at any accompanying illustrations.
3. Make sure all parts have been included.

4. Assemble all necessary tools and materials or ingredients.
5. Read and follow each step, using any accompanying illus-trations as an aid.

Other activities that provide natural practice in following directions are planting seeds, caring for classroom animals or plants, using a computer pro-gram, and following recipes. The best thing about real-life exercises is that they are self-checking. A computer program that is not used correctly will flash an error message, recipes incorrectly followed result in inedible food, and devices improperly constructed do not work.

SUMMARIZING

What is the most effective comprehension strategy of all? When five experts in learning examined the research on comprehension in order to discover which strategies seemed to have the greatest payoff and were the most solidly grounded in research, they listed summarization first (Pressley, Johnson, Symons, Mc-Goldrick, & Kurita, 1989). Summarization, which builds on the organizational strategy of determining main ideas and supporting details, improves compre-hension and increases retention. It is also a metacognitive means of **monitoring,** through which students can evaluate their understanding of a passage that they have just read. If a student has not comprehended a selection, she or he is almost certain to have difficulty summarizing it.

Summarizing is a complex skill that takes years to develop. Even college students may have difficulty summarizing. Young children realize that a summary is a condensation of material; however, they have difficulty determining what points should be included in a summary. The view of young students seems to be egocentric: They choose details that are personally interesting rather than select-ing details that seem important from the author's point of view. Young students also have difficulty with the procedures necessary to summarize (Hidi & Anderson, 1986): They delete information but do not combine or condense de-tails; they also tend to use a copy strategy. Until about grade 5 or 6, students record details word for word in their summaries. At that point, they begin com-bining and condensing.

In a study of fifth-grade students, K. K. Taylor (1986) found that proficient summarizers sift information and combine details as they read, using the title and organization of the material to help them. They have a good understanding of the demands of the task and see it in terms of searching out and constructing the most important ideas. They also monitor their work, checking their own written sum-maries against the original.

Introducing Summarizing.
Summaries need not be written. All of us make oral summaries of movie and book plots, events, conversations, and so on. Since writing summaries can be difficult (Brown & Day, 1983; Hare & Borchardt, 1984), teachers should first develop students' ability to summarize orally.

Retelling is a natural way to lead into summarizing. Young children tend to recount every incident in a story and give every detail about a topic. Help them structure their retellings so as to emphasize major events and main ideas. Ask

---

Affective factors play an important role in comprehen-sion. Often, students ask ques-tions about directions because they are unsure of themselves or are afraid of making a mis-take. These children need to build their self-confidence, and they also require an atmos-phere in which they can feel free to risk failure.

Monitoring is being aware of or checking one's cognitive processes. In reading compre-hension, the reader monitors his or her understanding of the text.

Although summarizing is a complex skill, its development begins early. Young children summarize when they describe a real event or retell a story.

questions like these: "What were the two most important things that the main character did? What were the three main things that happened in the story? What are the main things you learned about robots? What are the main ways in which robots are used?" (See Chapter 7 for a fuller discussion of retelling.)

From kindergarten on, teachers can model the process of summarizing by providing summaries of selections read, especially nonfiction, and of discussions and directions. As students get into content area material, they can be directed to pay special attention to chapter summaries. Although they may not be capable of writing well-formed summaries until the upper elementary school grades, they can begin learning the skill in ways appropriate to their level of development from their very first years of school.

Several activities can build summarizing or its underlying skills. Encourage students to use titles, illustrations, topic sentences, headings, and other textual clues. In Taylor's (1986) study, many students failed to use the title and topic sentence when composing their summaries, although both contained the main idea of the selection. Teach students how to read expository text. Ineffectual summarizers read such works as though they are fiction and so fail to note textual cues that could help them create better summaries (Taylor, 1986). Have students compose oral summaries of stories, articles, and class discussions.

To create a group summary, read an informational article aloud and ask students what the most important points are. After listing the points on the board, have the class summarize them. Group summaries provide preparation for the creation of independent summaries (Moore, Moore, Cunningham, & Cunningham, 1986).

Summarizing can be an excellent device for checking comprehension. Encourage students to stop after reading key sections of expository text and mentally summarize the materials. Once they have some ability to identify relevant details, make use of structural cues, and identify and construct main ideas, they are ready for a more formal type of instruction in summarizing.

Presenting Summarizing Skills.   When teaching summarizing, begin with shorter, easier text. Texts that are shorter and easier to comprehend are easier to summarize. Also, start off with narrative text, which is easier than expository text to summarize (Hidi & Anderson, 1986). Focus on the content rather than the form of the summaries. After students become accustomed to summarizing essential details, stress the need for well-formed, polished summaries. Since many students have great difficulty determining which details are important, have them list important details. Discuss these lists before they compose their summaries. Also have students create semantic maps before writing summaries. In addition to helping students select important information, such maps may help them detect important relationships among key ideas. In a study conducted with older students, those who constructed maps before summarizing used a greater number of cohesive ties than those who did not (Ruddell & Boyle, 1989).

Students should know why summarizing is important and how it might benefit them. For instance, in a study conducted by Rinehart, Stahl, and Erickson (1986), the teacher demonstrated to students that summarizing could improve their understanding and retention of content area material and so result in higher grades on tests. Using the steps of direct instruction, the teacher presented summa-

Being able to determine the relative importance of information is essential for summarizing. However, in addition to sifting out the important ideas, the summarizer must synthesize those ideas into a coherent whole, which makes summarizing a difficult, complex skill (Dole, Duffy, Roehler, & Pearson, 1991).

rization strategies over a period of five days. The instruction focused on teaching and reinforcing summarization operations. According to Brown & Day (1983) and Rinehart, Stahl, and Erickson (1986), there are five such operations:

1. Selecting or constructing the overall (main) idea
2. Selecting important information that supports the main idea
3. Deleting information that is not important or is repeated
4. Combining and condensing information
5. Polishing the summary

Lesson 6.3
Introduction to summarization

Step 1. Explaining the skill

Emphasize that a summary includes the most important ideas or information in a text. Students may have erroneous notions about summaries. For instance, they may tend to highlight the most interesting or the most difficult details, or sentences that are richly detailed (Taylor, 1986; Winograd, 1984). Give examples of summaries, and tell why they are useful and when they should be written.

Step 2. Modeling the process

Model the process of constructing a summary. In the beginning, focus on the first three operations: selecting or constructing the overall idea, selecting supporting details, and taking out details that are not important or repeated. Choose a brief, well-formed paragraph, such as the following:

> The New World turned out to be a good place to find new foods. Potatoes were first grown by the Incas of South America. Corn, a main food throughout America, was also first grown in Central or South America. The tomato is a third American food. It, too, was first grown in Central America. And if it hadn't been for America, there would be no vanilla ice cream. The vanilla bean was first grown in Mexico.

Explain that you will read it, and as you read, you will be asking yourself: "What is this paragraph all about?" Have students read the paragraph silently as you read it aloud. Then, think aloud. Demonstrate to students the process you use to select the overall idea and supporting details. Explain that the paragraph is all about foods that were first grown in America, so the first sentence of your summary will be "Many foods were grown first in America." Then, search out supporting details. Explain that since you are writing a summary, you want to write the details as briefly as possible; so you write, "Potatoes came from South America. Corn and tomatoes came from Central America. And the vanilla bean came from Mexico." Explain that the third operation is to take out unimportant or repeated details. Note for the students that you are not including the statement that corn was a main food because this detail is not important: It does not support the main idea but simply gives extra information. Note, too, that the detail that states "if it hadn't been for America, there would be no vanilla ice cream" is unimportant and therefore should be taken out.

Model the summarization of two or three additional brief and well-constructed paragraphs. As students catch on to the concept of summarization, involve them in the process. Have them help decide what the overall idea is and help choose important details. Have them help, too, with the wording of the summaries. Stress that the wording of summaries will vary, as will decisions about what to include and what to omit. As students become more adept at summarizing, model the processes of combining and condensing information and polishing summaries. Students should also be shown how to check their summaries against the original text to ensure that they are accurate and complete. A checklist for summaries that students can use is presented in Figure 6.5.

Step 3. Guided practice

Provide ample practice opportunities for students. Have them start with brief, well-constructed paragraphs about relatively familiar topics and gradually work up to more complex materials. For younger students and poorer readers, emphasis can be placed on oral summaries or retellings. Students who are struggling with summarizing might use text frames like that shown in Figure 6.6, in which the format of a general summary is provided. Aided by this structure, students only have to fill in the blanks with the specific elements.

Step 4. Independent practice and application

Have students summarize both fiction and nonfiction selections orally and/or in writing. Class discussions, demonstrations, stories read aloud, films, and other nonprint sources of information can and should be summarized.

Hidi and Anderson (1986) distinguished between reader-based and writer-based summaries. Reader-based summaries are written for the reader. They tend to be longer and not quite as well formed, but easier to compose. Writer-based summaries are written for someone else and so are better written and include more details, but they are more difficult to create. Initial efforts at summarizing might be focused on writer-based versions. Both types of summaries should have a practical payoff—preparation for a test or oral report, for instance.

FIGURE 6.5 | **Student checklist for summaries**

Put a check before the question if your answer is "yes."
Put an X if your answer is "no."

_____ Does the summary state the main idea?

_____ Is the main idea stated first?

_____ Does the summary state *all* the important ideas?

_____ Does the summary state *only* the most important information?

_____ Are details combined so that the summary is brief?

_____ Is the summary clear?

Three main toxic hazards can be found in homes.

Asbestos is _____. It can cause _____.

Radon is _____. It can cause _____.

Household chemicals include _____. They can cause _____.

Text adapted from *Toxic Waste* (pp. 32–33), by S. D. Gold, 1990, New York: Crestwood House.

Step 5. Extending the concept

For several lessons, review the concept of summarizing. Gradually provide students with somewhat longer paragraphs. Once they have a grasp of summarizing brief paragraphs, demonstrate how selections with several paragraphs can be summarized. This can be done in two phases. Students first write a summary of each individual paragraph; they then write a summary of the paragraph summaries. Once students have become adept at writing these two-part summaries, have them compose the overall idea for the group of paragraphs and then include the most important ideas. Once students are able to write summaries of a series of paragraphs, have them summarize sections of texts.

Adapting instruction for disabled readers
Some students might do better with strategies that help them visualize information. They might find semantic maps and webs and other graphic methods of organizing information to be especially helpful.

Mapping.   Idea maps can be used to summarize text (Berkowitz, 1986), and they are somewhat easier to compose than a traditional summary. To create a map summary, students write the title or heading of the chapter or section they are reading in the center of an 8½-by-11 sheet of paper, which has been placed horizontally. They use subheadings or skim the text to locate major topics, which are then numbered and placed in blocks arranged clockwise around the title. After reading each section, students fill in the appropriate block with the most important details, stated concisely, as illustrated in Figure 6.7. The teacher should emphasize that each map will be slightly different, since each person will have her or his own idea about which details are important (Taylor, 1986).

Elaboration refers to additional processing of text by the reader, which may result in improved comprehension and meaning. Elaboration involves building connections between one's background knowledge and the text or integrating these two sources through manipulating or transforming information.

ELABORATION STRATEGIES

Elaboration is a generative activity in which the reader constructs connections between information from text and prior knowledge. Like organizational strategies, elaboration strategies are employed during reading but may also be put into operation after reading. The reader generates inferences, images, questions, judgments, and other elaborations. A powerful strategy, elaboration increased comprehension by 50 percent in a number of studies (Linden & Wittrock, 1981).

MAKING INFERENCES

Although children have the cognitive ability to draw inferences, some do not do so spontaneously. A probable cause of this deficiency is a lack of background information about the topic or the failure to process information in the text that would foster drawing inferences. Two approaches enhance the ability to make inferences: building background and teaching specific strategies for making inferences. However, sustained instruction is required. When students were taught processes for making inferences, no significant change was noted until after four weeks of teaching. The effects were long-lasting, and, as a side benefit, literal comprehension improved (Dewitz, Carr, & Patberg, 1987).

There are two kinds of inferences: schema-based and text-based (Winne, Graham, & Prock, 1993). Schema-based inferences depend on prior knowledge. For instance, reading the sentence "They rode into the sunset," inferring that it was late in the day and the riders were heading west is schema-based. The reader uses her or his schema for the position of the sun to infer approximate time and direction. Schema-based inferences allow the reader to elaborate on the text by adding information that has been implied by the author. A text-based inference is one that requires putting together two or more pieces of information. Reading that peanuts have more food energy than sugar and that a pound of peanut butter has more protein than thirty-two eggs but more fat than ice cream, the reader might put all this information together to infer that peanuts are nutritious but fattening.

Making inferences is the most important elaboration strategy. Much of the information in a piece, especially fiction, is implied. Authors show and dramatize rather than tell. Instead of directly stating that a main character is a liar, the author

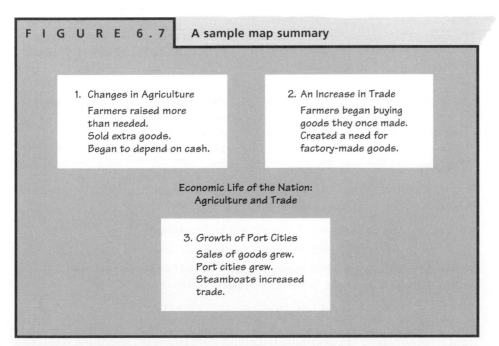

FIGURE 6.7 A sample map summary

1. Changes in Agriculture
   Farmers raised more than needed.
   Sold extra goods.
   Began to depend on cash.

2. An Increase in Trade
   Farmers began buying goods they once made.
   Created a need for factory-made goods.

Economic Life of the Nation: Agriculture and Trade

3. Growth of Port Cities
   Sales of goods grew.
   Port cities grew.
   Steamboats increased trade.

Text summarized from *Houghton Mifflin Social Studies: American Will Be,* by B. J. Armento, G. B. Nash, C. L. Salter, and K. K. Wixson, 1991, Boston: Houghton Mifflin.

As Dole, Duffy, Roehler, and Pearson (1991) noted, "Inference is the heart of the comprehension process" (p. 245). As readers and listeners construct meaning from what they read or hear, they use inferencing to fill in the unspoken or unwritten details. Because of its vital importance, inferencing should be taught from the very beginning of the literacy program.

Although making inferences is more difficult than literal comprehension, it is not necessary for students to master literal comprehension before they are instructed in making inferences. The two can and should be taught simultaneously.

In order to make inferences, two conditions have to be met: First, students must have access to the information necessary to make the inference; second, students must be able to implement inference-making procedures such as combining several pieces of text information or combining text information and prior knowledge. Other vital prerequisites for making inferences are knowing what kinds of information are required and explicit, thorough instruction (Winne, Graham, & Prock, 1993).

dramatizes situations in which the character lies. This is true even in the simplest of stories. For instance, in the third paragraph of *The Tale of Peter Rabbit*, Beatrix Potter (1908) wrote:

> "Now, my dears," said old Mrs. Rabbit one morning, "you may go into the field or down the lane, but don't go into Mr. McGregor's garden. Your Father had an accident there. He was put in a pie by Mrs. McGregor."

The reader must infer that Father was killed by Mr. McGregor and that Mr. McGregor will harm any rabbits that he catches in his garden. The reader might also infer that the reason Mr. McGregor does not like rabbits is that they eat the vegetables in his garden. None of this is stated, so the reader must use his schema for rabbits and gardens, together with his comprehension of the story, to produce a series of inferences. In a sense, the author erects the story's framework, and the reader must construct the full meaning by filling in the missing parts.

Activating prior knowledge helps students make inferences. For instance, if the teacher discusses the fact that rabbits anger gardeners by nibbling their vegetables before the students read *The Tale of Peter Rabbit*, they will be much more likely to draw appropriate inferences from the passage previously cited. Asking questions that require students to make inferences also helps. It increases both their ability and their inclination to make inferences (Hansen, 1981).

Although above-average students make more inferences than average ones (Carr, 1983), below-average readers can be taught the skill. Hansen and Pearson (1982) combined activation of prior knowledge, direct instruction in an inference-making strategy, posing of inferential questions, and predicting to create a series of lessons in which poor readers improved to such an extent that their inferential comprehension became equal to that of good readers. Here is how Hansen and Pearson's prior knowledge–prediction strategy works:

1. The teacher reads the story and analyzes it for two or three important ideas.
2. For each important idea, the teacher creates a previous-experience question that elicits from students any similar experiences that they may have had. This is a have-you-ever question (Pearson, 1985).
3. For each previous-experience question, an accompanying prediction question is created. This is a what-do-you-think-will-happen question.
4. Students read the selection to check their predictions.
5. Students discuss their predictions. Inferential questions, especially those related to the key ideas, are discussed.

The following important ideas, previous-experience questions, and prediction questions were used in the study (Pearson, 1985, Appendix B):

Important idea number 1: Even adults can be afraid of things.

Previous-experience question: Tell something an adult you know is afraid of.

Prediction question: In the story, Cousin Alma is afraid of something even though she is an adult. What do you think it is?

Important idea number 2: People sometimes act more bravely than they feel.

Previous-experience question: Tell about how you acted sometime when you were afraid and tried not to show it.

Prediction question: How do you think that Fats, the boy in the story, will act when he is afraid and tries not to show it?

Important idea number 3: Our experience sometimes convinces us that we are capable of doing things we thought we couldn't do.

Previous-experience question: Tell about a time that you were able to do something you thought you couldn't do.

Prediction question: In the story, what do you think Cousin Alma is able to do that she thought she couldn't do?

An important element of the technique is the discussion, with students' responses acting as a catalyst. One student's answer reminds others of similar experiences that they have had but do not think apply. For example, a girl mentioning that her uncle is afraid of snakes might trigger in another student the memory that his grandfather is afraid of dogs, even small ones. The teacher also emphasizes that students should compare their real-life experiences with events in the story.

Together with having background activated and being asked inferential questions, students should be taught a strategy for making inferences. Gordon (1985) mapped out a five-step process, which is outlined in Lesson 6.4.

Lesson 6.4
Making inferences

Step 1. Explaining the skill

The teacher explains what the skill is, why it is important, and when it is used. This explanation might be illustrated with examples.

Step 2. Modeling the process

While modeling the process of making inferences with a brief piece of text written on the chalkboard, the teacher reveals her or his thinking processes: "It says here that Jim thought Fred would make a great center when he first saw him walk into the classroom. The center is usually the tallest person on a basketball team, so I inferred that Fred is tall." The teacher also models the process with several other selections, so students see that inferences can be drawn from a variety of materials.

Step 3. Sharing the task

Students are asked to take part in the inferencing process. The teacher asks an inferential question about a brief sample paragraph or excerpt and then answers it. The students supply supporting evidence for the inference from the selection itself and from their background knowledge. The reasoning processes involved in making the inference are discussed. The teacher stresses the need to substantiate inferences with details from the story.

Step 4. Reversing the process

The teacher asks an inferential question and the students supply the inference. The teacher provides the evidence. As an alternative, the teacher might supply

Adapting instruction for poor readers
As Hansen and Pearson (1982) noted, one reason their strategy works so well with poor readers is that the good readers are already making inferences and so instruction does not help that much. Also, poor readers are typically asked literal questions, so their inferential skills are underdeveloped. Hansen and Pearson's research pointed out that, if carefully taught, lower-achieving readers can be successful.

the evidence and have the students draw an inference based on it. Either way, a discussion of reasoning processes follows.

Step 5. Integrating the process

The teacher just asks the inferential question. The students both make the inference and supply the evidence. As a final step, students might create their own inferential questions and then supply the answers and evidence. Basically, the procedure turns responsibility for the strategy over to students.

Using QAR.   Some students are text-bound and may not realize that answers to some questions require putting together several pieces of information from the reading or using their background of experience plus that information to draw inferences. Teachers frequently hear students lament that the answer is not in the book; those students do not know how to construct the answer from prior knowledge and textual content (Carr, Dewitz, & Patberg, 1989). Such readers may benefit from using QAR (question-answer relationship) in which questions are described as having the following four levels, based on where the answers are found (International Reading Association, 1988):

1. *Right there*. The answer is found within a single sentence in the text.
2. *Putting it together*. The answer is found in several sentences in the text.
3. *On my own*. The answer is in the student's background of knowledge.
4. *Writer and me*. A combination of information from the text and the reader's background is required to answer the question.

In a series of studies, Raphael (1984) observed that students' comprehension improved when they were introduced to the concept of QAR and given extensive training in locating the source of the answer. Initially, they worked with sentences

Students learn to locate evidence for inferences that they have made.

and very short paragraphs, but they progressed to 400-word selections. Raphael (1986) recommended starting with two categories of answers: "in the book" and "in my head." This would be especially helpful when working with elementary students. "In the book" includes answers that are "right there" or require "putting it together." "In my head" items are "on my own" and "writer and me" answers. Based on Raphael's (1986) suggestions, QAR might be presented in the manner described in Lesson 6.5.

Lesson 6.5
Presenting QAR

Step 1. Introducing the concept of QAR

Introduce the concept by writing on the board a paragraph similar to the following:

> Andy let the first pitch go by. It was too low. The second pitch was too high. But the third toss was letter high. Andy lined it over the left field-er's outstretched glove.

Ask a series of literal questions: "Which pitch did Andy hit? Where did the ball go? Why didn't Andy swing at the first pitch? The second pitch?" Lead students to see that the answers to these questions are "in the book."

Next, ask a series of questions that depend on the readers' background: "What game was Andy playing? What do you think Andy did after he hit the ball? Do you think he scored a run? Why or why not?" Show students that the answers to these questions depend on their knowledge of baseball. Discuss the fact that these answers are "in my head."

Step 2. Extending the concept of QAR

After students have mastered the concept of "in the book" and "in my head," extend the in-the-book category to include both "right there" and "putting it together." Once students have a solid working knowledge of these, expand the in-my-head category to include both "on my own" and "writer and me." The major difference between these two is whether the student has to read the text for the question to make sense. For instance, the question "Do you think Andy's hit was a home run?" requires knowledge of baseball and information from the story. The question "How do you feel when you get a hit?" involves only experience in hitting a baseball.

Step 3. Providing practice

Provide ample opportunity for guided and independent practice. Also refine and extend students' awareness of sources for answers and methods for constructing responses.

Although easy to implement, the QAR taxonomy may be oversimplified. As Alvermann and Phelps (1994) explain, the QAR taxonomy suggests a progression that is not based on the reality of what actually happens when children read. Readers do not begin by comprehending information that is right there, then move on to putting it together, and end up with on-my-own or writer-and-me responses. All of these processes operate simultaneously and, in fact, interact with each other. However, QAR is still a useful way of viewing the process of question answering. QAR helps students become more aware of sources of information for questions and thus become more strategic readers and better comprehenders. The putting-it-together and writer-and-me questions help students interrelate ideas within the text and also relate text information to their own background knowledge. In addition, Alvermann and Phelps (1994) have found that using QAR helps teachers "strike a balance between literal questions and more thought-provoking questions" (p. 158).

Difficulties in Making Inferences.   Some students' responses to inference questions are too specific. In addition to knowing that they can use both text and background knowledge as sources of information, students need to learn to gather *all* the information that is pertinent (McCormick, 1992). They need to base their inferences on several pieces of textual or background information. Some students choose the wrong information on which to base their inferences, and others do not use the text at all. They overrely on prior knowledge or do not recall or use sufficient pertinent text to make valid inferences (McCormick, 1992). This is especially true of poor readers.

Applying the Skill.   Inferencing is a cognitive skill that can be used in all areas of learning. Have students apply it in class discussions and when reading in the content areas. Emphasize the need to go beyond facts and details in order to make inferences.

IMAGING

Imaging refers to creating sensory representations of items in text.

Dual coding theory is the idea that text can be processed both verbally and nonverbally. Nonverbal coding focuses on imaging.

Although readers rely heavily on verbal abilities to comprehend text, they also use **imaging.** According to a **dual coding theory** of cognitive processing, information can be coded verbally or nonverbally. Verbal processing seems especially well suited to abstract and sequential text and tends to be characterized by order, logic, and organization. Nonverbal processing, or imaging, tends to be more holistic, less bound by constraints of logic, and better for dealing with concrete aspects of reality. These systems can perform independently, in parallel, or in a complementary, integrated fashion in which verbal input can stimulate the creation of a nonverbal image and a nonverbal image can stimulate a verbal response (Gambrell & Javitz, 1993; Sadoski & Paivio, 1994). Creating mental images has been shown to have many benefits. It promotes the use of prior knowledge and improves the ability to make predictions and draw inferences. In addition to aiding overall comprehension, imaging aids retention.

One reason that imaging is effective is that it is an active, generative process. In a study comparing fourth-graders who read a story without illustrations and created their own images with fourth-graders who made use of text illustrations, the group that created images remembered more of the story (Gambrell & Javitz, 1993). Apparently, creating one's own images works better than using someone else's creations.

For some passages, imaging is not just an aid to comprehension, it is the only way to grasp the author's meaning:

The sea became a wildcat now, and the galleon her prey. She stalked the ship and drove her off course. She slapped at her, rolling her victim from side to side. She knocked the spars out of her and used them to ram holes in her sides. She clawed the rudder from its sternpost and threw it into the sea. She cracked the ship's ribs as if they were brittle bones. Then she hissed and spat through the seam. (Henry, 1947, p. 11)

The meaning of this passage is in seeing, hearing, and even feeling the ship being smashed by the storm. After students have read such a passage, encourage them to imagine the scene and tell what they see, hear, and feel. Talk over how the metaphor of the sea as a wildcat might influence how they sense the passage. Have them identify words that paint pictures in their minds and create sound effects in their imaginations.

Imaging is relatively easy to teach. In one study, students' comprehension increased after just thirty minutes of instruction (Gambrell & Bales, 1986). The increase was not large, but it was significant. One way of enhancing imaging is to read high-imagery selections to children and ask them to try to picture the main character, a setting, or a scene. Good starting stories for younger children include Burton's (1942) *The Little House,* Sendak's (1963) *Where the Wild Things Are,* and Williams's (1926) *The Velveteen Rabbit.* For older students, use Byars's (1970) *Summer of the Swans* or Lewis's (1950) *The Lion, the Witch, and the Wardrobe,* either of which contains numerous high-imagery passages.

When teaching students to create images, start with single sentences and then move on to short paragraphs and, later, longer pieces. Have students read

Exemplary Teaching

Using Imaging

Creating images is a powerful strategy for enhancing both comprehension and memory of text. Maria (1990) encouraged fourth-graders to construct images to foster their understanding of a social studies passage that described an Iroquois village. Maria started the lesson by having students study a detailed drawing of an Iroquois village. After shutting their eyes and visualizing the scene, students discussed what they had seen. Their images varied.

Students were then directed to close their eyes as Maria described a scene laden with sensory images and asked image-evoking questions:

You are at an Iroquois village in New York State about the year 1650. It is winter. Feel how cold you are. Feel the snow crunch under your feet. The wind is blowing. You can hear it and feel it right through your clothes. See yourself walk through the gate into the village. See the tall fence all around the village. . . . (p. 198)

After discussing what they saw, heard, and felt, the students read a passage in their social studies textbook about life in an Iroquois longhouse. After each paragraph, they stopped and created images of what they had read and discussed the images. In the discussion, Maria asked questions that focused on the important details so that when students later created images on their own, they, too, would focus on these elements. The images that students created demonstrated that their comprehension was indeed enriched. Best of all, many of the students who responded were those who usually had little to say in class discussions.

Many people are concerned that television will destroy children's imaginations by depriving them of the opportunity to picture characters and scenes in their minds. One technique for encouraging image creation is to read aloud to children and encourage them to visualize scenes and characters. Later, a comparison can be made between the students' mental images and the illustrator's depictions.

the sentence or paragraph first, and then ask them to form a picture of it. The following are good examples of brief paragraphs that lend themselves to creation of images:

> The Little House was very sad and lonely. Her paint was cracked and dirty. Her windows were broken and her shutters hung crookedly. She looked shabby. . . . (Burton, 1942, p. 31)

> The six swans seemed motionless on the water, their necks all arched at the same angle, so that it seemed there was only one swan mirrored five times. (Byars, 1970, p. 33)

> There was a crisp, dry snow under his feet and more snow lying on the branches of the trees. Overhead, there was a pale blue sky, the sort of sky one sees on a fine winter day in the morning. Straight ahead of him he saw between the tree trunks the sun, just rising, very red and clear. (Lewis, 1950, p. 22)

Creating images serves three functions: fostering understanding, retaining information, and monitoring for meaning. If students are unable to form an image or if it is incomplete or inaccurate, encourage them to reread the section and then add to the picture in their minds or create a new one. As a comprehension strategy, imaging can help students who are having difficulty understanding a high-imagery passage. For example, it might be effective for comprehending the following highly visual description:

> A comet is like a dirty snowcone. A comet has three parts: a head, coma, and tail. The head is made of ice, gases, and particles of rocks. The heads of most comets are only a few kilometers wide. As a comet nears the sun, gases escape from the head. A large, fuzzy, ball-shaped cloud is formed. This ball-shaped cloud is the coma. The tail is present only when the coma is heated by the sun. The tail is made of fine dust and gas. A comet's tail always points away from the sun. The tail can be millions of kilometers long. (Hackett, Moyer, & Adams, 1989, p. 108)

Imaging can also be used as a pictorial summary. After reading a paragraph similar to the one about comets, students can review what they have read by trying to picture a comet and all its parts. A next step might be to draw a comet based on their visual summary. They might then compare their drawing with an illustration in the text or an encyclopedia and also with the text itself to make sure that they have included all the major components.

Like other elaboration strategies, imaging should be taught directly. The teacher should explain and model the strategy; discuss when, where, and under what conditions it might be used, and provide guided practice and application. From time to time, the teacher should review the strategy and encourage students to apply it.

Questions that ask students to create visual images should become a natural part of postreading discussions. Auditory and kinesthetic or tactile imaging should also be fostered. Students might be asked to tell how the hurricane in the story sounded, or what the velvet seats in the limousine they read about felt like. In discussing images that children have formed, remind them that each of us makes our own individual picture in our mind. Ask a variety of students to tell what pictures they formed.

Whether used with fiction or nonfiction, imaging should follow these guidelines (Fredericks, 1986):

- Students create images based on their backgrounds. Images will differ.
- Teachers should not alter students' images but might suggest that students reread a selection and then decide if they want to change their images.
- Students should be given sufficient time to form images.
- Teachers should encourage students to elaborate on or expand their images through careful questioning: "What did the truck look like? Was it old or new? What model was it? What color? Did it have any special features?"

Using Illustrations as an Aid.   One way of using imagery is to have students draw pictures of concepts or topics rather than use words to describe or talk about them. This works especially well with students who are still learning English or other students who might have difficulty expressing their ideas through words alone.

Working first with an adult class and then with primary-level pupils, McConnell (1992–1993) used drawings as a way of having students convey and refine their concepts of a rain forest and the greenhouse effect. When students seemed unable to convey in words their concepts of a rain forest, McConnell asked them to draw their impressions of it. Other students were asked to sketch their concepts of the greenhouse effect. The results were startling. Students' concepts varied widely, as did their perspectives. Some focused on the causes of the greenhouse effect; others on the effects; still others depicted what the greenhouse effect meant to them personally. The students shared their drawings in a small group and noted similarities and differences. Later, the class as a whole discussed the drawings.

After the class discussed the features of the drawings and the teacher listed them on the board, she and the class created a semantic map of the topic. Students then read an article about rain forests. After discussing the article, students revised their drawings in light of what they had learned. Because they had learned so much, some students created entirely new drawings.

As a final step, students discussed changes in their drawings and the differences between before and after depictions. Students frequently justified or clarified their changes by reading pertinent passages from the text. Students also sought out other books on rain forests for additional information about the topic to help them with their drawings.

Using drawings as a springboard and integrating them with discussion and reading of the text, the students activated schema, set a purpose for reading, and created a framework for organizing new knowledge. As McConnell (1992–1993) noted, drawings provide "a visible and explicit record of learning which can be reflected upon, altered, and developed" (p. 269). In addition to helping students explore prior knowledge and develop purposes for reading, drawings also foster comprehension and language use and help clarify concepts that are easily misunderstood. And they do all this in a novel, interesting way.

QUESTION GENERATION

Accustomed to answering questions posed by teachers and texts, students enjoy composing questions of their own. In addition to being a novel and interesting activity, question generation is also an effective strategy for fostering comprehension. It transforms the reader from passive observer to active participant. It also encourages the reader to set purposes for reading and to note important segments of text so that questions can be asked about them and possible answers considered. Creating questions also fosters active awareness of the comprehension process. Students who create questions are likely to be more aware of whether they are understanding the text and are more likely to take corrective action if their comprehension is inadequate (Andre & Anderson, 1978–1979).

Like other effective strategies, question generation requires careful, extensive instruction. Davey and McBride (1986) created a procedure for teaching sixth-graders how to generate and answer questions. The major elements of instruction are as follows:

1. *Overview of question generation.* The teacher explains how creating questions helps students improve and check their understanding of what they read. Students are taught that if they cannot answer a question they create, they need to reread the selection. The teacher also explains that creating questions helps students remember what they read and predict what might be asked on upcoming tests. Students are also taught the difference between locate (literal) and think-type (inferential) questions.
2. *Generating questions.* Students are taught how to generate questions, especially think-type ones. Words such as *similarities, differences,* and *comparison,* which might be used in questions relating one part of a selection to another, are introduced.
3. *Determining the most important information.* The teacher shows the class how to determine the most important information in a passage and how to compose questions that inquire about that information.
4. *Checking questions.* Students are supplied with five monitoring questions to respond to as they compose questions:

   How well did I identify important information?

   How well did I link information together?

   How well can I answer my questions?

   Did my "think" questions use different language from the text?

   Do I use good signal words? (p. 258)

   Students are given lots of guided practice identifying important information, generating questions, and responding to the monitoring questions.

Other elaboration strategies include applying information that has been obtained from reading, creating analogies to explain it, and evaluating text (covered in Chapter 7). A general operating principle of elaboration is that the more readers do with or to text, the better they will understand and retain it.

MONITORING

Summarizing, inferring, creating images, predicting, and other strategies are valuable tools for enhancing comprehension. Knowing how to use them is not enough, however; it is also essential to know when and where to use them. For example, visualizing works best with materials that are concrete and lend themselves to being pictured in the imagination (Prawat, 1989). Predictions work best when the reader has a good background of knowledge about the topic. Knowing when and where to use these and other strategies is part of monitoring, which is also known as **metacognition,** or **metacognitive awareness.**

Metacognition, or **metacognitive awareness,** means being conscious of one's own mental processes.

Monitoring also means recognizing what one does and does not know, which is a valuable asset in reading. If a reader mouths the words of a passage without comprehending their meaning and does not recognize his or her lack of comprehension, the reader will not reread the passage or take other steps to understand it; the reader is not even aware that there is a problem. "Metacognitive awareness is the ability to reflect on one's own cognitive processes, to be aware of one's own activities while reading, solving problems, and so on" (Baker & Brown, 1984, p. 353). An abstract ability, metacognition develops gradually; some types of awareness may not be present until students are in their teens. For example, in one study both fourth- and eighth-graders were able to skim a passage, but it was not until eighth grade that the majority of students could describe how to skim (Kobasigawa, Ransom, & Holland, 1980, cited in Baker & Brown, 1984).

The four major aspects of metacognition in reading are knowing oneself as a learner, regulating, checking, and repairing (Baker & Brown, 1984; McNeil, 1987).

KNOWING ONESELF AS A LEARNER

The student is aware of what he or she knows and his or her reading abilities and is able to activate his or her prior knowledge in preparation for reading a selection:

> I know that Theodore Roosevelt was a president a long time ago. Was it during the late 1800s or early 1900s? I'm not sure. I remember reading a story about how he was weak as a child and had bad eyesight. I'll read about him in the encyclopedia. I'll try *World Book* instead of *Encyclopedia Britannica*. *Encyclopedia Britannica* is too hard, but I can handle *World Book*.

A strategic reader knows what to read and how to read and is able to put that knowledge to use when reading content area material.

REGULATING

Regulating is a metacognitive process in which the reader guides his or her own reading processes.

In **regulating,** the student knows what to read and how to read it and is able to put that knowledge to use. He or she surveys the material, gets a sense of organization, sets a purpose, and then chooses and implements an effective strategy:

> Wow! This is a long article about Roosevelt. But I don't have to read all of it. I just need information about his boyhood. These headings will tell me which section I should read. Here's one that says "Early Life." I'll read it to find out what his childhood was like. After I read it, I'll make notes on the important points.

CHECKING

Adapting instruction for poor readers

A major difference between good and poor readers lies in their monitoring skills. Poor readers are less likely to detect lapses in comprehension and, when they do detect them, are less able to repair them. When instructed, however, poor readers can and do learn to become effective monitors (Palinscar, Winn, David, Snyder, & Stevens, 1993).

The student is able to evaluate his or her performance. He or she is aware when comprehension suffers because an unknown term is interfering with meaning or an idea is confusing. Checking also involves noting whether the focus is on important, relevant information and engaging in self-questioning to determine whether goals are being achieved (Baker & Brown, 1984):

> The part about Roosevelt's ancestors isn't important. I'll skim over it. I wonder what *puny* and *asthma* mean. I've heard of asthma, but I don't know what it is. This is confusing, too. It says, "He studied under tutors." What does that mean? Let's see if I have all this straight. Roosevelt's family was wealthy. He was sickly, but then he worked out in the gym until he became strong. He liked studying nature and he was determined. I don't know about his early schooling, though, and I ought to know what *asthma* and *puny* mean.

REPAIRING

Repairing refers to taking steps to correct faulty comprehension.

In **repairing,** the student takes corrective action when comprehension falters. He or she is not only aware that there is a problem in understanding the text but does something about it:

> I'll look up *asthma, puny,* and *tutor* in the glossary. Okay, I see that *tutor* means "a private teacher." Oh, yeah, it's like when my brother Bill had trouble with math and Mom got him a private teacher. Did Roosevelt have trouble in school? Is that why he had tutors? I'm still confused about his early schooling. I think I'll ask the teacher about it.

Failure to comprehend might be caused by a problem at any level of reading (Collins & Smith, 1980):

- Words may be unknown or may be known but used in an unfamiliar way.
- Concepts are unknown.
- Sentences are ambiguous or contorted.
- Punctuation is misread.
- Words or phrases are given the wrong emphasis.
- Paragraph organization is difficult to follow.
- Pronouns and antecedent relationships are confused. Relationships among ideas are unclear.
- Relationships among paragraphs and sections are not established. The reader becomes lost in details. Key ideas are misinterpreted.
- The reader has inadequate prior knowledge, or a conflict exists between that knowledge and the text.

Repair strategies (Baker & Brown, 1984; Harris & Sipay, 1990) include the following:

- Rereading the sentence or paragraph may clear up a confusing point or provide context for a difficult word.
- Reading to the end of the page or section might provide clarification.
- Having failed to grasp the gist of a section, the student might reread the preceding section.
- If there are specific details that a student cannot remember, then she or he should skim back through the material to find them.
- The text may be difficult or require closer reading, so the student might have to slow down, adjusting his or her rate of reading.
- Consulting a map, diagram, photo, chart, or illustration might provide clarification of a puzzling passage.
- Using a glossary or dictionary will provide meaning for an unknown word.
- Consulting an encyclopedia or similar reference might clarify a confusing concept.

Figure 6.8 shows a series of questions that students might ask themselves if they encounter difficulties as they read. The questions provide prompts for the major repair strategies and should be posted in a prominent spot in the classroom.

Lookbacks. Students may not realize that they can look back at a text when they cannot recall a specific bit of information or do not understand a passage (Garner, Hare, Alexander, Haynes & Winograd, 1984). If students' overall comprehension of a passage is faulty, they will need to reread the entire passage. If, however, they have simply forgotten or misunderstood a detail, they may use the **lookback strategy,** skimming back over the text and locating the portion that contains the information they need.

A lookback strategy involves skimming back over a selection that has already been read in order to obtain information that was missed, forgotten, or misunderstood.

F I G U R E   6 . 8 | **Repair strategies**

What to Do When I Don't Understand

What is keeping me from understanding?

Should I read the sentence or paragraph again?

Will looking at maps, charts, photos, or drawings help?

Should I look up key words?

Should I keep on reading and see if my problem is cleared up?

Should I slow down?

Should I ask for help?

To present the strategy, the teacher should explain why it is needed: It is not possible to remember everything (Garner, Maccready, & Wagoner, 1984). Therefore, it is often necessary to go back over a story. The teacher should then model the strategy by showing what he or she does when unable to respond to a question. The teacher should demonstrate how he or she skims through an article to find pertinent information and then uses that information to answer a difficult question. Guided practice and application opportunities should be provided. When students are unable to respond to questions during class discussions or on study sheets or similar projects, remind them to use lookbacks. As they learn how to use lookbacks, students should discover when and where to use them. Lookbacks, for instance, are useful only when the information needed to answer the question is present in the text.

INSTRUCTION IN METACOGNITIVE STRATEGIES

For most students, metacognitive awareness develops automatically over time; however, instruction is also helpful (Anthony, Pearson, & Raphael, 1989). In fact, it should be a part of every reading strategy lesson.

During each part of the lesson, the teacher should make explicit the cognitive processes involved. In the early stages, for instance, the teacher might model how he or she recalls prior knowledge, sets a purpose, decides on a reading strategy, executes the strategy, monitors for meaning, organizes information, takes corrective action when necessary, and applies knowledge gained from reading. Later, the teacher should discuss these elements with students, asking them what they know about a topic, how they plan to read a selection, and what they might do if they do not understand what they are reading. The ultimate aim is to have metacognitive processes become automatic. In the past, teachers have not made their thinking processes explicit. The teaching of reading now follows the novice-expert or master craftsperson–apprentice model. The student learns from the teacher's modeling and guidance as she or he progresses from novice reader/writer to expert.

One way of reminding students of metacognitive strategies is to make a list of those that have been introduced and place them in a prominent spot in the classroom. A sample list of metacognitive strategies appears in Figure 6.9.

To reinforce the use of metacognition, ask process, as well as product, questions. Product questions get at the content of a story. You might ask who the main character is, what problem he had in the story, and how he felt. A process question attempts to uncover how a student arrived at an answer. After a student responds that the main character was angry, ask, "How do you know that?" Other process questions are "How did you figure out that word? How did you find the answer? What did you do when you realized that you had forgotten some main facts?"

Metacognitive awareness has to be built into virtually all reading instruction; "any attempt to comprehend must involve comprehension monitoring" (Baker & Brown, 1984, p. 385). This monitoring need not be on a conscious level. The skilled reader operates on automatic pilot until some sort of triggering event signals that comprehension is not taking place. At that point, the reader slows down, focuses on the problem, and decides how to deal with it (Baker & Brown, 1984).

FIGURE 6.9 | Some metacognitive strategies

Think Ahead

What is this selection about?

What do I already know about the topic?

What do I want to find out?

What is my goal?

How should I go about reading in order to meet my goal?

Think While Reading

What have I read about so far?

Do I understand it?

If not, what should I do?

What is the author saying, and what do I think about it?

Think Back

Have I learned what I wanted to learn?

How can I use what I read?

From Alvermann, Bridge, Schmidt, Searfoss, Winograd, Paris, Priestly, & Santeusanio, 1989, *Heath Reading,* Lexington MA: D. C. Heath, p. R8.

As might be expected, younger readers and poorer readers are less aware of the purpose of reading and the most effective reading strategies. They may see reading primarily as a decoding task and fail to search for meaning. They may not notice when the text fails to make sense (Bransford, Stein, Shelton, & Owings, 1981). In other words, they don't know when they don't know. Therefore, metacognitive skills have to be taught early. Children should be informed early in their schooling that the purpose of reading is to construct meaning and not just to sound out words. In addition to being taught how to use skills, students should be told why, where, and when to use skills so as to acquire cognitive command of them.

Students should monitor how effectively they apply new strategies, perhaps by using before-and-after comparisons. For instance, if they have learned to use predicting, they might note that it improves their comprehension and provides deeper involvement in reading. Students might also discuss ways in which they have made especially good use of the strategy; if they were involved in preparing for a test, they could show how their performance improved. Thus, metacognition becomes a motivating device, as students are more likely to use a strategy if

Since metacognition is a developmental process, young students are far less adept than older readers. However, research and experience suggest that developmentally appropriate instruction in metacognition is effective.

Fix-up strategies involve taking corrective action when comprehension is faulty.

Adapting instruction for poor readers

The research on metacognitive processes strongly suggests that poor readers find it especially difficult to monitor or repair their reading. One reason may be that they often read materials with difficult words and concepts that are far beyond their comprehension. Their time and energy are completely taken up with decoding problems. It is essential that all readers, but especially students reading below grade level, be given material that they can read with relative ease.

they are convinced of its value and have faith in their ability to employ it effectively (Schunk & Rice, 1987).

In addition to scheduling lessons devoted to teaching monitoring and **fix-up strategies,** be alert for opportunities to do on-the-spot teaching or reinforcement. When a student is reading orally and makes an error, do not correct her or him. Give the student the opportunity to monitor her or his own reading and apply a fix-up strategy. In fact, if the miscue makes sense in the sentence, you might ignore it. If it changes the meaning of the sentence and the student does not correct it, ask questions like these: "Did that sentence make sense? What might you do to read the sentence correctly?" If the student cannot make the correction after a reasonable effort, supply the correct word. However, it is important that students be given a chance to correct their errors. To develop monitoring and fix-up strategies, students need ample opportunity to apply them. They also need an environment in which they are encouraged to take risks and in which they are not afraid to make mistakes.

To promote monitoring and use of repair strategies during silent reading, review these strategies from time to time. During their silent reading, when it is not possible for students to get help with comprehension difficulties, have them make a note of problems they encounter. A sticky note might be put under the word or passage that poses a problem. As part of every postreading discussion, talk over any difficulties that students may have had while reading the text. Also make sure that the text is not too difficult for students. They will have difficulty monitoring for meaning if they are unable to construct a coherent mental model of the text (Paris, Wasik, & Turner, 1991).

PUTTING IT ALL TOGETHER: APPLYING STRATEGIES

RECIPROCAL TEACHING

Comprehension strategies present an embarrassment of riches: There are so many strategies available. Which ones should be chosen? How might those chosen be integrated into some sort of coordinated technique? Highly effective preparational and elaboration strategies have been combined with monitoring in an ingenious approach known as **reciprocal teaching.**

Reciprocal teaching is a form of cooperative learning in which students learn to use four key strategies in order to achieve improved comprehension. Culturally diverse students do especially well in cooperative learning situations.

As a form of cooperative learning and cognitive apprenticeship in which students gradually learn key comprehension strategies by imitating and working along with the teacher, reciprocal teaching introduces group discussion techniques created to improve understanding and retention of the main points of a selection. Reciprocal teaching also has built-in monitoring devices that enable students to check their understanding of what they are reading and to take steps to improve their comprehension if it is found wanting.

In a reciprocal teaching situation, the group reads a story and then discusses it. Members of the group take turns leading the discussion. They use four tried-and-true techniques for building comprehension and for monitoring for meaning—predicting, question generating, clarifying, and summarizing (Palincsar & Brown, 1986):

1. *Predicting.* Students predict what information a section of text will present based on what they read in a prior section. If they are just starting a selection, their prediction is based on illustrations, headings, or an introductory paragraph. They must activate their background knowledge to guess what the author is going to say next. Predicting makes them active readers and gives them a purpose for reading.

2. *Question generating.* Students must seek out the kinds of information in a text that provide a basis for well-formed questions. Not being able to formulate a question may be a sign that they have failed to understand the significant points in the text and so must reread or take other corrective action.

3. *Clarifying.* Students note words, concepts, expressions, or other items that hinder comprehension, and they ask for explanations during discussion.

4. *Summarizing.* The discussion leader, with or without the help of the group, retells the selection, highlighting the main points. This retelling reviews and integrates the information and is also a monitoring device. Inability to paraphrase is a sign that comprehension is poor and rereading is in order (Brown, 1985). Summarizing also becomes a springboard for making predictions about the content of the next section.

Using direct instruction, the teacher introduces reciprocal teaching over approximately a week's time but may take longer if necessary. Lesson 6.6 outlines the teacher's role in reciprocal teaching.

Lesson 6.6
Reciprocal teaching

Step 1. Introduce reciprocal teaching

Ask students if they have ever wanted to switch places with the teacher. Tell them that they will be using a new method to help them read with better understanding and that each student will have a chance to lead a discussion of a story that the class has read. Outline for the students the four parts of the method: predicting what will happen; making up questions; clarifying, or clearing up details that are hard to understand; and summarizing.

Step 2. Explain the four basic parts

(a) Explain that predicting helps readers think what a story might be about, and that it gives them a purpose for reading. Students will want to see if their predictions are correct, so they will read with greater interest and understanding. Model the process, and give students a chance to try it out.

(b) Explain to students that asking questions will help them read with better understanding. Model the process by reading a selection and constructing questions. Emphasize the need to ask questions about the important parts of the selection, and provide guided practice in constructing some questions.

(c) Explain what clarifying is. Tell students that it is important to notice words or ideas that make it hard to understand a selection. Explain that

Accustomed to teacher-constructed questions, some students may have difficulty composing questions of their own. Supply these students with model questions at first. As they begin to catch on to the process, provide prompts or partial questions until they are able to create questions on their own.

clarifying hard parts of a selection will help them get more meaning out of what they are reading. Have them locate which words, sentences, or ideas in a sample selection need clarifying. Explain that what is clear to one person may not be clear to another.

(d) Explain why summarizing is an important skill. Tell students that summarizing a paragraph helps them concentrate on important points while reading. Demonstrate creating a summary for a model paragraph. Explain that if students summarize, they will better understand what they read and remember it longer.

Depending on students' age, ability, and previous experience with the strategies, the teacher might introduce the strategies all at once, one a day, or even one a week. It is not expected that students will become proficient in their use or even fully understand them at this point. That will come when the strategies are applied in a reciprocal teaching lesson. At first, the teacher plays a major role in the application of reciprocal teaching, modeling the four strategies, making corrections, and providing guidance when necessary. Gradually, the students take more responsibility for leading discussions and applying the strategies.

The following is a sample reciprocal teaching lesson based on the reading of a selection about Daisy Low, the founder of the Girl Scouts of America.

(Lead-in question)

Carmen (student discussion leader): My question is, how did Daisy Low help people and animals?

Paula: She fed stray cats and dogs.

Frank: She got clothes for needy children.

(Clarification request)

Charles: I think we should clarify *needy*.

Ann: I think needy children need stuff, like clothes and maybe food.

Teacher: What would be another word for *needy*?

James: Poor. I think *poor* means the same thing as *needy*.

Teacher: Good answer. *Poor* and *needy* mean just about the same thing. I have another question. Why did Daisy put a blanket on the cow?

Paula: She was afraid it would get cold.

James: I think that should be clarified. Do cows get cold?

Teacher: Does anybody know? Did any of you ever live on a farm? How can we find out?

Paula: We could look in the encyclopedia.

John: My grandfather raised cows. He's visiting us. I could ask him.

Teacher: That's a great idea. You ask him and report back to us. Maybe your grandfather could come in and talk to the class about life on a farm. By the way, Carmen, do you feel that your question has been answered?

Carmen: I think the story tells about some more things that Daisy Low did to help people. Can anyone tell me what they were?

Ann: Yes, she started a children's group called Helping Hands.

Frank: And the first sentence says that she was the founder of the Girl Scouts in America.

Teacher: Those are good answers. Can you summarize this section of the story, Carmen?

(Summary)

Carmen: The paragraph tells how Daisy Low helped animals and children who were in need.

(Prediction)

Teacher: Good summary. What do you predict will happen next?

Carmen: I think the story will tell how Daisy Low started the Girl Scouts.

Teacher: Does anyone have a different prediction? Okay. Let's read the next section to see how our prediction works out. Who would like to be the leader for this section?

During the session, the teacher provides guidance where needed and also models the four strategies. Ultimately, students should be able to apply the comprehension and strategy lessons they have learned. Research suggests that this does happen: Students who were trained in the use of the strategies were apparently able to apply them to their social studies and science reading; their rankings in content area evaluations shot up from the twentieth to the fiftieth percentile (Brown, 1985).

Reciprocal teaching can be used with nonreaders, the major difference being that the teacher reads the selection to the students. The process can also be adapted to a peer-tutoring situation in which a good reader is trained in the strategies and works with a poor reader. In one such case, both tutor and tutee improved in comprehension after just twenty days of instruction (Palinscar & Brown, 1986).

An entire class can use the method if it is adapted in the following two ways. First, students use the headings to make two predictions about the content of the text they are about to read. Second, after reading a segment, they write two questions and a summary, as well as list any items that require clarification. The predictions, summaries, and clarification requests are discussed after the selection has been read. Even with these whole group adaptations, comprehension improved 20 percent after using the approach for just one month (Palinscar & Brown, 1986).

Some classroom teachers have adapted reciprocal teaching to fit their particular situations. In a study of a first-grade teacher, a special education teacher, and a high school teacher, all of whom had been using reciprocal teaching for at least a year, several modifications were noted (Marks, Pressley, Cooley, Craig, Gardner, DePinto, & Rose, 1993). In the first-grade class, students were divided into groups consisting of four pairs. Each pair took responsibility for one of the four strategies. The discussion of the story was aided by notes that the students brought with them. In the special education class, students also read the story and prepared responses before the discussion was held. The discussion leader used a laminated card with the four strategy questions printed on it. In the high school class, students gathered in small student-led groups to discuss the selection. The three teachers provided additional instruction in question construction because they felt too many low-level questions were being asked. In addition, the teachers sought to increase the engagement of students who were not student leaders. In

Reciprocal teaching is based on four highly regarded learning procedures: expert scaffolding, cooperative learning, guided learning, and Vygotsky's zone of proximal development.

traditional reciprocal teaching, students join in the discussion spontaneously. However, the teachers felt that there was more participation when students prepared questions, clarification requests, and summaries beforehand. And one teacher allowed all students, not just the leader, to ask questions. The teachers also reported that considerable time was needed before students were able to fully participate in reciprocal teaching. All three teachers enjoyed using reciprocal teaching and felt it to be a valuable technique.

LEARNING ENVIRONMENT

The comprehension strategies that students learn and their general concept of what it means to understand text are affected by the overall learning context. For instance, students who apply comprehension strategies to informational books and real-world materials construct a different sense of what reading is than do students whose comprehension instruction is associated with workbooks and skills sheets (Dole, Duffy, Roehler, and Pearson, 1991). Students who are taught comprehension through teacher- or text-generated questions associate comprehension with answering questions. On the other hand, students who are taught through a discussion approach, such as reciprocal teaching, see reading comprehension as the application of predicting, question generating, clarifying, and summarizing strategies. They might also see comprehension as a group activity (Dole, Duffy, Roehler, & Pearson, 1991).

To provide students with a broad-based understanding of comprehension, it is essential that you use a variety of techniques and materials, putting emphasis on the ways in which expert readers comprehend texts. You should also establish an environment conducive to learning and applying strategies, one that provides for both integration of strategies and good information processing.

INTEGRATION OF STRATEGIES

For the sake of clarity, the major comprehension strategies presented in this chapter have been discussed in isolation. However, it should be emphasized that reading is a holistic act. Often, several interacting strategies are being applied simultaneously. As Pressley, Borkowski, Forrest-Pressley, Gaskin, & Wile (1993) explained,

> Strategies are rarely used in isolation. Rather, they are integrated into higher-order sequences that accomplish complex cognitive goals. For example, good reading may begin with previewing, activation of prior knowledge about the topic of a to-be-read text, and self-questioning about what might be presented in the text. These prereading activities are then followed by careful reading, reviewing, and rereading as necessary. General strategies (e.g., self-testing) are used to monitor whether subgoals have been accomplished, prompting the reader to move on when it is appropriate to do so or motivating reprocessing when subgoals have not been met. That is, good strategy users evaluate whether the strategies they are using are producing progress toward goals they have set for themselves. (p. 9)

Learning to use a strategy is a long process. Although researchers may get positive results after twenty lessons on predicting or summarizing, it may actually take students many months to master a particular strategy (Pressley, 1994).

GOOD INFORMATION PROCESSING

Because many factors are involved in strategy use, Pressley et al. (1993) preferred to use the term *good information processing*, to include not only strategies but the conditions that foster their effective use. One such condition is background knowledge. If students have little background knowledge on a topic, activating prior knowledge will not be of much benefit. In addition, the more readers know about a topic, the better able they are to relate new information to their own background of information. With a well-developed framework of knowledge, they are also better able to determine what is important. If readers know very little about a topic, everything may seem important (Pressley, 1994). Motivation is also a key factor in good information processing. If students believe that the strategies they possess can help improve their performance, they are more inclined to use them. Another important factor is a cognitive style that enables students to put forth their best cognitive efforts. The students are then planful and aspire to improve; they are reflective, attentive, and not overly anxious (Pressley et al., 1990; 1993).

SUMMARY

1. One key to comprehension is prior knowledge. Comprehending involves activating a schema, which is an organized package or network of information, and creating meaning by filling in slots with specific instances or examples. Comprehension can also be viewed as a process of constructing mental models. While processing text, the reader continually reconstructs or updates the mental model. According to a third view of comprehension, propositional theory, the structure of text is an important component of comprehension.

2. Major types of comprehension strategies include preparational, organizational, elaboration, and monitoring. Preparational strategies are activities in which a reader engages just before reading a selection. They include activating prior knowledge, setting a purpose and goal for reading, predicting the content of the selection, and surveying. Organizational strategies involve selecting the most important details in a piece and constructing relationships among them. Key organizational strategies are determining the most important details and relating the details to main ideas and summarizing. Elaboration strategies involve constructing relationships between prior knowledge and knowledge obtained from print. This is done through inferring, evaluating, imaging, and question generating. Monitoring strategies include being aware of oneself as a learner and of the learning task, regulating and planning comprehension activities, monitoring one's comprehension, and repairing it when it is faulty.

3. Reciprocal teaching is a well-researched technique that integrates predicting, question generating, clarifying, and summarizing.

4. Strategies are best applied within the context of good information processing, which considers students' motivation, background knowledge, and other factors. Integrating strategies and establishing an environment conducive to learning also foster comprehension.

CLASSROOM APPLICATIONS

1. In order to more fully understand comprehension strategies, create a semantic map depicting the main strategies covered in this chapter and their major characteristics.

2. In your own reading, try out for at least a week one of the strategies that was introduced in this chapter. Note its effectiveness. Did you encounter any difficulties implementing it?

FIELD APPLICATIONS

1. Plan a direct instruction lesson for teaching one of the comprehension strategies. If possible, teach it and evaluate its effectiveness.
2. Obtain information about an older elementary school student's use of comprehension strategies. Ask the student what she or he does to prepare for reading. Then ask what the student does if she or he is reading a selection and discovers that she or he does not understand it.
3. Introduce the reciprocal teaching approach to a group of elementary students or try it out with a group of classmates. What seem to be its advantages and disadvantages?

Summarizing information seems to be most difficult pg 210-214.

c h a p t e r 7

Comprehension: Text Structures and Teaching Procedures

For each of the following statements related to the chapter you are about to read, put a check under "Agree" or "Disagree" to show how you feel. Discuss your responses with classmates before you read the chapter.

Agree

Disagree

1. The structure of a piece of writing influences its level of difficulty.

2. Talking about the structure of a story ruins the fun of reading it.

3. Questioning is an art rather than a science.

4. Slower students should be asked mainly lower-level questions.

5. Students should play the most important role in class discussions.

6. Structured reading lessons work best.

7. All students should be taught to read critically.

8. Students should be aware that some of their textbooks may be biased.

Using What You Know

The emphasis in Chapter 6 was on learners and the strategies they might use to construct meaning. Of course, strategies have to be integrated with text, which has an effect on the types of strategies that can be applied. This chapter emphasizes the role of text, both narrative and expository, in comprehension. A number of teaching procedures are explored, such as the use of questions and techniques for asking them, reading lessons, and the cloze procedure, which consists of supplying missing words. This chapter also includes a section on critical reading.

What information are you bringing to this material? What do you already know about text structure? How might that knowledge improve your comprehension? What kinds of questions might foster comprehension? How should questions be asked? Think back on lessons that were used to introduce reading selections when you were in elementary school. What procedures did the teacher use? What aspects of those procedures worked best? What is the cloze procedure? What are some techniques that students might use to read critically?

NATURE OF THE TEXT

A major component of the comprehension process is the nature of the text. A text has both content and organization. Students are prepared for the content when the teacher activates schema or builds background; however, they also have to interact with the structure. Therefore, they develop another schema for organizational patterns. Knowledge of structure provides a blueprint for constructing a mental model of a story or informational piece.

NARRATIVE TEXT AND STORY SCHEMA

Hearing the phrase "Once upon a time . . ." triggers an immediate expectation in both children and adults: They expect to hear a story, most likely a traditional tale that took place many years ago, in some far-off land. It will probably have a hero or heroine and some sort of evil character. A problem or conflict will most likely develop and be resolved, perhaps with the help of magic. The story might end with the phrase ". . . and they all lived happily ever after."

Having heard a variety of stories over a period of years, children as young as 4 develop a schema for them—that is, an internal representation or sense of story. This sense of story continues to grow, and students use it to guide them through a tale, remember the selection, and write stories of their own. They "use a sort of structural outline of the major story categories in their minds to make predictions and hypotheses about forthcoming information" (Fitzgerald, 1989, p. 19). To put it another way, the reader uses structure to construct a mental model of the story.

Various **story grammars,** or schemes, are available for analyzing a story into its parts. Although each may use different terminology, they all tend to concentrate on setting, characters, and plot. Plot is divided into the story problem and/or the main character's goal, the principal episodes, and the resolution of the problem. In most story grammars, characters are included in the setting; however, as *setting* is a literary word that has long been used to indicate only time and place, it is used in that sense in this book.

Different types of stories have different types of structures, and, as students progress through the grades, both stories and structures become more complex. Goals and motivations of major characters become more important. Settings may be exotic and include mood as well as time and place.

What can be done to build a sense of story? The most effective strategy is to read aloud to students from a variety of materials, from kindergarten right through high school. Most children gain a sense of story simply from this exposure, but it is also helpful to highlight major structural elements. This can be done by discussing the story's setting, characters, plot, and main problem. Story structure can be used to guide discussions through questions such as the following (Sadow, 1982):

When and where does the story take place?

Who are the characters?

What problem does the main character face?

What does the main character do about the problem? Or what happens to the main character as a result of the problem?

How is the problem resolved?

Students can also be asked other kinds of questions, including those on higher levels of thinking. However, they will be better prepared to answer higher-level questions when they have a firm grasp of the story. Discussions should also include an opportunity for students to construct personal responses. The structure is the skeleton of a story. The reader's response is the heart of the piece.

Another technique for reinforcing story structure is having students fill out generic guide sheets. Students reading significantly below grade level found that guide sheets and maps based on story structure helped them better understand the selections they read (Cunningham & Foster, 1978; Idol & Croll, 1985). In their review of the research, Davis and McPherson (1989) concluded that **story maps** are effective because they require students to read actively to complete the maps and also require self-monitoring. Generic guide sheets can be used to help students better understand works that they are reading independently and so would be of value in a program of individualized reading.

A generic story map based on McGee and Tompkins's (1981) simplified version of Thorndyke's (1977) story grammar is presented in Figure 7.1. As students meet increasingly complex stories, other elements can be added—for example, theme, conflict, and multiple episodes. Maps can be filled in by students working alone or in small groups, with each student having a different part to work on. They can also be used in the prereading portion of the lesson. The teacher might give students a partially completed map and ask them to finish it after reading.

A **story grammar** is a series of rules designed to show how the parts of a story are interrelated.

A **story map** provides an overview of a story: characters, setting, problem, plot, and ending.

FIGURE 7.1 | **A generic story map**

Setting   Where does the story take place?
                   When does the story take place?
                   _____
                   _____

Characters   Who are the main people in the story?
                   _____
                   _____

Problem   What problems does the main character face?
                   _____
                   _____

Goal   What is the main character's goal?
                   What is he or she trying to do?
                   _____
                   _____

Plot   What are the main things that happened in the story?
                   _____
                   _____

Outcome   How was the story problem resolved?
                   _____
                   _____

RETELLING

One of the best devices for developing both comprehension and awareness of **text structure** has been around since the dawn of speech but is seldom used in classrooms—**retelling**. It has proved to be effective in improving comprehension and providing a sense of text structure for average learners and learning-disabled students (Koskinen, Gambrell, Kapinus, & Heathington, 1988; Rose, Cundick, & Higbee, 1983); it also develops language skills. According to research by Morrow (1985), children who retell stories use syntactically more complex sentences, gain a greater sense of story structure, and evidence better comprehension than those who simply draw pictures of the stories that are read to them. Combining questions with retelling enhances the effectiveness of the technique. This was especially true in Morrow's study when the questions prompted students whose retelling was

Text structure is the way a piece of writing is organized: main idea/details, comparison/contrast, problem/solution, etc.

Retelling is the process of telling a story that one has read or heard. It is used to check comprehension or gain insight into a student's reading processes.

flagging or helped students elaborate. Kindergarten students who retold stories and answered questions did better than those who only retold stories or only answered questions. They also seemed to grow in confidence and were better at story-sequencing tasks. Koskinen, Gambrell, Kapinus, and Heathington (1988) suggested the direct teaching approach for presenting retelling outlined in Lesson 7.1.

Lesson 7.1
Retelling

Step 1. Introduction

Explain what retelling is and give an example. Discuss why it is a useful skill: We often tell stories to friends and family; retelling will help us do this better. It will also help us understand and remember stories better. Model a retelling.

Step 2. Explanation of technique for retelling

Stress that only the main elements will be retold. For fiction, this might include a narration of the story problem, the main plot episodes, resolution of the problem, and the ending. For nonfiction, it might include a statement of the main idea and details, a sequential presentation of a process, or perhaps a description. After explaining the process, again model a retelling, choosing a brief selection so that students will be better able to grasp the procedure.

Step 3. Guided practice

Lead students through a guided practice of brief selections. Use prompts, if necessary. For fiction, such prompts might include the following:

Where and when does the story take place?

Who are the main characters?

What action starts the story?

What is the story problem?

What happens next? or What does _____ do next?

How does the story end?

For nonfiction, prompts might include the following:

What is the main thing that the author is trying to tell you?

What details, facts, happenings, or examples are used to explain the main idea?

Step 4. Independent application

Students working in pairs read and retell passages. The listener should take an active role, asking questions about any details that are not clear, or requesting additional information. To keep the interchange positive, the listener might tell what she or he liked best about the piece that the listener's partner retold.

There are several steps that can be taken to enhance students' retellings. Before students read or listen to a story they will be asked to retell, tell them they

Bartlett (1932), a British psychologist, asked subjects to read and then retell an old Indian folk tale, which contained an unfamiliar structure. In the retelling, aspects of the tale were changed so that the reconstructed tale was more like a traditional English tale. Bartlett concluded that we tend to reinterpret tales in terms of our own experience.

A retelling has several advantages over the traditional question-answer discussion format: It is more holistic, it avoids the fragmentation of questions and answers about specific parts of a story, and it helps students assimilate the concept of story structure (Morrow, 1994).

Narrative structures are easier to understand because children typically acquire familiarity with narratives before coming to school, narrative structures are similar to oral language, and narratives incorporate one or several sequences of events. A sequence of events is an easier system to understand than main idea/details or other more abstract organizational systems (Grasser, Golding, & Long, 1991).

will be asked to retell it. If you will be focusing on a specific aspect of the retelling, inform them of this; if you will be focusing on plot and sequence, ask them to note the main things that happen in the story and then try to remember them in order (Morrow, 1994). Also, use props; puppets or feltboard figures are a visual reminder of main characters and also help shy children, who tend to forget themselves and assume the identities of the puppets. Other visual aids include drawing a series of pictures of the main episodes in the tale and using these as a way of structuring the story.

Students might also use a retelling storybook (Yopp & Yopp, 1992). In a retelling storybook, scenes from the tale are drawn, painted, or pasted and then assembled in a booklet. Characters are drawn on tagboard (file folders work fine) and cut out. The characters are then moved to the appropriate scene as the story is told. Characters may be attached to the booklet with ribbons or long strands of yarn.

To give students additional insight into the structure of a story, have them create their own stories by using wordless picture books, in which the story is told entirely through illustrations. After several sessions in which you tell a story based on a wordless picture book, invite students to create stories to go along with the pictures. Use prompting and probing questions to help them elaborate and clarify their ideas: "What kind of dog is that? What is the dog doing? How does the dog help out?" (Searfoss & Readence, 1994).

In time, retelling can be a learning strategy. Students can be encouraged to retell stories or informational selections in their heads to help them better understand and remember what they have read (Koskinen, Gambrell, Kapinus, & Heathington, 1988).

WRITING STORIES

Story structure can also be used as a framework for composing stories. Laura Pessah, a staff developer at P.S. 148 in New York City, introduced students to the fact that picture books have different patterns of development (Calkins & Harwayne, 1991). Students discovered that some are a series of snapshots; others are circular, as the ending returns to the beginning; still others embody contrasts. Studying these structures gave students ideas about how they might organize picture books they were creating. However, students should be encouraged to follow the dictates of their own imaginations. As Calkins and Harwayne noted, too strict an adherence to structure could limit individual visions. Fitzgerald (1989) cautioned, "Strict adherence to a particular story structure could have a detrimental effect, resulting in formulaic stories" (p. 20).

EXPOSITORY TEXT

Expository text is writing that is designed to explain or provide information.

Generally speaking, stories are easier to read than science articles, how-to features, and descriptions of historical events (Grasser, Golding, & Long, 1991). Children's schema for **expository text** develops later than that for narration. Expository text has a greater variety of organizational patterns, and, typically, young students have limited experience hearing and reading it. Narrative text is linear; there is generally an initiating event and a series of following episodes

Knowledge of narrative structure helps students compose stories; writing stories, in turn, helps develop greater awareness of story structure.

which lead to a climax or high point, a resolution of the story problem, and the ending. Because of its structure and linear quality, narrative text is generally more predictable than expository text. If children are presented with narrative text only, they tend to focus on linear thinking (Trussell-Cullen, 1994). A mix of narrative and expository text is needed to promote a full range of thinking and comprehension skills.

One key to improved comprehension of expository text is understanding the text's structure—that is, the way the author has organized her or his ideas. The author may develop an idea by listing a series of reasons, describing a location, supplying causes, or using some other technique. Often content dictates structure. In science texts, students expect to see both descriptive passages that tell, for example, what a nerve cell is or what an anteater looks like and explanatory paragraphs that tell how a nerve cell passes on impulses or how an anteater obtains food.

Knowledge of structure has a three-way payoff. It focuses attention on individual ideas, it provides a clearer view of the relationship among ideas, and it is a framework to aid retention of information (Slater & Graves, 1989). The reader can use text structure to organize information from the text.

TYPES OF EXPOSITORY TEXT STRUCTURE

Listed below are some of the most important types of text structure (Armbruster & Anderson, 1981; Meyer & Rice, 1984):

1. *Enumeration/description.* This type of structure is a listing of details about a subject without any cause/effect or time relationship among them. Included in this category are structures that describe, give examples, and define concepts. It uses no specific signal words except in pieces that provide examples, where *for example* and *for instance* may be used as signals.

Adapting instruction for ESL students

Students who are still learning English can transfer their ability to use text structure in their native language to English. However, two conditions are important for that transfer to take effect: Students must be proficient readers in their native language, and they must be fairly proficient in reading English (Hague, 1989). A lack of proficiency in English "short circuits" the transfer process.

2. *Time sequence.* This type of structure is similar to enumeration; however, time order is specified. Signal words include the following:

after	*first*	*and then*
today	*next*	*finally*
afterward	*second*	*earlier*
tomorrow	*then*	*dates*
before	*third*	*later*

3. *Explanation/process.* An explanation tells how something works, such as how coal is formed, how a diesel engine works, or how a bill becomes law. Sequence may be involved, but steps in a process rather than time order are stressed. An explanation structure may include some of the same signal words as those found in a time sequence structure.

4. *Comparison/contrast.* This type of structure presents differences and/or similarities. Signal words and terms include the following:

although	*similar*	*on the one hand*
but	*different*	*on the other hand*
however	*different from*	

5. *Problem/solution.* A statement of a problem is followed by a possible solution or series of solutions. Signal words are *problem* and *solution*.

6. *Cause/effect.* An effect is presented along with a single cause or a series of causes. Signal words and terms include the following:

because	*therefore*	*thus*
cause	*since*	*for this reason*
effect	*as a result*	*consequently*

Although cause/effect structure aids comprehension, elementary school students may be less familiar with it (Richgels, McGee, & Slaton, 1989).

Some kinds of text structure can facilitate comprehension and retention. Readers understand more and retain information better from text written in cause/effect or comparison/contrast patterns than they do when the text is written in an enumeration/description frame (Pearson & Camperell, 1994). These structures apparently provide readers with "additional schemata to help them understand and remember the information. . . . [A comparison/contrast structure] indicates that the information will be about opposing views. . . . Cause-effect structures indicate that the information will be about problems and solutions. . . . [Enumeration/description structures] are more loosely organized, however, and do not provide additional information" (p. 460). It is encouraging that students can be taught to recognize and use text patterns and comprehension improves as a result.

Roller (1990) concluded that a reader-friendly text structure is especially important when the content is moderately unfamiliar because the text helps the reader establish relationships among the ideas it contains.

When reading, students need to activate two kinds of schema: prior knowledge and text structure. The content of a text cannot be separated from the way that content is expressed. Teachers are "well advised to model for students how to figure out what the author's general framework or structure is and allow students to practice finding it on their own" (Pearson & Camperell, 1994, p. 463).

TEACHING EXPOSITORY TEXT STRUCTURE

One way to teach expository text structure is simply to have students read a variety of expository materials. This may include periodicals, trade books, content area textbooks, recipes, sets of directions, and other real-world materials. Teachers should also read expository prose aloud to students, beginning in kindergarten.

Before preparing students to read an expository piece, examine it for content and structure. Usually the two will go together. Purpose questions and discussion questions should also reflect both features. For example, a brief biography of Abraham Lincoln may highlight the main events of his life and use a time sequence structure. You might instruct students to note these events and their dates to help keep them in order.

Text patterns should be introduced one at a time. Start off with well-organized, single paragraphs that reflect the structure being taught. Signal words used in that structure should be presented. To provide practice in the recognition of signal words, use a cut-up paragraph or article and have students recreate the piece by using signal words and the sense of the piece as guides. For instance, students might use dates to help them rearrange a chronologically organized piece. Or they might use the signal words *first, second, next,* and *last* to arrange sentences or paragraphs explaining a step-by-step process.

Gradually work up to longer selections. Whole articles and chapters often use several text structures, and students should be aware of that. However, in many cases a particular structure dominates.

Using Graphic Organizers.

As a postreading activity, students might fill in a time line, as in Figure 7.2, to capitalize on both content and structure. Or they may use a graphic organizer, in which concepts are written in circles, rectangles, or triangles, and interrelationships are shown with lines and arrows. Generally, the more important ideas are shown at the top of the display and subordinate concepts are

To foster awareness of paragraph organization, divide a bulletin board into six segments, one for each type of paragraph organization. Encourage students to locate and bring in examples of different types of paragraphs. Before placing the sample on the board, read it aloud and have the class discuss in which category it should be placed. Students should note that some kinds of organization are more common than others and that writers may mix two or more patterns (Devine, 1986).

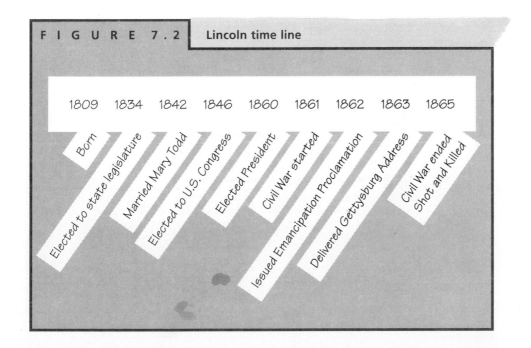

FIGURE 7.2 Lincoln time line

| 1809 | 1834 | 1842 | 1846 | 1860 | 1861 | 1862 | 1863 | 1865 |

Born
Elected to state legislature
Married Mary Todd
Elected to U.S. Congress
Elected President
Civil War started
Issued Emancipation Proclamation
Delivered Gettysburg Address
Civil War ended
Shot and Killed

shown at the bottom. The organizers can be constructed to reflect a variety of patterns (Sinatra, Stahl-Gemeke, & Berg, 1984; Sinatra, Stahl-Gemeke, & Morgan, 1986). After reading a selection, students complete an appropriate graphic organizer and, in so doing, organize the major concepts in a text and discover its underlying structural pattern. Graphic organizers for two major types of text structures, enumeration/description and time sequence, are presented in Figures 7.3 and 7.4.

Using Questions to Make Connections. Identifying the structure of a text is only a first step. The reader must then make two kinds of connections: internal (how ideas in text are related to each other) and external (how text ideas are related to the reader's background) (Muth, 1987). The right kinds of questions can help students detect relationships among ideas in a text. For instance, if the text has a cause/effect relationship, you can ask questions that highlight that relationship. Your questions can seek out causes or effects. Questions can also help the students relate ideas in the text to their own backgrounds. Here are some questions (adapted from Muth, 1987) that might be asked to help students who have read a piece about the process of rusting make internal connections:

What causes rusting?

What are some effects of rusting?

Under what conditions does rusting take place fastest? Why?

These questions focus on external connections:

What kinds of things rust in your house? Why?

In what areas of the house do things rust? Why?

What can be done to prevent rusting? Why would these preventive steps work?

Note that all these questions require students to establish internal or external cause/effect relationships. Questions can also be posed that facilitate establishing

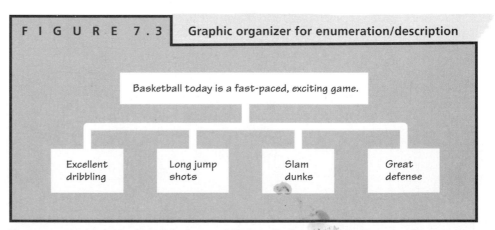

FIGURE 7.3 | **Graphic organizer for enumeration/description**

Basketball today is a fast-paced, exciting game.

| Excellent dribbling | Long jump shots | Slam dunks | Great defense |

Text summarized from *Basketball for Boys and Girls,* by B. Gutman, 1990, Freeport, NY: Gary Castle Press.

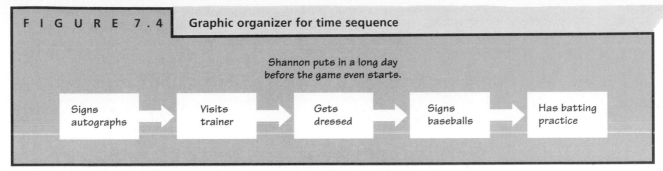

F I G U R E   7 . 4   Graphic organizer for time sequence

Shannon puts in a long day
before the game even starts.

| Signs autographs | → | Visits trainer | → | Gets dressed | → | Signs baseballs | → | Has batting practice |

Text summarized from "Game Day," by G. Rolfer, 1990, *Sports Illustrated for Kids, 2*(8), p. 25.

relationships in comparison/contrast, problem/solution, or other kinds of patterns. Once students have grasped the concept, have them create their own connection questions.

Writing for Organization.   Another way to teach expository text structure is to encourage students to compose pieces that employ comparison/contrast and other types of structures. After reading a text that has an explanation/process structure, students might write an explanation of a process they find intriguing. Over time, they should have the opportunity to practice with all the major types of structures.

Students might also use photos or drawings to help them grasp a selection's organizational pattern. For time sequence, they might arrange photos of a vacation trip they have taken with their family. For explanation/process, they might create a series of drawings showing how to plant tomato seeds. They might use a series of

There are various ways of helping students incorporate structure in their writing. You might use frames in which students fill in the blanks with details or planning sheets that lead students step by step through the writing of a well-organized piece. Both are covered in detail in Chapter 11.

One way of teaching expository text structure is by having students use a variety of structures in their writing.

photos to compare or contrast two vehicles, two countries, or two animals. After arranging the graphics, students can add a title, headings, and captions.

THE ROLE OF QUESTIONS IN COMPREHENSION

When asked inferential questions during the reading of a story, third-graders generated inferences and included this information in a later retelling. The inferences they generated became a part of their memory for the story (Sundbye, 1987). Through questioning, they had constructed an elaborated version of the tale.

Questions play a central role in facilitating comprehension. They can be used to develop concepts, build background, clarify reasoning processes, and even lead students to higher levels of thinking. In one study, second-graders became more adept at making inferences simply by being asked inferential questions (Hansen & Pearson, 1980).

Questions foster understanding and retention. When questions are asked about information in text, that information is remembered longer. Asking higher-level questions is especially helpful. Questioning that demands integrating information in a text "will promote deeper processing, and therefore more learning and better remembering than questions that require recall of specific facts only" (Sundbye, 1987, p. 85). As Wixson (1983) put it, "What you ask about is what children learn" (p. 287). If you ask questions about trivial facts, then those facts are what children will focus on and remember. The questions we ask shape students' comprehension and also their concept of what is important in a text.

Wixson (1983) suggests that when asking questions, it is important to consider the interaction between the reader and the text. In an experiment with fifth-graders, Wixson asked the three kinds of questions noted by Raphael in her QAR framework, as described in Chapter 6: textually explicit (answer is directly stated in the text), textually implicit (answer is implied in the text), and schema-implicit (answer must come from the reader's schema). The different types of questions had a dramatic effect on students' comprehension. Asking textually explicit questions resulted in verbatim recall of text. Responding to textually implicit queries fostered the creation of text-based inferences. Schema-implicit questions promoted the production of inferences based on the reader's prior knowledge. Wixson made the following recommendations for use of questions: When students are reading texts such as recipes or directions that require literal comprehension, stress textually explicit questions. When you want students to integrate information within a text or see connections, as when drawing conclusions about a main character, ask textually implicit questions. When you want students to integrate text information with their background knowledge, as when applying information about the causes of pollution to their own lives, ask schema-implicit questions.

PLANNING QUESTIONS

Because of their importance, questions need to be planned carefully. They should be used to establish the main elements in a story or the main concepts in a nonfiction selection (Beck, Omanson, & McKeown, 1982). Poor readers benefit from questions that elicit the basic elements in a selection (Medley, 1977). Once the basic plot of a story or the main facts in an article are established, students can be led into a deeper understanding of the material. It is important to ask questions that help children see relationships among ideas, relate new information to their background of experience, and modify their schema. Students must have opportunities to respond in a personal way to literary pieces—to judge the material and apply the information they gather to their own lives.

PLACEMENT OF QUESTIONS

The placement of questions has an impact upon their effect. Questions posed before a text is read have a different impact from that of questions asked during the reading of a text or after a text has been read. Questions asked before reading help readers activate schema and set a purpose (Harris & Sipay, 1990). They guide readers into the text and tell them what information to seek. Questions that are asked after reading help readers organize and summarize the text. Questions asked during reading help readers process text. During-reading questions are especially prevalent in the primary grades. Teachers may stop the reading of a selection halfway through or even at the end of each page and pose questions. Such questioning can clarify any confusing elements in text just read and prepare students to read the upcoming segment.

TYPES OF QUESTIONS

One way of looking at questions is to examine the kinds of thinking processes involved in asking and answering them. An arrangement of skills from least demanding to those that require the highest mental powers is known as a **taxonomy**.

A **taxonomy** is a classification of objectives, types of questions, or other items.

Table 7.1 presents a taxonomy of comprehension tasks based on the work of Bloom (1957). Although it has been around for some time, it is still apparently the

TABLE 7.1 Taxonomy of comprehension tasks

Knowledge	Recognizing and recalling vocabulary and details on a literal level.
Comprehension	Being able to put answers in one's own words or in a nonverbal form. Includes seeing relationships among ideas; inferring consequences, effects, main ideas, summarizing, and generalizing; and making predictions based on information.
Application	Applying theories or ideas to a new circumstance or event.
Analysis	Analyzing information so as to note relevant details, identify conclusions and supporting details, detect assumptions, and discriminate between a fact and an opinion. Basically involves the ability to read critically.
Synthesis	Putting information together in a new way. Composing a story, poem, plan, or essay. Inventing a creative solution to a problem.
Evaluation	Using a set of standards to make a judgment about a piece of writing, work of art, plan, and so on. Could involve detecting illogical reasoning, noting inconsistencies, or applying external standards to the judgment. Because evaluation requires a set of standards, it is not simply giving an opinion.

One of the simplest taxonomies describes comprehension in terms of the reader's interaction with the text: literal, interpretive, and applied. Literal comprehension entails understanding the basic meaning of the text. Interpretive comprehension entails making inferences by putting together several pieces of information. In applied comprehension, the reader synthesizes ideas from multiple sources or makes use of ideas found in the text.

most widely used such listing. The first two levels, Knowledge and Comprehension, mainly involve the comprehension strategies of selecting and organizing. The four higher levels—Application, Analysis, Synthesis, and Evaluation—are primarily elaborative comprehension strategies.

Taxonomies are approximate indicators of the relative positions questions occupy on a scale of complexity, but some may overlap. Undoubtedly, some knowledge questions are more difficult than some analysis questions. Being asked to recall a complex set of details would be more difficult than drawing a simple inference, for example. Still, taxonomies are useful for looking at questions. Discussion and test questions should be examined to make sure that higher as well as lower levels of thinking are being tapped. Taxonomic descriptions can help clarify the levels of questions being asked. For example, some questions that might be labeled evaluative simply ask the student to supply an unsupported opinion. By checking the description in a taxonomy, one can readily see that many of the what-do-you-think questions frequently seen in school textbooks are not on the evaluative level.

NUMBER OF QUESTIONS

Although questions are important in developing comprehension and thinking skills, research suggests that teachers ask too many of them. In one study, forty-two questions were asked in a half-hour (Susskind, 1969). In a more recent study, second-grade teachers asked an average of twenty-seven questions during a reading lesson (Weber & Shake, 1988). These large numbers suggest that teachers concentrate on lower-level skills. Answering thought-provoking questions would have taken the students more time. Concentrate on quality rather than quantity. Ask fewer questions, making sure that several of them require higher-level thinking and extended responses.

Discussions should be considered opportunities to expand students' background and enhance their verbal and thinking skills. All too often, however, discussions become oral quizzes with a focus on correct answers, when emphasis should be on helping the child. If a student is unable to provide an answer, it may be the fault of the question—rephrase it, or ask an easier one (Pearson & Johnson, 1978). Some students, because of shyness or because they come from an environment that does not prepare them for the types of questions asked in school, have difficulty answering higher-level questions (Heath, 1991). They may know the answers but must be prompted to help shape their responses.

USING WAIT TIME

Wait time is a period of silence between asking a question and repeating or rephrasing the question, calling on another student, or making some sort of comment.

One way of extending responses is to make use of **wait time.** Often teachers expect an immediate answer and, when none is forthcoming, call on another student. Waiting five seconds results in longer, more elaborative responses, higher-level thought processes, and fewer no-responses and I-don't-knows. Teachers who use wait time become more proficient at helping students clarify and expand their responses (Dillon, 1983; Gambrell, 1980). It would be difficult to find a better instructional use of five seconds of silence.

Silence after an answer is given also helps. Used to rapid-fire responding, teachers tend to call on another pupil the second the respondent stops talking. Often, however, students have more to say if given a few moments to catch their mental breath. Dillon (1983) suggested waiting from three to five seconds when a student pauses, seems to be unable to continue, or seems to be finished speaking. Often the student will resume talking and may even supply the most thoughtful part of the response at that point. Such postresponse wait time must be a genuine grace period. Maintain eye contact and do not turn away. Failing to maintain eye contact and turning away are cues that your attention is being diverted and will shut down any additional response that the student is about to make (Christenbury & Kelly, 1983).

Although highly useful and effective, wait time requires practice and patience; you will have to make a conscious effort to implement it. Try counting to five thousand by thousands after asking a question or after a student has halted an initial response. You might ask a colleague to evaluate your beginning attempts so that you are aware of how you are doing. Arrange for that person to review your performance periodically so that you do not slip back into bad habits.

CLASSROOM ATMOSPHERE

Even more important than using wait time or asking thought-provoking questions is establishing the right classroom atmosphere. The spirit of inquiry and exploration should be obvious. The teacher must be warm and accepting, so students will feel free to speculate, go out on an intellectual limb, or take an unpopular stand without being criticized. Criticism by teachers or classmates actually leads to lowered performance. Less emphasis should be placed on the rightness or wrongness of an answer and more on the reasons supporting the response.

Questions should be democratic, with everyone's contribution valued. That means calling on slower students as often as brighter ones, and giving introverts as much opportunity to respond as extroverts. Ironically, research suggests that not only are bright students asked more questions than slow students, but they are also given more prompts (Brophy & Good, 1970). All too often, the teacher calls on another student as soon as a slower learner begins to falter. Thus, the ones who would profit the most from prompting receive the least.

TECHNIQUES FOR ASKING QUESTIONS

FELS

A useful, research-based technique for using questions to evoke higher-level thinking processes was devised by Taba (1965). Known by the acronym FELS, it consists of asking questions that are *f*ocusing, *e*xtending, *l*ifting, and *s*ubstantiating.

Focusing questions, as the name implies, direct the student's attention to a particular topic—for example, the peculiar behavior of Sam, a character in a story. The teacher asks literal questions designed to help students describe that behavior.

Extending questions are designed to elicit clarification and elaboration. By extending the student's thoughts on the same level, they might seek additional information about a character or event and clear up points of confusion. Extending

Teacher's guides may include an excessive number of questions; ask only the most relevant ones. Note the major concepts or ideas that you want students to take away from their reading and then restrict your questions to the ones that lead to those learnings.

Middle-class adults conversing with their children often ask questions that focus the children's "attention on labels, require that they learn to say what they mean, and insist on the recounting of shared and known knowledge in prescribed ways" (Heath, 1991, p. 19). In some other cultures, language takes on a more functional role. Children learn labels in the context of their daily lives and not through questions or discussions initiated by adults. Questions from adults are frequently of the yes-no variety and not of the type that encourages the children to organize and express knowledge. Teachers need to be aware of these culturally determined experiences in order to plan accordingly. Some students may need additional guidance in asking questions and elaborating responses.

Hyman (1978) described the plateaus approach, a technique similar to FELS. The questioner asks at least three questions on one level of cognition (establishing a plateau) before asking a higher-level question (moving to a higher plateau). For example, after students have read *Dinosaur Time* (Parish, 1974), ask the following questions: "What are the names of some of the dinosaurs that you read about? What did the dinosaurs eat? How big were they? In what ways were brontosaurus and brachiosaurus alike?" The first three literal questions prepare the student for the fourth question, which involves putting together several pieces of information.

Searfoss and Readence (1994) caution against asking questions that are too diffuse. A question such as "What is the main idea of the selection?" is so general that it fails to provide the kind of structure that helps prompt a response. Rather than asking a single general question, ask several specific questions that provide better support.

is important because it prepares students for the next step and also provides slower students with an opportunity to become involved.

Lifting is the crucial stage. Through questioning or other means, the teacher lifts the discussion to a higher level. Through focusing and extending, the teacher has established that Sam refused to go into the reptile house on the class trip to the zoo, would not get out of the car when the family stopped for a picnic in the woods, and has not visited his friend Joe since Joe obtained a pet snake. The teacher asks, "What do all these actions tell us about Sam?" Now, instead of just giving factual responses, students are asked to draw the conclusion that Sam is afraid of snakes.

Substantiating questions ask students what evidence they found or what standards or criteria they used to draw a conclusion, make a judgment, or prove a point—for example, the evidence that Sam is afraid of snakes.

The following example shows how FELS might be used to build higher-level comprehension. The questions are based on a selection about Andrea, a knowledgeable backpacker who is trekking through the forest.

Focusing

Teacher: Where was Andrea?

Student: Forest.

Teacher: What did she watch out for?

Student: Snakes.

Teacher: What was she wearing?

Student: Shirt and jeans.

Extending

Teacher: What else did she watch out for besides snakes?

Student: I don't know.

Teacher: Let's look back over the story.

Student: Oh, I see. She was watching out for poison ivy.

Teacher: What kind of shirt was she wearing?

Student: Old.

Teacher: What kind of sleeves did it have?

Student: Long.

Lifting

Teacher: We usually judge people by their actions. Think over Andrea's actions. What do they tell us about her? What kind of person does she seem to be?

Student: Careful.

Substantiating

Teacher: Which actions led you to believe that Andrea is careful?

Student: She watched out for snakes and poison ivy. She wore a shirt with long sleeves so she wouldn't get poison ivy or insect bites.

Taba (1965) cautioned that FELS should be used with care. Frequent shifting from level to level may produce lack of sustained achievement at any level and result in a return to a more basic level. It is also important for teachers to encourage students to reason out and substantiate their answers. If teachers do the students' thinking for them, the strategy is ineffective. Timing and pacing are also important. The teacher has to know, for example, when to proceed to a higher level. Moving to lifting before building a solid understanding of the selection through focusing and extending hinders students' progress. It is also important that the FELS procedure be individualized, as some students require more time on a level than others (Taba, 1965).

REQUEST

One of the simplest and most effective devices for getting children to create questions is **ReQuest,** or reciprocal questioning (Manzo, 1969; Manzo & Manzo, 1993). Although originally designed for one-on-one instruction of remedial pupils, ReQuest has been adapted for use with groups of students and whole classes. In ReQuest, the teacher and students take turns asking questions. ReQuest can be implemented by following the steps outlined in Lesson 7.2.

ReQuest is a procedure in which the teacher and student(s) take turns asking and answering questions.

Lesson 7.2
ReQuest procedure

Step 1. Choose a text that is on the students' level but is fairly dense so that it is possible to ask a number of questions about it.

Step 2. Explain the ReQuest procedure to students. Tell them that they will be using a teaching technique that will help them better understand what they read. Explain that in ReQuest they get a chance to be the teacher because they and you take turns asking questions.

Step 3. Survey the text. Read the title, examine any illustrations that are part of the introduction, and discuss what the selection might be about.

Step 4. Direct students to read the first significant segment of text. This could be the first sentence or the first paragraph but should not be any longer than a paragraph. Explain that as they read, they are to think up questions to ask you. Students can make up as many questions as they wish. Tell them to ask the kinds of questions that a teacher might ask (Manzo & Manzo, 1993). Read the segment with the students.

Step 5. Students ask their questions. The teacher's book is placed face down. However, students may refer to their texts. If necessary, questions are restated or clarified. Answers can be checked by referring back to the text.

Step 6. After student questions have been asked, ask your questions. You might model higher-level questioning by asking for responses that require integrating several details in the text. If difficult concepts or vocabulary words are encountered, they should be discussed.

Step 7. The questioning proceeds until enough information has been gathered to set a purpose for reading the remainder of the text. This could be in the form of a prediction: "What do you think the rest of the article will be about?" Manzo and Manzo (1993) recommended that the questioning be concluded as soon as a logical purpose can be set but no longer than ten minutes after beginning.

Step 8. After the rest of the selection has been read silently, the purpose question and any related questions are discussed.

Students enjoy reversing roles and asking questions. Initially, they may ask lower-level questions but with coaching and modeling will soon ask higher-level ones. ReQuest is especially effective with lower-achieving readers.

RESPONSIVE ELABORATION

Responsive elaboration is a process in which a teacher uses an on-the-spot analysis of the student's reasoning to help guide the student to modify a response.

Despite a carefully constructed questioning procedure like FELS or ReQuest, students' thought processes sometimes go astray. They may have misinterpreted instructions or may be misapplying a strategy. A procedure that works well in these instances is **responsive elaboration** (Duffy & Roehler, 1987). Responsive elaboration is not an introduction to or a new explanation of a strategy or skill, but an elaboration. It is responsive because it is based on students' answers, using them as guides to students' thought processes.

To use responsive elaboration, teachers listen to answers to determine how students arrived at those responses. Instead of asking, "Is this answer right or wrong?" they ask, "What thought processes led the student to this response?" And, if the answer is wrong, "How can those thought processes be redirected?" Instead of calling on another student, telling where the answer might be found, or giving obvious hints, teachers ask questions or make statements that help put students' thinking back on the right track. The key to using responsive elaboration is asking yourself two questions: "What has gone wrong with the student's thinking?" and "What can I ask or state that would guide the student's thinking to the right thought processes and correct answer?"

The following is a scripted example of how a teacher might use responsive elaboration with a student who has inferred a main idea that is too narrow in scope:

Student (giving incorrect main idea): Getting new words from Indians.

Teacher: Well, let's test it. Is the first sentence talking about new words from the Indians?

Student: Yes.

Teacher: Is the next?

Student: Yes.

Teacher: How about the next?

Student: No.

Teacher: No. It says that Indians also learned new words from the settlers, right? Can you fit that into your main idea?

Student: The Indians taught the settlers words and the settlers taught the Indians words.

Teacher: Good. You see, you have to think about all the ideas in the paragraph to decide on the main idea. (Duffy & Roehler, 1987, p. 517)

WHY QUESTIONS

Simply asking "Why?" can significantly increase retention of information (Menke & Pressley, 1994). One group of students in grades 4 through 8 were given paragraphs about animals and told to study the information in the paragraph. A second group were given the same paragraphs but were instructed to ask why after each piece of information. For instance, after reading that grey seals sleep in shallow water, the students in the second group asked, "Why do grey seals sleep in shallow water?" Although both groups spent the same amount of time with the paragraphs, the group that asked why remembered significantly more. Overall, asking why questions increased retention about as much as creating mental images of the paragraph—picturing a grey seal sleeping in shallow water, for instance.

FRAMEWORKS FOR FOSTERING COMPREHENSION

Asking the right kinds of questions, building background, activating schema, learning to use strategies, and monitoring one's cognitive processes are all essential elements in fostering comprehension. Systematic but unified approaches that incorporate all these elements are required so that building background and vocabulary and prereading and postreading questions are all related to the selection's major concepts and the students' needs. Two such frameworks are the directed reading activity and the directed reading–thinking activity.

DIRECTED READING ACTIVITY

The **directed reading activity (DRA)** is probably the most widely used and the most highly respected instructional procedure used in reading. A flexible procedure, the DRA is the basis for a number of teaching techniques, including the directed reading–thinking activity and the instructional framework. The DRA is also the foundation for the informal reading inventory, the most widely used and most thoroughly documented diagnostic/evaluative instrument. The traditional DRA has five steps: preparation or readiness, silent reading, discussion and skill development, rereading, and follow-up. Today's DRA also incorporates schema theory, metacognition, and text analysis (Adoption Guidelines Project, 1990b). Although the steps are the same, their implementation has been revised.

Directed reading activity is a traditional five-step lesson plan, designed to assist students in the reading of a selection.

STEPS IN A DIRECTED READING ACTIVITY

An updated DRA proceeds as follows.

Preparation.   Through discussion, demonstration, use of audiovisual aids, and/or simulations, students are given guidance in the following areas:

- *Experiential background/concepts.* Experiential gaps that impede understanding of the selection's major concepts are filled in. If students are about to read a piece about solar power but have no experience with the subject, the teacher might demonstrate the workings of a solar calculator. Concepts or ideas crucial to understanding the selection are also developed. *Batteries* would be an important concept in this instance; however, in the discussion students might indicate that they know that batteries are necessary to make certain devices run, but they do not know why. The battery's use as a device for storing energy would then be discussed.

- *Critical vocabulary.* Vocabulary necessary for understanding the selection is presented. For a factual article about Australia's animals, the words *kangaroos, marsupials,* and *carnivores* are presented. Care is taken to show how these words are related to each other.

- *Reading strategies.* Students have to know how a selection is to be read. Most selections require a mix of preparational, organizational, and elaboration strategies. However, some strategies work better than others with certain kinds of materials. An editorial, for example, requires evaluation. A fictional story might require students to visualize the setting. At times, the format might be unfamiliar. For example, before tackling a play, students should be given tips on techniques for reading stage directions and dialogue.

- *Purpose for reading.* Whether set by the teacher or the class, the purpose for reading usually embraces the overall significance of the selection. It may grow out of the preparatory discussion. Students discussing hearing-ear dogs might want to find out how they are chosen, and that would become the purpose for reading. On other occasions, the teacher might set the reading purpose.

- *Interest.* Last but not least, the teacher tries to create interest in the selection. To do this in a piece about an explorer lost in a jungle, the teacher might read the portion of the selection that describes the dangers the explorer faced.

For the purpose of clarity, the elements in the preparation step have been described separately, but in actual practice they are merged. For instance, background concepts and the vocabulary used to label them are presented at the same time. The purpose for reading flows from the overall discussion, and throughout the discussion, the teacher tries to create an interest in the selection. Reading strategies might become a part of the purpose: "Read the story straight through, but read it carefully, to find out how the Great Brain solved the mystery" (reading purpose); "Look for clues as you read the story and try to figure out what they mean" (reading strategy).

Silent Reading.   The first reading is usually silent. Reading is a meaning-gaining process rather than a speech activity. What a student understands is more important than how the selection's words are pronounced. During the silent reading, the teacher should be alert to any problems that students might be having. If the class is listless, the piece may be too difficult or too boring. If it is humorous and no one is chuckling, perhaps the humor is too sophisticated or too childish. Finger pointing and lip movement are signs that individuals are having difficulty with the selection. The teacher should also be available to give assistance as needed, making note of who requested help and what kinds of help were supplied. Those students can then be scheduled for added instruction or practice in those areas. Reading speed should also be noted. Very fast reading with good comprehension might be a sign that materials are too easy. Very slow reading might be a sign that they are too difficult.

During the silent reading, students should monitor their comprehension to check whether they adequately understand what they are reading and, if necessary, take appropriate steps to correct the difficulties. The teacher should note these monitoring and repair strategies. In some classrooms, steps for attacking unfamiliar words or repairing comprehension failure are posted in prominent spots.

Discussion.   The discussion complements the purpose for reading. Students read a selection for a specific purpose; the discussion begins with the purpose question. If the students read about how hearing-ear dogs are trained, the purpose question is "How are hearing-ear dogs trained?" During the discussion, concepts are clarified and expanded, background is built, and relationships between known and unknown, new and old are reinforced.

Difficulties applying comprehension and word-attack strategies are corrected spontaneously, if possible. The teacher also evaluates students' performance, noting whether they were able to consider evidence carefully and make deductive conclusions and noting weaknesses in concepts, comprehension, word attack, and application. Any difficulties noted provide direction not only for immediate help for those that can be resolved on the spot, but also for future lessons for those that require more work. Although the discussion is partly evaluative, it should not be regarded as an oral quiz. Its main purpose is to build understanding, not test it.

Rereading.   In most lessons, rereading blends in naturally with the discussion. It may be done to correct misinformation, to obtain additional data, to enhance appreciation or deepen understanding, and to give students opportunities for purposeful oral reading. During the discussion of hearing-ear dogs, students might indicate that they believe the dogs are easy to train (a mistaken notion). Students can then be directed to locate and read aloud passages that describe how long training takes. If students disagree as to what main character traits such dogs should possess, they can be asked to locate and read orally passages that support their assertions.

On occasion, rereading may be an entirely separate step. For instance, students might dramatize a story that has a substantial amount of dialogue or reread a selection to gain a deeper appreciation of the author's style. A separate reading is generally undertaken for a new purpose, although it may be for a purpose that grows out of the discussion. Rereading is not a necessary step. Some selections are not worth reading a second time, or students might grasp the essence in the first reading.

In the rereading stage, oral reading should not be overemphasized. Unless a selection is being dramatized, it is generally a poor practice to have students reread an entire selection orally. Oral rereading should be for specific purposes: to clarify a point, to listen to a humorous passage or enjoy an especially vivid description, and to substantiate a conclusion or an answer to a question.

Follow-up.   Follow-up activities offer excellent opportunities to work on comprehension or word-attack weaknesses evidenced during the discussion phase, to provide additional practice, to extend concepts introduced in the selection, or to apply skills and strategies. These activities may involve any or all of the language arts or creative arts. Students might read a selection on the same topic or by the same author, draw illustrations for the selection, hold a panel discussion on a controversial idea, create an advertisement for the text, or write a letter to the author. The possibilities are virtually limitless, but the follow-up should grow out of the selection and should encompass worthwhile language or creative arts activities. As with rereading, it is not necessary to have follow-up or extension activities for every reading.

PREPARING A DIRECTED READING ACTIVITY

Creating a DRA starts with an analysis of the selection to be read. After reading the selection, the teacher decides what she or he wants the students to learn from it. Content analysis of fiction may result in statements about plot, theme, character, setting, or author's style. For nonfiction, the statements concern the main principles, ideas, concepts, rules, or whatever the children are expected to learn.

After analyzing the selection, the teacher chooses three to five ideas or story elements that she or he feels are most important. The piece may be saturated with important concepts; however, more than three to five cannot be handled in any depth at one time and could diffuse the focus of the activity. Even if an accompanying teacher's guide lists important concepts or provides key story events, the teacher should still complete a content analysis. That way, the teacher, not the textbook author, decides what is important for the class to learn. For example, for a piece entitled "Dream Cars for the 2000s," the teacher composes the following major learnings. These will provide the focus for prereading and postreading activities and strategies for prereading, during reading, and postreading.

The T-2008 will be easier to care for, repair, and guide.

The T-2008 will be safer and more flexible.

The Express will be faster.

After selecting these major ideas, the teacher lists vocabulary necessary to understand them. If the list contains a dozen terms, the teacher knows that is too many to attempt to cover. As a rule of thumb, no more than seven or eight vocabulary words should be chosen, and five or six would probably be more effective. Seven is said to be the largest number of distinct items that the average person can hold in short-term memory or working memory (Atkinson, Atkinson, Smith, & Hilgard, 1987). An excessive number of difficult words may be a sign that the selection is too difficult.

The teacher selects the words that will be difficult for the students. From the list of difficult words, those most essential to an understanding of the selection are chosen. For example, the following words are chosen as most essential to understanding the three learnings listed for the dream cars selection, and as being ones that students are likely to find difficult: *turbine engine, protective devices, sensors, communicate,* and *satellites.* Examining these words gives the teacher a sense of what prior knowledge or schema the passage requires. A mental assessment of the students helps the teacher decide if additional background has to be built. For example, poor urban children whose families do not own a car may have very limited experience with cars and so would require more background than middle-class children whose families own one or two cars.

Once the major understandings and difficult vocabulary words have been chosen, the teacher looks over the selection to decide what major cognitive and reading strategies are necessary to understand it. For the dream cars selection, visualizing and using illustrations would be helpful strategies. Comprehension should be improved if students visualize the futuristic vehicles and their major capabilities and characteristics. In addition, the photos illustrating the cars being described should help students understand the text.

Building background and vocabulary, activating schema, piquing interest, setting purposes, and giving guidance in reading and cognitive strategies are all done in the preparatory segment of the lesson. Generally, this takes the form of a discussion. Key vocabulary words are written on the board. When discussing each word, the teacher points to it on the board so that students become familiar with it in print.

Lesson 7.3 presents a sample DRA for "Dream Cars for the 2000s."

Lesson 7.3
A sample DRA

Step 1. Preparation

The teacher asks, "What is your favorite car? What do you like best about that car? If you were a designer of cars for the future, what kind of a dream car would you build? What kind of an engine would you put in it? A *turbine engine*? Why or why not? [Explain that a turbine engine is used on jets.] How many passengers would your car hold? What kind of *protective devices* would it have? *Protective devices* are things like air bags and seat belts that help keep passengers safe in case of a crash. Would you have any devices that would help you *communicate*? What do we do when we *communicate*? Would your car make use of *satellites*? What are *satellites*, and how might they help car drivers in the future? What kind of *sensors* might the car have? What do *sensors* do? [Although judged to be difficult for students, the key words *module* and *guidance system* are not introduced since it is felt that they are adequately explained in the selection.] Now that we have talked over some of the parts of a future car, put all your ideas together, close your eyes, and picture your dream car and its main parts. [Students are given a few minutes to picture their dream cars.] What do your dream cars look like? [Discussion.] Read 'Dream Cars for the 2000s.' Find out what two of tomorrow's dream cars, the T-2008 and the Express, are like. As you read, try to picture in your mind what the car or car part looks like or what's happening in the car. Also look at the pictures of the T-2008 and Express. They will help you to understand the selection."

In a DRA the key vocabulary words (italicized in Step 1 of the sample DRA) are defined as a natural part of the preparatory discussion. As they are being discussed, the teacher should write them on the board or point to them if they have already been written there. Students will thereby get a view of the written forms of the words.

Step 2. Silent reading

During silent reading, the teacher looks around to get a sense of the students' reactions to the story. Their silence suggests that they are intrigued. She notes that most of them are glancing at the photos as they read. One student raises his hand and asks for help with the word *ambulance*. The teacher suggests that he look for pronounceable word parts and put them together; when he is unable to do so successfully, she tells him the word. Another student has difficulty with *anniversary*, a third with *efficiently*, and a fourth with *kilometers*. The teacher makes a note to work with polysyllabic words in the future.

Step 3. Discussion

The teacher begins the discussion with the purpose question "What are the T-2008 and Express like?" Additional questions flow from the students' responses; however, the teacher keeps in mind the three major understandings that she wants students to learn and will make sure that they are explored: "Why might a variety of people buy the T-2008? What could an owner do who needed more passenger room? How many passengers will the T-2008 hold?" There is some disagreement, and the teacher asks the class to go back over the story to find a passage that will answer the question. Then she asks, "How will the T-2008 use a satellite link?" The class seems confused. *Satellite link* is an important concept. The teacher decides that it is worth some in-depth teaching. She directs the class to go back over the part that tells about it. She reminds students to try to picture in their minds how the satellite link operates and suggests that after rereading the section, they make a drawing showing how it works. The drawings are discussed, demonstrating students' improved understanding. The teacher asks further questions: "How will the driver and the car use the satellite link? Why will the T-2008 be hard to steal? Why do you think there will be fewer accidents with a T-2008? In case of an accident, would the passengers be safer than if they were in a regular car? What is the Express like? Which car do you like better? How do these cars compare with your dream car?"

Step 4. Rereading

During the discussion, the teacher notes that the students had difficulty scanning through the selection to find facts that would justify their responses. The next day, she reviews the skill of scanning. She models the process and explains why it is important and when it is used. She gives the class a series of questions whose answers are numerals, alerting them to this fact so they know to look for numerals rather than words. The questions are "What does *T-2008* stand for? How fast does the Express go? When will cars like the Express be seen?"

The teacher also reviews methods for attacking multisyllabic words and stresses the importance of both syllabication and context. Students scan to find the words *information, ambulance, notified, location, kilometers,* and *anniversary,* which are examined in context. Students use both syllabication and context clues to figure them out. As a review of vocabulary, students create and then discuss maps for words they learned in "Dream Cars for the 2000s."

Step 5. Follow-up

Some students design their own dream cars and create ads for them. Others read books about transportation in the future or other books about cars. Still others elect to read about satellites. A few write to auto manufacturers to obtain information about the newest experimental cars. The class also makes plans to visit the auto show.

Teaching reading is a personal activity. The DRA in Lesson 7.3 is just one of many possible lessons. Another teacher might choose to stress different understandings and would tailor discussion and other activities to match her or his teaching style and the abilities, backgrounds, and interests of the students. The teacher might also choose different purposes for rereading or elect not to have any follow-up. The DRA is a flexible method and works best when teachers alter it to suit their own circumstances.

DRA FOR FICTION

The sample DRA in Lesson 7.3 was written for informational text. A lesson for a piece of fiction would incorporate the same features; however, it might use a story elements map instead of a list of main concepts as the framework. Created by Beck, Omanson, and McKeown (1982), story elements maps result in better questions and improved comprehension. A story elements map provides a sense of the most important elements in a story, allowing the teacher to gear preparatory and postreading activities to understanding those elements. Preliminary questions lead up to the story; postreading questions enhance understanding of its main elements. Questions about style and questions that lead to appreciation of the author's craft are asked after the reader has a grasp of the essentials. However, some provision should be made for eliciting a personal response.

Basically the teacher asks him or herself, "What is the core of this story?" and then gears questions for students to it. To reach the core, the teacher uses a story elements map, which is constructed by deciding what the starting point is and then listing "the major events and ideas that constitute the plot or gist of the story, being sure to include implied ideas that are part of the story though not part of the text, and the links between events and ideas that unify the story" (Beck, Omanson, & McKeown, 1982, p. 479). A sample story elements map is presented in Figure 7.5.

One way of creating a story elements map is to begin by noting the problem or the conflict and then listing the major events leading up to the resolution. Then use that information to compose the story's theme or moral. You might also list the key characters and identify any vocabulary or concepts needed to understand the key elements of the story. Then create questions that focus on the central elements of the story.

DIRECTED READING–THINKING ACTIVITY

The DRA is basically a teacher-directed lesson. The DR-TA (*Directed Reading–Thinking Activity*) has been designed to help students begin to take responsibility for their own learning. Although based on the DRA, the DR-TA puts the ball in the students' court. The teacher leads them to establish their own purposes for reading, to decide when these purposes have been fulfilled, and to attack unfamiliar words independently.

Stauffer (1970), the creator of the DR-TA, based the approach on our penchant for predicting and hypothesizing. By nature, we have an innate tendency to look ahead. We are also decision-making creatures who need opportunities as well as the freedom to make decisions. Building on these propensities, Stauffer structured a predict-read strategy that has the following facets:

Directed reading–thinking activity (DR-TA) is an adaptation of the directed reading activity in which readers use preview and prediction strategies to set their own purposes for reading.

- *Setting purposes.* Students have to know how to ask questions about text they are about to read.

FIGURE 7.5   A story elements map

Title:	*Leo the Late Bloomer*
Author:	Robert Kraus
Theme:	Some people take longer than others to develop.
Problem:	Leo can't do the things that others his age can do.
Plot:	Leo can't do anything right.
	Leo's mom says he is a late bloomer.
	Leo's father watches for signs of blooming but nothing happens.
	Leo's mother tells the father to stop watching, but nothing happens.
	At last, Leo can do things.
Ending:	Leo says, "I made it."
Needed Concepts or Ideas:	*Bloom* means "to grow and develop." Late bloomers are people who take longer to develop.

- *Obtaining information.* Students have to know how to sift through reading material to get the information they need to answer a question.
- *Keeping goals in mind.* Students must be able to work within the constraints of their goals, noting information that fits in with these goals and not being led astray by information that does not.
- *Keeping personal feelings in bounds.* Students have to be able to suspend personal judgments when reading a piece that contains ideas with which they might not agree, at least until they have finished the piece and have a good grasp of what the author is trying to say.
- *Considering options.* Students must be able to consider a number of choices as they make their predictions and also be flexible enough to change or refine a prediction in the light of new information.

Like the DRA, the DR-TA has five steps, as outlined in Lesson 7.4. The major difference is that students are given a more active role in the DR-TA (Stauffer, 1969).

Lesson 7.4
A DR-TA

Step 1. Preparation stage

Students are led to create their own purposes for reading. The title of the selection, headings and subheads, illustrations, and/or the beginning paragraph are used to stimulate predictions about the content of the selection. For example, in preparation for reading "Live Cargo!" which is the first chapter of *Misty of Chincoteague* (Henry, 1947), the teacher might have the students examine the first illustration—a Spanish galleon. After discussing it, the teacher would have the students read the title of the chapter and then ask them what they think the chapter might be about. Responses, which might include slaves, prisoners, horses, and cattle, would be written on the board. Since the DR-TA is an active process, all students are encouraged to make a prediction or at least to indicate a preference for one of the predictions made by others. The teacher reads the predictions aloud and asks students to raise their hand to show which one they think is best.

One potential problem with using the DR-TA is the possibility of neglecting to develop students' background knowledge and vocabulary prior to reading a selection (Tierney, Readence, & Dishner, 1995). To build essential background and vocabulary, spend additional time with the title, illustrations, and other elements needed to make predictions. One indicator that students may not have adequate background is difficulty in making reasonable predictions.

Step 2. Silent reading

Students read silently until they are able to evaluate their predictions; this might mean a single page, several pages, or a whole chapter. Students are encouraged to modify their initial predictions if they find information that runs counter to them.

Step 3. Discussion

This stage is almost identical to Step 3 of the DRA, except that it begins with the consideration of the class's predictions. After reading just one page of "Live Cargo!" students should be able to evaluate their predictions and identify which ones were correct and which required rethinking. Additional questions flowing from the sense of the selection are then asked: "Where were the ponies being taken? Why was the captain headed for trouble? What is a stallion?" During the discussion, students offer proof of the adequacy of their predictions or clarify disputed points by reading passages orally. As in the DRA, the teacher develops comprehension, background, and concepts as the need arises and the opportunity presents itself. The discussion also leads students into making further predictions, as the teacher asks, "Why do you think the captain is angry with the stallion? What do you think will happen next?" If students do not respond to these prediction-making questions, the questions should be rephrased or altered. For instance, after getting no response to the question "What do you think will happen next?" the teacher might ask, "What do you think will happen to the stallion and the ponies?" The teacher might also read a few paragraphs aloud to stimulate predictions. As in Step 1, predictions are written on the board and students select the ones they believe are best.

Step 4. Rereading

This is the same as Step 4 of the DRA.

Step 5. Follow-up

This is the same as Step 5 of the DRA.

The DR-TA should be used with both fiction and nonfiction. If students only apply the strategies of predicting, sifting, and verifying to fiction, they may not develop the ability to transfer these to nonfiction. In time, some of the strategies practiced in DR-TA should become automatic.

THE CLOZE PROCEDURE

Cloze is a procedure in which the reader demonstrates comprehension by supplying missing words. *Cloze* is short for *closure,* referring to the tendency to fill in missing or incomplete information.

Another approach used to foster comprehension is **cloze**; it is illustrated in the following exercise. As you read the paragraph, supply the missing words.

> If we see a part of a person or object, we tend to fill in the missing portions. If someone omits the final word of a sentence, we supply it _____ her or him. There is something about the human _____ that can't _____ incompleteness. This tendency to fill in what's _____ is the basis of cloze, a technique by which readers achieve closure by filling in the _____ words in a selection. Based on the concept of gestalt _____, cloze was first proposed as a _____ for measuring the difficulty _____ of reading material. Today it is used to assess readability, to test reading ability, and to build comprehension.

Cloze is an excellent device for building comprehension. Filling in missing words forces a reader to use semantic and syntactic clues together with symbol-sound information, and to predict meaning. It also activates the reader's background knowledge. The reader's knowledge of the world must be used to figure out which words should be put in the blanks. Cloze works especially well with students who are concentrating so hard on sounding out words that they fail to read for meaning. Cloze leads students to integrate semantic and syntactic clues along with symbol-sound information. It also has been used to build students' ability to make inferences (Carr, Dewitz, & Patberg, 1989).

Dewitz, Carr, and Patberg (1987) theorized that completing cloze exercises is similar to drawing inferences. In their study, after learning to complete cloze exercises, students applied the technique to intact social studies passages. After reading a passage, students used the same strategies they had used to complete the cloze exercises. They were shown how to use their prior knowledge and clues in the passage, just as they had done when completing the cloze exercises. "In both instances the reader becomes accustomed to looking at text carefully while monitoring knowledge and searching for additional information across text" (p. 102).

CLASSIC CLOZE

In classic cloze, the teacher deletes words at random from a narrative or expository passage. The first and last sentences are left intact, and no proper nouns are removed; otherwise, every fifth, sixth, seventh, eighth, ninth, or tenth word is deleted. (Generally, the interval for word deletion should be no more than every fifth and no fewer than every tenth.)

The teacher explains the purpose of cloze and gives some tips for completing the exercise:

- Read the whole exercise first.
- Use all the clues given in a passage.
- Read past the blank to the end of the sentence. Sometimes the best clues come after a blank.
- If necessary, read a sentence or two ahead to get additional clues.
- Spell as best you can. You lose no points for misspelled words.

- Do your best, but do not worry if you cannot correctly complete each blank. Most readers will be able to fill in fewer than half the blanks correctly.
- After you have filled in as many blanks as you can, reread the selection. Make any changes that you think are necessary.

SCORING CLOZE

EXACT REPLACEMENT

There are two ways of scoring a cloze exercise. When it is used as a test, only exact replacements are counted as correct. Otherwise, marking becomes both time-consuming and subjective. Scores are noticeably lower on cloze exercises than they are on multiple-choice activities; a score of 50 percent is adequate. Criteria for scoring a cloze procedure using exact replacement are shown below.

Level	Percentage
Independent	> 57
Instructional	44–57
Frustration	< 44

SUBSTITUTION SCORING

When cloze is used for instructional purposes, substitution scoring is generally used. A response is considered correct if it fits both semantically and syntactically. Thus, the following sentence would have a number of correct responses, such as *wagon, toy, ball, bike, coat,* and *dress:*

The child pointed to the red _____ and cried, "I want that!"

DISCUSSION FOR COMPREHENSION

Discussion enhances the value of cloze as a comprehension building technique (Jongsma, 1980). Discussions can be led by the teacher or pupils. During the discussion, participants talk over their responses and give reasons for their choices, thus justifying their responses and clarifying their thinking processes. They also compare their answers; in the process, they broaden vocabulary, concepts, and experience and learn to consider and value different perspectives. Of course, before students guide discussions, the teacher should model how to do it, and ground rules should be established. Discussion groups should be large enough to encompass several perspectives but small enough to allow plenty of opportunity for each member to participate (Rye, 1982).

CONSTRUCTING CLOZE EXERCISES

The first rule for constructing cloze exercises is to choose selections that are interesting so that students will be motivated to complete them. It is best to start with easier exercises and progress to more difficult ones. In general, the following items affect the difficulty of a cloze exercise (Rye, 1982):

- *Number of deletions.* The fewer the deletions, the easier the task.

- *Types of words deleted.* Content words such as nouns, verbs, adverbs, and, to a lesser degree, adjectives are more difficult to replace than structure words such as articles, prepositions, and conjunctions.
- *Location of deletion.* Deletions in the beginning of a sentence are more difficult to replace than those in the middle or end.

In early exercises, the teacher may want to delete just one word out of ten—mainly structure words that occur in the second half of a sentence. In time, the number of deletions can be increased, more content words can be omitted, and a proportion of words can be taken out of the beginnings of sentences. The kinds of deletions will be dictated by instructional objectives. If the teacher wants students to work on seeing relationships, he or she may delete structure words such as *if, then, and, but, moreover,* and *however.* Deleting nouns and verbs and, to a lesser extent, adjectives and adverbs will place the focus on content. Deleting adjectives and adverbs could be a device for having students note how modifiers alter a selection.

VARIATIONS ON CLOZE

Traditional cloze exercises are not recommended until students are in fourth grade and/or have achieved a fourth-grade reading level. However, with modification, related activities can be introduced as early as kindergarten.

ORAL CLOZE

Very young students can complete cloze exercises orally. The teacher reads a story, hesitates before a word that students have a good chance of supplying because of its predictability, and asks them to tell what word comes next. For example, when reading *The Little House* (Burton, 1943) aloud, the teacher would pause upon reaching the italicized words:

> Once upon a time there was a Little House way out in the *country.* She was a pretty Little *House* and she was strong and well built. The men who built her so well said, "This Little House shall never be sold for gold or *silver* and she will live to see our great-great-grandchildren's great-great-grandchildren living in *her.*" (p. 1)

Oral cloze is greeted enthusiastically by students and occasions lively discussion of alternatives (Blachowicz, 1977). It also introduces children to predicting.

WORD MASKING

As children begin to acquire some reading skills, word masking is used. A rhyme such as "Baa, baa, black sheep" is shared with students. Students follow along as the teacher reads the selection in a big book. During the second reading, some of the words are covered over. When the teacher gets to one of them, he or she pauses and the children predict what it might be. After they respond, the word is uncovered, and students are asked if they were correct. Comprehension and word-reading skills are combined (Hornsby, Sukarna, & Parry, 1986).

MODIFIED CLOZE

In modified cloze, each blank is accompanied by answer choices so that students do not have to supply the word; they simply identify the best of three or four possible choices. This is a format employed by a number of commercial workbooks. Although they provide valuable practice, these exercises shift the focus from predicting a word to considering which alternative is best. The task is changed from being one of constructing meaning to recognizing meaning, a subtle but significant alteration. However, modified cloze can be good preparation for completing classic cloze exercises.

CRITICAL READING

Today's students are barraged with an overwhelming number of sophisticated, slick television and print ads. Even the youngest readers encounter slanted writing, illogical arguments, and persuasive techniques of all types. The ability to evaluate what one hears and reads has never been more important.

When reading critically, children judge what they read. This judgment is not a mere opinion but an evaluation based on either internal or external standards. In the process of learning to evaluate what they read, students deal critically with words, statements, and whole selections.

The tendency is to reserve **critical reading** for the brightest students because of the feeling that average or slower students cannot handle it or require instruction in more basic skills. Although some may catch on to critical reading faster than others, all students can learn it. According to a classic study of twenty-four classrooms, students of diverse abilities in grades 1 through 6 learned to read critically; the key was teacher training (Wolf, King, & Huck, 1968). Teachers in the experimental group were trained to ask questions that required children to think critically. As a result, they asked many questions that involved analyzing and

Critical reading is a type of reading in which the reader evaluates or judges the accuracy and truthfulness of the content.

Today's students should be taught how to read advertisements critically.

evaluating information. Students' responses, in turn, rose to high levels and their thinking reflected the questions they were asked. Students also seemed to feel better about themselves as learners and showed some evidence of applying critical thinking skills to their everyday lives. Some time after a session on making logical generalizations, one teacher chastised her class for being noisy:

> Coming into the classroom after recess, the teacher said, "Quiet please! Everyone is talking!" One child replied, "Oh no, Mrs. Smith, we're not *all* talking. I'm not talking, Suzie isn't talking. Mary isn't talking. . . ." (p. 487)

Obviously, the student had learned her lessons on generalizations well. The authors also reported transfers of critical thinking and reading to other content areas and to radio and television.

Critical reading is an affective as well as a cognitive skill. To read critically, students must be able to suspend judgment and consider other viewpoints. Generally, people tend to interpret what they read in light of their beliefs. Some readers, and this seems to be especially true of poor readers, reject information that contradicts their beliefs. On the other hand, some readers suffer from a malady that one educator called the "Guttenburg syndrome" (J. Rothermich, personal communication, January 1980): If a statement appears in print, it must be true. Students have to challenge what they read and realize that a printed statement might be erroneous or simply be someone else's opinion.

To encourage critical reading, the teacher must create a spirit of inquiry. Students must feel free to challenge statements, support controversial ideas, offer divergent viewpoints, and venture statements that conflict with the majority view. When they see that their own ideas are accepted, they are better able to accept the ideas of others. The program, of course, must be balanced. The idea is not to turn students into mistrustful young cynics but to create judicious thinkers.

SCOPE AND SEQUENCE OF CRITICAL READING SKILLS

Few agree on which critical reading skills should be taught. The suggested skills listed in Table 7.2 are based on examination of professional materials and analysis of critical reading tasks. No time table is suggested for these skills.

USES OF LANGUAGE

A good starting point for a study of critical reading is to examine how language is used. What do words do? What functions do statements fulfill? Words are used in four main ways: to describe, to evaluate, to point out, and to interject (Wilson, 1960). The words *car, take,* and *dog* describe bits of reality. The words *evil* and *dull* evaluate, going beyond mere description to judgment. Some words both describe and evaluate: *Jalopy, steal,* and *mutt* describe objects and actions, but they also incorporate unfavorable evaluations. A key strategy in critical reading is to note whether words offer neutral descriptions, evaluations, or both. Pointing out and interjecting do not call for critical reading. Words that point out include conjunctions, prepositions, and articles—*and, on, a*—and so have little or no meaning. Interjections express feelings—*hurrah! wow!*—rather than thoughts or ideas.

TABLE 7.2 Critical reading skills

Distinguishing between facts and opinions
Identifying words that signal opinions
Verifying factual statements
Identifying the uses of words (e.g., to describe, to judge)
Recognizing denotations and connotations
Identifying persuasive language
Identifying an author's purpose
Drawing logical conclusions
Supporting conclusions
Judging sources of information
Identifying slanted or biased writing
Identifying major propaganda techniques
Recognizing assumptions

To introduce the concept of the uses of words, write a series of sentences similar to the following on the board:

The horse weighs 950 pounds.

The horse is black with white spots.

The horse is lazy.

The horse is wonderful.

Discuss which words just tell about the horse and which judge it. Guide students as they locate words in their texts that describe, judge, or do both. While discussing selections that students have read, note words that are used to judge. To extend the concept of uses of words, introduce the concept of connotations; have students note words that have favorable connotations (*thrifty, slim*) and those that have unfavorable ones (*selfish, skinny*). For younger students, you may want to use phrases like "sounds better" and "sounds worse," instead of "favorable connotations" and "unfavorable connotations."

Introduce the concept of persuasive language by bringing in ads and package labels. Have students locate words that sell or persuade in television and print ads—*fresh, delicious, new,* and *improved*. They can even compose their own persuasive advertising.

UNDERSTANDING FACTS AND OPINIONS

To introduce the concept of facts and opinions, place sentences similar to the following on the board:

We have twenty-five players on our soccer team.

We have won twelve games in a row.

Our uniforms are red.

Soccer is the best sport.

Show students that the first three sentences can be proved in some way, but the last one cannot. It is simply an opinion, a statement that tells how someone feels. Help students locate statements of fact and opinion in their texts. To reinforce and extend this concept, plan lessons and activities such as the following.

Reinforcement Activities
Extending the concept of facts and opinions

- Present words that signal opinions, such as *good, bad, worse, terrible, wonderful,* and *awful.* Ask students to use these and other signal words in differentiating between facts and opinions.
- Introduce the concept of verifying factual statements. Explain to students that factual statements can be proved in some way—by measuring, weighing, observing, touching, hearing, counting, and so on. Bring in a kiwi or other unusual fruit, and encourage students to make factual statements about it—for example, *The kiwi is brown* and *It has fuzzy skin.* Discuss how each statement might be proved. Bring in a scale and a measuring tape so that the kiwi can be weighed and measured. Have students make other factual statements and tell how they might prove them; that is, whether they would mainly count, measure, weigh, touch, listen, or observe to prove the statements.
- Let students examine an object and make at least five factual statements about it based on counting, measuring, weighing, touching, listening, observing, or checking a reference book. Then ask them to write down their personal opinions about that object. This might be an opportunity for them to be especially imaginative and creative.
- Ask students whether a particular statement in a reading selection is a fact or an opinion. Take special note of opinions that might be mistaken for facts.

RECOGNIZING THE AUTHOR'S PURPOSE

In addition to being a key critical reading skill, recognizing the author's purpose is an essential general comprehension skill. According to Spearitt (1972), it is one of only four distinct skills involved in comprehension.

The three main purposes for writing are to inform, entertain, and persuade. Recognizing which one applies to a particular selection enables students to match their strategy to their reading. For example, knowing that a writer is attempting to persuade, they will look at the piece with a critical eye. To introduce the concept of purpose, read aloud an ad or an editorial, an encyclopedia article, and a short story, and discuss each author's purpose. Help students suggest other writings that are designed to inform, entertain, and persuade.

To extend the concept, have students predict the author's purpose before reading a selection and then discuss their predictions after reading. For each book report that students complete, have them identify the author's purpose. Students can also decide what their own purpose is before writing a piece. Let them write editorials for the school newspaper or letters to the editor. Bring in persuasive pieces, and discuss them with the class. Help the class see what persuasive techniques are being used.

DRAWING LOGICAL CONCLUSIONS

Drawing a conclusion is a type of inference. It usually entails examining several facts or details and coming to some sort of conclusion based on the information. In critical reading, stress is placed on drawing conclusions that are logical, have sufficient support, and consider all the evidence. In many instances, different conclusions can be applied to a set of facts. Students should be shown that they should reach the most likely conclusion while keeping an open mind, since other conclusions are possible.

To introduce drawing logical conclusions, model the process and provide guided practice. Have students apply the skill to all content areas, drawing conclusions about the main character in a piece of fiction, about experiments in science, and about historical events and figures in social studies. Stress the need to consider the evidence very carefully.

JUDGING SOURCES

Because students tend to believe everything they read, they should understand that some sources are better than others. Three main criteria are used to judge a source: whether it has expert knowledge about the subject, whether the information is up to date, and whether the source is unbiased.

Encourage students to examine their textbooks to see if they are written by experts and are up to date. When students read nonfiction, have them note who wrote the book and then examine the book jacket or another source of information to see if the author seems to be an expert. Students also should check the date of publication. Also discuss the issue of author bias. For instance, talk over why a book on coal mining written by someone who works for a coal company might be considered to be written by an expert but could be biased in favor of the coal industry.

Slanted Writing.   Slanted, or biased, writing uses emotionally toned words and specially chosen details to create an unfairly favorable or unfavorable impression about a person, place, object, or idea. It is found in political speeches, personal opinion columns in magazines and newspapers, sports articles, biographies and autobiographies, and history texts.

Show students how words and details can be selected in such a way as to shape readers' opinions. Discuss why it is important to recognize slanted writing. Assign selections, some of which are slanted and some of which are neutral, and ask students to decide which are which. They should take note of techniques used to slant writing. Most importantly, they must be able to detect it in their reading. To reinforce this skill, keep a file of examples of slanted writing, and from time to time, share and discuss some of them with the class. Encourage students to bring in examples of slanted writing, and discuss these also. Have students look for examples of slanted writing in their own written pieces.

Detecting Assumptions.   Assumptions are statements that are neither proved nor supported. They may be directly stated or implied. The problem with assumptions is that young readers often accept them as facts.

To introduce the concept, present paragraphs similar to the following to students:

> When I went to school, we did our math problems in our heads. It may have taken longer to do the problems, but we learned how to add, subtract, divide, and multiply. Many of today's students use calculators or computers to do their adding, subtracting, dividing, and multiplying. We were much better at math than today's kids are. (Gunning, 1989, p. 18)

Discuss the paragraph and lead students to see that it makes a statement for which the author offers no proof: "We were much better at math than today's kids are." Also discuss the implied assumption: Students learn better if they do problems in their heads rather than use calculators.

Model the process of identifying assumptions, and discuss why it is important to question them. The reader must decide whether assumptions are true, and whether to accept them or withhold judgment. Students should examine and discuss additional examples of assumptions. Once they have grasped the concept, have them note assumptions in periodicals and expository books that they read and in their textbooks.

Student Strategy
Judging sources

Once students seem to grasp the concept of judging sources for fairness, help them develop a set of questions that they might use to assess texts they read:

Is the text up to date?

Who is the author?

Is the author an expert?

Is the author unbiased? Is there any reason that the author would be in favor of one side or one position?

Is the writing fair, or does it seem to be slanted?

Does the author make assumptions?

Does the author give enough proof for all conclusions?

You might post the questions as a reminder for students to use them when they are reading. In adapted form, the questions might also be used for evaluating speeches and informational TV programs.

DETECTING PROPAGANDA

Propaganda is any systematic effort to persuade others to accept certain beliefs or opinions.

Propaganda is the deliberate, organized attempt to use words and nonverbal symbols to persuade others to accept an idea, adopt an attitude, or take a certain action. Although propaganda seems to have an unfavorable connotation, it may be used for both selfish and unselfish reasons. Politicians use it to get elected on the basis of emotion rather than reason; conservation groups use it to save endangered animals.

For better or for worse, propaganda is here to stay. Readers must be able to recognize the technique and realize it is a device to sway their judgment. Armed with this realization, they are in a better position to make a reasoned decision or sift out the emotional appeals as they read and consider an issue strictly on its merits. Although there are dozens of propaganda techniques, the following seven techniques are most frequently taught in schools:

- *Testimonial*. Well-known personalities testify or speak out for an idea or product. This technique is frequently used in advertisements in which a sports star endorses a shampoo, or a TV star urges consumers to buy a certain brand of toothpaste.
- *Bandwagon*. Playing on the natural desire to be part of the crowd, this technique tries to convince by stating that because so many others are buying a product or taking a certain action, we should too.
- *Card stacking*. This method lists all the good points or advantages of an idea or product, but none of its bad points or disadvantages.
- *Plain folks*. To win our trust, a person of power or wealth tries to convince us that she or he is an ordinary person just like us.
- *Name calling*. Words that may have unfavorable connotations such as *tightwad, liberal,* or *spendthrift* are used to describe opposing political candidates, competing products, or rival ideas. Responding emotionally to the name, we fail to consider the persons, products, or ideas rationally.
- *Glittering generalities*. The near opposite of name calling, glittering generalities are favorable-sounding abstract terms or scientific words that usually evoke a positive response. Examples are *justice, honesty, new, miracle ingredient*, and scientific-sounding names like *benzoyl peroxide*.
- *Transfer*. In this device, the favorable feeling we have for a symbol, person, or object is carried over or transferred to an idea or product someone is trying to sell. A candidate for political office is seen standing next to a flag with his family, which includes a big friendly collie. The positive feelings that we associate with our country's flag, our family, and our pets are transferred to the man.

Since testimonials are widely used and seem to be the easiest of these techniques to understand, introduce propaganda by discussing them. Display print ads in which sports stars or other famous people endorse items, and discuss their appeal. Ask students if they have ever bought or asked their parents to buy a product because a person they admired was advertising it. Underline the double fallacy of this technique: The person endorsing the product is probably not an expert on toothpaste, shampoo, or whatever is being advertised and, even if the person is an expert, she or he is being paid to speak highly of the product.

Introduce the other techniques one by one, discussing how they are frequently used and why it is important to be able to identify them. To provide additional practice, bring in examples of propaganda and ask students to identify the technique being used. Have them note when a combination of techniques is used. Discuss which examples are most convincing and why. When students encounter examples of propaganda in their reading in textbooks or other classroom materials, discuss them with the class.

Student Strategy
Using ALERT

An intriguing approach that uses commercials to present critical thinking skills is ALERT (Allen, Wright, & Laminack, 1988). Combining language experience techniques with listening, viewing, and reading, it demonstrates the specifics of an ad: the item being sold; word(s) repeated or used to sell it; and special effects, such as music and cartoon characters. The following procedure may be used by students to evaluate an ad:

1. Focusing on the propaganda techniques listed previously, children examine the ad critically, asking such questions as the following:

   Were any claims, promises, or persuasive statements made? If so, what were they?

   What "commercial" words or phrases did you hear?

   What do they mean?

   Were there any special sound effects or pictures? (p. 907)

2. After carefully considering an ad, students summarize and interpret it. This helps as children "further develop . . . evaluative thinking as they strive to restate as accurately as possible their perceptions of the message" (p. 907).

3. As a final step, students test out the product's claims. They might assess whether one brand of peanut butter is smoother than another or try a taste test to see whether more classmates prefer brand Y or brand X.

The outcome of ALERT is awareness. Children become aware that "they have the power to evaluate and critically analyze information received via listening or reading" (pp. 909–910). ALERT is a powerful technique that teaches a powerful lesson.

The key to developing critical thinkers is to build their confidence in their ability to interpret text and spoken and visual messages. If these interpretations are valued and discussed, students acquire both the skill and the faith in their own judgment to evaluate what they read, hear, and see.

IMPORTANCE OF THE LEARNING ENVIRONMENT

The learning environment can have a dramatic impact on students' ability to construct meaning. As noted earlier, reading is an interaction of the characteristics of the reader, the text, and the setting. As Mosenthal (1990) pointed out, certain of these factors can have a negative effect on efforts to improve comprehension. These include extreme range of ability within a classroom, large number of low-achievers, lack of materials of appropriate level of difficulty, large class size, and an inexperienced teacher.

In an experiment with a class of thirty-two fourth-graders in an elementary school that was part of a public housing project, Mosenthal (1990) noted that all thirty-two youngsters received whole class instruction and read from a text that was on grade level, even though some children were reading below grade level. Selecting the seven lowest-achieving students, Mosenthal and the children's teacher, who was highly experienced, obtained materials on a second-grade level and provided the children with supplementary comprehension instruction that consisted of directed reading–thinking activities and written retellings. Retellings were chosen because they offered insights into the children's changing ability to comprehend narrative text.

Over a period of three months, the students' retellings improved dramatically. They became more complete and began to reflect the most important elements in the tales that they read. Although instruction and practice were undoubtedly essential factors in the children's improvement, setting may have been even more important than the quality of instruction. As the children's teacher noted, "I know at times in the beginning that they [the students in the reading/writing group] were elated that they were part of a small group. I think the stories helped. They were stories they could read and they could enjoy" (Mosenthal, 1990, p. 282). Although reluctant to write at first, the children's attitude changed because they were praised for their efforts. Over time, they also felt better about themselves. As their teacher remarked, "They saw improvement and I think they felt better about what they were doing" (Mosenthal, 1990, p. 283).

As the researchers noted, improved learning environment interacted with direct instruction in reading and writing. Being given materials they could read, tasks they could perform, and a positive can-do atmosphere, students were able to make the most of instruction.

The reader's information-processing capabilities have an impact on comprehension. Both short-term memory and capacity to pay attention are limited. If a student has to devote too much attention to difficult vocabulary or convoluted syntax, she or he may not have sufficient memory or attentional resources for forming a coherent macrostructure (Weaver & Kintsch, 1991).

SUMMARY

1. Through hearing stories, children develop a schema for narrative tales. This becomes a kind of structural outline that helps students construct meaning from narrative text. It also aids memory.

2. Generally, expository works are harder to read than narratives, but understanding expository text structure results in increased comprehension and memory. Major types of text structures are enumeration/description, time sequence, explanation/process, problem/solution, comparison/contrast, and cause/effect.

3. Questions play a vital role in facilitating comprehension. They can be used to develop concepts, build vocabulary, clarify reasoning, redirect cognitive processes, and lead students to higher levels of thinking. A taxonomy is a useful guide for constructing questions on a variety of thinking levels and for judging questions that have already been created. Allowing plenty of time to answer questions and establishing an accepting atmosphere enhance students' responses.

4. The DRA (directed reading activity), modified to include greater emphasis on schema activation and use

of learning strategies, is a highly useful framework for conducting reading lessons with both fiction and nonfiction. The DR-TA (directed reading–thinking activity), an adaptation of the DRA, gives students more responsibility for their learning.

5. Story elements maps can be used by the teacher to analyze fictional selections and create a discussion that flows from the structure of the piece, thereby making the lesson more coherent.

6. Cloze is an exercise in which students fill in missing words in selections. Although it can be used for testing and assessing readability, cloze is valuable for building comprehension, as it forces students to read for meaning, use context, and make predictions.

7. Faced with a barrage of ads and other biased sources of information, students must be able to read critically. An affective as well as cognitive skill, critical reading involves willingness to suspend judgment, consider another point of view, and think carefully about what one reads. Thoughtful reading and discussion also promote critical thinking.

8. The total class setting has an impact on comprehension. Students do better when materials are on the proper level of difficulty, when assignments seem workable, and when there is a positive can-do atmosphere.

CLASSROOM APPLICATIONS

1. Collect samples of propaganda and other forms of biased writing from children's periodicals and textbooks.

2. Examine a lesson from a basal series that is no more than three or four years old. Examine the questions for

three selections, and classify them according to Bloom's taxonomy. What percentage are on a knowledge level? On a comprehension level? Beyond the comprehension level?

FIELD APPLICATIONS

1. Plan a DRA for a chapter of a children's book, a short story, or an informational piece. Teach the lesson and evaluate its effectiveness. Also plan a DR-TA and evaluate its effectiveness.

2. Create and teach a cloze lesson. Evaluate its effectiveness.

3. Try out the FELS system for asking questions with a class. Also use wait time, and create an accepting atmosphere. Do this for a week. Have a colleague observe your performance and give you objective feedback.

c h a p t e r 8

Reading and Writing in the Content Areas and Study Skills

ANTICIPATION GUIDE

For each of the following statements related to the chapter you are about to read, put a check under "Agree" or "Disagree" to show how you feel. Discuss your responses with classmates before you read the chapter.

Agree

Disagree

1. Content area textbooks should be simplified.

2. Instead of using content area texts, students should use informational children's books.

3. The strategies that are most effective in promoting comprehension of content area material are those that are used after the text has been read.

4. Strategies that help readers relate new information to their own backgrounds are more effective than those that simply help readers organize new information.

5. When teaching reading of content area material, the teacher should stress strategies rather than content.

6. Writing is one of the most effective ways to learn content area material.

7. Content area teachers should be responsible for teaching the reading skills necessary to use their subjects' texts.

8. Content area information should be presented to poor readers through discussions, experiments, and audiovisual aids rather than through texts that might be too difficult for them.

9. Students who are good readers generally turn out to be proficient learners.

10. Most students learn effective study techniques without any formal instruction.

Using What You Know

Chapters 6 and 7 presented a variety of strategies for improving comprehension of narrative and expository text. This chapter focuses on applying those strategies to improve reading in the content areas. Additional aids to comprehension are introduced, and some special difficulties inherent in reading in the content areas are explained. It also explores studying and techniques for remembering content area and other material.

Before reading this chapter, reflect on your knowledge of reading in science, history, and other content areas. Do you use any special strategies to comprehend what you read in the content areas? If so, what are they? How well do they work for you? Do you have any problems reading in the content areas? Do you have any problems studying? How might you improve your comprehension and retention of the material? How might you help students improve their reading in the content areas? How might you help them improve their studying?

OVERALL GOALS OF LITERACY INSTRUCTION IN THE CONTENT AREAS

The overall goal of content area instruction is to help students construct their own understanding of key concepts. Students bring their own unique backgrounds and perspectives to each reading selection and use them to create an understanding of the content area. No longer are students seen as passive recipients of knowledge. Rather, they actively seek to make sense of new information by relating it to what they know about a topic. This type of learning requires time to discuss and reflect. In addition to thoughtful demonstrations and explanations by the teacher and in the text, the students need opportunities to interact with the information, to mull it over, talk about it, and make it their own. This is in stark contrast to the concept of coverage in which topics are presented but not explored and reflected upon, leaving students without the opportunity to interact with the information, to discuss it, see its implications for their lives, and, if appropriate, apply it (Brandt, 1992).

THE TEACHER'S ROLE

Peer interaction also helps students organize and evaluate information from content area textbooks. It enhances their understanding and motivates them to read more (Alvermann, O'Brien, & Dillon, 1990).

In the initial stages of content area instruction, the teacher plays the dominant role. Since the topic is new, the teacher provides information and structures explanations and demonstrations that help the students construct an understanding of the information. However, just as in teaching students new strategies, there is a gradual release of responsibility. As students develop expertise, they also develop their growing knowledge through discussion, asking questions, and applying that knowledge. The teacher's role changes from being the source of information to being the guide who helps students refine, clarify, and deepen their understanding.

The teacher's role is to select the key concepts that he or she wants to emphasize. Since conceptual, student-constructed learning takes time, not all topics typically taught in science or social studies can be presented in depth; therefore, the teacher will have to make choices. Unless a decision is made to restrict the amount of material covered, less important topics will have to be presented through overviews. In terms of instruction, teachers must not only present information, but must also help students become actively engaged with the material. They must arrange for opportunities for students to question, discuss, clarify, explore, and apply. In presenting a concept or topic, teachers must be prepared to go beyond the text. They must be prepared to present an in-depth look and careful consideration of a topic. However, textbooks typically present quick coverage. In an interview with Brandt (1992), Gardner cautioned:

> The greatest enemy of understanding is coverage. As long as you are determined to cover everything, you actually ensure that most kids are not going to understand. You've got to take time enough to get kids deeply involved in something so they can think about it in lots of different ways and apply it not just at school but at home and on the street and so on. (p. 7)

HIGHER-ORDER THINKING SKILLS

Teaching for understanding requires both lower- and higher-order thinking skills. Using lower-order thinking skills, students memorize or recite facts and concepts. Using higher-order thinking skills, students construct meaning by combining facts, drawing conclusions, explaining, or hypothesizing (Newmann & Wehlage, 1993). Although both lower- and higher-order thinking skills are required, there should be a substantial proportion of higher-order thinking skills in every lesson. Teaching for understanding also requires a depth of knowledge, an intensive look at a topic. Depth of knowledge is achieved by focusing on the big ideas or key concepts in a content area. Depth of knowledge also has to do with how the material is covered. Comparing, contrasting, organizing, evaluating, and applying key concepts develop depth. Students need time to construct understanding and to clarify misconceptions. New knowledge should also be connected to the real world. Students need to relate new information to what they already know and see how it applies to the world outside school.

BUILDING ON STUDENTS' STRENGTHS

To help students become active learners, teachers should build on their strengths. Prior knowledge and the ability to reason, communicate, and work with others are definite strengths that students bring to a content area. To take advantage of students' prior knowledge, Herber and Herber (1993) recommended that teachers construct an organizing idea for each unit or lesson and then express that organizing idea broadly enough so that the students can relate their prior knowledge to it.

The organizing idea states which major concepts students should learn. For instance, for a study of unions, Herber and Herber (1993) expressed the organizing idea as "Protests take many forms and produce many outcomes" (p. 21). They

In their study of social studies textbooks, Chall and Conrad (1991) noted that so many topics are covered that most are only mentioned in passing. This, of course, makes the material more difficult to comprehend.

Adapting instruction for ESL students
Learning involves integrating new knowledge with old. Because old concepts may be encapsulated in their first language and new knowledge is presented in English, children who are still learning English as a second language (ESL) may have difficulty integrating the two. Allowing students to discuss in their first language what they already know may help them relate new concepts with old (Barba, 1995). Peer tutoring and small cooperative groups help students who are still learning English cope with the language requirements of content area classes. They acquire more concepts and improve their attitudes toward the subject matter (Watson, 1991).

As students move through the grades, reading and writing in the content areas take on more importance.

Adapting instruction for ESL students

Barba (1995) theorizes that science fails to connect with diverse cultures. Some bilingual students may not have acquired the technical, academic language that science demands. Programs may fail to build on what students bring to the classroom and may not use procedures that fully engage students. Using experiences, examples, and analogies that are familiar to students fosters understanding. For instance, when investigating nutrition, use as examples the foods that the children and their parents eat (Barba, 1995).

speculated that students might know very little about unions but would have knowledge of protests. Building on that knowledge, they were able to help students study unions and relate what they learned to their prior knowledge of protests.

USING CONTENT AREA TEXTBOOKS

Although children's books are being used with increasing frequency to present and reinforce concepts in the content areas, content area textbooks account for an estimated 75–90 percent of the learning that takes place in subject matter classes. However, content area textbooks present several hurdles to overcome. Stories are emphasized in the early years, so children may have little experience with informational text. Often, the informational text that they do read in their basals has a strong narrative thread. Content area text has a different, more complex structure. Instead of following a narrative, readers must understand complex processes and identify causes and effects as well as problems and solutions.

Readers must also cope with increased density of ideas and technical vocabulary and concepts for which they may have a very limited background. However, what really sets content area reading apart from other reading is its purpose, which is to learn and, ultimately, to be able to apply what is learned.

Fortunately, content area textbooks offer plenty of comprehension aids: chapter overviews; headings that outline the text; helpful graphics such as maps, charts, tables, graphs, diagrams, photos, and drawings; difficult words defined in context; summaries; and review questions. Also on the positive side, research suggests that students' reading of content area materials can be improved. In a review of the research, Wade (1983) concluded that students perform better in both social studies and reading when provided with an instructional program that includes an active teacher and varied activities and materials.

As teachers provide instruction in the use of social studies materials, they should build independent learning strategies. As Herber (1970) commented,

> If we fail to help students develop skills for independent learning, then "education" will cease when they leave school. This understanding sets the *teaching of reading in content areas* in its proper perspective. Its purpose is to help students acquire the skills they need for adequate study of all materials required in their subjects. Using subject-related material, regularly assigned, as the vehicle for this instruction, content teachers can provide for the simultaneous teaching of reading skills and course content. Neither has to be sacrificed to the other. (p. v)

CHOOSING TEXTBOOKS

The first order of business is to decide what content to teach. The teacher should decide on his or her objectives and the topics to be covered and then select the materials. Typically, a single textbook is the major source and sometimes the only one. It should be supplemented with informational children's books, periodicals, primary sources, audiovisual aids, computer software, and, possibly, videodiscs.

TEXTUAL FEATURES THAT FOSTER LEARNING

From a reading standpoint, a number of features promote learning from a textbook. As noted in Chapter 6, the five major groups of strategies (excluding rehearsal) are preparing to read; selecting and organizing relevant information; elaborating the information once it has been selected, which means integrating the new information with existing knowledge structures or schemata; monitoring for meaning; and affective or motivational strategies. Table 8.1 presents textual features that foster these processes.

Finding a well-organized textbook that contains helpful features should be easier these days. According to Conrad (1990) and Chall and Conrad (1991), newer content area textbooks are longer and contain more information but are also more colorful, have more illustrations per page, and pay more attention to overall organization of topics and to the organization and cohesion of the writing.

Finding a textbook that is on the appropriate level of difficulty is another matter. Conrad (1990) suggested that 57 percent of the best-selling content area textbooks are above the grade level for which they were written. On the fourth-grade level, for example, the average social studies textbook is written for grade 5 or 6, and the average science textbook for grade 7 or 8. Of course, this is not true of all textbooks.

ESTIMATING READABILITY

Readability levels of textbooks are available from publishers. For most textbooks, they are also contained in a publication called *Readability of Textbooks* (Touchstone Applied Science Associates, latest edition). You can also use a formula to estimate readability. According to numerous studies (see, for example, Chall, 1958; Chall & Dale, 1995; Klare, 1984), the two factors that correlate most

Adapting instruction for ESL students

Activities that help ESL students activate schema and build concepts and also provide the teacher with information about students' background knowledge are especially effective. For instance, students with the ability to put their thoughts down on paper can use an activity known as quick-write. In quick-write, students quickly write down what they know about a topic and then discuss what they wrote. The teacher can help students clarify misinformation or fill in gaps (Farnan, Flood, & Lapp, 1994). PReP and KWL might also be used.

Adapting instruction for ESL students

ESL students may have special difficulty learning from content area textbooks. They may lack the technical vocabulary required by such texts, or they may not have the background knowledge assumed by them. In addition, their English reading skills may not be up to the demands of the textbook. To prepare these students to cope with content area textbooks, the teacher might analyze the text, select key vocabulary, and help students construct meaning for those words (Kang, 1994). Instruction should focus on the relationships among the key terms and full development of any words that might represent new concepts. Care should also be taken to build background knowledge and relate the selection to students' prior knowledge.

TABLE 8.1 Textual features that foster use of learning strategies

Feature	Examples
Help students prepare	Chapter overview that lets student activate schema
	Semantic maps or other graphic organizers
	Heading and illustrations to make predictions
	Key terms and explanations
	Glossary
Help readers select relevant information and organize it	Introduction and summaries to highlight important information
	Headings and subheadings highlighting main ideas
	Details that clearly support main ideas
	Topics developed in sufficient detail but not so much as to overwhelm readers
	Clear, well-written text with connectives and transitions where needed
	Graphic aids
	Questions and activities at the end of the chapter
Help readers elaborate or integrate important information	Explanations to relate new knowledge to readers' background
	Questions or activities that help readers relate what they have read to their prior knowledge or experience
Help students monitor reading	Questions at the end of the chapter or interspersed throughout the chapter that ask students to check their understanding
Foster motivation	Illustrations and other graphic devices that give the text an appealing look
	Interesting style that engages the reader; use of anecdotes
	Relationships drawn between content and students' lives

Adapted from *Textual Features That Aid Learning from Text*, unpublished manuscript by B. Armbruster, 1987. Champaign, IL: Center for the Study of Reading.

Adapting instruction for ESL students

Activity-based science is recommended for all children, but it is especially effective for bilingual youngsters who may have difficulty following lengthy abstract explanations or reading text replete with technical terms (Martin, Sexton, Wagner, & Gerlovich, 1994). However, this does not suggest that children who are still learning English should not be taught essential abstract principles of science or a basic scientific vocabulary. It simply means that activities and experiments build a solid foundation and an interest in science.

Readability formulas are devices that generally measure sentence complexity and word difficulty and are used to estimate the difficulty level of text.

closely with level of difficulty are vocabulary and sentence complexity. The greater the proportion of difficult words and the longer the sentences, the harder the selection tends to be. In their calculations, **readability formulas** do not allow for complexity of topic, organization, students' background knowledge and interest, or use of graphic aids or instructional devices such as summaries and prequestions or postquestions. Many of these factors are assessed subjectively by the New

Dale-Chall Readability Formula (Chall & Dale, 1995). These are the factors that affect the likelihood that a particular student will be able to comprehend a particular textbook. They should be evaluated subjectively by the teacher. (Table 8.1 can be used to evaluate textual features that foster learning.) Despite obvious limitations, readability formulas do have value: They provide useful, objective evidence about the difficulty level of a text (Fry, 1989).

Several formulas can be used to estimate readability levels of elementary school textbooks. These include the Spache (1974) for grades 1 through 4, the New Dale-Chall (1995) for grade 1 through adult, the Wide Range (Harris & Sipay, 1990) for grades 1 through 8, and the Fry (1977b) for grade 1 through adult. Of these, the easiest to use is the Fry readability graph, which is shown in Figure 8.1.

GROUP INVENTORY PLACEMENT

In order to provide students with the proper level of textbook, it is important to know what the student's reading level is. In a typical elementary school class, there is a wide range of abilities. Although most students might be reading on or near grade level, some may be reading two or more years above grade level and some may be reading two or more years below grade level. The best technique for matching students with textbooks they can handle is to try out the books. This can be done through administering individual informal reading inventories (as explained in Chapter 13). Group inventories (Johnson, Kress, & Pikulski, 1987) and cloze tests (Singer & Donlan, 1989) based on the target textbooks can also be employed.

USING MULTILEVEL BOOKS

In the typical elementary school classroom, the teacher makes provision for individual differences, so that students are given or are able to select reading books that are on their level. However, when this same teacher switches over to history or science lessons, the whole class usually reads the same textbook, generally one designed for the average student. In a typical class, however, such a book will be too difficult for approximately one child out of four or more. Singer and Donlan (1989) claimed that in the upper grades as many as 50 percent of students may have difficulty with their textbooks. Also, some children will be able to use a more challenging book. Some provision has to be made for these different reading abilities, especially for students reading significantly below the level of the textbook.

Some easy-to-read content area textbooks are listed below. If you do use an easy-to-read textbook, make sure that it covers all the essential content. If not, supplement the book you do use with easy-to-read children's books, discussions, audiovisual aids, and simulations.

America's Story. Bernstein, V. Austin, TX: Steck-Vaughn. Although designed for high school students, this text, which is written on a second- to third-grade level, could be used with upper elementary students.

Biographies from American History. Upper Battle River, MN: Globe Fearon. Thirty historical biographies written on a second-grade level. Subjects range from Susan B. Anthony to Frank Lloyd Wright.

Adapting instruction for ESL students
In sheltered instruction, content area teachers adjust their instruction so that it becomes more comprehensible for ESL students. Teachers try to use a simplified syntax, and they also attempt to use vocabulary that the students know. To make the instruction more understandable, they may repeat key words and ideas, clarify the meanings of words and expressions that might be misunderstood, and use gestures to help convey meaning (Lapp, Flood, & Tinajero, 1994). In addition, the teacher may rely heavily on visuals to convey information (Chamot & O'Malley, 1994).

To build background in social studies and science, try reading aloud books that have a strong narrative structure or detail the lives of scientists. By reading to students, you can acquaint them with works that they might not be able to read on their own. Some possibilities for social studies are Sewall's (1986) *The Pilgrims of Plimouth,* D. P. Brown's (1985) *Sybil Rides for Independence,* Blumberg's (1987) *The Incredible Journey of Lewis and Clark,* and Sewall's (1990) *People of the Breaking Day* (an account of the Wampanoags before the coming of the Pilgrims).

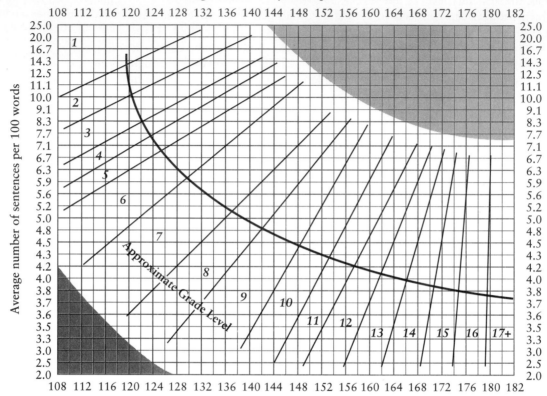

Average number of syllables per 100 words

Expanded Directions for Working Readability Graph

1. Randomly select three (3) sample passages and count out exactly 100 words each, beginning with the beginning of a sentence. Do not count proper nouns, initializations, and numerals.

2. Count the number of sentences in the hundred words, estimating length of the fraction of the last sentence to the nearest one-tenth.

3. Count the total number of syllables in the 100-word passage. If you don't have a hand counter available, an easy way is to simply put a mark above every syllable over one in each word, then when you get to the end of the passage, count the number of marks and add 100. Small calculators can also be used as counters by pushing numeral 1, then the + sign for each word or syllable when counting.

FIGURE 8.1 (continued)

4. Enter graph with *average* sentence length and *average* number of syllables; plot dot where the two lines intersect. Area where dot is plotted will give you the approximate grade level.

5. If a great deal of variability is found in syllable count or sentence count, putting more samples into the average is desirable.

6. A word is defined as a group of symbols with space on either side; thus, *Joe, IRA, 1945,* and *&* are each one word.

7. A syllable is defined as a phonetic syllable. Generally, there are as many syllables as vowel sounds. For example, *stopped* is one syllable and *wanted* is two syllables. When counting syllables for numerals and initializations, count one syllable for each symbol. For example, *1945* is four syllables, *IRA* is three syllables, and *&* is one syllable.

Note: This "extended graph" does not outmode or render the earlier (1968) version inoperative or inaccurate; it is an extension. (REPRODUCTION PERMITTED—NO COPYRIGHT)

From "Fry's Readability Graph: Clarifications, Validity, and Extension to Level 17," by E. Fry, 1977, *Journal of Reading, 21,* p. 249.

Rookie Read-about Science. Chicago: Children's Press. Easy readers that cover a wide range of topics, including seasons, weather, the five senses, mammals, and plants. Written on a first- and second-grade level.

Science in Action Series. Upper Battle River, MN: Globe Fearon. A series of twelve short texts that present major science topics on reading levels 2.5 to 4. Designed for middle school and high school students, they may be adapted for poor readers in the upper elementary grades.

Steck-Vaughn Social Studies. Austin, TX: Steck-Vaughn. Covering content traditionally presented in elementary social studies, this recently published series of six texts is written significantly below the grade levels for which they were intended.

The Wonders of Science. Gottlieb, J. Austin, TX: Steck-Vaughn. Six-book series is written at grade level 2–3 and designed for middle school and high school students; many of the topics covered are presented in the upper elementary grades. Titles in the series include *The Human Body; Water Life; The Earth and Beyond; Land Animals; Matter, Motion and Machines;* and *Plant Life.*

World History. Hart, D. Upper Battle River, MN: Globe Fearon. Although designed for middle and high school students, this text, which is written on a third- to fourth-grade level, may be used with upper elementary students.

Adapting instruction for poor readers

One technique for helping poor readers is to use the textbook in a limited way, mainly for diagrams, photos, and other illustrations. Since science topics are spiraled, a fourth-grade teacher working with students reading on a second-grade level might use the chapter on electricity from a second-grade textbook. It would be a good idea to use a book from a different series so that students would not be forced to reread a textbook that they used two years earlier. To make up for the lack of depth of material, the teacher could supplement the text with discussion, activities, and audiovisual materials. Of course, the teacher could use easy-to-read trade books.

LITERATURE IN THE CONTENT AREAS

Adapting instruction for ESL students

Bilingual youngsters, whose grasp of English may be rudimentary, do better with materials in which illustrations convey much of the information. A particularly helpful format is the fotonovela, in which illustrations and balloons containing simple text explain a process or convey a story. More advanced text at the bottom of the page is written at a higher level and goes into more detail. The text is actually written on three levels: picture or nonreading, easy reading, and intermediate or advanced reading (Barba, 1995).

Adapting instruction for poor readers

The typical sequence for handling the reading of content area textbooks is read-listen-discuss. Students read a chapter or section of text, which the teacher then explains. After the explanation, the class discusses the text. Often, a more effective sequence is listen-read-discuss, in which the teacher gives a five-to-fifteen minute explanation of the material, directs the students to read it, and then has the class discuss it. Because the explanation precedes the reading of the text, the students are much better prepared to read it (Manzo & Manzo, 1990).

In addition to or instead of using content area textbooks with poor readers, you might use easy-to-read children's books written on the topic being studied. For instance, when studying slavery, students might read *Harriet Tubman: Guide to Freedom* (Epstein & Epstein, 1968), which is written on a second-grade level. When studying the Revolutionary War, students could read *Meet George Washington* (Heilbroner, 1964), which is also written on a second-grade level. Another excellent source of brief, heavily illustrated, easy-to-read children's books is the *Young Discovery Library,* published by Charlesbridge, which includes thirty-six titles on a variety of science and social studies topics. Harper's *Trophy* series and Random House's *Step into Reading* series feature a variety of lively, easy-to-read books on dinosaurs, whales, dolphins, sharks, and historical figures.

Of course, literature can make the content areas come alive for all students—good readers as well as poor readers. For instance, it can give drama and human faces to events and people briefly described in the history textbook. Through reading *Watch the Stars Come Out* (Levinson, 1985) or *The Cat Who Escaped from Steerage* (Mayerson, 1990), students can feel what it must have been like to leave all that was familiar, crowd aboard a ship, and set sail for America. Instead of a dry paragraph or two in a history textbook, emigration becomes a lived-through experience that breathes life into long-ago events.

Literature can be brought into the content area class in a number of ways (Smith & Johnson, 1994). It can be as simple as reading for ten minutes a day one of Jean Fritz's biographies of the heroes of the fight for independence—*And Then What Happened, Paul Revere?* (1973) or *Will You Sign Here, John Hancock?* (1982). Or it could mean setting aside time once a week for the reading of books related to the Revolutionary War. Other possibilities include having the class read one or a series of books that complement information in the text—*The American Revolutionaries: A History in Their Own Words* (Meltzer, 1987), *Black Heroes of the American Revolution* (Davis, 1976), *Buttons for General Washington* (Roop & Roop, 1986), or *Can't You Make Them Behave, King George?* (Fritz, 1977). Or, a notable children's book such as *Johnny Tremain* (Forbes, 1943) could be the core of an integrated unit.

Children's books can add a multicultural perspective to content area study. When exploring inventions, students who read a biography of Thomas Edison have a deeper understanding of the process of inventing. However, along with reading about inventors traditionally presented in textbooks, students might read about black inventors in Haskin's (1991) *Outward Dreams: Black Inventors and Their Inventions.* When studying explorers, include a biography of DuSable along with those of Columbus and Magellan (Sims, 1994).

Be sure to discuss multicultural perspectives. What was the impact of the Westward Movement on Native Americans? What is their perspective on this historical event? When studying math look at the number systems created by other cultures. Look, too, at the contributions made in science by other cultures (Sims, 1994).

Exemplary Teaching

Using Literature in the Content Areas

To make history come alive in her multicultural sixth-grade classroom in New York City, Lila Alexander, working with Queens University associate professor Myra Zarnowski, used literature sets. The sets incorporated five issues: poverty, human rights, immigration, the environment, and civil rights. The literature sets included novels, photo essays, picture books, and informational texts.

Each of the five sets of books was discussed, and students chose which set they wanted to read. Students read their books and kept journals in which they recorded interesting information and their feelings about this information. Meeting in groups of five several times a week, they discussed their journal entries and related questions. During discussions Alexander and Zarnowski moved among the groups. As active participants, they encouraged children to raise important questions and make connections among the books read. They expanded students' understanding of the issues under consideration. In the following exchange, for instance, Alexander helped the group investigating immigration construct an important generalization about the way immigrants were treated:

> *Paula:* I was reading about the Irish. If America is the land of freedom, why are immigrants treated so badly?
> *Bruce:* They don't shoot them.
> *Alexander:* Paula's point was that they were badly treated.
> *Ellen:* The same thing happened to the Chinese.
> *John:* The West Indians—it was the same.
> *Alexander:* Is there a pattern here? (Zarnowski & Gallagher, 1993, p. 38).

With a little prodding and through the reading and discussion of a number of texts on the same theme, students were able to construct their own understandings of immigration, past and present. Their comprehension of immigration was richer, deeper, and far more personal than it would have been if they had simply read a brief textbook account of immigration.

INSTRUCTIONAL TECHNIQUES

The first principle of content area reading instruction is to help students construct meaning from text. The second principle is to have students focus on the big ideas. As students may not be familiar with the organizational patterns of science and social studies, a third principle is to include instruction in how to use organizational patterns to aid reading comprehension and writing. A fourth principle is to activate students' prior knowledge. Because content area subjects have their own specialized vocabularies, a fifth principle is to help students develop vocabulary and concepts. Strategy instruction is also important. Although students may have been introduced to strategies, they do not always transfer this knowledge. A sixth principle is to stress instruction in the application of learning strategies. These six principles are incorporated in the instructional techniques described in this section. Techniques for teaching students to read content area material, many of which were introduced in Chapters 6 and 7, fall in one or more of the following categories: before reading, during reading, and after reading.

BEFORE READING

In preparing to read a text, strategic readers survey the selection, activate appropriate prior knowledge, predict what the text will be about, set goals, and decide how to read the material. To help the reader learn and apply these strategies independently, the teacher uses the DRA and DR-TA, which were introduced in Chapter 7, and the following instructional procedures: PReP, anticipation guides, survey technique, and structured overviews.

PREP

PReP (prereading plan) is a diagnostic and instructional technique designed to help the teacher build background knowledge and prepare instruction.

The **prereading plan (PReP)** is both a diagnostic and an instructional device. It helps the teacher diagnose students' prior knowledge and provide necessary instruction to prepare them for comprehending the main concept in an upcoming selection (Langer, 1981). For students who already know a great deal about the topic, PReP can help them determine which information is relevant. For those who do not realize that they are familiar with the subject, PReP can help them activate prior knowledge. For students who have a limited background, the technique can be used to expand what knowledge they do have. It can also help the teacher decide whether the students have adequate knowledge to bring to a selection or whether some additional concept building is required (Tierney, Readence, & Dishner, 1995). PReP has four main steps, which are described in Lesson 8.1.

Lesson 8.1
Using PReP

Step 1. Preparation

Examining the text, the teacher decides on the key concept that she or he wishes to stress. The teacher then chooses a word, phrase, or picture to initiate a discussion. In preparation for reading the first section of *Exploring the Sky by Day* (Dickinson, 1988), for example, the teacher might decide that the concept to be stressed is that each of the four layers of the atmosphere has certain characteristics.

Step 2. Initial association

The teacher invites the class to brainstorm about the topic. She says, "Tell what comes to mind when you hear the word *atmosphere*." Responses are written on the board. Brainstorming enables students to make associations between their prior knowledge and the key concept. Associations might include *clouds, sky, rain,* and *pilot.*

Step 3. Reflections

Students reflect on their initial associations. The teacher asks what it was that made them think of these words. In this second stage of the discussion, students "develop awareness of their network of associations" (Langer, 1981, p. 154). They also listen to the responses of others. This helps them evaluate and organize their associations and, perhaps, think of additional ones.

Step 4. Reformulation

Students refine and expand their concepts. The teacher asks if, based on the discussion, students have any new ideas about the atmosphere. Responses are generally clearer and more fully developed. Students have had a chance to search their memories for related knowledge and to learn from their peers.

Throughout the discussion, the teacher uses directed questions to help students clarify and elaborate responses and make connections. The teacher also evaluates students' prior knowledge to determine whether it is adequate to build a bridge between what they know and the content of the text. If it is adequate, the discussion can lead into a purpose for reading, one that builds on students' knowledge. In this instance, the teacher judges the students' background to be adequate and has them read the selection. The teacher's purpose question is "What are the main characteristics of each level of the atmosphere?" If students' background seems inadequate, the teacher might decide to do some spot teaching or decide that more extensive preparation is needed.

ANTICIPATION GUIDES

There is nothing like a good old-fashioned debate to perk up a class. Everyone, young and old, enjoys expressing opinions on controversial subjects. One device that capitalizes on this predilection is the **anticipation guide**—a simple listing of three or more debatable statements about a topic that students indicate whether they agree with before they read about the topic. (An adapted anticipation guide introduces each chapter in this book.)

Besides building interest, the anticipation guide activates prior knowledge. Readers have to activate information that they possess to decide whether they agree or disagree with each statement. The guide also gives students a purpose for reading: to evaluate their responses. In addition, it opens the students' minds. Some students, especially those who are younger and poor readers, tend to reject statements in print that contradict concepts they might have (Lipson, 1984; Maria & MacGinitie, 1987). By comparing their responses with what the author said and by listening to the class discussion of the statements, they can correct and clarify these ideas.

The anticipation guide can be used with any age group and works best when students have some familiarity with the subject. If they do not know anything about it, they do not have much to agree or disagree with. The guide is also most effective when used with subjects about which students have misconceptions—for example, diet, pollution, legal rights, snakes, and insects. The recommended steps for constructing an anticipation guide are described in Lesson 8.2 (Head & Readence, 1986).

> An **anticipation guide** is an instructional technique designed to activate prior knowledge and have students reflect on it.

> The anticipation guide should help students refine erroneous concepts since it involves confronting misconceptions.

Lesson 8.2
Using an anticipation guide

Step 1. Identification of major concepts

List three or four major concepts that you wish students to learn.

Step 2. Determination of students' background

Consider the experiential and cultural backgrounds of your students. Ask yourself how their backgrounds will affect their knowledge and beliefs about the topic under study. What misconceptions might they have?

Step 3. Creation of statements for the guide

Write three to five statements (or more) that are sufficiently open-ended or general to encourage a discussion. Do not choose simple, factual statements. Instead, think of those that might touch on students' misconceptions or involve areas in which students have partial knowledge. The statements can be arranged in the order in which the concepts they reflect appear in the selection or from simplest to most complex. They may be written on the chalkboard or on paper.

Step 4. Introduction of the guide

Introduce and explain the guide, and have students respond to the statements. Emphasize that they should think about their responses because they will be asked to defend them.

Step 5. Discussion of responses

Talk over each statement. You might begin by having students raise their hands if they agree with it. Ask volunteers to tell why they agreed or disagreed.

Step 6. Reading of the text

Sum up the main points of the discussion and have students read the text to compare their responses with what the material states. In some instances, the text may contain information that proves or disproves a statement. However, if the statements have been constructed carefully, they will be sufficiently open-ended that students will find information that may support a position but will not prove it one way or another.

Step 7. Discussion of text and statements

Talk over each statement in light of the information in the text. Ask students if they changed their responses because of information in the text. Ask what that information was and why they changed their minds. Responses can be discussed in small or large groups. If small groups are used, bring the whole class together for a summary after the groups have finished their discussions. At this point, you might want to go over at greater length any statements that seem especially controversial or confusing.

SURVEY TECHNIQUE

Survey is a study strategy that students use to get an overview of a selection.

The **survey** is a near duplicate of the first stage of SQ3R, a study technique that is explained later in this chapter. It, too, orients the reader to the material to be read and sets up purposes for reading. It is so useful that students are able to answer 20–30 percent of the chapter's review questions just on the basis of completing the survey (Tierney, Readence, & Dishner, 1995). The advantage of the survey is that it requires little time and effort. It can be used as preliminary instruction before SQ3R or as a stand-alone method for children who might not use SQ3R. The survey technique has six steps, as outlined below (Aukerman, 1972).

1. *Analysis of the chapter title.* The chapter title is analyzed fairly thoroughly with questions such as these: "What do you think this chapter will be about? What do you know about the topic in this chapter?"
2. *Analysis of subheads.* Subheads are turned into questions, as in the SQ3R. Questions are placed on the chalkboard so that they can serve as guides to the selection.
3. *Analysis of graphics.* Photos, graphs, maps, charts, tables, and other illustrative materials are examined and discussed. Particular attention is paid to elements that students might have difficulty interpreting, such as a map or graph.
4. *Discussion of introductory paragraph.* Students read and discuss the introductory paragraph. Information contained there is compared with information garnered from analysis of the title, subheads, and graphics.
5. *Discussion of summary.* Students read and discuss the summary. A well-written summary will highlight the main points covered in the selection.
6. *Construction of main idea.* Based on the previous steps, students can construct a main idea statement about the selection's contents.

STRUCTURED OVERVIEWS

Students learn new concepts more easily if they can relate them to old ones. It is also helpful if students have an overview of what is to be learned so that they can see this relationship and how the new concepts are related to each other. For example, it is easier to understand the new concepts *gavials* and *caimans* once one sees that these creatures are related to alligators and crocodiles and that they all belong to the group known as *crocodilians*.

Adapting a strategy devised by Ausubel (1960) known as the advanced organizer, Barron (1969) created the **structured overview,** which uses vocabulary words to relate new materials to old materials and to show interrelationships among both old and new concepts. The overview should provide a structure "so that it does not appear to students that they are being taught a series of unrelated or equally important words" (Estes, Mills, & Barron, 1969, p. 41). To construct an overview, follow the six steps listed below (Barron, 1969).

A **structured overview** is a technique designed to help students relate new words and concepts to known ones.

1. *Selection of concepts.* Analyze the selection to be read or unit to be introduced, and select two to four concepts that you think are important.
2. *Analysis of vocabulary.* Analyze and list the vocabulary necessary to understand the concepts.
3. *Arrangement of words.* Arrange the list of words into a diagram that shows their interrelationships.
4. *Addition of known words.* Add vocabulary words that you think students already understand so that they can see how the new words relate to them.
5. *Evaluation of overview.* Evaluate the overview. Ask if the major relationships are clearly shown. Can the overview be simplified and still do a good job?
6. *Introduction of overview.* Introduce students to the learning task. Display the structured overview, and explain why you arranged the words the way you

did. Have students suggest any words they want to add. During the learning task, use the overview as a guide. As the new words are encountered, refer to their position on the overview and discuss how they are related to the other words. Also feel free to add new words.

An example of how an organizer might be constructed and used follows: Using *Merrill Science* (Hackett, Moyer, & Adams, 1989), a popular textbook series, a fifth-grade class has just finished a unit on invertebrates and are now tackling a unit on vertebrates. The teacher examines the textbook chapter and thinks about what students already know about vertebrates, and what he would like them to learn. The teacher decides to emphasize the following concepts:

1. Vertebrates have a skeleton.
2. There are seven main groups of vertebrates.

The teacher then lists the following words that he thinks would be necessary to understand the two concepts about vertebrates:

vertebrates	fish	reptiles	amphibians	warm-blooded
backbone	jawless fish	lizards	newts	cold-blooded
mammals	cartilage fish	turtles		metamorphosis
birds	bony fish	crocodilians		

The teacher organizes the words in a structured overview. He then examines the overview and adds *animals, invertebrates,* and *no backbones,* so that students can see how the information on vertebrates fits in with the information on invertebrates. Believing that the word *amphibian* would be unknown, the teacher adds *frogs* to the list so that students will have an example of an amphibian.

The teacher evaluates the overview. The words *metamorphosis* and *newts* are important; however, they seem to be making the display too complex, so he removes them. The revised structured overview is shown in Figure 8.2.

The teacher presents the overview. The class discusses the fact that there are two main types of animals: vertebrates and invertebrates. Various interrelationships are discussed. A question is raised about *cartilage;* its meaning is discussed.

The overview becomes a unifying element for the unit. As each group of vertebrates is discussed, the class refers to the overview. It is expanded to include other examples of amphibians, reptiles, birds, mammals, and the three kinds of fish. Thus students are able to see how these new words relate to the ones already contained in the structured overview.

As students gain skill in seeing relationships, they take part in constructing the overviews. They might construct overviews in cooperative learning groups. Eventually, they should be guided to use these tools as a study aid. Although designed to be used at the beginning of a unit or lesson, overviews can also be used as a summary at its conclusion.

DURING READING

During reading, strategic readers construct meaning. They distinguish between important and unimportant details and organize information from text. They also integrate information from text with prior knowledge, make inferences, check

FIGURE 8.2 | A sample structured overview

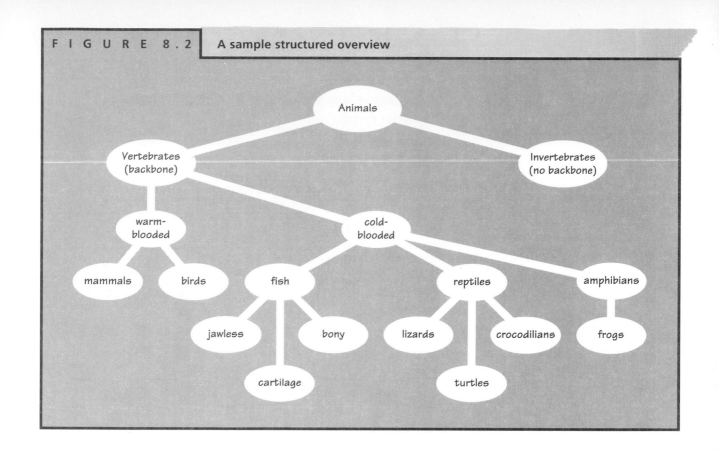

predictions, seek clarification, and, perhaps, create images of scenes and events portrayed by the text. They use the structure of the text as an aid to comprehension. Strategic readers also regulate their rate of reading and monitor their understanding of the passage. They may reread or seek clarification if their comprehension breaks down.

During-reading strategies include using chapter organization, text structure, and think-alouds. Study guides, which are teacher-created devices designed to foster comprehension, are also presented. One during-reading strategy, imaging, was discussed in Chapter 6. Although not discussed in this section, it should be noted that imaging works just as well with content area text as it does with fiction. Students can create a sensory image of what it was like to travel west in the 1850s or visualize the parts of a plant.

CHAPTER ORGANIZATION AND TEXT STRUCTURE

Along with visuals, numerous typographical aids are generally included in most content area textbooks to assist the reader in determining organization and noting important points. These include the title, subheads, colored panels, sidebars, bullets, use of color type, and words printed in italics or boldface. Questions might

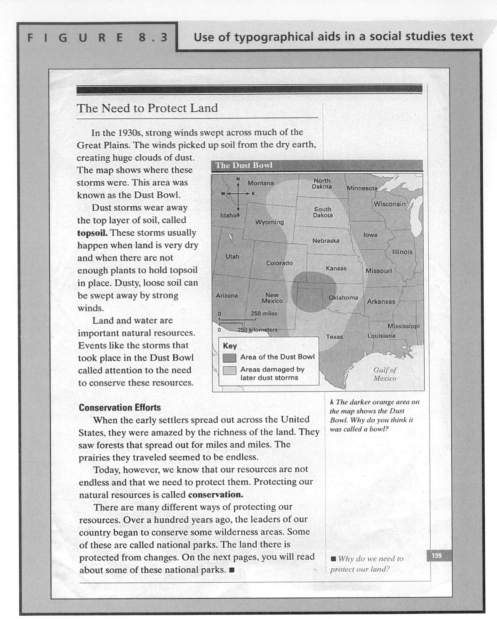

The Need to Protect Land

In the 1930s, strong winds swept across much of the Great Plains. The winds picked up soil from the dry earth, creating huge clouds of dust. The map shows where these storms were. This area was known as the Dust Bowl.

Dust storms wear away the top layer of soil, called **topsoil.** These storms usually happen when land is very dry and when there are not enough plants to hold topsoil in place. Dusty, loose soil can be swept away by strong winds.

Land and water are important natural resources. Events like the storms that took place in the Dust Bowl called attention to the need to conserve these resources.

Conservation Efforts

When the early settlers spread out across the United States, they were amazed by the richness of the land. They saw forests that spread out for miles and miles. The prairies they traveled seemed to be endless.

Today, however, we know that our resources are not endless and that we need to protect them. Protecting our natural resources is called **conservation.**

There are many different ways of protecting our resources. Over a hundred years ago, the leaders of our country began to conserve some wilderness areas. Some of these are called national parks. The land there is protected from changes. On the next pages, you will read about some of these national parks. ■

▲ *The darker orange area on the map shows the Dust Bowl. Why do you think it was called a bowl?*

■ *Why do we need to protect our land?*

From *Houghton Mifflin Social Studies: From Sea to Shining Sea* (p. 199), by B. J. Armento, G. B. Nash, C. L. Salter, and K. K. Wixson, 1991, Boston: Houghton Mifflin. Copyright © 1991 by Houghton Mifflin Company. Reprinted by permission of Houghton Mifflin Company.

also be posed in the margins. Figure 8.3 displays a page that uses a number of these devices. Although typographical aids are often used to preview a chapter, they should also be used as the reader interacts with the reading. Personal observation and experience suggest that they are given only limited attention, however. Perhaps students do not realize their full value. With the help of a textbook that makes especially good use of these elements, explain the purpose and value of each one. Then model how you might use them to aid your understanding of the content.

THINK-ALOUDS

Think-alouds are just what their name suggests. The teacher models a silent reading strategy by thinking aloud as she or he processes a text, thus making explicit skills that normally cannot be observed. Originally a research technique for studying reading processes, think-alouds are used to model comprehension processes such as making predictions, creating images, linking information in text with prior knowledge, monitoring comprehension, and using a fix-up strategy when there is a problem with word recognition or comprehension. In addition to being a demonstration technique, think-alouds can be used by students to become more aware of their reading processes and to make needed changes in the way they read. Lesson 8.3 illustrates how the technique is put into operation as a repair strategy when comprehension has failed.

Think-alouds follow the expert-apprentice model. As the expert, the teacher demonstrates how he or she reads text so that the pupil-apprentice can gain insight into the process. Cooperative learning is also involved as students work on their think-alouds with partners.

Lesson 8.3
Think-alouds

Step 1. Modeling

The teacher reads a brief passage aloud, showing what her or his thoughts are when the text does not make sense and what repair strategies she or he might implement:

> Like a camera, the picture of the outside world which lands on the retina is upside down. The brain turns it the right way up as it interprets the messages from the retina. (Baldwin & Lister, 1984, p. 9)

Then the teacher thinks aloud, "I don't get this. I don't know where the retina is. I'll take a look at the diagram. There it is; it's the lining at the back of the eyeball, and there's the optic nerve. The optic nerve goes from the retina to the brain. Now I understand."

Step 2. Working with partners

Students take turns reading brief passages orally to each other. The selections should be fairly difficult or contain problems. The reader thinks aloud to show what processes he or she is using, what problems he or she is encountering, and how he or she is attempting to solve those problems. The partner is encouraged to ask questions: "Are you trying to picture the main character as you read? Do you see any words you don't know?"

Step 3. Practicing

Students practice thinking through materials as they read them silently. Self-questionnaires or checklists are used to encourage readers to use active processes and to monitor their reading. A sample self-questionnaire, in which students may answer the questions orally or in writing, is shown in Figure 8.4.

As an alternative to a self-questionnaire, you might use a checklist such as the one in Figure 8.5 (Davey, 1983). It assesses use of predictions (made

FIGURE 8.4   A think-aloud self-questionnaire

A. Before reading
   1. How do I prepare for reading?

B. During reading
   1. What do I do to improve my understanding of what I am reading?
   2. What do I do if I come across a word I don't know?
   3. What do I do if the selection doesn't make sense?

C. After reading
   1. Do I do anything special with the information I just read? If so, what?

predictions), images (formed pictures), analogies ("like-a"), monitoring of difficulties (problems), and repair strategies (fix-ups). The "like-a" strategy is especially useful. Students think of a link between an earlier experience (prior knowledge) and information in the text: "This is like the time I thought I knew all my spelling words and I didn't study, and I got half the words wrong."

A technique recommended by Smith and Dauer (1984) is having students code material. As students read content area material, they make notations

FIGURE 8.5   Think-aloud checklist

During my reading, I did the following: (Circle one word in each row.)

Made predictions	Never	Sometimes	Often
Formed pictures in my mind	Never	Sometimes	Often
Thought of "like-a" times	Never	Sometimes	Often
Found problems in my reading	Never	Sometimes	Often
Used fix-ups	Never	Sometimes	Often

Adapted from "Thinking Aloud—Modeling the Cognitive Processes of Reading Comprehension," by B. Davey, 1983, *Journal of Reading, 27,* p. 46.

on accompanying slips of paper: A = agree, B = bored, C = clear, D = disagree, H = hard, I = important, M = main idea, N = not clear, and so on. The teacher models the technique and provides guided practice before asking students to undertake coding. Teachers who have used the codes report that students' comprehension and attitude improve as teachers gain insight into specific problems that students are having with the text, which include difficulties with word meaning, concepts, and comprehension of certain types of sentences and structures, and are able to focus on those problems. The teachers also report that the method is easy to implement.

Step 4. Applying think-alouds

Students apply the strategy to everyday and content area material. From time to time, the teacher models predicting, visualizing, or other strategies. Discussion questions address both content and process as the teacher discusses means that students used to cope with reading material: "What pictures did you create in your mind as you read? Were there any confusing passages? How did you handle them?"

STUDY GUIDES

Study guides are flexible, time-tested devices that help students during as well as after reading. They can take a variety of forms, such as asking students to respond mentally to a series of questions, to match items, to indicate whether statements are true or false, to fill in blanks, to complete a time line, a semantic map, a structured overview, or a comparison-contrast chart, to list the steps of a process, or to work a crossword puzzle. The best guides help students organize information and reflect on it. Follow the procedure outlined below when creating a study guide.

A **study guide** is a teacher-prepared set of questions or other activities designed to foster understanding of a selection that students read independently.

1. Analyze the selection to be read. Note the major concepts or principles that you think students should learn. Make a note of the sections that students must read to grasp the concepts. The chapter may cover concepts that you do not think are important. Indicate those pages so that students can skip unnecessary parts.
2. Consider elements of the text that might pose problems for students, such as difficult vocabulary, figurative language, confusing explanations, or complex organization.
3. Assess the organizational patterns of the chapter, such as enumeration/description, sequential, process/explanation, or other (see Chapter 7 for a description of patterns). Keep in mind that more than one pattern may be used.
4. Note strategies or skills that students might use to get the most out of the reading.
5. Construct a study guide that leads students to critical content, aids them in overcoming potential hindrances to comprehension, and directs them in the use of appropriate strategies and skills.

Study guides can be constructed for aiding comprehension, highlighting key concepts, providing extra help for poor readers, examining both sides of a controversial subject, and so on.

Several sample guides are described in the following pages. Figure 8.6 presents a general all-purpose content guide that focuses on the key information in a chapter.

FIGURE 8.6 | A content study guide

The section tells about the founding of Jamestown, the first successful colony. Read it to find out how Jamestown became a successful colony.

A. Find the answers to the following questions. The page and column numbers where answers can be found are written on the left.

p. 117, cols. 1 & 2   Where and when was Jamestown started?

p. 119, cols. 1 & 2   What problems did the Jamestown settlers have?

p. 119, col. 2   What rule did Captain John Smith make up?

p. 119, col. 2   Why was tobacco important to the settlers?

p. 120, col. 2   Who were the indentured servants?

p. 121, cols. 1 & 2   How do you know that Jamestown became a success?

B. Match the following by drawing a line between the item on the right and the item on the left that it identifies.

Pocahontas	First person to grow tobacco
John Smith	Saved John Smith
James I	Sent expeditions to Roanoke Island
Sir Walter Raleigh	King of England
Elizabeth Dare	Leader of Jamestown
John Rolfe	First English child born in the New World

C. Using the dates and events listed below, create a time line.

1584   1586   1607   1608   1614   1619

Settlers were given the right to own land.

The colonists were given the right to make their own laws.

Jamestown was founded.

John Smith was chosen to be the leader of Jamestown.

Sir Walter Raleigh sent the first expedition to Roanoke.

Sir Walter Raleigh sent a second expedition to Roanoke.

D. Fill in the blanks with the following vocabulary words: *burgess, indentured, peninsula, profits, stock.*

1. At first, the Virginia Company lost money and so there were no _____ .
2. The people who bought _____ in the Virginia Company became the company's owners.
3. After the seven years were up, many of the _____ servants started small farms.
4. Settlers who wanted new laws passed would speak to the _____ from their area.
5. Because it was built on a _____ , Jamestown was nearly surrounded by water.

E. Discuss the following statements. Be able to give reasons for your responses.

Captain John Smith was a good leader.

Jamestown's first settlers were well prepared for life in the New World.

Knowing what I know now, I would have sailed to Jamestown with Captain Christopher Newport/I would have stayed home in England.

Text drawn from *The United States Yesterday and Today* (pp. 117–121), by T. M. Helmus, E. A. Toppin, N. J. G. Pounds, and V. E. Arnsdorf, 1988, Morristown, NJ: Silver Burdett & Ginn.

PATTERN GUIDES

Detecting the pattern of writing in a piece fosters both understanding and retention (Herber, 1970). For example, if readers realize that the author is using a comparison pattern to discuss U.S. Presidents Harry Truman and Franklin D. Roosevelt, they can mentally sort the information into the proper categories. If readers know that a piece has a main idea/details organization, they can mentally file the details under the main idea.

A pattern guide can take various forms. It may be a partially completed outline in which just the main ideas are included. Or it may involve matching causes and effects or a compare/contrast pattern (Estes & Vaughn, 1985). The sample pattern guide in Figure 8.7 not only helps students obtain essential information

Adapting instruction for ESL students
Study guides can be constructed in such a way as to provide assistance with key vocabulary, difficult syntactic structures, figures of speech, and any language elements that might hinder students' comprehension. This would be especially helpful for ESL students. The guides can also highlight illustrations and diagrams that students might use to further their understanding of the passage.

FIGURE 8.7 | **A pattern guide on food makers**

All living creatures must have food to stay alive, even plants. Plants make food for themselves, for animals, and for us. Read "Food Makers," pp. 350–353. Find out where plants store their food, what kinds of food-producing plants there are, and what forms of food plants make. After reading the section, complete the outline by listing supporting details under main ideas.

A. Where food is stored in plants
   1. Roots—carrots
   2.
   3.

B. Types of food producers in a water community
   1. Plants with roots—cattails
   2.
   3.
   4.

C. Types of food producers in a forest community
   1. Ground layer—mosses
   2.
   3.

D. Forms of food made by plants
   1. Starch—beans
   2.

Guide designed for use with *Holt Science 4* (pp. 350–353), by J. Abruscato, J. Fusco, D. Peck, and J. Strange, 1989, New York: Holt, Rinehart and Winston.

---

from the section, it also assists them in organizing that information so they can note the main ideas and see how the details relate to them.

AFTER READING

After completing reading, strategic readers reflect on what they have read, continue to integrate new information with old information, may evaluate the new information or use it in some way, and may seek additional information on the topic. To help students learn to use after-reading strategies, the teacher can apply several instructional procedures in addition to summarizing, retelling, and other postreading strategies covered in previous chapters. These additional procedures include constructing analogies, creating graphic organizers, and applying and extending.

CONSTRUCTING ANALOGIES

Analogies can foster comprehension. Students better understand an article about the game of cricket when given analogies between cricket and baseball, or other information from which they can construct their own analogies (Hayes & Tierney, 1982). An analogy between the functioning of cells in the body and the operation of a factory will also lead to improved comprehension.

Recognizing and constructing analogies is one way of helping students bridge the gap between the new and the old. Point out analogies when they appear. Traditional analogies include the eye and a camera, the heart and a pump, the brain and a computer, and the memory and a file cabinet. Help students create their own analogies by comparing old information and new concepts. Self-created analogies are generally more effective than those made up by others.

CREATING GRAPHIC ORGANIZERS

Graphic organizers are visual devices designed to help readers note relationships between key concepts or events in a selection.

One of the most effective ways to understand and retain complex content area information is to use some sort of **graphic organizer** to represent key concepts, main points, or basic steps. The content and structure of material and the teaching-learning purpose dictate the type of organizer used: structured overview, time line, or an organizer that highlights the steps in a process, contrasts elements, or identifies causes.

One of the most useful graphic organizers is the structured overview because it shows subordinate relationships. Figure 8.8 shows a structured overview for the concept of galaxies. Earlier in this chapter, the structured overview was presented as a device for preparing students to read. It also can be created or added to as an after-reading strategy. It then becomes a method to enhance understanding and retention, especially if students play an active role in creating it. After the selection has been read, its elements would be discussed again. Information obtained from reading might be placed on lines beneath each element. For example, a brief definition of the word *galaxy* might be given, together with descriptions of irregular, spiral, and elliptical galaxies.

If given their own copies of the overview, students can add information about the elements as they read. They can also use drawings to illustrate concepts, such as irregular, spiral, and elliptical galaxies. In time, they can aid in constructing

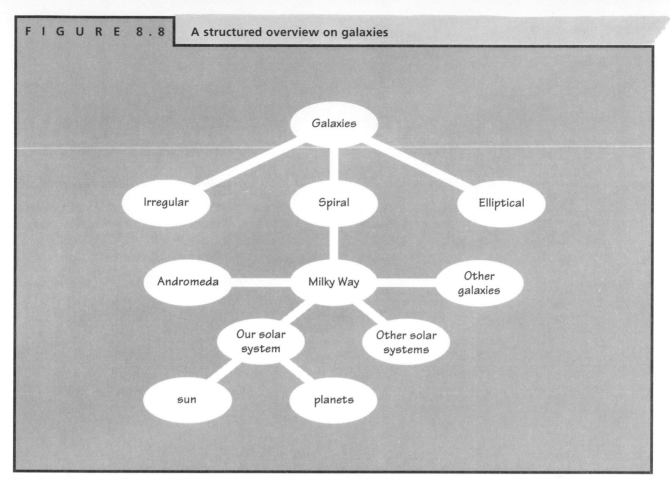

Text drawn from *Merrill Science 5* (pp. 98–99), by J. K. Hackett, R. H. Moyer, and D. K. Adams, 1989, Columbus, OH: Merrill.

overviews or make their own. Through creation of graphic organizers, students achieve better understanding of essential processes and concepts. Retention is also aided. A structured overview may also be created in its entirety after a selection has been read, in which case it functions as a summary of major concepts.

Another kind of graphic organizer that can be used as a postreading aid was presented in Chapter 7—an organizer that reflects the actual structure of the text (enumeration/description, time sequence, explanation/process, comparison/ contrast, problem/solution, or cause/effect). Building as it does on structure, this kind of organizer enhances understanding of the interrelationships of the ideas covered in the text or the process being explained. For instance, an explanation/process organizer can be used to show how an engine operates, how solar cells turn sunlight into energy, how the water cycle operates, or how numerous other systems work (see Figure 8.9). Boxes or circles containing explanatory text show the steps in the process, with arrows indicating the flow of the process.

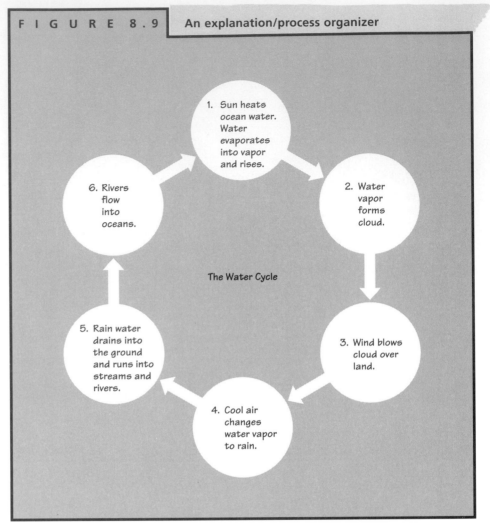

FIGURE 8.9 An explanation/process organizer

Based on text from *Fearon's United States Geography*, by W. Lefkowitz, 1990, Belmont, CA: Fearon Education.

For some elements, the best graphic organizer is a diagram. For example, a diagram is the best way to show the parts of the eye (see Figure 8.10). Initially, a diagram can be drawn or traced by the teacher. However, having students create their own diagram makes reading an active process.

For reading material that has a chronological organization, a time chart is a useful way to highlight major events (see Figure 8.11 for an example). A time line serves the same function and may be used instead of a time chart. Often, two or more kinds of graphic organizers can be combined. For instance, a map showing the voyages of the French explorers might be used together with the time chart in Figure 8.11.

FIGURE 8.10 Diagram of the eye

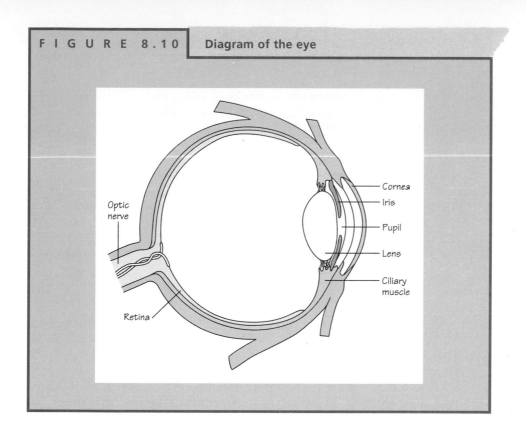

APPLYING AND EXTENDING

A particularly effective way of deepening comprehension is to reflect on one's own reading, which often results in a sense of not knowing enough or wanting to know more. Encourage students to use and extend what they know by expanding their knowledge. They can do this by reading books that explore a particular topic in detail or ones that provide enjoyment while increasing knowledge—for example, a book of math puzzles, one on bird watching, or a piece of historical fiction.

Reinforcement Activities
After-reading strategies

- Putting knowledge to use expands and enhances it. After completing a unit on the heart and circulation, encourage students to exercise regularly and eat a balanced diet. A unit on geology may encourage some children to become rock collectors. A unit on weather could provide the impetus for some readers to set up a weather-watchers' club. A study of plants may inspire others to become novice gardeners. Provide encouragement and printed materials that explain how to turn interests into hobbies.

| FIGURE 8.11 | A time chart |

1524—Verrazano explored the eastern coast of North America.

1535—Jacques Cartier sailed up the Saint Lawrence River and claimed that area for France.

1608—Samuel de Champlain founded Quebec, the first permanent French colony in the Americas.

1673—Father Marquette and Louis Joliet set out on a journey that took them to the Mississippi River.

1682—Robert de La Salle reached the Gulf of Mexico after canoeing down the Mississippi River. He claimed the area for France.

■ Provide students with project book kits. Recently, an enterprising publisher packaged an easy-to-read book on bird watching with a clear plastic birdfeeder. With the feeder as a motivating device and means of application, readers can apply knowledge obtained from the book to identify the birds that visit the feeder. Other possibilities for project kits include a book on magnets and a set of magnets, a book on plants with packets of seeds and soil in a tray, a book on stamp collecting and some canceled stamps, and a book on robots and a kit for building a model robot. ● ● ● ●

KWL PLUS: A TECHNIQUE FOR BEFORE, DURING, AND AFTER READING

KWL Plus (*K*now, *W*ant to know, and *L*earn) is a technique designed to help readers build and organize background as well as seek out and reflect on key elements in a reading selection.

A lesson designed to give students an active role before, during, and after reading is **KWL Plus:** Know, Want to know, and Learn. According to Ogle (1989), KWL evolved as she and a number of classroom teachers searched for a way to "build active personal reading of expository text" (p. 206).

The before-reading stage of KWL consists of four steps: brainstorming, categorizing, anticipating or predicting, and questioning. Brainstorming begins when the teacher asks the class what they know about a topic. If they are about to read a selection about camels, for example, the teacher asks what they know about camels. Responses are written on the board and discussed. If a disagreement occurs or students seem puzzled by a statement, this cognitive conflict can be used to create a what-we-want-to-know question. The group brainstorming activates prior knowledge so that students become more aware of what they know. The students would then write about their personal knowledge of camels in the first column of a KWL worksheet.

Next, in a step similar to semantic mapping, students categorize their prior knowledge. The process of categorization is modeled. Brainstormed items already

FIGURE 8.12 | KWL Plus

Name: _____ Topic: _Army ants_ Date: _____

What we know	What we want to find out	What we learned	What we still have to learn
H Live in the jungle	How large a	Tens of thousands	Do army ants
C Are fierce	group do army	form a group.	harm people?
H Live in	ants form?	The queen lays	What are larvae
the ground	Why are there so	100,000 to	and pupae?
F Eat plants	many army ants	300,000 eggs	
C Work together	in a group?	at a time.	
F Eat insects	Why do the ants	Form armies to get	
	form armies?	food for larvae	
	What do army ants	and pupae	
	eat?	Kill other insects	
		and small animals	
		and take them	
		back to their	
		home	
		Live in the ground	
		or in trees in the	
		jungles of South	
		America	

Categories of information we expect to see

Habitat
Food
Characteristics
Society
Travel
Appearance

written on the board are placed in appropriate categories. Students then label the items in the *what we know* column with letters that indicate category names as shown in Figure 8.12: H = habitat, C = characteristics, and F = food. Students also anticipate what categories of information the author will provide. This helps them both anticipate the content of the text and organize the information as they read it. The process of anticipating categories is modeled. The teacher might ask, for example, what kinds of information an author might provide about camels. Students then write these items at the bottom of the KWL worksheet.

In the third step, questions are created. As a group, the class discusses what they want to know about camels. Questions are written on the chalkboard. Each student then records in the second column of the worksheet her or his personal questions.

With these questions in mind, the class reads the text. After reading, students discuss what they learned and the teacher writes their responses on the chalkboard. Information is organized, misconceptions are clarified, and emerging concepts are developed more fully. After the discussion, students enter what they learned personally in the third column. In light of this information, they cross out any misconceptions that were written in the first column. They may find that they still have questions about the topic, so a fourth column—with the heading *what we still want to know*—could be added to the worksheet. You might also discuss with the class how they might go about finding the answers to the questions they still have. A completed KWL worksheet is presented in Figure 8.12. Ogle (1989) presents a fuller description of KWL, including a sample lesson.

The KWL approach can be simplified by omitting the category phase. Primary-grade teachers might use it strictly as a group technique until students have sufficient writing ability to fill out the worksheet individually. However, teachers have found that just discussing what we know, what we want to find out, and what we have learned is helpful. The ultimate purpose is to lead students to ask these questions automatically as they read.

TEACHING CONTENT AREA KNOWLEDGE

Throughout this book, using strategies has been stressed; however, content and strategies must be integrated, as the former often dictates the latter (Peters, 1990). Each discipline has its own structure and tools of inquiry. Historians, for example, use diaries, original documents, journals, and so on; history texts involve time sequence and cause/effect structures. Geographers use maps, graphs, and charts; their writings reflect descriptive and process structures. Learning to read and write in the content areas requires adjusting strategies to structures.

Cooperative learning groups can foster content area learning, especially for students who are still learning English.

A second key requirement is an adequate base of knowledge. Peters (1990) commented, "Without sufficient domain knowledge, comprehension is impeded, strategies cannot be used appropriately, learning is fragmented, and transfer of knowledge is impaired" (p. 69). "The most sophisticated processing strategies will not be of much help if a text deals with a totally foreign domain" (Weaver & Kintsch, 1991, p. 237).

Knowing assorted facts about a content area is not sufficient. What is needed to enhance comprehension is a depth of knowledge about a topic (Pressley, 1994). It is not enough to simply tell students about the food pyramid; students must process that information. They must understand the significance of the food pyramid, why carbohydrates are at the bottom and fats are at the top. Of course, they should know what carbohydrates and fats are. Students should also be thinking about the foods they eat and how their own diet stacks up in terms of the food pyramid.

Moreover, reading in the content areas involves reading to learn and may require going beyond comprehension. For instance, a reader may be able to answer a series of questions about a selection in a computer manual but still be unable to carry out the instructions it contains. In his research, Kintsch found that some students could answer questions about math problems but could not solve the problems. When reading to learn, readers must go beyond comprehension to a level where they can construct a mental map of a math procedure or create an image of a procedure or problem. Their performance will depend more on that mental model than it will on their memory of the text itself. Integrated into a student's model of a procedure, for example, will be the student's prior knowledge and experience with the procedure as well as information from the text.

This is the key question the teacher should ask: "What must students be able to do as a result of reading this text?" This is a step beyond merely remembering, so the teacher must go beyond merely fostering comprehension. She or he must plan for and assist in the creation of the mental model of the situation, problem, or concept. Instead of simply asking whether the student can answer a series of questions about the text, the teacher must inquire whether the student can perform the actual and/or mental operation the text requires.

One of the great dangers of content area instruction is overreliance on strategies and neglect of content. This book espouses the schema and mental models concepts of reading, both of which emphasize the importance of the reader's background. It is important to balance strategy instruction with background building.

READING FOR CONCEPTUAL CHANGE

When students read in the content areas, they must be prepared to modify their schemata to reflect new knowledge. This can be especially difficult in science. Students' ideas about natural phenomena are often deeply entrenched but erroneous. Their naturalistic explanations seem logical and are hard to change. For instance, many elementary school students believe that plants get their food from the soil (Roth, 1991; Smith & Anderson, 1984). Moreover, even after reading that plants produce their own food, students do not alter this belief. Left on their own, most of them, slow as well as bright students, use ineffective strategies to read science texts and so fail to grasp essential information on a conceptual level.

Some students memorize technical terms, or isolate facts without integrating them with each other or with prior knowledge. Others interpret the material in terms of their own ideas, which they fail to revise in light of information from the text. Even better students expect that the text will confirm their misconceptions and are unable to reconstruct their schema in terms of the facts. They end up distorting what they read so that it fits in with their schema. C. W. Anderson (1987) commented, "With prior knowledge taking the driver's seat in the process, learning was often quite different from what was intended by the authors" (p. 83).

Successful readers are those who use a conceptual change strategy. They integrate their prior knowledge with information from the text but use facts in the text to reconstruct their schema. In other words, they adapt or accommodate their schema so that it fits what they read, rather than vice versa. This proves to be an intellectually demanding task. Students may report that the text is confusing and difficult. Successful students are aware of the conflict between their beliefs and text and understand that they are changing their beliefs to conform to information in the book.

When students are reading science or other material that may conflict with their personal views, steps have to be taken to ensure conceptual change. Prior knowledge should be activated so that students become aware of what they know about a given topic. Equally important, they have to realize what they do not know, what they are unsure of, and what they should know. Techniques such as brainstorming, structured overviews, KWL, anticipation guides, and, of course, prereading discussions can help. Any preparatory activities used should include a discussion of key concepts and other areas that are likely to be misunderstood.

Unfortunately, many of students' commonsense beliefs about the real world are erroneous. Deeply entrenched, they are difficult to dislodge and demand direct confrontation.

During reading, key concepts should be highlighted in some way. A study guide could prepare students for material that may contradict what they believe. The teacher might also model his or her actions when reading something that runs counter to his or her ideas. Students should be alerted to look for such information and to try to correct the difficulty by reconstructing their schema. It is not a bad idea to have them write out these reconstructions, by using KWL, for example.

After reading, discussion can focus on clarifying confusing information and straightening out conflicts. Students should be supported as they reconstruct their schema to accommodate new knowledge. There should also be ample opportunity for application. C. W. Anderson (1987) cautioned that "students cannot fully master a concept until they have successfully used it in a variety of different contexts" (p. 87).

USING CHILDREN'S BOOKS AND PERIODICALS

How do students become proficient readers in a field such as social studies that is both broad and diverse? The answer is quite simple: They read. Although the strategies described above should increase comprehension of their reading, students have to build a broad base of knowledge so they have a schema to draw from and to build on. Knowing why the Civil War was fought, for instance, makes a biography of Abraham Lincoln more meaningful. Using trade books in the teaching of social studies provides many advantages:

> Instead of a single perspective on a topic, trade books offer multiple perspectives. They show children that an event or an idea can be interpreted many ways. Instead of short, superficial accounts, trade books enable children to slow down and explore topics in depth. (Zarnowski & Gallagher, 1993, p. 35)

Literally thousands of children's books can be used to explore social studies topics. A good source of current high-quality materials is the annual listing of "Notable Children's Trade Books in the Field of Social Studies," which is published in the April/May issue of *Social Education.* Categories of notable books include American history, culture, and life; world history and cultures; folklore, myths, legends, stories, and storytelling; poetry and song; biography and autobiography; and understanding oneself and others. Another excellent source of appropriate children's books is *Literature-Based Social Studies: Children's Books and Activities to Enrich the K–5 Curriculum* (Laughlin & Kardaleff, 1991), which provides both suggested readings and activities to accompany social studies units commonly taught in grades K–5. Additional collections of children's books that might be used in the content areas include *Children's Literature and Social Studies: Selecting and Using Notable Books in the Classroom* (Zarnowski & Gallagher, 1993) and *The Story of Ourselves: Teaching History Through Children's Literature* (Tunnell & Ammon, 1993).

Periodicals are especially important in social studies since they usually present current events; Table 8.2 shows some examples. For a more complete listing of periodicals for young people, see *Magazines for Kids and Teens* (Stoll, 1994), which is published by the International Reading Association.

Just as in social studies, wide reading of children's informational books is one of the best ways to build science concepts and reading skills. A list of excellent science books is published each year in the March issue of *Science and Children.* A good source of recommended science books for elementary school students is *Science and Technology in Fact and Fiction: A Guide to Children's Books* (Kennedy, Spangler, & Vanderwerf, 1990). This text lists 350 books, including fiction and nonfiction, that explore science topics. Summaries and estimated reading levels are provided. In such a fast-changing field, keeping up to date means reading periodicals as well as books. Table 8.3 lists periodicals that explore science topics.

TABLE 8.2 Social studies periodicals

Periodical	Appropriate Grades	Content
Cobblestone: The History Magazine for Young People	4–9	American history
Junior Scholastic	6–8	Current events and general social studies topics
Current Events	7–10	Current national and world events
Faces: The Magazine About People	4–9	People from diverse lands and cultures
Scholastic News	K–6	Social studies, science, and other topics of interest to children
Time for Kids	4–6	Current events
U*S* Kids	1–5	Children in other lands
Weekly Reader	K–6	Social studies, science, and other topics of interest to children

TABLE 8.3 Science periodicals

Periodical	Appropriate Grades	Content
Chicadee	K–4	General science
Child Life	1–4	General interest, with focus on health
Children's Digest	1–6	General interest, with emphasis on health
Children's Playmate	1–6	General interest and health topics
Current Health I	4–7	Health topics typically taught in schools
Current Science	5–8	General science
Dolphin Log	2–8	Emphasis on marine sciences
National Geographic World	3–6	General interest, with emphasis on nature and ecology
Odyssey	3–8	Emphasis on astronomy and space
Owl Magazine	4–7	General science, with emphasis on nature
Ranger Rick	1–6	Wildlife and ecology
Science Weekly	1–8	General science and math
Superscience, Red Edition	1–3	General science
Superscience, Blue Edition	4–6	General science
3-2-1 Contact	3–8	General interest, with emphasis on science

A sampling of children's books that might be used to reinforce or expand math concepts is presented in the Children's Book List. An excellent source of additional books is *Wonderful World of Mathematics* (Thiessen & Matthias, 1992), which contains an annotated bibliography of more than five hundred children's books.

Children's Book List
Math puzzles and riddles

Anno, M. *Anno's Math Games*. New York: Philomel (1982). Basic math concepts are explored through illustrations, puzzles, and questions.

Arnold, C. *Measurements: Fun Facts and Activities*. New York: Watts (1984). A variety of devices are used to measure height, weight, distance, speed, time, temperature, etc.

Carona, P. *Numbers*. Chicago: Children's Press (1982). The history and uses of numbers are explained.

Crawford, J. *How Do Octopi Eat Pizza Pie?* Alexandria, VA: Time-Life (1992). A collection of stories, poems, games, and activities, all focusing on food, introduce basic mathematical skills, including addition, subtraction, and estimation.

Gantz, D. *The David Gantz Wacky World of Numbers.* New York: Checkerboard (1988). Humorous rhymes and illustrations introduce numbers 1 to 100.

Gardner, T. *Math in Science and Nature.* New York: Watts (1991). Patterns in the world around us are shown.

Markle, S. *Math Mini-Mysteries.* New York: Atheneum (1993). Challenging problems, which can be solved using suggested problem-solving techniques and basic math, are presented.

McMillan, B. *Eating Fractions.* New York: Scholastic (1991). Food is cut into halves, quarters,and thirds to illustrate how parts make a whole. A good introduction to fractions.

Schwartz, D. M. *How Much Is a Million?* New York: Lothrop (1985). Intriguing examples are provided to illustrate the concepts of million, billion, and trillion.

Schwartz, D. M. *If You Made a Million.* New York: Lothrop (1989). Various forms of money are described, including coins, paper money, and personal checks. How money can be used to make purchases, pay off loans, or build interest is also discussed.

WRITING TO LEARN

Writing is a way of learning as well as a method of communication. Zinsser (1988), a professional writer and teacher of writing, observed,

> We write to find out what we know and want to say. I thought of how often as a writer I had made clear to myself some subject I had previously known nothing about by just putting one sentence after another—by reasoning my way in sequential steps to its meaning. (pp. viii–ix)

Writing activities, such as the following, can help clarify complex topics:

- Writing summaries after reading chapters
- Writing reports on famous people or events
- Summarizing and interpreting the results of a science experiment conducted in class
- Writing an essay on a social studies or science topic: What does the Bill of Rights mean to me? What can we do to clean up our home, the earth?

Insofar as possible, help students relate what they are studying to their personal lives. For example, make the Bill of Rights provisions more concrete by having students write about how they exercise their rights every day or about an incident that made them appreciate their freedom to use their rights.

Students' writing in the content areas often consists of simply retelling information. One solution is to have them make first-hand investigations and report the results. They might undertake activities such as the following:

- Writing observations about a natural phenomenon (for example, changes in plants that are being grown from seed)
- Describing birds that visit a bird feeder, changes in a tree from season to season, or changes in a puppy or kitten as it develops over a period of months
- Summarizing the results of a classroom poll
- Interviewing older family members about life when they were growing up

A writing activity that can be used in any content area class is having students explain a process to someone who has no knowledge of it. Processes include finding the area of a rectangle, how magnets work, how the president is elected, and how to find a particular state on a map. Students might also use graphics to help explain a process. Where appropriate, the explanation might be oral, instead of written.

Other kinds of writing-to-learn activities include the following (Noyce & Christie, 1989):

- Writing letters to convey personal reactions or request information on a topic
- Writing scripts to dramatize key events in history
- Writing historical fiction
- Writing a children's book on an interesting social studies or science topic
- Writing an editorial or commentary about a social issue
- Writing an illustrated glossary of key terms
- Creating captions for photos of a scientific experiment
- Creating a puzzle for key terms

LEARNING LOGS

A **learning log** is a type of journal in which students record and reflect upon concepts and skills that they are studying.

One easy device that combines personal reaction with exploration of content is the **learning log.** It consists of a notebook that is

> . . . informal, tentative, first draft, and brief, usually consisting of no more than ten minutes of focused free writing. The teacher poses questions and situations or sets themes that invite students to observe, speculate, list, chart, web, brainstorm, role-play, ask questions, activate prior knowledge, collaborate, correspond, summarize, predict, or shift to a new perspective: in short, to participate in their own learning. (Atwell, 1990, p. xvii)

The class can discuss their learning logs, or the teacher can collect them and respond to them in writing. Following is a learning log from a third-grader who drew up a summary based on the teacher's reading of *Squirrels* (Wildsmith, 1988):

> Squirrels nests are called dreys. Squirrels tails are used for leaps, a parachute, change directions, swim, balance, blanket. Sometimes squirrels steal eggs. (Thompson, 1990, p. 48)

The main purpose of logs is to have students examine and express what they are learning, not to air their personal matters (Atwell, 1990). Logs can also be used to ask questions. Calkins (1986) suggested that before viewing a film or reading a selection, students might record the questions they have about that topic. Later, they can evaluate how well their questions were answered. On other occasions students might record what they know about a topic before reading a selection or undertaking a unit of study.

Whether students pose a question, jot down a reaction, or create a semantic map, the writing stimulus should help them think as scientists, historians, or mathematicians and think about what they are learning. At times, they can draft free responses in their learning logs; at other times, the teacher might want to provide prompts. Log-writing prompts for a unit on weather might include the following, only one of which would be provided for any one session:

What do I know about weather forecasting?

What questions do I have about weather?

What is the worst kind of storm? Why?

What kind of weather do I like best? Least? Why?

How does weather affect my life?

What kinds of people might be most affected by the weather?

What causes fog?

What are some of the ways in which people who are not scientists predict the weather?

Students can also write pre-learning and post-learning entries in their logs. Before studying snakes, they might write what they know about snakes and then share their knowledge with a partner. Talking to a partner helps them to elicit more information. Students then read the selection and make journal entries indicating what they know now. Pre-learning and post-learning entries help students become more metacognitive, more aware of what they know and are learning (Santa, 1994).

Learning logs help a teacher keep in touch with her class. Nancy Chard (1990), a fourth-grade teacher in Maine, uses them to find out what her students know at the beginning of a unit and what kinds of misunderstandings crop up. One night while reading the entries, she noted that her class knew virtually nothing about Antarctica. The next day, she read Lynn Stone's (1985) *Antarctica* to them.

The major advantage of learning logs is that they provide students with the opportunity to reflect on their learning and raise questions about concepts that puzzle them and issues that are of special concern.

READING TO REMEMBER

Marge, a fifth-grader, is feeling anxious. She has been told to study the chapter on the Revolutionary War for a unit test the next day. Marge is a good reader and usually does well in school, but she is having trouble with history. She understands what she reads, but she does not remember the dates and names that the tests ask for. She remembers most of the main ideas but not the details. Marge's

Otto (1990) noted that students often don't know how they will be tested. When testing students, be sure to inform them, well in advance, of the nature of the test and how they might prepare for it.

problem is a common one. She knows how to read for understanding, but she has no strategies for reading for retention. Marge has another problem, too. Whereas she reads for main ideas, the test will concentrate on details. Marge has to gear her studying for the type of test she will be given. Research suggests that knowing the type of test to be taken is an important factor in effective studying (Anderson & Armbruster, 1984).

Some students seem to learn on their own how to study for different types of tests, while others require instruction. Teachers should let students know what types of tests they intend to give and should explain how to study for each one. For example, essay tests require knowing the main ideas of the material; objective tests require more attention to details. Teachers should also discuss the difference between studying for multiple-choice tests, which require only that one recognize correct answers, and studying for fill-in-the-blank exams, which require recalling names, dates, or terms. Recognizing is, of course, far easier than recalling.

Studying also has an affective component. Up to 75 percent of academic failure is attributed to poor study habits or strategies. However, a number of studies conducted over the years indicate that when students are taught these skills, their performance improves significantly (Richardson & Morgan, 1994). A key element, however, is motivation. When students are convinced of the value of study skills, they are more likely to use them (Schunk & Rice, 1987). A crucial element in study strategy instruction is proving to students that these strategies work—they need to see that better studying leads to better grades.

In elementary school, the focus is on teaching children to read. Emphasis is typically on the reading of narrative text. Reading informational text and using study skills are often neglected. However, study habits develop early, and effective study skills take many years to learn. Locating, organizing, and taking steps to retain information should be an integral part of elementary school curriculum. From the very beginning, students should be taught how to preview a book to get an overview of its contents and how to use the table of contents. Students should also be taught in the earliest grades how to preview a section of text, make predictions, create questions, summarize, and then apply what they read. Instruction in these strategies will help build a solid foundation for effective study skills. This instruction will pave the way for the teaching of more formal study strategies such as SQ3R.

Learning to learn begins when children observe parents performing such tasks as memorizing a phone number, looking up a word in the dictionary, or taking notes during a telephone call.

FOSTERING RETENTION

In studying, comprehension is important but not sufficient. Students must also remember the material. They might have a flawless understanding of what they read as they read it but forget much of the information soon after. Knowing how the memory works is the key to devising techniques to improve retention. Memory has three stages: encoding, storing, and retrieving. Encoding should be clear and purposeful; text that is vaguely understood will be quickly forgotten. Storage works best when the material is meaningful. Students will remember a piece of information better if they concentrate on its meaning rather than on the exact words used, which is why it is best to respond to questions in one's own words.

Elaborating on the information also helps. For example, a student reads and might want to remember the following three facts from a selection about anteaters:

1. They have a long, thin snout.
2. They have sharp claws.
3. They have sticky tongues.

The student then elaborates on the text by asking herself or himself why anteaters have a long and thin snout, sharp claws, and a sticky tongue, and determines that it can use its long snout to poke into underground ant nests, its claws can rip open the nests, and it can pick up the ants with its sticky tongue. This elaboration aids long-term storage. It also helps retrieval.

The more connections that are constructed between items of information in memory, the greater the number of retrieval paths (Atkinson, Atkinson, Smith, & Hilgard, 1987). "Questions about the causes and consequences of an event are particularly effective elaborations because each question sets up a meaningful connection, or retrieval path, to the event" (p. 269).

PRINCIPLES OF MEMORY

The following principles are based on the way that memory is believed to work and should aid retention:

- Get a clear, meaningful encoding of the material to be learned.
- Have a purposeful intention to learn. Activate strategies that will aid retention.
- Organize and elaborate information so that it will have a greater number of meaningful connections and thus will be easier to store and retrieve. Creating outlines, summaries, and maps, taking notes, reflecting, and applying information promote retention.
- Overlearning aids retention. **Overlearning** means that a person continues to study after the material has been learned. This extra practice pays off in longer-lasting retention. Novice students often make the mistake of halting their study efforts as soon as they are able to recite the desired material. Added practice sessions should help maintain the level of performance.
- When it is not possible to structure meaningful connections between material to be learned and prior knowledge, use mnemonic and other memory devices to create connections. Some popular memory, or rehearsal, devices are described in the following section.
- Give your mind a rest. After intensive studying, take a break, rest, and get enough sleep. Sleep, it is believed, gives the brain the opportunity to organize information.

Overlearning refers to the practice of continuing to study after the material has been learned in order to foster increased retention.

Adapting instruction for above-average students

Used to learning most material with ease, bright students may balk at memorizing and/or stop as soon as they can recite the information they have been studying. Demonstrate the benefits of using memory strategies.

MEMORY DEVICES

CONCEPTUAL UNDERSTANDING

The best way to remember new material is to achieve conceptual understanding. Bransford (1994) gives an example of a student who is studying arteries and veins for a test: The student knows that one type of blood vessel is thick and elastic, and one is thin and nonelastic, but he is not sure which is which. He can use a number of strategies to help him remember. He could use simple rehearsal and just say, "artery, thick, elastic" over and over. But a far better approach would be to seek conceptual understanding and ask, "Why are arteries thick and elastic?" The student has read that blood is pumped from the heart through the arteries in spurts and reasons, therefore, that the arteries must be elastic so that they can contract and expand for pumping. They have to be thick because they must withstand the pressure of the blood. If the explanation that enables the learner to see the significance of the information is not provided in the reading, the learner must seek it out. As Bransford and Stein (1984) explained,

> Our learner realizes the need to obtain additional information. The learner's activities are not unlike those employed by good detectives or researchers when they confront a new problem. Although their initial assumptions about the significance of various facts may ultimately be found to be incorrect, the act of seeking clarification is fundamental to the development of new expertise. In contrast, the person who simply concentrates on techniques for memorizing facts does not know whether there is something more to be understood. (p. 57)

REHEARSAL

Rehearsal is the process of repeating over and over information to be memorized.

The simplest memory device of all is **rehearsal.** Rehearsal may be used when conceptual understanding is not feasible or possible. For instance, one has to memorize a list of arbitrary dates. In its most basic form, rehearsal involves saying the item to be memorized over and over again. It is the way students learn the names of the letters of the alphabet, the names of the vowels, and their home addresses and telephone numbers. Rehearsal works because it focuses the learner's attention on the items to be learned and transfers material into long-term memory (Weinstein & Mayer, 1986).

Young children use rehearsal strategies, but they may not do so spontaneously. They may have to be taught how to use such strategies, and then they may have to be reminded to apply them. Natural development is also a factor. Older children, even when not instructed to do so, tend to use rehearsal more frequently than younger children do. A program of study skills for elementary school students would have to balance students' development with careful instruction. As students grow older, they can learn to use more complex rehearsal strategies, such as rereading text aloud or silently. They also learn how to test themselves.

MNEMONIC METHOD

Mnemonics are artificial devices, such as rhymes, which are used to aid memory.

Rehearsal is an inefficient way to remember material. If at all possible, a more meaningful approach should be used. If conceptual understanding is not possible, learners might use a mnemonic method that constructs connections that are artificially meaningful. **Mnemonics** are artificial memory devices, such as using verses to remember how many days there are in each month ("30 days has September, April, June, and November"). Mnemonics are used when it is not possible to create more meaningful connections. One especially useful mnemonic device is the key word technique.

The Key Word Technique.　The **key word technique** uses visual images to build associations. This technique was explained in Chapter 6 as a device for remembering vocabulary; however, it can also be used to remember facts (Peters & Levin, 1986).

To use the key word technique, students follow a two-step procedure. First, they create a key word that sounds like the item they wish to remember. For instance, to remember the name of James Smithson, who helped establish the Smithsonian Institution, students might choose the word *smile*. Then, students create an interactive image that involves both the key word and the person's accomplishment. For Smithson, the interactive image might be of a family smiling as they view the dinosaur exhibit in a museum. The dinosaurs are also smiling (Peters & Levin, 1986). The key word technique aids memory because when students see the name *Smithson,* they think of *smile,* which begins like *Smithson,* and picture people and animals smiling in a museum. Conversely, when students see the word *museum,* they think of people smiling in a museum and then think of *Smithson* because it has the same beginning letters and sounds as *smile.*

The **key word technique** is a memory device in which the learner associates a new word with a key word and a visual image that incorporates the key word and a portion of the target word.

Try the key word technique with some difficult terms that you have to learn for this or another class. Note any difficulties that you encounter. Assess the effectiveness and utility of the technique.

OTHER MNEMONIC DEVICES

An assortment of devices are used to aid in the memorization of facts and details. Many traditional rhymes were written specifically to help school children with memory tasks:

> In fourteen hundred and ninety-two
> Columbus sailed the ocean blue. . . .

> Use *i* before *e* except after *c*
> or when sounded like *a* as in *neighbor* and *weigh.*

Acronyms.　Words made from the first letter of a series of words are often used to assist memory. Common **acronyms** include ROY G. BIV for the colors of visible light in the order in which they appear in the spectrum (red, orange, yellow, green, blue, indigo, violet); and HOMES for the Great Lakes (Huron, Ontario, Michigan, Erie, and Superior).

An **acronym** is a mnemonic device made up of the first letters of a series of words.

Acrostics.　In **acrostics** a simple phrase is used to learn a series of unrelated words or letters. For instance, *Every Good Boy Does Fine* has long been used as an aid in memorizing the letters of the string chords (E, G, B, D, and F). Acrostics and acronyms work because they provide a way to organize information whose natural organization is essentially random.

An **acrostic** is a mnemonic device in which the first letters of a series of words or phrases, taken in order, spell out a word or phrase.

The best mnemonic devices are those that students create for themselves. Help the class create rhymes or other assists for remembering important dates, names, rules, or other items that have to be memorized.

FLASH CARDS

Memorizing dates, names, formulas, or terms is essential but can be tedious. In addition, some students simply do not know how to memorize. To use flash cards as an aid to memorization, have students put each item to be learned on one side of a three-by-five card and its explanation or definition on the other. Students can make a game of memorizing by studying the items and then testing themselves, with the goal of getting all items correct. They should not attempt to learn too many items at one time. For some, five might be plenty; others may be able to handle eight to ten. Students' performance should be the guide as to how many items they attempt to learn at one sitting. As additional motivation, students can work with partners and take turns testing each other.

CLUSTERING

The simple act of clustering or grouping data will help students remember it better (Richardson & Morgan, 1994). (An example of the use of clustering is grouping the digits in your phone number by area code, exchange, and individual number.)

Try the following experiment with your students. Distribute list A to half the class and list B to the other half. Give the students two minutes to study the lists. Then have them jot down as many words as they can remember.

List A		
bread	celery	cream
eggs	cake	tomatoes
broccoli	cheese	pastry
rolls	spinach	lettuce
milk	pie	

List B		
Bakery	*Dairy*	*Produce (Vegetables)*
bread	eggs	broccoli
rolls	milk	celery
cake	cheese	lettuce
pie	cream	spinach
pastry		tomatoes

In virtually every case, students studying list B will remember more words. Have the students discuss why those studying list B remembered more words, even though both sides had the same words on their lists. Discuss the value of organizing information and clustering details to be learned.

Although associational learning, such as clustering and using mnemonic devices, is on a low cognitive level, students gain a sense of accomplishment and mastery when they have memorized the names of the planets, the oceans, the continents, and other essential bits of information:

> When students commit information to memory, the very act of knowing something increases their confidence, and often their self-image. This is especially important for students who may have gotten the idea that they do not know anything and that what they say has no value. The chief benefit of mnemonics and memory training is that, by making difficult study easier, they can kindle in the student a desire to learn. (Richardson & Morgan, 1994, p. 354)

METACOGNITIVE AWARENESS

In addition to learning how to use memory techniques, students must be able to recognize which techniques work best in certain circumstances. Acronyms and

Side notes (left column):

There are three basic reasons for students' inability to answer questions about materials that they have previously read or heard: (1) Although they may have encountered it, they didn't really understand it or didn't learn it; (2) they learned it but didn't take steps to retain it in memory; and (3) they learned it, and it's in memory but they can't retrieve it (Readence, Bean, & Baldwin, 1992). Understanding content material isn't sufficient. Since students must also be able to retain and retrieve new information, study skills are an essential part of the elementary school literacy curriculum.

Effective studying requires three kinds of awareness: task, strategy, and performance. Task awareness means that the student is aware of what is to be studied. Strategy awareness means that the student has command of study strategies and knows which ones to use in a particular situation. Performance awareness means that the student can gauge when the material is mastered or to what extent it is mastered (Alvermann & Phelps, 1994).

acrostics, for example, work best when memorizing lists of items. The key word technique works best for single words. Seeking conceptual understanding works best with meaningful material, such as key concepts. All strategies should be adapted to students' individual learning styles.

DISTRIBUTED VERSUS MASSED PRACTICE

Generally speaking, short practice sessions work better than long ones, especially when students are memorizing. Brief reviews are also important to forestall forgetting.

Distributed practice, or studying that is spread over a number of sessions, is often preferred over massed practice. Concentration can be best maintained for short periods, and there is less chance for the student to become bored. This is especially true when the student is engaged in rote tasks, such as studying spelling words or a list of dates. Massed practice, or studying for extended periods of time, works best when the material has a wholeness that would be lost if it were split into separate segments. Reading a long story or writing an essay would fall into this category. Lengthier study periods also seem to work better for students who have difficulty settling down and tend to fritter away the first fifteen minutes of a study session.

Distributed practice refers to studying or doing practice exercises at intervals.

Massed practice refers to studying or doing practice exercises all at one time.

SQ3R: A THEORY-BASED STUDY STRATEGY

A five-step technique known as **SQ3R**—Survey, Question, Read, Recite, and Review—implements many of the principles presented in the previous section. Devised in the 1930s, it is the most thoroughly documented and widely used study technique in the English language. SQ3R, or a method based on it, appears in nearly every text that discusses studying. It is very effective when properly applied (Caverly & Orlando, 1991).

SQ3R (Survey, Question, Read, Recite, Review) is a widely used and effective study strategy incorporating five steps.

PRINCIPLES OF SQ3R

SQ3R is based on the following principles, derived from Robinson's (1970) review of research on studying:

- Surveying headings and summaries increases speed of reading, helps students remember the text and, perhaps most importantly, provides an overview of the text.
- Asking a question before reading each section improves comprehension.
- Reciting from memory immediately after reading slows down forgetting. If asked questions immediately after reading, students are able to answer only about half of them. After just one day, 50 percent of what was learned is forgotten. Students are then able to answer just 25 percent of questions asked about a text. However, those who review the material have a retention rate of more than 80 percent one day later. In another study, students who spent 20 percent of their time reading and 80 percent reciting were able to answer twice as many questions as those who simply read the material (Gates, 1917).

- Understanding major ideas and seeing relationships among ideas helps comprehension and retention.
- Having short review sessions, outlining, and relating information to students' personal needs and interests are helpful.

A more recent review of the research on studying techniques confirms several of the principles cited by Robinson (1970). That is, taking notes, summarizing, paraphrasing, outlining, and creating questions increase retention (Anderson & Armbruster, 1984). However, in some instances, favorable results were found only when students were carefully trained in the use of the particular technique being researched.

Applying any one of Robinson's (1970) principles should result in more effective studying. However, Robinson based SQ3R on all of them. SQ3R consists of the procedure described below, which prepares students to read and helps them organize, elaborate, and rehearse information from text.

Student Strategy
Applying SQ3R

1. *Survey.* Survey the chapter that you are about to read for an overall picture of what it is about. Glance over the title and headings. Quickly read the overview and summary. Note what main ideas are covered. This quick survey will help you organize the information in the chapter as you read it.
2. *Question.* Turn each heading into a question. The heading "Causes of the Great Depression" would become "What were the causes of the Great Depression?" Answering the question you created gives you a purpose for reading.
3. *Read.* Read to answer the question. Having a question to answer focuses your attention and makes you a more active reader.
4. *Recite.* When you come to the end of the section, stop and test yourself. Try to answer your question. If you cannot, go back over the section and then try once again to answer the question. The answer may be oral or written. Note, however, that a written answer is preferable because it is more active and forces you to summarize what you have learned. The answer should also be brief; otherwise, SQ3R takes up too much time.

   Do not take notes until you have read the entire section. Taking notes before completing the section interrupts your reading and could interfere with your understanding of the section. Repeat steps 2, 3, and 4 until the entire selection has been read.
5. *Review.* When you have finished the assignment, spend a few minutes reviewing what you read. If you took notes, cover them up. Then, asking yourself the questions you created from the headings, try to recall the major points that support the headings. The review helps you put information together and remember it longer. ⫰⫰⫰⫰⫰

In general, special elements should be treated the same way as text. For graphs, tables, and maps the title is turned into a question and the information in the graph, table, or map is then used to answer the question (Robinson, 1970). A

Although devised nearly a half-century ago, SQ3R incorporates many of the strategies recently recommended by cognitive psychologists: for example, predicting or surveying, setting goals, constructing questions, summarizing, monitoring for meaning, and repairing.

Unless steps are taken to prevent it, the rate of forgetting is very rapid (60 percent or more of what is learned is forgotten in a few days). Students may not realize this and may believe that forgetting is a sign of a lack of ability. Explain to them that forgetting is natural, but they can enhance their memories through studying (Richardson & Morgan, 1994).

diagram may be as important as the text and merits special effort. After examining the diagram carefully, students should try to draw it from memory and then compare their drawings with the diagram in the book (Robinson, 1970). Drawing becomes a form of recitation.

TEACHING SQ3R

SQ3R cannot be mastered in a day or even a month. Each element requires extensive practice and guidance. Students also have to be able to recognize whether they are applying the technique correctly and, if they are not, what they can do about it.

WHEN TO BEGIN INSTRUCTION

Although originally designed for college students, SQ3R works well with elementary school students. In fact, if SQ3R or some of its elements are not taught in the early grades, college may be too late. By the upper elementary and middle school years, unless students have learned otherwise, they may have acquired inefficient study habits that are resistant to change (Early & Sawyer, 1984). Very young readers can and should be taught to survey material, make predictions, and read to answer questions they have composed or to check how accurate their predictions were. Answering questions and reacting to predictions is a form of recitation. Once students are reading large amounts of text (in fourth grade or so) and are expected to remember information for tests, they should be introduced to all the principles of SQ3R or some other effective study strategy. If students are to be tested, they must know how to prepare for tests.

> SQ3R is hard to teach because it requires not only the development of component skills but the replacement of old habits. Consider that most students—even the best of them—turn to the first page of a chapter and begin at the first word. It's the student in a hurry, sometimes the less conscientious one, who is sensible enough to turn first to the questions at the end to see what the authors consider important. The survey step requires skimming and scanning, which many students, again the better ones, shun. (Early & Sawyer, 1984, p. 422)

Teaching SQ3R requires a commitment of time and effort. Each step must be taught carefully, with ample opportunity provided for practice and application. Early and Sawyer (1984) recommended spending at least a semester using it with older students. Slower students require additional instruction and practice time (Caverly & Orlando, 1991). Even after it has been taught carefully and practiced conscientiously, SQ3R requires periodic review and reteaching.

In addition to needing lots of opportunity for application, students using SQ3R require individual feedback so that they can make necessary adjustments in the way they apply the technique.

ADAPTATIONS OF SQ3R

Over the years, numerous adaptations have been made to SQ3R. A step that several practitioners advocate adding is reflecting (Pauk, 1989; Thomas & Robinson, 1972; Vacca & Vacca, 1986). After reading, students are encouraged to think about the material and how they might use it. Vacca and Vacca (1986) also recommend that before reading, students reflect on what they already know about the topic.

TEST-TAKING STRATEGIES

In addition to teaching students study strategies, teach them how to take a test. Of course, the best way to prepare for a test is to study conscientiously and strategically and to be fully aware of what will be tested and how it will be tested. A systematic way of teaching test-taking strategies is to implement PLAE: Preplanning, Listing, Activity, and Evaluating (Nist & Simpson, 1989).

Adapting instruction for lower-achieving readers

Students will have difficulty studying texts that are significantly above their reading levels. For children with severe reading difficulties, obtain taped versions of texts and review ways of studying information from an oral source.

- *Preplanning.* In the preplanning stage, students describe the study task, asking questions such as these: What will the test cover? What kind of questions will be asked? What will be the format of the questions?
- *Listing.* Based on preplanning information, students list the steps they will take to prepare for the test. They will answer the following or similar questions: How will I get ready for the test? When will I study? How long will I study? Which study strategies will I use?
- *Activity.* Students activate their plans and monitor them. They ask whether they are using the right strategies and spending the right amount of time studying. They might ask the following or similar questions: Am I following my plan? If not, why not? Is my plan working? Am I learning what I need to learn? If not, what changes do I need to make in my plan? Am I using the best study strategies?
- *Evaluating.* Based on their performance on the test, students evaluate the effectiveness of their study plans. They might ask questions such as these: Which questions did I miss? Why? Did I study all the material that the questions were based on? Did I remember the material? How could I have studied to get more questions right?

To help students develop realistic study strategies, arrange for practice study sessions and practice tests. Focus on the kinds of tests that students are most often required to take. Choose a selection that is representative of the type of material they will be tested on. Discuss the criterion task—the topic of the test to be given—and ways in which the material might be studied. Also discuss how students can self-test to assess how well they have studied (performance awareness). Then administer the test, and discuss the results. Discuss with students how effective their studying was and what might be done to improve it. Provide practice with several test formats, and acquaint students with any formats, such as cloze, that may be unfamiliar to them.

TEST-TAKING TIPS

In addition to learning a test-taking strategy such as PLAE, students should be advised to get a good night's rest the night before a test, eat a good breakfast, and bring all necessary supplies. Other test-taking strategies include the following:

- Surveying the test to see what is involved
- Reading directions carefully
- Using time well and not spending too much time on any one item
- Doing known or easy items first
- In a multiple-choice test, making careful guesses, especially if points are not taken off for wrong answers

STUDY HABITS

Some people have such intense powers of concentration that they seem to be able to study almost anywhere. As a child, the Nobel prize-winning scientist Madame Curie became so engrossed in a book that she was not aware that her siblings had constructed a pyramid of chairs over her until she had completed her reading and the pyramid collapsed (Curie, 1937). Most students do not have such a remarkable ability to concentrate and will study best under certain controlled conditions. Ideally, each student should have a quiet place to study that is free of distractions. The area should be well lit, contain a desk or other writing surface, and be supplied with paper, pens, pencils, and a few basic reference books, such as a dictionary and an almanac. Of course, not every child has the luxury of such a retreat, but children should be advised to find the best study spot they can. In even the most crowded homes, there is a time when quiet prevails. One member of a ten-person family did his studying early in the morning while everyone else was asleep.

Studying, however, is more a matter of attitude than place. Research and common practice suggest that students study best when they meet the following conditions:

- They know how to study.
- They know why they are studying. The assignment has value and the students understand what that value is.
- They know what type of test they are studying for and how to adjust their efforts to meet its demands.
- They have a routine. Studying requires discipline. Students should determine the best time for them to study and then study at that time every day. Generally, study should precede recreation.

Although procrastination is natural and many students put off studying until the evening before a test, distributed practice, or spreading out studying over a period of time, is more effective than massed practice, or cramming.

Discuss study habits and strategies with the class. Invite students to tell how, when, and where they study. Highlight the successful strategies and habits.

Ideally, each student should have a quiet place to study that is free of distractions.

- Studying is active and purposeful. An hour of concentrated study is better than two hours of studying in which the student takes many breaks and lets her or his attention wander.

Another condition that fosters effective studying includes rewarding oneself. Suggest that students reward themselves for a job well done. For instance, they might treat themselves to a snack or to watching a favorite TV show after forty-five minutes of concentrated study. Having an interest in the material also makes it easier to study and learn. Some material is intrinsically interesting; in other cases, interest has to be built. Students should be encouraged to envision how a certain subject might fit in with their personal needs and goals. If that fails, they can remember the extrinsic rewards—studying the material will result in a higher grade, for example.

Students need to see a payoff for studying. Those who study hard but get poor grades on tests will become discouraged. In order to increase the chance that their studying will pay off in higher grades, students should be told exactly what type of test they will be given and how to study for that test. Tests should reflect the content that has been emphasized and should take the form that you, as the teacher, indicated they would take. They should contain no trick questions. You might also model how you go about studying for a test and then provide guided practice. Observe students as they study and discuss the procedures that they use. Lead them to use efficient study strategies.

Help students make a detailed study plan. This should include not only what they will study and why, but where, when, how long, and under what circumstances. Study plans should be individualized, so encourage students to try different techniques. Part of learning to study is discovering how, when, and where one studies best.

The use of portfolio assessment now places more emphasis on students' work samples or actual classroom performance. This may help reduce test anxiety. However, students still need to know how to study because tests will undoubtedly be a significant part of their formal education. In addition, they will need to learn new information for projects they undertake and as a part of their work and family responsibilities.

EXPRESSIVE STUDY SKILLS

A key part of studying is recording information in some way. This might take the form of traditional or simplified notes or various kinds of graphic organizers.

TAKING NOTES

Taking notes is an essential study skill. It is also a very practical one. Writing telephone messages is a form of note taking, as is jotting down a series of complex details. Teaching students how to take phone messages provides them with a practical skill and can also be an effective introduction to note taking. Model the process of taking messages. Emphasize that it is necessary to obtain only the essential information: who called, whom the call was for, and the caller's message. Pretend that you are a caller and have students take notes. Discuss the clarity and conciseness of their notes. Have pairs of students role-play, with one student playing the part of the caller, the other the message taker. Also discuss real-life cases in which students have taken notes.

As students begin writing expository reports, a natural need arises for note taking. They have to have some method for preserving information drawn from a variety of sources. As they prepare to write reports, share with them experiences you have had taking notes. Model how you might take notes from an encyclopedia or other source. Teach students a tried-and-true procedure that might include the steps outlined in the Student Strategy below.

Student Strategy
Taking notes

1. Write the name of the topic on the top line of the card: for example, "Camels—how they help people." Turn the topic into a question: "How do camels help people?"
2. Search for information that answers the question. You do not have to read every word of each article that you locate on your topic. You can skim through to find the relevant facts, and you can skip parts that do not contain what you are looking for.
3. Take notes on details that answer your question. Put the notes in your own words. The best way to do this is to read a brief section and write the important facts from memory. To save time and space, leave out words that are not important like *the, a,* and *an.* Write in phrases instead of sentences, and do not bother with punctuation except in quotations.
4. Check back over the section. Make sure that you have taken all the notes that answer your question and that you have put them in your own words. Sometimes you may want to quote someone's exact words. Maybe a famous scientist said something interesting about camels. If you use exact words, make sure that you put quotation marks around them. Also make sure that you write exactly what the person said.
5. Fill in identifying information. At the bottom of the card, write the page number where you got your information. At the top, write the author's name, title of the article, title of the book or periodical, volume number if it has one, publisher's name, place where the publisher is located, and date of publication. (Younger students may use a simplified bibliographic reference.) The finished notes might look like those in Figure 8.13.

A major problem with elementary school students' research reports is that often they are verbatim copies of encyclopedia articles. Having students take notes in their own words is one way to eliminate this. Another is to request that students obtain information from at least two sources. Actually, encyclopedias should be only a starting point. Their information is limited and often dated. Encourage students to find other sources from the large number of high-quality informational books published each year. Students should also be encouraged to think over the information they have collected and to select only the most interesting details for inclusion in their reports. The ultimate solution to this problem is to have students explore areas in which they have a genuine interest. Calkins and Harwayne (1991) called this "writing with voice": "We will write with voice when we have read, questioned, dreamed, argued, worried, wept, gossiped, and

FIGURE 8.13 | Example of note taking

Camels—how they help people

Dagg, Ann Innis. Camel. *World Book Encyclopedia,*
Vol. 3, Chicago: World Book, 1994, pp. 75–78.

Pull plows
Turn water wheels to work pumps
Carry grain to market
Carry people and their goods
Meat of young camels is eaten—can be tough
Fat from hump used as butter
Can drink camel's milk and make cheese
Camel's milk is very rich
Hair made into cloth and blankets
Skin used to make tents
Skin used to make leather for shoes, saddles, saddlebags
Bones used for decorations and as cooking and eating utensils

laughed over a topic" (p. 201). These authors recommended that student writers use many different sources of information, including interviews and observation, and record their thoughts, feelings, and ideas in notebooks.

OUTLINING

A complex skill, outlining requires that students note the relative importance of major and minor details. As Anderson and Armbruster (1984) observed, "A potential problem with outlining as a study aid is that it is very time consuming to think through the logical relationships in text and represent the meaning in outline form" (p. 673).

Full outlining is probably beyond the capabilities of most elementary school students. However, simple outlining can be a valuable study aid. Santa (1988) devised proposition/support and opinion/proof outlines (see Figure 8.14) that may be used with younger students. In these two-level outlines, students state a proposition or an opinion and then list supporting statements. The main steps in introducing this procedure are detailed in Lesson 8.4.

Lesson 8.4
Introducing simple outlining

Step 1. Explain and model the procedure. Read a brief selection and construct a proposition or thesis. Then search out proof or supporting details.

Place the proposition and proof on the chalkboard or an overhead projector, explaining the process as you go along.

Step 2. Have students divide their papers into two columns as in Figure 8.14, or supply sheets on which columns have been created.

Step 3. After reading a brief selection, help students develop a proposition.

Step 4. Help students find proof for the proposition and list the proof in the outline.

Step 5. Check over the outline to ensure that all the important supporting details have been included and that the outline is clear. As an extension, students might use their outlines as a basis for drawing conclusions or writing expository pieces.

Step 6. Have students develop proposition/support outlines independently.

I-CHARTS

I-Charts, which can be used by individuals, small groups, or the whole class, can also help students prepare reports (Hoffman, 1992). After selecting a topic, the teacher creates a series of three or four key questions to which students will seek answers. (Once students become familiar with I-Charts, they might create their own questions.) The topic and questions are listed at the top of a large chart, as shown in Figure 8.15. Once the questions are written, students talk about what they already know or believe about the topic and list known information and beliefs on the chart. Students' information and beliefs are recorded, even if inaccurate. Students then discuss possible sources of answers to their questions, such as books, articles, and CD-ROM databases, and list these on the chart. Students consult the sources and list their findings in the appropriate blocks. Information

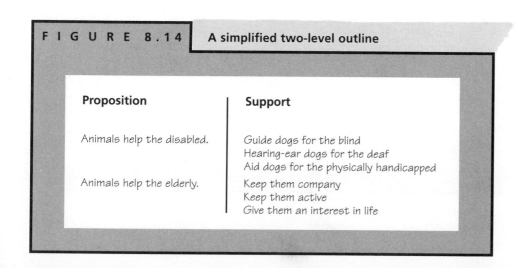

FIGURE 8.14 **A simplified two-level outline**

Proposition	Support
Animals help the disabled.	Guide dogs for the blind Hearing-ear dogs for the deaf Aid dogs for the physically handicapped
Animals help the elderly.	Keep them company Keep them active Give them an interest in life

Guiding Questions

Topic Penguins	What are penguins like?	How many different kinds are there?	What do penguins eat?	Where do penguins live?	Other Interesting Facts	New Questions
What We Know	Penguins are birds that walk funny.		fish	South Pole	Slide on their stomachs	Do penguins have enemies?
Children's Britannica, Vol. 13, Britannica Corporation, 1995.	Have webbed feet	Many kinds of penguins	fish	Antarctic Continent and Antarctic islands		How do chicks learn to swim?
World Book Encyclopedia, Vol. 15, World Book, 1994.	Have rolls of fat to keep them warm			Southern half of world in areas touched by cold water	Have rookeries of 1,000,000	How do chicks learn to get food?
Looking at Penguins, Dorothy Hinshaw Patent, New York: Holiday House, 1993.	Bodies are shaped like torpedoes; have powerful flippers; breathe air.	Smallest is blue penguin; largest is emperor. 17 species.	krill, squid, and fish		Rockhoppers hop on both feet.	Leopard seals, killer whales, and pollution kill penguins.
Summary	Penguins are birds that are built like torpedoes and have strong flippers and webbed feet so they swim fast. Rolls of fat keep them warm.	There are 17 kinds of penguins. Smallest is blue penguin; largest is emperor.	Eat fish, krill, and squid	Live on Antarctic Continent and islands; Live only in southern part of world in areas touched by cold water.	Penguins gather in large groups to lay and hatch eggs. Penguins have funny ways of moving.	Found out that seals, killer whales, and pollution kill penguins. Find out how chicks learn to swim and get food.

Sources

that seems important but does not address the original questions is listed under "Other Interesting Facts." New questions that arise from students' reading are listed under "New Questions." This provides students with the opportunity to seek answers to questions not posed by the teacher. Information about each question is summarized and recorded. As students summarize information, they must reconcile conflicting data and revise any misconceptions they have. A major purpose of I-Charts is to foster critical thinking. The summaries can be used as a basis for a written or an oral report. Unanswered questions in the New Questions column can be researched by individuals or small groups.

METACOGNITIVE STUDY STRATEGIES

The key to teaching children how to direct their study is to present metacognitive study strategies within the context of material to be read or a project to be undertaken. Although presented in context, the strategies must be taught in such a way that they transfer to other texts and other situations. As with the comprehension strategies introduced in earlier chapters, it is essential that the metacognitive demands be presented and integrated with cognitive and affective factors.

Metacognitive strategies that apply to virtually all study tasks are listed in Table 8.4 (Nisbet & Shucksmith, 1986). Students involved in writing reports and other long-term projects should learn to go through the six stages of asking ques-

TABLE 8.4   Metacognitive study strategies

Strategy	Examples
Asking questions: What do I want to learn?	This includes setting up hypotheses, setting aims, defining boundaries of area to be explored, discovering audience, and relating task to previous work.
Planning: How will I go about the task?	This includes deciding on tactics and subdividing the overall task into subtasks.
Monitoring: Am I answering my questions?	This is a continuing attempt to see if the results of one's efforts are matching the questions posed or purposes set.
Checking: How have I done so far?	This is a preliminary check to assess results and tactics.
Revising: What do I have to change?	Tactics, results, or goals may have to be changed.
Self-testing: How did I do? What did I learn?	In this final evaluation, both the results and method of achieving them are assessed.

tions, planning, monitoring, checking, revising, and self-testing, as shown in the table. These stages, in adapted, abbreviated form, can also be used in studying for tests and completing daily homework assignments. Initially, you should walk the students step by step through these stages. Gradually, they will assume responsibility for each stage on their own; ideally, this will become automatic.

SUMMARY

1. The general goal of content area instruction is to help students construct an understanding of key concepts. Content area textbooks, which account for most of the teaching and learning of subject matter, pose special problems because they are more complex than narrative materials and may contain a high proportion of difficult concepts and technical vocabulary. In addition, they require reading to learn, which is a step beyond reading to comprehend. Children's books enliven content area instruction and can be used along with or instead of content area textbooks. Children's books can also be used to provide multicultural perspectives.

2. Numerous strategies can be used to prepare students for content area textbooks. Those discussed in this chapter include PReP, anticipation guides, the survey technique, and structured overviews.

3. During-reading strategies recommended for fostering comprehension of content area material include imaging, graphic aids, textual aids, think-alouds, and study guides.

4. After-reading strategies feature construction of analogies, graphic organizers, and application and extension. A special technique—KWL Plus—can be used during all three phases of reading.

5. Content and strategies should be combined. The nature of the content determines choice of strategies. Increased content knowledge also makes strategies easier to apply.

6. Concepts that run counter to students' commonsense ideas pose a special problem, because students' erroneous concepts may remain unchanged. To counter students' misconceptions, it is important to teach for conceptual change.

7. Writing is a powerful way to promote learning in the content area. In addition to traditional reports, students might record first-hand observations of experiments or surveys, create picture books or other texts

about subjects studied. Learning logs are also an effective device for recording observations and raising questions about content area topics.

8. Even students who are good readers may not know how to study. Studying requires remembering in addition to understanding material. Retention of materials depends on clear, active encoding and on structuring connections between details being learned and older information. Material that is well organized aids memory storage. Retrieval is also improved by organization and elaboration, because the increased number of connections means a greater number of retrieval pathways. Connections that involve causes and effects are especially helpful. Having an intention to learn, overlearning, and resting at appropriate times enhance retention.

9. Material is most easily learned and retained when students bring to their reading a firm foundation of understanding, and when meaningful relationships are established. Rehearsal is an appropriate strategy for learning materials that lack meaningful connections. If possible, however, memory devices such as the key word technique, rhymes, acronyms, and acrostics should be used with materials that lack meaningful connections, since they create artificial connections. Young students may not spontaneously use study strategies; they must be taught such strategies and reminded to use them.

10. A study strategy that has been effective with a variety of students is SQ3R (Study, Question, Read, Recite, Review), which is based on a number of learning strategies that involve preparing, organizing, and elaborating, as well as metacognition. In addition to learning how to study, students should also learn how to take tests. An effective technique for taking tests is PLAE (Preplanning, Listing, Activity, and Evaluating).

11. Good study habits include finding an appropriate time and place to study and studying purposefully as part of a regular routine.

12. Metacognitive strategies essential to studying include asking questions, planning, monitoring, checking, revising, and self-testing.

CLASSROOM APPLICATIONS

1. Examine an up-to-date content area book. Using the Fry readability graph (Figure 8.1) on at least three separate passages of one hundred words or more, obtain an estimate of the readability of the book. How does the book shape up? What are its strengths and weaknesses?
2. Choose a grade level and a subject matter area, and start a collection of bibliography cards on books that might be used to supplement or replace the textbook. Try to locate books on easy, average, and challenging levels.
3. Create a mnemonic device for learning the names of the planets in order of their distance from the sun.

FIELD APPLICATIONS

1. Try out one of the strategies described in this chapter for at least a week. Use a learning log to keep a running record of your experience. How well did it work? How hard was it to use? How practical is it?
2. Create a lesson showing how you would introduce KWL or another strategy to a class. If possible, teach the lesson and evaluate its effectiveness.
3. Prepare a study guide for a chapter in a science or social studies textbook or children's book. If possible, use the guide with a class. Have students react to the guide, telling how it helped them and how it might be changed to make it better.

c h a p t e r 9

Reading Literature

For each of the following statements related to the chapter you are about to read, put a check under "Agree" or "Disagree" to show how you feel. Discuss your responses with classmates before you read the chapter.

Agree   **Disagree**

1. Children should read the classics—works that have stood the test of time.

2. Good literature teaches us how to live.

3. The primary goal of reading must be enjoyment.

4. The main danger of a literature approach to reading is that selections will be over-analyzed.

5. Teachers should not waste their time covering literary lightweights. Students deserve the best.

6. Students should have some say in choosing the literature they read.

7. It does not really matter what children read just as long as they read something.

8. Class time is too precious to be spent on free reading.

When reading literature, students use many of the same processes that they use when reading more mundane materials; word-attack and comprehension strategies and skills are necessary. However, reading literature involves going beyond mere comprehension. The focus is on appreciation, enjoyment, and reader response. This chapter explores ideas for building understanding and appreciation of folklore, myths, poems, plays, and novels and ends with suggestions for promoting voluntary reading.

What are your favorite kinds of literature? What experiences have you had that created a love of literature? What experiences have you had that may have created negative feelings about literature? How might literature be taught so that students learn to understand and appreciate it without losing the fun of reading it? What might be done to make students lifelong readers of high-quality novels, poetry, plays, and biographies?

EXPERIENCING LITERATURE

Until recently, reading was considered a skills subject. It did not really matter what students read. After all, they could practice sequencing skills on a set of directions as well as on a short story. Today, content is paramount, the idea being that students' minds and lives will be greatly enriched if they read the best that has been written.

Huck (1989) stated, "Most of what children learn in school is concerned with *knowing*; literature is concerned with *feeling* . . . " (p. 254). As Lukens (1995) explains,

> Literature at its best gives both pleasure and understanding. It explores the nature of human being, the conditions of humankind. If these phrases seem too pompous and abstract for children's literature, rephrase them in children's terms: What are people like? Why are they like that? What do they need? What makes them do what they do? (p. 8)

Reading literature involves a dimension beyond reading ordinary material. If read properly, a classic tale draws out a feeling of wholeness or oneness, a carefully drawn character or situation evokes a feeling of recognition, and a poem that speaks to the heart engenders a feeling of tranquility. Louise Rosenblatt (1978) called this the aesthetic response: "In aesthetic reading, the reader's attention is centered directly on what he is living through during his relationship with that particular text" (p. 25).

In contrast to aesthetic reading is efferent reading, in which the reader's attention is directed to "concepts to be refined, ideas to be tested, actions to be performed after the reading" (Rosenblatt, 1978, p. 24). In efferent reading, the

The way in which literature is taught affects how and why students read literature. Using literature is currently seen as a better way of teaching reading; it is also considered a way of modeling process writing and motivating students. However, literature is more than just a means for teaching reading and writing; it has value in its own right.

The study of literature has a number of possible values. Literature can be viewed as having moral force: We are inspired by reading the best of what has been written; we are challenged to explore major moral issues (Purves, 1993). Literature also has aesthetic force: It evokes a deep personal response (this is the basis of reader response). The two can be combined so that the purpose of literature becomes "to teach and to please." Literature is also seen as having a force for enlightenment, allowing us to respond to universal themes and so come to understand ourselves and others better. However, literature is also "an expression of and a lens into . . . cultures" (Purves, 1993, p. 358), thereby allowing the reader to view "literary works in their historical and cultural context rather than as disembodied texts" (p. 358).

Speaking of the power of literature, teacher and author Mem Fox (1994) explains that a story may touch children, may even make them weep, but this is not to be avoided: "Something in print will have touched them at last. Something in print will have made them aware—perhaps for the first time—that within the pages of a book it is occasionally possible to find a story worth thinking about, a story with an impact that lasts for years rather than minutes, a story that makes reading seem like a possible attraction rather than a likely chore. It's the stories that make us think and feel, laugh aloud or cry, gasp or shiver, snuggle in, or want to share that which makes us *want* to read, and keep on reading"(p. 154).

reader "carries away" meaning. In aesthetic reading, the reader is carried away by feelings evoked by the text. Text can be read efferently or aesthetically, depending on the reader's stance. For example, we could read an essay efferently for ideas or information, but if we respond to its biting satire or subtle humor, our stance becomes aesthetic. Thus it is not an either/or proposition but falls on a continuum, with the reader moving closer to one stance or the other depending on her or his expectations and focus (Dias, 1990). As Rosenblatt (1991) explained, "We read for information, but we are conscious of emotions about it and feel pleasure when the words we call up arouse vivid images and are rhythmic to the inner ear" (p. 445).

Rosenblatt cautioned that it is important to have a clear sense of purpose when asking children to read a particular piece. The purpose should fit in with the nature of the piece and the objective for presenting it. By its nature, for instance, poetry generally demands an aesthetic reading. But if the focus of the reading is on literal comprehension, then the experience will be efferent. The reading is aesthetic if the focus is on experiencing the poem or story and savoring the sounds, sights, and emotions that the words conjure up.

According to Dias (1990), school reading tends to be efferent, even when students encounter literary selections, because the teacher's stance and activities tend to be efferent. The teacher, therefore, must also adopt an aesthetic stance, to encourage students to enjoy, wonder, feel, and respond to the literature they read. Literature should be treated as literature and not as an exercise in comprehension.

Reading aesthetically results in a deeper level of involvement for students (Cox & Many, 1992). As they read aesthetically, children tend to picture the story in their minds. They imagine scenes, actions, and characters. As they become more deeply involved, they may enter the world that they have constructed and try to understand events and characters "in terms of how people in their world would act in similar circumstances" (Cox & Many, 1992, p. 30). Aesthetic readers also extend and hypothesize. They might wonder what happens to the characters after the story is over and imagine possible scenarios or create alternative endings. Students might also identify with a particular character and wonder how they might act if they were that character and experienced the story events.

An aesthetic response may also elicit a network of feelings. A child who feels sad at the end of a tragic tale might relate the story-elicited feeling of sadness to a time in real life when she or he felt sad. The child might relive the personal experience that caused sadness. Reading about a story character's death, for example, the student might recall the recent death of a relative and the sadness this death occasioned.

How might students' responses be fostered? The research suggests several possibilities. Students might be allowed to choose the form of their response: It could be a poem, a story, a letter, a journal entry, or, simply an oral reaction. It is important that students be encouraged to make connections with their personal lives and other texts that they have read. Children also need time to respond, with ample opportunity to share and discuss. As Cox and Many (1992) commented, "A lot of groping goes on during this talking and again seems necessary to provide for quick flashes of personal understanding that come suddenly and quickly during informal, open discussions" (p. 32).

READER RESPONSE THEORY

To illustrate **reader response theory,** Probst (1988) described observing a class discussion of a story about a student who, feeling pressured to succeed, yielded to a temptation to cheat on a test. The tale hit home. Not even waiting for the teacher to initiate the discussion, one student remarked, "I know exactly how he felt" (p. 32). The student then explained how, because of parental pressure, she would feel compelled to cheat if she felt she were going to fail a test. A lively, spontaneous discussion erupted. However, the teacher's purpose for the lesson was to review with her class the literary devices for revealing character. Persisting with her question "Now there are three ways an author reveals character—can you tell me what they are?" (p. 33), the teacher succeeded in quelling the discussion and extracting the correct answer from the subdued group. The teacher missed a wonderful opportunity to lead the students to experience the power of literature and how its themes often relate to their lives. Ironically, she could also have fostered a deeper understanding of some literary techniques, including ways to reveal character, thereby achieving her original purpose. If she had allowed the students to respond fully to the piece, they would have been more interested in how the author had crafted such a gripping tale.

As Probst (1988) pointed out, the teacher had an erroneous vision of the purpose of literature. To her, it was a series of technical terms and techniques to be grasped, which is a little like trying to understand the workings of the mind by memorizing the parts of the brain. However, the ultimate purpose of literature is to touch our inner lives in some way. Unless we feel that touch, we do not truly experience literature. Rosenblatt (1990) explained that there are a number of practices which hinder an aesthetic response:

> The habit of explaining the literary qualities of the work by pointing to elements in the text (such as rhythm, imagery, metaphor, and departures from ordinary diction) has prevented the realization that the reader must first of all adopt what I term an "aesthetic stance"—that is, focus on the private, as well as the public aspects of meaning. Reading to find the answer to a factual question requires attention only to the public aspects of meaning, and excludes, pushes into the periphery, any personal feelings or ideas activated. (p. 104)

The teacher's first purpose, then, should be to evoke a response. Because literature is a **transaction** between reader and writer, that response must be personal. Using a poem, story, novel, or other literary work as a blueprint, readers can create their own work. A class of twenty-five students reading *Charlotte's Web* (White, 1952) will create twenty-five different versions of that classic story. This does not mean that readers are free to interpret a literary selection in any way that they want. Their interpretations must be based on the blueprint, which is the text. However, to build from that blueprint, readers bring their life experience, perspective, experience in reading literature, cognitive ability, attitudes, and values, all of which become part of the final meaning that they construct. As a practical matter, readers often agree on some common meaning in their response to a piece of literature. However, there is also considerable personal interpretation and reaction (Beach & Hynds, 1991).

Essentially, therefore, teaching literature is a matter of structuring activities in which students respond to a selection and then clarify the impact of the selection

Reader response theory is a view of reading in which the reader plays a central role in constructing the meaning of a text. The meaning is not found in the text or the reader but is found in the relationship or transaction between the two.

Purves (1990) commented that although elementary school teachers have put literature into the curriculum, the types of questions they ask and the way they focus on comprehension reflect an efferent approach. "It is the bottle that has changed, not the wine" (p. 82).

To promote aesthetic reading, "teachers should recognize, support, and further encourage signs that the reader's focus of attention is on the lived-through experience of the literary evocation. . . . Signs of the aesthetic response may include picturing and imagining while reading or viewing; describing a strongly felt sense of . . . the reality of being there; imagining oneself in a character's place or in story events; questioning or hypothesizing about a story; extending a story or creating new stories; making associations with other stories and one's own life experiences; and mentioning feelings evoked" (Cox & Many, 1992, pp. 32–33).

A **transaction** is the process whereby the reader is part of the reading act so that the reader is affected by the text and the text, in turn, is affected by the reader. The reader, the text, and the act of reading all have an impact on each other.

Drawing is one way of responding to literature.

in terms of itself and its meaning in their lives. It is important to create an environment in which students feel free to first deal with their own reactions and then work out, through reflection and discussion, a personal meaning for the piece. Although in the early stages the reader's response to literature may be highly personal, readers gradually learn to become more evaluative. As Rosenblatt (1990) explained, personal response becomes the basis for "growth toward more and more balanced, self-critical, knowledgeable interpretation" (p. 100).

Traditionally, there has been a sense in the classroom that a poem or other piece of literature has a certain meaning, and that the teacher is the final judge as to what that meaning is. Realizing now that children are active constructors of meaning, we know that they are the ultimate interpreters. They must be helped to see that a story or poem does not have a right or wrong interpretation but takes on meaning in light of their experiences and subjective feelings. Students who have lived in a foster home will have a much different reaction to *The Pinballs* (Byars, 1977), a tale of foster children, than students who have not. The foster children's interpretation of the book's characters, theme, and events will reflect their experiences. Students' individual interpretations and responses should not only be accepted but actively encouraged. Although there is no single, correct interpretation, those interpretations that are made should be grounded in text. Students should be prepared to justify them; a response could be based on a misreading or erroneous information and would have to be revised.

How does one go about eliciting reader response? Probst (1988) described the following general steps:

1. *Creating a reader response environment.* Establish a setting in which students feel free to respond and each response is valued, so that students are free of worry about rightness or wrongness.

2. *Preparing to read the literary piece.* Preparation for reading a literary piece is basically the same as that for reading any text: A DRA framework is used. In the preparatory stage, a schema is activated, new concepts and vocabulary words are taught, interest in reading the selection is engendered, and a purpose is set. The purpose generally is open-ended, to evoke a response.

3. *Reading the literary piece.* The work is read silently by students. However, if it is a poem, you may elect to read it aloud, as the sound of poetry is essential to its impact.

4. *Small-group discussion.* The literary piece is discussed by groups consisting of four or five students. In small groups, each student has a better opportunity to express her or his response to the piece and compare it with that of others. Discussion is essential because it leads to deeper exploration of a piece.

Students need assistance in holding discussions. Set ground rules, and have a group role-play the process. To foster a fuller discussion, students might be asked to take a few moments to jot down their responses before they discuss them. Writing facilitates careful consideration. Questions that might be used to evoke a response include the following, some of which were suggested by Probst (1988):

- Which part of the selection stands out in your mind the most?
- Picture a part of the piece in your mind. Which part did you picture? Why?
- Was there anything in the selection that bothered you?
- Was there anything in it that surprised you?
- What main feeling did it stir up?
- What is the best line or paragraph in the piece?
- Does this selection make you think of anything that has happened in your life?
- As you read, did your feelings change? If so, how?
- Does this piece remind you of anything else that you have read?
- If the author were here, what would you say to her or him? What questions would you ask?
- What do you think the writer was trying to say?
- What special words, expressions, or writing devices did the author use?
- Which of these did you like best? Least?
- If you were grading the author, what mark would you give her or him? Why? What comments might you write on the author's paper?

5. *Class discussion.* After the small groups have discussed the piece for about ten minutes, extend the discussion to the whole class. The discussion should center on the responses, beginning with those made in the small groups. Ask, "How did your group respond to the piece? In what way were responses the same? Is there anything about the work that we can agree on? How were the responses different? Did your response change as your group discussed the piece? If so, how?"

Throughout the discussion, you, as the teacher, must remain neutral and not intervene with your interpretation. Students have to be empowered to construct their own interpretations, and they need opportunities to develop their interpretive skills.

Readers who make aesthetic responses enjoy a richer experience and produce more elaborated written responses. When elementary school students write from an aesthetic stance, their responses are more fully developed and more likely to show connections between the text and their lives. Efferent responses often consist of a barebones retelling of the tale and a brief evaluation of literary elements (Many, 1990, 1991).

This is a menu of questions. Choose those that are most appropriate for your circumstances; do not attempt to ask them all.

Rosenblatt (1991) commented: "Textbooks and teachers' questions too often hurry students away from the lived-through experience. After the reading, the experience should be recaptured, reflected on. It can be the subject of further aesthetic activities—drawing, dancing, miming, talking, writing, role-playing, or oral interpretation. It can be discussed and analyzed efferently. Or it can yield information. But first, if it is indeed to be literature for these students, it must be experienced"(p. 447).

Meyers (1988) cautioned, "Students are used to looking to teachers for answers. They are seldom asked to reflect on what they think about what they read, or even less so, why they think what they think" (p. 65).

Students grow in their ability to respond to reading and explain their responses (Purves & Monson, 1984). Some adaptation may be necessary in the reader response procedure, as some students may benefit from more structure. However, all students should construct their own personal responses, and those responses should be respected. Students must see that they are truly constructors of meaning. Poetry works especially well with the reader response method because it typically evokes a wide range of responses. Lesson 9.1 shows how a reader response lesson might be presented using the poem "Zinnias" (Worth, 1972).

Lesson 9.1
Reader response

Step 1. Preparing to read the literary piece

Reader response theory may be used with any piece of literature but works especially well with poetry.

If possible, show students a bunch of zinnias or a large color picture of zinnias. Ask the class to say the name of the flowers. Write the name on the chalkboard. Ask students what their favorite flower is and why.

Step 2. Reading the literary piece

Have students read "Zinnias," or listen as you read it. Their purpose should be to see what feelings, thoughts, or images the poem brings to mind.

Zinnias, stout and stiff,
Stand no nonsense: their colors
Stare, their leaves
Grow straight out, their petals
Jut like clipped cardboard
Round, in neat flat rings.

Even cut and bunched,
Arranged to please us
In the house, in water, they
Will hardly wilt—I know
Someone like zinnias; I wish
I were like zinnias. (Worth, 1972)

Step 3. Responding to the literary piece

Have students write a brief response to each of the following questions, using their thoughts and feelings:

- What feelings, thoughts, or pictures come to mind as you read or listen to the poem?
- After reading the poem, what stands out most in your mind?
- Was there anything in the poem that bothered you or surprised you?
- Do you know anyone who is like a zinnia? How is that person like a zinnia?

Step 4. Small-group discussion

Have students talk over their responses in groups of four or five. Each question should be discussed. Students will have been taught previously to accept everyone's responses, but they can ask for explanations or justifications. Each group should have a discussion leader and a spokesperson. The leader keeps the discussion moving and on track. The spokesperson sums up the group's reactions.

Step 5. Whole-class discussion

Have the whole class discuss the responses. Being careful not to inject your own interpretation, guide the discussion to obtain a full range of responses, thereby making it possible for students to hear them all. You can first take a quick survey of reactions by calling on the spokespeople for each group. Probe and develop those responses by calling on other members of the class. Encourage students to justify their responses by reading phrases or lines from the poem. As the opportunity presents itself, discuss how the language of the poem—the use of alliteration, for example—helps create feelings, images, and thoughts. Also talk about the mental pictures the poem evokes. Students might want to discuss mental pictures they have formed of zinnias. They might also want to discuss why the author chose to write about zinnias. Why not roses or buttercups? Students might talk about what kind of flower or other plant they might like to be.

Step 6. Extension

Have students read other poems about inner feelings. A selection of such poems is included in Joanne Cole's *A New Treasury of Children's Poetry* (1984). Or students might write an "I wish" poem, story, letter, or essay in which they explain or express feelings about something in their lives that they would like to change.

USING JOURNALS TO ELICIT RESPONSES

Response journals, or literary logs, can also be used to evoke personal responses to literature. After reading a chapter in a novel, students might write their thoughts and reactions in a literary log. These responses could be open-ended or could be the result of a prompt. Parsons (1990) suggested the following types of questions, some of which have been altered slightly:

- What surprised you about the section that you read today? How does it affect what might happen next in the story?
- As you read today, what feelings did you experience in response to events or characters; for example, did you feel anger, surprise, irritation, or disappointment? Why do you think you responded that way?
- What startling, unusual, or effective words, phrases, expressions, or images did you come across in your reading that you would like to have explained or clarified?
- What characters and situations in the story reminded you of people and situations in your own life? How are they similar, and how do they differ?

Generally, students would be provided with just one or two prompts but should feel free to respond to other concerns or situations. Gradually, the prompts should be faded so that students can come up with their own concerns. Responses in the logs become the basis for the next day's discussion of the selection read. In supplying prompts for literary journals, Meyers (1988) took a different tack. She supplied

A **response journal** is a notebook in which students write down their feelings or reactions to a selection they have read. They may also jot down questions that they have about the selection.

Responses need not be written. Young children may respond by drawing their favorite character, favorite part of the story, funniest or scariest event, and so on. The drawings then become a basis for response-oriented discussions.

students with a list of twenty questions, similar to those listed above and earlier in this chapter. They were free to choose two or three questions from the list.

USING LITERATURE CIRCLES TO ELICIT RESPONSES

A **literature circle** is a small discussion group composed of students who meet to discuss a piece that they all have read.

Literature circles are also an effective means for eliciting responses. Basically, they consist of discussion groups composed of students who talk over material they all have read, whether it is a short selection, an entire book, or just specific chapters. The teacher initiates the discussion by asking an open-ended question, such as "What is the chapter about?" or "Talk about this book while I listen" (Harste, Short, & Burke, 1988, p. 245). The teacher need not be the discussion leader but can function as an interested participant, asking thought-provoking questions to keep the discussion going as well as questions to help children relate the selection to their own lives. After the initial session, students can conduct the discussion. The group might discuss their reactions to the book, talk over favorite parts, or ask questions about parts that they did not understand. If some members use literary logs, their entries could be used as the focal point. The group might also decide on issues or questions to be explored during subsequent meetings.

Questions designed to elicit a genuine response from a reader are similar to those that might occur in a conversation between two adults discussing a book. McClure and Kristo (1994) provide the following example of a book conversation. "Thus a conversation about Patricia MacLachlan's *Sarah, Plain and Tall* (1985) might go like this: 'Sarah made me think of the time I moved to the Midwest from New England. I missed the ocean and landscape, much as Sarah did. Have any of you had a similar kind of experience?' " (pp. xv–xvi).

It is important that the teacher actively encourage students to respond with their personal interpretations and reactions. One teacher, who has been using reader response for years, asks at least some questions for which she herself has no answers. In this way, she does not signal consciously or subconsciously that students are supplying or failing to supply the answer she was expecting. Harste, Short, and Burke (1988) advised,

> For literature circles to be successful, there needs to be a classroom environment already established that supports risk taking and varied constructions of meaning from reading. If the students feel that they must reproduce what the teacher thinks is *the* meaning of a piece of literature, the literature circles will not be productive. (p. 296)

In literature circles, students talk over books or stories that they have all read.

These authors suggested the following strategies for students who are used to traditional discussions in which the focus is on "the right answer" and thus might not be responsive to literary circles at first:

- *Sketch to stretch.* Each student makes a drawing to show what a story means to her or him, and then small groups discuss the drawings.
- *Say something.* Working in pairs, students read a segment of a selection, stopping periodically to discuss what it means. Later, they discuss it as a group.
- *Save the last word for me.* As they read a selection, students write on one side of a note card words, phrases, or sentences that they find particularly interesting or intriguing. On the other side, they write their reactions to the quotations, which might take the form of questions or statements of agreement or disagreement. Cards are shared in small groups.

Literature can evoke deep feelings. When using a reader response approach, be sensitive to students' emotional states and their right to privacy. Care must be taken not to upset children or elicit personal information that might be embarrassing to them. Because of its power and personal nature, the reader response approach should be handled with professional discretion.

Asking *why* after a reader has described her or his response requires that the student justify his or her reaction to a piece and suggests that you may be challenging his or her response. Instead, request that the student tell you more about what he or she is thinking" (McClure & Kristo, 1994).

PRINCIPLES OF TEACHING FROM AN AESTHETIC STANCE

There are several basic principles of teaching literature from an aesthetic stance. The first is to expose children to a wide variety of literary texts such as novels, short stories, essays, poems, and plays. These may be read aloud by the teacher or silently by the students. Also, emphasize activities that lead to an aesthetic rather than an efferent response. Stress enjoyment and appreciation. Do not pepper students with a series of who, what, where, and when questions or load them down with worksheets. Whenever possible, allow them to select the books they read. Also keep in mind that an aesthetic response is highly individualized.

Give students an opportunity to discuss texts without your supervision, perhaps in a round table format. Dias (1990) advised, "The best teacher is experience, a variety of reading experiences with opportunities to talk with other readers about these experiences in order to make sense of them" (p. 291). Freed from teacher supervision, students can react more freely. They will not feel compelled to supply answers that they think the teacher is looking for or that will earn them the highest grade.

Finally, activate the work. Make it come alive by having choral readings of poems, putting on plays, dramatizing stories, and using art and music to extend the experience.

In an aesthetic stance, the reader becomes personally involved with the text.

DEVELOPING AESTHETIC JUDGMENT

As children gain depth in their response to literature, they should also develop standards by which to judge what they read. For a piece of fiction, they should judge the quality of the character development, plot, theme, author's style, and setting.

- *Character development.* In most pieces of fiction, character development is key. As Lukens (1995) notes, "If literature is to help children understand the nature of human beings, we need reality in the study of character. Nothing—not style, nor conflict, nor adventure, nor suspense, nor vivid setting, nor laughter, nor tears—nothing can substitute for solid character development in creating a pleasurable and lasting literature for children as well as adults" (p. 59). As Lukens explains, well-developed characters are rounded; they are not flat or one-dimensional, nor are they all good or all bad. They seem real enough to readers that they can identify with their struggles, bemoan their defeats, and glory in their victories. Most of all, they are memorable—they stay with us long after the final page has been read.

- *Plot.* Children thrive on action and adventure, so well-plotted stories will gain and maintain their interest. Twists and turns in a story grab children's attention, but plot developments must be plausible and have a measure of originality. Predictable plots are boring, but contrived plots leave readers feeling tricked or cheated.

The **theme** is the main idea or central meaning of a work.

- *Theme.* The **theme** may be implicit or directly stated, but as the main idea or central meaning of a work (Lukens, 1995), it provides coherence to a story that otherwise would simply be a collection of episodes. Themes are most evident in traditional tales in which love conquers all, virtue is rewarded, and evil is punished. However, a theme should not be preachy. A tale written to demonstrate the evils of drugs or selfishness falls flat. Genuine themes arise out of the credible actions of believable characters.

- *Author's style.* In writing, style is simply the way an author writes. Authors may have a simple style, an ornate or flowing style, a plodding style, or a brisk style. Good writing is distinguished from poor writing by its forcefulness and originality of style, including choice of words, aptness of description, presence of original figures of speech, and imagery used to create pictures in our minds. As readers, we wish to be transported above the mundane, the trite, and the hackneyed.

- *Setting.* Setting includes the time and place of a story and the mood that the author creates. For example, in a horror story, the author must create a sense of impending supernatural occurrence as well as depicting a deserted castle in a far-off place. When the setting is an integral part of a story, as it would be in a survival tale set in the Arctic, the author must make the setting come alive.

As they progress through the grades, students should develop standards for judging the quality of books. Over time, they should be able to recognize a well-plotted book, original style, universality of theme, well-developed characters, and—above all—how all the elements work together to produce a superior work. However, response and enjoyment should be at the heart of instruction. Analysis and critical evaluation should only come after students have personally interpreted and responded to the text. Moreover, not all of their reading needs to meet the highest literary standards. There should be a place in the reading program for books like the Baby-Sitters Club series or sports biographies—books that do not have literary quality but that young people enjoy reading and that can serve an important function in their personal and literacy development.

TYPES OF LITERATURE

FOLKLORE

A good place to start the study of literature is with **folklore,** which includes folk-tales, myths, rituals, superstitions, songs, and jokes. Folklore follows an oral tradition. As M. A. Taylor (1990) put it, "The tales of the tongue are a good introduction to the tales of the pen." Having stood the test of time, folklore has universal appeal.

Folklore refers to tales, rituals, superstitions, nursery rhymes, and other oral works.

FOLKTALES

One popular form of folklore is the **folktale.** Although created for all ages, today folktales are primarily read by or to children. It is natural that children should be the primary audience since the qualities that are universally found in the folktales are those to which children respond in any story:

> The folktale starts briskly and continues to be filled with action; it often has humor; it appeals to children's sense of justice, since many tales reward good and punish evil; it has little nuance of characterization, so the characters are presented as entirely good, bad, obedient, lazy, and so on; it often includes rhyme or repetition; it is usually concise; it usually has a satisfying and definite conclusion. In other words, the folktale has all the things that children, especially small children, like. And if it has magic—and most do—so much the better. (Sutherland & Arbuthnot, 1986, p. 163)

A **folktale** is a story handed down orally from generation to generation. Folktales include fairy tales, myths, legends, and tall tales.

As the product of people who could neither read nor write, folktales originally were not conveyed by print but were told and retold by countless storytellers in a variety of versions. According to Cole (1982),

> The tales served not only to entertain but to transmit the values and wisdom of the culture, imbue a strong sense of right and wrong, and provide a reservoir of vivid images that became part of the individual's imagination and even of his everyday language. (p. xvi)

Since they are part of an oral tradition, reading folktales to students is an excellent way to introduce them. Even kindergarten children enjoy hearing "The Three Little Pigs," "The Three Billy Goats Gruff," and "Little Red Riding Hood." Because folktales often have repeated elements, they are especially appropriate for shared or choral readings. Students whose reading skills are limited can join in and read the part of the wolf in "The Three Little Pigs" or the part of Baby Bear in "The Story of the Three Bears."

With their emphasis on what happens rather than on character development, folktales focus on strong plots. When discussing folktales with students, stress the story line, how the story started, the problem or conflict, and the resolution; but be sure to emphasize activities that lead to genuine enjoyment and appreciation of folktales.

Have students compare different versions of the same folktale—for example, Janet Stevens's (1987) and Paul Galdone's (1973) versions of *The Three Billy Goats Gruff*. Students can read several modern versions and compare them with the original. Point out that the stories were often reshaped to fit the times. Let students try their hand at retelling a folktale to make it fit their world. Give students the opportunity to choose their own folktales to read and discuss with others who have read similar ones. One discussion group may talk about fairy tales; a second group, tall tales; a third group, trickster tales.

Every culture has produced its own folktales. Students can investigate those drawn from the culture of their ancestors. African American students might look into one of Aardema's works, such as *Why Mosquitoes Buzz in People's Ears: A West African Folk Tale* (1975), or one of Harold Courlander's collections of African tales. Closer to home is Virginia Hamilton's (1985) *The People Could Fly: American Black Folktales*. Students of Polish ancestry might want to read *Polish Fairy Tales* by Zajdler (1968). Other outstanding sources of materials about diverse cultures are *Kaleidoscope: A Multicultural Booklist for Grades K–8* (Bishop, 1994), *Multicultural Literature for Children and Young Adults* (Kruse & Horning, 1991), and *Multicultural Teaching* (Tiedt & Tiedt, 1990). To provide additional follow-up, use the following reinforcement activities.

Reinforcement Activities
Folktales

- Since folktales were meant to be told orally, have a volunteer retell a tale. Students can pretend to be members of the storyteller's family or village. They can decide when and where the tale was told and how the listeners might have reacted. Have a storytelling festival, with students retelling a tale that they located on their own.
- Have older students create a semantic map of major types of folktales and their elements.
- Encourage students to ask parents and grandparents about any favorite folktales they remember hearing. If possible, parents or grandparents might tell the stories to the class.
- Students can retell folktales through puppet shows and other dramatizations. Older students might put on shows for primary-grade students.
- Point out allusions to folktales as these occur in newspapers, magazines, or books. Discuss, for instance, terms like *cried wolf* and *Cinderella team*.
- Above all, acquire collections of folktales for the classroom library so that students may have easy access to them. Also continue to read folktales aloud to the class.

MYTHS

Myths are stories based on the beliefs of a culture that explain how things were created or came into being.

Pourquoi tales are myths that have been designed for young people to explain such natural phenomena as how the leopard got its spots or how the elephant got its trunk.

Although both are part of folklore, **myths** are distinguished from folktales as being rooted in the beliefs of a culture. Myths explain "cosmic forces and the natural order" (Benét, 1987, p. 688). The themes of mythology include "creation, divinity, the significance of life and death, natural phenomena, and the adventures of mythical heroes" (p. 678).

Pourquoi tales (*pourquoi* is French for "why") explain the origin of natural phenomena: the origin of fire, how the beaver got its tail, why the sun rises and sets as it does. Some pourquoi tales explain customs—for instance, why certain people became shepherds rather than farmers (Purves & Monson, 1984). Because myths deal with some of the most profound themes, many are not suitable for young readers. However, most pourquoi tales can be both grasped and enjoyed by primary-grade students.

LEGENDS AND HERO TALES

Legends also embody the important elements in a culture. However, unlike myths, they are based on history rather than the supernatural. Students might enjoy the legends, **hero tales,** and myths listed in the Children's Book List.

Children's Book List
Myths, legends, and hero tales

Aardema, V. *Borreguita and the Coyote: A Tale from Ayutla, Mexico.* New York: Knopf (1991). Presents the tale of a coyote who is tricked by Borreguita (a lamb).

Aliki. *The Gods and Goddesses of Olympus.* New York: HarperCollins (1994). Tells about the legends, loves, and battles of the gods, goddesses, monsters, and heroes of Greek mythology.

D'Aulaire, I. & D'Aulaire, P. *Book of Greek Myths.* New York: Macmillan (1985). Retells a number of the most famous Greek myths.

Francesca, M. *The Honey Hunters: A Traditional African Tale.* Boston: Candlewick Press (1992). Explains why animals who were friends became enemies.

Goble, P. *Dream Wolf.* New York: Bradbury (1990). Tells a tale of friendship between Native Americans and wolves.

Haviland, V. (Ed.). *North American Legends.* New York: Collins (1978). Presents a variety of legends.

Kellogg, S. *Johnny Appleseed: A Tall Tale.* New York: Morrow (1988). Tells the story of John Chapman, who planted apple seeds across the land.

Kellogg, S. *Mike Fink.* New York: Morrow (1992). Relates the extraordinary deeds of the frontiersman who became king of keelboatmen on the Mississippi River.

Kellogg, S. *Paul Bunyan.* New York: Mulberry (1993). Recounts the life of the extraordinary lumberjack whose unusual size and strength brought him many fantastic adventures.

Lester, J. *John Henry.* New York: Dial (1994). Retells the life of the legendary African-American hero who raced against a steam drill to cut through a mountain.

Mahey, M. *The Seven Chinese Brothers.* New York: Scholastic (1990). Tells the story of brothers who help each other when threatened by an evil emperor.

Miles, B. *Robin Hood: His Life and Legend.* Chicago: Rand McNally (1979). Provides a somewhat revised version of a traditional tale.

Legends are traditional tales passed down as being based in fact.

Hero tales are stories in which the central character does grand deeds and, in so doing, serves as an inspiration for the culture. Hero tales may be fictional or based on real characters, like the tale of John Henry.

Since hero tales and legends are based in history, they might be coordinated with the social studies curriculum.

Mollel, T. M. *A Promise to the Sun: An African Story*. Boston: Little Brown (1992). Explains why bats are seen only at night.

Osborne, M. *American Tall Tales*. New York: Knopf (1991). Features Sally Ann Thunder, Ann Whirlwind, Pecos Bill, John Henry, and Paul Bunyan.

Philip, N. *The Tale of Sir Gawain*. New York: Philomel (1987). Tells of the many adventures of King Arthur and the Knights of the Round Table, as seen by Sir Gawain.

Rockwell, A. *The Robber Baby*. New York: Greenwillow (1994). Retells fifteen tales from Greek mythology, including those of Hermes, Daedalus, Pandora, and Atlanta.

POETRY

Ironically, the highest form of literary expression is the least liked by the majority of students. According to McClure, Harrison, and Reed (1990), poetry is viewed by many children as the literary equivalent of liver. Why do children rank poetry at or near the bottom of their list of literary preferences? One reason may be that it is sorely neglected in elementary classrooms. According to a survey of forty-two upper-elementary teachers, three-fourths of them read poetry to their students once a month or less. Furthermore, most students read poetry "only occasionally" or "very seldom" (Terry, 1974).

Teachers may also fail to provide students with the kinds of poetry they most enjoy. In Terry's (1974) study, 113 recorded poems were played for 422 fourth-,

Exemplary Teaching

From Basals to Books

Sensing that her second-graders at Calhoun South Elementary School in Chicago were bored with their basal readers, Marva Collins decided to try using children's books:

> I stopped using the required reader and brought in books from the library and from bookstores. My children read from *Aesop's Fables, Grimm's Fairy Tales,* Hans Christian Andersen, La Fontaine's *Fables,* and Leo Tolstoy's *Fables and Fairytales.* I chose these stories because they teach values and morals and lessons about life. Fairy tales and fables allow children to put things in perspective—greed, trouble, happiness, meanness, and joy. After reading those stories, you have something to think over and discuss. More than anything, I wanted my students to be excited about reading. I wanted ed them to understand that reading is not an exercise in memorizing words but a way to bring ideas to light.
>
> I had my students draw their own pictures to illustrate the stories. Sometimes we acted out the fables, or we made up our own ending. We even composed our own fables. I would start and then each child would add a sentence. I felt my way along, trying out new ideas and experimenting with different methods and lessons. And I loved it. I loved watching my students' faces when they recognized on their own the parallel between two stories. There was an effervescent quality to their excitement. (Collins & Tamarkin, 1982, p. 21)

fifth-, and sixth-graders over a ten-day period. Students were asked to list their favorite and least-liked works. Their favorites tended to be contemporary and humorous and included poems that rhymed, were easy to understand, and had a pleasing rhythm. Limericks and poems with a narrative element were also favored. The least-preferred poems included works that were older, that lacked rhyme, that tended to be abstract or primarily painted an image, or that were hard to understand. The least-liked poem was William Carlos Williams's "The Red Wheelbarrow," which creates an image and lacks rhyme. A number of **haiku** also made the list of the twenty-five most disliked pieces. Students said they were too short, did not rhyme, and did not make much sense. A study of first-, second, and third-graders' preferences tended to confirm these results (Fisher & Natarelli, 1982).

> **Haiku** is a form of poetry that consists of seventeen syllables divided into three lines. The subject is usually nature.

Choosing poems that students have a difficult time relating to and providing activities that students dislike will, of course, hinder their enjoyment and appreciation of poetry. Asking them to memorize poems and spending excessive time on analysis and interpretation also contribute to a dislike of poetry (McClure, Harrison, & Reed, 1990).

TEACHING POETRY

Research suggests that teachers' enthusiasm for particular poems can influence what children like (Terry, 1974). The first step that teachers should take is to become acquainted or reacquainted with children's poetry, as presented in the following sources:

Bauer, C. F. *The Poetry Break, an Annotated Anthology for Introducing Children to Poetry.* New York: H. W. Wilson (1995). More than 240 poems and suggestions for presenting them.

Cole, J. *A New Treasury of Children's Poetry: Old Favorites and New Discoveries.* New York: Doubleday (1984). A breathtaking array of children's poems from Shakespeare to Prelutsky.

Harrison, M. & Stuart-Clark, C. *The Oxford Treasury of Children's Poems.* New York: Oxford (1988). A number of classic works.

Hopkins, L. B. *Pass the Poetry, Please!* New York: Harper & Row (1987). Good, solid information about poets and poetry and many excellent suggestions for teaching poetry.

Prelutsky, J. *The Random House Book of Poetry for Children.* New York: Random House (1983). Poems that younger children will enjoy hearing.

Read poems as though you were the same age as the students in your class. Read those that you most enjoy to your students. Remember that children like poetry that has humor and a narrative element and that rhymes. Include both light verse and more thoughtful pieces. Before reading a poem to the class, practice it so that your reading is strong and dramatic. Briefly discuss vocabulary words or concepts that might interfere with students' understanding or enjoyment. Give students a purpose for listening, such as creating images in their mind, awaiting a surprise ending, or hearing unusual words.

After reading the poem, discuss it but do not overanalyze it. In fact, you might emphasize questions that evoke a personal response: "What about the poem stands out most in your mind? What pictures came to mind as you listened?

Which line do you like best? How does the poem make you feel? Is there anything in the poem that you do not like? Is there anything in it that surprises you?" Better yet, invite students to ask questions about anything in the poem that may have confused them. Gear discussions toward personal responses and interpretations. The emphasis should be "upon delight rather than dissection" (Sloan, 1984, p. 86). Reactions to poetry are very personal. One student's favorite could be another student's least liked. For example, in Terry's (1974) study of preferences, a sixth-grade boy had a special feeling for Edwin Hoey's "Foul Shot" because it reminded him of something that happened in a game in which he had played. A fourth-grade girl, however, disliked the poem because she had difficulty making shots.

The teacher should model how he or she reads a poem, especially one that is complex. The teacher should explain how the images create a certain mood or meaning for him or her. Much of the magic of poetry arises from its language. Read alliterative verse such as Eleanor Farejon's "Mrs. Peck Pigeon" or Rachel Field's "Something Told the Wild Geese," as well as poems that contain excellent examples of onomatopoeia, such as Rhoda Bracemesseter's "Galoshes" and David McCord's "Song of the Train." Also, help students discover how poets use sensory words, as in Mary O'Neil's "Sound of Water" or Polly Chase Boyden's "Mud." Through becoming aware of its language, students will develop an ear for poetry.

Help students discover the richness of metaphor in poetry. Discuss, for instance, how metaphors are used to describe the color white (Sloan, 1984) in the following excerpt from a poem in Mary Le Duc O'Neill's (1961) book *Hailstones and Halibut Bones:*

What is White?
White is a dove
And lily of the valley
And a puddle of milk
Spilled in an alley—
A ship's sail
A kite's tail
A wedding veil
Hailstones and
Halibut bones
And some people's telephones. . . . (p. 35)

Using figurative language, poets can create powerful images. Some of these are visual, as in "The Eagle" by Tennyson (Denman, 1988):

He clasps the crag with crooked hands;
Close to the sun in lonely lands,
Ringed with the azure world, he stands.
The wrinkled sea beneath him crawls;
He watches from his mountain walls,
And like a thunderbolt he falls.

Help students see the universality of images (Sloan, 1984) by using, for example, images that contain allusions to the seasons. Show students that spring is often used to symbolize new life and hope. Winter, on the other hand, is often a symbol of old age, illness, grief, or death.

Contrast the rhythms of poems like David McCord's "Song of the Train" and "Base Stealer" by Robert Francis. Discuss how the beats match the poems' mood and meaning. For older students, show how free verse uses the rhythm of natural speech, whereas bound verse retains the beat of poetic patterns. Although students prefer to read bound verse, free verse may be easier to write as it is not held to traditional formats (Calkins, 1986).

Discussions of poetry are important, and students should be encouraged to create their own meanings. Painter (1970) explained,

> Carl Sandburg in his introduction to *Early Moon* and Walter de la Mare in *Come Hither* maintain that poetry is personal; it has as many different meanings as the different minds that read it. A reader may make out of a poem anything he will and, therefore, make a poem his poem. As a reader changes with the years, the poem changes for him, too, and may take on new meanings. Reinterpretation is constant. (p. 40)

Of course, your ultimate goal is to have students sample a wide variety of poetic forms and become readers of poetry. To promote exploration, encourage students to check out books of poetry from the library, and include such books in the classroom collection. If funds are limited, purchase one or two anthologies. Choose those that seem to have the greatest number of poems that might appeal to your students. Create your own anthologies by obtaining poems from basals or other sources, including selections that students bring in. Some students may want to make their own anthology or folder in which to keep their favorite poems. The Children's Book List presents a sampling of some of the many fine poetry anthologies available for young people.

Children's Book List
Poetry

Bruchac, J. and London, J. *Thirteen Moons on Turtle's Back*. New York: Philomel (1992). Poems based on Native American legends.

Ciardi, J. *You Read to Me, I'll Read to You*. New York: Harper (1962). Features thirty-five lighthearted poems.

dePaola, T. *Tomie dePaola's Book of Poems*. New York: Putnam (1988). A variety of poems especially appropriate for the primary grades.

de Regniers, B. S., Moore, E., White, M. M., & Carr, J. (Eds.). *Sing a Song of Popcorn: Every Child's Book of Poems*. New York: Scholastic (1988). A wide range of poems illustrated by nine award-winning artists.

Greenfield, E. *Night on Neighborhood Street*. New York: Dial (1991). A collection of seventeen poems that focuses on life in an African American neighborhood.

Hoberman, M. *My Song Is Beautiful: Poems and Pictures in Many Voices*. Boston: Little, Brown (1994). Celebration of the power of childhood from the perspectives of a rich variety of authors.

Hopkins, L. B. (Ed.). *Surprises*. New York: Harper (1986). Thirty-eight easy-to-read poems on a variety of subjects ranging from pets to flying.

Hudson, W. *Pass It On: African-American Poetry for Children*. New York: Scholastic (1993). An illustrated collection of poetry by such African American poets as Langston Hughes, Nikki Giovanni, Eloise Greenfield, and Lucille Clifton.

Hughes, L. *The Dream Keeper and Other Poems*. New York: Knopf (1993). A collection of sixty-six poems selected by the author for young readers, including lyrical poems and songs, many of which explore the African American tradition.

Knudson, R. R. & Swenson, M. *American Sports Poems*. New York: Orchard (1988). A collection that should be welcomed by sports fans.

Lewis, J. *Earth Verses and Water Rhymes*. New York: Atheneum (1991). A collection of poems celebrating the natural world around us.

From Sea to Shining Sea. New York: Scholastic (1993). A compilation of more than 140 folk songs, folktales, poems, and stories telling the history of America and reflecting its multicultural society. Illustrated by eleven Caldecott award-winning artists.

Reinforcement Activities
Poetry appreciation

- Set aside time for students to talk about their favorite poems in small groups. Groups can be arranged by topic or author.
- Students can give dramatic readings of their favorite poems. These can be simply animated recitations or more elaborate events with background music and costumes. Some poems lend themselves to choral readings.
- Tie poetry in with the study of content area subjects. For instance, students can read "Arithmetic" in connection with the study of math. While studying insects, read poems about bugs. In *A Pocketful of Poetry*, Sharan Gibson (1989) included a number of poems about insects, such as "I Like Bugs" by Margaret Wise Brown, "Dragonfly" by Florence Page Jaques, and "Firefly" by Elizabeth Madox Roberts.
- Last, but not least, encourage children to write poetry. Smith (1985) and McClure, Harrison, and Reed (1990) offer suggestions.

CHAPTER BOOKS AND NOVELS

As students grow from reading picture books to chapter books and novels, they progress from a focus on fantasy, in which animals talk and magical deeds are performed, to realistic works that deal with divorce, drugs, and growing up.

PREPARATION FOR READING CHAPTER BOOKS AND NOVELS

In a literature-based program, chapter books or novels are often set aside as a separate unit of study. Before embarking on a chapter book or novel, students should receive some guidance to build background essential for understanding the text. Their interest in the book should also be piqued. Place particular emphasis on understanding the first chapter. If students, especially the poorer readers, have a thorough understanding of the first chapter, they will have a solid foundation for comprehending the rest of the text. It will also build their confidence in their ability to read the rest of the text (Ford, 1994).

Generally, students are asked to read a chapter or more each day. Questions to be considered during reading can be provided, or students might make predictions and read to evaluate them. Students might also keep a response journal for their reading. Responses might be open-ended, with students jotting down their general reactions to the segment being read, or students might react to response questions posed by the teacher.

After a segment has been read, it is discussed. Students might also do some rereading to clarify confusing points or might dramatize exciting parts. A cumulative plot outline or story map could be constructed to keep track of the main events. If the story involves a long journey, the characters' progress might be charted on a map. Extension activities can be undertaken once the book has been completed. In general, the work is presented within the framework of an extended directed reading activity or directed reading–thinking activity. The emphasis, however, is on building enjoyment and appreciation and evoking a response; skills are secondary.

Both content and form should be discussed. Design questions to help students understand what is happening in the story and to see how the setting, plot, characters, theme, point of view, and author's style work together. However, take care that you do not overanalyze a piece or ask too many questions at any one time. Balance analysis with eliciting personal responses. Response should precede analysis and general discussion. Once the reader's response is ended, she or he is in better position to analyze the piece. Part of the analysis might involve discovering what elements in the piece caused the student to respond (see the earlier section on reader response for some questions). Some general questions for novels are outlined in Table 9.1. Do not attempt to ask all the questions that have been listed. Choose only those that seem most appropriate for your students.

STORY ELEMENT ACTIVITIES

Several activities help students gain a deeper understanding and appreciation of the story elements.

Character Analysis. A number of devices can be used to analyze characters in a story. One such device is an opinion/proof, in which readers write an opinion about a character and cite proof to back it up. The proof could be the character's actions or comments made about the person by other characters or the author (Santa, 1988). Figure 9.1 presents an opinion/proof for Chibi from *Crow Boy* (Yashima, 1955).

A literary sociogram can be constructed to show how the characters relate to each other. The name of the main character is written in a circle in the middle and other characters' names are written in circles surrounding it. Arrows are drawn between the circles. On the arrows are written words that describe how the characters feel about each other, how they get along, or how they are related (Santa, 1988). Figure 9.2 is a literary sociogram of the characters in *Summer of the Swans* (Byars, 1970). It represents the interrelationships that exist in the first portion of

In addition to their personal background knowledge, readers bring to the reading of literature a knowledge of the procedures of reading. The way they read is determined, in part, by the context of the reading. The reading of an assigned text in school differs from the way a student might voluntarily read this same book. In school, the student knows that she or he will read for a certain period of time and will be expected to focus on certain aspects of the text (the plot or characters, perhaps), and that the discussion afterwards will follow a certain format. As the student moves through the grades, discussions of the text become less personal and more analytical. There is more emphasis on noting motives and drawing inferences (Purves, 1993).

In their study of elementary school children's reading stance, Cox and Zarillo (1993) noted that the children had a variety of ways of responding aesthetically. The children talked about their favorite part, discussed what pictures the selection brought to mind, or made connections between the piece and their own lives or another piece that they had read. Younger children sometimes got so involved in the story that they acted it out. They would talk like one of the characters, make sound effects, or dramatize an episode.

TABLE 9.1 Possible questions for novels

Setting	Characters	Plot
Where does the story take place?	Who are the main characters?	What event started the story?
When does the story take place?	What kinds of people are they?	What is the main problem?
How important is the setting to the story?	Do they seem like real people? Why or why not?	What is making the problem better?
Could the story have happened in a different place at a different time? Why or why not?	How does the author let you know what the main characters are like?	What is making the problem worse?
When you close your eyes and imagine the setting, what do you see?	Did the characters change? If so, how?	What has been the most exciting part of the story so far?
How does the author give you a "you-are-there" feeling?	Were these changes unexpected? Did they surprise you? Why or why not?	Could you guess what was going to happen, or did the author surprise you? How?
	Can you picture the characters in your mind? What do they look like? What do they do? What do they say?	How is the problem resolved?
	Do you know anyone like them?	How does the story end?
	Would you like to meet them? Why or why not?	

Point of view	Theme	Style
How is the story told?	What seems to be the main or most important idea in the story?	What are some especially well-written passages?
Is it told by a narrator who is a part of the story and who calls himself "I"?	What main idea do you take away from the story?	What are some examples of colorful words that the author uses?
Is it told in the second person, using the pronoun "you"?		Does the author use figures of speech or images? If so, give some examples.
Is the story told by someone outside, a person who can see all and tell all?		What special writing techniques does the author use? Give some examples.
How does the author seem to feel about the characters? Who seems to be the author's favorite?		Does this story remind you of any other stories that you have read? If so, which one(s)? In what ways are they similar?
		Does this author remind you of any other authors you have read? If so, who? How are they similar?
		Would you like to read another book by this same author or about this same subject? Why or why not?
		Would you recommend this book to a friend? Why or why not?
		If you could, would you make changes in this book? Why or why not? Give some changes you would make.
		Do you think this book would make a good movie or a good television show? Why or why not?

FIGURE 9.1 | Opinion/proof for Chibi from *Crow Boy*

Opinion	Proof
Chibi knew the ways of nature.	He could hold insects in his hand.
	He knew where wild grapes and wild potatoes grew.
	He knew about flowers.
	He could imitate the voices of crows.

FIGURE 9.2 | Literary sociogram for *Summer of the Swans*

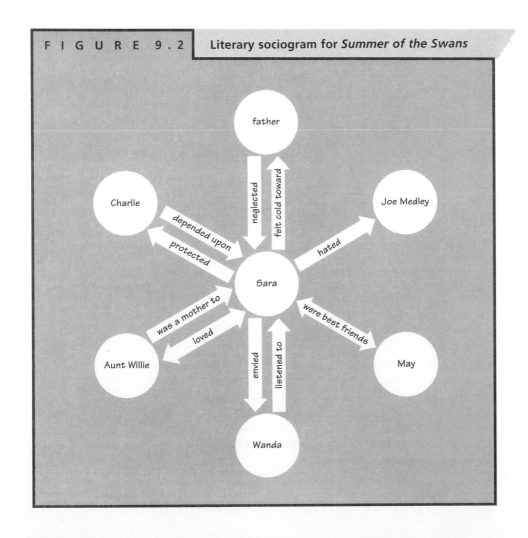

FIGURE 9.3 | SFA chart for *Charlotte's Web*

	Animal	Person	Young	Old	Foolish	Wise	Kind	Selfish	Lonely	Afraid
Fern	–	+	+	–	–	?	+	–	–	–
Wilbur	+	–	+	–	+	–	?	–	+	+
Charlotte	+	–	–	+	–	+	+	–	–	–
Talking sheep	+	–	–	+	–	+	?	–	–	–
Templeton	+	–	–	+	–	?	–	+	–	–
Mr. Arable	–	+	–	+	–	+	+	–	–	–

the book. For longer works, it is a good idea to draw up literary sociograms that represent interrelationships at different points in the story.

Compare/contrast or semantic feature analysis charts might also be constructed to highlight characters' relationships or traits. A semantic feature analysis chart of the characters in *Charlotte's Web* (White, 1952) is shown in Figure 9.3.

On a simplified level, a semantic map can be created for the main character. The character's name is written in the center circle, with his or her major attributes written in surrounding circles. Figure 9.4 is a semantic map for Sara in *Summer of the Swans*.

Plot Analysis.   Understanding the structure of a story aids comprehension and gives students a framework for composing their own stories. A plot chart shows the story problem, the main actions or events leading up to the climax, the climax, the resolution of the problem, and the ending. It could be a series of rectangles, a diagram, or a picture. Figure 9.5 provides an example of a plot chart.

Students might also draw the major events of a story or put the events on a time line. Acting out key scenes or putting on a puppet show would highlight the action. To help them choose the most exciting parts of the story, have students pretend that they are making a movie of the book and must decide which scenes to depict in a preview of coming attractions and which scene to show on a poster advertising the movie.

Most books lend themselves to a variety of follow-up activities. Plan activities such as the following to deepen students' understanding and appreciation of the book and to promote the development of language arts skills.

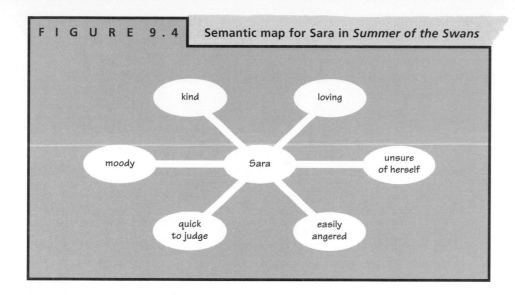

FIGURE 9.4 Semantic map for Sara in *Summer of the Swans*

Reinforcement Activities
Chapter books and novels

- Read a sequel or another book by the same author, or a book that develops the same theme or can be contrasted with the book just completed.
- Dramatize portions of the book.
- Create a print or TV ad for the book.
- Create a dust cover for the book, complete with blurbs that highlight the story and that tell about the author.
- View a movie based on the book, and then compare the two.
- Create a montage, diorama, or other piece of art related to the book.
- Write a review of the book for the school newspaper.
- Have a Characters' Day during which students dress up and act the parts of characters in the book.
- Arrange for a panel discussion of the book. The panel might be composed of the book's characters.

Remember that the goal in reading a book is to have students understand, enjoy, and appreciate it. Do not assign so many activities that the life is squeezed out of the book. Some teachers report spending a month or more with a novel. For most books, two weeks should be adequate.

DRAMA

Plays are a welcome change of pace but require some special reading skills. Although designed to be acted out or at least read orally, plays should first be read silently so that students get the gist of the work. Students need to be taught to read stage directions so that they can picture the setting. They also require practice in

FIGURE 9.5 | **Illustrated plot chart for *Crow Boy***

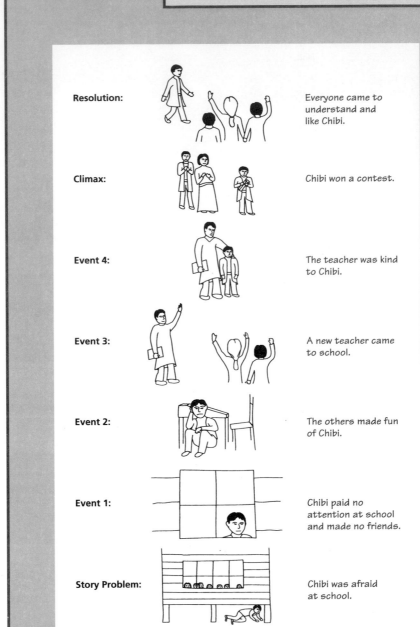

Resolution: Everyone came to understand and like Chibi.

Climax: Chibi won a contest.

Event 4: The teacher was kind to Chibi.

Event 3: A new teacher came to school.

Event 2: The others made fun of Chibi.

Event 1: Chibi paid no attention at school and made no friends.

Story Problem: Chibi was afraid at school.

reading dialogue, which does not contain the familiar transitions and descriptive passages of their usual reading. If possible, students should see plays put on by local professional or amateur groups to give them first-hand experience with theater.

Acting out plays provides a legitimate opportunity for students to read orally. Give them ample time to rehearse their parts, however. A drama could be presented as a radio play. Sound effects and background music might be used, but no costumes would be required. If students tape record the play, other classes might enjoy their efforts.

Plays are found in many basal readers. Scripts from TV shows and movies are often included in children's magazines. The magazine *Plays* is, of course, an excellent source. The Children's Book List identifies a number of anthologies of children's plays.

Children's Book List
Drama

Adorjan, C. & Rasorisky, Y. *WKID: Easy Radio Plays*. New York: Whitman (1988). Four plays suitable for being produced on the radio.

Alexander, S. *Small Plays for Special Days*. New York: Seabury (1977). Dramatizations of holidays and other special days.

Bland, J. *Stage Plays from the Classics*. Boston: Plays (1988). Classic tales transformed into one-act plays.

Jennings, C. A. & Harris, A. (Eds.). *Plays Children Love*. New York: St. Martin's Press (1981). A variety of plays drawn from traditional tales, and patriotic and contemporary themes.

Jennings, C. A. & Harris, A. (Eds.). *Plays Children Love*, Vol. II. New York: St. Martin's Press (1988). Includes plays based on *Charlotte's Web* and African folklore.

Kamerman, S. E. (Ed.). *Holiday Plays Round the Year*. Boston: Plays (1983). A variety of plays on holiday themes.

Kamerman, S. E. (Ed.). *Patriotic and Historical Plays for Young People: One-Act Plays and Programs About the People and Events That Made Our Country Great*. Boston: Plays (1987). Twenty-five plays and choral readings that dramatize key historical events.

Kamerman, S. E. (Ed.). *Plays of Black Americans*. Boston: Plays (1987). Plays featuring Harriet Tubman, Martin Luther King, Jr., and other famous African Americans.

Leedy, L. *The Bunny Play*. New York: Holiday (1988). Bunnies stage "Little Red Riding Hood."

Marks, B. *Puppet Plays and Puppet-Making: The Plays—The Puppets—The Production*. Boston: Plays (1982). Explanation of how to create puppet productions.

DRAMATIZATIONS

To dramatize a story, actors must understand the action and must think carefully about the characters they are portraying. Instead of passive comprehension, readers as actors must put themselves into the piece. They must make the characters come alive by giving them voice, expression, and motivation. This requires that readers think carefully and creatively about what they have read.

Story theater is a form of dramatization in which participants pantomime a selection while a narrator reads it aloud.

Story Theater. In **story theater**, readers pantomime a selection—a folktale, a realistic story, or a poem—while a narrator reads it aloud. Their actions need not be limited to those performed by human characters. For example, the sun, the wind, trees swaying in the breeze, and a babbling brook can all be pantomimed. The teacher will probably have to help students organize the production, at least in the beginning. As students become familiar with the technique, they should be able to work out production details for themselves. Working out the details encourages cooperative learning and also involves all the language arts.

Reader's theater is a form of dramatization in which the participants read aloud a selection as though it were a play.

Reader's Theater. In **reader's theater**, participants dramatize a selection by reading it aloud. A whole selection can be dramatized or just one portion of it. Pieces with a generous amount of dialogue work best. A narrator reads the portions not spoken by characters. Parts are not memorized but are read from the text. Even though they do not have to memorize their parts, readers should spend time developing their interpretation of the dialogue and rehearsing. A reader's

 One way of interpreting literature is by dramatizing it.

theater production might be implemented in the following way (Pike, Compain, & Mumper, 1994):

1. *Select or write the script.* In starting out, it might be helpful to use scripts that have already been prepared for reader's theater. They are available from Reader's Theater Script Service (P.O. Box 178333, San Diego, CA 92117). Spotlight on Reader's Theater (Phoenix Learning Resources, 2349 Chaffee Drive, St. Louis, MO 63146) features a series of twenty-seven plays organized around nine themes. Designed to integrate social studies and language arts, most of the plays focus on famous people or multicultural topics. Speaking parts vary in difficulty so that even poor readers will be able to participate. Scripts can also be written by the class, but this takes more time and effort. They should include extensive dialogue, be interesting to your students, and be on the appropriate level of difficulty. The script should have from three to eight participants. Composing a script could be a fruitful cooperative learning project. However, students would need some guidance.

2. *Assign parts.* The parts can be either assigned by the teacher or decided upon by students.

3. *Rehearse the script.* Although the scripts are read aloud, they should be rehearsed. Before students rehearse the scripts, they should have read and discussed the selection. As a group, students should decide how each part is to be read. Focus should be on interpreting the character's mood and feelings. Should a character sound angry, sad, or frightened? How are these emotions to be portrayed? Students then rehearse individually and as a group.

4. *Plan a performance.* Students decide where they want to stage their performance. Although no props are needed, they may want to place their scripts in colorful folders. They may use stools if they are available, or they may stand.

Other Dramatic Activities. Students might also like to try improvisation, role-playing, and use of puppets. Role-playing works well with all ages, but seems to work best with younger children, whereas improvisation seems to suit older children better. Using improvisation, students spontaneously dramatize a story or situation. Improvisation might be used to portray a character in a tale or extend a story. It might also be used to dramatize a concept in science or social studies.

NONFICTION

BIOGRAPHIES

Although biographies generally rank poorly when students are asked to tell what types of books they like best, the lives of interesting and relevant subjects are often runaway favorites. Biographies of sports heroes and singing stars are among some of the most heavily circulated books in the children's departments of libraries.

When properly motivated, students show an intense, long-lasting interest in historical figures. In one elementary school, students were involved in reading and

Introduce students to a variety of types of reading: short stories, novels, biographies, poems, plays, and informational pieces. Students may have a favored genre or may exclude informational text from their reading. They need to experience a full range of literary types. Squire (1994) fears that the current emphasis on literature-based reading instruction may neglect informational text.

writing biographies for as long as three months. One fourth-grader, who was completing an intensive study of Benjamin Franklin, commented,

> I started writing this book in March and here I am still writing it. And believe me this is no piece of cake. I have to write it over and over to get it right. It's taking me a long time, but it's worth it. (Zarnowski, 1990, p. 18)

The key to motivating children to become interested in biography is to choose the right subject. Above all, the subject should have led an interesting life and should be someone that the students can relate to and care about. Zarnowski (1990) chose such people as Benjamin Franklin, Martin Luther King, Jr., and Eleanor Roosevelt.

In Zarnowski's (1990) study the teacher first read biographical material aloud to give students an overview of a subject. Students then read several easy biographies that acted as stepping stones to more difficult books. Students were also introduced to primary materials, such as magazine and newspaper articles, letters, and films. As they read and wrote about their subjects, students formed a relationship with them. Entries in their journals proved that the subjects came alive. Instead of vague historical figures, they became real people with real problems that had to be overcome:

> As they read about a person, children not only learn information, they also develop feelings of sympathy and empathy, and sometimes anger and aversion. . . . As they develop both emotional and intellectual understanding, children begin to strongly connect with figures from the past. Ultimately, these connections enable children to connect with the larger scope of history. (Zarnowski, 1990, p. 5)

The Children's Book List provides the titles of some high-quality biographies.

Children's Book List
Biographies

Adler, D. A. *Thomas Jefferson: Father of Our Democracy.* New York: Holiday House (1987).

Adler, D. A. *A Picture Book of Eleanor Roosevelt.* New York: Holiday House (1991).

Freedman, R. *Lincoln: A Photobiography.* New York: Clarion (1987).

Fritz, J. *Can't You Make Them Behave, King George?* New York: Coward, McCann & Geoghegan (1977).

Haskins, J. *The Life and Death of Martin Luther King, Jr.* New York: Lothrop (1977).

Meltzer, M. *Dorothea Lange: Life Through the Camera.* New York: Viking (1985).

Meltzer, M. *Mary McLeod Bethune: Voice of Black Hope.* New York: Viking (1987).

Monjo, F. N. *The One Bad Thing About Father.* New York: Harper (1970).

Peare, C. O. *The Helen Keller Story.* New York: Crowell (1959).

Walker, A. *Langston Hughes: American Poet.* New York: Crowell (1974).

Walker, P. R. *Pride of Puerto Rico: The Life of Roberto Clemente*. New York: Harcourt (1988).

HOW-TO AND INFORMATIONAL BOOKS

A balanced reading program, even one that is literature-based, must include nonfiction. Children need to learn at an early age that books contain a treasury of interesting and useful information on subjects that range from how to play baseball to how the brain works. Informational books build background, concepts, and vocabulary; expand interests; help students understand and solve problems; and, most importantly, expand their horizons and lead to new interests.

Reading informational books requires a different approach from that for reading fiction. In fiction, students have a narrative thread to follow. In nonfiction, students build bridges between what they know and what they read. A good way to handle informational books would be to use the KWL strategy explained in Chapter 8 or a similar technique. The author's style should also be discussed. Activities should be designed that help students discover especially apt descriptions, clear explanations, interesting examples, figurative language, and skillful use of prose. In addition to content questions, you might ask students the following questions:

- How did the author make the subject clear?
- How did the author make the subject interesting?
- What are some especially original similes or metaphors that the author used?
- Did the author use exciting or interesting examples? If so, give some of these examples.
- What are your favorite descriptions?
- Can you find any other examples of imaginative use of language? If so, what are they?

There are a number of ways of incorporating literature into the literacy program. See Chapter 10 for suggestions for organizing a literature-based program.

VOLUNTARY READING

The key to improved reading achievement in elementary school is very simple: Encourage students to read ten minutes a day on their own. According to carefully conducted research, these extra ten minutes result in significant improvements in reading (Fielding, Wilson, & Anderson, 1986). Unfortunately, a nationally administered questionnaire revealed that fewer than half the nation's fourth-graders read for fun every day, and 13 percent never or hardly ever read for fun on their own time (Mullis, Campbell, & Farstrup, 1993). A study of fifth-graders had an even gloomier finding: Only 30 percent of the students read for ten minutes or more a day (Anderson, Wilson, & Fielding, 1988). What can be done to motivate children to read? Again, the answer is a simple one. Demonstrate that reading is both personally fulfilling and fun, and put children in contact with books that they will enjoy.

Children generally like to read about characters who are their own age or who are facing problems and situations that are similar to theirs (Harris & Sipay, 1990). Humor is also enjoyed by children of all ages. Funny stories were the top choice of primary-grade children, and the second choice of upper-grade students (Greenlaw, 1983). However, clear differences in interests exist depending on age. Animals and make-believe are ranked high by primary-grade students; upper-grade students, on the other hand, have a distinct preference for mystery, adventure, and sports. The dominant conclusions to be drawn from the research are that children's interests are wide-ranging and change with age. Each child has her or his own pattern of interests. Whereas humor is a top choice for many children, adventure or how-to books may be preferred by others.

DETERMINING INTERESTS AND ATTITUDES

A good starting point for creating a voluntary reading program is to determine students' reading interests and their attitudes toward reading. Close observation of your students yields useful information about these areas—you probably have a good sense of who likes to read and who does not. Through observation, classroom discussions, and conversations with individual children, you probably also know who likes sports, who prefers mysteries, and who is interested in animals. An easy way to obtain an overview of the kinds of books your students might enjoy reading voluntarily is to duplicate several pages at their grade level from the catalog of a distributor of paperbacks or children's library books. Ask students to circle the ones that interest them. One experienced librarian recommended indirect questioning when exploring children's interests:

> The best way to learn what any child likes to read is to ask, but a direct question may not elicit clear information. A bit of probing may be necessary. What does he do with leisure time? What are his favorite television programs? The last good book he read? (Halstead, 1988, p. 35)

THE CLASSROOM LIBRARY

Once you have a sense of what your class might like to read, start building a classroom library and involve students in the process. Propinquity is a primary principle in promoting voluntary reading. When books are close by and easy to check out, students will read more. The goal is to build a community of readers (Fielding, Wilson, & Anderson, 1986). If students feel they have a stake in the classroom library, they will be more highly motivated to read.

Invite students, their parents, and the community at large to contribute books to your classroom library. You might also be able to obtain some volumes from the school librarian and other local librarians. Students, as they get older, find paperbacks especially appealing. Paperbacks are also cheaper to buy and to replace if lost or damaged.

OBTAINING BOOKS ON A VARIETY OF LEVELS

Students need reading material they can handle. Many attempt to read books that are too difficult for them (May, 1990). Although students will read books that are beyond their level if they have a special interest in the subject, a steady diet of such books can be discouraging. Students are more likely to read a book all the way through if it is on their level. A study of sixth-graders found that both good and poor readers chose books on the same level; however, a higher percentage of good readers finished their books (Anderson, Higgins, & Wurster, 1985). Perhaps, if the less able readers had selected books closer to their ability, they would have completed them.

SETTING UP THE CLASSROOM LIBRARY

Make the classroom library as appealing as possible. Display books with their covers showing. You might also have special displays of books on high-interest topics. Update the collection periodically—at least once a month, add new titles to keep children interested.

One of the essentials that students learn from a classroom library is how to choose books. In informal research, Wilson (1992) noted that many students have difficulty selecting books during classroom visits to the library. They do not seem to know how to browse. Browsers are very selective about the books they read. They typically look through five books before choosing one and may later decide not to read the books that they have chosen. Children, especially poor readers, need to learn how to select a book. Having a classroom library with sufficient books to provide children with a genuine choice is important. Another way to promote wise selection among your students is to obtain books that children are genuinely interested in.

MANAGING THE CLASSROOM LIBRARY

Wilson (1992) suggested that the teacher involve the poorest readers in helping with the management of the classroom collection. By helping display, advertise, and keep track of the collection, poor readers become familiar with its contents.

Involve students in setting up check-out procedures and rules. Keep the rules simple; if they are complicated and punitive, they will discourage borrowing (Wilson, 1986). Inevitably, some books will be lost or damaged. Consider this as part of the cost of "doing business." Do not charge late fines or fees for lost or damaged books; these could be a genuine hardship for poor children. Instead, have a talk with students about being more responsible. If it is not a hardship, students could contribute replacement books, which do not necessarily have to have the same titles as the lost books. Put students in charge of keeping track of books; they can handle checking in, checking out, and putting books away.

SETTING ASIDE TIME FOR VOLUNTARY READING

When provided with time for recreational reading, students learn that reading is important. Initially, the time set aside for voluntary reading may only be five minutes (Fader, 1977), but it can be lengthened gradually up to thirty minutes. Some classrooms, and even entire schools, adopt a program known as SSR. Although SSR originally stood for **Sustained Silent Reading**, it should probably be changed to *Self-Selected Reading*. Research suggests (Manning and Manning, 1984; Wilson, 1992) that students get more out of their reading and read more when they can

Sustained Silent Reading (SSR) is a period of time during which all students and teachers in a class or entire school read materials of their own choosing.

In addition to setting aside time for reading, set aside a special place. A corner of the classroom might be furnished with some throw rugs, small bookcases, and a comfortable chair or two, if space allows.

share with their peers. Students should be allowed to discuss books in small groups, read with a buddy, dramatize the reading of a book in a small group, view a CD-ROM version of a book or listen to a taped version, or silently read a book in the traditional way. Adapted rules for SSR are listed below:

1. Each student is involved in reading.
2. The teacher reads.
3. Books to be read should be chosen before the session starts. (Students should choose two or three books, in case the original selection does not work out.)
4. A timer is used.
5. Absolutely no book reports are required.

Young children may require special provisions during SSR. Kaissen (1987) observed that SSR works well with first-graders if several books are available to them, including those that have been read to them previously. In addition, preprimers and wordless picture books should be available. Kindergarteners showed a preference for books that had been read to them that morning or earlier in the week (Gutkin, 1990).

MODELING THE PROCESS OF SELECTING AND DISCUSSING BOOKS

Some students have little experience choosing or discussing books. From time to time, tell them how you happened to select a book that you are reading. Discuss how you got a sense of its contents by examining the cover, finding out who the author is, reading the blurb on the jacket, glancing through the book, and reading selected parts. Talk about your book with students, and ask about their books, so they realize that in a community of readers people share their reading.

THE IMPORTANCE OF SHARING AND INSTRUCTION IN DEVELOPING AVID READERS

How do children become avid readers? First of all, they must have someone to talk to about books. In their study of fifth-graders who read at least thirty minutes a day, Fielding, Wilson, and Anderson (1986) found that most of these students had someone at home with whom they could discuss books and who made suggestions about what they might read next. In their large-scale study of a national sample of 9-, 13-, and 17-year-olds, Guthrie, Schafer, Wang, and Afflerbach (1995) also report that the students who read the most talked about their reading with family and friends.

Systematic teaching fosters voluntary reading. Students who are taught a variety of comprehension strategies (such as those presented in this book) read more. Carefully taught strategies enable students to comprehend materials that they encounter at school and at home. Because reading is a successful experience, they are motivated to read on their own. In addition, teachers "who emphasized the importance of comprehending and learning from books probably created greater interest in books and fostered students' motivation to read" (Guthrie et al., 1995, p. 23).

Although reading might seem like a solitary, silent activity, the opportunity to talk about reading is highly motivating. In a study comparing sustained silent reading with individualized reading in which students have conferences with the teacher and also with individualized reading in which students have conferences with each other, the students who discussed books with peers did significantly better on reading achievement tests. You should note, however, that both teacher conference and peer conference groups evidenced improved attitudes toward reading. For the peer conference group, reading became an important activity, at least in part, because it was something that these students shared with other students (Manning & Manning, 1984). As Wilson (1992) commented,

> Reading becomes something that students do because of friendship, because their friends read. More important, sharing their thoughts and feelings about books becomes part of the intellectual currency of their social relations within the classroom. Reading becomes part of the culture of the classroom. (p. 163)

A major benefit of sharing is that students recommend books to each other. Children are more likely to read a book when it is recommended by a friend than when it is suggested by a parent, teacher, or librarian (Gallo, 1985). Therefore it is important to provide students with time to talk over their books in informal groups once a week or so. Students reading books by Judy Blume or those reading mystery books or books about baseball might meet to discuss their common interests and share their responses.

ACTIVITIES FOR MOTIVATING VOLUNTARY READING

To motivate voluntary reading, be enthusiastic, accepting, and flexible. Present reading as an interesting, vital activity. Include a wide range of material from comics to classics. Do not present books as vitamins, saying, "Read them. They're good for you." Share reading with students in the same way that you might share with friends. By doing so, you are accepting students as serious readers. Above all, be a reader yourself. Some activities for motivating voluntary reading follow:

- Match books with interests. Make casual, personal recommendations. For a basketball fan, you might say, "Joe, I know you enjoy watching professional basketball. The town library has a new book about Shaquille O'Neal. I read it, and it's very interesting."
- Use the indirect approach. Choose a book that would be appropriate for your students and that you would enjoy reading. Carry the book to class with you. Mention that it is interesting to read. Tell students that they can borrow it when you're finished. Or you may just want to carry the book around and see how many inquiries you get.
- Pique students' interest. Read a portion of a book and stop at a cliff-hanging moment; then tell students that they can read the rest themselves if they want to find out what happened.
- Use videotapes to preview books. Show a portion of a videotape of a book that has been made into a movie; then encourage students to find out what happened by reading the book. (First, be sure that the book is available to students.)

As teachers, we want children to read the best that has been written. However, students must be allowed to choose what they wish to read. As Wilson (1992) noted, "If we have to choose between the reading we want to require and the reading that the children prefer, we must honor the children's choices. To do otherwise would be to seriously impede the development of avid reading" (p. 167).

- Substitute voluntary reading for workbook or other seatwork assignments. The Center for the Study of Reading (1990) made the following statement: "Independent, silent reading can fulfill many of the same functions as workbook activities—it permits students to practice what they are learning, and it keeps the rest of the class occupied while you meet with a small group of students. A surprising amount of time for independent reading can be freed if workbook assignments are trimmed down to an essential core that gives students sound practice on newly taught concepts and a review of important information" (p. 5).

- Encourage partner reading. Young and less able readers might be willing to attempt a challenging book if they get some help and support from a partner. Such readers might also be more willing to read on their own if given a "running start" that gets them solidly into the book (Castle, 1994).

- Recommend books by a popular series author. Students who have enjoyed Beverly Cleary's *Ramona* or *Henry* might not be aware that other equally funny books feature these same characters.

- Book clubs that cater to school-age populations offer a variety of interesting books at bargain prices. When students choose and pay money for a book, it is highly likely that they will read it. Make alternative provisions for economically disadvantaged children.

- Community resources should not be overlooked. Invite the public librarian and a representative from a local bookstore to visit the class and tell students what is "hot" in children's books. Inform speakers beforehand about the reading levels and interests of students so that they can suggest suitable titles.

- Present books as sources of interesting information. Include the *Guinness Book of World Records* (McFarlan, 1995), *Famous First Facts* (Kane, 1981), *World Almanac* (Lane, 1995), books on trivia, and other collections. When students disagree about the best quarterback, the tallest building, or the longest fingernails, refer them to one of these references.

- Encourage students to build personal libraries with a few inexpensive paperbacks. They can add to their collection by requesting books as gifts.

- Once a month, give students the opportunity to trade books they have read. Before the trading session, students might want to post a list or announce titles that they will swap. You might also have a trading shelf in the classroom from which students may take any book they wish, as long as they put one in its place.

- Suggest and have on hand books that relate to people or subjects being taught in the content areas. Reading a brief biography of John F. Kennedy, for instance, could help shed light on his presidency and the early 1960s.

- Encourage students to obtain library cards. Pave the way by acquainting them with the locations of public libraries and their regulations. Also secure applications and have them filled out in class, if the library permits this. Make sure students are familiar with the expanded services of today's libraries. Many, for example, loan audiotapes and videotapes. Students who visit the library primarily to look over these collections might end up checking out a book or two.

To help children build personal libraries, use books as awards for winners of food drives, writing competitions, and other school contests.

A simple but effective reinforcer for voluntary reading is to have students keep a record of their reading, such as a simple list, a wheel, or a graph showing number of books read or number of minutes spent reading. Since students differ in reading speed, and since the number of words in a book varies, the fairest measurement might be number of minutes spent reading rather than number of books read.

- In his study of the reading habits of disadvantaged children, Hamilton (1976) found that students preferred TV tie-ins two to one over regular books. Those who watched a lot of television tended to read books used in tie-ins and did not see them as being difficult. Exploit this interest: After a featured documentary on the Loch Ness monster, for example, give students a list of books about the monster that can be easily obtained. Also be aware of books being recommended on television. Librarians report a flood of requests for books that have been featured on public television's "Reading Rainbow."

- The school librarian can be asked to describe new acquisitions during morning or afternoon announcements. These descriptions could also be included in the daily bulletin. School librarian Pamela Spencer (1984) obtained five paperback copies of the title she talked about over the public address each morning so as to be prepared for the demand.

- If all else fails, try extrinsic reinforcers. In the past, pizza chains, local restaurants, and fast-food establishments have supplied free pizza and other rewards to students who read a certain number of books. A teacher in New Jersey offered his students tickets to a wrestling match if they read their quota of books. In a follow-up discussion with students, the teacher discovered that the students read not for the prize but because he had tried so hard to find them books they liked (Freeland, 1986).

SUMMARY

1. Although teachers have always promoted reading worthwhile literature, until recently reading was looked upon as primarily being a skills subject. Practice was the focus, and it did not really matter what kind of material students practiced on. Today, the emphasis is definitely on reading quality material.

2. Reading literature involves fostering appreciation and enjoyment as well as understanding. The teacher's stance becomes an aesthetic one. Focus is on eliciting a personal response and valuing students' interpretations.

3. Folklore, because of its universal quality and appeal to young people, is a good place to start the study of literature. Other literary forms include mythology, poetry, novels, drama, and high-quality informational books.

4. The least-liked literary form is poetry. Teachers rarely read poetry to their students, and students seldom read it on their own or as part of their reading program. Enthusiastically reading to the class poems that they can enjoy and providing ample opportunity to explore poetry are two steps that can be taken to increase students' enjoyment and appreciation.

5. Chapter books and novels are often set aside for a separate unit of study. Although content and style should be explored, personal response should come first. If possible, students should be allowed some self-selection.

6. One way to interpret literature is to dramatize it. Story theater and reader's theater can be used to make selections come alive.

7. A balanced literature program should include biography as well as other forms of informational text. In well-written informational books, students should be made aware of the author's style as well as content.

8. Just ten minutes a day of voluntary reading results in significant gains in reading achievement. To promote voluntary reading, demonstrate that it is enjoyable and personally fulfilling. Through discussion, involvement, and modeling build a community of readers. Make sure that interesting material is available and that voluntary reading occupies a prominent place in your program.

CLASSROOM APPLICATIONS

1. Read at least three current anthologies of children's poetry. Which poems did you like best? Which do you think would appeal to your students?
2. Keep a card file of high-quality chapter books and novels that you feel would appeal to students you are teaching or plan to teach. Include bibliographic information, summaries of the selections, some questions you might ask about the work, and some ideas for extension activities.
3. With a group of classmates, start a literature circle in which you discuss children's books.

FIELD APPLICATIONS

1. Create a lesson in which you introduce a poem, play, or other literary piece. In your lesson, stress appreciation, enjoyment, and personal response. Teach the lesson and evaluate it.
2. Try out one of the suggestions listed in this chapter or an idea of your own for increasing voluntary reading. Implement the idea and evaluate its effectiveness.

chapter 10

Approaches to Teaching Reading

ANTICIPATION GUIDE

For each of the following statements related to the chapter you are about to read, put a check under "Agree" or "Disagree" to show how you feel. Discuss your responses with classmates before you read the chapter.

Agree   **Disagree**

1. A structured approach to reading works best.

2. Extensive reading of children's books should be a part of every elementary school reading program.

3. It is the teacher, not the method, that counts.

4. The language-experience approach works best with young children.

5. An individualized reading program would be hard to manage.

6. The basal approach is best for new teachers because it shows them step by step how to teach reading.

7. Teachers should combine the best parts of each reading approach.

8. Teachers should be free to choose the approach to reading that they feel works best.

Using What You Know

There are really just two main ways of learning to read: by reading and by writing, or some combination of the two. The approach that uses writing is known as language experience. Reading approaches use textbooks (including basals and linguistic reading series) and children's books. Children's books are used in the individualized and literature-based approaches. However, whole language, which is typically described as a philosophy rather than an approach, also advocates using children's literature. Of course, these approaches can also be combined in various ways. Teachers who use basals often supplement their programs with language-experience stories and children's books.

Which of these approaches are you familiar with? What are the characteristics of the approaches? What are their advantages? Their disadvantages?

CHARACTERISTICS OF EFFECTIVE READING APPROACHES

A little more than a decade ago, Aukerman (1984) described more than a hundred different programs for teaching reading. Some of these programs have disappeared, but new ones have arrived to replace them. Although reading can be taught in a variety of ways, the most effective approaches incorporate the basic principles of teaching literacy that have been emphasized throughout this book:

- Children become readers and writers by reading and writing. Reading programs should include a rich variety of interesting, appropriate material and should stress lots of reading and writing.
- Strategies should be presented that promote independence in word recognition and comprehension.
- Reading programs should be language-based. Provision should be made for developing speaking and listening as well as reading and writing skills.
- Since reading fosters writing development and writing fosters reading development, literacy programs should develop both.
- Provision should be made for individual differences. Since students differ in terms of interests, abilities, learning rate, experiential background, and culture, the approach used should take into consideration the needs of all students.
- Students' progress should be monitored, and provision should be made for helping students fully develop their potential.

As a practical matter, you may not be able to choose the approach to reading that you wish to use. Although some schools allow and even encourage teachers to choose their own methods and materials, for the sake of continuity, many schools and even whole school districts adopt a program and expect all teachers to implement it. This chapter examines the major approaches to teaching reading and writing. Each approach has its strengths and weaknesses. Suggestions are made for adapting each of the approaches to take advantage of its strengths and compensate for its weaknesses. For instance, suggestions are made for making the basal approach more holistic. Thus, if it has been mandated that you use a basal but you prefer a whole language approach, you can adapt your instruction to make the program more holistic and still keep within the guidelines of the school or school district that employs you.

BASAL APPROACH

At one time, up to 95 percent of schoolchildren in the United States were instructed using **basal reading programs** (Anderson, Hiebert, Scott, & Wilkinson, 1985; Langer, Applebee, Mullis, & Foertsch, 1990). A complex package based on a relatively simple concept, the basal program includes a series of readers, or anthologies, and supplementary materials that gradually increase in difficulty and act as stepping stones along a path that begins with emergent literacy and extends through eighth-grade reading. Accompanying teacher's manuals provide guidance so that the classroom teacher can lead students upward.

With the advent of **whole language** and literature-based instruction, the role of basals changed dramatically. Fewer teachers are now using basals, and those who do use them use them in a different way. Instead of being virtually the entire reading program, basals are now just one component of most teachers' literacy programs. Many teachers now use children's books along with basal readers or instead of them (Mullis, Campbell, & Farstrup, 1993).

Basals themselves have also changed. Although the core of the basal program is still the anthology, today those texts comprise high-quality fiction and nonfiction selections. The contrived selections with their carefully controlled vocabulary that made up much of the content in beginning basal readers have been replaced by enticing children's literature. Also, recognizing the importance of personal choice and wide reading, all basal readers offer libraries of children's books to supplement the anthologies. The concept of emergent literacy is fully embraced by basal programs, and all of them suggest techniques such as reading aloud to students and shared reading. In addition, many of the basals feature some degree of integrated language arts instruction. All include writing process, and there is a growing tendency to integrate spelling, handwriting, and language study as part of the basal package.

The list of authors for basal series reads like a who's who of experts in reading and language arts. As a result, the instructional programs suggest the use of the latest teaching techniques and educational innovations. Inclusion, authentic assessment, cooperative and alternative grouping, and diversity in the classroom are addressed by all of the basals.

Basal systems offer an embarrassment of riches. In addition to anthologies, related workbooks, and detailed teacher's manuals packed with teaching suggestions, basals offer big books, supplementary libraries of the best in children's

A **basal reading program** is a comprehensive program for teaching reading that includes readers, or anthologies, that gradually increase in difficulty, teacher's manuals, workbooks, and assessment measures.

Whole language is a philosophy of teaching reading and writing that is based on the way in which oral language is learned. Students learn to read and write for real purposes and are taught in natural, whole-part fashion.

At one time, up to 95 percent of schoolchildren in the United States were instructed using basal reading programs.

The latest basals, which are in a cycle of almost constant revision, attempt to implement recent research and feature the most popular children's authors. The major series include high-quality literature, elaborate illustrations, and up-to-date teaching strategies.

books, read-aloud books, a wide array of games and manipulatives, audiotapes, regular and CD-ROM software, videodiscs, inservice programs, posters and charts, supplementary spelling and language books, a wide variety of unit and end-of-book tests, placement tests, observation guides, portfolio systems, and more.

Clearly, today's basals are bigger and better than ever. But the real question is "Are today's basals good enough?" Considering all that is known about reading and writing, have basal publishers composed the kinds of programs that will help children reach their fullest potential? Have the basals done an effective job implementing research and promising practices? The answer is yes and no. Basals have many advantages, but they also have some shortcomings.

ADVANTAGES OF BASALS

Basals offer teachers a convenient package of materials, techniques, and assessment devices, as well as a plan for orchestrating the various components of a total literacy program. In their anthologies, which gradually increase in difficulty, basals offer students a steady progression from emergent literacy through an eighth-grade reading level. They also offer varied reading selections, an abundance of practice material, carefully planned units and lessons, and a wealth of follow-up and enrichment activities.

Although basals often offer excerpts, their teacher's manuals feature bibliographies, so interested children can read the whole book on their own. Each series also includes supplementary libraries of whole texts.

DISADVANTAGES OF BASALS

Despite a major overhaul, basals are still driven by the same engine. The core of the basal program is the trio of anthology, workbook, and manual. Although the contents of the anthology are much improved, its function remains the same—to provide a base of materials for all students to move through. However, students have diverse interests and abilities and progress at different rates. Although basal selections are meant to be of high quality, they will not all be of interest to all students. The sports biography that delights one child is a total bore to another. A second shortcoming has to do with the way basal readers are assembled: They are anthologies and often contain excerpts from whole books. For example, the fourth-grade reader from a typical series contains "The Diary of Leigh Botts," a delightful tale of a budding young writer that is excerpted from Beverly Cleary's 1983 Newbury Award winner, *Dear Mr. Henshaw.* If reading the excerpt is worthwhile, reading the whole book should be even better.

There is also the question of pacing and time spent with a selection. Whereas some students are able to move through a piece quickly, others are barely able to keep up. A related disadvantage of basal use is the difficulty that arises in providing for *all* readers. Bobbi Fisher (1994), a first-grade teacher, switched from basals to whole language for just that reason; she cites two examples. In a basal classroom, Jerry, who was an emergent reader just beginning to get some insight into the alphabetic system, would not have been good enough for the low group. But, in Fisher's room, he wrote, participated in shared reading, and felt good about himself as a learner. And then there was Allison. On the first day of school, she wrote a letter expressing an interest in Egypt and the Revolutionary War. In a basal classroom, she would have been too advanced for the top group, but in a whole language classroom, she was provided with many opportunities for learning.

Students often move through basals in lockstep fashion. Part of the problem is the nature of the teacher's guides; they offer too much of a good thing. Stories and even poems are overtaught. There are too many questions asked before a selection is read, too many asked after the piece has been read, and too many follow-up activities. A class might spend three to five days on a thousand-word story! For instance, in a sample third-grade lesson from Macmillan/McGraw Hill's *A New View* (1993), there are so many activities covering Chris Van Allsburg's *Two Bad Ants* that the teacher can easily spend a week on the selection. To be fair, the guide does present activities as choices. Teachers can choose those that they wish to undertake and omit the others. Teachers are even provided a choice of three ways of presenting the story: interactively with the teacher modeling strategies, independently with the teacher providing a minimum of assistance, or with literary support, which means that students follow along as the teacher reads the story. All in all, the lesson has many fine suggestions, but the ideas are "canned," that is, created by someone in an editorial office far from the classroom. Designed to be all things to all third-grade teachers, the activities are not designed for a specific class of children having specific needs and interests.

Perhaps the greatest concern or criticism expressed about basal programs is the overreliance by teachers on these instructional tools. Some teachers see the basal as the only reading material that they need to provide for students. They are reluctant to abandon the basal even for a short time, for fear that their students will somehow lose out if they miss a workbook page or skip a story. So much is included in a typical basal program that teachers never run out of things to do, and many feel compelled to finish the program. When that type of thinking dominates classroom activities, children are provided with very little reading material beyond the basal.

As a new teacher in a large urban school system, I had the good fortune to work for administrators who encouraged the integration of language arts and the use of themed units but frowned on the use of teacher's manuals and workbooks. In fact, a manual was not available for the basal that I used. Not having a teacher's manual, I planned my own units and my own lessons. In retrospect, I realize that some of my lessons fell flat. However, others worked extremely well. I still recall with pride being asked to present a model lesson for other new teachers at one of our monthly meetings. Good, bad, or indifferent, I owned the lessons and so had made a commitment to them. When I planned my lessons, I kept in mind the needs and interests of my students. I especially enjoyed building interest in a story so that they really wanted to read it. And I did not teach any stories I disliked or I thought the students would not like. My management skills were marginal that first year, and one of the ways I kept the lid on was to keep the students interested. A few years later, when I moved to another school and manuals were available, I used them selectively.

USING MANUALS FLEXIBLY

One of the major criticisms of basal readers has been that they dictate programs. However, basals are simply sets of materials that should be used with teacher discretion. Basal author Peter Winograd (1989) stated that basal readers are most effective when they are used flexibly as part of a comprehensive, balanced program of reading instruction.

Although basal manuals have been criticized as being too didactic (Goodman, 1994), the fault may be with the professionals who use them. Manuals and, in fact, the entire basal program should be viewed as a resource. The manual is a treasure chest of ideas, and the anthologies are good, representative collections of children's literature. As professionals, we should feel free to use those selections that seem appropriate and to use the manual as a resource rather than a guide. Select only those suggestions and activities that seem appropriate and effective. For instance, if I were presenting *Two Bad Ants,* I would not introduce it in the way suggested by the manual, which is to have students read about the author: The blurb about the author gives the story away. I like to build suspense and would rather have the students predict how the ants got into and out of trouble. I also disagree with the vocabulary that the manual's authors choose to preteach. I would have included the word *crystal* because it is important in understanding the story, and it is a word that the third-graders I've taught probably would not know. However, I would use the background information about ants provided by the manual. There are also some excellent suggestions for several very worthwhile activities in the manual.

SELECTING A BASAL

Selecting a basal is a major decision. An excellent set of guidelines for evaluating basals is *A Guide to Selecting Basal Reading Programs* (Adoption Guidelines Project, 1990a–d). Ideally, the selection should be made by a committee that includes teachers, students, parents, administrators, and the school's reading/language arts specialist. One of the best ways to assess a set of materials is to try it out before making a final decision.

ADAPTING BASALS

Despite the criticisms voiced here and elsewhere, there is nothing intrinsically wrong with basals. Over the years, thousands of teachers have successfully used basals to teach millions of children. However, in keeping with today's research and promising practices, basals should be adapted in the following ways:

1. Use basal readers selectively as a resource. Teach only those selections that seem appropriate for your students.
2. Plan your own lessons and units. Use the teacher's manuals as a resource, but tailor your lessons to the needs and interests of your students.
3. Emphasize real writing and real reading. Many of the activities promoted in basals are practice exercises. According to Edelsky (1994), language is learned by using it for some real purpose. Because reading and writing are forms of language, they too should be learned through real use. Students should therefore read directions to find out how to operate a new computer, read a story for pleasure, make a list in preparation for shopping, or write a letter to a friend. Basal activities in which children write a letter to a story-book character or read a story to practice reading in phrases or to reinforce new vocabulary words are exercises (Edelsky, 1994). They do not constitute reading and writing for real purposes. Where feasible, students should write letters that get mailed and respond openly to stories and poems. They should also be involved in setting their own purposes for reading and writing.
4. Workbooks should be used judiciously. They play both management and instructional roles. Students can work in them independently, while the teacher meets with a small group or individual children. Workbooks can also provide students with additional practice and yield information that the teacher can use to assess children's progress (Adoption Guidelines Project, 1990c). If a workbook exercise fails to measure up, it should be skipped. The teacher should provide alternative activities, such as having the students read children's books. Reading builds background and gives students an opportunity to integrate and apply skills. Instead of just practicing for the main event, they

A few years ago, students spent up to 70 percent of their time in school doing seat work and, on average, completed one thousand workbook pages a year (Anderson, 1981). According to a study completed in 1992, workbook usage has decreased dramatically, whereas the reading of children's books has increased significantly (Mullis, Campbell, & Farstrup, 1993).

Reading easy books independently provides students with much needed practice. "Clocking up reading mileage on easy materials is one of the most important aspects of independent reading" (Learning Media, 1991, p. 76).

 As students read silently, supply individual help as needed.

are taking part in it. In fact, students get far better practice reading children's books than they do completing workbook exercises. Writing, drawing, discussing, and preparing a presentation also provide superior alternatives to workbook exercises.

5. Emphasize wide reading of a variety of materials. No matter how well the basal has been put together, students need to read a broad range of fiction and nonfiction materials, including books, magazines, newspapers, sets of directions, brochures, ads, menus, schedules, and other real-world materials. Make use of the extensive libraries of children's books offered by basal publishers to supplement the basal materials; excellent suggestions for additional reading are also provided in basal manuals.

6. Focus on a few key skills or strategies. Teach and use these in context. Today's basal readers offer instruction in as many as 190 skills or strategies (Crawford & Shannon, 1994). In trying to cover so many areas, they typically spread themselves too thin and so fail to present crucial skills in sufficient depth. It may take twenty lessons or more before students are able to draw inferences or infer main ideas.

7. Gradually take control of your program. Decide what your philosophy of teaching literacy is. List the objectives that you feel are important, aligning them, of course, with the requirements of your school and school district. If possible, work with other professionals to create a reading program that makes sense for your situation. Consider basals as only one source of materials and teaching ideas. Basals are neither a method nor an approach to teaching reading. They are simply a carefully crafted set of materials. The core of the reading program is the teacher. It is the teacher who should decide how and when to use basals and whether to choose alternative materials.

MAKING THE TRANSITION TO A LITERATURE-BASED APPROACH

Some teachers want to trade in their basals for a literature-based approach to reading. Others are reluctant to switch but are being urged to do so by colleagues or administrators. When any change is contemplated, the unknown can be a bit daunting. Teachers know where they are going with their basals. By switching to children's books, they may feel that they are moving into uncharted territory.

The transition to a literature-based approach can be made in a number of ways. Begin by adapting your basal program as discussed in the previous section. Start supplementing your instruction by using children's literature. As you get a feel for using children's books and a sense of which books students prefer, begin adding these books to your curriculum. Create activities to accompany the children's books that you use. Phase out worksheets and workbooks. Use instead the reading of children's books, writing, or other suitable activities. The skills or strategies that you teach should be learned and applied in the context of real reading and writing. As Edelsky (1994) has noted, when children apply skills to practice exercises, there is a transfer problem. Lacking valid context, the skills seem to transfer only to other worksheets.

As you shift into children's books, adopt the kinds of holistic practices described in earlier chapters. Basals typically use a DRA approach to present a reading selection. In addition to the DRA, employ the DR-TA, KWL Plus, a cooperative learning format such as reciprocal teaching or a reading or writing work-shop, or some sort of balanced mixture. Use a reader response approach. Do not trivialize literature. As you become accustomed to the changes you are making, aim for a greater integration of the language arts and, eventually, some integra-tion with the content areas.

As Reggie Routman (1991) noted, the transition to holistic teaching is "a very slow process. Most teachers seem to need to hang on to their basals for a while as they gradually move toward a literature and meaning-centered approach" (pp. 26–27). Ultimately, the basal is not to blame for fragmented, ineffective in-struction. It is the way the materials are used:

> It is not unusual to see classrooms with no basals but where books of literature are read whole class, round-robin style. Seatwork consists of packets of vocabu-lary words to look up and lots of questions to answer in written form for each chapter. Even though literature is being used, children have few actual choices during reading time. Using literature, reading Big Books, and doing journal writing are not enough. Unless we also know why we are doing what we are doing, the way we do these activities may be no different from the skills-based, fragmented, teacher-directed basals we have set aside. Conversely, it is possible to take a basal story and use it meaningfully. (Routman, 1991, pp. 25–26)

HOLISTIC MATERIALS

Although originally created for use in New Zealand, there are a number of holis-tic beginning reading programs that enjoy wide usage in regular classrooms in the United States and are increasingly being used in remedial and special education: Ready to Read, Story Box, Sunshine, and Literacy 2000. Materials from these pro-grams are used instead of or along with basals. U.S. publishers are now produc-ing similar materials.

READY TO READ

Unlike the United States, New Zealand does not use basals. Instead, students have traditionally been taught to read children's books, an approach that is becoming increasingly popular in the United States. In New Zealand, a state-sponsored pro-gram, Ready to Read, provides a series of books graded in difficulty that can be used to ease children into reading and move them from emergent to fluent read-ing. Since most children's books are too difficult for beginning readers to read on their own, the Ready to Read series was designed to "enable beginning readers to make use of context through reading stories which were close to the experiences of New Zealand children, and which included language that they would use in conversation and hear in the stories read to them" (Learning Media, 1991, p. 33).

In addition to a handbook for the teacher and a variety of supplementary materials, Ready to Read consists of forty titles classified into nine levels of diffi-culty: emergent; early 1, 2, 3, 4; and fluency 1, 2, 3, 4. These nine levels range from very beginning reading through the first half of second grade.

Books at the emergent stage are designed so that students can enjoy books before they can actually read them. Illustrations help children predict what the text might say. The text itself is brief, often consisting of a single sentence that contains a repetitive phrase. Each page of the book might contain the same repeated phrase. The books are read through shared reading, and eventually students can, with the help of illustrations, read the books on their own. At this point, students are primarily "reading" pictures rather than text. The intent is to emphasize reading for enjoyment and meaning. Of course, they are also picking up concepts about print.

After students have enjoyed a number of books and shown an interest in reading print, text reading strategies are introduced. Difficulty and length of text are carefully controlled so that students are eased into reading. As students gain in skill, they move into the early reading and fluency stages.

STORY BOX (THE WRIGHT GROUP)

Originally published in New Zealand, Story Box has been revised for students in the United States. Designed as a whole language program, it is very similar in philosophy, approach, and organization to Ready to Read. Story Box consists of a manual, a series of little books similar to those in Ready to Read, and big books. The books, which are housed in boxes, range from the emergent to early fluency levels, similar to the levels used in the Ready to Read program.

SUNSHINE SERIES (THE WRIGHT GROUP)

Similar to Ready to Read, the Sunshine Series ranges in levels of difficulty from emergent literacy to grade 3 and features more than a hundred titles.

LITERACY 2000 (RIGBY)

Also similar in philosophy and approach to Ready to Read and the Sunshine Series, Literacy 2000 has eight stages, ranging from emergent literacy through grade 3 reading. Featuring a balance of fiction and informational texts, Literacy 2000 includes approximately 500 books and numerous supplementary materials.

For many primary-grade teachers, programs such as these are replacing basals that have traditionally been the mainstay of reading instruction. Many teachers combine materials from two or more of the programs so as to have a wide assortment of books for their students. Individual books may be purchased.

LITERATURE-BASED APPROACH

A **literature-based approach** is a way of teaching reading in which literary selections are the main instructional materials.

More and more teachers are using literature as the core of their program. Today's basal anthologies comprise high-quality selections drawn from children's literature. Increasingly, basals are including children's books in their entirety as an integral part of the package or a recommended component. Although there is some overlap between a basal program and a literature-based approach, the term **literature-based approach** is typically used to describe programs in which teachers use sets of children's books as a basis for providing instruction in literacy. A major advantage of this approach is that teachers, independently or in committees, choose the books they wish to use with their students so the reading material can be tailored to students' interests and needs.

A literature-based program may be organized in a variety of ways. Three popular models of organizing literature instruction include core books, text sets, and thematic units.

CORE BOOKS

Core literature is defined as those selections "that are to be taught in the classroom, are given close reading and intensive consideration, and are likely to be an important stimulus for writing and discussion." These are works of "compelling intellectual, social, or moral content . . ." (California State Department of Education, 1986, p. ix). Core literature pieces might include such children's classics as *The Little House* (Burton, 1942), *Grimm's Fairy Tales, Aesop's Fables,* or more recent works, like *Shiloh* (Naylor, 1991) or *Number the Stars* (Lowry, 1990).

In addition to providing students with a rich foundation in the best of children's literature, the use of core books also builds community (Ford, 1994). It gives students a common experience, thereby providing the class with common ground for conversations about books and also a point of reference for comparing and contrasting other books. The use of core literature should help boost the self-esteem of the poorer readers, who are often given less mature or less significant reading material. As Cox and Zarillo (1993) noted, in the core book model, "no child is denied access to the best of children's literature" (p. 109).

However, there are some obvious problems with the core literature approach. Children are diverse in interests and abilities. What is exciting to one child may be boring to another. An easy read for one child may be an overwhelming task for another. Careful selection of core books with universal appeal should take care of the interest factor. It is difficult, for instance, to imagine any child not being intrigued by E. B. White's *Charlotte's Web* (1952). Selections can also be presented in such a way as to be accessible to all. Suggestions for presenting texts to students of varying abilities can be found in Chapter 14.

Pace yourself when working with core books. Do not move so slowly that the book becomes boring. But do not rush through the book so that slower readers cannot keep up. Do allow students to read ahead if they want to. If they finish the text early, they might read related books or books of their own choosing. Also avoid assigning too many activities. Activities should build reading and writing skills or background knowledge and should deepen or extend students' understanding of the text. In addition, if you do use core books, make sure that students are provided with other opportunities to select books so that teacher selection of texts is balanced by student selection. Also make sure that low-achieving readers have ample opportunity to read books on their level. If core books are too difficult for some students, provide additional assistance, or, if necessary, read the books to them or obtain audiotapes of the texts. If audiotapes are available for all to use, there will be no stigma attached to using them.

TEXT SETS

Text sets are related books. Reading text sets fosters the making of connections. When connections are made, the reading of all related texts is enriched (Harste, Short, & Burke, 1988). In addition to deepening readers' background, text sets

Core literature is a selection of works to be read and analyzed by the entire class. In a core book approach students read the same book.

A text set is a series of related books. Because the books are related, reading and comparing them deepens the reader's understanding of the theme or topic of the text set.

broaden readers' framework for thinking about literature. Having read two or more related books, they can compare and contrast them. Discussions are also enlivened since students have more to talk about. If students read books on the same topic, understanding can be developed in greater depth.

Texts can be related in various ways. They may cover the same theme, such as sports or hobbies. They may cover the same genre, such as biography or mystery. They may include the same cast of characters, such as in the Frog and Toad series or the Henry and Mudge series. They may contrast different versions of the same tale, such as Galdone's (1974) *Little Red Riding Hood* versus Goodall's (1988) version versus Hyman's (1982) version. Or they may present cultural versions of the same basic plot, such as the traditional Cinderella tale and the Chinese version of the story, as in Louie's (1982) *Yeh-Shen: A Cinderella Story from China*. A text set may be composed of books on the same topic or even books written with a similar structure—**cumulative tales,** for instance.

Text sets may initially consist of groups of three or four books but may later include a larger number. Students might read all the books in a text set and then discuss them with a sharing group, or they might make individual selections. If students have read the same books, they can compare and contrast them. If they have not read the same books, they can share with each other the contents of the books that they have read. Harste, Short, and Burke (1988) recommended the use of text sets in literature circles because they promote discussion, especially among students who are reluctant to share.

Cumulative tales are stories in which one detail or event is added to a previous one and the entire list is recited after each addition.

THEMATIC UNITS

Another model of literature-based instruction is the **unit,** which has a theme or other unifying element. Its unifying element may be the study of a particular author, a genre—mystery or picture books, for example—or a theme. (Actually, a core book or a text set could also be the focus of a unit. The unit would then consist of the reading of the core book or text set and the completion of related activities.) Themes might include such diverse topics as heroes, distant places, sports and hobbies, animals, teddy bears, friendship, plants, or the Westward Movement. A unit's theme may involve only the language arts, or it may cut across the curriculum and include social studies, science, math, and the visual and performing arts.

Thematic organization has a number of advantages, the principal one being that it helps students make connections among reading, writing, listening, speaking, and viewing activities and among different pieces of literature. If there is integration with other subjects, even broader and more numerous connections can be constructed. However, Routman (1991) cautioned that before the language arts are integrated with content area subjects, they should first be integrated with each other.

Routman (1991) also warned that some thematic units lack depth and "are nothing more than suggested activities clustered around a central focus or topic" (p. 277). In her judgment, this is correlation rather than integration. In order for true integration to occur, there must be some overall concepts or understandings that the unit develops, with activities to support those concepts or understandings. For instance, a unit may revolve around famous people, with students reading and writing about such people, but the unit would not be truly integrated

A **unit** is a way of organizing instruction around a central idea, topic or focus.

As you plan a unit, focus on the theme rather than activities. Ask yourself, "What activities will best help students acquire an understanding of the unit's theme and major concepts?" (Lipson, Valencia, Wixson, & Peters, 1993).

unless the reading and related activities developed a genuine theme or core idea. "Famous people" is a topic rather than a theme because it does not express a unifying idea. Some unifying ideas include "Successful people have had to overcome obstacles on their way to success" or "Successful people have many characteristics in common." An excellent way to integrate such a unit is to create broad questions to be answered by students: "What are the secrets of success?" or "What are successful people like?" Ideally, these are questions that students have had a hand in creating. As part of the unit's activities, students read about successful people, then interview and write about them in order to integrate information from the unit and answer broad questions. They might also look at successful people in science, social studies, and the arts. The suggested procedure for creating and implementing a thematic unit follows:

1. Select a topic or theme that you wish to explore. When deciding upon a theme, select one that encompasses concepts that are an important part of the curriculum and that will facilitate the development of essential language arts goals. The theme should be significant and interesting to students. The unit "Westward Wagons" was planned by the fifth-grade teacher, the librarian, and the reading consultant in an elementary school in North Scituate, Rhode Island (DiLuglio, Eaton, & de Tarnowsky, 1988). This unit on the Westward Movement is appropriate for fifth-graders, since it is a topic typically presented in that grade and it lends itself to a wide variety of language arts, science, social studies, and art activities.

2. Involve students in the planning. Determine through a modified KWL or similar technique what they know about the topic and what they would like to learn.

3. State the overall ideas that you wish the unit to emphasize. Include questions that your students might have about the topic (Routman, 1991). The teachers who created the "Westward Wagons" unit decided on four overall or big ideas: reasons for moving west, problems encountered during the move, transportation in the west, and life in a frontier settlement. Also, compose a list of language arts objectives. What literary appreciations and comprehension, study, and writing or other skills/strategies will the unit develop? These objectives should tie in with the unit's big ideas. They should help students understand the nature of the Westward Movement. Included in the list of skill/strategy objectives are reading skills, such as summarizing, and writing skills, such as report writing, that students need in order to investigate the Westward Movement. Since the unit is interdisciplinary, objectives are listed for each content area.

4. Decide on the reading materials and activities that will be included in the unit. You may wish to focus on a core book that will become the center of the unit. Using a semantic map or web, show how you might integrate each of the language arts. Show, too, how you might integrate science, social studies, and other areas. Each activity should advance the theme of the unit. Activities should also promote skill/strategy development in the language arts and other areas. For instance, in the "Westward Wagons" unit students simulated a journey west. As part of the simulation, they wrote journal entries and tracked their progress on a map.

Themes enable students to discover connections. However, in order to do so, themes "must be coherent . . . and . . . make genuine connections through thoughtful responses to literature. The right theme gives the work of the classroom a *focus* and provides a rubric for making decisions about what to teach. . . ." (Lipson, Valencia, Wixson, & Peters, 1993, p. 253).

For a unit on trees, the major understandings that second-grade teacher Elaine Weiner wanted to emphasize were "We cannot live on earth without trees" and "Trees provide shade, beauty, paper, homes for animals, and more" (Routman, 1991, p. 278). Weiner's students observed trees as they changed, and each child kept a detailed observation record of a tree that she or he had adopted. Students also read and wrote about trees.

Units may encompass a single area, such as language arts or social studies, or they may be integrated and cut across subject matter areas. Advocated by whole language theorists, the integrated unit applies the language arts to one or more content areas. The focus is on a theme, problem, or central question. Curriculum lines are dropped, and all activities are devoted to that topic. The theme is usually a broad one so that language, social studies, science, math, and art activities can be included.

5. List and gather resources, including materials to be read, centers to be set up, audiovisual aids, and guest speakers or resource personnel. Be sure to work closely with school and town librarians if students will be doing outside reading or research. In the "Westward Wagons" unit, *Sarah, Plain and Tall* (MacLachlan, 1985), *Caddie Woodlawn* (Brink, 1935), *A Gathering of Days* (Blos, 1979), and other high-quality selections were listed. These texts varied in difficulty level from grades 3–4 to grades 6–7, so all the students might have materials on an appropriate level of difficulty.

6. Plan a unit opener that will set the stage for the unit. It could be the showing of a film or video, a reading of a poem or the first chapter of the core book, or it might be a simulation. For the "Westward Wagons" unit, students could picture how it might feel if they were making a long, dangerous trip across the country. The opener might involve brainstorming with students to decide which aspect of the topic they would like to explore.

7. Evaluate. Evaluation should be broad-based and keyed into the objectives that you have set for your students or that they have set for themselves in collaboration with you. It should include the unit's major concepts or understandings as well as skills and strategies that were emphasized. For example, if the ability to visualize was emphasized, it needs to be assessed. If you emphasized ability to take notes or write journals, that might be assessed through holistic evaluation of students' written pieces. As part of the evaluation, you must decide whether students learned the concepts and skills or strategies listed in the objectives. If not, then reteaching is in order. In addition,

Exemplary Teaching

Teaching a Multicultural Unit

The students in Ms. Curiel's nongraded class ranged in age from 6 to 10 and hailed from nine different Asian countries. Some spoke no English, while others were proficient in both English and their native language. In order to obtain a better knowledge of all the cultures represented in the class, Curiel and her students decided to create an Asian Museum.

Pursuing the theme of understanding cultural diversity, the students chose as their first activity using a map and a globe to find out how far their ancestors had come. Other activities included creating a map that showed their countries of origin, reading books about those countries, and planning the museum. Work groups were created to set up various exhibits in the museum: oral and written language samples and literature, toys, foods, arts, landscapes, and music.

In order to set up exhibits, the groups researched their areas, wrote descriptions for their exhibits and created signs and a brochure for the museum. The students also obtained artifacts and mementos from their families and, of course, used them as an essential resource. When completed, the museum included maps, stories, signs, science experiments, time lines, and artwork, in addition to artifacts and mementos. The students also put on plays, gave speeches, sang songs, and played games. They sold tickets, acted as guides, and prepared foods from many cultures for the visitors. In addition to learning valuable literary skills while integrating knowledge from many subject matter areas in order to achieve a greater understanding of cultural diversity, the students learned how to run a museum (Lapp & Flood, 1994).

you should evaluate the unit itself and determine what might be done to improve the unit. You might take out activities or materials that proved boring or ineffective and revise other elements as necessary.

SELF-SELECTION

Reading a chapter book, novel, or full-length biography is a major commitment of time. Students will be more willing to put forth the necessary effort if they enjoy the book and have some say in its selection. Even when working with groups, it is possible to allow some **self-selection.** Obtain several copies of a number of appropriate books. Give a brief overview of each, and have students list them in order of preference. Group students by their preferences into literary circles or similar groups. You can even allow some self-selection when using a core book approach with the entire class. Give the students a choice of two or three core books from which to select. If it is necessary for the entire class to read a particular book, plan some activities in which students can select their own reading materials. You might also alternate teacher selection with self-selection: After teaching a unit that revolves around a core book, plan a unit in which students select books.

Self-selection means that students choose their own reading material.

SHAPING THE PROGRAM

A literature-based program can use sets of children's books or anthologies or some sort of combination thereof. Today's basal readers are mainly literature anthologies. The major advantage of the basal anthology is that a variety of materials are contained in one volume—it typically includes short stories, poems, essays, plays, and excerpts from a chapter book or novel. The disadvantages are that many pieces are excerpts of longer works rather than complete works and that some of the selections included may not be the best choice for your class.

Some teachers use literature to complement the basal. The basal might be used three days a week, the literature books two days a week. Or three weeks of basal-based instruction might be followed by three weeks of reading a novel or chapter book. Some programs use only children's books.

CREATING LITERATURE GUIDES

One advantage of using basals is that lessons and extension activities have already been planned. When teachers use children's books, they must obtain or create their own lessons. Commercially prepared units and **literature guides** are available from a number of publishers and range in size from a few pages to a small booklet. For instance, one guide for *Frog and Toad Are Friends* (Lobel, 1970), which is a book for first-graders, is just four pages long, whereas a second guide is thirty-two pages long (Helper, 1989). The question then becomes how much time a first-grade teacher wants to spend with a single book.

Apart from length, literary guides should be examined from the perspectives of format, assumptions about reading instruction, and usability (Helper, 1989). Of three guides published for *Sarah, Plain and Tall* (MacLachlan, 1985), one emphasized inferential thinking and substantiating opinions; the second, much longer, guide emphasized analysis of the structure of the book and careful reading of the text; and the third presented the book in the context of a thematic unit (Helper, 1989). Buying a guide could mean buying into the author's philosophy of teaching literature and view of the relationship between reader and text. Thus a key issue in selecting guides is whether questions and activities foster students'

Literature guides are teaching aids that may include questions and activities for a text as well as background information.

construction of meaning and response or lean toward a single interpretation, with the teacher (or the guide) being the ultimate authority.

A valuable resource for planning a guide or unit for primary-level books is *Primaryplots 2* (Thomas, 1993). Designed to help librarians plan book talks, *Primaryplots* provides bibliographic information—including readability level, a plot summary, and a description of the theme—for the best picture books published between 1988 and 1992 and appropriate for children from ages 4 to 8. Also included are a list of audiovisual aids, related titles, and sources of information about each author. An especially helpful feature is a list of suggested activities: curriculum correlations, ideas for writing, dramatizing, and creating paintings, murals, and puppets. Hints for introducing and discussing each book are also presented. All of the suggested activities have been tried out with elementary school children. Although written for librarians, *Primaryplots* contains a wealth of information for planning and teaching literature units.

Similar in intent to *Primaryplots* is *Introducing Book Plots 4* (Spirt, 1994), which provides suggestions for presenting books that are appropriate for students aged 8 to 12.

An excellent compilation of guides is *Response Guides for Teaching Children's Books* (Somers & Worthington, 1979). It includes twenty-six brief but carefully planned guides for timeless works ranging from Sendak's (1963) *Where the Wild Things Are* to L'Engle's (1962) *A Wrinkle in Time*. A more recent compilation is *Inviting Children's Responses to Literature* (McClure & Kristo, 1994), which presents brief guides for fifty-seven notable books. Reading guides for many of the most popular children's books are also available free from publishers. When using a ready-made guide, it is important that you tailor it to your teaching style and the personality of your class.

The best guides, of course, are the ones teachers create themselves. The classroom teacher is in the best position to decide which approaches and activities are right for her or his students. A sense of ownership and pride is also involved: Through creating their own guides, teachers put more of themselves into their work. In some schools, teachers share the job of creating lessons and guides. In a school district in which there are five fourth-grade teachers, each one might agree to compile a guide for one book. In that way, they can prepare five guides with a minimum of work.

In whatever way they are prepared, the guides should be flexible so that teachers are able to choose among activities and suggestions. In addition, they should be evaluated and updated to eliminate or revise activities that do not work well and to include new suggestions. The list of books to be read should also be updated and revised.

A SAMPLE PROGRAM

The school district in Clovis, California has a three-pronged literature program: core literature, extended literature, and recreational reading. Core literature is presented to all students, is closely analyzed, and is the basis for classroom discussion and writing. It includes such favorites as *Make Way for Ducklings* (McCloskey, 1941), *Leo the Late Bloomer* (Kraus, 1971), *Misty of Chincoteaque* (Henry, 1947), and Kipling's (1912) *Just So Stories*. Extended literature consists of materials that can be either correlated with the core literature or simply recommended for individual reading. Recreational reading includes materials that might be termed escapist—works that are interesting but will not win any awards for literary merit. Study guides have been created for the core literature books. Comprehension activities are structured according to Bloom's taxonomy. Questions are asked at each level from knowledge or factual recall to evaluation or making judgments about the material.

CHOOSING MATERIALS

One of the most important tasks in structuring a literature-based program is choosing the books. If the program is to be schoolwide or districtwide, teachers at each grade level must meet and decide which books should be offered at each grade level. Quality and appeal of the materials must be considered. Teachers also have to think about students' reading abilities, with easy, average, and challenging books provided for each grade. All genres should be included: novels, short stories, poems, plays, myths, and well-written informational books.

A wealth of children's books exists. The latest edition of *Children's Books in Print* (1995) lists nearly 70,000 titles. In addition, thousands of high-quality books have gone out of print but can be found in school and public libraries across the country. It is almost too much of a good thing. How does a busy teacher keep up with the latest and the best in children's books? The following journals regularly provide information about children's books:

> *Booklist*. Published biweekly by the American Library Association. Includes reviews of books and other media on all levels.
>
> *Bulletin of the Center for Children's Books*. Published monthly except August. Reviews children's books.
>
> *The Horn Book*. Published six times a year. Includes articles about authors and illustrators, together with reviews.
>
> *Language Arts*. Published monthly during the school year. Features articles about teaching language arts in elementary school. Regularly reviews children's books.
>
> *The Reading Teacher*. Published monthly during the school year. Features articles on teaching reading and reviews children's books.
>
> *School Library Journal*. Issued monthly except June and July. Reviews more than one hundred children's books in each issue.

Other sources of information about children's books include the following:

> Burke, E. *Literature for the Young Child* (2nd ed.). Boston: Allyn & Bacon (1990). Contains numerous titles suitable for children between ages 3 and 8.
>
> Huck, C. S., Helper, S., & Hickman, J. *Children's Literature in the Elementary School* (5th ed.). New York: Holt (1993). Known for both its extensive bibliographies and its teaching suggestions, this is a favorite among teachers.
>
> Jensen, J. M., & Roser, N. L. *Adventuring with Books: A Booklist for Grades Pre-K–Grade 6* (10th ed.). Urbana, IL: National Council of Teachers of English

An example of a recently published literature series is *The Jamestown Heritage Readers* (Mountain, Crawley, & Fry, 1991, 1995). Designed for grades 1 through 8, it includes both traditional authors, such as Nathaniel Hawthorne and Mark Twain, and contemporary writers, including Beverly Cleary and Shel Silverstein.

(1993). Contains annotations on nearly 2000 recommended children's books published between 1988 and 1992.

Lima, C. W. *A to Zoo: Subject Access to Children's Picture Books* (4th ed.). New York: Bowker (1993). Categorizes thousands of picture books by subject, author, and title.

Routman, R. *The Blue Pages, Resources for Teachers from Invitations*. Portsmouth, NH: Heinemann (1994). Includes an extensive annotated bibliography of trade books at all levels.

ADVANTAGES AND DISADVANTAGES OF A LITERATURE-BASED APPROACH

The primary advantage of a literature-based approach is that books can be chosen to meet students' needs and interests. The major disadvantage of a literature-based program is that fine literature may be misused, by being made simply a means for developing reading skills rather than a basis for fostering personal response and an aesthetic sense. A second major disadvantage is that the books chosen may not be equally appealing to all students.

ADAPTING A LITERATURE-BASED APPROACH

In a literature-based approach, selections can be read in one of three ways: whole class, small group, or individually. Whole class reading creates a sense of community and builds a common background of knowledge but neglects individual differences in reading ability and interest. Working in small groups does not build a sense of larger community but allows for some self-selection. Individualized reading, which is described in the next section, fosters self-selection and provides for

As part of a literature-based unit, students might conduct a study of an author.

individual differences but may be inefficient. If you do use whole class reading, use it on a limited basis and complement it with small groups or an individualized approach and self-selection.

Planning and implementing a literature-based program can be time-consuming, especially when you are initiating the program. You might want to introduce the approach gradually or use it in conjunction with a basal reading program.

INDIVIDUALIZED READING

According to the latest data, schoolchildren in the United States are learning the skills of reading (at least the low-level ones), but they are not learning the joys of reading. Although 61 percent of the nation's fourth-graders watch three hours or more of television every day, only 44 percent read for fun on a daily basis (Mullis, Campbell, & Farstrup, 1993). By eighth grade, the proportion of students who read for daily enjoyment drops to one in four.

The **individualized reading approach** is designed to create readers who can and do read. Each child chooses her or his own reading material and has periodic conferences with the teacher to discuss it. Originated a half-century ago and highly popular in the 1950s, individualized reading is enjoying a rebirth in the 1990s. It is based on three principles—seeking, self-selection, and pacing—that are just as valid today as they were four decades ago (Olson, 1949):

1. *Seeking.* Children naturally seek out experiences that are consistent with their maturity levels and needs. For example, 8-year-olds, who are at a stage of development where they are curious about the wider world, tend to seek out books about distant places.
2. *Self-selection.* Even at young ages, children's interests vary. Self-selection allows them to choose materials that they want to read. A child will be motivated to read a book he or she has chosen because the material is of interest and also because the child has a personal stake in it.
3. *Pacing.* Children grow and develop at different rates. Whereas one child might finish a hundred books in a school year, another in the same class might barely finish ten. In an individualized program, the faster child is not held back; the slower child is not pressured or pushed ahead before he or she is ready.

> The **individualized reading approach** is a method for teaching reading in which students select their own reading material, read at their own pace, and are instructed in individual conferences and whole class or small-group lessons.

> **Adapting instruction for poor readers**
> Because students select their own books and read at their own pace, individualized reading works extremely well with students reading below grade. No longer are they stigmatized by being put in the lowest group or forced to read material that is too difficult for them.

MATERIALS

An individualized approach requires a large collection of materials. As a rule of thumb, it has been suggested that initially there should be at least three times as many books as children in the class, with more books being added over time (Barbe & Abbott, 1975). However, teachers should not let lack of materials stand in their way. School and local libraries might loan a classroom collection, children might bring in books from home, or the community might be asked to contribute. Old basals can be a part of the collection. What is necessary is a wide variety of materials to reflect children's personal interests and reading ability; there should be suitable materials for the slowest student as well as the brightest.

ORGANIZING THE PROGRAM

The classroom must be organized carefully. Just as in a library, it should have an inviting browsing area where students can choose books and settle down comfortably to read. The individualized reading program should be organized from a management standpoint. Routines must be established for selecting books, keeping track of books circulated, taking part in conferences, and completing independent activities. The nature of the activity should determine the types of rules and routines (Barbe & Abbott, 1975). Since they are expected to follow these procedures, students should have a role in formulating them. The teacher might describe the situation and have students suggest ways to make it work.

The following basic conditions must be managed: (1) The teacher must be able to hold individual conferences with students that are free from interruptions; (2) students must be able to work on their own without disturbing others; and (3) students must be responsible for choosing books on their own and reading them. Some commonsense rules and routines might include the following:

- *Book selection.* The number of students choosing books at one time is limited to five; students may select two books at one time; students may make one exchange.
- *Circulation.* Students are responsible for the books they check out; a card, sign-out sheet, or computerized system is used to keep track of books; students are in charge of the circulation system; books may be taken home.
- *Conference time.* No one may interrupt the teacher during conferences; students must come prepared to conferences; students (or the teacher) must arrange for periodic conferences.

IMPLEMENTING INDIVIDUALIZED READING

The six basic components of an updated individualized reading program are introduction, direct instruction of skills and strategies, silent reading, conferences, sharing, and strategies/skills grouping. The six components provide a good mix of individual and group work with direct instruction, practice, and application.

INTRODUCTION

The introduction is a brief warm-up activity designed to get the students in a reading frame of mind. It may consist of oral reading of a poem or story or a shared reading.

DIRECT INSTRUCTION OF SKILLS AND STRATEGIES

The program should include a period of direct instruction each day. The instruction should be broad in scope and sequential. It should include all the essential strategies and skills that students need: using phonics and context, predicting, summarizing, skimming, monitoring, and so forth. Ideally, the strategy or skill being taught should prepare the students for the pieces they are about to read. It can also address a need that the teacher has detected. For example, students may be having difficulty with words that contain prefixes and suffixes, or perhaps they are not monitoring for meaning and are not aware when a passage does not make sense. A series of lessons on affixes or using metacognitive strategies is then in order. These lessons should follow the direct instruction model described in this book. For whole class guided practice, the teacher can construct exercises or use selections from basals, workbooks, periodicals, or content area material. Since students read on a variety of levels, it is recommended that easy material be used for guided practice so that everyone can handle it, or, if it is too difficult for some, the teacher should read it aloud.

Once the skill or strategy has been taught and practiced under teacher guidance, students can apply it to whatever they are reading. During direct instruction, ways of applying the new strategy should be discussed. During ensuing direct instruction lessons and conferences, students should indicate how they used it and any problems they may have had with it.

SELF-SELECTED READING

Students read their self-selected books for at least thirty minutes. If time is available, this period can be extended. Students may also select books at this time but must do so according to classroom rules. Because students will be reading their self-selected books independently, they should be encouraged to use appropriate strategies. Before reading, they should survey, predict, and set a purpose for reading. As they read, they should use summarizing, inferential, and imaging strategies—if appropriate—and should monitor for meaning. As they read, students can use sticky notes to indicate a difficult word or puzzling passage. Or, as suggested by Atwell (1987), they can record difficult words and the page numbers of puzzling passages on a bookmark. A full bookmark could be a sign that a book is too difficult. After reading, students should evaluate their original prediction and judge whether they can retell the selection and relate it to their own experiences.

CONFERENCES

Conferences are the core of the individualized reading program. Both individual and group conferences are recommended, each having distinct advantages.

Individual Conferences. Although time-consuming, the individual conference allows each student to have the teacher's full attention and direct guidance and instruction for at least a brief period. It builds a warm relationship between teacher and student and provides the teacher with valuable insights into each child and her or his needs. While individual conferences are being held, other students are engaged in silent reading. No interruption of the conference is allowed, and those involved in silent reading are not to be disturbed.

An individual conference begins with some questions designed to put the student at ease and to get a general sense of the student's understanding of the book. Through questioning, the teacher also attempts to elicit the child's personal response to the text and encourages the child to relate the text to her or his own life. The teacher poses questions to clear up difficulties and to build comprehension—and concepts, if necessary—and reviews difficult vocabulary. In addition, the teacher assesses how well the student understood the book, whether she or he enjoyed it, and whether she or he is able to apply the strategies and skills that have been taught. The teacher notes any needs the student has and may provide spontaneous instruction or give help later.

After holding a conference, be sure to summarize it. Include date, selection read, and student's reaction to the text. Did the student enjoy it? Was she or he able to respond to it? Was the book too difficult or too easy? Did you note any needs? If so, how will these be provided for? Will the student engage in an extension or enrichment activity? Will she or he read another book? Keep the notes brief but include any information that is pertinent. Have the student read a brief passage orally. Note whether the student was able to read correctly at least 95 percent of the words. If not, the book may be too difficult.

To prepare for individual conferences, students choose a favorite part of the book to read to the teacher and also give a personal assessment of the book, telling why they did or did not like it or what they learned from it. Students also bring words, ideas, or items they want clarified or questions that they have about the text. In addition, students may be asked to complete a generic response sheet or a specific response sheet geared to the book they have read. Figures 10.1 and 10.2 present generic response forms that include items designed to elicit a personal response from students. To avoid having students do an excessive amount of writing, you might focus on just a few of the personal response questions or have students respond to the questions orally rather than in writing.

Another way that students can prepare for an individual conference is to keep track of their reading in journals. Students note the date, title and author of the book, and their personal response to the piece, answering questions such as these: How does the selection make me feel? What will I most remember about it? Was there anything in it that bothered me (Gage, 1990)? Did it remind me of a person or event in my life? Do I have any questions about the piece (Parsons, 1990)? For an informational book, students answer such questions as these: Which details did I find most interesting? How might I use the information? What questions do I still have about the topic? Questions should not be so time-consuming or arduous that children avoid reading so they will not have to answer them. As an alternative, you might have students keep a dialogue journal as described later in this chapter. And younger children may respond to a book by drawing a picture. Whatever form the response takes, it should be geared to the maturity level of the child and the nature of the text.

Students should keep a record of all books that they read. While helping the teacher keep track of students' reading, such records are also motivational. Students get a sense of accomplishment from seeing their list grow. A simple record like the log in Figure 10.3 would suffice.

Individual conferences can last anywhere from five to fifteen minutes. At least one conference should be held each week. Not every book needs a conference. A student who is reading two or three books a week should decide on one book to talk about. On the other hand, if the student is a slow reader, a conference may be held when she or he is halfway through the book. Conferences should be scheduled. A simple way to do this is to have students who are ready for conferences list their names on the chalkboard. The teacher can then fill in the times for the conferences.

After the conference is over, the teacher should make brief notes in the student's folder, including date, title of book read, assessment of student's understanding and satisfaction with the book, strategies or skills introduced or reinforced, student's present and future needs, and student's future plans. A sample conference report form is presented in Figure 10.4.

Group Conferences. Group conferences are an efficient use of time. The teacher has the opportunity to work with five or six students rather than just one. Conferences can be held to discuss books by the same author, those with a common theme, or those in the same genre. Group conferences work best when students have read the same book. If several copies of a book are available, they can be given to interested students, who then confer.

In the past, some teachers found individualized reading unmanageable because of the demand that conferences made on their time. However, with group conferences and the experience gained from writing conferences, lack of time should no longer be a major hindrance.

Name: _____   Date: _____

Title of book: _____   Publisher: _____

Author: _____   Date of publication: _____

Plot

Problem: _____

_____

Main happenings: _____

_____

_____

_____

Climax: _____

_____

Outcome: _____

_____

Answer any three of the following questions:

1. What did you like best about the book?

_____

_____

_____

2. Is there anything in the book that you would like to change? If so, what? Also tell why you would like to make changes.

_____

_____

_____

3. Is there anything in the book that puzzled you or bothered you?

_____

_____

_____

4. Would you like to be friends with any of the characters in the book? Why or why not?

_____

_____

_____

5. If other students your age asked whether you thought they might like to read this book, what would you tell them?

_____

_____

_____

FIGURE 10.2 | **Response sheet for informational books**

Name: _____ Date: _____

Title of book: _____ Publisher: _____

Author: _____ Date of publication: _____

Topic of book: _____

Main things I learned: _____

_____

_____

_____

Most interesting thing I learned: _____

_____

Questions I still have about the topic: _____

_____

_____

_____

Recommendation to others: _____

_____

FIGURE 10.3 | **A reading log**

Name: _____

Title of book: _____

Author: _____

Publisher: _____

Date of publication: _____

Number of pages: _____

Subject: _____

Date started: _____

Date completed: _____

Recommendation to others: _____

_____

_____

_____

_____

An individualized reading conference report

Name: *Althea S.*   Date: *10/19*

Title: *Owl at Home*   Author: *Arnold Lobel*

Understanding of text and personal response:
Discussion of Ch. 1 of text: Saw humor in story. Remembered time when furnace broke and apartment was cold but became cozy again.

Oral reading:
Fairly smooth. Good interpretation. Some difficulty reading dialogue. 97% accuracy.

Needs:
Read behav for behave. Needs to integrate context and phonics.

Future plans:
Plans to finish book by end of week. Will join Arnold Lobel Literature Circle and compare Owl books with Frog and Toad books. Will share funniest incident with whole class.

A group conference includes three types of questions: an opening question to get the discussion started, following questions to keep the discussion moving, and process questions to "help the children focus on particular elements of the text" (Hornsby, Sukarna, & Parry, 1986, p. 62). Process questions focus on comprehending and appreciating a piece and are similar to those asked in the discussion and rereading portions of a DRA. They are often related to reading strategies and might ask students to summarize a passage, compare characters, predict events, clarify difficult terms, or locate proof for an inference. Students should also have the opportunity to respond personally to the text. Process and response questions might be interwoven. The teacher should lead the discussion, although students eventually may take on that role. Just as in individual conferences, the teacher evaluates students' performance, notes needs, and plans future activities based on those needs.

Follow-up Activities.   Extension activities to follow group or individual conferences grow out of the nature of the book read and are similar to the activities that can follow a DRA. Possible extension activities include creating a time line of main events, a drawing of the main character, a map of a journey undertaken by a character, a drawing of the setting, or a story map of the plot, writing a letter to the author, reading another book by the same author or on the same subject, performing a procedure explained in a how-to book, and watching a VCR or CD-ROM version of the book and comparing the two.

Group conferences are important educationally. They allow students to clarify their ideas, compare their interpretations and responses, learn from the experiences of others, and see ideas from different perspectives. Literature circles, which are a form of group conference, give students the opportunity to "explore half-formed ideas with others and to revise their understandings of a piece of literature through hearing other readers' interpretations" (Short & Kauffman, 1988, p. 107). Students learn to participate in group discussion, hone their listening skills, and work cooperatively.

SHARING

Although one-on-one and small-group activities are beneficial, it is also important that the class function as a whole. Sharing helps bring the whole class together. During sharing time, which might take only ten minutes of the day, children demonstrate activities they have completed, dramatize or talk over the books they are currently reading, or discuss projects in which they are engaged. The teacher should join in the sharing and tell students about some good books that he or she is reading. New additions to the classroom library can also be presented at this time.

Some activities that might be used as means for sharing a book include a panel discussion, dramatizing a book, creating puppets of the main characters and dramatizing a portion of the book, writing an ad for the book, putting on a skit in which the main character is interviewed (this takes two students who have both read the book), and conducting a survey to see which books and authors are most popular with the class.

STRATEGIES/SKILLS GROUPING

When it is evident that four or five students have a common need—for example, difficulty with consonant-vowel-consonant words or problems making inferences—the teacher can call the students together to work on the problem. Instruction should not be limited to the poorest readers; otherwise a stigma will be attached to the skills group. Needs of the average and best readers should also be addressed. These temporary skills groups are in addition to the whole class teaching and/or review that occurs every day.

ADVANTAGES AND DISADVANTAGES OF INDIVIDUALIZED READING

The major advantage of individualized reading is that students select their own material. In addition, each student can move at her or his own pace, and slower students are not stigmatized. With all students reading on their own level and choosing their own books, there is no need to divide the class into the traditional three groups—that is, there are no "owls," "bluebirds," or "turkeys."

Individualized reading should have a positive payoff for children's self-esteem. It is also just as effective in building skills and strategies as a basal series (Austin & Morrison, 1963; Sartain, 1972), and, in the hands of an excellent teacher, it might be better (Skolnick, 1963). With its emphasis on self-selection, use of children's books, wide reading, discussion groups in a cooperative learning style, the empowerment of teachers and learners, and integration of the language arts, individualized reading has the potential to be especially effective.

However, the individualized approach does have some disadvantages. Working one-on-one with students can spread the teacher so thin that students do not get enough instruction. Acquiring sufficient materials can also be a problem. The teacher should be knowledgeable about children's books and techniques for teaching reading. Good management and record-keeping skills are also prerequisites.

Individualized reading is not an all or nothing approach. It can be the heart of the reading program or can be used along with a basal series and/or literature-based approach. It can be done every day, three days a week, or just once a week.

Children should have some say in what they read. Regardless of what type of approach you use, self-selection should be a vital feature. As a group, teachers apparently agree with this recommendation. More than half of a representative sample of fourth-grade teachers had their students read books on a daily basis that the students themselves chose. More than 80 percent of the teachers arranged for self-selected reading on a weekly basis (Langer, Applebee, Mullis, & Foertsch, 1990).

Exemplary Teaching

Implementing Individualized Reading

As an experienced second-grade teacher who realized that the biggest threat to an individualized reading program is getting bogged down in paperwork and conferences, Ms. White enlisted the help of her students. After a child proved in her conference with White that she understood the book she had read, she became the class "expert" on the book. The next student who read it conferred with the expert. Children were also encouraged to make up quizzes for books they had read. After trying out a student-constructed quiz and helping the child revise it, White used it as a way for other students to respond to the book.

Another way that White's students demonstrated comprehension of a book was to describe a charac-

ter. The other members of the class were then asked to guess who the character was and give the title of the book in which the person appeared. In addition, as a book-of-the-month activity, the students created books for the classroom library.

White knew how to seize the moment to teach a strategy, expand knowledge, or keep the spark of wonder alive in her young charges' minds. Whenever something especially interesting came up in a conference, she would ring a bell and a mini-lesson or discussion on homonyms, a vivid description, an unusual word, or a strange fact would ensue. It is small wonder that years later students would recall second grade with the comment "That's the year I learned to read" (Parsons, 1985, pp. 60–61).

Another potential weakness of individualized reading is that skills and strategies may be neglected. Use the word recognition and comprehension skills and strategies presented in this book as a base for your skills/strategies groups. (A summary of learning strategies is presented in Table 14.2.) Provide both systematic instruction and instruction as the need arises.

ADAPTING INDIVIDUALIZED READING

With its emphasis on working one on one with students, individualized reading can be very time-consuming. One way of correcting this situation is to use a more group-oriented approach along with individualized reading so that students spend some time working in groups and some time working alone. Individualized reading might be used along with a basal or literature-based approach, for instance. An approach that includes some of the best features of individualized reading but also provides for small-group and whole-class activities, thereby making a more efficient use of time, is reading workshop.

READING WORKSHOP

Although the focus of **reading workshop** is self-selected reading, the workshop has three major components: preparation time, self-selected reading and responding, and student sharing (Atwell, 1987; Cooper, 1993; Reutzel and Cooter, 1991).

Reading workshop is a form of individualized reading in which students choose their own books and have group or individual conferences and may meet in groups to discuss books or work on projects. There may also be whole class or small-group lessons, and students may work in dialogue journals.

PREPARATION TIME

Reading workshop begins with preparation time, which includes a mini-lesson and a state-of-the-class conference. In the mini-lesson, the teacher presents a skill/strategy lesson based on a need evidenced by the whole class. It could be a lesson on making inferences, predicting, using context clues, deciphering multi-syllabic words, or interpreting metaphors. The mini-lesson might be drawn from the basal reader or literature resource book or might be created by the teacher (Cooper, 1993). It should be presented within the framework of a story or article that students have read or listened to, and it should be applicable to the reading that they will do that day. The mini-lesson should last approximately ten minutes.

The state-of-the-class conference is a housekeeping procedure and can be as brief as a minute or two. During this time, the schedule for the workshop is set, as students note what they will be doing. The students' plans are recorded on a chart (see Figure 10.5), which allows the teacher to keep track of who is doing what and who may need some guidance. Some students, for instance, may not be signing up for conferences or may be spending an inordinate amount of time on one book.

SELF-SELECTED READING AND RESPONDING

At the heart of the workshop is the time when students read self-selected books, respond to their reading, or engage in group or individual conferences. Self-selected reading may last from fifteen to thirty minutes or longer. Response time may also last from fifteen to thirty minutes. During response time, students may meet in a literature circle to discuss their reading, write in their journals, work on an extension activity, plan a reader's theater or other type of presentation, work at one of the classroom's centers, continue to read, or attend a conference. During response time, hold individual and/or group conferences as you do with individualized reading. If time allows, circulate around the room, giving help and guidance as needed. Visiting literature circles should be a priority.

USING DIALOGUE JOURNALS

A **dialogue journal** is a written record of the student's reactions and observations about reading selections or other topics and the teacher's responses.

If you are working with older students, you might try **dialogue journals** as an alternative to conferences or along with conferences. After Nancy Atwell (1987) instituted self-selection and time to read in her classroom, her students read an average of thirty-five books. She commented, "Last year's average of thirty-five books per student grew as much from students' power to choose as from the time I made for them to read. I heard again and again from students of every ability that freedom of choice had turned them into readers" (p. 161). Although providing students with time to read and freedom to choose started them reading, Atwell was not satisfied. She realized that response was needed to allow students to reflect on their reading and deepen their understanding and appreciation. Because individual conferences were so brief, they did not lend themselves to an in-depth discussion of the text. To provide the framework for response, Atwell used dialogue journals to initiate an exchange with the students.

Name	M	T	W	Th	F
Angel	IC, SSR	LTC			
Amy	LTC	SSR, GC			
James	LTC	SSR, GC			
Keisha	SSR, GC	LC, EX			
Maria	LTC	GC, LC			
Marsha	PR	IC, SSR			
Robert	J, GC	WC			
Stephanie	SSR, GC	LTC			
Tiffany	IC, SSR	LTC			
William	PR	IC, SSR			

Key

SSR: Self-selected reading
IC: Individual conference
GC: Group conference
LTC: Literature circle
J: Journal
EX: Extension

PR: Paired reading
RT: Reader's theater center
WC: Writing center
LC: Listening center
TC: Technology center

Having the opportunity to write about their reading gave students time to reflect and led to deeper insights. With the "give and take" of dialogue, they were led to develop their thoughts and reconsider interpretations. Atwell commented:

I initiated written dialogues about literature because I had some hunches about the combined possibilities of writing as a way of reflecting on reading, and teacher-learner correspondence as a way of extending and enriching reflection

One of the primary advantages of dialogue journals is that teachers can model and scaffold more mature expression (Atwell, 1987). Through thoughtful comments and careful questioning, they can elicit lengthier, more elaborated responses and they can direct students to look at essential aspects of the texts being discussed. Closed questions such as "Which character did you like best?" tend to elicit a limited response. Open-ended questions such as "The story sounds interesting—tell me about it" tend to elicit a fuller response.

through collaboration. I suspected kids' written responses to books would go deeper than their talk; that writing would give them time to consider their thinking and that thoughts captured would spark new insights. I also suspected that a written exchange between two readers, student and adult expert, would move readers even deeper inside written texts, with the give and take of the dialogue helping them to consider and develop their thoughts. Finally, I believed this special context—a teacher initiating and inviting first-draft chat—would provide a way for me to be responsive to every reader as well as creating a specific occasion for them to write and reflect: a genuine and genuinely interested audience who was going to write back. (p. 165)

In addition to providing students with an opportunity to respond, dialogue journals yield insight into students' growth as readers. Thus, they offer the teacher a rich source of ideas for teaching lessons. Although, at first, the dialogue was between teacher and individual students, Atwell discovered students passing notes about poems they had read. She extended an invitation to dialogue, and students began exchanging their responses with each other.

STUDENT SHARING

During the student-sharing portion of reading workshop, which should last from ten to twenty minutes, students share their reading with the entire class. They might give the highlights of a book they especially enjoyed, read an exciting passage, share a poem, make a recommendation, enact a reader's theater performance, or share in some other way. "Sharing time advertises and promotes the excitement of literacy learning and helps to promote the class as a community of readers" (Cooper, 1993, p. 389). As an alternative to whole class sharing, the teacher might arrange for small-group sharing with four or so students in a group. The teacher can then visit with the groups as a participant or observer (Cooper, 1993).

ADVANTAGES AND DISADVANTAGES OF READING WORKSHOP

Self-selection, moving at one's own pace, using group processes, and relating reading and writing are the major advantages of reading workshop. Disadvantages include potential neglect of skills and the possibility that the teacher might spread herself or himself too thin in an attempt to meet with a variety of groups and individuals and respond to students' journal entries. Also, reading workshop might be unsuitable for students who have a hard time working independently or whose skills are so limited that there are few books they can read on their own.

ADAPTING READING WORKSHOP

Reading workshop can be used instead of a basal series or along with it. Use whole class instruction as appropriate. For instance, teach book selection and strategies needed by all students to the whole class. Use small-group instruction for those children who evidence a specific need for additional help. Obtain multiple copies of selected titles, just as you might do for a literature-based approach, and periodically invite students to choose one of the titles and read it as part of a small group. Use efficient management techniques, and do not overextend yourself.

If you use reading workshop with younger students whose writing skills are still rather limited, gradually lead them into the use of dialogue journals. They might begin by drawing pictures in response to selections read.

LANGUAGE-EXPERIENCE APPROACH

The **language-experience approach** is very personal. Children's experiences expressed in their own language and written down by the teacher or an aide become their reading material. Because both the language and the experience are familiar, this method presents fewer difficulties for children who are learning to read. It also integrates thinking, listening, speaking, reading, and writing. Roach Van Allen (1961) explained the basic tenets for the language-experience approach from the learner's point of view: "What I can think about, I can talk about. What I can say, I can write—or someone can write for me. What I write, I can read" (p. 109).

Through discussion, the teacher can lead students to organize and reflect on their experiences. If time order is garbled, the teacher can ask, "What happened first? What happened next?" If details are scant, the teacher can request the children to tell more or can ask open-ended questions, such as "How do you think the dinosaur tracks got there? What do the tracks tell us about dinosaurs?" Through comments that show an interest in the children and the topic, the teacher affirms them and encourages them to elaborate.

Whereas the teacher should affirm, support, encourage, and scaffold, she or he needs to be careful not to take over. The teacher should draw language from the children—not put words in their mouths. It is also important for teachers to be aware of the students' cultural customs of conversation. In some cultures, children have been taught not to speak until spoken to. In others, children have been taught to speak their minds.

When recording students' stories, it is important to write their exact words. Rephrasing what they have dictated shows a lack of acceptance for the language used. In addition, if the story is expressed in words that the child does not normally use, the child may have difficulty reading it. For instance, if the child dictates, "I been over my grandma's house," and the teacher rewords it as "I have been to my grandma's house," the child might stumble over the unfamiliar syntax. As Cunningham and Allington (1994) have observed,

> If language experience is being used with an individual child to help the child understand what reading and writing are and that the child can write and read what he or she can say, then the child's exact words must be written down. To do anything else will hopelessly confuse the child about the very things you are trying to clarify by using individual language experience. (p. 92)

However, when a group story is being written, the situation is somewhat different. The story and the way it is written reflect the language structures that the group typically uses. To record a nonstandard structure might confuse some members of the group and result in criticism for the child who volunteered the structure. Displaying group stories containing nonstandard structures might

The **language-experience approach** is a method for teaching reading in which students dictate a story based on an experience they have had. The dictated story is written down by a teacher or an aide and used to instruct the students in reading.

When students talk about a visit to an aquarium, a science experiment, planting a tree, or other experience as part of composing a language-experience story, the teacher is provided with the opportunity to help them think about the experience and clarify and extend their understanding of it (Reutzel & Cooter, 1992).

Adapting instruction
for ESL students
Because the language-
experience approach is based
on children's language, it is a
very effective technique to
use with students who are
still learning English. It also
provides the teacher with an
opportunity to learn about the
child's language and culture.

also result in protests from parents and administrators (Cunningham & Allington, 1994).

Because language experience is based on students' individual backgrounds, it allows each student to share her or his culture, experience, and mode of self-expression. By valuing each child's language and experiences, this approach lends itself to affirming diversity in the classroom. It also has the power to promote understanding and community among students whose backgrounds may differ.

The language-experience approach can be used with individuals or groups. Lesson 10.1 describes the steps for a group activity that extends over three days.

Lesson 10.1
Group language-experience chart

Day 1

Step 1. Building experiential background for the story

The students have an experience that they share as a group and that they can write about. It might be a field trip, the acquisition of a pet for the classroom, the baking of bread, or similar experience.

Step 2. Discussing the experience

Students reflect on their experience and talk about it. During the discussion, the teacher helps them organize the experience. In discussing a visit to the circus, the teacher might ask them to tell what they liked best so that they do not get lost in details. If they baked bread, the teacher would pose questions in such a way that the children would list in order the steps involved.

Step 3. Dictating the story

When initiating the language-
experience approach, start
with group stories so that the
class becomes familiar with the
procedure. As students share
experiences and learn about
each other, this also builds a
sense of community.

The children dictate the story. The teacher writes it on large lined paper, an overhead transparency, or on the chalkboard, or might even type it on a computer that has an attachment to magnify the input and project it on a screen. The teacher reads aloud what she or he is writing so that children can see the spoken words being written. The teacher reads each sentence to make sure it is what the child who volunteered the sentence wanted to say. The teacher sweeps her or his hand under the print being read so that students can see where each word begins and ends and that reading is done from left to right. For students just learning to read, each sentence is written on a separate line, when possible.

Step 4. Reviewing the story

After the whole story has been written, the teacher reads it aloud once more. Children listen to see that the story says what they want it to say. They are invited to make changes.

Step 5. Reading of story by teacher and students

The teacher reads the story, running her or his hand under each word as it is read. The children read along with the teacher.

Step 6. Reading of familiar parts by students

Volunteers are asked to read sentences or words that they know. The teacher notes those children who are learning words and phrases and those who are just getting a sense of what reading is all about.

Day 2

Step 1. Rereading of story

The story is reread by the teacher, who points to each word as it is read. The children read along. The story might then be read in unison by the teacher and students. The teacher continues to point to each word. Volunteers might be able to read some familiar words or phrases.

Step 2. Matching of story parts

The teacher has duplicated the story and cut it into strips. The teacher points to a line in the master story, and students find the duplicated strip that matches it. Individual words might also be matched. A volunteer reads the strip, with the teacher helping out as necessary.

For students who can go beyond matching, the teacher plans activities that involve reading, asking questions like the following: Which strip tells where we went? Which strip tells what we saw? Students identify and read the strips. On a still more advanced level, students assemble the strips in correct order. This works best with stories that have no more than four or five sentences.

Individual sentences can also be cut up into words that students assemble into sentences. This can be done as a pocket chart activity. The scrambled words are displayed, and volunteers read each one. Then a volunteer reads the word that should come first, puts it in its place, and reads it once more. A second volunteer reads the word that should come next and places it after the first word. The teacher reads the two words that have been correctly placed or calls on a volunteer to do so. This continues until the sentence has been assembled correctly. Once the entire strip has been assembled, the teacher or a volunteer reads it. The class listens to see whether the sentence has been put together correctly. Once students agree that it has, they read it in unison. This technique works best with short sentences.

Working with individual words helps both the least able and the most able readers. It helps poor readers see where words begin and end, and more advanced readers learn to read words at sight. When words are looked at individually, students note their characteristics, such as which letter comes first and the length of the word. Sentence construction helps all students see how words are put together. During this activity, the teacher might note that the first word in a sentence has a capital letter. The concept of end punctuation can also be introduced.

Day 3

Step 1. Rereading of story

A copy of the story is distributed to each student. The story is discussed and read in unison.

Word banks are collections of words that students have learned to read or that they are in the process of learning.

Group language-experience stories can be used beyond the beginning or early reading level to demonstrate writing techniques. One way of showing students how to write a letter to the editor, a persuasive essay, or a story is to arrange for them to compose such items as group-experience stories.

If your students are creating individual language-experience stories, it's helpful if you have an aide or volunteers to assist with dictation. First explain the process to your helpers and then let them observe you until they feel they can undertake it on their own.

Step 2. Identification of familiar words

Students underline words that they know. Known words are placed in **word banks** or otherwise saved for further study and use in other activities (see sections on high-frequency words and phonics).

PERSONALIZING GROUP STORIES

One way to personalize group language-experience stories is to identify the name of each contributor. After a volunteer has supplied a sentence, the teacher writes the student's name and the sentence, as shown in Figure 10.6. When the story is reread, each student can read the sentence that she or he contributed originally. Seeing their names in print gives students a sense of ownership of the product. It also helps them remember the sentences that they supplied.

AN INDIVIDUAL APPROACH

Individual language-experience stories are similar to group stories, except that they are more personalized. (Figure 2.2 is an individual language-experience story about a trip to an apple orchard.) Just as in the group approach, the child dictates a story and the teacher, an aide, or a volunteer writes it down and uses it as the basis for teaching reading. Often, an individual language-experience story starts out as a drawing. The child then dictates a story that tells about the drawing. A photo can also be used to illustrate a story or as a stimulus for dictating one.

When dictating a language-experience story, a child may bring up experiences that are highly personal or that reveal private family matters. Affirm the child's feelings, but suggest a more appropriate way for the child to relate the experience. "I'm pleased that you trusted me enough to share that with me, but I think maybe you should tell your mom or dad about it." If the child uses language that is unsuitable for the classroom, have her or him use more appropriate language:

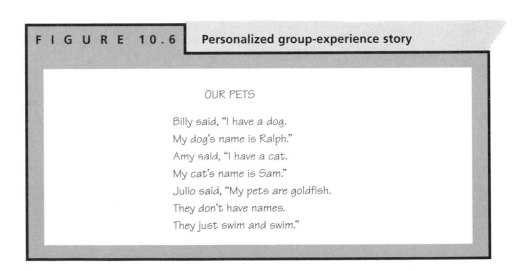

F I G U R E   1 0 . 6   Personalized group-experience story

OUR PETS

Billy said, "I have a dog.
My dog's name is Ralph."
Amy said, "I have a cat.
My cat's name is Sam."
Julio said, "My pets are goldfish.
They don't have names.
They just swim and swim."

"Can you think of another way to say it?" (Tierney et al., 1995). Maintaining the child's dignity and self-concept is of primary importance. Handle delicate situations with sensitivity and careful professional judgment.

INTRODUCING SKILLS AND STRATEGIES

Whether group or individual, language-experience stories can be used to introduce and reinforce a host of reading strategies and concepts about reading. By explaining what is being done as he or she writes down a story and runs his or her hand under a line as it is being read, the teacher is introducing basic concepts that include the ideas that spoken words can be written down and read, that one reads from left to right and top to bottom, and that sentences are made up of words. Students also learn where words begin and end.

HIGH-FREQUENCY WORDS

As they read language-experience stories, most students automatically memorize some words. The teacher might ask students which words they would like to learn, or she or he might set aside certain high-frequency words, such as *I* and *can,* for instruction. To ensure that *I* and *can* have been learned, the teacher might present activities that include having the students write individual "I can" stories, reading big books that contain *I* and *can,* having words printed on cards and placed in word banks, and completing a variety of reinforcement activities. Working in pairs, students can quiz each other on *I* and *can* and other words from their word banks. Using word-bank cards, they might make a list of things they can do. They can categorize words, by placing color words in one pile, action words in another, and animal words in a third. They can search out opposites or write stories about individual words. For concrete nouns or some action words, students might draw an illustration of the word on the reverse side of the paper or card. They might then quiz themselves by attempting to read the word, turning the card or paper over to see if they got it right.

After students have accumulated a number of words in their word banks, they can keep them in alphabetical order by first letter. This will reinforce the use of the alphabet and also help them locate words. In time, the word bank becomes a kind of dictionary as well as a source of motivation: Word banks that are growing signal to the children that they are learning.

Word walls can also be used to reinforce new words and known words from the language-experience stories. Being on the wall, the words become a resource for students' writing activities, and their location makes them useful for quick reinforcement activities whenever there are a few spare moments (Cunningham & Allington, 1994).

Word walls are displays on the classroom wall on which words have been placed for reference or study.

PHONICS

Phonics can be introduced through a language-experience story. For example, the teacher might help the class see that *bike, ball, bake, Barbara,* and *Bob* all begin with the same letter and sound and that the letter *b* stands for the sound /b/ at the beginning of *ball.* When rereading the selection, the teacher might mask *-ike* in *bike, -all* in *ball,* or *-ake* in *bake* in a sentence and have students guess what word that begins with the letter *b* might be used to complete the sentence. Word-bank cards can also be used as a basis for teaching phonics. The teacher can have students group words that rhyme or begin with the same sound and then guide them in a study of the letter-sound correspondence or vowel pattern.

COMPREHENSION SKILLS

Comprehension skills are introduced when students answer questions about the stories. Answering questions about significant details helps students determine what is important. Putting sentence strips in order reinforces sequencing skills, while supplying a title involves grasping the main idea of a piece. Questions might also involve relating the main idea and details. In addition, the language-experience story is an excellent device for introducing print conventions, such as end punctuation, quotation marks, and capitalization.

CONCEPTS

Language-experience stories can be used to build concepts, too. Individual stories about animals, colors, weather, plants, community helpers, or any other topic can be stapled or sewn into books. These handmade books can then become a part of the classroom or school library.

THE LANGUAGE-EXPERIENCE APPROACH AND ESL STUDENTS

Because it uses a child's own language and can draw on aspects of the child's culture, the language-experience approach can be especially helpful for ESL students. Even a bilingual child who has learned enough English to read a little may have difficulty with idiomatic expressions, many syntactical structures, and, of course, some words.

Teachers often wonder whether they should edit an ESL student's dictation if it contains unconventional or nonstandard items. As with native speakers of English, the best advice is to accept the child's language and show that it is valued. If the teacher edits it, it becomes the teacher's language, not the child's. This is especially true when children are in the initial stages of learning to read. In general, students' words should be written exactly as they are dictated; however, even if mispronounced, they should be spelled correctly, for example:

Dictation: I happy. My dog do'an be sick.
Written: I happy. My dog don't be sick.

As children grow in language, they will have opportunities to develop fuller knowledge of verbs, contractions, and pronunciation. The teacher might work on these patterns at appropriate times or consult with the ESL teacher if the child is taking part in such a program. However, focus at this point should be on introducing reading in English. Since the child is demonstrating a basic grasp of English, waiting for further refinement is an unnecessary delay.

A **dialect** is a variation of a language that may differ somewhat in pronunciation, grammar, and vocabulary.

VARIANT DIALECTS

Some students may speak a **dialect** that is somewhat different from that typically expected by the school. It is important to accept that language: It will be confusing if the children say one thing and you write another, and constant correction will turn them off. At this point, children are rapidly acquiring vocabulary and developing their understanding of increasingly complex constructions. The last thing a teacher wants to do is to cut off the flow of language and risk interfering with their development. Introducing a standard dialect and correcting variant English should not be a part of early reading instruction.

THE LANGUAGE-EXPERIENCE APPROACH IN THE CONTENT AREAS

Science and social studies topics are often covered in the primary grades without books. Group-experience stories can be used to summarize main concepts or events. After studying mammals, for example, the teacher can discuss the main ideas and have the class dictate an experience story that highlights them. Duplicated copies of the stories can be distributed and collected into a science booklet; students can then illustrate their booklets.

In the intermediate grades, science and social studies textbooks might be too difficult for some students. Discussion projects, filmstrips, and experiments can be used to present the subject matter. Although these activities build concepts, they do not call for reading in the content areas. Language-experience stories can be used to summarize key topics so that students have a text—their own—to read.

How to handle dialect is a controversial issue. Shuy (1973) made the point that it is developmentally inappropriate to introduce another dialect to a young child. The child will be confused and will not pick up the second dialect. As children grow older, however, they may choose to use other dialects in order to be able to communicate more effectively with diverse groups of people. This does not mean, however, that they will need to surrender their home dialect.

Display language-experience stories on the wall. When students have free time, encourage them to "read the walls." They might do this alone or with a buddy (Pike, Compain, & Mumper, 1994).

OTHER USES FOR THE LANGUAGE-EXPERIENCE APPROACH

The language-experience approach does not have to be confined to narratives or summaries of content area textbooks. Thank-you notes to a visiting author, a letter to a classmate who is hospitalized, an invitation to a guest speaker, recipes, a set of directions for the computer, class rules, charts, lists, captions, diaries, booklets, plays, and similar items are suitable for the language-experience approach. When possible, the pieces should be written for real purposes.

Shared writing is another way in which the language-experience approach might be used. **Shared writing** is a cooperative venture involving teacher and students. In a regular language-experience story, the teacher records students' exact words. In shared writing, the teacher draws from the children the substance of what they want to say but may rephrase it (Cunningham & Allington, 1994). For instance, at the end of the day, the teacher may ask the students what they learned that day. Summarizing the contributions of many children, the teacher records the day's highlights. In doing so, the teacher is modeling how spoken language is transformed into written language.

Shared writing is a type of language-experience story that the teacher and the class work together to create. In shared writing, the teacher draws from the children the substance of what they want to say but may rephrase it.

Adapting instruction for low-achieving readers

The language-experience approach is frequently used with older students who have difficulty reading. Obtaining suitable materials for an older student who is reading on a very low level can be a problem. In such a situation, a language-experience story is an excellent solution to the problem.

A HIGH-TECH LANGUAGE-EXPERIENCE APPROACH

Writing to Read (Martin & Friedburg, 1986) employs IBM personal computers and software and electric typewriters. However, it is basically a language-experience approach to learning to read and may be used without computers or electric typewriters. In fact, its creators used paper and pencil when devising the program.

Based on a practice implemented years ago by Maria Montessori, *Writing to Read* is a method for teaching reading through writing. Until recently, the conventional wisdom was that children learn to listen, speak, read, and write in that

Altering spelling patterns seems to be a mistake. For instance, the *e* at the end of *home* marks the *o* as being long. The *e* at the end of *face* serves a double function—it marks the *a* as being long and the *c* as having an *s* sound. Using a macron and substituting *s* for *c* deprives students of the opportunity to learn how the English spelling-sound system works. Use of an artificial system also creates an inconsistency, in that the spellings students learn in their reading are different from those they will experience in the wider world.

Based on a two-year evaluation that involved thousands of students, Educational Testing Service (Murphy & Appel, 1984) concluded that *Writing to Read* works. Kindergarteners and first-graders using the program made better-than-average progress and did significantly better on writing tasks than control groups. Kindergateners also performed significantly better than control groups in reading. However, there was no significant difference between *Writing to Read* and control groups in reading at the end of first grade.

Based on a review of twenty-nine evaluations, Slavin (1990) expressed reservations about *Writing to Read*. He was concerned about the lack of significant difference between the *Writing to Read* students and controls in first grade, especially in view of the high cost of the program. Although admitting that children liked the program, that their parents were pleased, and that it had a positive impact on writing, Slavin wondered whether there were not cheaper alternatives.

order. However, Martin and Friedburg (1986) claimed that children should write before reading. Writing is a self-motivating, active task, whereas reading is passive. When children write, they can see what they are doing. Writing also seems to be the key that unlocks the mystery of written language. Children learn that what they say, they can write, and that what they write represents what they say.

In an attempt to remove spelling as an obstacle, Martin and Friedburg created their own spelling system for *Writing to Read* in which certain sounds are spelled phonemically rather than conventionally. For instance, final *e* as a long vowel marker is omitted and a single vowel letter with a macron (-) is used to indicate the sound of the long vowel, as in *hōm* and *pīp*. In the word *face*, the letter *s* is used instead of *c: fās*. The forty-two phonemes and their altered spellings are presented by sophisticated software at the computer station. However, the computer station is just one of six work stations. Other stations include the writing/typing station, the work-journal station, the listening-library station, the multisensory-materials station, and the make-words station. Except for the listening-library station where the children listen to and read along with tapes of literary classics, most of the stations' activities are designed to reinforce the particular lesson that has been presented. However, as they progress, children compose original stories at the writing/typing station.

ADVANTAGES AND DISADVANTAGES OF THE LANGUAGE-EXPERIENCE APPROACH

The language-experience approach is most frequently used as a supplement to other programs and is especially useful in the beginning stages of learning to read. The major advantage of the approach is that it builds on children's language and experience. A major disadvantage of using it as the sole approach to teaching reading is that the child's reading will be limited to his or her own experiences.

ADAPTING THE LANGUAGE-EXPERIENCE APPROACH

Because it neglects published reading materials and because it limits children's reading experiences, language experience should not be the sole approach to reading instruction. However, it makes an excellent supplement to any of the other approaches presented in this chapter, especially at the emergent and early stages of reading.

LINGUISTIC APPROACH

The **linguistic approach** to reading is based on a principle that linguists use to distinguish speech sounds: minimal contrast. In linguistics, the phoneme is the smallest unit of sound that can be used to distinguish one word from another. The words *hat* and *hit* are said to have minimal contrast because the difference in a single sound—the vowel sound in this instance—causes them to be different words. Using the principle of minimal contrast, Fries, Wilson, and Rudolph (1986) created a program in which students learn to read by contrasting words. For example, students learn the minimally contrasting words *cat, sat,* and *mat* by hearing and seeing how they are the same and how they are different.

Fries (1962) believed that readers should respond to graphic patterns just as they respond to phonemic patterns—by responding to whole words and not just to individual sounds or letters. Therefore, in Fries's program, as presented in *Merrill Linguistic Readers,* the student responds only to whole words; no phonics of any type is ever introduced. Students are not taught that *b* represents /b/ or that *c* represents /k/ or /s/. No mention is made of long vowels or short vowels. Students inductively learn to deal with letter-sound elements by contrasting dozens of patterns.

Inspired by Bloomfield (1942; Bloomfield & Barnhart, 1961), who believed that students should learn regular spellings before learning irregular ones, Fries's program presents easy, regular spellings before discussing more complex or more variable elements. Patterns are also heavily reinforced; *Book A* of *Merrill Linguistic Readers* is devoted entirely to the short *a* pattern. A linguistic program that is similar to the *Merrill Linguistic Readers* is SRA's *Basic Reading Series* (Rasmussen & Goldberg, 1985).

The **linguistic approach** is a way of teaching reading that emphasizes the regularities of the language by presenting regularly spelled patterns first. It also presents patterns by comparing and contrasting words that have minimal differences (such as *pat* and *pan*) so that students can see how they differ.

ADVANTAGES AND DISADVANTAGES OF THE LINGUISTIC APPROACH

Merrill Linguistic Readers has a number of strengths. The patterns are carefully sequenced and heavily reinforced. After being introduced to patterns, students have the opportunity to apply their new knowledge by reading selections that contain the patterns. Although the series has been used with both average and bright students, it is now primarily used with poor readers, especially those with learning disabilities.

With their step-by-step introduction of spelling patterns, linguistic programs seem to offer an easier introduction to reading. Students read only words with which they are already familiar. However, this apparent strength is also the source of the greatest weakness of the approach. Restricted to pattern words, stories in the beginning stages tend to be artificial. Since the beginning selections are not written in familiar language patterns and are less meaningful than selections in children's books, students' opportunities to apply syntactic and semantic cues are limited.

Although linguistic programs aren't used in many classrooms, they are frequently employed by remedial specialists, especially in special education. By understanding these programs and how they work, you will be better prepared to work with resource teachers who might use them.

ADAPTING THE LINGUISTIC APPROACH

To offset the artificial selections in a linguistic program, have students read a wide variety of children's books. You might supplement the linguistic approach with a language-experience, individualized reading, or reading workshop approach.

WHOLE LANGUAGE

Whole language has been described as a grass roots movement that classroom teachers across the land embraced and pushed forward. To help each other apply a whole language philosophy, a number of vigorous support groups sprang up. These groups include national networks such as TAWL (Teachers Applying Whole Language).

Described as a philosophy of learning rather than a teaching approach, whole language incorporates a naturalistic, organic view of literacy learning. The basic premise is that children learn to read and write in much the same way that they learn to speak. Oral language is learned by being used for real purposes, not by completing artificial practice exercises that present it piecemeal—work on adjectives today, nouns tomorrow, verbs the day after. Since theorists see reading and writing as a part of the whole, they reason that they should be learned in the same way oral language is learned—through use and for real purposes. The basic belief underlying whole language is acquisition of all aspects of language, including reading and writing, "through use not exercise" (Altwerger, Edelsky, & Flores, 1987, p. 149).

BASIC PRINCIPLES OF WHOLE LANGUAGE

Since whole language is not a prescribed program or method, its implementation varies from setting to setting and is expected to evolve and change as more is learned about how literacy is acquired. Basically, it embodies the following principles.

First, reading is best learned through actual use. Children learn by reading whole stories, articles, and real-world materials. Because of the richness of these materials, children are able to use their sense of language and the three cueing systems of semantics, syntax, and letter-sound relationships to grow in reading.

In a whole language classroom, children read and write for real purposes. There are no letters written to aunts who do not exist, thanking them for gifts that were not sent, just so that students can practice the format of the friendly letter. They write letters to real people for real reasons and mail them. Nor are children given isolated skill exercises such as circling words that contain short *a*. Instead, they read a story that has short *a* words.

According to the whole language philosophy, literacy is a social undertaking best learned in the context of a group. Therefore, in whole language classrooms, one sees writing workshops, group conferences, peer editing, and other examples of cooperative learning.

Whole language teachers are reflective "kid watchers." By watching children acquire literacy and reflecting on the experience, teachers learn more about the process and about how to help their students. They examine their beliefs about teaching and plan activities that match their beliefs. In other words, they create their own curriculum and procedures. Since this is done in light of each teacher's own theory and teaching circumstances, each program will be different.

CONDITIONS OF LANGUAGE LEARNING

To plan their programs, whole language teachers must have a theory about how language is learned. Seven conditions account for oral language learning. These can be transferred to the classroom to foster the development of reading and writing (Brown & Cambourne, 1987):

1. *Immersion.* Children learn to speak by being immersed in language, that is, in reading and writing activities.

2. *Demonstration.* Children learn language by hearing parents and others demonstrate it. In the classroom, teachers demonstrate literacy activities by letting the children see them read a book for fun, read the directions for operating a new piece of computer software, or write notes to parents inviting them to an open house. Teachers explain and show what they are doing so that children can see how and why people read and write.

3. *Expectation.* Parents expect their children to learn to speak and they do. Teachers should hold the same kinds of expectations for their students for developing literacy skills.

4. *Responsibility.* Parents do not set up a program for teaching oral language to their children. The children take responsibility for their language acquisition. Children naturally select expressions and grammatical constructions that fit their development. In the classroom, they must be given a sense of ownership of the tasks of literacy development. Ultimately, they are responsible for their own learning.

5. *Approximation.* No one expects perfect pronunciation or mature sentence structure from toddlers. Through a series of approximations, children's language slowly approaches mature speech. Yet when children learn to read and write, teachers are dismayed by reversals, invented spellings, and dropped endings of words. Teachers must recognize that invented spellings, misread words, and other "errors" could be approximations that will gradually develop into standard spellings and accurate pronunciations.

6. *Employment.* Learning a complex task such as talking takes time and effort. So does learning to read and write.

7. *Feedback.* Learning language involves feedback. Children's speech approximations are accepted, but the correct forms are modeled with great patience. Students learning the complexities of reading and writing also need feedback that is accepting, caring, and patient.

In whole language classes, students take responsibility for their own learning. As Crafton (1991) explained, "When learners of any age initiate their own learning, the intent and purpose of the experience are clear. With self-initiation comes a greater degree of ownership, involvement, and commitment to the activity. The learning then really belongs to the participant" (p. 16). Students engage in self-selection of reading materials and writing topics. Also, the schedule must allow "the necessary time to read and reread, to revise one time or twenty, to talk things through at individual points of discovery or confusion. Sharing the decision-making and allowing students to direct their learning is paramount if teachers are to encourage independence and self-direction" (p. 17).

WHOLE LANGUAGE ACTIVITIES

In general, whole language teachers espouse the basic philosophical principles and are guided by the seven language-learning conditions or similar conceptions. They also typically support use of the following activities:

- Use children's books instead of basals. If basals are used, teachers adapt them, deciding which selections to present and how to present them.
- Integrate reading, writing, listening, and speaking with each other as well as with content areas. Reading and writing are considered to be tools for learning science and social studies. In addition, teachers take a process approach to writing and provide functional instruction in the mechanics of writing and other literacy learnings. Punctuation, for example, is taught when needed.
- Empower students as learners. Teachers make available the resources—dictionaries, reference books, and children's books—as well as writing tools and strategies that students must have to learn to read, write, and explore. Teachers also make wide use of group work.
- Emphasize the use of all language systems in decoding words. Phonics should be taught in combination with semantic and syntactical cues.

To capture the essence of whole language, see *The Whole Language Catalog* (Goodman, Bird, & Goodman, 1991), which is a compilation of contributions from more than five hundred educators from the United States and other countries. Along with articles about the philosophy and history of whole language, there are hundreds of examples of imaginative, inspiring teaching ideas and hundreds of resources that will enliven your teaching, regardless of your particular educational philosophy.

- Evaluate students continuously, primarily through observing classroom behavior and work samples. Evaluation is a guide to understanding children's learning processes and structuring activities that fit their needs. Students can be a part of the evaluation process.
- View oneself as a learner. Teachers learn with their students. They learn about the students' learning process, as well as about themselves as teachers.

Whole language is often misinterpreted as being a set of teaching practices: emergent literacy, literature-based instruction, and process writing, for instance. While it is true that these practices are associated with whole language, the important question for whole language is not "What am I doing?" but "Why am I doing this?" (Church, 1994, p. 364). Adopting a whole language perspective means trying out techniques and practices in terms of one's beliefs about teaching and learning. It also means recognizing that there is no one right way to teach. "Instead, there is a constant process of inquiry into both beliefs and practices" (Church, 1994, p. 369).

MAKING THE TRANSITION TO HOLISTIC TEACHING

What steps might you take if you wish to implement a whole language program? First, clarify your beliefs about how children learn. Take a little time to write them down. Then list the kinds of teaching techniques that you use. Also list the learning activities that you typically assign and the materials that you use. Are you walking your talk? Does what you do in your classroom match what you believe about teaching and learning? If not, start aligning the two. Ken Goodman (1991), in an open letter to teachers new to whole language, suggested the following:

> My advice is to take your time and find your own path to whole language. Take a personal inventory and decide what you are already doing that fits. Then decide which parts of your teaching you are least happy with, such as using workbooks, grouping, organizing time, or giving weekly spelling tests. . . . Move at your own pace as you make the change. . . . Don't be discouraged by temporary setbacks. . . . Keep moving until you feel what you are doing is consistent with what you have come to believe, and keep moving some more as you see what you and your kids can accomplish. (p. 10)

After you have examined your beliefs and practices, start aligning the two. As Goodman (1991) suggested, if you want to make changes, pick the area that bothers you the most. But select an area that is easy to change. For instance, if you make all the instructional decisions in the class, you might want to start involving students in the planning process. Start asking them what kinds of activities they want to pursue, what kinds of books they want to read, and what kinds of topics they want to write about. If you have been doing more talking than listening, focus on listening. If you have been telling students what they should learn, start involving them in setting instructional goals.

Building on your strengths as a teacher, gradually refine your instruction so that it becomes more holistic. Implement the practices recommended in this book. Although this book does not advocate a strictly whole language philosophy, the techniques recommended are holistic. By all means, meet with other professionals for support and advice. Also read professional literature and attend conferences.

ADVANTAGES AND DISADVANTAGES OF WHOLE LANGUAGE

The major advantages of whole language are that it stresses real reading and real writing for real purposes and a functional, contextual approach to skills instruction, thus eliminating tedious artificial skill-and-drill activities. A major disadvantage of whole language is a lack of systematic instruction. Teachers teach skills and strategies incidentally, as the occasion calls for it. However, as Manzo and Manzo (1995) note, whole language "tends to be a 'top down' approach with only slight provision for those individuals whose learning style is more 'sequential' and rule-guided than 'simultaneous' or intuitive and meaning-driven" (p. 48).

ADAPTING WHOLE LANGUAGE

To adapt whole language, first do as Goodman (1991) suggests. Construct your own philosophy about teaching literacy skills. Then create a program that is built on your convictions. If, for instance, you believe in direct instruction, then keep that as a part of your program, gradually introducing holistic practices. Start first with practices that will make the biggest difference in your students' learning but that are easiest to implement, such as self-selected reading. As you master one aspect, then introduce another.

A basic issue in the analysis by Stahl and Miller (1989) was whether the language-experience and whole language approaches can be grouped into the same category.

COMBINING APPROACHES

A large-scale comparison of approaches to teaching reading in the 1960s came up with no clear winner (Bond & Dykstra, 1967). All of the approaches evaluated were effective in some cases. However, some children experienced difficulty with each one. The study suggested that the teacher is more important than the method, and that a method successful in one situation may not be successful in all. Combinations of approaches were recommended. Adding language experience to a basal program seemed to strengthen the program. A word-attack element also seemed to be an important component, a conclusion that was reached repeatedly in a number of studies and research reviews (Anderson, Hiebert, Scott, & Wilkinson, 1985; Chall, 1967, 1983a; Dykstra, 1974).

A more recent comparison of whole language and the language-experience approach with basal programs observed that the former approaches duplicate the kinds of literacy activities that parents might engage in with their children: reading aloud, sharing books, encouraging writing, fostering language development, and supplying the tools of literacy (Stahl & Miller, 1989). Understandably, these methods work better in kindergarten. Basal programs, especially those with a strong decoding component, do a better job of helping students master reading skills typically taught in first grade. They also seem to work better with children who require a more directed approach.

Another interpretation of the research strongly suggests that what is really most effective is using the best features of all approaches. Draw from whole language the emphasis on functional/contextual instruction, the use of children's

Stahl and Miller (1989) recommended a combination of approaches, commenting that some authorities "trichotomize the practice of reading, separating practices into either phonics approaches, skills approaches, or whole language approaches. In this scheme, whole language approaches involve increased use of quality children's literature, writing, and ensuring that all skills are applied in the context of reading, rather than treated as isolated exercises. These are virtues that should be part of any reading program. It would be wrong to interpret the indifferent effects found for whole language/language experience programs at the first grade level as supporting the banality of some basal reading series, the excessive use of worksheets, or other aspects of the basal reading program" (p. 109).

literature, and integration of language arts. From basal programs, adopt some of the structure built into skills/strategies components. From individualized approaches, take the emphasis on self-selection of students' reading material. From the language-experience approach, adopt the practice of using experience stories to build and extend literacy skills.

Above all else, use your professional judgment. This book presents a core of essential skills and strategies in word recognition, comprehension, reading in the content areas, and study skills. Use this core of skills as a foundation when implementing your literacy program, regardless of which approach or approaches you use. If a skill or strategy is omitted or neglected, then add it or strengthen it. For instance, not all basals recommend the use of pronounceable word parts or analogy strategies. If you are using a basal and these elements are missing, add them.

In actual practice, teachers tend to use whatever works. Slaughter (1988) reported observing whole language teachers using direct skills instruction and skills-oriented teachers using children's literature. The most effective program might be the one that has achieved the best balance.

SUMMARY

1. There are a number of approaches to teaching reading. Language experience uses writing to teach reading. Approaches that use a textbook to teach reading include basal and linguistic. The literature-based approach, individualized reading, and reading workshop use children's books, as does whole language, which is more a philosophy than a method.

2. Basal readers are used to teach reading in a majority of this nation's classrooms. Today's basals incorporate high-quality literature, integrated language arts, comprehension strategies, emphasis on activation of schemata, and a process approach to writing, although they use a structured approach to reading. Basals neglect self-selection, often provide fragments rather than whole pieces of literature, and may suggest excessive practice with worksheets. Teachers can adapt basal series by being more selective about the pieces students read and the exercises assigned and by planning their own lessons rather than relying on the manual. In the early grades, kits of books specifically written for beginning readers are being used instead of or along with basals by a number of regular and remedial teachers.

3. A literature-based program can take many forms. Often, a unit approach is used. Core books or text sets might be at the center of the program. The program may take an individualized, group, or combination approach and may use anthologies, individual books, or both. Materials selection should be flexible to provide for students' interests and abilities. If possible, students should be given some choice in the selections to be read.

4. Designed to foster a love of reading, the individualized reading approach is based on self-selection of materials, seeking experiences that are appropriate in terms of each student's maturity level and needs, and proceeding at each reader's own pace.

5. Reading workshop, which includes group discussion of selections read, group and/or individual conferences, and dialogue journals, is based on the individualized reading approach but may be more efficient.

6. Based on the premise that reading is easier if the reading material incorporates students' language and experience, the language-experience approach uses as reading material stories dictated by the children about familiar experiences. Skills and strategies are related to the selection. Word banks may be used to develop word-recognition skills. As students grow in literacy, they begin writing their own stories instead of dictating them. *Writing to Read,* a high-tech program based on the language-experience approach, uses computers and software and electric typewriters.

7. The linguistic approach is based on the concept of minimal contrast. Students learn to decode words by contrasting dozens of patterns in which words vary by just one sound (such as *cat, hat,* and *fat*).

8. Described as a philosophy of learning rather than a teaching method, whole language is based on the premise that reading and writing are learned in much the same way as language is. That is, they are learned holistically as students read and write for real purposes.

9. According to research, no one approach to teaching reading yields consistently superior results. A combination is probably best. Teachers should use their professional judgment and know-how to adapt any program to fit the needs of their students.

CLASSROOM APPLICATIONS

1. Examine your philosophy of teaching literacy. Make a list of your beliefs and your teaching practices. Do your practices fit in with your beliefs? If not, what might you do to align the two?

2. Examine a current basal series. Look at a particular level and assess the interest of the selections, the kinds of strategies and teaching suggestions presented in the manual, and the usefulness of the workbook exercises. Summarize your findings.

3. Prepare conference cards for three children's books that you might use to teach reading. Include bibliographic information, a summary of the selection, a series of questions that you might ask about the book, and a description of some possible extension activities.

FIELD APPLICATIONS

1. Plan a series of language-experience lessons, either for an individual or for a group of students, in which an experience story is written and used to present or reinforce appropriate literacy understandings or skills and strategies. Evaluate the effectiveness of your lessons.

2. Adapt a lesson in a basal reader to fit the needs of a group of students you are teaching. Teach the lesson and assess its appropriateness. In what ways was the manual a helpful resource? What adaptations did you have to make?

c h a p t e r 11

Writing and Reading

ANTICIPATION GUIDE

For each of the following statements related to the chapter you are about to read, put a check under "Agree" or "Disagree" to show how you feel. Discuss your responses with classmates before you read the chapter.

Agree
Disagree

1. Reading and writing are two sides of the same coin.

2. New writers should write short pieces to keep their mistakes to a minimum.

3. Students should be allowed to choose their own topics.

4. Completing endings for unfinished stories written by others is good practice for budding fiction writers.

5. Students should try various types of writing.

6. The most time-consuming part of the writing process is revising.

7. Teachers should mark all uncorrected errors after a piece has been edited by a student.

8. Emphasis in a writing program for elementary school students should be on content rather than form.

Using What You Know

Writing and reading are related processes that are mutually supportive. Reading improves writing, and vice versa. The last two decades have witnessed a revolution in writing instruction, which today is based on the processes that expert student and professional writers use as they compose pieces.

What is your writing process? What steps do you take before you begin writing? What elements do you consider when you choose a topic? How do you plan your writing? How do you go about revising and editing your writing? How are your reading and writing related? What impact does your reading have on your writing? What impact does writing have on your reading?

THE ROOTS OF WRITING

The roots of writing go deep and begin their growth early. Writing evolves from the prespeech gestures children make and from the language they hear and later use, as well as from the developing realization that the spoken word is not the only way to represent reality.

Children discover pictures and words in storybooks that are read aloud to them. They draw pictures of mommy and daddy and their house. They scribble for the fun of it. In time, these scribbles become invested with meaning. Ultimately, children discover that not only can they draw pictures of people and objects, but they can represent people and objects with words. Many children make this crucial discovery about writing before they reach kindergarten; for other kindergarteners, the concept is still emerging.

It is important to determine where children are on the writing continuum to know how best to help them. Writing development generally follows the stages listed below. However, it should be noted that children can and do move back and forth between stages.

- *Age 18 months.* Children spontaneously scribble when given paper and pencils, and may do so even earlier if shown how (Gibson & Yonas, 1968, cited in Gibson & Levin, 1974).
- *Age 3 years.* Children begin to discriminate between writing and drawing, may create letterlike shapes, and have a budding sense of story.
- *Age 4.* Children can distinguish between letters written to people and stories. When asked to write letters and stories, they create pieces that differ in appearance. Although it may be composed of apparent scribbles, the letter looks like a letter; the story has the general appearance of a story. Some children may begin to form alphabet letters.
- *Kindergarten.* Writing ranges from drawing or scribbling to creating invented spellings. In a study by Applebee (1978), nearly half of the 5-year-olds used

Moving back and forth between stages, young children at times may use letterlike forms and at other times regress to scribbling. The demands of the task may determine their mode of writing (Sulzby, 1989). When writing a long piece, the child may scribble, whereas the same child may use letterlike forms for a shorter piece.

the past tense when telling a story, opening traditionally with "Once upon a time," and concluding traditionally with "They lived happily ever after."

- *First grade.* Writing is a motor activity. Children enjoy the feel of a pencil or crayon gliding across a sheet of paper. Their writing is immediate and spontaneous. They are more involved in the process than the product. Children in this stage may prepare for their writing by drawing, but their drawings are often an important part of what they are attempting to express (Calkins, 1986). First-graders make few or no revisions but can be encouraged to reread what they have written and do some gross editing. They typically use invented spellings, but these become more conventional during the course of the year.
- *Grade 2.* Children progress from writing for the sake of the activity to writing to create a finished piece. They are better able to focus on the end product and are becoming more fluent. However, being more conscious of form and correctness, they are more restricted and less willing to improvise. Talking over ideas with classmates or teachers is the preferred method of preparing for writing. The revision process begins to take hold, especially when encouraged and guided (Calkins, 1986).
- *Grade 3.* Concern for correctness intensifies. Students also gain a sense of audience. Personal narratives continue to be topics of choice. Students' revisions are more concerned with editing for correctness than with genuine reworking (Calkins, 1986).
- *Intermediate grades.* Writing is more complex and flexible. Students are better able to mentally compose a piece and may think through several ideas before committing one to paper. They are also better able to revise the substance of their pieces (Calkins, 1986).

PROCESS APPROACH TO WRITING

Writing process is an approach to teaching writing that is based on the way students and professionals write.

Besides fostering emergent literacy, writing instruction has changed dramatically in other ways. Today, it is based on the **writing process** that professional writers and students actually use. From the research of Graves (1983), Emig (1971), and others, a series of steps has been described that attempts to tell how writers write. The steps are prewriting, composing, revising, editing, and publishing.

PREWRITING

Easily the most important step, prewriting encompasses all necessary preparation for writing, including topic selection, researching the topic, and gathering ideas.

TOPIC SELECTION

Topic selection is the hallmark of the process approach. In the past, students were supplied with topics and story starters. The intent was to help, but the result was writing that was wooden, contrived, and lacking in substance and feeling because the topics were ones in which the students had no interest. Letting students choose their own topics is one of the keys to good writing because there is a greater chance that students will invest more of themselves in a piece that means something to them. When a group of 7-year-olds were allowed to choose their topics, they wrote four times as much as a peer group who were assigned subjects (Graves, 1975).

D. H. Graves (1982) recounted the story of a teacher who left Graves's weekly workshop filled with enthusiasm for the process approach but returned to the next session angry and discouraged. The problem? Hearing that they were to choose their own topics, the students demanded that the teacher supply them with suitable subjects. They felt that it was bad enough they had been asked to write; having to decide on their own subject matter was adding insult to injury. According to Graves, these students were unable to choose topics because they had never been taught how to do so. In previous years, well-meaning teachers had always provided them with topics. There was an implicit message in the teachers' act: These students had nothing worth writing about and thus had to be fed a diet of story starters, topic sentences, finish-the-story exercises, and other canned activities. Undoubtedly, some of these topics were quite creative. However, the best writing is about something that matters to the writer—a question that the writer wants to answer, a discovery or adventure that the writer wants to share, or a humorous episode that the writer wants to recount.

Murray (1989) suggested that teaching writing is mainly a matter of helping students discover what they have to say and how to say it. The teacher should model the process of selecting a topic and begin by discussing what he or she has done, seen, or knows that he or she would like to tell others. The teacher then jots down three or four topics on the chalkboard. They might be similar to the following:

I saw a real whale close up.

I saw the tallest building in the world.

I saw the longest baseball game ever played.

As the class listens, the teacher goes through the process of choosing a topic. The teacher rejects the first two because many people have seen whales and the tallest building, but only a handful of fans watched the longest game ever played. Most importantly, that is the topic that holds the greatest interest for the teacher.

Once the teacher has demonstrated the process, he or she asks the class to **brainstorm** topics and then lists them on the board. This helps others discover subjects of interest. After a discussion, each student lists three or four tentative topics and, later, chooses one to develop. In group discussions and one-on-one conversations or conferences with the teacher, children discover additional topics. With the teacher's questioning as a stimulus, they find subjects in which they have expertise, that they would like to explore, and that they would like to share. Knowing that they will be writing nearly every day and so must have many subjects to write about, students search for topics continuously. They find them on television, in their reading, in their other classes, in their homes, in writing notebooks, and in outside activities. They can keep lists of topics in their folders or in special notebooks or journals (Calkins & Harwayne, 1991).

To **brainstorm** is to attempt to accomplish a task as a group by having members submit ideas spontaneously. It also refers to individual efforts to accomplish a task by rapidly producing ideas.

It isn't necessary for students to have a piece planned in their minds before they begin writing. Writing can be an exploration—writers may not be sure what they want to say until they've said it.

Adapting instruction for ESL students

If ESL students can write in their first language, they will be able to transfer many of these writing skills to English. However, in addition to learning English vocabulary and syntax, these students may also be faced with learning a new orthography. For some, it may mean learning the entire alphabet. For others, it might mean learning a few letters or punctuation marks that are formed differently.

Writing is not a linear process. We don't plan and then write and then revise. As we write, we plan and revise. When author Tom Clancy was asked in an interview about the ending to a novel he was writing, he responded that he didn't know what the ending would be because he hadn't written it yet. Another author stated in an interview that he couldn't wait to get started writing each day because he wanted to see what his main character was going to do.

Journals are a favorite repository for writers' observations and ideas. In their writing journals, students can list topic ideas, outline observations they have made, or explore ideas. They can also record passages from their reading that were especially memorable or that contained distinctive language. Students might also use their journals to test out writing techniques or experiment with story ideas. Writing journals keep ideas germinating until they are ready to flower.

With students, establish guidelines for journals. If you plan to read the journals, make that known to students so that the journals do not become private diaries. Reading students' writing journals has several advantages. It makes the journals part of the writing program and encourages students to make entries. It also provides you with the opportunity to gain insight into students' thoughts about writing and to respond. Students could highlight any items that they would like you to focus on, and they can mark as private or fold over a page containing any item that they do not want you to see. Journals are not graded, and corrections are not made, because doing so will shut off the flow of ideas. However, you should write a response.

One of the shortcomings of journals is that they can, over time, become a diary of mundane events. Encourage students to take a broader look at the world and also to dig beneath the surface. The observation that "I struck out three times in the Little League game" might be expanded in a number of ways. Your response might be, "What were the consequences of striking out? Why do you think you struck out? What might you do about it? Could this be the start of a story?"

Another excellent repository of possible topics is the idea folder. Idea folders hold newspaper clippings, notes, or magazine articles that could become stories. For example, intriguing newspaper articles about flying snakes or the return of monarch butterflies can be stored for future reference. Students need to realize that topic ideas are everywhere; they just have to be alert to possibilities.

Time expended on collecting and selecting topics is time well spent. Children discover that they have stories to tell. Their writing becomes better and less time-consuming to produce. In one study, as children learned to choose and limit topics, fewer drafts were required (Graves, 1983).

PLANNING

Research and preparation are also essential parts of prewriting. For older students, preparation might take the form of discussing, brainstorming, creating semantic maps or webs, reading, viewing films or filmstrips, or devising a plot outline or general outline. For younger students, it could be discussing topics or drawing a picture. Drawing is especially useful, as it provides a frame of reference. Drawing also helps older students who have difficulty expressing themselves verbally. Distressed that a number of her students typically produced brief paragraphs almost totally devoid of detail, J. L. Olson (1987) encouraged them to draw a picture of their subjects. After discussing the drawings with her, the students then wrote. The improvement was dramatic; the resulting pieces were rich in detail. Apparently, the act of drawing helped students retrieve details about their subjects.

A particularly effective prewriting strategy is to have students brainstorm words that they think they might use to develop their topics. Brainstorming is a free-flowing, spontaneous activity. All ideas should be accepted and recorded but not critiqued. Everyone should contribute. After brainstorming, ideas generated can be discussed, elaborated on, and clarified. Related ideas can also be introduced.

Brainstorming helps students note details to include in their pieces (Bereiter & Scardamalia, 1982). D'Arcy (1989) recommended several different kinds of brainstorming. The simplest form involves writing down names—of birds, famous people, or mystery places, for example. Students jot down the results of their brainstorming rather than simply thinking aloud. This gives them a written record of their associations as well as concrete proof of the power of brainstorming to draw out items. Students then share their lists with partners, which may result in additional items. At this point, students might circle the name of a bird, famous person, or place that they know the most about and brainstorm that item. Later, they brainstorm questions about the item they have chosen: Where do bald eagles live? What kinds of nests do they have? Are they in danger of becoming extinct? What do they eat? How fast do they fly? The questions can be the basis for exploring and writing pieces about the topic.

Memories, feelings, images, and scenes can also be brainstormed. For instance, students might go down their list of items and note the one that drew the strongest feelings or created the sharpest image. Words to describe the feelings or details that describe the image could be brainstormed and listed.

Clustering and free writing are versions of brainstorming. Clustering is a kind of mapping in which students jot down the associations evoked by a word. Lines and circles are used to show relationships. In **free writing,** students write freely for approximately ten minutes on an assigned or self-selected topic, about a real event or an imagined one. The idea is to have children catch the flow of their thoughts and feelings by writing nonstop. Ideas or themes generated can then become the basis for more focused work. In some instances, free writing might be an end in itself—an exercise that promotes spontaneity in writing.

Orally sharing ideas is another form of preparing for writing. Discussing helps students "order their thoughts and generate many more ideas and angles for writing" (Muschla, 1993, p. 37). This technique is especially effective when students work in pairs. After students have generated ideas through brainstorming, clustering, or some other method, have them talk over their ideas with their partners. The listener should summarize what the speaker has said, ask the speaker to clarify any parts that are not clear, and answer questions that the speaker might have, thereby helping the speaker shape and clarify his or her ideas.

Role-playing can be an effective way to draw out ideas (Muschla, 1993). Students can role-play fictional or real-life events, including historical happenings or events that they have personally experienced. Role-playing can also help students elaborate on and clarify what they want to say. For instance, if students are about to write a letter to a classmate who has moved away, they might divide up into pairs and role-play the writer of the letter and the intended receiver. Students might role-play situations that they intend to write about: persuading the town to fix up the park or requesting that the local health department get rid of rats in the neighborhood. Students might also role-play Washington's crossing of the Delaware, the landing of astronauts on the moon, or other historical occasions. Or they could role-play a Little League coach giving her team a pep talk, the principal confronting two students who have been arguing, or a zookeeper answering questions about the newly acquired giraffe.

Clustering is a form of brainstorming in which students use mapping to show the associations evoked by a word.

Free writing is a form of writing in which participants write for a brief period of time on an assigned or self-selected topic without prior planning and without stopping. Free writing can be used as a warm-up activity or a way of freeing up the participant's writing ability.

REHEARSING

Rehearsing is the part of the writing process in which the author thinks over or mentally composes a piece of writing.

Experienced writers do a lot of **rehearsing**, or writing in their heads, composing articles, stories, and even parts of books at odd moments during the day or before going to sleep. Professional writers, if they can avoid it, do not write "cold." They are ready to write down ideas that they have been rehearsing in their minds when they finally sit down at their desks. How important is rehearsal? Donald Murray (1989), Pulitzer Prize–winning journalist, commented, "When the writing goes well, it usually means I have mulled over the idea and the material for quite a long time" (p. 250).

COMPOSING

Composing is the part of the writing process in which the writer creates a piece.

Composing is difficult because the writer must produce the whole message without the prompts supplied in conversation, create a context so that the message is understandable, and write for an unseen audience. Prewriting activities and conferences help supply the writer with some of the support that is provided in conversation.

Composing is also an uneven process. At times, we cannot get our ideas down fast enough. At other times, we labor just to write a few words so the paper won't look so blank. Composing requires focus, discipline, and time. Make the writing period as long as possible, and, if your schedule permits, allow students whose writing is flowing to continue for a longer stretch of time. For instance, if a reading workshop or self-selected reading follows the writing workshop, perhaps those students could continue writing or be given a choice of continuing to write or read self-selected books.

Composing is the act of writing a piece. The idea is for the writer to put her or his thoughts down on paper without concern for neatness, spelling, or the mechanics. A writer who is concerned about spelling is taking valuable time away from the more important job of creating. Reassure students that they will have time later to revise and edit.

Experienced writers generally do not tell all they know in any one piece. They have far more information than they can use, and they discard much of it either before or after it is put on the page. However, elementary school students often do not seem to have enough to say. According to Scardamalia and Bereiter (1986), "For young writers finding enough content is frequently a problem and they cannot imagine discarding anything that would fit" (p. 785).

Of course, young writers know less than more mature writers do, but finding enough to say may be essentially a problem of access (Scardamalia & Bereiter, 1986). Younger students are used to oral conversations in which the responses of the listener act as cues for retrieving knowledge. When the speaker fails to supply enough information, the listener's blank look or questions ferret out more talk:

> Written speech is more abstract than oral speech. . . . It is speech without an interlocutor. This creates a situation completely foreign to the conversation the child is accustomed to. In written speech, those to whom the speech is directed are either absent or out of contact with the writer. Written speech is speech with a white sheet of paper, with an imaginary or conceptualized interlocutor. Still, like oral speech, it is a conversational situation. Written speech requires a dual abstraction from the child. (Vygotsky, 1987, pp. 202–203)

This need to supply the missing listener when writing explains, perhaps, why prewriting activities are so important and why postdrafting conferences are so helpful in evoking a full written response from younger students. Scardamalia, Bereiter, & Goelman (1982) found that just encouraging young writers, who claimed to have written everything they knew, doubled their output. What the children had apparently done was extract their top-level memories, which are the main ideas, the generalities. They had not mined the lower-level memories, the examples, details, and explanations, that give body to the general ideas. With encouragement, they proceeded to do so.

For novice writers, the mechanical production of letters and words may take an extraordinary amount of effort. Placing less emphasis on handwriting and mechanics are steps that can be taken to lessen the physical effort, and that should release additional time and energy for matters of content and style.

Composing is not a smooth process. If a writer is primed and the ideas flow, her or his pen might race ahead and produce page after page of text, in seemingly effortless, almost automatic fashion. Or the writer may simply stare at the page for endless moments before finally producing a tortured paragraph. Or the writer may write in fits and starts. An initial burst of writing is usually followed by intense reflection, which is then followed by another burst of writing.

Preparation can help the composing process, but perseverance is required. A writer must be prepared to overcome various obstacles and blocks. By using strategies that experienced writers employ, the writer can avoid certain pitfalls. A key pitfall for elementary school students is believing that the first **draft** is the last draft, thereby blocking their writing with an overconcern with correctness and neatness. As Calkins (1986) commented,

> By the time many unskilled writers have written three words . . . they already believe they have made an error. . . . They continually interrupt themselves to worry about spelling, to reread, and to fret. This "stuttering in writing" leads to tangled syntax and destroys fluency. (p. 16)

Students need to know that their first writing is a draft and that the focus should be on getting thoughts down. There is plenty of time for revising and correcting later.

Beginnings are often the most difficult part of a piece to create. If students are blocked by an inability to create an interesting beginning, advise them to write down the best beginning they can think of and then return to it after they have completed their first draft. This same principle applies to other aspects of composing. If students cannot remember a fact, a name, or how to spell a word, they can leave a blank or insert a question mark and come back later. Nothing should interrupt the forward flow of the composing process.

Some students freeze at the sight of a blank piece of paper. Discuss some possible opening sentences. If nothing else works, suggest to the students that they just start writing. Their first sentence might simply be a statement that they are having difficulty getting started. As they continue to write, it is very likely that other thoughts will kick in.

FOCUSING ON AUDIENCE

Although we make lists or diary entries strictly for ourselves, most of our writing is geared toward an audience. A sense of audience helps shape our writing. As we write, we consider the backgrounds and interests of our readers. We try to think of ways of making our writing appealing as well as informative. Young writers typically lack a sense of audience and may assume that the readers already know whatever they know. A first step in writing is to define whom one is writing for. To help young students write for a particular audience, help them ponder the following questions (Learning Media, 1991):

What is my topic?

Why am I writing this piece?

Who will read my piece?

A **draft** is the part of the writing process in which the writer composes a rough copy.

What makes writing difficult, especially for the novice? The writer must compose an entire story or message on his or her own. This is a far more difficult means of communication than speaking. In conversation, the speaker is aided by the verbal and nonverbal responses of the listener. In conversation, if something is not clear, or not enough information has been supplied, the listener will frown or ask a question. Context also aids communication. For example, if speaker and listener are on a baseball diamond watching a pitcher, context will reinforce a conversation about pitching.

What might they already know about the topic?

What do they need to know?

The answers to these questions should help sharpen students' focus and provide them with a plan for gathering information. As they look over what they need to know and what they want to tell their audience, students can begin collecting information from books, family members, computer databases, or experts. They might then use semantic webs or other diagrams to help them organize their information. Again, audience comes into play as students ask themselves, "How can I present this information so that my audience will understand it?" Teacher modeling, mini-lessons, and conferences with teacher and peers might be used to help students organize their material.

REVISING

Revising is that part of the writing process in which the author reconsiders and alters what she or he has written.

Professional writers often spend more time **revising** than they do composing. Although a fortunate few report running the story through the typewriter or word processor once, others talk of constant revision, going through as many as five drafts. The wife of humorist James Thurber typically dismissed his first draft of a story as "high school stuff." But his response was "Wait until the seventh draft, it'll work out all right" (Plimpton & Steele, 1977, cited in Grauer, 1994, p. xix).

For many students, revising means making mechanical corrections—putting in missing periods and capital letters, and checking suspicious spellings. Actually, revising goes to the heart of the piece and could involve adding or

Exemplary Teaching

Writing in Kindergarten

A teacher and teaching principal for thirty years, Judy Meagher of Bozeman, Montana, wisely allows her first-graders to spell as best they can. She explains:

> If I insist on correct spelling, they will be afraid to venture beyond a limited "The big dog can jump" or "I like to run and play." I know they have much more to say than that, and I want them to be able to express their ideas and feelings. That's why I also accept invented spelling at first. (Silberman, 1989, p. 93)

Released from the restriction of correct spelling, the children are able to write imaginative pieces that feature a rich vocabulary. As the year progresses,

students' spelling, with an assist from Meagher, gradually becomes more conventional.

Personal communication with a purpose is emphasized in the class. When students have a problem, they are encouraged to tell about it on a five-by-eight card and place the card on the teacher's desk. A quick reply from the teacher keeps the cards rolling in. Each week, one of the students is chosen to become the honored recipient of letters from the other members of the class. Each letter tells something that the writer likes about the student. The letters are then placed in a booklet, which the child can keep. At year's end, the members of Meagher's class write letters welcoming the kindergarteners to first grade. These letters reflect the first-graders' growing proficiency in writing and often contain remarks indicating how much they have enjoyed their learning.

deleting material, changing the sequence, getting a better lead, adding details, or substituting more vivid words for trite expressions. Revising means rethinking a work and can, in fact, lead to a total reworking of the piece. Revision may be aided by a peer conference or a conference with the teacher.

MODELING THE REVISION PROCESS

One way of conveying the concept of revision is for the teacher to model the process. The teacher puts an original draft that he or she has written on the chalkboard or overhead. She or he poses pertinent questions such as: "Does this piece say what I want it to say? Have I fully explained what I want to say? Is it clear? Is it interesting? Is it well organized?" The teacher can then show how to add details, clarify a confusing passage, or switch sentences around. The teacher might also model some of the more productive revising routines. Essential routines include rewriting for clarity, rewriting beginnings and endings to give them more impact, substituting more vivid or more appropriate words, rearranging sentences or paragraphs, and adding additional examples or details.

Over a series of lessons, the teacher shows students how to make revisions, as indicated by the kinds of writing challenges that students are meeting. One group might be grappling with lead sentences, whereas another group might not be fully developing ideas. In time, students can demonstrate to their peers how they successfully revised a piece. Having professional writers such as children's authors and newspaper reporters visit the class to demonstrate how they revise will emphasize the importance of revision and the fact that virtually everyone who writes must do it.

Instruction should also include the mechanical techniques of revision. Students can cross out, cut and paste, and use carets to insert to their hearts' content. Long insertions may be indicated with an asterisk and placed on a separate sheet of paper. Students should be encouraged to revise as much as they feel they have to. To remind students of the kinds of things they should be doing when they revise, you might develop a revision checklist. Figure 11.1 presents a sample checklist.

Revising takes objectivity. To distance themselves from their writing, professional writers usually let a piece sit for at least twenty-four hours and then take a good, hard look at it. Often, ideas for changes will occur to them that they would not have thought of immediately after writing.

Students have five areas of concern in writing: spelling, motor aesthetic (handwriting and appearance), convention, topic information, and revision (Graves, 1983). Although they operate in all five areas from the very first stages of writing, early emphasis is on the lower-level processes: spelling, motor aesthetic, and convention. New writers find it most difficult to revise content. However, what the teacher stresses in class also has an effect on what the child emphasizes. Given good teaching, children will put aside concern about spelling, handwriting, and appearance and concentrate on improving content and expression. Spelling, handwriting, and conventions must be taught but in perspective. Mechanical issues usually recede into the background by the time a child is 7 years old or so, but if overemphasized, they could "last a lifetime" (Graves, 1983, p. 237). From an early concern with spelling and handwriting, children can be led to add information to

Be sure to model the revision process. Show students how you read and reread a draft and decide what changes need to be made. With the class, devise a revision checklist, one that fits the students' abilities and needs. A key question to ask is "Does it sound right?" In addition to developing ownership, students should develop an "ear" for good writing.

See the section "Technology and Writing" later in this chapter for suggestions on revising with a word processor.

FIGURE 11.1   A sample revision checklist

_____ Does the piece say what I want it to say?

_____ Will the audience understand it?

_____ Is it interesting?

_____ What might I do to make it more interesting?

_____ Did I give enough details or examples?

_____ Does it sound right?

their pieces and, later, to making more complex revisions such as reordering sentences or clarifying confusing points. One of the last revision skills to develop is the ability—and willingness—to delete material that should be left out.

Conferences help children move beyond mechanical revisions. "Revisions that children make as a result of the conference can be at a much higher level than those made when the child is working and reading alone" (Graves, 1983, p. 153). This is an excellent manifestation of Vygotsky's (1987) concept of zone of proximal development, which states that with the support of adults, children can operate on a higher level and, ultimately, perform higher-level tasks on their own. In other words, what students ask for help with now, they will be able to do on their own in the future.

As with other cognitive activities, younger students are less likely to monitor their writing. For example, they may fail to consider the background or interests of their intended audience (Maimon & Nodine, 1979). Through skillful questioning in conferences, the teacher can help students see their writing from the point of view of the audience. This helps them figure out what they want to say and how to say it so others will understand. The teacher provides an executive structure to help students revise effectively (Scardamalia & Bereiter, 1986). In time, students internalize such a structure, allowing them to monitor their writing just as they learn with experience and instruction to monitor their reading.

There is some danger in overemphasizing revising. Although all pieces should be reread carefully, they may not have to be revised or may require only minor changes. This is especially true if the writer is experienced and has prepared carefully before writing. Knowing when to revise and when not to revise is an important skill.

EDITING

In the editing stage, students check carefully for mechanical errors, adding commas and question marks and correcting misspelled words. Ideally, all mechanical errors should be corrected. Realistically, the teacher should stress certain major elements. For some students, correcting all errors could be a very discouraging process. The degree of editing depends on students' maturity and proficiency.

Editing can begin as early as kindergarten, with children checking to make sure they put names, dates, and page numbers on their pieces (Calkins, 1986). As new skills are acquired, the items to be checked increase to include spelling, punctuation, capitalization, and so on.

FIGURE 11.2   A sample editing checklist

_____ Is my story clear? Will readers be able to understand it?

_____ Did I write in complete sentences?

_____ Did I capitalize the first word of every sentence?

_____ Did I capitalize the names of people, cities, towns, and other places?

_____ Did I end each sentence with a period, question mark, or exclamation point?

_____ Did I spell all the words correctly?

Just as with revision, editing should be modeled. Children should also have access to its tools: pencils, a dictionary, easy style guides, and editing checklists. Such checklists help support students' evolving executive function and encourage them to focus on the conventions of writing, which require looking at writing objectively and abstractly. Such a checklist should be geared to the students' expertise and experience; a sample is presented in Figure 11.2. Peer editing can also be employed. However, this is just an additional check. The authors should realize that ultimately it is their responsibility to correct errors.

As part of learning the editing process, students should be introduced to the use of a writer's indispensable tool—the dictionary. Although students may understand that the dictionary is used to look up the meanings and spellings of unfamiliar words, they may not realize that dictionaries can be used to check capitalization and usage and that most dictionaries contain sections on grammar, punctuation, forming endings, ways to address dignitaries, and correct forms for business and friendly letters and thank-you notes. Model the various ways in which the dictionary can be used in editing and, as the need arises, encourage and guide students in their use of the dictionary. If possible, each student should have a copy of a dictionary on the appropriate level. Also model and encourage the use of style guides and thesauruses. If these tools are available on word-processing programs used by the class, show how the computerized versions are used.

When deciding which editing skills to introduce, examine students' current writing and see what is most needed. Sometimes, the nature of the writing will dictate the skill. If students are writing pieces in which they will be talking about titles of books, introduce italicizing and underlining. After you have taught a skill, have students add it to their editing checklists. Also display a brief explanation or example of the skill's use on the bulletin board, as shown in Figure 11.3, so that students have a reminder of it (Muschla, 1993).

As a final editing check, the teacher should examine the piece before approving it for copying onto good paper or typing. The teacher might decide to note _all_ errors for an advanced student and only focus on one or two areas for a less

Underline the titles of books, magazines, newpapers, and movies:
<u>Charlotte's Web</u>, <u>Weekly Reader</u>, <u>Sports Illustrated for Kids</u>, <u>Jurassic Park</u>.
(If you are using a word processor, italicize instead of underlining.
Underlining is used to tell printers to use italics.)

Publishing gives a writing program vitality. As teachers in New Zealand commented, "Where publication has not been part of the writing [programs], or has been treated in a casual manner, there has been a general lack of interest in writing. The [programs] lacked impact because no purpose and audience had been determined for the writing. As a result, children tended to see writing as a neat copy produced to order. Classrooms that allowed children to negotiate time to reach a published form of work seemed to achieve higher overall standards of writing" (Learning Media, 1991, p. 71).

advanced student. If the piece is to be published, however, all errors should be corrected. The corrections should be handled in such a way that the child is not deprived of pride in his product. Making such corrections must be recognized for the lower-level, mechanical skill that it is.

The writing process has been described step by step to make it more understandable; however, in reality, many steps may be operating at the same time, and the steps are not necessarily executed in order. For example, writers mentally plan and revise and edit as they compose (Scardamalia & Bereiter, 1986). Books designed to assist young writers are listed in the Children's Book List.

Children's Book List
Books for young writers

Asher, S. *Where Do You Get Your Ideas?* New York: Walker (1987). Practical suggestions for thinking up and developing topic ideas.

James, E., & Barkin, C. *Sincerely Yours: How to Write Great Letters.* New York: Clarion (1993). Discussion of the general purposes of writing letters and the elements of different types of personal and business letters. Includes information on pen pals.

Juster, N. *As: A Surfeit of Similes.* New York: W. W. Morrow (1989). Explanations of dozens of similes.

Leedy, L. *Messages in the Mailbox.* New York: Holiday House (1991). Discussion of different kinds of letters and the parts of a letter with examples.

Livingstone, M. C. *Poem-Making: Ways to Begin Writing Poetry.* New York: HarperCollins (1991). Discussion of poetry and how to write it by a poet.

Maberry, D. L. *Tell Me about Yourself: How to Interview Anyone from Your Friends to Famous People.* Minneapolis: Lerner (1985). How to plan and conduct an interview, and how to use and integrate the information from an interview into a report.

Otfinoski, S. *The Scholastic Guide to Putting It in Writing.* New York: Scholastic (1993). Examples, models, and advice for writing letters to friends, relatives, and businesses or preparing school reports.

Ryan, E. A. *How to Be a Better Writer.* Mahwah, NJ: Troll (1992). Suggestions for practical techniques for improving one's writing.

PUBLISHING

As Emig (1971) noted in her landmark study, students all too often write for an audience of one—the teacher—which limits their style. Students tend to write in a way they think will be most appealing to the teacher and so never gain a true sense of audience. In the writing process approach, the emphasis is on writing for real purposes and real audiences, and on going public with the works. Poems are collected in anthologies. Stories are bound in books, which are placed in the library. Essays and reports are shared and placed on classroom and school bulletin boards. Scripts are dramatized. Essays and stories are entered in contests and printed in class and school publications, or submitted to children's magazines that print young people's works. Other ways of **publishing** include creating charts, posters, ads, brochures, announcements, sets of directions, book reviews, and video- or audiotapes.

To emphasize the importance of the writer, the teacher might arrange to have a student share his or her writing orally through use of the **author's chair.** Seated in this special chair, the author reads her or his piece to the class and invites comments. Special assemblies are also held to honor authors. Professional writers are invited to share with the other writers in the class. With publication and celebration, children put their hearts into their writing.

Publishing is the part of the writing process in which the author makes his or her writing public.

Author's chair is an activity in which a student author shares his or her work with the rest of the class.

Exemplary Teaching

Making the Switch to Writing Process

Cynthia Holton had an outstanding reading program for her second-graders that included a substantial classroom library and the use of drama. But her writing program was another story. Trained in traditional ways, she taught writing as she had been taught. Emphasis was on turning in a correct piece on an assigned topic on the first try. After attending workshops on the process approach, she encouraged students to choose topics, at least some of the time, and she stressed the idea of writing drafts in which the author tries out ideas that may then be revised. But one of the main changes was that she was no longer the primary audience for her students' writing:

As Holton explained, before she had served as an audience of one. "The kids always wanted to know what I wanted because I was the only person who mattered." No more. Today she and all the children in the class respond to a writer's work. "In a few minutes, you'll see the class gather on the rug in the back of the room," Holton told an observer. "Today Stephanie will be sitting in the author's chair, reading a piece that she's having a problem finishing. With twenty-five writing 'teachers' realizing that she is writing to attract their interests, not just my comments, I think she'll get the help she needs." (Silberman, 1989, p. 107)

CONFERENCES

Conferences are conversations between teacher and student(s) or among students, which are designed to foster the development of one or more aspects of the writing process.

Wanting to improve her writing, Lucy McCormick Calkins (1986) wrote to Donald Murray, a well-known writing teacher, and asked if he could help her. Murray agreed to hold **conferences** with her once a month. For two years, Calkins made the five-hour round trip from Connecticut to the University of New Hampshire for a fifteen-minute conference, which was primarily a conversation about her writing. Was the drive worth it? According to Calkins, yes: "He taught me I had something to say" (p. 124).

If a conference does not show writers that they have something to say, it fails to achieve its purpose. Through encouraging, gentle questioning and responding, the teacher tells the writer, "You have a story to tell!" A conference is an affirmation. A belief in young people is the only unbreakable rule for conducting conferences. If we have a fundamental faith that everyone has a story to tell, we do not supply topics. Students must search within themselves and their experiences for subjects to write about. If we start directing and shaping, we are taking over the topic. Written under our direction, the piece may actually sound better, but it will be our piece—we will have stolen it from the student. Through careful questioning and responding, help students discover their stories and techniques for telling them. According to Turbill (1982), the teacher "is advised to develop the art of questioning; instead of telling what to do, [the teacher] uses questions to move the child to find answers" (p. 35).

CONFERENCE QUESTIONS

In a typical conference, three types of questions are asked: opening, following, and process. They are nonjudgmental and are intended to evoke an open and honest response. Opening questions might take one of the following forms: How is it going? How is your piece coming? What are you working on today? The student's response provides clues for following questions, which are asked to find out more about how the child's writing is progressing. Process questions such as "What will you do next?" prompt students to make plans or take action. However, do not be so concerned about asking questions that you forget to listen. Calkins (1986) cautioned, "Our first job in a conference, then, is to be a person, not just a teacher. It is to enjoy, to care, and to respond" (p. 119).

Sometimes, a human response is all that is necessary. At other times, the teacher reflects the child's line of thinking but gently nudges the child forward. The student might say, for example, "I'm not sure how to describe my dog. My dog isn't a purebred." The teacher reflects that concern by saying, "You're not sure how to describe your dog because he is just an ordinary dog?" The repetition is a gentle expression of interest that encourages the child to elaborate and continue the flow. If that does not work, more directed responses might include such questions as "You say your dog isn't a purebred, but is there anything special about him? What does your dog look like? Can you think of anything about the way your dog acts or looks that might set him apart from other dogs?" Care must be taken that questions are not too directed, or there may be the danger that the teacher is taking over the writing. The purpose of the questioning is to have writers explore ways in which they might develop their work.

If a piece is confusing, the teacher might say, "I liked the way you talked about the funny things your dog did, but I don't understand how you taught him

TABLE 11.1 Teacher prompts for common writing difficulties

Writing Difficulty	Teacher Prompts
Topic is too broad or lacks focus.	What is your purpose in writing this? What's the most important or most interesting idea here? How might you develop that?
Piece lacks details or examples.	I like your piece about _____. But I don't know very much about _____. Can you tell more about it?
Needs a beginning sentence	How might you start this off? What might you say to pull your reader into this story?
Inadequate conclusion or lack of ending	How might you sum up what you've said? What thought or idea do you want your reader to take away from this?
Lack of coherence or unity	What is your main purpose here? Do all your ideas fit? Are your ideas in the best order?

Adapted from *Writing Workshop Survival Kit* by G. R. Muschla, 1993, West Nyack, NY: The Center for Applied Research in Education.

to roll over." The child will then tell how she or he taught the dog to roll over and most likely realize that this is an element to be included in the piece. If not, the teacher leads the child in that direction.

If a child has not developed a piece adequately, the teacher might say, "You said your dog was always getting into trouble. Can you tell me what kind of trouble he gets into?" Often, the response will be an oral rehearsal for what to write in the next draft. "They tell me what they are going to write in the next draft, and they hear their own voices telling me. I listen and they learn" (Murray, 1979, p. 16). Table 11.1 presents some common writing difficulties that students encounter and teacher prompts that might be used to help them focus on these difficulties. At times, students will reject the teacher's hints or suggestions, preferring to take a piece in a different direction. That is their prerogative. After each conference, note the student's writing strengths, needs, plans, and other pertinent information. A sample writing conference summary sheet is shown in Figure 11.4.

PEER CONFERENCES

Conferences with peers can also be very helpful. Effective peer conferencing is a learned behavior. Discuss the ingredients of a successful conference and then model and supervise the process. In addition to being effective and producing improved writing, conferences must be humane and should build a sense of community and respect. Some general principles of conferencing include the following:

- Students should learn to listen carefully.
- Students should lead off with a positive comment about the piece.
- Students should make concrete suggestions.
- Suggestions should be put in positive terms.

Name	Date	Topic	Strengths	Needs	Plans
Angel	11/15	Football game	Exciting opening.	Key part not clear.	Tell how he caught pass.
Amy	11/15	Pet rabbit	Interesting subject.	Not developed enough.	Give examples of pet's tricks.
James		Little sister			
Keisha		Making friends			
Maria		Dream vacation			
Marsha		Recycling trash			
Robert		Letter to sports star			
Stephanie		New bicycle			

Adapted from *Writing Workshop Survival Kit* by G. R. Muschla, 1993, West Nyack, NY: The Center for Applied Research in Education.

Working with a student, model a peer conference and show how suggestions can be used to make revisions.

AUTHORS' CIRCLE

Authors' circle is a form of peer conferencing in which students meet to discuss their drafts and obtain suggestions for possible revision.

One form of peer conference is the **authors' circle.** When students have pieces they wish to share, they gather at an authors' table and read their works to each other. The teacher may join the circle. The only requirement is that everyone in the circle have a work he or she wishes to read (Harste, Short, & Burke, 1988).

The authors' circle is designed for rough drafts rather than edited pieces. By seeking and listening to the reactions of others, students can determine whether their works need clarification and which parts might have to be revised. Both authors and listeners benefit from the circle. Harste, Short, and Burke (1988) commented:

> As they shared their stories with others through informal interactions and authors' circles, the children shifted from taking the perspective of an author to taking the perspective of reader and critic. These shifts occurred as they read their pieces aloud and listened to the comments other authors made about their stories. As children became aware of their audience, they were able to see their writing in a different light. (p. 32)

WRITING WORKSHOP

Just as students learn to read by reading, they learn to write by writing. The **writing workshop** is a way of organizing writing instruction that fosters active engagement of pen, pencil, magic marker, word processor, or whatever writing instrument students choose to use. The writing workshop combines whole class instruction, individual and group conferences, and opportunity to write. Although the workshop lends itself to a flexible organization, it typically has three major parts: mini-lesson, writing time (during which conferences are held), and sharing. If possible, the workshop should be held every day.

Writing workshop is a way of organizing writing instruction that includes a mini-lesson, time for students to write and participate in individual and group conferences, and whole class sharing.

MINI-LESSON

The purpose of the mini-lesson is to present a needed writing skill or concept. The skill could be writing interesting beginnings, capitalizing titles, selecting topics, taking notes, providing convincing examples, using correct letter form, or any one

In the authors' circle, students who have pieces to share gather at an authors' table and read their works to each other.

of a dozen other skills. Ideally, the skill or topic covered is one for which the class has demonstrated a need and one that they will be able to apply during the upcoming workshop. Although time is somewhat flexible, the mini-lesson should be limited to five to ten minutes. During the writing session, the teacher can guide students as they apply the skill that has just been taught and can supply needed clarification or elaboration.

WRITING TIME

Writing time, which is the core of the workshop, lasts for twenty to thirty minutes or longer. During that time, students work on their individual pieces, have peer or teacher conferences, or meet in small groups to discuss their writing. Before beginning this portion of the lesson, you may want to check with students to see what their plans are for this period.

As students write, circulate in the classroom and supply on-the-spot help or encouragement as needed. You might show one student how to use the spell checker, applaud another who has just finished a piece, encourage a third who is searching for just the right ending, and discuss topic possibilities with a student who cannot seem to decide what to write about. You might also have scheduled conferences with several students or sit in on a peer conference that students have convened.

GROUP SHARING

At appropriate times, such as the end of the day, students gather for group sharing. Volunteers read their pieces. The atmosphere is positive, and other students listen attentively and tell the author what they like about the piece. They also ask questions, make suggestions, and might inquire about the author's future plans for writing. Through large-group sharing, a sense of community is built. Student writers are shown appreciation by their audience. They also have the opportunity to hear what their peers are writing about, what techniques their peers are using, and what struggles they are having.

MANAGEMENT OF THE WRITING WORKSHOP

Active and multifaceted, the writing workshop requires careful management. The room should be well organized. Professional writers have offices, studies, or at least desks at which to work. They also have access to the tools of writing. The classroom should be set up as a writer's workshop. Younger students need an assortment of soft lead pencils, crayons, magic markers, and sheets of unlined paper. Older students can get by with pencil and paper but should have some choices, too. At times, they might feel the need to write on a yellow legal pad or with a pink magic marker. You should have a round table or two for group meetings, a word-processing or editing corner, and a reference corner that contains a dictionary, style guide, almanac, and other references. Staplers, paper, and writing instruments of various kinds should be placed in the supply corner. Writing folders or portfolios should be arranged alphabetically in cartons. Involve students in helping with housekeeping chores. They can take turns seeing that materials are put away and that writing folders are in order.

Before starting the workshop, explain the setup of the room and show where supplies and materials are located. With the class, develop a series of rules and routines. Before students engage in peer conferences or small sharing groups, discuss and model these activities.

Be aware of students' productivity. Students should have specific plans for each day's workshop: revise a piece, confer with the teacher, obtain additional information about a topic, start a new piece. Make sure that peer conferences are devoted to writing and not last night's TV programs. Also note students who do more conferencing than writing, those who never seem to confer, and those who have been on the same piece for weeks. You might keep a record of students' activities in a daily log. A sample daily log, adapted from Muschla (1993), is presented in Figure 11.5.

As you circulate in the room, note students' strengths and weaknesses. During the mini-lesson or sharing period, call attention to the positive things that you saw: Mary Lou's colorful use of language, Fred's title, Jamie's interesting topic. Needs that you note might be the basis for a future mini-lesson or a brief, on-the-spot, one-on-one lesson or—if several students display a common need—a small-group lesson.

Most of all, serious writing demands time. Even professionals need a warm-up period to get into their writing. Once the thoughts begin to flow on paper, however, writers have to keep on writing. If possible, at least thirty minutes to an hour a day, three to five days a week, should be set aside for writing.

INTERACTIVE WRITING

A highly motivating method for eliciting writing from students is **interactive writing,** which is a written dialogue or conversation. It can be conducted between teacher and student, two students, student and pen pal, or student and grandparent or other adult. Interactive writing most often takes the form of dialogue journals but can be embodied in letters, notes, messages left in computer mailboxes, or written conversations.

Interactive writing is writing that is exchanged and responded to by two participants over a period of time.

In a **written conversation,** two students or a student and a teacher converse by writing to each other. Either party may initiate the conversation, which may be conducted at a table or other convenient spot and include the teacher and one or more students. The teacher might start with a statement or a question such as, "How is your new puppy?" The student responds, and then the teacher replies. As one student is responding, the teacher can initiate a written conversation with a second student, and then a third.

Written conversation is a type of writing in which teacher and student or two students carry on a conversation by writing a series of notes to each other.

Written conversations provide practice in both reading and writing. The teacher's writing is geared to the student's reading level. If the student's reading level is very limited, the teacher can read her letter to the student. If a student's writing ability is so rudimentary that the teacher cannot understand it, the student is asked to read it.

FIGURE 11.5   Daily log: Students' plans for writing workshop

Name	Topic	M	T	W	Th	F
Angel	Football game	D-1, TC	RE			
Amy	Pet rabbit	E, TC	PE			
James	Little sister	AC	R, TC			
Keisha	Making friends	AC	M			
Maria	Dream vacation	TC, D-2	E			
Marsha	Recycling trash	M	P, S			
Robert	Letter to sports star	AC	R			
Stephanie	New bicycle	R	D-3, TC			

Key

P: Planning	PE: Peer editing	PC: Peer conference
D: Drafting	P: Publishing	TC: Teacher conference
R: Revising	M: Making final copy	AC: Authors' circle
E: Editing	RE: Researching	S: Sharing

Adapted from *Writing Workshop Survival Kit* by G. R. Muschla, 1993, West Nyack, NY: The Center for Applied Research in Education.

Written conversation has been used successfully with students of varied ages and abilities. Duffy (1994) used written conversation with primary-grade students. When visiting a writing group, she would jot down an initiating sentence in each of their journals. As they wrote responses, Duffy would visit another group and then return to the first group to reply to their responses. The activity was both productive and enjoyable. Prompted by the teacher's writing, typical student responses might produce up to one hundred words, far more than would normally be written. The students also enjoyed the written conversations. According to Duffy, the activity was special because "it offers them the individual attention of the teacher, and it offers the teacher as a person rather than as a teacher" (p. 41).

Written conversations have also been used with older learning-disabled children. With these students, both reading and writing fluency increased (Rhodes & Dudley-Marling, 1988).

The use of interactive writing does raise several issues. Students' privacy must be respected. Teacher responses need to be genuine, caring, and sensitive. If health or safety concerns are raised because of information revealed by students, consult with the school principal regarding your legal and ethical responsibilities.

KEEPING TRACK

Students should have a place to store and keep track of their completed works, works in progress, and future writing plans. File folders make convenient, inexpensive portfolios. Two for each student are recommended—one for completed works and one for works in progress. The works-in-progress folder should also contain an editing checklist, a list of skills mastered, a list of topics attempted, and a list of possible topics.

The works-completed folder, or portfolio, provides a means for examining the student's development. If all drafts of a piece are saved, the teacher can see how the student progressed through the writing steps. A comparison of current works with beginning pieces will show how the writer has developed over the course of the year. Careful examination of the portfolio's contents should reveal strengths and weaknesses and provide insights into interests and abilities. While

One of the main benefits of using portfolio assessment is that it provides the student with a means for examining and reflecting upon her or his work. To get the most out of portfolios, students should set goals, periodically reflect upon their work, and evaluate their portfolios in light of their goals.

Students should have specific plans for each day's writing workshop.

reading through the portfolio, the teacher might try to ascertain whether a student is finding his or her own voice, has a pattern of interests, is showing a bent for certain kinds of writing, is applying certain techniques, and is being challenged to grow and develop. The teacher then decides what will best help the student progress further.

Students should also examine their portfolios with a critical eye. What have they learned? What topics have they explored? What pieces do they like best? What kinds of writing do they enjoy most? What are some signs of growth? What questions do they have about their writing? What would help them become better writers? Are there some kinds of writing that they have not yet attempted but would like to try? Of course, teacher and student should confer about the portfolio, reviewing past accomplishments, planning future goals, discussing current concerns, and setting up future goals and projects. (For more information on portfolio assessment, see Chapter 13.)

TECHNOLOGY AND WRITING

The invention of the printing press revolutionized the world's reading and writing habits. To a lesser extent, so did the availability of cheap paper and the invention of inexpensive, easy-to-use writing instruments, such as pencils with erasers and ballpoint pens. Today, the computer is making significant changes in the ways in which we record our ideas.

WORD-PROCESSING PROGRAMS

Word processing is the use of a computer and software to perform the typing and correction of manuscript.

The computer's primary use is for **word processing.** Word-processing programs have taken the drudgery out of revising. No longer is it necessary to recopy a piece just because a revision has been made. Computer editing programs allow the user to move words, phrases, sentences, or whole passages; eliminate unwanted words and other elements; and revise elements with a minimum of effort. Many programs also contain spell checkers that alert students to possible spelling and typing errors. Some programs include a thesaurus so student writers can seek substitutes for overworked words. The more sophisticated programs will even check grammar, indicate average sentence length, and note certain characteristics of style that might require alteration, such as overusing certain words and writing mostly in simple sentences.

Text-to-speech word-processing programs such as *Dr. Peet's Talk/Writer* (Hartley) or *Special Writer Coach* (Tom Snyder) say the words that students type in. These programs are especially helpful for students with impaired vision and very young students. They can also be used by students who have difficulty detecting errors in their writing. Students who reread a written piece without detecting a dropped *-ed* or *-ing,* missing words, or awkward phrases often notice these errors when they hear the computer read the piece aloud.

To obtain full benefit from a word-processing system, students must be instructed in its use. The following are some key elements that should be covered:

- Learning the keyboard
- Starting up the program
- Making editing changes, beginning with the easiest and progressing to the most difficult. These editing changes would generally follow the sequence of eliminating a letter, word, or sentence; substituting a letter, word, or sentence; adding a letter, word, or sentence; moving a whole sentence or paragraph; using a single command to change a word that appears in several places; and using the spell checker, thesaurus, and grammar checker.
- Formatting a disk on which to save writing
- Saving one's writing on a disk
- Printing out a piece using various options
- Changing fonts and type size and using boldface and italic

Generally, it is advisable for students to compose their first drafts with pencil and paper because they are faster at writing than they are at typing. In addition, computers are in short supply in most elementary schools. Restricting word processing to revised and final drafts increases availability of the computer.

Word-processing programs come with a host of features, and there are dozens of programs to choose from. Some are general-purpose; others are designed for school use and contain features that help with the writing process, such as suggestions for planning. Teachers in a school or district might want to get together to decide on one word-processing program so that students do not have to relearn a new program in each grade. As students progress through the grades, they can also learn to use more advanced features, such as the grammar checker and italicizing. Here is a sampling of word-processing programs:

Bank Street Writer for the Macintosh by Scholastic (Mac only): The program contains a built-in spell checker and thesaurus, as well as a graphic gallery for adding illustrations. It also has a series of hypertext operations: note buttons, so that students can add notes to their piece; a file button, which allows students to store relevant information; and sound buttons, so that students can include oral notes or a commentary, or just for thinking aloud. The network version allows you to set up an e-mail community.

Dr. Peet's Talk/Writer by Hartley (Apple II, PC, Mac): This program teaches letter identification and how to find letters on the keyboard. It can be used by very young students. A talking word processor, it says words and gives spoken directions.

Microsoft Word by Microsoft (Mac, PC): Although designed for adults, Microsoft Word can be used by primary-grade children if they stick with the basic features and functions. As students grow in writing and word-processing skills, they can use more advanced features. One feature that elementary students will enjoy is the import capability, which allows them to insert illustrations in their pieces.

Special Writer Coach by Tom Snyder (Mac): This software was specifically designed for students who have difficulty writing. It features speech capability, error detection, and prompts that can be customized.

Adapting instruction for students with disabilities

With the help of computers, students with a variety of physical and learning disabilities can become writers. For students who have difficulty with keyboarding or spelling, word-prediction and abbreviation-expansion software can be used to ease the burden of keyboarding. When the first letter of a word is typed, the software predicts what the full word might be and inserts it. If the prediction is wrong, the student chooses from a list of alternatives or types in the second letter.

Word-processing programs encourage experimentation. With the MOVE function, for instance, it is relatively easy to shift sentences or paragraphs and to compare the original with altered versions to see which sounds best.

Adapting instruction for students with disabilities

There are various adaptive input devices that can be used as long as the student can make a consistent, reliable movement (Zorfass, Corley, & Remey, 1994). For students who are unable to keyboard, voice-activated software is available. One such piece, *Dragon Dictate,* has been specifically designed for schools. *Dragon Dictate* is only about 90 percent accurate, so it will supply some incorrect words.

DESKTOP PUBLISHING

Desktop publishing is a system that combines word processing with layout and other graphic design features so that the user can place print and graphic elements on a page.

One advantage of word processing is that it makes students' text readily visible, thereby making it easier for the teacher to take a quick look at their work. This visibility also makes peer conferencing and collaboration easier (Zorfass, Corley, & Remey, 1994).

As the last step in the writing process, publishing is often ignored. However, it is the step that gives purpose to writing. **Desktop publishing,** as its name suggests, provides publishing opportunities where none existed before. With it, students can produce high-quality posters, banners, signs, forms, brochures, résumés, classroom or school newspapers, and newsletters for clubs. They can also illustrate stories or write stories based on illustrations.

In addition to motivating writing and providing a means of disseminating students' works, desktop publishing combines the visual with the verbal arts. Students not only write their pieces, they design them and select or create illustrations for them. They also learn to work cooperatively; children who have a way with words team up with those who have an eye for visual elements. The two groups learn from each other.

Perhaps desktop publishing's greatest advantage is that it leads to more polished writing. Without any coercion by the teacher, students take one last look at their pieces before having them printed out. Often, they discover a misspelled word, an awkward phrase, or erroneous punctuation that would have gone unnoticed.

Three popular desktop publishing systems are as follows:

The Children's Writing and Publishing Center by the Learning Company (Apple II, PC, Mac): This system features word processing, page design, and illustration capabilities. It is available in an English or a Spanish version, and the Bilingual Writing Center features both versions.

Kid Works II by Davidson (Mac, PC): This system combines a word processor, speech capabilities, and story illustration features. Students can create, illustrate, and have their stories read aloud. In addition, it has a dictionary of several hundred pictured nouns, verbs, and adjectives. Students can, therefore, include in their writing words that they might not have used because of their inability to spell them. The program features a manuscript font on a screen that looks like double-lined primary writing paper, so the program's printing is very similar to students' manuscript writing and would be most appropriate in the primary grades.

Kids' Stories by Storm Software (Mac, PC): In addition to full-feature word-processing and page design, this system contains a library of nearly one thousand pictures that students can use to help tell stories. In the CD-ROM version, students can insert their own photos by first having their 35-mm film digitized and placed on a CD-ROM disc (a service available at stores that process Kodak film).

In addition to these general systems, there are number of desktop publishing systems that can be used for specialized tasks:

The Amazing Writing Machine by Broderbund (Mac): This system helps students generate ideas and designs to illustrate their pieces.

Dinosaur Days Plus by Pelican (Mac): This system allows students to create their own dinosaurs by using clip art of dinosaurs. Using conversation bubbles, which have speech capability, students can show the dinosaurs talking or making dinosaur noises.

My Media Text Workshop by Wings for Learning/Sunburst (Mac): This highly motivating package enables students to put together a multimedia presentation by integrating print, graphics, animation, film, and sound clips.

Pelican Press for the Macintosh by Pelican (Mac): This system is designed to create posters, signs, cards, and even calendars. It features an extensive library of illustrations, borders, and backgrounds.

Storybook Weaver by MECC (Mac): This system includes 650 images from cultures around the world, which students can use to prompt or illustrate their writing.

TEACHING FORM

In helping young writers, teachers tend to stress content, which is as it should be. However, some attention has to be paid to form, especially when children are exploring new modes, such as a first attempt to write an informational piece or a mystery. Instruction in form can actually improve content. Paris (cited in Scardamalia & Bereiter, 1986) taught a group of children the structure for an opinion/proof piece. Included in the instruction were ways to recognize beliefs and supporting ideas as well as examples of both sides of an argument in persuasive pieces that the students were reading. Although students were not instructed to use these elements in their writing, they did. Their compositions showed increased use of reasons and examples to buttress statements of belief. It was an intriguing demonstration that form can improve content.

Although some students seem to have a natural bent for narrative and others prefer composing expository text, all students should become acquainted with all major structures, learning how each is written and developed. Part of that instruction simply involves having children read widely in order to acquire a rich background of comparison/contrast, problem/solution, and other expository and narrative structures. However, instruction should also include explaining each structure, modeling the writing of it, and having students compose similar structures.

In a program known as **Cognitive Strategy Instruction in Writing**, Raphael, Englert, and Kirschner (1989) combined instruction in text structure and writing strategies to improve students' composing skills. Based on tryouts and experiments that spanned a number of years, these researchers devised strategies that help students make use of text structure to both understand and produce expository prose. In addition to instruction, scaffolding is provided through the use of a series of guides that students might use to plan, compose, and revise their pieces. These guides are dubbed "think sheets" and correspond to the major types of text organization; there are sheets for narrative pieces, compare/contrast structures, explanation, and other text forms. The think sheets are designed to be "concrete

Cognitive Strategy Instruction in Writing is an approach to writing that emphasizes instruction in writing process and text structure and uses think sheets as a scaffolding device. It has been especially useful for students with learning disabilities.

FIGURE 11.6   Planning think sheet

Author's Name: _____   Date: _____

Topic: _Echolocation_____

Who: Who am I writing for?
The kids in my group.

Why: Why am I writing this?
Our group is making a book on dolphins.

What: What is being explained?
How dolphins find objects.

What are the steps?

First,   _Dolphin sends out clicks._

Next,   _Clicks bounce off object._

Third,   _Clicks return to dolphin._

Then,   _Dolphin senses how long it took clicks to return._

Finally,   _Dolphin can tell how far away object is._

Adapted from *Cognitive Strategy Instruction in Writing Project* by C. S. Englert, T. E. Raphael, L. M. Anderson, 1989, East Lansing, MI: Institute for Research on Teaching.

reminders of appropriate strategies to use and of the times when particular strategies might be relevant" (Raphael & Englert, 1990, p. 242).

The first think sheet (shown in Figure 11.6) prompts students to plan their writing by noting their audience and reason for writing and to list details that might be included in the piece. Students might also be asked to group ideas or show how they might be organized: steps in a process, comparison/contrast, or problem/ solution, for instance. Having shown which ideas they will include and how they will organize their writing, students must then consider an interesting beginning and suitable closing. These can be created as students compose a rough draft, or they can be noted at the bottom of the planning think sheet.

After composing their pieces, students use a self-edit think sheet (shown in Figure 11.7) to assess their piece. This think sheet prompts them through the first stage of the revising process and asks them to note if the paper is clear, interesting, and well organized. Since the think sheet will be used by a peer editor to

FIGURE 11.7 | Self-edit think sheet

Author's Name: _____ Date: _____

First, reread my paper. Then answer the following:

What do I like best about my paper? *Gives a good explanation*

Why? *Has all the steps*

What parts are not clear?

Why not?

Did I . . .

1. Tell what was being explained?	(Yes)	Sort of	No
2. Make the steps clear?	(Yes)	Sort of	No
3. Use keywords to make it clear?	(Yes)	Sort of	No
4. Make it interesting to my reader?	Yes	(Sort of)	No

What parts do I want to change?

Make a more interesting beginning

What questions do I have for my editor?

Is the explanation clear?
Is the ending OK?

Keywords such as *first*, *next*, and *last* signal the organization of a piece.

Adapted from *Cognitive Strategy Instruction in Writing Project* by C. S. Englert, T. E. Raphael, L. M. Anderson, 1989, East Lansing, MI: Institute for Research on Teaching.

examine the first draft, the student also notes changes that she or he plans to make or questions for the editor. The peer editor uses the sheet to make recommendations for changes. The editor lists changes that might be made and can also offer suggestions for making the paper more interesting.

After a conference with the peer editor, the student lists the editor's suggestions, decides which ones to use, lists ways of making the paper more interesting, completes a revision think sheet (as shown in Figure 11.8), and then revises the paper.

In real writing, some of the subprocesses presented separately are combined and some may be skipped. Others, such as revision, may be repeated several times. However, it is recommended that students go through all the steps of the process and use the suggested think sheets. Later, as students no longer need scaffolding to use appropriate writing strategies, they may adapt the process. Like

FIGURE 11.8 | Revision think sheet

Suggestions from My Editor

List all the suggestions your editor has given you:

X 1. Use a question as a beginning sentence.

X 2. Use more key words.

X 3. Write a good closing.

   4.

Put an X next to all the suggestions you would like to use in revising your paper. Also think of ideas of your own that might make your paper clearer or more interesting. Read your paper once more, and ask yourself:

Is my beginning interesting? Will it make people want to read my paper? Not exactly

Are the steps in my explanation clear? Yes

Did I write down all the steps? Yes

Are the steps in the right order? Yes

Do I have a good closing sentence? No

Returning to My Draft

On your draft, make all the changes you think will help your paper. Use ideas from the list above, those from your self-edit think sheet, and any other ideas you may have for your paper. When you are ready, you can write your revised copy.

Adapted from *Cognitive Strategy Instruction in Writing Project* by C. S. Englert, T. E. Raphael, L. M. Anderson, 1989, East Lansing, MI: Institute for Research on Teaching.

other forms of scaffolding, think sheets are only intended to be used until students are able to use the strategies without being prompted to do so. Having incorporated the strategies prompted by the think sheets, the students will no longer need them.

SKILLS LESSONS

One problem with a strictly functional approach to teaching writing skills is that essential skills may not receive as much attention as they deserve or may be ignored completely. Functional, opportunistic teaching should be balanced with systematic instruction.

In conferences with teachers and peers, students receive a great deal of informal, fix-it-on-the-spot instruction. However, time also must be set aside in each writing period for more extended instruction in techniques and mechanics. The instruction should be functional and contextual. Skills and strategies taught should be those that students need and can apply to pieces that they are planning or working on. For example, the best time to teach vivid adjectives is when students are working on descriptive pieces. An opportune time to teach commas is when many of the students have been observed misusing them. Instead of inserting commas in sentences on exercise sheets, students concentrate on using commas in their written pieces.

Does this functional approach work? A study of two primary-grade classes revealed that children who were taught punctuation marks when they had to use them in their writing knew more about punctuation and were better able to use the marks than a group of their peers who learned them through drill exercises (Calkins, 1980). Although skills instruction is functional, it should also be systematic and ongoing. Each day, using perhaps fifteen to twenty minutes at the beginning of each writing session, teachers should instruct students in the major skills and techniques appropriate for their level of development.

READING HELPS WRITING

Frequent reading is associated with superior writing. This fact was borne out by the results of several studies reviewed by Stotsky (1983). Students who were assigned additional reading improved as much or more in expository writing as those who studied grammar or who were assigned extra writing practice. It should be noted that the students who improved did engage in writing tasks. Improved writing resulted only when students also engaged in writing.

Reading also has an impact on fiction writing. At the end of a four-year longitudinal study, fourth-graders who had listened to, read, and talked about children's literature in preparation for writing performed better than a control group (Mills, 1974). At the first-grade level, poetry was used to sharpen the students' observations and oral descriptions. Sequence was presented through a dramatization of "The Three Little Pigs," and later, students retold the story. At the third-grade level, the students discussed the settings in *Crow Boy* (Yashima, 1955), *Evan's Corner* (Hill, 1967), and *Little Toot* (Gramatky, 1939), and then created a fictional piece with an emphasis on setting.

Ken Kesey (1989), an accomplished writer who teaches writing courses at the University of Oregon, advises his students to begin writing fiction with a character. His contention is that "it's hard to create any sort of righteous plot without some character" (p. 22).

Mills's research suggests that the quality of reading affects the quality of writing. In a later study, Eckhoff (1983) examined the effects on children's writing of two different basals: one written in a simplified style, the other composed primarily of children's literature. Students who read the simplified basal tended to write in simplified style. Those who read basal stories written in a more elaborate style wrote more complex pieces. Students also picked up the stylistic devices that they encountered. For instance, the words *and* at the beginning of sentences and *too* at the end of sentences appeared frequently in the simplified basals and cropped up often in the writing of the children who used those books. Imitation is a strategy even young children use to learn to write.

One of the most fundamental ways in which reading enhances writing is by providing a model of form. Children's writing reflects the forms with which they are familiar. Calkins (1986) described how a group of sixth-graders moved from reading mysteries to writing their own. Through a discussion of the books they were reading, they came to understand and appreciate the components of a mys-

Poems and stories that students have read can become models for their writing.

tery and believed that the authors were showing them how to write in this genre. One of the members of the group explained it this way:

> Everybody's authors are different. When we have writing conferences, we teach each other what we learn from our authors. . . . I pick a book that has a famous author because if you read famous books, not goofies, you learn to be a better author. In an excellent book like Alfred Hitchcock, I pick out things to put in my story. . . . My writing got better because I started reading more better books and it was like talking with other authors, when I read their books. (p. 257)

Students can also learn stylistic features from their reading. After a trip to the zoo, one first-grade teacher read *The Day Jimmy's Boa Ate the Wash* (Noble, 1980) to the class. The book begins with the query "How was your trip to the zoo?" and goes on to recount a series of amazing and amusing incidents. A student also began his piece with "How was your trip to the zoo?" However, the rest of his work told how one class member became lost and was found watching the tigers. The boy used *The Day Jimmy's Boa Ate the Wash* to shape his piece but not to determine its content (Franklin, 1988). The stylistic device of using an opening question was borrowed, but the content was original.

SWITCHING FROM NARRATIVE TO EXPOSITORY

Reading can help writers make the switch from narrative to expository. Butler and Turbill (1984) described an 8-year-old whose informational piece about animals was a jumble because it was written in narrative style. The child lacked the expository discourse schema and therefore had no background knowledge or mental structure for framing an informational piece. Wisely, the teacher gave him a series of beginning science books to read. Within six weeks, the student had incorporated the patterns of expository text into his own writing.

The key to picking up writing techniques from one's reading is to read like a writer, which means perceiving oneself as a writer (Smith, 1983). Students perceive themselves as writers when they are treated like writers, when their writing is valued, when it is published or made public, and when others respond to it in individual conferences and in group sharing. It also helps if students take note of authors' techniques during discussions of books read. Teachers might make specific recommendations of pieces that students could use as models or sources of techniques. For example, one of Beverly Cleary's or Betsy Byars's works might help a student who is attempting to write conversational prose.

In addition to being a source of ideas, books and articles can also provide model formats. For instance, the *A Day in the Life of* series published by Troll features books describing a typical day in the life of a seeing-eye dog trainer, a museum curator, and other interesting occupations. Students can investigate those occupations in which they have some interest and create books using a similar format. They can also use the format to compose their autobiographies, perhaps including photos or drawings—a day in the life of a fifth-grader, a little sister, or a Little League pitcher.

Reading can also help with topic selection. For instance, reading about some funny incidents that happened to Ramona Quimby, one of Beverly Cleary's characters, may remind students of humorous happenings in their lives. Students can also read books in which one of the characters is a writer (Noyce & Christie, 1989). Beverly Cleary's (1983) *Dear Mr. Henshaw* would be an excellent choice for intermediate students exploring the use of journals.

When students see the connection between published authors and their writing, they become more attuned to devices and modes of writing that they might use in their own work.

As students collect information, they need to ask, "What is the best way to express this information?" Possible forms include verbal essays, photo essays, picture books, letters, plays, and so on. The form should fit the content, the audience, and the author's goals. Forms can be changed. As more information is uncovered about a topic, what might have started out as a brief article, for instance, might grow into a picture book.

A FULL MENU

Students should engage in a full range of writing activities. With guidance, everyone can and should write poetry, plays, and stories. How can we tell what our limits are unless we try? Exploring a new genre helps students understand that particular form and provides them with a different kind of writing experience. Another advantage is that the skills learned in one mode often transfer to other modes. Writing poetry improves word choice and figurative language. Writing plays helps improve dialogue when writing fiction. Fictional techniques enliven expository writing.

Budding writers need a full menu of writing experiences. They should write everything from postcards and thank-you notes to poetry, the most demanding kind of writing. Table 11.2 contains some of the kinds of writing activities that might be introduced in elementary school. It is not a definitive list and offers only suggestions. It should be adapted to fit the needs of your students and your school district's curriculum.

TABLE 11.2 Suggested writing activities

Academic	**Social**	**Creative**
Book review/book report	Friendly letters	Story
Essay test	Postcards	Poem/verse
State competency test	Thank-you notes	Essay (humorous or serious)
	Get-well cards and notes	Play/script
Business/economic	Special occasion cards and notes	
Business letter	Invitations	**Personal**
Consumer complaint	Fan letters	Diary
Correcting a mistake		Journal
Seeking information	**General communication**	
Ordering a product	Announcements	**Writing to learn**
	Newsletters	Comparisons of characters, places, events, issues, processes
Civic/personal development letters		
Letter to the editor	**Newspapers**	Descriptions of characters, persons, places, events, experiments
Making a suggestion	Ads	
Protesting a government decision	Editorial	Diary of events
Requesting help	Features	Journal of observation
Seeking information	Letter to editor	Explanation of processes, events, movements, causes, and effects
	News stories	
Everyday/practical	Photo essay/captions	Summaries of information
Directions		Synthesis of several sources of information
Lists		
Messages (computer, telephone)		Critiquing a story, play, movie, or TV program
Notices		
Signs		

SUMMARY

1. Writing develops from a child's gestures and experiences with language, evolving from scribbles and drawings to letterlike forms, invented spelling, and conventional spelling. Heavily influenced by selections that have been read to them or that they have read, children incorporate storytelling conventions into their earliest writing. More concerned with process than product in the early stages, students gradually learn to consider their audience and find their personal writing style, or voice. Expository writing generally follows narrative writing. The ability to step back from their work and revise increases as students progress through the grades.

2. Once viewed primarily as a product, writing today is viewed as both process and product. Major processes involved in writing include prewriting (topic selection, planning, and rehearsing), composing, revising, editing, and publishing. Publishing and sharing are essential extensions of the writing process. Through sharing, students' writing is celebrated. As writers, students learn to view their writing from the perspective of an audience; as listeners, they come to writing from the perspectives of both audience and editor.

3. Essential techniques for teaching writing include modeling, conferencing, sharing, and direct teaching of skills and strategies. Students confer with both class-

mates and teachers. A major purpose of conferences is to show students that they have something to say.

4. Portfolios in the form of file folders are recommended for storing students' writing and keeping track of it. Each portfolio should be examined periodically by both teacher and student to assess the student's writing development and to plan for the future.

5. Although the emphasis in writing instruction is on content, form is also important. Good form improves content. A balanced writing program should include instruction and exploration of a variety of narrative and expository forms.

6. Instruction in composing and mechanical skills should be geared to students' current needs and should be continuing and systematic, including daily instruction as well as on-the-spot aid when problems arise.

7. Good readers tend to be good writers, and vice versa. Also, students who read more tend to be better at writing. Their writing reflects structures and stylistic elements learned through reading. Through reading, they also pick up ideas for topics.

CLASSROOM APPLICATIONS

1. Observe a group of elementary school students as they write. Note how they go about prewriting, composing, revising, and editing. What strategies do they use? How effectively do they employ them? What other strategies might they use?

2. Try writing for a short period of time three to five days a week to gain insight into the process. If possible, have conferences with a classmate, friend, or colleague. Note your strengths and areas that need work.

FIELD APPLICATIONS

1. Examine a student's permanent writing folder. Track the student's growth. Note gains and needs, as well as the types of topics the student has explored and the kinds of writing the student has done. With the student, make plans for future activities.

2. Plan a writing lesson. Using the process approach, focus on topic selection and planning. If possible, teach the lesson. Give an overview of the results of the lesson.

c h a p t e r 12

Diversity in the Classroom

For each of the following statements related to the chapter you are about to read, put a check under "Agree" or "Disagree" to show how you feel. Discuss your responses with classmates before you read the chapter.

Agree **Disagree**

1. By and large, techniques used to teach average students also work with those who have special needs.

2. Labeling students as mentally retarded, learning disabled, or at risk is harmful.

3. Materials and techniques used to teach students from diverse cultures should reflect their cultures.

4. Economically disadvantaged children may have difficulty learning to read because their language is inadequate when they begin school.

5. One of the major problems that children with mental retardation and learning disabilities face is low self-esteem.

6. Of all the special needs students, gifted children require the least help.

7. After they learn to read English, bilingual students should be discouraged from reading their native language because that would confuse them.

8. Students with serious reading or other learning disabilities should be taught in a resource room.

Using What You Know

Our nation is the most culturally diverse in the world. Dozens of languages are spoken in our schools, and dozens of cultures are represented. Adding to that diversity is the trend toward inclusion. Increasingly, students who have learning or reading disabilities, visual or hearing impairments, or other disabilities are being taught in regular classrooms. Because these children have special needs, adjustments may have to be made in their programs so that they can reach their full potential. Adjustments also need to be made for children who are economically disadvantaged or who are still learning English. Without adjustments in their programs, these students may not reach their full potential in reading/language arts. The gifted and talented also have special needs and require assistance to reach their full potential.

What has been your experience teaching children from other cultures or children who are just learning to speak English? What has been your experience with students who have special needs? Think of some special needs students you have known. What provisions did the school make for these students? Could the school have done more? If so, what? What are some adjustments that you make now or might make in the future for such students?

TEACHING ALL STUDENTS

Flood and Lapp (1994) describe a classroom in which the students represented nine cultural groups; the students' ability to speak English ranged from no English to bilingual. Although most classrooms do not include as wide a range of backgrounds, U.S. schools are becoming increasingly diverse. When a report recently predicted that by the year 2000 the traditional work force, now made up predominantly of white males, would be composed of a far more diverse group of employees, forward-looking companies began planning for the day when their workers might no longer arrive sharing the same social and cultural backgrounds. Business leaders were quick to conclude that the success of their enterprise would depend, in no small part, on the way they planned and provided for diversity (Noble, 1994).

Increasingly, the success of the nation's schools also depends on the way that we plan for all our children. As a first step, we can put children at the center of the learning process (Crawford, 1993). If, as educators, we focus on *all* children and use caring and common sense in dealing with their needs, then we will have gone a long way toward establishing equity in our schools. Two movements designed to affirm **diversity** and foster equity in the schools are multicultural education and inclusion.

"A multicultural approach is based on the assumption that all groups have strengths that contribute to the fabric of U.S. society. The United States is one of the most unique countries on the globe because of its diversity. As such we have the opportunity to meld the values, perspectives, practices, and genius of many cultures into a heterogeneous, yet compatible environment" (Shade & New, 1993, p. 328).

Diversity refers to the presence of students of varying ethnic, cultural, religious, and racial backgrounds, students of varying abilities, and students who are mentally, emotionally, or physically disabled.

MULTICULTURAL EDUCATION

Multicultural education is an educational reform movement that attempts to affirm in children an understanding and appreciation of their culture and the cultures of others. It also attempts to achieve equality of education for all students.

Multicultural education is "an educational reform movement designed to restructure schools and other educational institutions so that students from all social-class, racial, cultural, and gender groups will have an equal opportunity to learn" (Banks, 1994b, p. 10). Also included in the multicultural education reform movement is a push for equal educational opportunities for exceptional students. Exceptional students include "both children who have difficulty learning and children whose performance is so advanced that an individualized educational program is necessary to meet their needs. Thus *exceptional* is an inclusive term that includes both students who are severely disabled and students who are gifted and talented" (Heward & Cavanaugh, 1993, p. 239).

Banks (1994b), a leading authority on multiculturalism, suggests the use of five dimensions to implement and assess multicultural education: content integration, knowledge construction, prejudice reduction, equitable pedagogy, and social structure. The first four dimensions are discussed in the following subsections; the fifth is beyond the scope of this text. See Banks (1994b) for a discussion of the social structure dimension.

CONTENT INTEGRATION

Content integration refers to the inclusion of the study of diverse cultures, which can be accomplished through four approaches: contributions, additive, transformation, and social action. The contributions approach includes "heroes and holidays"; special occasions such as Cinqo de Mayo or Martin Luther King's birthday may be celebrated or important African Americans, Latinos, or women studied (Banks, 1994a). In the additive approach, a unit on women or African Americans is added, but the basic structure of the curriculum remains the same.

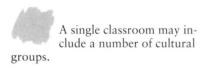
A single classroom may include a number of cultural groups.

In the transformation approach, "the structure of the curriculum is changed to enable students to view concepts, issues, events, and themes from the perspective of diverse ethnic and cultural groups" (Banks, 1994b, p. 25). For instance, the Westward Movement might be considered from the viewpoint of the women on the journey west as well as that of the men and from the viewpoint of Native Americans as well as settlers. The social action approach involves an extension and application of the transformation curriculum. Knowing what they know, students attempt to put their knowledge into action. For instance, having looked at the Westward Movement from the perspective of women, students may want to read diaries of women from that era and try to appreciate the contributions they made.

KNOWLEDGE CONSTRUCTION

Teachers help students understand that various texts are written from the perspectives of their authors and that to get a complete overview of an event or issue, they should have multiple perspectives. Ultimately, students should be led to form their own conclusions and to become critical, independent readers, writers, and thinkers. The Children's Book List provides titles of books that offer multicultural perspectives.

Multicultural education benefits all students. One of its purposes is to "help all students, including white mainstream students, to develop the knowledge, skills, and attitudes they will need to survive and function effectively in a future U.S. society in which one out of every three people will be a person of color. Our survival as a strong and democratic nation will be seriously imperiled if we do not help our students attain the knowledge and skills they need to function in a culturally diverse future society and world" (Banks, 1994b, p. 17).

Children's Book List
Multicultural books

Baer, E. *This Is the Way We Go to School*. New York: Scholastic (1990). The many different modes of transportation children all over the world use to get to school are described in text and illustrations.

Choi, S. *Halmoni and the Picnic*. Boston: Houghton Mifflin (1993). A Korean American girl's third-grade class helps her newly arrived grandmother feel more comfortable with her new life in the United States.

Dorros, A. *Abuela*. New York: Dutton (1991). While riding on a bus with her grandmother, a little girl imagines that they are carried up into the sky and fly over the sights of New York City.

Hoffman, M. *Amazing Grace*. New York: Dial (1991). Although a classmate says that she cannot play Peter Pan in the school play because she is black and a girl, Grace discovers that she can do anything she sets her mind to do.

Keegan, M. *Pueblo Boy: Growing Up in Two Worlds*. New York: Cobblehill (1991). Text and photographs depict the home, school, and cultural life of a young Indian boy growing up in the San Ildefonso Pueblo in New Mexico.

Mora, P. *Pablo's Tree*. New York: Macmillan (1994). Each year on his birthday, a young Mexican American boy looks forward to seeing how his grandfather has decorated the tree that he planted on the day the boy was adopted.

Ringgold, F. *Tar Beach*. New York: Crown (1991). A young girl dreams of flying above her Harlem home, claiming all she sees for herself and her family.

Say, A. *Grandfather's Journey*. Boston: Houghton Mifflin (1993). A Japanese American man recounts his grandfather's journey to America, which he later also undertakes, and the feelings of being torn by a love for two different countries.

Soto, G. *Too Many Tamales*. New York: Putnam (1993). Maria tries on her mother's wedding ring while helping make tamales for a Christmas family gathering and later realizes that the ring is missing.

PREJUDICE REDUCTION

Schools can be effective in reducing negative stereotypes that students hold. One means of doing this is providing students with reading materials that present positive images of all cultures. On a more active level, cooperative learning also has the potential to reduce prejudices. When African American, Mexican American, and white students work in cooperative groups, they display more positive racial attributes and make more friends outside the group. Achievement for students of color also increases (Banks, 1994b).

EQUITABLE PEDAGOGY

Equitable pedagogy means modifying the instructional program so that all students have an opportunity to learn to their fullest potential. That means choosing from the techniques advocated in this book and other techniques that you may have learned about those that best meet the needs of your students. If some students are not profiting, try other materials or techniques until you find an approach that works. Each student is a unique individual, and there are no sure-fire methods that work with everyone all the time. However, there are some basic principles that research and practice have shown to work well with students from diverse cultures and other students who have special needs. This chapter will discuss programs and possible modifications for students who are at risk, economically disadvantaged, linguistically and culturally diverse, mentally and physically disabled, and gifted and talented. There is some overlapping among groups. A student may be poor, speak a language other than English, have a learning disability, and be gifted. However, for the sake of coherence and emphasis, each of these groups has been addressed separately.

STUDENTS AT RISK

At-risk students are those who have been judged as likely to have difficulty at school because of poverty, low grades, retention in a grade, excessive absence, mental or physical disabilities, or other potentially limiting factors.

At-risk students have been identified as those who are likely to fail either at life or in school (Frymier & Gansneder, 1989). This group includes 25 to 35 percent of the country's schoolchildren. Children have been said to be at risk if they are identified as having any six of some forty-five factors. The list includes such diverse factors as parents or peers who use drugs and alcohol, retention in a grade, low marks, low scores on standardized tests, IQ below 90, membership in a special education class, negative self-image, illness, excessive absence from school, frequent changes of schools, and a home where English is not the principal language.

Although widely used, the term *at risk* is avoided by some because it has a negative connotation. "By focusing primarily on characteristics of the students, their families and their communities, the accompanying responsibility and blame for the at-risk condition is placed on the population themselves. . . . Instead . . . attention should be focused on the educational situation and on the sociocultural factors that have contributed to the at-risk condition" (García, Pearson, & Jiménez, 1994, p. 4). Moreover, if educators blame the victims or their background, they may lower their expectations for these students.

Ironically, in their desire to provide at-risk children with an effective program, educators may offer a program that focuses on lower-level reading and thinking skills. In her study of fifth-grade classes, Anyon (1980) found that instruction in low-income schools emphasizes rote learning, minimal student involvement, and low expectations, whereas the programs in more affluent schools stress higher-level skills, student involvement, and high expectations. Studies of lower-achieving readers have found that these students read less, are less likely to be taught comprehension strategies, and are not assigned out-of-class reading because the teachers feel they would not do it (García, Pearson, & Jiménez, 1994).

However, when poor and middle-class African American and white students are given similar reading instruction, their achievement is similar. Neither race nor social-economic status is a factor. This is a key point that cannot be overemphasized. When carefully taught with effective methods and materials, the vast majority of children learn to read and write. This has been proved dramatically and conclusively by Reading Recovery and other early intervention programs, which are described later in the chapter.

ECONOMICALLY DISADVANTAGED STUDENTS

Approximately one elementary school student in five lives in poverty. The poor are found everywhere: cities, small towns, and suburbs. Contrary to popular opinion, the largest percentage are in small towns and rural areas; approximately two-thirds are white, and one white child of every seven is poor. Minority groups have an even higher rate of poverty. Three of every eight Hispanic children live in poverty. The proportion for African Americans is four of nine (Wright, 1991). The characteristics of poverty are fairly obvious: poor health; possibly reduced self-esteem; inadequate food, clothing, and shelter; more frequent school absences; less stability in the home; and fewer literacy-promoting materials in the home. In addition, increasing numbers of children are homeless.

Unfortunately, many of the schools attended by children of poverty are also impoverished. Slightly fewer than half the teachers in urban communities where the population is **economically disadvantaged** feel that they have all the resources they need. In advantaged urban communities, the percentage is 75 percent (Langer, Applebee, Mullis, & Foertsch, 1990).

Poverty in and of itself does not mean that children cannot and will not be successful in school. However, it does make getting an education more difficult, and many students who live in poverty experience lowered achievement in literacy skills. By age 17, economically disadvantaged children lag about four years behind more affluent students (Langer, Applebee, Mullis, & Foertsch, 1990). Even so, many children do achieve success despite poverty, especially if their homes are achievement oriented (Dave, 1964).

Economically disadvantaged means that people's lives and opportunities are limited or put at risk by having insufficient economic resources.

Exemplary Teaching

Building Self-Esteem

Being poor can be hard on one's self-esteem. Billie Davis (1972), who worked as a migrant worker during her childhood years, remembers how her teacher set aside a bottle of milk for her in a refrigerator in the teacher's lounge. Having fainted from malnutrition, Billie was supposed to go to the teacher's lounge twice a day, during specially arranged times when no one was there, and drink a glass of milk. She made her scheduled visits, but instead of drinking the milk she poured it down the sink. Her wounded pride would not allow her to drink it.

Then Billie met a teacher who knew how to turn a receiver into a giver, not only salvaging self-esteem but building it. Noting that Billie literally put her nose into the book she was reading, the teacher arranged for an eye examination for Billie and later presented her with a pair of glasses. Billie explains what happened next:

Then I began to protest, embarrassed, "I can't take them. I can't pay for them."

She told me a little story. "When I was a child, a neighbor bought glasses for me. She told me that I should pay for them someday by getting glasses for some other little girl. So you see, the glasses were paid for before you were born."

Then the teacher said the most welcome words that anyone had ever said to me. "Someday you will buy glasses for another little girl."

She saw me as a giver. She made me responsible. She believed that I might have something to offer someone else. She accepted me as a member of the same world she lived in. I walked out of that room, clutching the glasses, not the recipient of charity, but a trusted courier. (Davis, 1972, pp. 20–21)

PRINCIPLES FOR TEACHING THE ECONOMICALLY DISADVANTAGED

Start Early.   The principles for teaching children of poverty are similar to those for teaching any child. However, it is important to start early. As a group, these children may lack some of the background knowledge and skills that spell success in school. Based on data from several long-term studies, Stallings and Stipek (1986) concluded that preschool programs have a number of beneficial results. Compared to students who do not attend these programs, those who do have higher achievement in math and reading, which continues throughout the elementary school grades and into secondary school. Attendees also have more positive feelings about themselves as learners, are retained less often, are less likely to be placed in special education classes, and are less likely to drop out of school. A greater proportion attend college or obtain employment.

Build Background.   It is important that background in reading be developed for all children. For some economically disadvantaged children, this background will have to be extensive. Limited incomes generally mean limited travel and lack of opportunity for vacations, summer camps, and other expensive activities. However, the teacher should not assume that children do not have the necessary background for a particular selection they are about to read. One teacher was somewhat surprised to learn that a group of low-income sixth-graders with whom she was working had a fairly large amount of knowledge about the feudal system (Maria,

1990). Use a technique such as brainstorming or simple questioning to probe students' background to avoid making unwarranted assumptions about knowledge.

Create an Atmosphere of Success.

As teachers, we sometimes emphasize problems, not successes. MacArthur Award recipient L. D. Delpit (1990) said that teachers must maintain visions of success for the disadvantaged. We have to help them get As, not just pass. Our aim should be to create leaders. Because the disadvantaged often fall behind, they must catch up and then move ahead.

Make Instruction Explicit.

Middle-class children are more likely to be taught strategies at home that will help them achieve success in school and are more likely to receive help at home if they have difficulty or fail to understand implicit instruction at school. Low-income children need direct, explicit instruction. If they do not learn skills at school, the home will be less likely to supply or obtain remedial help for them. The disadvantaged must have better teaching and more of it (Delpit, 1990).

Provide a Balanced Program.

Since the economically disadvantaged as a group do less well on norm-referenced skills tests, teachers may overemphasize basic skills (Garcia, 1990). These skills should be taught in context with plenty of opportunity to apply them to high-quality reading materials and real life. And higher-level skills should not be neglected.

Counteract the Fourth-Grade Slump.

In their study of children of poverty, Chall, Jacobs, and Baldwin (1990) observed a phenomenon known as the fourth-grade slump: "It is not a difference in kind, only a difference in amount" (p. 149). Students perform well in grades 2 and 3 on measures of reading and language although, in writing, form lags behind content. However, beginning in fourth grade, many students slump in several areas. They have particular difficulty defining abstract, more academically oriented words. In addition to vocabulary, word recognition and spelling scores begin to slip. These are the skills that undergird achievement in reading and writing. They are also the skills for which the schools bear primary responsibility.

Why the slump? The authors concluded that parents are able to supply their children with the help and intellectual stimulation they need to do well in grades 1 through 3, but as children reach the higher grades and vocabulary and concepts grow more abstract, poorly educated parents are no longer able to provide that assistance and support.

From grade 4 on, the school's role in the development of low-income children's literacy capabilities becomes especially important. The school must teach the vocabulary and concepts necessary to cope with subject matter texts. Middle-class children also need this instruction, but economically disadvantaged children must be given extra or more thorough instruction in this area because they are less likely to get help at home. Chall, Jacobs, & Baldwin (1990) recommended systematic teaching of word-recognition skills in the primary grades and the use of children's books, both informational and fictional in all grades. "Exposure to books on a variety of subjects and on a wide range of difficulty levels was particularly effective in the development of vocabulary . . ." (p. 155).

Added opportunity for writing and reading in the content areas was also recommended. The researchers noted that children who wrote more comprehended

Poor children are three times more likely to drop out of school (García, Pearson, & Jiménez, 1994).

better, and those who were in classes where the teachers taught content area reading had higher vocabulary scores.

LINGUISTICALLY AND CULTURALLY DIVERSE STUDENTS

It is important to discover how literacy is used in the students' culture. How do they use reading and writing in their lives? What reading and writing skills might they use to improve the quality of their lives? The skills might include knowing how to write a letter to a grandmother in a distant city or learning how to follow a recipe.

Both African American and Mexican American children seem to benefit from cooperative learning groups. In fact, cooperative learning was first initiated to enhance the achievement of students from diverse cultures.

It is important to value and build on every student's culture. Children from diverse cultures may not see the connection between their culture and school. First and foremost, it is essential that teachers become acquainted with the children's culture, especially if the teachers' backgrounds are different from those of the children they teach. Reading, discussions with the children, visits to homes, and interaction with those who are knowledgeable about the various cultures represented in the classroom are some informal ways of obtaining information. The teacher should constantly seek to know the literary heritage of the cultures, especially how literacy is used. For example, according to Taylor & Dorsey-Gaines (1988), African American families may read for a wide range of purposes, but the school often fails to reinforce the purposes for reading and writing taught in the home. According to Goldenberg (1994), parents of Hispanic students have high academic aspirations for their children, but the school may not realize this.

Reading books to children and having them read books about their heritage is another way of incorporating their cultural background into the classroom. (See Chapter 9 for suggested sources.) Other cultural aspects that might be inves-

Exemplary Teaching

Understanding Cultural Differences

As a teacher instructing second-graders who had recently arrived from El Salvador, South America, Ethiopia, the Caribbean, the Philippines, Korea, Vietnam, Portugal, Saudi Arabia, Guam, Canada, and Lebanon, Sonia Arono remembered the day she and her family went to the courthouse in Los Angeles to become citizens. She was 8 years old at the time. To celebrate the day, the family had lunch in the courthouse cafeteria. Also seated at the table were a group of white businessmen who looked on in disgust as Arono ate her mashed potatoes with her fingers, as is the custom in her village in the Philippines. The sense of shame and humiliation she felt that day was still a vivid memory. After reading aloud *People* (Spier, 1980), a text that depicts the diverse ways in which people eat, play, and live, and *How My Parents Learned to Eat* (Friedman, 1984), a story about a child who learns to eat Japanese- and American-style because her father is American

and her mother is Japanese, Arono shared her experience with her students. The students were quick to respond by discussing and writing about some of the difficulties, such as learning English or learning to tie shoes, that they had experienced. A subsequent lesson focused on the children's cultural heritage (Cox & Zarillo, 1993).

The second-graders in Arono's class explored their heritage through a thematic unit on grandparents. If grandparents were deceased or not available, the children obtained information about them through interviews with parents. As part of the unit, children constructed family trees, made time lines showing when their families came to the United States, and drew family shields and flags from the family's country of origin. As the children learned more about their own cultures and their appreciation of their heritage grew, they became more interested in the cultures of others. Learning to understand and value one's own heritage is a prerequisite for appreciating other cultures.

tigated are foods, geography, fashions, music, songs, poetry, names, etymology, history, art, and crafts (Hale-Benson, 1986).

MAKING USE OF DIVERSE WAYS OF RESPONDING

Culture is not just content. It determines how we respond and express ourselves, and even how we learn. In the typical classroom, the teacher asks a question, calls on a child, and the child responds. Emphasis is on the individual. In some cultures, however, children use a shared response style in discussion. Hawaiian children, for example, use a discussion style known as story talk in which two or more respond to a question simultaneously (Au & Mason, 1981). When a teacher allows children to respond in story talk, their time is spent more productively. Discussions center on the story and are much more effective than those led by a teacher who uses traditional structure and devotes much time to management issues such as keeping children from "talking out of turn."

Banks (1994b) notes that "a large number of low-income, linguistic minority Hispanic, Native American, and African American students have learning, cultural, and motivational styles that differ from the teaching styles that are used most frequently in the schools . . ." (p. 11). For instance, based on her review of the research, Guild (1994) concludes that middle-class, white students value independence, analytic thinking, objectivity, and accuracy. The typical classroom focuses on information, texts, grades, and linear logic, which fits in with the students' cultural characteristics. However, African American students value oral language, physical activity, and interpersonal relationships. Discussion, collaborative work, active learning, and an oral style would seem to work best with these children. Mexican American students also seem to be people-oriented and seem to prefer generalizations and broad concepts, rather than specifics. Native American students seem especially adept with visual symbols and might do well with instruction that is visually oriented. Of course, there is great variation among individuals within a group. Just because a student is Native American does not mean that she or he will have a special proficiency in visual learning.

However, what this and other research indicates is that traditional classroom instruction was established for the average middle-class, English-speaking, white student. Given the cultural diversity of the United States, it is essential that the teacher be prepared to accept a variety of **learning styles** and ways of structuring the classroom. Just as it is essential to find out what students are interested in and what they know, it is also important to find out how they learn best and what their preferred modes of response are.

In developing teaching techniques that are appropriate for diverse learning styles, we have to be aware of the ways in which students think and process information, which means that our teaching needs to be more collaborative. We have to ask children how they construct meaning and figure out hard words so that we can gain insight into their thinking processes. We need to try varied approaches to teaching and organizing classes to learn which ones work best. We also need to give students choices to determine the kinds of activities they prefer. Many of the suggestions for increasing the achievement of ethnic and linguistic minority children—such as cooperative learning and being sensitive to learning styles—should help all children learn better (Banks, 1994b).

Adapting instruction for African American students
Based on her research and an extensive review of the literature, Hale-Benson (1986) concluded that African American children are accustomed to a conversational style in which they and adults contribute equally. She suggested that their teachers structure discussions in which the children do half the talking. In addition, she concluded that African American children, as a group, are better at learning holistically, are more people-oriented and empathetic, and make fuller use of body language than white children. Individual children's learning styles, of course, vary.

Learning styles are individual preferences in acquiring, remembering, and applying new information. Learning styles include auditory, visual, or hands-on learning, learning in wholes or parts, and learning alone or with others.

Research on effective teaching indicates that the amount of time on task, or academically engaged time, is closely related to achievement (Rosenshine & Berliner, 1978). If the teacher can increase productive time by adapting instruction to conform to the learning and responding styles of the students, the result should be an increase in achievement.

Based on their research, Shade and New (1993) recommend the use of games that provide social interaction and intellectual stimulation. They suggest that brainstorming words or word problems or using a TV game-show format can meet "students' needs for cooperative affiliation, varying and exuberant communication styles, the freedom to think out loud, and the opportunity to learn from peers" (p. 326).

A child's language is part of who she or he is. Rejecting it is interpreted as a personal rejection. Everyone speaks a dialect, which is determined by place of birth, socioeconomic status, and other factors. Some African American children speak a dialect known as Black English. It is very similar to standard English. The differences between the two dialects are minor and include features such as dropping the suffixes *-ing* and *-ed*, omitting the word *is* ("He busy"), and some variations in pronunciation such as "pin" for *pen* (Shuy, 1973).

No research suggests that Black English hampers a child's reading in any significant way (Goodman & Goodman, 1978; Melmed, 1973). In fact, the opposite might be true. Stopping a discussion to correct a child's dialect may cause the student to reduce her or his participation in class. In their study of minority children, Au and Mason (1981) mentioned that the students who were superior responders were given "breathing room":

> The term "breathing room" referred to the teacher's willingness to let the children respond as best they could at the moment, without criticism that reflected on their abilities. Responses given in dialect were always accepted, as long as their content was appropriate. (p. 124)

Dialect then has no negative effect on reading achievement with the possible exception of teacher attitude (Goodman & Goodman, 1978). Teachers who form unfavorable opinions on the basis of variant dialects can convey those feelings and associated lowered expectations to students. If they constantly correct the language, teachers might also be hindering communication between themselves and their students. Brown (1988) warned,

> When students are told constantly that their verb forms are incorrect, their syntax is awkward, their modifiers are misplaced, or their speech is unacceptable for school, they decide that the risks associated with attempts to communicate with teachers outweigh the benefits. This *decision* results in limited interacting with teachers *and* ultimately, limited opportunities to engage actively in planned learning experiences. (p. 13)

Even when reading orally, a child who uses a variant dialect should not be corrected. In fact, translation of printed symbols into one's dialect is a positive sign (Goodman & Goodman, 1978). It indicates that the student is reading for meaning and not just making sounds. Black English pronunciations can cause some slight difficulty in phonics. Students might not perceive some final consonant clustering and may confuse word parts, as in *toll* and *told*, and *coal* and *cold*. The use of context and added work on auditory discrimination will help take care of this minor interference.

Teachers should use standard English, thus providing a model for children who speak a variant dialect. Although all dialects are equally acceptable, the use of standard English can be a factor in vocational success. Rather than correcting or eradicating the variant dialect, J. J. Brown (1988) recommended that standard English be presented as a second dialect that students may use if they wish.

BILINGUAL LEARNERS

There are currently more than 2 million elementary schoolchildren whose native language is not English. By the year 2000, the number is expected to reach 3.4 million (Lara, 1994).

Some children come to school speaking no English at all. Others have some degree of proficiency in English. Although these students are sometimes referred to as LEP (Limited in English Proficiency), this term has a negative connotation, so the terms **SAE** (Still Acquiring English) and **ESL** (English as a Second Language) are used in this book. A disproportionate number of SAE students live in poverty. And Hispanic students have lower-than-average achievement in school and high dropout rates; only a little more than half complete high school. Hispanic students also read significantly below average as a group (Williams, Reese, Campbell, Mazzeo, & Phillips, 1995).

SAE is an acronym for Still Acquiring English. **ESL** is short for English as a Second Language.

OVERVIEW OF A PROGRAM FOR SAE STUDENTS

The question of how SAE students should be taught to read and write strikes at the core of what reading is, that is, a language activity. Using prior experience and knowledge of language, the reader constructs meaning. Common sense and research (Fillmore & Valdez, 1986) dictate that the best way to teach reading and writing to SAE children is to teach them in their native language. Learning to read and write are complex tasks that involve the total language system: the semantic, syntactic, and phonological. Until children have a basic grasp of the meaning of a language, they will be unable to read it. Even if they are able to sound out the words, they have no meaning for them.

A general plan for teaching SAE students to read is to teach them in their native language while, at the same time, teaching them to speak English as a second language. Once they have a sufficient grasp of English and of basic reading in their native language, they can then learn to read in English. This type of program has several advantages. First of all, children build a solid foundation in their native tongue. With language development, thinking skills are enhanced, concepts are clarified and organized, and children learn to use language in an abstract way. Since they are also learning math, science, and social studies in their native language, background experience is being developed.

Thinking skills, background of knowledge, and reading skills learned in students' native language transfer to reading and writing in English. One objection to a **bilingual approach** is that it delays instruction in reading and writing in English, thereby causing children to lose ground. Research clearly indicates that this is not the case. In several studies, students taught to read in their native language and then later in a second language outperformed those taught to read in the second language (Modiano, 1968). What's more, as they progressed through the grades, the difference between the two groups increased (Rosier, 1977). Learning to read in their native language provides SAE students with a solid foundation for learning to read in another language. In addition, many of the literacy skills transfer from one language to another.

A **bilingual approach** refers to a teaching program that uses more than one language.

The key to a successful bilingual reading program may lie in knowing when to start instruction in the second language. Students should first read relatively

Tregar and Wong (cited in García, Pearson, & Jiménez, 1994) found that bilingual elementary school students who were able to read in their first language became more proficient in reading English than those who were unable to read in their first language. However, oral-language proficiency in the second language is also a factor, especially for older students. Students who were proficient in speaking English were likely to become proficient readers of English. In fact, limited proficiency in English exerts a ceiling effect for reading (García, Pearson, & Jiménez, 1994). Second-language readers may have special difficulty with vocabulary and syntax and may also lack necessary background information.

proficiently in their native language. Thonis (cited in Fillmore & Valdez, 1986) cautioned that reading in a second language should not be attempted until students have reached a level where they can interpret the text and draw inferences. This indicates that they have developed higher-level comprehension skills, which can then be transferred to reading in the second language. A number of bilingual Spanish/English reading systems include a component in Spanish and one in English. Some also include a transitional component that eases the transfer from Spanish into English.

ESL Only. According to current law, school systems are required to offer bilingual programs only if twenty or more students speak the same minority language. Many school systems go beyond the letter of the law and try to provide a program for only one or two students. However, in some instances, because of a lack of funds or because no one can be found who speaks the students' language, the only program offered is one that teaches the students English as a second language. In that instance, it is best to delay formal reading instruction until the children have a reasonable command of English. However, students can engage in shared reading, complete language-experience stories, and read predictable books. They should also be encouraged to write as best they can. As they gain proficiency in oral English, they can tackle increasingly complex reading and writing tasks. Their oral-language skills will support their reading and writing, and their reading and writing will reinforce and build oral-language skills.

The classroom teacher's role is to support the efforts of these bilingual and/or ESL professionals by meeting regularly with them and mutually planning activities that will enhance students' progress. Even after students have finished the ESL program, they still require special language-development activities. Some adjust-

If possible, students should be taught to read and write in their native language.

ments that might be made to adapt the classroom instruction to SAE students' needs are described in the paragraphs that follow.

Build Language.

The SAE students' greatest need is to develop skills in understanding and using English. Special emphasis should be placed on school-type language. Through their ESL program and interaction with peers, these children learn the language needed to cope in the everyday world. However, they may not learn the more abstract vocabulary and structures of the language of instruction. It may take years to gain the level of proficiency in English necessary to succeed in academic areas. Mastery of conversational English may mask deficiencies in important higher-level language skills (Sutton, 1989).

As students learn English, they first acquire functional structures that allow them to greet others, make conversational statements, and ask questions. This type of everyday communication is heavily contextualized and is augmented by gestures, pointing at objects, and pantomiming. It takes approximately two years for students to become socially proficient in English (Cummins, 1994). However, schooling demands academic language, which is more varied and abstract and relatively decontextualized. This is the language in which math procedures and subject matter concepts are explained. Proficiency in academic English may take five years. Even though SAE students may seem proficient in oral English, they may have difficulty with academic language. Because of the time required to acquire academic language, SAE students may not demonstrate their true abilities on achievement and cognitive ability tests administered in English.

Increasing the amount of oral language in the classroom enhances English speaking. Structure conversations at the beginning of the school day and at other convenient times to talk about current events, weather, hobbies, sports, or other topics of interest. Encourage students to participate in discussions and provide opportunities for them to use "language for a broad variety of functions, both social and academic" (Allen, 1991, p. 362). SAE students are currently being taught a second language through a communicative approach. A communicative approach emphasizes learning language through using it to communicate rather than through rote memorization. Students use role-playing, simulation games, small-group work, and similar activities. Students also read functional materials, such as ads, signs, and menus (Chamot & O'Malley, 1994).

A reading program for ESL students should include children's books. "Children's books can provide a rich input of cohesive language, made comprehensible by patterned language, predictable structure, and strong, supportive illustrations" (Allen, 1994, pp. 117–118). Children's books can be used as a stimulus for discussion, show objects that ESL students may not be familiar with, and build concepts. Books that are well illustrated and whose illustrations support the text are especially helpful. A predictable book such as *Cat on a Mat* (Wildsmith, 1982) repeats the simple pattern "The _____ sat on the mat." Eric Carle's *Have You Seen My Cat?* repeats the question pattern "Have you seen my _____?" Such books build knowledge of basic syntactical patterns as well as vocabulary. After reading texts of this type, students might use the patterns in their oral language and writing.

The speed with which students learn English will be determined in part by the quality of their English-learning experiences. Students learn English faster if there

Adapting instruction for ESL students

The social environment of a classroom is very important for language learning. Wong (cited in Cummins, 1994, p. 4) recommended: "Those situations that promote frequent contacts are the best, especially if the contacts last long enough to give learners ample opportunity to observe people using the language for a variety of communication purposes. Those which permit learners to engage in the frequent use of the language with speakers are even better" (p. 54).

To develop language, provide opportunities for students to engage in small-group activities, such as projects, discussions, paired sharing, and cooperative learning.

Adapting instruction for ESL students

When working with students who are not native speakers of English, it is important to focus on their understanding of what they read. Because of limited English, ESL students may have difficulty fully explaining what they know about a selection they have read. In addition, they may mispronounce words whose meanings they know. The key element is whether students are getting meaning from these words, not whether they are pronouncing them correctly. In one study, students who were good readers in Spanish and apparently becoming proficient readers in English were not given instruction in comprehension because the teachers wrongly believed that their mispronunciations were a sign of weak decoding skills (Moll, Estrada, Diaz, & Lopez, cited in García, Pearson, & Jiménez, 1994).

is ample comprehensible input, which means that the level of English is such that the students can make sense of it (Cummins, 1994). Students learn more English when they have confidence in their ability to learn it. Instruction that accepts students' language and culture and builds on their knowledge fosters language development. Students also learn English faster in classes that are student centered. Working with buddies and in small groups provides additional context and fosters language learning (Cummins, 1994).

To facilitate understanding of oral language, add illustrative elements to discussions. Use objects, models, and pictures to illustrate vocabulary words that might be difficult. Role-play situations and pantomime activities. When talking about rocks in a geology unit, bring some in and hold them up when mentioning their names. When discussing a story about a tiger, point to a picture of the tiger. When introducing a unit on magnets, hold up a magnet every time you use the word; point to the poles each time you mention them. Supplement oral directions with gestures and demonstrations. Think of yourself as an actor in a silent movie who must use body language to convey meaning.

Shared readings from a big book, choral readings, and songs can be used to develop oral-language fluency. Scripts, dramatized stories, and readers' theater might also be used. Puppets stimulate oral language and are especially useful for children who are shy or reluctant speakers.

Use Print.   Use print to support and expand the oral-language learning of SAE students. Label items in the room. Write directions, schedules, and similar information about routines on the chalkboard. As you write them, read them orally (Sutton, 1989). Also encourage students to write:

> Provide experiences in which language is greatly contextualized (as, for example, a field trip, a science experiment, role playing, planning a class party, solving a puzzle). Use print materials with these activities as a natural extension of the oral language generated: write a class language experience report about the field trip; record information on a science chart; write dialogues or captions for a set of pictures; make lists of party items needed; follow written directions to find a hidden treasure. (p. 686)

Adapt Instruction.   Compare the child's native language with English and note features that might cause difficulty; then provide help in those areas. For example, some major differences between Spanish and English are noted in Table 12.1 (O'Brien, 1973). Other differences between Spanish and English include a lack of contractions in Spanish and confusion caused by idiomatic expressions, such as "shoot down the street," and "call up a friend." Another difference has to do with relationships between speakers and listeners. In Hispanic cultures, for example, it is customary to avert one's eyes when speaking to persons in authority. However, for many cultural groups, the opposite is true. Students learning English should learn the cultural expectations of the language along with vocabulary and syntax.

Adapt lessons to meet the needs of SAE students. For example, when teaching phonics, start with sound-symbol relationships that are the same in both languages. For Spanish-speaking children, you might start with long *o*, since that sound is common in both English and Spanish. Before teaching elements that are not present in Spanish—short *i*, for instance—make sure that these elements have been introduced in the ESL class. For easily confused auditory items—long *e* and

TABLE 12.1 Areas of special difficulty for native speakers of Spanish

Phonological	Morphological	Syntactical
Fewer vowel sounds: no short *a* (hat), short *i* (fish), short *u* (up), short double *o* (took), or schwa (sofa)	*de* (of) used to show possession: *Joe's pen* becomes *the pen of Joe*	use of *no* for *not*: He no do his homework.
	mas (more) used to show comparison: *faster* becomes *more fast*	no *s* for plural: my two friend
Fewer consonant sounds: no /j/ (jump), /v/ (vase), /z/ (zipper), /sh/ (shoe), /ŋ/ (sing), /hw/ (when), /zh/ (beige)		no auxiliary verbs: She no play soccer.
Some possible confusions:		adjectives after nouns: the car blue
/b/ pronounced /p/: *cab* becomes *cap*		agreement of adjectives: the elephants bigs
/ǰ/ pronounced /y/: *jet* becomes *yet*		no inversion of question: Anna is here?
/ŋ/ pronounced as /n/: *thing* becomes *thin*		articles with professional titles: I went to the Dr. Rodriguez.
/ch/ pronounced as /sh/: *chin* becomes *shin*		
/v/ pronounced as /b/: *vote* becomes *boat*		
/y/ pronounced as /ǰ/: *yes* becomes *jes*		
/sk/, /sp/, /st/ pronounced as /esk/, /esp/, /est/: *speak* becomes *espeak*		
/a/ pronounced as /e/: *bat* becomes *bet*		
/i/ pronounced as /ē/: *hit* becomes *heat*		
/ē/ pronounced as /i/: *heal* becomes *hill*		
/u/ pronounced as /o/: *hut* becomes *hot*		
/o͝o/ pronounced as /o͞o/: *look* becomes *Luke*		

Adapted from C. A. O'Brien, *Teaching the Language-Different Child to Read.* Columbus, OH: Merrill, 1973.

short *i,* for example—provide added auditory-discrimination exercises. Also use the items in context or use real objects or pictures to illustrate them. When discussing *shoes,* for example, point to them.

When teaching a reading lesson, examine the text for items that might cause special problems. Pay particular attention to the following items:

- *Syntax.* Does the selection use sentence patterns that the student might have difficulty with? Is there a heavy use of contractions?
- *Semantics.* Might certain figures of speech or idiomatic expressions cause confusion?
- *Culture.* What cultural items might cause problems in understanding the selection? For instance, some ESL students from traditional cultures might have difficulty understanding the casual relationship that children in the mainstream culture have with authority figures.

The teacher does not have to attempt to present all potentially confusing items. Those most important to a basic understanding of the selection should be chosen. Some potentially difficult items might be discussed after the story has been read.

Of course, as with any group of students, care must be taken to explain to SAE students concepts and vocabulary that could hinder their understanding, as well as to build background and activate schemata. Before students read a piece, activate their prior knowledge. Because of cultural and linguistic differences, students might not realize that they have background to bring to a story or article.

The first reading of a selection should be silent. Because SAE students are still learning English, the temptation is to have them read orally. However, this turns the reading lesson into a speech lesson. Plan legitimate activities for purposeful oral rereading after the selection has been read silently and discussed. Also emphasize comprehension over pronunciation (Chamot & O'Malley, 1994). Although SAE students may mispronounce words, they may know their meanings; however, you may want to note pronunciation difficulties and work on them later.

Use a Language-Experience Approach. A language-experience approach avoids the problem of unfamiliar syntax and vocabulary since children read selections that they dictate. Some students might dictate stories that contain words in both English and their native tongue. This should be allowed and could be an aid as the child makes the transition to English.

Although students are learning to read in English, they should still be encouraged to read in their native tongue if they are literate in that language. In the classroom library, include books written in the various languages of SAE students. Since Spanish is spoken by a large proportion of the U.S. population, a number of books are published in Spanish, including both translations and original works. Most of the major educational and children's book publishers offer translations of favorite books.

> Reading in a second language makes greater cognitive demands on students. In addition to using reading skills and strategies, they must meet the demands of coping with words and sentence structures that may not be familiar to them (Chamot & O'Malley, 1994).

> Respect and reinforce the child's culture. Plan activities in which students share their cultural heritages (see Tiedt and Tiedt, 1990, for suggestions).

STUDENTS WITH DISABILITIES

STUDENTS WITH LEARNING DISABILITIES

One of the largest categories of special needs students is represented by the group identified as learning disabled. Slightly more than 4.5 percent of all students have been determined to be learning disabled. This group is also the most controversial; experts disagree as to what constitutes a **learning disability.** The most widely followed definition is that used by the federal government in the Education for All Handicapped Children Act (PL 94–142), which was recently revised and is now known as the Individuals with Disabilities Education Act, or IDEA (PL 101–476):

> Specific learning disability means a disorder in one or more of the basic psychological processes involved in understanding or in using language, spoken or written, which may manifest itself in an imperfect ability to listen, think, speak, read, write, spell, or to do mathematical calculations. The term includes such conditions as perceptual handicaps, brain injury, minimal brain dysfunction, dyslexia, and developmental aphasia. The term does not include children who

> **Learning disability** is a general term used to refer to a group of disorders that are evidenced by difficulty in learning to read, write, speak, listen, or do math. Speaking and listening difficulties of students with learning disabilities are not caused by articulation disorders or impaired hearing.

have learning problems which are primarily the result of visual, hearing, or motor handicaps, of mental retardation, or of environmental, cultural, or economic disadvantage. [PL 94–142, section 5(b)(4)]

Accompanying regulations further define a student with learning disabilities as one who evidences a serious discrepancy between ability and achievement in one of the following areas: "oral expression, listening comprehension, written expression, basic reading skills, reading comprehension, mathematics calculation, and mathematics reasoning" (Wallace & McLoughlin, 1988, p. 6). Although students can be classified as learning disabled for a variety of reasons, approximately 80–85 percent of learning-disabled students have a reading problem (Smith, 1994).

In other words, a learning-disabled child has adequate intellectual ability but displays a significant gap between level of ability and achievement. Moreover, as far as can be determined, this gap is not caused by mental retardation, emotional problems, physical handicaps, or poverty. Although some sort of dysfunction in the central nervous system is suspected as being at the root of the problem, no cause has been identified, which is one of the reasons why this category is both mysterious and controversial.

CHARACTERISTICS OF STUDENTS WITH LEARNING DISABILITIES

Because of the vague definition, the learning-disabled group is quite heterogeneous. It includes students who have visual- or auditory-perceptual dysfunction, difficulty paying attention, memory deficits, problems using language to learn, or all of these conditions. Students may have an underlying problem that manifests itself in all school subjects, or the problem may be restricted to a single area, such as reading, writing, or math.

Students with reading disabilities may have a number of weaknesses in language development. They may have difficulty comprehending and/or using language. Poor language skills may be the cause of difficulty in remembering printed words and other items.

LITERACY PROGRAM FOR STUDENTS WITH LEARNING DISABILITIES

Based on the major behavioral and academic characteristics noted, a literacy program for learning-disabled students should include several important features. These students should be provided with reading materials at their instructional level so that they can experience success and begin to see themselves as learners.

Learning-disabled students, especially those with reading difficulties, often experience problems with basic decoding skills. Having difficulty with phonemic awareness, these children might miss out on rudimentary phonics instruction when it is provided in primary grades. As they move through the grades, it might be assumed that they have mastered these skills. Through an IRI, a word-list test, or observation, find out where struggling readers are and provide instruction in basic decoding skills if necessary. Word Building, discussed in Chapter 4, is a very thorough approach. Relate the skills taught to books and stories students are reading. Provide plenty of reinforcement in the form of books and materials that incorporate the phonics elements or patterns you have taught.

Beyond Picture Books: A Guide to First Readers, 2nd ed., by Barstow and Riggle (1995) profiles more than 2500 books for students reading on a first-through second-grade level. Reading levels are provided.

Some disabled readers have been taught a full range of decoding skills but at too rapid a pace, so the skills never became automatic. What these students need is ample opportunity to apply their skills with texts that are relatively easy for them to read. Some students need more practice time than others, perhaps because they never got sufficient opportunity to apply their skills. If students do not respond to your best efforts, seek help from the reading teacher or specialist in learning disabilities.

MATERIALS FOR STUDENTS WITH LEARNING DISABILITIES

Since they frequently read below grade level, students with learning disabilities often need high-interest, low-readability books and periodicals. Two excellent bibliographies of easy-to-read books are as follows:

Libretto, E. V. *High/Low Handbook* (2nd ed.). New York: Bowker (1990). Describes 412 books that would be appropriate for disabled and/or reluctant readers in the upper elementary grades and beyond.

Pilla, M. A. *The Best: High/Low Books for Reluctant Readers*. Englewood, CO: Libraries Unlimited (1990). Features 374 books for reluctant and/or disabled readers in grades 3 through 12.

There are also periodicals specifically designed for older disabled readers:

Know Your World Extra (Field Publications, Subscriber Services, P. O. Box 16673, Columbus, OH 43216). Written on grade levels 2–3, this is designed for poor readers in grades 5 and up. It is a well-rounded periodical that includes news and science articles, recreational features, puzzles, and word games and is published eighteen times a year.

Scholastic Sprint (Scholastic Classroom Magazines, P. O. Box 644, Lyndhurst, NJ 07071). Written on grade levels 2–3, this is a sixteen-page periodical designed for poor readers in grades 4–6. It features news and recreational and general interest features and often contains a TV script. It is published fourteen times a year.

WRITING AND STUDENTS WITH LEARNING DISABILITIES

Writing is an area in which symptoms of a learning disability show up dramatically. Unlike silent reading, the end product of writing is there for all to see. Learning-disabled students often experience difficulty with the higher-level composing aspects of writing as well as with the lower-level mechanical processes. Some have more difficulty than average children with letter formation, spacing, letter orientation, and letter order. (Reversals are normal until about the age of 7. Research is not clear about what they signify beyond that age. Since reversing letters is normal for beginning readers, it is also normal for older students who are still in the beginning stages of reading.) Others have difficulty organizing their thoughts when composing. For some, disorganized writing reflects disorganized speaking patterns. However, a number of learning-disabled writers have average or superior oral-language expression but still have difficulty putting their thoughts down on paper.

As with average students, writing instruction for students with learning disabilities should emphasize the expressive function. Mechanics should be especially deemphasized for these students. Graves (1985) described the strengths displayed by Billy, a third-grader, as he attempted to record his thoughts on paper. Billy's paper was smudged and blackened, showing evidence of many valiant efforts to spell correctly the few words he had managed to write. However, as Graves wisely

Cohen (1983) found that learning-disabled writers had a less adequate sense of audience than average students who had a comparable reading level. They were less able to figure out what their readers needed to know. To help such students better understand these needs, Bereiter (1980) taught them to ask themselves a series of questions that would help them keep the audience in mind while they wrote; it is also helpful if they form a mental picture of their readers. The think sheets discussed in Chapter 11 should be especially helpful for these students.

observed, spelling and handwriting were the least of Billy's writing problems. Billy had diagnosed himself as a poor writer because of a perceived lack of worthwhile ideas and experiences; he was well versed in what he could not do. Billy had been skilled and drilled on handwriting and spelling in isolation. There was no question that he needed expert help in these areas; however, the mechanical skills should have been connected to the total writing process so that he could see the true function of handwriting and spelling. Most of all, Billy needed to know that he had something worthwhile to say so that he could see himself as a writer. Otherwise, he would not be able to make full use of the mechanical skills that he was being taught.

STUDENTS WITH ATTENTION DEFICIT DISORDER

Attention deficit disorder (ADD) has as its primary symptom difficulty in sutaining attention. This may be due to a chemical imbalance and is frequently accompanied by **hyperactivity** or **impulsivity**. According to the DSM-IV (*Diagnostic and Statistical Manual of Mental Disorders*, 4th ed., American Psychiatric Association, 1994), there are three types of ADD: combined attention deficit/hyperactivity disorder, predominantly attention deficit disorder, and predominantly hyperactivity/impulsivity disorder. Table 12.2 lists diagnostic criteria for ADD.

ADD is not classified as a learning or reading disorder. A student can have ADD but demonstrate no difficulty learning. However, there is considerable overlap between the two categories. Many students diagnosed as having a learning disability also have difficulty with attention.

Attention deficit disorder refers to a difficulty focusing and maintaining attention.

Hyperactivity is the condition of being overly active or easily distracted. **Impulsivity** is the tendency to act on the spur of the moment without thinking of the consequences.

ASSISTING STUDENTS WITH ADD

Whether ADD is a valid disorder is still being debated. However, it is clear that there are large numbers of students who have difficulty learning because of a problem with their attention. Whole language advocate Constance Weaver (1994), whose son has been diagnosed as having ADHD (the H stands for hyperactivity), has a number of humane and practical suggestions for helping these children. Her chief concern is that we not blame the victim. Instead, she suggests that we look at ways in which we can help the student perform better in school and in which the school can adjust to the student's characteristics. For instance, ADHD children, by definition, have difficulty sitting still. Why not allow them stretch breaks or the opportunity to participate in projects that provide freedom of movement? Instead of just focusing on trying to change the child, we need to work with him or her and modify the program.

Other suggestions include the following, many of which would be beneficial to all students:

- Provide students with tasks that are meaningful and interesting.
- Give students a choice of materials and activities.
- Allow mobility in the classroom; use writing, reading, and other learning centers.
- Allow students to confer with peers.
- Minimize formal tests.

Although PL 94–142 and PL 101–476, which promise services to special education students, do not specifically mention ADD, many children with ADD have other handicapping conditions and are therefore provided for under these laws. In addition, those with ADD may be provided services under Section 504 of the Rehabilitative Act of 1973 if their disorder limits their ability to benefit from regular education. They may also qualify for help under the "other health-impaired" category of the Individuals with Disabilities Education Act (Weaver, 1994).

A. Either (1) or (2):

   (1) Six (or more) of the following symptoms of **inattention** have persisted for at least six months to a degree that is maladaptive and inconsistent with developmental level:

Inattention

   (a) often fails to give close attention to details or makes careless mistakes in schoolwork, work, or other activities

   (b) often has difficulty sustaining attention in task or play activities

   (c) often does not seem to listen when spoken to directly

   (d) often does not follow through on instructions and fails to finish schoolwork, chores, or duties in the workplace (not due to oppositional behavior or failure to understand instructions)

   (e) often has difficulty organizing tasks and activities

   (f) often avoids, dislikes, or is reluctant to engage in tasks that require sustained mental effort (such as schoolwork or homework)

   (g) often loses things necessary for tasks or activities (e.g., toys, school assignments, pencils, books, or tools)

   (h) is often easily distracted by extraneous stimuli

   (i) is often forgetful in daily activities

   (2) Six (or more) of the following symptoms of **hyperactivity** or **impulsivity** have persisted for at least six months to a degree that is maladaptive and inconsistent with developmental level:

Hyperactivity

   (a) often fidgets with hands or feet or squirms in seat

   (b) often leaves seat in classroom or in other situations in which remaining seated is expected

   (c) often runs about or climbs excessively in situations in which it is inappropriate (in adolescents or adults, may be limited to subjective feelings of restlessness)

   (d) often has difficulty playing or engaging in leisure activities quietly

   (e) is often "on the go" or often acts as if "driven by a motor"

   (f) often talks excessively

Impulsivity

   (g) often blurts out answers before questions have been completed

   (h) often has difficulty awaiting turn

   (i) often interrupts or intrudes on others (e.g., butts into conversation or games)

B. Some hyperactive/impulsive or inattentive symptoms that caused impairment were present before age 7 years.

C. Some impairment from the symptoms is present in two or more settings (e.g., at school [or work] and at home).

D. There must be clear evidence of clinically significant impairment in social, academic, or occupational functioning.

E. The symptoms do not occur exclusively during the course of a Pervasive Development Disorder, Schizophrenia, or other Psychotic Disorder and are not better accounted for by another mental disorder (e.g., Mood Disorder, Anxiety Disorder, Disassociative Disorder, or a Personality Disorder).

From the American Psychiatric Association, *Diagnostic and Statistical Manual of Mental Disorders,* 4th ed., Washington, DC: American Psychiatric Association, 1994, (pp. 83–85).

- Make sure students understand directions. Establish eye contact. Give directions one step at a time, writing them on the board as you do so. Make sure that the students have copied the directions accurately and understand them.
- When students have homework assignments, make sure they leave with all the necessary materials and directions.
- Help them keep a schedule for major assignments. Break the assignment down into a series of smaller steps. Check to see that each step is completed.
- Work closely with parents so that the home supports the school's efforts, and vice versa.

STUDENTS WITH MENTAL RETARDATION

Robert, a 12-year-old sixth-grader, had little difficulty pronouncing the words at the fifth-grade level of the word recognition test being administered. He seemed to have a natural bent for translating printed words into their spoken equivalents. When asked the meaning of the words, however, he was unable to respond. When asked questions about a series of reading passages that increased in difficulty, he also had problems with passages beyond the second-grade level. Robert's pattern of good decoding and poor comprehension was not surprising. Robert has mild mental retardation. A hard worker who was blessed with outstanding teachers, he was able to master the lower-level skill of sounding out words but had difficulty with the higher-level cognitive skill of understanding what he had read.

About 2 percent of the population might be classified as mentally retarded. **Mental retardation** is determined by two criteria: low level of intellectual functioning and deficits in adaptive behavior. Low level of intellectual functioning translates into an IQ score of approximately 70 or below or two standard deviations below the mean.

Deficits in adaptive behavior cause the child to have difficulty meeting the demands of society and to function adequately. For a six-year-old, this might mean the inability to use the toilet without assistance; for a sixth-grader, it might mean the inability to function in a school setting. The two criteria highlight the importance of considering the whole child when making educational decisions. Because children with mental retardation often have adjustment problems, social as well as intellectual factors have to be considered when planning a program.

IMPLICATIONS FOR READING INSTRUCTION

A top priority in a program for students who are mentally retarded is providing successful experiences and empowerment. Such students need to see themselves as active, competent readers and writers who control the process. The program should be adapted to the students' strengths and weaknesses and geared to their needs and goals. Actually, mildly retarded youngsters can benefit from the same kind of program recommended for average children, with some adaptations.

Full-Language Approach.   Mentally retarded children should be immersed in reading, writing, listening, and speaking. They should be read to daily, express themselves in writing as best they can, and begin reading instruction through a language-experience approach and shared reading of big books. The advantage of

Judgments about cognitive capacity must be made with great care. Current measures of ability assess only a narrow range of skills. They do not tap creativity or the ability to respond to one's environment. In addition, students who have not had equal opportunity to learn or who are still learning English may be assessed unfairly. Moreover, labeling children may lead to lowered expectations, a less challenging program, and, therefore, lower achievement.

Mental retardation refers to a condition of low-level mental functioning that affects approximately 2 percent of the population.

IQ scores are further broken down to indicate degree of intellectual retardation (Cartwright, Cartwright, & Ward, 1989): mild (educable), 56 to 70; moderate (trainable), 41 to 55; and severe and profound, below 41. The vast majority of those classified as mentally retarded fall into the mild or moderate category. Most are taught in separate classes or separate schools. Students who are mildly retarded might achieve on a second- to fifth-grade level and might also reach a degree of social independence. Chances of partial or total self-support are good (Hardman, Drew, Egan, & Wolf, 1993).

Currently, there are about a half-million students classified as having mental retardation. This represents a decrease of 300,000 students over the past two decades. The cutoff IQ score for classifying children as mentally retarded was lowered from 80 or below to 70 or below. In addition, many children who are mildly retarded have been classified as learning disabled because that label is felt to be less stigmatizing (Hardman, Drew, Egan, & Wolf, 1993).

the full-language approach is that it builds on students' language and experience. This helps to ensure success, as the children will not be meeting unfamiliar concepts or vocabulary.

A Process Approach to Language.   A primary problem for mentally retarded students is limited reasoning ability. Through modeling and other techniques, the teacher must make explicit the processes of reading and writing that average students often pick up on their own. Book selection and the use of decoding, comprehension, study, and writing skills have to be modeled carefully and continually. The teacher must also model processes that underlie learning: paying attention, staying on task, listening, and determining relevant information.

For most mentally retarded children, the major obstacles to reading achievement are vocabulary and conceptual development. Because of lessened cognitive ability and, perhaps, lack of experiential background, they may have difficulty comprehending what they read. They need to have concepts and background built in functional, concrete ways.

Strategy Instruction.   Strategy instruction grows naturally out of modeling and explaining the basic processes of literacy. After instruction, students may successfully use learning and literacy strategies such as the following:

- *Before reading.* Activating prior knowledge, predicting, setting purposes
- *During reading.* Predicting and confirming, determining relevant ideas, inferring, summarizing, using graphic aids, monitoring for comprehension
- *After reading.* Summarizing, relating new information to prior knowledge, evaluating, rehearsing

Of course, students with mental retardation may have to learn the strategies in smaller steps and in simplified form. These students also need more guidance and more practice. Above all, they must have instruction in when and where to apply strategies, since executive control, or the ability to manage and organize their learning, is one of their weakest areas.

Appropriate Materials.   A 12-year-old, mentally retarded sixth-grader may be reading on a second- or even a first-grade level. This student needs materials that appeal to her or his age but that consist of short sentences and easy words. In addition, the language should be straightforward and concrete and on a conceptual level that the student can handle. A fairly wide variety of high-interest, low-readability materials is available, including fiction, content area materials, and even periodicals. The bibliographic sources of materials for learning-disabled students can be used for locating such materials.

Some students with mental retardation may never read beyond a second-grade level. Others will never be able to do any sustained reading. Because their literacy development is so limited, it is important that they be taught the literacy skills they need to function in society. These skills include reading traffic and warning signs, labels, simple cooking directions, and common forms. They also have to know how to write their name, address, telephone number, date of birth, names of family members, and other information frequently requested on forms. A list of survival signs for such students is presented in Table 12.3.

TABLE 12.3 Survival signs for students with mental retardation

General	Building Signs	Warnings
Beware	Airport	Do not inhale fumes.
Beware of Dog	Bus Station	Do not refreeze.
Caution	Dentist	Do not use near heat.
Closed	Doctor	Do not use near open flame.
Danger	Down	Keep out of reach of children.
Deep Water	Elevator	
Dynamite	Emergency Exit	Keep refrigerated.
Explosives	Employees Only	Replace cap.
Flammable	Entrance	Shake well before using.
Fragile	Exit	Use before (date).
Gasoline	First Aid	
High Voltage	Information	
Inflammable	Men	
Information	Nurse	
Keep off the Grass	Office	
Live Wires	Police Station	
Lost and Found	Private	
No Diving	Pull	
No Fishing	Push	
No Hunting	Up	
No Swimming	Use Other Door	
No Trespassing	Watch Your Step	
Open	Women	
Out of Order		
Poison		
Poisonous		
Private Property		
Thin Ice		
Wet Paint		

Maryland State Department of Education (1976–1977). *Functional Reading: A Resource Guide for Teachers*. Baltimore: Author.

Students with mental retardation should also be taught how to read the newspaper, especially for functional items like weather, movie times, want ads, and grocery and other ads. They must know, too, how to use the white, blue, and yellow pages of the telephone book. Stress should be placed on locating emergency numbers. An overview of a functional reading curriculum is presented in Table 12.4.

TABLE 12.4 Overview of a functional reading curriculum

Following Directions	Locating Information	Acquiring Information	Understanding and Completing Forms

Basic directions
    Road, building, and
    other signs
    Medicine
Sequential directions
    Emergency
    Games
    Computer software
    Put-together toys
    Finding a location
    Cooking directions
    Recipes
    General
	White and blue pages of
	telephone book
	Yellow pages of telephone
	book
	Television guide
	Cookbook
	Newspaper
	Catalogs
		Newspaper
		Announcements
		Notices
			Order forms
			    Subscription
			    Record/tape club
			    Merchandise
			General forms
			    General identifying
			    information
			    Library card

Adapted from Maryland State Department of Education (1976–1977). *Functional Reading: A Resource Guide for Teachers.* Baltimore: Author.

SLOW LEARNERS

Slow learners have below average ability but do not have mental retardation. In general, IQ's for slow learners range between 71 and 85.

Functioning generally on a higher level than mentally retarded students but on a lower level than average students are a large number of students known as **slow learners.** They make up approximately 14 percent of the school population. Because they have IQ scores between 71 and 85, they function on too high a level to be classified as retarded but are frequently excluded from learning-disabled and remedial reading programs because their scores are too low. Although they have some special needs, slow learners are often denied special services.

Slow learners manifest some of the same characteristics that mentally retarded students display, but to a lesser degree. They tend to be concrete in their thinking, need help with strategies and organization, and are eager for success. Their executive functioning is on a higher level than that of children with mental retardation. They are better able to decide when and where to use strategies and are better able to classify and group information. They also are more aware of their mental processes and can take more responsibility for their learning.

All students need instruction in higher-order thinking skills. Be sure to include higher-level questions when discussing selections. Provide prompts and scaffolding as needed.

In terms of instruction, these are "more so" students; they need the same instruction that regular students need, but more so. They must be given more guidance, more practice, and more time to complete learning tasks. One of their greatest needs is to have materials and instruction on their level. (The bibliographic sources of materials for learning-disabled students can also be used for slow learners.) All too often, slow learners are given a basal that is below grade level but still above their reading level, or a content area textbook that is on grade level and well above their reading level. This is frustrating and leads to lowered self-concept and lowered achievement.

STUDENTS WITH PHYSICAL DISABILITIES

Reading and writing are essentially mental activities. Children who have impaired sight, profound hearing loss, or other physical disability can and do learn to read and write. Because of advances in technology and techniques for teaching the physically disabled, most of these children can be taught in regular classrooms. Computers can be adapted so that they can be operated by a child's breathing into a straw or simply blinking an eye. Other devices magnify type or read print aloud. Talking keyboards make it possible for the blind to hear what they type. Teaching the physically disabled is partly a matter of adapting technology and techniques. More importantly, however, it is an issue of caring and acceptance.

STUDENTS WITH HEARING LOSS

Hearing loss ranges from mild to profound. Children with a mild loss may be unable to hear distant sounds; those with moderate to severe losses need hearing aids and training; those with a severe or profound loss have virtually no hearing and may only feel vibrations.

Reading achievement is seriously affected by hearing impairment, especially if impairment occurs before age 3 (Jensema, 1975). The effect is especially negative in children with severe or profound deafness. Even a temporary loss of hearing can cause difficulties. Otitis media, an infection of the middle ear that is common among young children, can cause loss of hearing if not treated (Kavanagh, 1986). Even after the infection clears, fluid may still be present in the middle ear and may impair hearing if not attended to, thereby hindering language development and school progress (Neu, 1989).

One issue that has to be addressed is the difference between a disability and handicap. The term *disability* refers to an objective, measurable organic dysfunction or impairment, such as the loss of a hand or paralysis of speech muscles or legs. The term *handicap* refers to a limitation arising from environmental or functional demands placed upon a person with a disability in a given situation (Cartwright, Cartwright, & Ward, 1989, p. 67). A disability is always present, whereas a handicap need not be. A child who is unable to walk because of a spinal injury is not handicapped when it comes to learning to read because the disability does not interfere with reading, but she or he would be handicapped in tasks that involve mobility. Insofar as possible, teachers must make adjustments so that disabilities do not become handicaps.

As inclusion becomes more widespread, greater numbers of students with mild or moderate hearing loss will be taught in the regular classroom.

Teachers should note whether children display problems with their hearing or ears and should make referrals or recommendations for testing to the school nurse or parents, depending on school policy. Common signs of possible difficulty are presented in the hearing checklist in Figure 12.1.

Children with serious hearing impairment will most likely have a special education placement. However, as inclusion becomes more prominent, greater numbers of students with mild or moderate hearing impairment will be taught in the regular classroom.

Hearing-impaired students need help in all language areas, but especially in vocabulary, figurative language, and syntax; they may also need additional help with conceptual development. Because their ability to learn through language is restricted, hearing-impaired children may lag behind in conceptual development (Hardman, Drew, Egan, & Wolf, 1993).

| FIGURE 12.1 | Hearing checklist: Signs of possible difficulty |

_____ Inattention

_____ Turning head or ear to speaker

_____ Cupping the ear

_____ Difficulty following spoken directions

_____ Frequent requests to repeat directions

_____ Speech difficulties

_____ Withdrawn behavior

_____ Concentration on speaker's lips

_____ Inconsistent or inappropriate responses

_____ Use of gestures

_____ Relying on classmates to explain directions and assignments

_____ Earaches

_____ Ringing or buzzing in ears

_____ Sores in ears or discharge

_____ Head noise

_____ Frequent colds, sore throats, or tonsillitis

Adapted from "Hearing Problems" by A. Berlin, 1972, in G. P. Cartwright & C. A. Cartwright (Eds.), _Care: Early Identification of Handicapped Children_, University Park, PA: Pennsylvania State University and "Teacher Judgment of Hearing Loss in Children" by M. L. Geyer and A. Yankaver, 1971, in I. M. Ventry, J. B. Chaiklin, and K. F. Dixon (Eds.), _Hearing Measurement: A Book of Readings_, New York: Appleton-Century-Crofts as compiled in _Educating Special Learners_, 3rd ed. (p. 129) by G. P. Cartwright, C. A. Cartwright, and M. E. Ward, 1989, Belmont, CA: Wadsworth. Copyright © 1989 by Wadsworth, Inc. Adapted by permission.

Because reading depends so heavily on language ability, it is the area in which hearing-impaired students have the most difficulty. Although they do fairly well in the primary grades, achievement starts to lag as students encounter materials that have more complex syntax and more advanced vocabulary. By the time they reach their teens, average hearing-impaired students are reading on a fifth-grade level (Hardman, Drew, Egan, & Wolf, 1993).

Hearing-impaired children must be given directions very clearly and explicitly. The teacher should use gestures, pantomime, pictures, and real objects to illustrate directions and explanations. She or he should also make generous use of the chalkboard. Hearing-impaired children should be seated in the front of the class with an unimpeded view of the board. The teacher must speak distinctly and face the students directly, especially if they can read lips. The teacher might use some sign language if students understand it.

In teaching reading, use a whole word approach rather than phonics, and also a language-experience approach (Carlsen, 1985). Have a generous supply of heavily illustrated, easy-to-read materials. Encourage students to watch suitable closed-captioned TV shows and also to obtain a library of captioned videocassettes. Depending on the severity of the students' deficits, consider using *Reading Milestones* (Quigley & King, 1981), a reading series specifically designed for hearing-impaired students. In addition to controlling syntax, *Reading Milestones* features a carefully paced introduction of new vocabulary and new concepts.

STUDENTS WITH LANGUAGE AND SPEECH DISORDERS

A language disorder is "the impairment or deviant development of comprehension and/or use of a spoken, written, and/or other symbol system" (Rice, 1988, p. 238). Language disorders that involve deficiencies in comprehension of speech also have a direct impact on reading, since reading involves understanding language.

Speech problems generally involve difficulties with production of oral symbols. Speech is said to be disordered when "it deviates so far from the speech of other people that it calls attention to itself, interferes with communication, or causes the speaker or his listener to be distressed" (Van Riper & Emerick, 1984, p. 34). Many speech disorders are developmental and disappear as the child grows older, but others require intervention. The most prevalent speech disorder is difficulty articulating particular sounds. For example, children may say "Wobert the wabbit" for "Robert the rabbit." Other disorders involve fluency, or flow, of speech and include stuttering and cluttering, which is disorganized speech or slurring.

Speech impairments do not directly affect reading or writing. The teacher's role is primarily one of being sensitive to the difficulty and helping the child apply skills in the classroom that she or he learned while working with a speech therapist. The teacher should also be supportive and help the child build confidence, providing opportunities for the child to take part in discussions and purposeful oral reading. Consultation with the speech therapist and "promotion of a classroom atmosphere conducive to unpressured verbal interaction" (Cartwright, Cartwright, & Ward, 1989, p. 174) are also recommended.

Although articulation difficulties do not generally impair the acquisition of reading and writing skills, other less noticeable language difficulties may pose

Teachers are more comfortable working with disabled children in their classrooms if they have had a special education course and feel confident about their ability to help these students (Schulz, 1993).

significant problems. Some children's language development follows a normal path but is slow. These children may experience a delay acquiring basic reading and writing skills.

Students who suffer from language disorders experience a disruption in the language development process (Hardman, Drew, Egan, & Wolf, 1993). The disruption may be expressive or receptive or a combination of the two. Receptive language disorders affect students' understanding of language. Expressive disorders hinder the ability to communicate. Students with an expressive disorder may possess information but have difficulty communicating it. One subtle but relatively common expressive disorder is difficulty with word finding, that is, finding the words to express what one wants to say. For instance, unable to retrieve the word *bat*, a student might say "the thing that you hit a ball with." The speech of these students is marked by hesitations, roundabout expressions, and "You knows." They may have difficulty using picture and context clues because they cannot retrieve from memory the name of the object shown in the picture or think of the word that might fit the context. Students with word-finding difficulties are helped by techniques that develop language and vocabulary and that help them to organize information so that it is easier to retrieve.

STUDENTS WITH VISUAL IMPAIRMENTS

Visually impaired students include children who are blind and those who have low vision. Children with low vision can see print but, even when their vision is corrected with glasses, their ability to see is less than that of average children. Only about one child in a thousand has a vision impairment (Kirk & Gallagher, 1986); however, a number of correctible deficiencies may cause difficulties. Deficiencies in acuity, which is the ability to see clearly at all working distances, can hinder reading. In addition, a deficiency in the efficiency with which the eyes work together can also hinder reading.

Because of their visual impairments, these children may not fully develop their concepts about events and objects that are primarily visual. Reviewing the research, Warren (1984) commented, "The new work of the past several years strongly suggests that, while blind children may use words with the same frequency count as sighted children, the meanings of the words for the blind are not as rich or as elaborated" (p. 278).

As with hearing impairment, the impact of visual impairment depends upon the degree of the loss and the time of its onset. If children lose vision before the age of 5, for instance, they may lose the ability to construct visual images. Depending on the degree of loss, children may have more difficulty learning new words because they cannot see the objects that the words name. On average, visually impaired students are two grades behind their peers (Hardman, Drew, Egan, & Wolf, 1993). The classroom teacher should be alert for possible vision problems. Note whether a child can read from the chalkboard or has obvious vision problems with other classroom or play activities. Some signs of visual difficulties are listed in Figure 12.2.

For the benefit of all children, but especially for the visually impaired, the teacher should ensure that the room has adequate lighting with no glare. Students who need to sit up close should do so. The teacher should also check to see that students who have glasses are wearing them and those who need magnifying glasses or other special equipment are using it. Avoid using materials that have small print or fuzzy dittos that are hard to see. Supplement visual presentations with oral explanations. When explaining a diagram on the board, for instance, describe it. If possible, make the diagram extra large. Also obtain objects that

---

FIGURE 12.2 | **Vision checklist: Signs of possible difficulty**

____ Reddened eyes or lids

____ Frequent sties

____ Frequent tearing

____ Squinting

Headaches

____ Burning or itching sensation in eyes after reading or writing

____ Rubbing eyes while reading or writing

____ Excessive blinking while reading or writing

____ Double vision

____ Closing or covering one eye while reading or writing

____ Tilting head while reading or writing

____ Holding printed material too close

____ Frequently changing distance between eyes and printed material

____ Difficulty copying from board

____ Skipping or rereading lines

____ Omitting words

____ Using finger to keep his or her place

____ Difficulty writing on lines when writing or staying in lines when coloring

____ Writing with ragged left margin

____ Writing or doing math problems crookedly on page

Adapted from *Your Child's Vision Is Important* (pp. 10–11) by C. Beverstock, 1991, Newark, DE: International Reading Association.

depend on the sense of touch. Start a collection of real objects, and encourage visually handicapped children to use them. When discussing different types of fabric, for example, encourage students to use their sense of touch to analyze the difference among cotton, silk, and wool.

Provide appropriate materials, such as three-dimensional maps and large-print books accompanied by tapes. Many of the most popular children's books come in large-print editions. These should be used with discretion, however, as some students find that the books draw unwanted attention to their disability (Tuttle, 1988).

STUDENTS WITH OTHER PHYSICAL IMPAIRMENTS

A wide variety of physical and health conditions, such as spinal injuries and cystic fibrosis, place limits on children's ability to participate fully or without assistance in school activities. Some restrict motor skills, including mobility and degree of self-care; others require medication; and still others may result in intermittent and/or long absences from school.

The teacher's role is to become familiar with the physically impaired child's condition and make necessary adjustments in the classroom. Field trips, visits to the library, and even the physical setup of the classroom will have to be planned so as to accommodate the child's needs. Reading and writing skills will probably only be affected if the child has difficulty holding a book or using a pencil. Adjustments might have to be made to allow the child to use an adaptive device to type her or his work instead of writing it.

Promote understanding of disabilities. Until recently, most children with serious physical disabilities did not have access to regular classrooms, so many nondisabled children have little knowledge or understanding of these conditions. Through discussion, reading, and writing, stress what the disabled child *can* do. Be considerate but not overprotective. Because of their condition, some physically disabled students may miss school for extended periods of time. Encourage their classmates to send get-well cards or perhaps a newsletter informing them of classroom activities. When a child returns, plan a welcoming activity. Keep the child "involved in as many activities as her condition allows" (Kirk & Gallagher, 1986). The Children's Book List includes a number of recently published books that deal with disabilities.

Children's Book List
People with disabilities

Adler, A. *A Picture Book of Helen Keller*. New York: Holiday House (1990). A brief biography of the woman who overcame being both blind and deaf.

Alexander, S. *Mom Can't See Me*. New York: Macmillan (1990). A 9-year-old girl describes how her mother leads an active and rich life despite being blind.

Booth, B. *Mandy*. New York: Lothrop, Lee & Shepard (1991). Hearing-impaired Mandy risks going out into the scary night during an impending storm, to look for her beloved grandmother's lost pin.

Fleming, V. *Be Good to Eddie Lee*. New York: Philomel (1993). Although Christy considers him a pest, Eddie Lee, a boy with Down syndrome, shares several discoveries with her when he follows her into the woods.

Roby, C. *When Learning Is Tough*. Morton Grove, IL: Whitman (1993). Children describe their learning disabilities, talents, learning techniques, as well as misconceptions associated with learning disabilities.

Rosenberg, M. *My Friend, Leslie*. New York: Lothrop, Lee & Shepard (1983). A multi-handicapped kindergarten child, who is well-accepted by her classmates, is presented in various situations within the school setting.

GIFTED OR TALENTED STUDENTS

A basic goal of reading instruction is that all students should be taught to read up to their capacity. That is, average students should read up to grade level; gifted and talented students should be reading beyond grade level.

CHARACTERISTICS OF GIFTED AND TALENTED STUDENTS

Giftedness has been defined in many different ways. In the past, it was defined as superior intellectual ability but, more recently, special talents have been included in the definition. In PL 100–297, the Jacob K. Javits Gifted and Talented Students Education Act, the gifted are defined as follows:

> Children who give evidence of higher performance capability in such areas as intellectual, creative, artistic, leadership capacity, or in specific academic fields; and who require services or activities not ordinarily provided by the school in order to fully develop such capabilities. (Title V, Part 13, 1988)

Although a number of factors are mentioned in the above definition, the gifted are typically identified through an IQ test, norm-referenced achievement test results, rating scales, and teacher observation. The cutoff IQ score varies from approximately 120 to 130. Achievement is expected to be at the 90th percentile or better, and these children might also be expected to display characteristics of leadership, creative thinking, and abstract reasoning as measured by a behavioral checklist. Students may be recommended for gifted programs on the basis of classroom performance or manifestation of special talents in art, drama, or leadership. Recommendations could come from parents, guidance counselors, and peers as well as from teachers. Final selection of students is frequently made on the basis of a combination of factors.

FEATURES OF GIFTED PROGRAMS

A reading and writing program for gifted students should take into account the individual characteristics of the children. About 50 percent of the gifted come to school already reading (Terman, 1954). Provision should be made for them and for those reading above grade level. Some school programs have a policy that forbids students to read a basal meant for the next grade. The teacher might instead obtain an alternative basal, a supplementary reading series, or children's books. Gifted second-graders reading on a fifth- or sixth-grade level should not be restricted to second-grade material. The materials they read should be on their instructional and interest levels.

Tasks should also be commensurate with students' ability and achievement. One second-grader who was reading a simplified version of the Bible at home was assigned the second-grade supplementary phonics workbook. Obviously, the child had excellent word recognition skills or she would not have been able to read on such an advanced level. Practicing phonics skills that she was already applying was a waste of time.

Giftedness is a term for persons who have mental or other talents that are well above the ordinary. Approximately the top 2 percent of the population is classified as being gifted or talented.

Gifted students from diverse cultures may manifest their abilities in different ways. Each culture emphasizes those abilities that it values most.

Renzulli (1978) defined giftedness as the interaction of above-average ability, a high-level task commitment, and a high level of creativity brought to bear on a particular problem area.

Gifted children may also have problems. Their interests may be narrow, and they may be bored by having to work on skills that they have already mastered. They may also have problems accepting their ability because it sets them off from their peers. Not wishing to be perceived as different, many hide their talents, often quite successfully. They may also have learning disabilities and may experience serious difficulties reading and writing, despite their intellectual ability. They often fail to get help with their learning problems because their ability enables them to compensate for deficits (Wallace & McLoughlin, 1988).

Gifted students can, of course, be disadvantaged. Their giftedness may be masked by poverty and lack of opportunity to develop and display their gifts. Special care must be taken to identify talented, economically disadvantaged children.

The children chosen for a gifted program will depend, in part, on the school system's definition of intelligence. One of the broadest definitions of intelligence is Gardner's (1983) concept of multiple intelligences, which includes linguistic, logical-mathematical, spatial, bodily-kinesthetic, musical, interpersonal, and intrapersonal intelligences. A gifted student would be one who had exceptional ability in one or more of the intelligences.

Even though they possess superior cognitive ability, gifted students still need plenty of encouragement and guidance. And, even though they may be gifted, they may need help coming to terms with their talents and responsibilities. Being different, they also need acceptance and understanding by their peers. Despite their abilities and distinct needs, gifted students are frequently overlooked or neglected.

Inclusion is the practice of educating within the regular classroom all students, including those with special needs. In full inclusion, all support services are provided within the classroom setting. In partial inclusion, the student may be pulled out of the classroom for special instruction.

Because they master basic reading skills early and may not be sufficiently challenged by the classroom collections of books, gifted students should learn how to select books from the school library. To enable them to investigate areas of special interest, provide early instruction in the use of the dictionary, encyclopedia, and other basic references, as well as in the use of research skills. These students may also need help with study skills as they progress through the grades. Some are able to get by in the lower grades because of their ability, but as they reach more advanced grades, they may not have acquired the study habits and skills that will enable them to work up to their abilities.

Reading and writing workshops work quite well for the gifted. Through self-selected reading in reading workshop, gifted students are free to pursue advanced work at an accelerated pace. Through writing workshop, gifted students can also explore a broad range of writing genres. In creating reports on subjects of interest, they can investigate topics in depth and apply a host of practical research skills. Gifted students might also attempt some of the more difficult kinds of writing such as poetry, drama, and short pieces of fiction. One program that works exceptionally well with the gifted is Junior Great Books.

Junior Great Books is a program in which students from grade 2 on read literary classics and discuss them using a technique known as shared inquiry. The group leader, who is trained by the Great Books Foundation, initiates and guides the discussion, but it is up to the group to interpret the reading and validate its interpretation with evidence from the text. In addition to developing skill in the careful reading of complex materials, the shared inquiry program is designed to develop discussion and thinking skills and "a deeper understanding of self and others, as well as the motivation and desire to be life-long learners" (Tierney, Readence, & Dishner, 1995, p. 144). Although the Junior Great Books' shared inquiry program can be used with any student who has the skill to read the books, it is frequently used with gifted readers. It could be a part of the classroom program or an after-school or out-of-class activity. The discussion leader need not be a teacher but should be someone trained by the Great Books Foundation.

INCLUSION

For more than fifty years, there has been a movement to integrate disabled students into the classroom so that they might enter the mainstream of life (Reynolds & Birch, 1988). In order to accelerate the trend toward educating special education students within the regular classroom, the concept of **inclusion** has been widely adopted. Inclusion is more than just an organizational pattern. It is a philosophy that values diversity and the worth and potential of each individual (Hardman, 1994). Inclusion is also a collaborative, cooperative venture, with professionals working together and students helping each other. For inclusion to work, the competitive atmosphere of the traditional classroom must give way to the caring, collaborative spirit of the inclusive classroom where students and teachers learn from one another.

Inclusion fits in with current trends in teaching literacy. The stress on self-selected reading, workshop approach to writing, and various types of cooperative learning lend themselves to inclusion. In addition, adaptive technology has made it possible for students to compensate for a variety of handicapping conditions. A common observation from visitors to inclusive classrooms is that they cannot tell who is disabled and who is not.

How should teachers handle the increased diversity of the classroom? The National Association of State Boards of Education (1992) recommended the following:

- Seek out assistance in your classroom from other professionals, emphasizing a cooperative or team teaching approach.
- Explore/observe a variety of teaching methods to learn different ways to tailor instruction to the multiple needs and learning styles of your students.
- Accept that not all students will cover the same material at the same time.
- Above all, be flexible. This type of change takes time, and every teacher makes mistakes along the way as he or she learns to work with increasingly diverse students. (p. 29)

What adjustments should teachers make to help integrate students with disabilities into the classroom? Effective teachers report individualizing instruction and receiving support from the special education resource teacher (Schulz, 1993). Depending upon the disability, they also use shortened assignments, study buddies, oral tests, easier materials, and preferential seating.

TITLE 1 AND REMEDIAL PROGRAMS

Increasingly, Title 1 and remedial specialists are also moving towards an inclusive model, which means that remedial instruction is often conducted within the classroom instead of in a resource room. To obtain the best results for the children in Title 1 or remedial programs, it is important for teachers and specialists to confer regularly. All involved benefit from these conferences. The classroom teacher obtains insight into the child's problem and techniques for later use in the classroom; the specialist learns information about the child's functioning in a group and can enlist the classroom teacher's help in providing opportunities for having the child apply skills. The child, of course, benefits by getting the best from both professionals. Conducting remediation in the classroom has many advantages. The classroom teacher is less isolated and spends more time working with other professionals. In addition, disabled readers prefer working in the regular classroom and spend more time reading books and less time on worksheets. Having additional assistance in the classroom also means greater individualization (Gelzheiser & Meyers, 1990).

EARLY INTERVENTION PROGRAMS

An ounce of prevention is worth a pound of cure. Over the last decade, a number of programs have been created that are designed to help those students who are most at risk of failing to learn to read and write. Because of its dramatic but well-documented success, one such program, Reading Recovery, is now being implemented in every state.

READING RECOVERY

The basic intent of many remedial programs is to help students catch up so that they can then learn with their peers. However, some practices represent a "slow-it-down, make-it-more-concrete" approach. Having a low estimate of students' ability to progress, the pace of the work is slowed and students might even be retained. Programs like Reading Recovery, on the other hand, have as their main purpose accelerating students' progress so that they catch up and stay caught up (McGill-Franzen, 1994).

Devised by Marie Clay (1993b) and colleagues in New Zealand, Reading Recovery is based on a series of highly effective procedures that the group, through discussion and experimentation, assembled. The idea behind Reading Recovery is to intervene early, before students are discouraged by failure and before they pick up unproductive reading strategies. A program that ignores labels, Reading Recovery is designed for the lowest-achieving 20 percent of a class. The success rate has been phenomenal. In New Zealand, approximately 95 percent of the students complete the program reading as well as average children in their classes. Moreover, these children continue to do well when retested several years later (Clay, 1993b). In the United States, the success rate is approximately 80–86 percent (Smith-Burke, 1994; Dunkeld, 1991).

In thirty-minute, one-on-one daily sessions, students read whole books, write, and are taught how to use a variety of decoding strategies and how to monitor their reading. Instructors are highly trained. A key element in Reading Recovery's success is the teacher's guidance, which is based on close observation of the student and a thorough knowledge of the reading process.

Careful monitoring of students' progress, working with parents, having high expectations for the students, and building students' control of strategies so that they can apply them independently are other key factors in the success of Reading Recovery. In addition, students are provided with carefully selected materials. Reading Recovery teachers have a listing of more than a thousand books that are sequenced in order of difficulty into twenty levels, which range from an emergent or picture-reading level to early second grade. Table 12.5 presents an overview of a Reading Recovery lesson. For a complete description of Reading Recovery, see *Reading Recovery: A Guidebook for Teachers in Training* (Clay, 1993b).

OTHER EARLY INTERVENTION PROGRAMS

Although Reading Recovery is an outstanding program, it is costly to implement. However, there are a number of other highly successful early intervention programs which do not require extensive training and may be implemented with small groups of students by the classroom teacher, Title 1 instructor, or remedial specialist. These include Early Intervention in Reading, a program in which the first-grade teacher spends twenty minutes a day working with five to seven of the lowest-achieving students (Taylor, Strait, & Medo, 1994), and the Boulder Project, in which Title 1 teachers work with small groups of low-achieving students (Hiebert, 1994). Both programs have encouragingly high success rates.

Unlike other early intervention programs, Success for All is designed for an entire elementary school. Success for All stresses prevention of reading problems and teaching in such a way that children are successful. "Getting reading right the first time is a kind of a motto for the program, which is rooted in the research-based finding that a reading failure in the early grades is fundamentally preventable" (Slavin, Madden, Karweit, Dolan, & Wasik, 1994, p. 126). Originally

TABLE 12.5 Overview of a Reading Recovery lesson

Reading familiar stories	Student reads one or more familiar books to build fluency.
Taking a running record of yesterday's book	The teacher analyzes the student's performance as she or he reads the book introduced in yesterday's lesson.
Working with letters	Magnetic letters are used at various points in the lesson to provide instruction in letter-sound relationships.
Writing a story or message	The student, under the teacher's guidance, composes a one-sentence or longer story related to an experience the student has had or a book read during the lesson. The story is cut up and taken home to be read for practice.
Reading a new book	Carefully chosen so as to present an appropriate level of challenge, the new book is introduced by the teacher before being read orally by the student.

Drawn from *Partners in Learning: Teachers and Children in Reading Recovery* by C. A. Lyons, G. S. Pinnell, and D. E. DeFord, New York: Teachers College Press, 1993.

implemented in Baltimore's most impoverished schools, Success for All is now used in a number of urban areas. In addition to improved reading achievement, Success for All refers fewer students to special education classes and has retained very few students.

In his description of a reading program for Spanish-speaking students, Goldenberg (1994) describes what happens when teachers switch from low to high expectations. At the elementary school where he was working, the teachers progressed slowly through the basal readers because it was felt that the children could not move any faster. By year's end, 49 percent of the first-graders were still in the beginning book of the basal series; only 7 percent were on grade level. The program was revised to include emergent literacy instruction in kindergarten, and a parent program was initiated. In addition, conferences were held with teachers to discuss the pace of the students' progress. The program also was balanced to include more comprehension. Within three years, only 1 percent of the children were still in the first book at year's end and 25 percent were reading at or above grade level. Higher expectations plus an improved program resulted in higher achievement.

LESSONS FROM EARLY INTERVENTION PROGRAMS

What lessons can be learned from these intervention programs? Although they differ on specifics, all stress the importance of providing ample opportunity for students to read materials on the appropriate level, teaching students to be strategic readers, monitoring their progress, training staff, evaluating the program, providing inservice training, and having strong leadership. Each program also has a strong decoding component. Most important of all, the programs have a strong belief in the ability of at-risk children to succeed, a belief that the programs have convincingly confirmed.

SUMMARY

1. Because of the multicultural nature of our nation and the trend to include disabled students in the regular classroom, schools are becoming increasingly diverse. Multiculturalism and inclusion require a focus on the diverse background and needs of all children.

2. Between 25 and 35 percent of U.S. schoolchildren are at risk of failing either in life or in school. These include economically disadvantaged children, linguistically and culturally diverse children, mentally retarded children, slow learners, learning-disabled children, and children with physical disabilities.

3. Approximately one elementary schoolchild in five is economically disadvantaged. With inadequate housing, substandard medical care, poor diet, and restricted opportunities because of a lack of money, such children as a group do not perform as well in reading and writing as more advantaged children. Necessary program adjustments include building background knowledge and the kind of abstract vocabulary that school demands, especially in the content areas. Starting early, involving parents, reflecting the child's culture, having high expectations, and valuing the child's language are additional recommended program adjustments.

4. Teaching culturally diverse children requires understanding of and building on the students' culture and accepting the students' language. If possible, students who are not native speakers of English should generally be taught to read in their first language. Classroom teachers should support the efforts of the bilingual and ESL teachers. Encouraging students, building language, and engaging in a variety of supportive reading and writing activities, such as shared reading and language-experience stories, are some of the ways in which classroom teachers can assist SAE (Still Acquiring English) students.

5. Nearly one child in twenty has been identified as being learning disabled. A common characteristic of learning-disabled students is evidenced by a significant discrepancy between performance and ability. These students may have difficulty in underlying processes such as language, attention, memory, or perception. About 85 percent of children classified as learning disabled have a reading difficulty. It is estimated that from 3 to 5 percent of all children have an attention deficit disorder. Although not technically classified as a learning disability, attention deficit disorder can interfere with the learning process.

6. Approximately 2 percent of the population is mentally retarded. Mental retardation is defined as an IQ of 70 or below and deficient adaptive behavior. Severely retarded children cannot learn to read. However, mildy and moderately retarded children are able to acquire some skill in reading. Because they have difficulty with executive functioning and central processing, they tend to do better with word attack than they do with comprehension, which requires higher-level skills.

7. Slow learners, who make up approximately 14 percent of the school population, tend to be concrete in their thinking and need help with organization. Although they function on a higher level than mentally retarded children, they need some adaptations in their instruction and materials on the appropriate level.

8. Except for children with hearing and vision impairments, those with physical disabilities do not necessarily have trouble learning to read and write. However, physical adjustments might have to be made so that these students can take part in all activities. Cut off from oral language, hearing-impaired students may experience difficulty with reading and writing, depending on the severity of their loss. Vision-impaired children generally experience less difficulty learning to read but may lack an adequate understanding of concepts about objects and events that are primarily visual.

9. Because of new legislation and advances in technology, more and more disabled students will be taught within the classroom. Working closely with special education resource personnel, the classroom teacher will have to make adjustments in the physical environment and/or program so that these students learn to read and write to their full capacities. The classroom teacher should also work closely with Title 1 teachers and reading specialists as more and more remedial students are taught in the classroom.

10. Reading Recovery and other early intervention programs have demonstrated conclusively the effectiveness of preventing reading failure. The programs have proved that, given the right kind of instruction, children at risk for failure can be successful.

CLASSROOM APPLICATIONS

1. Select and read five books that you think might be appropriate for culturally diverse students. Choose from those listed in one of the resource books or select books on your own. For each book create a conference card containing bibliographic information, a summary of the book, discussion questions, and extension activities.

2. Select and read five books that you think might be used to help students better understand the handicaps of others. Construct conference cards.

3. Interview the special education, Title 1, or remedial reading specialist at the school where you teach or at a nearby elementary school. Find out what kinds of programs the school offers for special education, Title 1, and remedial students.

4. Observe a classroom in which remedial or special education instruction is offered. What arrangements have the specialist and the classroom teacher made for working together? What are the advantages of this type of arrangement? What are some of the disadvantages?

FIELD APPLICATIONS

1. Investigate the culture of a minority group that is represented in a class you are now teaching or that you may be teaching in the future. Find out information about the group's literature, language, and customs. How might you use this information to plan more effective instruction for the class? Plan a lesson using this information. If possible, teach the lesson and evaluate its effectiveness.

2. Plan a reading lesson for some students with moderate mental retardation that is designed to teach them how to read a series of warning signs. Talk over your plan with a special education teacher. If possible, teach the lesson and comment on its effectiveness.

Evaluation

For each of the following statements related to the chapter you are about to read, put a check under "Agree" or "Disagree" to show how you feel. Discuss your responses with classmates before you read the chapter.

Agree   **Disagree**

_____ 1. Nationwide achievement tests are essential for the assessment of reading. _____

_____ 2. Current tests do not fairly measure whole language programs. _____

_____ 3. Most writing assessments are too subjective. _____

_____ 4. Elementary school students take too many tests. _____

_____ 5. The community has a right to know how its schools are doing. _____

_____ 6. Tests should not be used to determine what is taught in a reading program. _____

_____ 7. If students are taking tests mandated by the state or school district, they should be taught the skills that are tested. _____

_____ 8. Observation yields more about a student's progress in reading and writing than a standardized test does. _____

Using What You Know

Evaluation is an essential part of literacy learning. It is a judgment by teachers, children, parents, administrators, and the wider community as to whether instructional goals have been met. Evaluation also helps teachers determine what is and is not working so that they can plan better programs. Self-evaluation gives students more control over their own learning.

What kinds of experiences have you had with evaluation? How has your school work been assessed? Do you agree with the assessments, or do you think they were off the mark? Keeping in mind the current emphasis on holistic reading and writing processes and integration of language arts, what might be some appropriate ways to evaluate the literacy development of today's students?

THE NATURE OF EVALUATION

In **evaluation,** we ask, "How am I doing?" so that we can do better. Evaluation is a value judgment. We can also ask, "How is the education program doing?" and base our evaluation on tests, quizzes, records, work samples, observations, anecdotal records, and similar information. The evaluation could be made by a student while reviewing her or his writing folder or by parents as they look over a report card. The evaluator could be a teacher, who, after examining a portfolio or collection of a student's work and thinking over recent observations of that student, concludes that the student has done well but could do better.

Evaluation should result in some kind of action. The evaluator must determine what that action should be, based on her or his judgment. The student may decide that he or she has been writing the same type of pieces and needs to branch out, the parents might decide that their child must study more, and the teacher might choose to add more silent reading time to the program.

Evaluation is a subjective process that uses the results of tests, observations, work samples, or other devices to judge the effectiveness of a program. A program is evaluated in terms of its objectives. The ultimate purpose of evaluation is to improve the program.

THE STARTING POINT

Evaluation starts with a set of goals. You cannot tell if you have reached your destination if you do not know where you were headed. For example, a teacher may decide that one of his or her goals will be to instill in children a love of reading. This is a worthy goal, one that is lacking in many programs. But how will the teacher decide whether the goal has been reached, and what will the teacher use as evidence? The goal has to be stated in terms of a specific objective that includes, if possible, observable behavior—for example, students will voluntarily read at least once a week or at least one book a month. The objective then becomes measurable, and the teacher can collect information that will provide evidence as to whether it has been met.

Evaluation should help students become more aware of where they are in their learning, where they want to go, and what they need to do to get there. It should help students become "more self-reflective and in control of their own learning" (Winograd, 1994, p. 420).

Evaluation of a reading program does not end with a judgment. An essential component is improvement of the program. Once strengths and weaknesses are noted, steps should be taken to build on the strengths and repair the weak spots. For example, if you administer an attitude survey whose results indicate that students do not enjoy reading, you would need to plan activities to help your students discover the satisfaction of reading. Farr and Carey (1986) commented:

> Most evaluators today consider the act of evaluating only to determine whether a program is adequate or inadequate to be a waste of time. What one wants to know is how to improve the program regardless of how good or how bad it is. What is true about programs is also true in the evaluation of individual students. The emphasis should be on obtaining information for planning instruction and not on labelling. (pp. 2–3)

THREE PERSPECTIVES OF EVALUATION

Evaluation has three perspectives: self, collaborative others, and society (Short, 1990). The self is the student. The collaborative others are all those who work with the child, including the teacher, peer editor, learning team, discussion groups. Society includes the parents, the community at large, and officials of the school or school district. Each group may have a different purpose for evaluating and may require different types of evidence. The school board, for instance, may want to examine norm-referenced, multiple-choice, standardized test scores; students may note that they are not doing well on science and social studies tests; and teachers may observe that students are having difficulty applying comprehension strategies to expository text. The students and teacher are using information as clues to improving students' immediate performance. The school board is more concerned with how the district's students are performing as compared with similar schools, or how the performance of this year's students compares to that of past students.

Because students, teachers, parents, and school boards have differing perspectives, they need different kinds of evaluation information. Although results of norm-referenced tests are frequently used by school boards and state departments of education as a basis for evaluation, they have limited usefulness for teachers. Instead, authentic measures are more helpful because they provide insight into students' learning strategies.

AUTHENTIC ASSESSMENT

Changing views of reading and writing have created a need for alternative methods of **assessment.** Traditional reading tests contain brief passages and multiple-choice questions that often assess subskills. The results are unrealistic on two counts: (1) The selections are briefer than those students normally read, and (2) the multiple-choice format measures recognition rather than construction of meaning. The tests tend to measure product rather than process. Guessing is also a factor, so it is difficult to be sure whether a student actually knows the answer to an item or has simply made a lucky guess.

Alternative forms of assessment are often called **authentic assessment.** The word *authentic* is used because these assessment procedures "reflect the actual

One danger of insisting that all objectives be observable and measurable is that the objectives will then be primarily lower-level ones because those lend themselves to measurement.

Farr (1991) argues for the creation of an assessment that would be useful for students, teachers, and external decision makers. If a test is going to be used by a principal, school board, or legislative body to judge students' performance, then this fact exerts pressure on the school and individual teachers to plan instruction in such a way that students do well on the test. In other words, the test determines the curriculum. Recognizing this fact, Connecticut, Michigan, and some other states have created tests that better reflect what is being taught in the most effective classrooms.

Assessment is the process of gathering data about an area of learning through tests, observations, samples, or other means.

Authentic assessment involves gathering data from tasks that are typical of the kinds of reading or writing that students perform in school and out.

learning and instructional activities of the classroom and out-of-school worlds" (Hiebert, Valencia, & Afflerbach, 1994, p. 11). In authentic assessment, students retell or summarize whole texts, as opposed to the kind of objective testing in which students respond to multiple-choice questions asked about short paragraphs. Observations, think-alouds, holistic scoring of writing, anecdotal records, and assembling and evaluating a portfolio are also examples of authentic assessment.

In the past, many assessment practices were not found to have been very helpful. Some have been downright misleading and, perhaps, even harmful. For instance, using **norm-referenced tests,** which compare one student with another or one school district with another, has fostered competition and a focus on high scores. The emphasis should be on developing each student's abilities to the fullest. If administrators and teachers are being judged by test results, there will be a natural tendency to gear instruction to the test. If the assessment measures only a portion of the curriculum, then the portion not measured may be neglected. Worse, the format of the test may influence instruction. For example, if the test features short paragraphs with multiple-choice responses, then the instructional reading program will tend to emphasize that format. Valuable instructional time that could have been devoted to reading literature and developing higher-order thinking skills may be allotted instead to low-level exercises designed to help students achieve higher scores. Moreover, the population most likely to be subjected to these lower-level activities is remedial and at-risk students, because the pressure to show improvement in the performance of these students is greatest (Herman, 1992).

However, when assessment is authentic and when students are judged on their ability to read whole selections and to respond by composing a written response, assessment practices can be very helpful. Teachers then emphasize these more holistic activities. As a result of holistic writing assessment in California, for instance, teachers began requiring their students to write more frequently and to attempt a greater variety of writing genres (Herman, 1992).

PRODUCT VERSUS PROCESS MEASURES

Authentic assessment emphasizes process rather than product. Product assessment is concerned with what the student has learned. Process assessment seeks to find out how the student learns. Product measures are the number of correct answers on a quiz, the stanine or percentile score on a norm-referenced test, the final copy of a composition, or the number of books read. They help teachers assess students' current and past levels of achievement. They provide information on students' reading and writing levels and abilities, the kinds of materials they can read, the kinds of writing they can do, and how well they can spell. Knowing where each child is, the teacher can plan instruction and activities that build on what students have already accomplished.

Process measures include observing students to see what strategies they use to arrive at a particular answer, to compose a piece of writing, or to study for a test. These measures seek to answer such questions as "How do students prepare to read an assignment? Do they monitor for meaning? What fix-up strategies do they use? Do students select, organize, and elaborate information as they read? If so, how?" Having this kind of insight, the teacher is able to redirect errant

A **norm-referenced test** is one for which a student's performance is compared to a representative sample of other students (a norm group) who have taken the test.

Many forms of authentic assessment are actually examples of performance assessment, which involves using the performance of an individual or a group on a literacy task as the basis of assessment. Performance assessment typically focuses directly on the task itself. It may involve observation and assessment of an individual or a group of students working on a project that requires reading and writing as well as thinking and discussion skills. For instance, small groups of students working together may be assessed on their ability to read several articles about recycling and to respond to their reading by writing editorials about recycling in the school newspaper. Performance assessment also includes evaluation of students' reading and writing logs, their oral or written responses to open-ended questions, and their portfolios. The key element in performance assessment is that it should be directly linked to learning goals and classroom activities (Tierney, Readence, & Dishner, 1995).

thought processes, correct poorly applied strategies, or teach needed strategies. Actually, both process and product measures provide useful information. Knowing where a child is and how he or she got there, the teacher is better prepared to map out a successful journey.

QUESTIONS TO BE ASKED

Essentially, evaluation is the process of asking a series of questions. Specific questions depend on a program's particular goals and objectives. However, some general questions that should be asked about every literacy program include the following:

- Where are students in their literacy development?
- At what level are they reading?
- Are they reading up to their ability level?
- How well do they comprehend what they read?
- Are they able to comprehend a variety of materials?
- How adequate are students' reading vocabularies?
- What comprehension and word-attack strategies do students use?
- Do they know how to study?
- What are their attitudes toward reading?
- What kinds of books do they like to read?
- Do they enjoy a variety of genres?
- Do they read on their own?
- Do they enjoy reading?
- How well do they write?
- What kinds of writing tasks have they attempted?
- Are students' reading and writing improving?
- Which students seem to have special needs in reading and writing?

Answers to these essential questions help teachers plan, revise, and improve their reading and writing programs. The rest of this chapter explores a number of techniques for gathering the assessment information necessary to answer them. Both traditional and alternative means will be used. However, one danger in evaluation is the temptation to gather too much information. Be economical. Do not waste time gathering information you are not going to use.

Harste (1991), a major figure in whole language, prefers the concept of *engagement* to that of objectives. He feels that objectives suggest fixed predictable outcomes, whereas learning is unpredictable. In an engagement, students can demonstrate key learnings in a variety of ways. Sample engagements include the following:

- As a result of reading a given book, students will be able to relate what they've read to their background experience.
- As a result of reading a given book, students will be able to plan new action (p. 24).

With engagement, instead of setting a single criterion, teachers can accept a variety of literacy behaviors as evidence of progress.

PLACEMENT INFORMATION

The first question the classroom teacher of reading has to have answered is "Where are the students?" If they are reading, assessment begins with determining the levels at which they are reading. One of the best placement devices is an **informal reading inventory** (IRI). In fact, if properly given, it will tell just about everything a teacher needs to know about a student's reading. It will also supply useful information about language development, work habits, interests, and personal development.

An **informal reading inventory** is an assessment device in which a student reads a series of selections that gradually increase in difficulty. The teacher records errors and assesses comprehension in order to determine the level of materials that a student can read.

INFORMAL READING INVENTORY

An informal reading inventory is a series of graded selections beginning at the very easiest level—preprimer—and extending up to grade 8 or beyond. Each level has two selections; one is silent and the other oral. Starting at an easy level, the student keeps on reading until it is obvious that the material has become too difficult.

An IRI yields information about four levels: independent, instructional, frustration, and listening capacity. The **independent level,** or the free-reading level, is the point at which students can read on their own without teacher assistance. The **instructional level** refers to the point at which students need assistance because the material contains too many unknown words or concepts, or their background of experience is insufficient. This is also the level of materials used for teaching. Material at the **frustration level** is so difficult that students cannot read it even with teacher assistance. The fourth level is **listening capacity,** the highest level at which students can understand what has been read to them. Listening capacity is an informal measure of ability to comprehend spoken language. Theoretically, it is the level at which students should be able to read if they have all the necessary decoding skills. In practice, a small percentage of students have listening deficiencies, so a listening test might underestimate their true capacity. Younger students also tend to read below capacity because they are still acquiring basic reading skills. As students progress through the grades, listening and reading levels grow closer together (Sticht & James, 1984).

DETERMINING PLACEMENT LEVELS

Placement levels are determined by having students read two selections, one orally and one silently, at appropriate grade levels. The percentages of oral-reading errors and comprehension questions answered correctly at each level are calculated. This information is then used to determine placement levels. Quantitative data for determining levels are contained in Table 13.1.

Standards for determining levels, marking symbols, types of misreadings that are counted as errors, and administration procedures vary, depending on the source consulted. The standards used in this book are taken from Johnson, Kress, and Pikulski (1987) and seem to be the most widely used. To be at the independent

The **independent level** is the level at which a student can read without any assistance. Comprehension is 90 percent or higher, and word recognition is 99 percent or higher.

The **instructional level** is the level at which a student needs teacher help in order to be able to read profitably. Comprehension is 75 percent or higher, and word recognition is 95 percent or higher.

The **frustration level** is the level at which reading material is so difficult that the student can't read it even with help. Word recognition is 90 percent or less, or comprehension is 50 percent or less.

Listening capacity is the highest level at which students can understand material that is read to them with 75 percent comprehension.

TABLE 13.1   Quantitative criteria for IRI

Level	Word Recognition in Context (%)	Average Comprehension (%)
Independent	99	90–100
Instructional	95–98	75–89
Frustration	≤ 90	≤ 50
Listening capacity		75

The standards listed in Table 13.1 are fairly conservative. Some examiners, in an attempt to be kind to students, disregard some errors or use a more liberal set of standards—for example, making 90 percent acceptable word recognition for the instructional level. According to Enz (1989), however, this is the type of kindness that kills. In her study of students placed by conservative versus liberal IRI standards, she found dramatic differences in students' attitudes and behaviors. Those placed conservatively tended to be on task most of the time, have a higher success rate, and have a better attitude toward reading than those placed by criteria that were too liberal.

Before administering the word-list test, explain to students that they will be reading lists of words that grow harder and harder. Explain that some of the words might be too hard for them, but they should try to do their best.

level, a reader must have both 99 percent word recognition and 90 percent comprehension. At the instructional level, the reader must have at least 95 percent word recognition and at least 75 percent comprehension. The frustration level is reached when word recognition drops to 90 percent or comprehension falls to 50 percent. Even with 80 percent comprehension and 90 percent word recognition, readers are at the frustration level because they are encountering too many words that they cannot decode. Listening capacity is the level at which students can understand 75 percent of the material that is read to them.

ADMINISTERING THE WORD-LIST TEST

Rather than guessing at what grade level to begin the inventory, a teacher can administer a word-list test to locate an approximate starting point. This test consists of a series of ten to twenty words at each grade level. Students read the words in isolation, starting with the easiest and continuing until they reach a level where they get half or more of the words wrong. In a simplified administration of the test, students read the words from their copy of the list and the teacher marks each response on her or his copy as being right or wrong.

In diagnostic administration, the teacher uses three-by-five cards to flash the words for one second each. When students respond correctly, the teacher moves on to the next word. If the answer is incorrect or if students fail to respond, the teacher stops and lets them look at the word for as long as they wish (within reason). While students examine the missed word, the teacher writes down their response or marks a symbol in the flash (timed) column. If students make a second erroneous response, it is written in the second, or untimed, column. Symbols used to mark word-list tests are presented in Table 13.2. A corrected word-list test is shown in Figure 13.1.

Although used to indicate the starting level for the IRI, a word-list test can yield valuable information about students' reading, especially if a diagnostic administration has been used. By comparing flash and untimed scores, teachers can assess the adequacy of students' sight vocabulary (their ability to recognize words immediately) and their proficiency with decoding. Teachers can note which decoding skills students are able to use and which must be taught. Looking at the performance depicted in Figure 13.1, it is clear that the student has a very limited sight

---

TABLE 13.2   Word-list marking symbols

Word	Teacher Mark	Meaning
the	✓	Correct
was	✓	Incorrect response or repeated error
have	o	No response
dog	boy	Mispronunciation
are	dk	Don't know

FIGURE 13.1 | A corrected word-list test

		Flash	Untimed
1.	their	the	✓
2.	wet	o	✓
3.	king	o	✓
4.	off	o	dk
5.	alone	uh	along
6.	hurt	✓	
7.	near	✓	
8.	tiger	tie	✓
9.	stick	sick	✓
10.	move	moo	more
11.	let	o	✓
12.	men	✓	
13.	shoe	o	✓
14.	wish	✓	
15.	apple	o	dk
16.	on	o	✓
17.	sign	o	o
18.	bit	o	✓
19.	smell	sell	✓
20.	floor	for	✓
	Percent correct	20%	60%

vocabulary. The flash column shows that the student recognized few of the words immediately; the untimed column gives an overall picture of the student's ability to apply decoding skills. The student was able to use initial and final consonants and short vowels to decode words; for example, the student was able to read *wet, king, let,* and *bit* when given time to decode them. However, the student had difficulty with initial clusters; note how the student read *sick* for *slick, sell* for *smell,* and *for* for *floor.*

One of the newest inventories, the *Flynt-Cooter Reading Inventory for the Classroom,* 2nd ed. (Flynt & Cooter, 1995), uses series of sentences rather than word lists to assess students' ability to read high-frequency words.

ADMINISTERING THE INVENTORY

The informal reading inventory is started at the level below the student's last perfect performance on the flash or timed portion of the word-list test. If that perfect performance was at the fourth-grade level, the inventory is started at the third-grade level.

An IRI is like a directed reading activity, except that its main purpose is to assess a student's reading. To administer an IRI, first explain to the student that she or he will be reading some stories and answering some questions so that you can get some information about her or his reading. Before each selection is read, have the student read its title and predict what it will be about (Johns, 1994). Doing this will help the student set a purpose for reading, and it will give you a sense of the student's prediction ability and background of experience.

The student reads the first selection orally. This is one of the few times in which reading orally without having first read the selection silently is valid. As the child reads, use the symbols shown in Table 13.3 to record her or his performance. Although many different kinds of misreadings are noted, only the following are counted as errors: mispronunciations, omissions, insertions, and words supplied by the examiner because the student asked the examiner to read them or apparently could not read them on her or his own. Self-corrected errors are not

TABLE 13.3 Oral-reading symbols

	Marking	Meaning
Quantitative errors	bad the ~~big~~ dog	Mispronounced
	the ~~big~~ dog	Omitted word
	the (ferocious) dog	Asked for word
	bad the big ∧ dog	Inserted word
	bad ✓ the ~~big~~ dog	Self-corrected
Qualitative errors	I hit the ball⊗ and George ran.	Omitted punctuation
	The |ferocious dog	Hesitation
	the <u>ferocious</u> dog	Repetition
	Good morning! ↑	Rising inflection
	Are you reading? ↓	Falling inflection
	W x W	Word-by-word reading
	HM	Head movement
	FP	Finger pointing
	PC	Use of picture clue

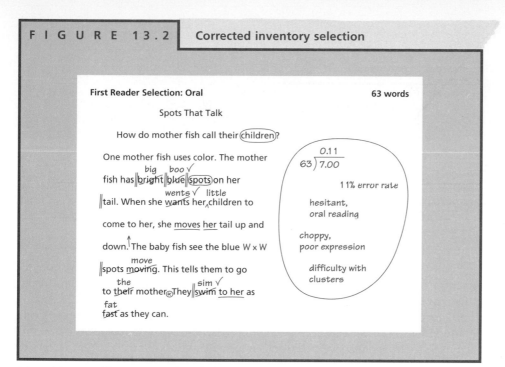

FIGURE 13.2 Corrected inventory selection

First Reader Selection: Oral   63 words

Spots That Talk

How do mother fish call their (children)?

One mother fish uses color. The mother
fish has ‖bright‖blue‖(spots) on her
tail. When she wants her children to

come to her, she moves her tail up and

down. The baby fish see the blue W x W
spots moving. This tells them to go
to their mother. They ‖swim‖ to her as
fast as they can.

$$63 \overline{\smash{)}7.00} \quad 0.11$$

11% error rate

hesitant,
oral reading

choppy,
poor expression

difficulty with
clusters

Adapted from *Building Basic Reading Skills: Main Idea and Details* (p. 23) by T. Gunning, 1982, Elizabethtown, PA: Continental Press.

counted. Hesitations, repetitions, and other qualitative misreadings are noted but not counted as errors. A corrected inventory selection is shown in Figure 13.2.

After the student finishes reading aloud, ask the series of comprehension questions that accompany the selection or ask for an oral retelling (see p. 508 for information on administering a retelling). Then introduce a silent selection on the same level. Just as with the oral selection, allow a very brief readiness phase and have the student make a prediction. During the silent reading, note finger pointing, head movement, lip movement, and subvocalizing. Symbols for these behaviors are given in Table 13.4. Ask comprehension questions when the student finishes reading. Proceeding level by level, continue to test until the student reaches a frustration level—that is, misreads 10 percent or more of the words or misses at least half the comprehension questions.

When the frustration level has been reached, read to the student the oral and silent selections at each level beyond the frustration level until the student reaches the highest level at which she or he can answer 75 percent of the comprehension questions. This is the student's listening capacity, and it indicates how well the student would be able to read if she or he had the necessary word-recognition skills and related print-processing skills. For children who have limited language skills or background of experience or deficient listening skills, you may have to backtrack and read selections at the frustration level and below. Since students will already have been exposed to the lower-level selections, you will have to use alternative selections to test listening comprehension.

The listening portion of the inventory provides only an approximate indication of children's capacity. It tends to be inaccurate with children who have difficulty paying attention or who lack good listening skills.

TABLE 13.4   Silent-reading symbols

Symbol	Meaning
HM	Head movement
FP	Finger pointing
LM	Lip movement
SV	Subvocalizing

After administering the inventory, enter the scores from each level on the inventory's summary sheet (see Figure 13.3). Word-recognition scores are determined by calculating the percentage of words read correctly on each oral selection (number of words read correctly divided by number of words in the selection). Comprehension is calculated by averaging comprehension scores for the oral and silent selections at each level. Using the numbers on the summary sheet, determine the placement levels. Refer to the criteria in Table 13.1.

INTERPRETING THE INVENTORY

After determining the student's levels, examine her or his performance on the inventory to determine word-recognition and comprehension strengths and weaknesses. What kinds of phonics skills can the student use? Is the student able to decode multisyllabic words? Could the student read words that have prefixes or suffixes? Did the student use context? Did the student integrate the use of decoding skills with context? How did the student's word recognition compare with her or his comprehension? How did the student handle literal and inferential questions? How did comprehension on oral passages compare with comprehension on silent passages? You can also note the quality of the student's responses as she or he answered questions and the way the student approached the tasks. What level of language did the student use to answer questions? What was the student's level of confidence and effort as she or he undertook each task? Through careful observation, you can gain insight into the student's reading processes. For example, you may observe the student decoding unfamiliar words sound by sound or using a combination of context and phonics to handle difficult words. Strengths and weaknesses as well as immediate needs can be noted on the IRI summary sheet.

Miscues are oral-reading responses that differ from the expected (correct) responses.

Miscue analysis is the process of determining which cueing system or combination of cueing systems (semantic, syntactic, or graphophonic) a student is using.

MISCUE ANALYSIS OF IRIs

As discussed in Chapter 3, students use three cueing systems to decode printed words: syntactic, semantic, and phonic (graphophonic). To determine how they are using these systems, analyze their word-recognition errors, or **miscues,** with a modified **miscue analysis.** On a sheet similar to the one in Figure 13.4, list the students' miscues. Try to list at least ten miscues, but do not analyze any that are at

Word-list Scores   Inventory Scores

Level	Flash	Untimed	Word recognition (in context)	Comprehension (oral)	(silent)	(avg.)	Listening capacity
PP	80	95	100	100	90	95	
P	70	80	96	100	80	90	
1	30	55	89	60	60	60	
2							90
3							80
4							50
5							
6							
7							
8							

Levels

Independent	P
Instructional	PP
Frustration	1
Listening capacity	3

or beyond the frustration level. Miscues can be chosen from the independent and instructional levels and from the buffer zone between the instructional and frustration levels (91–94 percent word recognition). Also list the correct version of each error. Put a check in the syntactic column if the miscue is syntactically correct—that is, if it is the same part of speech as the word in the text or could be used in that context. Put a check in the semantic column if the miscue makes sense in the sentence. In the graphic column, use a check to show whether the miscue is graphically and/or phonically similar to the text word. It is similar if it contains at least half the sounds in the text word. Also use a check to show whether the beginning, middle, and end of the miscue are similar to the text word. Put a check in the nonword column if the miscue is not a real word. Also indicate corrected miscues with a check in the self-correction column. Tally each column (as shown in Figure 13.4) and convert tallies to percentages. After tallying the columns,

FIGURE 13.4   Miscue analysis

Name: _____   Date: _____

Miscue	Text	Syntactic similarity	Semantic similarity	Graphic similarity	Beginning	Middle	End	Nonword	Self-correction
gots	gets	✓	✓	✓	✓	—	✓		
will	with	—	—	✓	✓	✓	—		
ran ✓	runs	✓	✓	✓	✓	—	✓		✓
balt	ball	—	—	✓	✓	✓	—	✓	
tricks	kicks	✓	—	✓	—	✓	✓		
my	me	—	✓	✓	✓		—		
trick	trust	✓	—	—	✓	—	✓		
bell	ball	✓	—	✓	✓	—	✓		
frain	five	—	—	—	✓	—	—	✓	
grain	gray	—	—	✓	✓	✓	—		
there	that	—	—	—	✓	—	—		
eak	each	—	—	✓	✓		—	✓	
Totals		5	3	9	11	4	4	3	1
Numbers of miscues analyzed		12	12	12					
Percentage		42	25	75				25	8

examine the numbers to see if the student is reading for meaning. Miscues that make sense in the context of the selection, self-corrections, and absence of non-words are positive signs. Conversely, the presence of nonwords is a negative sign, as are miscues that do not fit the sense of the passage or the syntax.

Compare the tallies to see if the cues are being used in balanced fashion or if one is being overused or underused. The student could be overusing phonics and underusing semantic context, or vice versa. Draw tentative conclusions about the strategies that the student uses in his or her word recognition. Double-check those conclusions as you observe the student read in the classroom.

As you can see from Figure 13.4, fewer than half of this student's miscues fit the context either syntactically or semantically. Moreover, three of them are nonwords, and the student had only one self-correction. All indications are that the student is failing to use context clues and is not reading for meaning. The student makes heavy use of phonics, especially at the beginning of words, but must also integrate his or her use of phonics with syntactic and semantic cues. The student also needs to improve his or her use of phonics skills, especially middle and ending elements.

Generally, IRIs are given at the beginning of the school year to obtain placement information, when a new student enters the class, or whenever a student's placement is in doubt. They may also be given as pretests and posttests and are often more sensitive indicators of progress than norm-referenced tests.

IRIs require training and practice to administer and interpret. They are best given by the school's reading specialist unless the classroom teacher has the required background and the time. Even if you, as a classroom teacher, never formally administer an IRI, it is still essential that you be familiar with the concept. Knowing the IRI standards for instructional and other levels, you have a basis for evaluating your students' reading performance. If students have difficulty orally reading more than five words out of a hundred, or if their oral and written comprehension seems closer to 50 percent than 75 percent, you may have to check the material they are reading to see if it is too difficult. On the other hand, if both word recognition and comprehension in everyday reading tasks are close to perfect, you may want to try more challenging materials.

As children struggle with difficult words, you may also want to conduct a mental miscue analysis. By closely observing miscues, you can sense whether students might need added instruction in using context, using phonics, or integrating the two.

RUNNING RECORDS

Similar to the informal reading inventory and based on Goodman's (1994) theory of analyzing students' miscues to determine what strategies they are using to decode words, the **running record** is becoming a popular device for assessing students' progress. Like the IRI, the running record is administered individually. However, only an oral-reading sample is obtained. The running record has two major purposes: to determine whether students' reading materials are on the proper level and to obtain information about the word-recognition processes students are using.

Although running records may be obtained from older readers, they are most often used to assess the performance of novice readers and are administered daily to Reading Recovery students. As used in Reading Recovery and recommended in Clay's (1993a) *An Observation Survey of Early Literacy Achievement,* running records are administered according to a standardized format in which students' errors and corrections are recorded on a separate sheet. As adapted for use by classroom teachers, running records may be recorded (as long as the fair-use provision of the copyright laws is adhered to or permission is obtained from the publisher) on a photocopy of the text that the student is using (Learning Media,

Some teachers create their own inventories, using basal series or trade books. Although time-consuming to devise, teacher-created inventories can be geared to the needs of particular students. If the same basal series is used for both the IRI and instruction, the content validity of the former is enhanced (as long as the students being tested have not read the test selections). Detailed directions for construction of an IRI can be found in *Informal Reading Inventories* (Johnson, Kress, & Pikulski, 1987).

A number of commercial inventories are available. These inventories vary somewhat in the procedures they incorporate.

Although not as precise or reliable as the IRI, group placement inventories do not require special training and can be administered to the whole class, so they do not take up as much time. They can be found in some basal series. See *Informal Reading Inventories* (Johnson, Kress, & Pikulski, 1987) for information on constructing and administering them.

A **running record** is an assessment device in which a student's oral-reading errors are noted and classified to determine whether the material is on the appropriate level of difficulty and which reading strategies the student is using.

Table 13.5 shows how miscues are recorded on a separate sheet.

1991). To assess whether materials are on a suitable level of difficulty and determine how well the child makes use of previously presented strategies, take a running record on a text that the student has recently read. To assess the student's ability to handle challenging materials and apply strategies independently, take a running record on material that the student has not read. If the book or article is very brief, take a running record of the whole piece. If the text is lengthy, select a sample of one hundred to two hundred words. As the student reads orally, record her or his performance with symbols, such as those presented in Table 13.5. However, you may use the IRI symbols if you are more familiar with them. After taking a running record, record the number of words in the selection, number of errors made, error rate, number of self-corrections made, and the accuracy rate.

Clay (1993a) accepts 90 percent as an adequate accuracy rate; however, 95 percent seems more realistic. Word recognition is emphasized in a running record, so comprehension is not generally checked. However, you may ask the child to retell the story if you wish to obtain information about comprehension.

It is essential that you analyze a student's miscues in order to determine what strategies she or he is using. As you examine the student's miscues, ask the following questions:

- Is the student reading for meaning? Do the student's miscues make sense?
- Is the student self-correcting miscues, especially those that do not fit the meaning of the sentence? Is the student using meaning cues?
- Is the student using visual or sound-symbol cues (phonics)? Are the student's miscues similar in appearance and sound to the target word?
- Is the student using picture cues?
- Is the student integrating cues? Is the student balancing the use of meaning and sound-symbol cues?
- Based on the student's performance, what strategies does she or he need to work on?

For younger readers in the very early stages, note whether they read from left to right or top to bottom and whether there is a voice-print match (the word the child says matches the one she or he is looking at). For detailed information on analyzing and interpreting running records, see Clay (1993a).

Norm-referenced tests provide information generally desired by school boards, policy makers, and the public at large. Ease and efficiency of administration and objectivity are appealing factors.

Although widely used, norm-referenced tests have a number of shortcomings. Because they typically use short passages and multiple-choice questions, they do not reflect the kind of reading students do or the manner in which they respond. In addition, they fail to provide useful information about the kinds of strategies students are using or failing to use. Perhaps worst of all, their scores invite comparison and competition. Because guessing is a factor and the tests are timed, norm-referenced tests might provide distorted scores for slow-moving students who are afraid to guess.

NORM-REFERENCED VERSUS CRITERION-REFERENCED TESTS

NORM-REFERENCED TESTS

Many traditional tests provide some sort of comparison. In a norm-referenced test, students are compared with a representative sample of others who are the same age or in the same grade. The scores indicate whether students did as well as the average, better than the average, or below the average. The norm group typically includes students from all sections of the country, from urban and nonurban

TABLE 13.5   Running record symbols

Symbol	Text	Example
Words read correctly are marked with a check mark.	Janice kicked the ball.	✓ ✓ ✓ ✓
Substitutions are written above the line.	A barn owl hooted.	✓ big ✓ ✓ 　 barn
Self-corrections are marked *SC*.	A barn owl hooted.	✓ big | sc ✓ ✓ · barn
A dash is used to indicate no response.	I saw her yesterday.	✓ ✓ ✓ — 　 yesterday
A dash is used to indicate an insertion of a word. The dash is placed beneath the inserted word.	We saw a big dog.	✓ ✓ ✓ bad ✓ 　　　 —
A *T* is used to indicate that a child has been told a word.	Her cat ran away yesterday.	✓ ✓ ✓ ✓ 　 T 　　　 yesterday
The letter *A* indicates that the child has asked for help.	A large moose appeared.	✓ ✓ ✓ 　　 A 　　 appeared
At times, the student becomes so confused by a misreading that it is suggested that she or he "try that again" (coded TTA). Brackets are put around the section that has been misread, the whole misreading is counted as one error, and the student reads it again for a new score.	The deer leaped over the fence.	[✓ ✓ landed ✓ ✓· field] TTA 　　　　 leaped 　　　 fence
A repetition is indicated with an *R*. Although not counted as errors, repetitions are often part of an attempt to puzzle out a difficult item. The point to which the student returns in the repetition is indicated with an arrow.	The deer leaped over the fence.	↓ ✓ ✓ landed | sc ✓ ✓ field | sc. R 　　 leaped 　　　 fence.

areas, and from a variety of racial or ethnic and socioeconomic groups. The group is chosen to be representative of the nation's total school population. However, norm-referenced tests can result in unfair comparisons. Urban schools, for example, should only be compared with other urban schools.

An excellent source for using scores from norm-referenced tests to help plan a reading program for groups and individuals is the third edition of the *Manual for Scoring and Interpretation of the Gates-MacGinitie Reading Tests*, (MacGinitie & MacGinitie, 1989). Although the manual was designed for use with the Gates-MacGinitie reading tests, its suggestions can be used with results from other tests or even informal measures.

Since norm-referenced tests yield comparative results that are generally used by school boards, school administrators, and the general public, they provide one source of information to assess the effectiveness of the school program. Classroom teachers can also make use of the data to complement information from quizzes, informal tests, and observations. Reading scores indicate an approximate level of achievement. If a measure of academic aptitude has been administered, results can be examined to see whether students are reading up to their expected or anticipated level of achievement. If they are not, the teacher can explore the problem.

The tests can also be used as a screening device. Very high-scoring students may be candidates for a gifted or enriched reading program. Low-scoring students may benefit from input from the reading or learning-disabilities specialist, especially if there is a marked difference between capacity and performance. Subtest scores of individuals can also be analyzed for patterns of strengths and weaknesses. A high-vocabulary, low-comprehension score, for example, is often a sign that a student needs extra instruction in the use of comprehension strategies. A low-vocabulary, high-comprehension score might indicate the need for language development.

This book does not recommend administering norm-referenced tests. However, in many school systems, their administration is mandated. If information from these tests is available, you should make use of it along with other sources of data.

CRITERION-REFERENCED TESTS

A **criterion-referenced test** is one in which a student's performance is compared to a criterion or standard.

In contrast to a norm-referenced test, a **criterion-referenced test** compares students' performance with some standard, or criterion. For instance, the criterion on a comprehension test might be answering 80 percent of the questions correctly. The informal reading inventory is criterion-referenced; a student must have at least 95 percent word recognition and 75 percent comprehension to be on the instructional level, for example. Tests that accompany basal readers also tend to be criterion-referenced. Many have a passing score, which is the criterion. The major weakness of criterion-referenced tests is that, all too often, the criterion is set arbitrarily. No one tests it to see if average students usually answer 80 percent of the items correctly, for example, or if 80 percent comprehension is adequate in most instances. A second major shortcoming of criterion-referenced tests is that all too often they do not assess reading skills and strategies in the way students actually use them. For instance, comprehension might be assessed as in norm-referenced tests, with brief passages and multiple-choice questions. Despite these limitations, criterion-referenced tests are generally more useful to teachers than are norm-referenced tests. They indicate whether students have mastered particular skills and so are useful for making instructional decisions.

Reliability is the degree to which a test yields consistent results.

Whether assessment is formal or informal, through paper-and-pencil testing or observation, reliability is essential. As Farr (1991) observed, "If a test or other means of assessment is not reliable, it's no good. . . . If you stand on the bathroom scale and it registers 132 lbs. one morning, but it's 147 the next morning, and 85 the morning after that, you conclude it's time for a new set of bathroom scales . . ." (p. 4).

JUDGING ASSESSMENT MEASURES

RELIABILITY

To be useful, tests and other assessment instruments, whether criterion- or norm-referenced, must be both reliable and valid. **Reliability** is a measure of consistency, which means that if the same test were given to the same students a number of times, the results would be approximately the same. Reliability is usually reported as a coefficient of correlation and ranges from 0.00 to 0.99 or −0.01 to −0.99. The higher the positive correlation, the more reliable the test. For tests on which individual decisions are being based, reliability should be in the 0.90s.

A test that is not reliable is of no value. It is the equivalent of an elastic yardstick—the results of measurement would be different each time.

VALIDITY

In general, **validity** means that a test measures what it says it measures: vocabulary knowledge or speed of reading, for instance. Ultimately, it means that a particular test will provide the information needed to make a decision, such as placing a student with an appropriate level book or indicating specific strengths and weaknesses in comprehension (Farr & Carey, 1986). Reading tests need content validity, meaning that skills and strategies tested must be the same as those taught. Calfee and Hiebert (1991) define validity with the following question: "Does assessment match what I have taught and the way I have taught it?" (p. 282).

To check for content validity, list the objectives of the program and note how closely a particular test's objectives match them. The test selections should be examined, too, to see whether they reflect the type of material that the students read. Also, determine how reading is tested. If a test assesses skills or strategies that you do not cover or assesses them in a way that is not suitable, the test is not valid for your class.

Closely tied to validity are the consequences or uses to which the assessment will be put. For instance, a statewide mastery assessment will almost surely be used by teachers as a kind of curriculum guide. If the test assesses only a narrow part of the curriculum, it will be detrimental and thus invalid (Joint Task Force on Assessment, 1994). Assessment measures should also be fair to all who take them. There should be no biased items, and the content should be such that all students have had an equal opportunity to learn it.

Validity is the degree to which a test measures what it is supposed to measure, or the extent to which a test will provide information needed to make a decision. Validity should be considered in terms of the consequences of the test results and the use to which the test results will be put.

Often, teachers change the content of their teaching to match the content of the test instead of switching to a more valid test. For example, teachers in one school taught an approach to reading that presented decoding through word patterns but did not include phonics of any kind. However, the test that their school was using required students to identify words with long vowels and those with short vowels. The teachers taught their students to discriminate between long and short vowels so that they would do well on that subtest. A better decision would have been to choose another test or ignore the subtest that did not match their objectives.

The assessment tasks should be interesting and of high quality. Reading and writing tasks should reflect the complexity of these processes by using more extensive passages and requiring the student to construct and extend the meaning of the passage. "The tasks selected to measure a given content domain should themselves be worthy of the time and efforts of students" (Herman, 1992, p. 76).

REPORTING PERFORMANCE

There are two primary ways of reporting scores: norm-referenced and criterion-referenced. In norm-referenced reporting, a student's performance is compared with that of other students. In criterion-referenced reporting, a student's performance might be described in terms of a standard or expected performance or in terms of the student's goals.

NORM-REFERENCED REPORTING

Tests and other assessment measures yield a number of possible scores. To interpret results correctly, it is important to know the significance of each score. Here are commonly used test scores:

A **raw score** is the number of correct answers or points earned on a test.

A **percentile rank** is the point on a scale of 1 to 99 that shows what percentage of students obtained an equal or lower score. A percentile rank of 75 means 75 percent of those who took the test received an equal or lower score.

A percentile rank can be a very cruel score. For instance, what might be the impact on parents who are told that 95 percent of the students who took a particular test did better than their child, who scored at the fifth percentile?

A **grade equivalent score** indicates the score that an average student at a certain grade level achieved.

A **normal curve equivalent** is the rank on a scale of 1 through 99 that a score is equal to.

A **stanine** is a point on a nine-point scale, with 5 being average.

A **scaled score** is a continuous ranking from 000 to 999 of a series of norm-referenced tests, from the lowest- to the highest-level test.

A **benchmark** is a standard of achievement or written description of performance against which a student's achievement might be assessed.

- *Raw score.* A **raw score** represents the total number of correct answers. It has no meaning until it is changed into a percentile rank or other score.
- *Percentile rank.* A **percentile rank** tells where a student's raw score falls on a scale of 1 to 99. A score at the first percentile means that the student did better than 1 percent of those who took the test. A score at the fiftieth percentile indicates that the student did better than half of those who took the test. A top score is the ninety-ninth percentile. Most norm-referenced test results are now reported in percentiles; however, the ranks are not equal units and should not be added, subtracted, divided, or used for subtest comparison.
- *Grade equivalent score.* The **grade equivalent score** characterizes a student's performance as being equivalent to that of other students in a particular grade. A grade equivalent score of 5.2 indicates that the student correctly answered the same number of items as the average fifth-grader in the second month of that grade. Note that the grade equivalent score does *not* tell on what level the student is operating; that is, a score of 5.2 does not mean that a student is reading on a fifth-grade level. Grade equivalent scores are more meaningful when the test students have taken is at the right level and when the score is not more than a year above or a year below average. Because grade equivalent scores are misleading and easily misunderstood, they should be used with great care or not at all.
- *Normal curve equivalents.* **Normal curve equivalents** (NCEs) rank students on a scale of 1 through 99. The main difference between NCEs and percentile ranks is that NCEs represent equal units and so can be added and subtracted and used for comparing performance on subtests.
- *Stanine.* **Stanine** is a combination of the words *standard* and *nine*. The stanines 4, 5, and 6 are average points, with 1, 2, and 3 being below average, and 7, 8, and 9 above average. Stanines are useful when making comparisons among the subtests of a norm-referenced test.
- *Scaled scores.* **Scaled scores** are a continuous ranking of scores from the lowest levels of a series of norm-referenced tests—first grade, for example—through the highest levels—high school. They start at 000 and end at 999. They are useful for tracking long-term reading development through the grades.

For additional information about tests, especially norm-referenced instruments, see the *Eleventh Mental Measurements Yearbook* (Conoley & Kramer, 1992), which contains thoughtful reviews of recent tests and also lists suggestions for choosing and using tests.

CRITERION-REFERENCED REPORTING

Criterion-referenced results are reported in terms of a standard or criterion: For example, the student answered 80 percent of the comprehension questions correctly. Two types of standards now being used in authentic assessment are the benchmark and the rubric, which are holistic forms of criterion-referenced reporting.

BENCHMARKS

The **benchmark** is a written description of a key task that students are expected to perform. For instance, a benchmark for word recognition might be "Uses both context and phonics to identify words unknown in print." Benchmarks are useful because they provide a concrete description of what students are expected to do. They provide students, teachers, parents, and administrators with an observable framework for assessing accomplishments and needs. Using benchmarks, the teacher can assess whether the student has mastered key skills/strategies and is ready to move on.

Benchmarks are often grouped around a certain level of development. For instance, the Green Bay (Wisconsin) Public Schools include the following benchmarks under Reading Strategies/Comprehension at the first-grade level: "Uses clues (e.g., pictures, meaning, word order, phonics) when reading; uses strategies to correct difficulties (e.g., rereading, reading ahead, pausing to reflect)" (Jett Simpson, 1990, p. 91).

A carefully developed set of benchmarks, known as literacy profiles, has been assembled by the Australian Ministry of Education (1990). The profiles were created by teachers who grouped them into bands so that related behaviors on approximately the same level are clustered. The bands extend from A, which is early emergent literacy, to I, which describes advanced literacy skills. Bands are divided into those devoted to reading and those focused on writing. Each band is described by a summary statement that features significant characteristics of students who are in that band. Major benchmarks are listed. Also provided is a listing of opportunities to observe the benchmark behaviors. For Reading Band B, the summary statement is as follows:

> These students recognize many familiar words and are game to try reading some unfamiliar text. They will retell what a book is about. They are showing signs of becoming quite active readers and are interested in the way their writing looks. (Australian Ministry of Education, 1990, p. 14)

Benchmark behaviors for Reading Band B are divided into Reading Strategies ("Takes risks when reading," " 'Reads' books with simple repetitive language patterns," "Uses pictures for clues to meaning of text") and Responses ("Recounts parts of text in writing, drama, or art work," "Retells with appropriate sequence") (p. 15).

Contexts for observing the benchmark behaviors include observing during shared reading, retelling, drama, writing activities, and conferences. Cloze, picture-sequencing activities, and parent conferences during which parents provide information about the child's reading and writing at home offer additional sources of data.

Allowing students a variety of ways in which to demonstrate benchmark performance seems more natural and is preferred by some educators. However, other educators choose to use standard tasks and standard materials so that the tasks are the same for all. For the primary grades, Weaver (1992) established a series of tasks and observational guidelines that can be used to assess primary students' progress. Her benchmarks include such activities as "Can use various cueing strategies while reading" and "Can write a simple story with an awareness of story sequence" (p. 55). For most benchmarks, the teacher uses one of a series of texts that gradually grow in difficulty. On the emergent literacy level, the teacher uses *Cat on the Mat* (Wildsmith, 1982) and suggestions contained in the *Benchmark Assessment Guide* to assess children's reading performance. The advantage of

At a meeting to present students' test scores to parents, one mother remarked that her son had scored in the sixtieth percentile because he had answered only 60 percent of the answers correctly. Later, using percentile ranks, the local newspaper reported that, on average, students had scored at the fiftieth percentile and so had answered half the questions wrong. Both the parent and the newspaper had misinterpreted percentile rank and were drawing false conclusions.

Grade equivalent scores have been officially criticized by the International Reading Association because they are misleading; however, they do seem more humane than percentile ranks. They are also relatively valid when students are given functional-level tests and when extrapolations are limited to a year or two beyond the target grade level. Schools are then able to avoid such reports as, "Johnny, a fourth-grader, scored a 9.4," which implies that Johnny can cope with ninth-grade materials.

The chief value of instruments such as the *Benchmark Assessment Guide* (Weaver, 1992) and *Literacy Profiles* (Australian Ministry of Education, 1990) is that they provide teachers with a framework for making observations. "Skilled observation is essential if teachers are to make accurate judgment about their students' literacy learning. Out of the numerous observations that teachers can and do make, it can be difficult, however, to know what to select and what is most significant" (Australian Ministry of Education, 1990, p. 5).

For more than three decades, teachers in Toronto's one hundred elementary schools used whatever methods they wished to report students' progress. In response to parents' requests for more systematic information, the Toronto Board of Education developed benchmarks for language arts and math. The concept was that the benchmark provided "information to which teachers, students, and parents can refer to daily as they teach, learn, and assess achievement" (Larter & Donnelly, 1993, p. 59). Benchmarks, then, become a means for integrating instruction, planning for students' learning, and assessment. As teachers construct benchmarks and ways to assess them, they also create learning activities for each benchmark.

A **rubric** is a description of the traits or characteristics of standards used to judge a process or product.

Devices that rely on judgment may be less reliable because assessors may interpret a rubric or benchmark differently. However, when assessors are well trained, their judgments tend to be similar (Joint Task Force on Assessment, 1994).

Functional level testing is the practice of assigning students to a test level on the basis of their reading ability rather than grade level.

using designated texts for the assessment of benchmark behaviors is that they provide material at the appropriate level of difficulty. If students are given material that is too difficult, they will be hampered in the use of various strategies.

RUBRICS

Another type of standard is the rubric. A **rubric** is a written description of what is expected in order to meet a certain level of performance and is accompanied by samples of typical performance. For assessing a piece of writing, such samples show the characteristics of an excellent, average, fair, and poor paper. A writing rubric is presented in Table 13.6. Although rubrics are typically used in the assessment of writing tasks, they can also be used to assess combined reading/writing tasks, portfolios, and other elements. The main advantage of a rubric is that it provides criteria for task assessment.

FUNCTIONAL LEVEL ASSESSMENT

The typical elementary school class will exhibit a wide range of reading ability. Just as students need appropriate levels of materials for instruction, they should have appropriate levels of materials for testing. A sixth-grader reading on a second-grade level should not be given a sixth-grade reading test. It would be frustrating to the student and would yield misleading results. The student should take a test that includes material on his or her level of reading ability; for example, a third-grade level test might include second-grade material. Similarly, a second-grade level test would probably not be appropriate for a second-grader reading on a fifth-grade level. It would probably lack an adequate ceiling and so would underestimate the student's true reading ability. Students should be tested at their **functional level,** which is not necessarily their grade level. Giving students a test at the wrong level results in erroneous, invalid information. This is true whether norm-referenced, criterion-referenced, or other assessment is being used. For more information on functional level testing, see Gunning (1982).

TESTS IN BASAL SERIES

Basal series are typically accompanied by an extensive assessment and placement system. Both group and individual inventories are usually available. Assessment devices may include periodic tests to be administered at the end of a unit, section, or book. Current basals feature holistic tests in which students read a fairly lengthy selection and write essay-type responses. Checklists, observation guides, and portfolios are also an important part of the basal assessment system.

TABLE 13.6 Rubric for assessing writing

	Level 4 Most successful	Level 3 Upper half	Level 2 Lower half (Basic)	Level 1 Least successful (Skill failure)
Content	Shows clear understanding of content. Develops the topic with appropriate detail in each paragraph.	Generally understands content. At least two paragraphs used. Details relate clearly to topic sentence.	Appears to understand the topic. If using more than one paragraph, relation to overall topic may be weak.	Some misunderstanding of topic. Usually only one paragraph. Includes material not related to topic.
Organization	Organization and sequence of ideas are clear and relate to one another in development of the overall topic.	Clear organization and sequences of detail. Relationship of paragraphs to major topic not fully developed.	Basically sequential. Some weakness in relating paragraph details to topic sentences.	Lacks coherence. Sequencing of ideas may be incorrect.
Sentence structure	Uses correct sentence structure, descriptive words, and phrases. Expands sentence patterns. Makes few grammatical errors.	Basic sentence patterns correct. Some difficulty with expanded sentence patterns and grammar.	Uses simple sentences. Errors in grammar when more complex structure is attempted. Some run-on and sentence fragments.	Uses basic simple sentences. Errors in noun-verb agreement. Infrequent use of modifiers.
Mechanics	Capitalization, punctuation, and spelling are generally correct.	Few problems with capitalization, punctuation, and spelling.	Errors in capitalization, punctuation, and spelling.	Frequent errors in capitalization, punctuation, and spelling of words.
Word choice	Vocabulary includes some words usually used at a higher level.	Average for grade level. Vocabulary words used correctly.	Simple vocabulary words used, some incorrectly.	Poor word choice.

From *The Writing Handbook* (p. 19) by the Reading and Communications Arts Department, 1983, Hartford, CT: Hartford Public Schools. Reprinted by permission of the Hartford Board of Education.

OTHER METHODS OF ASSESSMENT

RETELLING

Retelling has the potential for supplying more information about a student's comprehension than simply asking questions does. In a retelling, a student is asked to do what the name suggests: The student may retell a selection that has been read

Retelling is the process of summarizing or describing a story that one has read. The purpose of the retelling is to assess comprehension.

At the elementary school where I was a consultant a number of years ago, we had implemented functional level testing. However, when the school agreed to participate in the tryout of a standardized test, the publisher stated that all students had to be tested on grade level. Used to encountering tests that they could read, the lower-achieving students were visibly upset when they faced tasks that were far too difficult for them. One sixth-grader burst into tears. The incident was a powerful lesson for all of us that asking children to perform tasks that are far too difficult for them is not only educationally invalid, it is also inhumane.

Test publishers support the concept of functional level testing and offer guidelines for out-of-level assessment. A general practice is to use the teacher's estimate or a quick locator test provided by the publisher to obtain a rough estimate of the child's functional reading level and to test the child on that level.

In some statewide assessments, students are given materials on grade level to read and respond to. Since, in the typical population, as many as one child in four or even more will be reading significantly below grade level, this practice is unfair to under-achieving students and results in the same kind of misleading information yielded from wrong-level norm-referenced tests. Whatever form they take, assessment measures must provide all test takers with a fair and equitable opportunity to participate. For lower-achieving readers, this means providing at least some items that are on their instructional level.

to her or him or one that she or he has read. The student may do this orally or in writing. In addition to showing what the reader comprehended, retelling shows what she or he added to and inferred from the text (Irwin & Mitchell, 1983). Free from the influence of probes or questions, retelling demonstrates the student's construction of text and provides insight into her or his language and thought processes. It shows how the student organizes and shapes a response. The teacher can also assess the quality of language used by the student in the retelling.

To administer a retelling, explain to the student what she or he is supposed to do: Read a selection orally or silently, or listen to one read aloud. It may be a narrative or expository piece. Tell the student that she or he will be asked to retell the story in her or his own words. Use neutral phrasing, such as "Tell me about the story that you read." For a young child, say, "Pretend I haven't read the story, and tell it to me in your own words." A shy child can use props—such as a puppet—to facilitate the retelling.

If a child stops before retelling the whole selection, encourage her or him to continue or elaborate. When the student is finished, ask questions about any key elements that were not included in the retelling.

EVALUATING RETELLINGS

As the student retells the selection, record it on audiocassette and/or jot down brief notes on the major events or ideas in the order in which the child relates them. Note any recalls elicited by your questions. Tape recording provides a full and accurate rendition of the retelling but is time-consuming.

Retellings can be scored numerically by giving students credit for each major unit that they retell. However, this is a laborious process. Far less time-consuming but still useful is noting the major units in the retelling in one column, comments about it in a second column, and a summary and recommendations in a third. Since the main purpose of the retelling is to gain insight into students' reading processes, draw inferences about students' overall understanding of the selection and their ability to use strategies to construct the meaning of the piece. A sample retelling is presented in Figure 13.5.

WRITTEN RETELLINGS

Written retellings can be time savers, as the teacher can assess the class as a group. Using holistic scoring, the teacher can also assess the quality of the writing. It is important to keep in mind that, whether oral or written, the mode of expression will affect the information students convey. Students may have good knowledge of a selection but find it difficult to express orally and/or in writing. To obtain a better picture of that knowledge, the teacher might have a class discussion after students have completed their written retellings and compare impressions garnered from the discussion with those from the written versions.

STRUCTURED WRITTEN RETELLINGS

In a structured written retelling, the teacher might ask students to read a whole selection and write answers to a series of broad questions. The questions are constructed to assess students' ability to understand major aspects of the text, such

Name of student: _____ Jamie S. _____

	Retelling	Comments	Summary and recommendations
Elves and the shoemaker	Shoemaker said had only one piece of leather left. Elves made shoes.	Drew inference. Started with story problem.	Good grasp of story.
	Man in hat came in. Woman came in. Many people bought shoes. Shoemaker and wife waited up to see elves.	Told story in sequence.	Used structure of story to retell it.
	Elves had ragged clothes. Wife made new clothes. Elves thought new clothes looked funny.	Used picture to get information about elves. Misinterpreted passage.	Didn't go beyond story to suggest why elves started or stopped helping.
	Elves said would no longer be cobras. Never came back.	Missed <u>cobblers</u>.	Failed to use context to help with <u>cobblers.</u> Good average performance. Work on context and drawing conclusions.

Being less time-consuming, informal retellings are more practical for the classroom teacher. Of course, shy children may not perform up to their ability.

Retellings are available commercially. The *Qualitative Reading Inventory* (Leslie & Caldwell, 1995) and the latest edition of the *Basic Reading Inventory* (Johns, 1994) include retellings as an optional part of comprehension assessment. Another commercial retelling is contained in the *Durrell Analysis of Reading Difficulty* (Durrell & Catterson, 1980).

As an alternative to a strictly written retelling, invite students to use whatever form they choose to summarize a selection: semantic map or web, outline, flow chart, diagram, or other graphic organizers. Students, especially those in the early grades, might also respond by drawing an illustration of the selection.

A retelling that requires a written response is really assessing two areas: reading and writing. Some students with excellent comprehension may have difficulty composing a response. Research indicates that poor readers and hearing-impaired students have significant difficulty with tests that require written responses (Simmons, 1990).

Think-alouds are procedures in which students are asked to describe the processes they are using as they engage in reading or other cognitive activity.

as characters, plot, and setting. The questions can also be framed to provide some insight into the strategies students are using. They are scored and analyzed by the teacher.

THINK-ALOUD PROTOCOLS

As noted in Chapter 7, **think-alouds** are used to show readers the thought processes they can use to apply a particular strategy. They can also be used to look into students' processes as they attempt to construct meaning. During a think-aloud, the reader explains her or his thought processes while reading a text. These explanations might come after each sentence, at the end of each paragraph, or at the end of the whole selection. Students' thoughts might be expressed as "news

The purpose of evaluation will dictate the nature of the think-aloud. For example, you might assign students a section from a social studies text to study for a quiz and have students explain orally or in writing how they went about studying it. The results can be used to plan instruction in study skills for those who need it.

bulletins or play-by-play accounts" of what students do mentally as they read (Brown & Lytle, 1988, p. 113).

INFORMAL THINK-ALOUDS

Whereas formal think-aloud procedures might be too time-consuming, informal think-alouds can be incorporated into individual and small-group reading conferences and classroom activities. For example, the teacher might simply ask students to share their thoughts on a difficult passage or question, or tell what strategies they used. Think-aloud questions can include the following:

- Tell me how you figured out that hard word.
- Tell me how you got the answer to that question.
- What were you thinking about when you read that selection?
- Pretend that you are an announcer at a sports game. Tell me play by play what was going on in your mind as you read that sentence (or paragraph) (Brown & Lytle, 1988).
- What do you think will happen next in the selection? What makes you think that?
- How did you feel when you read that passage? What thoughts or pictures were going through your mind?

Think-alouds may also be expressed in writing. In their learning logs, students can note the difficulties they encountered in hard passages and describe the processes they used to comprehend the selections. In follow-up class discussions, they can compare their thought processes and strategies with those of other students (Brown & Lytle, 1988). A simple way to keep track of perplexing passages is to have students record comprehension problems on sticky notes and place them next to the passages.

As part of an informal think-aloud, the teacher might ask students to share their thoughts on a difficult question.

OBSERVATION

When evaluating, teachers often take on the role of classic anthropologists:

> Anthropologists alternate between participant-observers, detached observers and collectors of artifacts. At times, they observe . . . from a distance, recording their observations for later analysis. At other times, they ask questions of various informants about what they think and the ways they produce their artifacts, all the time recording their responses. These records become their stores of knowledge, from which they try to reconstruct what reality is for the tribe or culture which is being observed. (Brown and Cambourne, 1987, p. 113)

Teachers are detached observers when they complete checklists or anecdotal notes about children's behavior. At other times, they examine artifacts: students' compositions, learning logs, lists of books read. On still other occasions, it is nearly impossible to separate assessment from teaching, as in reciprocal teaching or responsive elaboration. The ultimate aim is to enhance students' learning. Teachers learn about children "by watching how they learn" (Goodman, 1985, p. 9). As "kidwatchers," teachers are better able to supply the necessary support or ask the kinds of questions that help students build on their evolving knowledge.

OPPORTUNITIES FOR OBSERVATIONS

Observations can be made any time students are involved in reading and writing. Some especially fruitful opportunities for observation include shared reading (What emergent literacy behaviors are students evidencing?), reading and writing conferences (What are the students' strengths and weaknesses in these areas? What is their level of development? How might their progress in these areas be characterized?), and sustained silent reading (Do students enjoy reading? Are they able to select appropriate materials? What kinds of materials do they like to read?). Other valuable observation opportunities include author's circle, literature circle, and sharing periods in general (Australian Ministry of Education, 1990).

ANECDOTAL RECORDS

Certain kinds of highly useful information will not appear in students' written work or show up on a retelling, checklist, quiz, or end-of-book test. This information is best captured in an **anecdotal record,** which is a kind of field note or description of a significant bit of student behavior. It is an observational technique long used by both anthropologists and teachers. Good teachers constantly engage in kidwatching but seldom record their observations, trusting instead to memory. But memory can be fragile and deceptive. Bush and Huebner (1979) cautioned:

An **anecdotal record** is the recording of a description of a significant incident in which the description and interpretation are kept separate.

> The record keeping is an absolute necessity because teachers may forget previous behaviors as new ones appear (psychological principle of recency), they may misinterpret if they jump to conclusions with insufficient data, or they may let one situation analysis overshadow numerous others. (p. 333)

Almost any observation that can shed light on a student's literacy endeavors is a suitable entry for an anecdotal record, including notes on strategies, miscues,

Exemplary Teaching

Making Observations

As a new teacher, Herbert Kohl (1967) was looking for a way to reach his sixth-graders. Careful observation helped him build bridges to the students:

> Stepping back momentarily from myself, forgetting my position and therefore my need to establish order, I observed the children and let them show me something of themselves. There were two clusters of boys and three of girls. There were also loners watching shyly or hovering eagerly about the peripheries of the group. One boy sat quietly drawing, oblivious to the world. . . .
>
> I am convinced that the teacher must be an observer of the class as well as a member of it. He must look at the children, discover how they relate to each other and the room around them. There must be enough free time and activity for the teacher to discover

the children's human preferences. Observing children at play and mischief is an invaluable source of knowledge about them—about leaders and groups, fear, warmth, courage, isolation. . . .

> There was Robert Jackson. I took time to look at his art, observe him working. He was good, accurate; he thought in terms of form and composition. (pp. 12–13, 16)

Later, observing how students took things away from Robert because of his passivity, Kohl determined to give him something that he could hold onto. Noting Robert's keen interest in myths and history, he presented him with a looseleaf binder full of blank paper and challenged him to write and illustrate a book. During the year, Robert wrote several books, refining his writing and artistic talent as he did so. Sensitive observation had made it possible for Kohl to provide the kind of guidance that Robert needed.

Teachers may resist keeping anecdotal or other written records, believing that they will remember important things that students do. However, memories are fallible. They may remember only the good things or not so good things that a student does and thus fail to obtain a balanced view of the child.

interests, interactions with others, and work habits (Rhodes, 1990). The anecdotal record should be "recordings of what the child said or did—not interpretations" (Bush & Huebner, 1979, p. 355). Interpretation comes later and is based on several records and other sources of information. It is important to keep in mind that when recording observations of strategy use, the way in which strategies are used may vary according to the nature of the task—the type of story being read, its relative difficulty, and the purpose for reading it. Therefore, it would be helpful to record several observations before coming to a conclusion (Tierney, Readence, & Dishner, 1995). In going over anecdotal records, the teacher should ask what this information reveals about the student and how it can be used to plan her or his instructional program.

RATINGS

Ratings are estimates of the quality of a learning process or product.

A structured and efficient way to collect data is through the use of **ratings**. Ratings generally indicate the "degree to which the child possesses a given trait or skill" (Bush & Huebner, 1979, p. 353). The three kinds of ratings are checklists, questionnaires, and interviews. Checklists can use a present-absent scale (a student has the trait or does not have it) or one that shows degrees of involvement. The present-absent scale might be used for traits for which there is no degree of possession, such as knowing one's home address and telephone number. The degree scale is appropriate for traits that vary in the extent to which they are

FIGURE 13.6 | **Observation checklist for voluntary reading**

Name of student: _____   Date: _____

	Never	Seldom	Occasionally	Frequently
Reads during free time	_____	_____	_____	_____
Visits the library	_____	_____	_____	_____
Reads books on a variety of topics	_____	_____	_____	_____
Recommends books to others in the class	_____	_____	_____	_____
Talks with others about books	_____	_____	_____	_____
Checks out books from the library	_____	_____	_____	_____

manifested, such as joining in class discussions. Figure 13.6 shows a sample observation checklist designed to assess voluntary reading.

QUESTIONNAIRES

A good example of a reading attitude **questionnaire** is the *Elementary Reading Attitude Survey (ERAS)* (McKenna & Kerr, 1990). It includes twenty items designed to measure how students feel about recreational and school reading. *ERAS* can be read to younger, less-skilled readers; older, more-skilled students can read it themselves. The questionnaire addresses such areas as how children feel when they read a book on a rainy Saturday and how they feel about reading in school. Students respond by circling one of four illustrations of Garfield, which range from a very happy to a very sad cat. Thanks to the generosity of the authors and Garfield's creator, Jim Davis, *ERAS* has not been copyrighted and was presented, ready to duplicate, in the May 1990 issue of *The Reading Teacher*.

Questionnaires can provide information about reading interests, study habits, strategy use, and other areas in reading and writing. They can be forced-choice like *ERAS* or open-ended and requiring a written response. Questionnaires assessing study habits and skills might cover such topics as how students go about studying for a test, where they study, and how much time they spend doing homework each night.

A **questionnaire** is an instrument in which a subject is asked to respond to a series of questions on some topic.

INTERVIEWS

An **interview** is the process of asking a subject a series of questions on a topic.

Interviews are simply oral questionnaires. Their advantage is that the teacher can probe a student's replies, rephrase questions, and encourage extended answers, and so obtain a wide range of information. An interview can focus on such topics as a student's likes and dislikes about a reading group, preferences with respect to reading materials, and reasons for these attitudes.

One kind of interview, the process interview, provides insight about the strategies students are using and also helps students become aware of their processes (Jett-Simpson, 1990). The process interview is best conducted informally on a one-to-one basis, but if time is limited, you might ask for written responses to your questions or hold sessions with small groups. Possible process interview questions include the following, which are adapted from Jett-Simpson (1990). Only one or two of these questions should be asked at one sitting.

1. How do you choose something to read?
2. How do you get ready for reading?
3. Where do you read/study at home?
4. When you come to a word you don't know, what do you do?
5. When a paragraph is confusing what do you do?
6. How do you check your reading?
7. What do you do to help you remember what you've read?
8. If a young child asked you how to read, what would you tell him/her to do?

Questionnaires, interviews, and ratings completed by students have a common weakness. Their usefulness depends on students' ability and willingness to supply accurate information. Children may, for example, give answers that they think the teacher wants to hear. Information gathered from these sources, therefore, should be verified with other data.

SELF-EVALUATION

As one way of helping their students reflect on their learning, Howell and Woodley (1992) asked them to complete "I learned" statements at key points in the day: "I learned that I . . ., I realized that I . . ., I discovered that I . . ., I was excited to learn that . . ."(p. 87).

The ultimate evaluation is, of course, self-evaluation. Students should be involved in all phases of the evaluation process and, insofar as possible, take responsibility for assessing their own work. Questionnaires and self-report checklists are especially useful for this. Figure 13.7 shows a self-report checklist in which students can assess their use of strategies in learning from text.

Self-assessment should begin early. Ahlmann (1992) noted that by October her first-graders are already evaluating their own work and that of authors they read. To self-assess, students reflect on their learning, assemble portfolios of their work, list their achievements, and, with the guidance of the teacher, put together a plan for what they hope to achieve.

In some classes, students complete exit slips on which they talk about what they have learned that day or raise questions that they did not have time to raise in class or were reluctant to raise. Learning logs and journals might perform a

	Usually	Often	Sometimes	Never
Before reading, do I				
1. Read the title, introductory paragraph, headings, and summary?	_____	_____	_____	_____
2. Look at photos, maps, charts, and graphs?	_____	_____	_____	_____
3. Think about what I know about the topic?	_____	_____	_____	_____
4. Predict what the text will be about or make up questions that the text might answer?	_____	_____	_____	_____
During reading, do I				
5. Read to answer questions that the teacher or I have made up?	_____	_____	_____	_____
6. Stop after each section and try to answer my questions?	_____	_____	_____	_____
7. Use headings, maps, charts, and graphs to help me understand the text?	_____	_____	_____	_____
8. Try to make pictures in my mind as I read?	_____	_____	_____	_____
9. Reread a sentence or get help if I don't understand what I am reading?	_____	_____	_____	_____
10. Use context or the glossary if I don't understand what I am reading?	_____	_____	_____	_____
After reading, do I				
11. Review the section to make sure that I know the most important information?	_____	_____	_____	_____
12. Try to organize the information in the text by creating a map, chart, time line, or summary?	_____	_____	_____	_____

similar function. As an alternative, the teacher and the class might design a form on which students tell what they learned in a certain class and list questions that they still have. In reading and writing conferences, part of the discussion should center on skills mastered and goals for the future, and how those goals might be met. These conferences, of course, should be genuinely collaborative efforts so that students' input is shown to be valued.

Some teachers have students keep a record of their reading or what they have done that day. As part of the record keeping, students might assess books read and activities completed, including statements that tell how they benefited. Portfolios, which are described later in this chapter, also offer opportunities for self-assessment.

LOGS AND JOURNALS

Reading logs and response journals can also be a part of students' self-evaluation, as well as a source of information for the teacher. Reading logs contain a list of books read and, perhaps, a brief summary or assessment. Response journals provide students with opportunities to record personal reactions to their reading. Both reading logs and response journals offer unique insights into students' growing ability to handle increasingly difficult books, their changing interests, and personal involvement with reading.

EVALUATING WRITING

HOLISTIC SCORING

Holistic scoring is a process for sorting written pieces on the basis of an overall impression of the piece. Description of standards (rubric) for rating the pieces might be used as guides, along with sample pieces (anchors).

What captures the essence of a piece of writing—its style, its theme, its development, its adherence to conventions, its originality? The answer is all of these elements and more. Because of the way the parts of the piece work together, it must be viewed as a whole. In **holistic scoring,** instead of noting specific strengths and weaknesses, a teacher evaluates a composition in terms of a limited number of general criteria. The criteria are used "only as a general guide . . . in reaching a holistic judgment" (Cooper & Odell, 1977, p. 4). The teacher does not stop to check the piece to see if it meets each of the criteria but simply forms a general impression.

The teacher can score a piece according to the presence or absence of key elements. There may be a scoring guide, which can be a checklist or a rubric. (A holistic scoring guide in the form of a rubric is shown in Table 13.6.) The teacher should also use anchor pieces along with the rubric to assess compositions. Anchor pieces, which may be drawn from the work of past classes or from the compositions that are currently being assessed, are writing samples that provide examples of poor, fair, good, and superior pieces. The teacher decides which of the anchor pieces a student's composition most closely resembles.

APPLYING HOLISTIC SCORING

Before scoring the pieces, the teacher should quickly read them all to get a sense of how well the class did overall. This prevents setting criteria that are too high or too low. After sorting the papers into four groups—poor, fair, good, and superior—the teacher rereads each work more carefully before confirming its placement. If possible, a second teacher should also evaluate the papers. This is especially important if the works are to be graded.

ANALYTIC SCORING

Analytic scoring is a type of scoring that uses a description of major features to be considered when assessing a written piece.

Analytic scoring involves analyzing pieces and noting specific strengths and weaknesses. It requires the teacher to create a set of specific scoring criteria. Instead of overwhelming students with corrections, it is best to decide on a lim-

FIGURE 13.8 Analytic scoring guide for a friendly letter

Name of student: _____   Date: _____

	Poor	Fair	Good	Superior
Content				
Has a natural but interesting beginning.				
Includes several topics of interest.	_____	_____	_____	_____
Develops each topic in sufficient detail.	_____	_____	_____	_____
Shows an interest in what's happening to the reader.	_____	_____	_____	_____
Has a friendly way of ending the letter.	_____	_____	_____	_____
Style				
Has a friendly, natural tone.	_____	_____	_____	_____
Form				
Follows friendly letter form.	_____	_____	_____	_____
Indents paragraphs.	_____	_____	_____	_____
Is neat and legible.	_____	_____	_____	_____
Mechanics				
Begins each sentence with a capital.	_____	_____	_____	_____
Uses correct end punctuation.	_____	_____	_____	_____
Spells words correctly.	_____	_____	_____	_____

ited number of key features, such as those that have been emphasized for a particular writing activity. Although more time-consuming than holistic scoring, analytic scoring allows the teacher to make constructive suggestions about students' writing. An analytic scoring guide for a friendly letter is presented in Figure 13.8.

USING A COMBINATION OF TECHNIQUES

In some cases, a combination of holistic and analytic scoring works best. Holistic scoring guards against the teacher's becoming overly caught up in mechanics or stylistics and neglecting the substance of the piece. Analytic scoring provides students with necessary direction for improving their work and becoming more proficient writers.

PORTFOLIOS

Artists, photographers, designers, and others assemble their work in **portfolios** for assessment. Portfolios are now being used in a somewhat modified fashion to assess the literacy growth of elementary school students. Portfolios have a number of advantages. They facilitate the assessment of growth over time. Because they provide the teacher with an opportunity to take a broad look at a student's literacy development, they are an appropriate method for assessing holistic approaches. Portfolio assessment can also lead to changes in the curriculum and teaching practices. In Au's (1994) study, for instance, teachers began emphasizing revision when portfolio assessment helped them see that they were neglecting that area.

TYPES OF PORTFOLIOS

There are five kinds of portfolios, each performing different functions and containing different kinds of materials: showcase, evaluation, documentation, process, and composite (Valencia & Place, 1994). Like the traditional portfolio used by artists to display their best works, the showcase is composed of works that students have selected as being their best. The focus in the evaluation portfolio is on obtaining representative works from key areas. The samples included might be standardized—that is, based on a common text or a common topic—so that results are comparable across students. A documentation portfolio is designed to provide evidence of students' growth and so might contain the greatest number and variety of work samples. The process portfolio is designed to show how students work, so it includes samples from various stages of a project along with students' comments about how the project is progressing. A composite portfolio contains elements from two or more types of portfolios. For instance, a portfolio designed for district evaluation might contain showcase and process items.

WRITING SAMPLES

Collecting representative pieces from several types of writing assignments gives the teacher a broad view of a student's development. Including pieces written at different times of the year allows the teacher to trace the student's growth. Rough drafts as well as final copies illustrate the student's writing progress and indicate how well the student handles the various processes. Each student might include in her or his portfolio lists of pieces written, major writing skills learned, and current goals. Both student and teacher should have access to the portfolio and should agree on which pieces should be included. Teacher and student should also agree on how to choose what goes into the portfolio. Giving students a say in the decision helps them maintain a sense of ownership (Simmons, 1990).

To help students reflect on their learning and make wise choices about the included pieces, you might have them explain their choices by completing a self-evaluative statement. The statement can be a brief explanation with the heading "Why I Chose This Piece." Initially, reasons for inclusion and comments tend to be vague (Tierney, Carter, & Desai, 1991). However, through classroom discussions and conferences, you should help students explore criteria for including

---

A **portfolio** is a collection of work samples, test results, checklists, or other data used to assess a student's performance.

More than any other assessment device, portfolios have the potential for demonstrating students' growth. As you assess them, note areas in which students have done especially well, along with areas of weaknesses. Portfolios also provide information that shows class, as well as individual, needs. If the class as a whole is evidencing difficulty with mechanics, then that might be an area in your curriculum that needs special attention.

A portfolio can demonstrate the power of a reader and a writer. Unbeknownst to the teacher, a student may read dozens or hundreds of books or be a budding author. A reading log or sampling of written pieces should reveal this. The portfolio should provide a sense of how much the student reads and writes (Tierney, Carter, & Desai, 1991).

Choosing selections for inclusion provides students with the opportunity to assess their strengths as readers and writers as they decide which selections to include. However, as this could lead to placing only those works that students think are their best, the sample would not be representative. A "mine/theirs/ours" system has been suggested in which the student and teacher each select a piece, and the two cooperatively choose a third.

certain pieces rather than others—it tells a good story, it has a beginning that grabs the reader, it has lots of interesting examples, it seems to flow, and so on.

READING SAMPLES

Some teachers use portfolios primarily to assess writing. If you wish to use portfolios to assess reading, include samples of reading. Samples to be included depend on the goals of the program. If a goal of reading instruction is to teach students to visualize, drawings of reading selections might be included. If you have been working on summaries, you may want to see sample summaries. A list of books read might be appropriate for a goal of wide reading. Valencia (1990) cautioned, "If the goals of instruction are not specified, portfolios have the potential to become reinforced holding files for odds and ends . . ." (p. 339).

At certain points, reading and writing will converge—written summaries of selections and research reports using several sources might count toward both reading and writing goals. Other items that might be placed in the portfolio are tape-recordings of oral reading or samples of inventory results, checklists, quizzes, standardized and informal test results, learning logs, written reactions to selections, and semantic maps.

You also need to decide how you will rate the portfolios and whether your assessment of the portfolios will be used as a grade. If they are used as a grade, how will you decide what kind of portfolio constitutes an A, a B, a C, and so on?

REVIEWING PORTFOLIOS

To check on students' progress, periodically review their portfolios. Farr and Farr (1990) suggested that this be done a minimum of four times a year. In order to make the best use of your time and to help students organize their work, you might have them prepare a list of the items included in the portfolio. The port-

There are some possible disadvantages in using portfolios. They can be difficult to manage and time-consuming to assess (Au, 1994). Portfolios can also lack focus.

Teachers periodically review students' portfolios with them.

Name: _____ Date: _____

Portfolio Evaluation

What were my goals in reading for this period?

What progress toward meeting these goals does my portfolio show?

What are my strengths?

What are my weaknesses?

What are my goals for improving as a reader?

How do I plan to meet those goals?

What were my goals in writing for this period?

What progress toward meeting these goals does my portfolio show?

What are my strengths as a writer?

What are my weaknesses?

What are my goals for improving as a writer?

How do I plan to meet those goals?

What questions do I have about my writing or my reading?

For average and above-average writers, results of portfolio assessments compare favorably with the holistic scoring of compositions that have been assigned as tests. These writers have similar results on the test compositions and on the portfolio assessment. However, the weakest writers achieve higher scores on the portfolios than they do on the tests, apparently needing more time to produce their best results (Simmons, 1990).

folio should also contain a list of students' learning objectives: Students might write a cover letter or fill out a form summarizing work they have done, explaining which goals they feel they have met, which areas might need improvement, and what their plans for the future are. A sample portfolio evaluation form is presented in Figure 13.9. Before you start to review a portfolio, decide what you want to focus on. It could be number of books read, changes in writing, or effort put into revisions. Your evaluation should, of course, consider the student's

Name of student: _____   Date: _____

Voluntary Reading
Number of books read   _____
Variety of books read   _____
Strengths   _____
Needs   _____

Reading Comprehension
Construction of meaning   _____
Extension of meaning   _____
Use of strategies   _____
Quality of responses   _____
Strengths   _____
Needs   _____

Writing
Amount of writing   _____
Variety of writing   _____
Planning   _____
Revising   _____
Self-editing   _____
Content   _____
Organization   _____
Style   _____
Mechanics   _____
Strengths   _____
Needs   _____

Comments: _____
_____
_____

stated goals; it is also important to emphasize the student's strengths. As you assess the portfolio, consider a variety of pieces and look at the work in terms of its changes over time. Ask yourself: "What does the student's work show about her or his progress over the time span covered? What might she or he do to make continued progress?"

To save time and help you organize your assessment of the portfolio, you may want to use a checklist that is supplemented with personal comments. A sample portfolio review checklist is presented in Figure 13.10. Since the objective of eval-

Portfolio raters must be in approximate agreement. Otherwise, the scores "are a measure of who does the scoring rather than the quality of the work" (Herman & Winters, 1994, p. 49). Agreement is highest when the criteria and rubrics are clear and the raters have been well trained and have a thorough understanding of the process.

By examining portfolios, parents get a broader view of their children's progress in school. If informed of the criteria for assessing portfolios, they can spot problem areas and work with the teacher to ameliorate these difficulties. They can also act as a sounding board when their child is deciding which piece to include in a portfolio.

As Winograd (1994) notes, the movement toward alternative or authentic assessment is motivated by the desire to make assessment procedures an integral part of the teaching-learning process so that students have greater involvement in their learning, and teachers have useful information on which to base instructional decisions.

uation is to improve instruction, students should be active partners in the process. "It follows that . . . assessment activities in which students are engaged in evaluating their own learning help them reflect on and understand their own strengths and needs, and it instills responsibility for their own learning" (Tierney, Carter, & Desai, 1991, p. 7).

Portfolios can be passed on from grade to grade and can even be used as part of a districtwide assessment system. Teachers in Orange County, Florida, place both core and supplementary items in students' portfolios. Core items provide consistency and feature (1) a reading development checklist that includes questions about the students' concepts about print, comprehension, word-recognition strategies, and attitudes toward reading; (2) writing samples, including rough drafts; (3) a list of books that students have read; and (4) a test of reading comprehension. The reading development checklist and list of books read could be added to each year, as both are indicators of students' continuous progress. The checklist highlights mastery of strategies; the book list provides insight into students' changing interests and indicates what kinds of materials they are able to handle. Optional elements include students' self-assessments, pages from reading logs, teacher notes from reading or writing conferences, or "other measures a teacher or student felt would illustrate the growth of the student as a language learner" (Matthews, 1990, p. 421). Ultimately, all sources of information should be integrated to obtain the fullest possible picture of the student, group, and program.

Used to traditional methods of assessment, parents may feel uncomfortable or even threatened by portfolios or benchmarks. When portfolios are carefully explained, parents prefer them to standardized tests (Tierney, Carter, & Desai, 1991). Tierney, Carter, and Desai (1991) suggested sitting down with parents and explaining the portfolio process to them. This not only helps parents understand the process, it also helps them to see what their role might be. Traditionally, report cards are sent home for parents to look at and sign or to receive at conferences. Having parents examine portfolios at the same time would provide the kind of positive, in-depth information that a report card cannot convey.

SUMMARY

1. Evaluation entails making a subjective judgment about the quality of students' work or the effectiveness of a program or some component of it. It is based on data from tests, work samples, and observations. An evaluation is made in terms of goals and objectives and should result in some sort of action to improve deficiencies that are noted or to build on strengths.

2. Placement information is necessary to indicate where the student is on the road to literacy. For a student

who is reading, the informal reading inventory is one of the best sources of such information. It taps word recognition and comprehension and yields information about language development and thought processes. It also yields information on four reading levels: independent, instructional, frustration, and listening capacity.

3. In norm-referenced tests, which are sometimes referred to as standardized tests, students are compared to a representative sample of children who are

the same age or in the same grade. Scores are reported in a variety of ways: raw scores, percentile ranks, grade equivalent scores, stanines, normal curve equivalents, and scaled scores.

4. In criterion-referenced tests, students' performance is assessed in terms of a criterion or standard. Because they indicate whether students have mastered a particular skill or strategy, these tests tend to be more valuable than norm-referenced tests for planning programs. Because neither norm-referenced nor criterion-referenced tests are adequate for today's holistic instruction and student-centered assessment in reading and writing, there has been a strong push for authentic assessment. In authentic assessment, students read whole texts and construct responses. Portfolios and observation are widely used components of authentic assessment.

5. Benchmarks, literacy profiles, and rubrics offer ways of holistically indicating performance. The benchmark is a written description of a key task that students would be expected to perform. Literacy profiles offer a device for summarizing students' performance in reading and writing through the use of a checklist of clusters of key literacy behaviors or benchmarks. Rubrics provide descriptions of expected or desirable performances as well as unsatisfactory ones.

6. Students should be given tests designed for the level on which they are reading. Tests that are too easy or too hard are invalid and yield erroneous information.

7. End-of-unit and end-of-book tests in basal series can help the teacher assess students' progress but should be supplemented with other data. Recent basal series include a variety of holistic assessment devices.

8. Assessment is beginning to catch up with evolving theories of reading and writing instruction. Oral and written retellings, think-alouds, observations, anecdotal records, questionnaires, interviews, and ratings are growing in popularity.

9. Holistic evaluation of writing is based on the premise that, to capture the essence of a piece, it is necessary to consider it as a whole and assess it by forming an overall impression. However, analytic assessment of key elements of the piece provides information that the teacher can use to make specific suggestions to the writer.

10. Portfolios provide a means of assembling a broad range of assessment data. They can include work samples, list of books read, results of observations, test scores, and other information.

Portfolio vs report cards.
Norm-reference vs. criterion reference. urban school kids compared to urban. suburban comp to suburban

CLASSROOM APPLICATIONS

1. Keep a file of observation guides, checklists, sample tests, think-aloud protocols, questionnaires, and other assessment devices that might be useful.

2. Examine the assessment devices in a basal series. Evaluate their content validity and format. Note whether all major areas of reading have been covered, whether guessing is a factor, and whether the devices have been tested and give information on validity and reliability.

3. After writing down the goals and objectives for your reading program, examine a recent norm-referenced test to see how closely it measures your objectives.

4. Create a portfolio system for evaluation. Decide what kinds of items might be included in the portfolio. Also devise a checklist or summary sheet that can be used to keep track of and summarize the items.

FIELD APPLICATIONS

1. Construct a checklist for an important area of reading: study strategies, comprehension strategies, participation in group discussions, work habits, or a similar area. If possible, try out the checklist in an elementary school classroom and revise it, if necessary.

2. Devise a think-aloud for a student who is having difficulty with comprehension. Administer the think-aloud, and analyze the results. How might you use the results of the think-aloud to plan a program of comprehension instruction for the student?

c h a p t e r 14

Constructing and Managing a Literacy Program

ANTICIPATION GUIDE

For each of the following statements related to the chapter you are about to read, put a check under "Agree" or "Disagree" to show how you feel. Discuss your responses with classmates before you read the chapter.

Agree   **Disagree**

_____ 1. Students should be heterogeneously rather than homogeneously grouped.   _____

_____ 2. A great deal of time is wasted in the typical elementary school classroom.   _____

_____ 3. Teaching small groups of students with common needs is just about the best way to provide for individual differences.   _____

_____ 4. It is mainly the responsibility of the classroom teacher to work collaboratively with the learning-disabilities specialist, the reading consultant, and other resource personnel.   _____

_____ 5. If parents do not want to be involved with the school, the teacher should respect their wishes.   _____

_____ 6. Computers should be a part of the literacy program.   _____

_____ 7. Teachers should have some say in the materials they use.   _____

Using What You Know

The best teachers are caring individuals who have solid knowledge of their field, broad knowledge of children and how they learn, and a firm grasp of effective teaching strategies. In addition, they must be skilled managers. They must have goals and objectives and the means to meet them. They must make wise and efficient use of their resources: time, materials, and professional assistance. They must also have positive interactions with students, administrative and supervising staff, resource personnel, parents, and the community at large. Clearly, a tall order.

Think of some teachers you have had who were excellent managers. What management strategies did they use? What routines did they devise to keep the class running smoothly? As you read this chapter, try to visualize how you might implement those strategies and principles. Also think about the components of a successful literacy program. What elements would such a program have?

CONSTRUCTING A LITERACY PROGRAM

Previous chapters provided the building blocks for a literacy program. Constructing a program means assembling the blocks in some logical way, and then reassembling them when necessary. Effective programs have some common features, such as a philosophy that all children can learn to read, high expectations for students, objectives that are specific and clearly stated, varied and appropriate materials, effective teaching strategies, efficient use of time, continuous monitoring of progress, involvement of parents, and a process for evaluating the program (Hoffman, 1991; Samuels, 1988).

Construction of a literacy program starts with the students. The program should be built on their interests, their cultures, their abilities, and the nature of the community in which they live. To build an effective program, you need to ask: "What are the children's needs? What are their interests? What aspirations do their parents have for them? What literacy skills do they need in order to survive and prosper now and in the future?"

After acquiring as much information as you can about your students and their community, you should consider your philosophy of teaching reading and writing. Do you prefer a top-down or bottom-up approach, or a combination? Will you use whole language, direct instruction, or a combination of methods?

SETTING GOALS

Once you have acquired some basic information about students and have clarified your philosophy of teaching reading and writing, you can start setting goals. Although research suggests that literacy programs should have specific objectives, teachers should take a broad view of literacy and also set broad goals (Au &

Mason, 1989). These goals should include reading for enjoyment as well as building reading skills to meet the demands of school and society. In addition, specific objectives should be established that lead to fulfilling the goals.

Ultimately, goals and objectives will be determined by the needs of the students. A goal for fourth-graders who will be reading a great deal of content area material, for example, may be to have them learn and apply study strategies. A goal for second-graders who are struggling with phonics might be to have them improve their automatic application of skills.

CHOOSING MATERIALS

Goals and philosophy lead naturally into a choice of materials and activities. For instance, one teacher might use shared reading with second-graders who are struggling with word recognition. A second teacher might use word building to introduce phonics patterns and then use children's books to reinforce the patterns. A third may choose a basal series that has a very structured phonics component, such as Open Court's *Collections for Young Scholars*. All three are setting out to accomplish the same goals, but their approaches reflect different philosophies.

Regardless of philosophy, materials should be varied and should include children's books, both fiction and informational. Numerous suggestions have been made throughout this book for appropriate children's books. Because children's interests and abilities are diverse, the selection should cover a wide variety of topics and include easy as well as challenging books. There should also be reference books, children's magazines and newspapers, pamphlets, menus, telephone books, and directions for activities as diverse as planting seeds and operating the classroom computer.

Supplementary materials, such as a VCR and videocassette library, tape recorders and audiocassettes, and computers and software, including CD-ROM and videodiscs, should also be available. (Additional information on the use of computers and today's technology in a literacy program is offered at the end of this chapter.) Basals and other commercial materials should be on hand if the teacher chooses to use them.

SELECTING TECHNIQUES AND STRATEGIES

The heart of the instructional program is the quality of the teaching. Effective teachers will have mastered a variety of techniques that they can adapt to fit the needs of their students. Some basic techniques for teaching literacy are listed in Table 14.1.

Teachers' knowledge of techniques should be metacognitive. Not only should they know how to teach the techniques, they should also know where and when to use them. For example, a group of students who need a maximum of structure and assistance should be taught within a DRA framework. As their work habits improve, the DR-TA can be introduced to foster independence. Later, reciprocal teaching might be employed.

Teachers must also decide when it is time to substitute one technique or approach for another. For instance, if regular inductive phonics lessons are not working, the teacher might try a word-building approach. If an analytic approach seems too roundabout for the students, the teacher might attempt a synthetic ap-

TABLE 14.1 Essential techniques for teaching literacy

Technique	Appropriate Grade Level
Reading to students	All grades
Shared/assisted reading	Primary grades/remedial
Language experience	Primary grades/remedial
Inductive phonics lesson	Primary grades/remedial
Word building	Primary grades/remedial
Pattern approach to syllabication	Grade 2 and up
Morphemic analysis	Grade 3 and up
Direct instructional lesson for skills and strategies	All grades
Modeling	All grades
Think-aloud lesson	All grades
DRA	All grades
DR-TA	All grades
Cooperative learning	All grades
Reciprocal teaching	All grades
KWL Plus	All grades
ReQuest	Grade 3 and up
I-Search	Grade 2 and up
Responsive elaboration	All grades
Process approach to writing	All grades

proach or a combined analytic-synthetic approach. The important point is that the teacher chooses the techniques to be used and makes adjustments when necessary.

Some key student strategies are listed in Table 14.2. It is important to teach students a variety of strategies: Research suggests that, because of the novelty factor, changing strategies enhances achievement.

BUILDING A SENSE OF COMMUNITY

In an effective literacy program, the teacher focuses on building a community of learners. Traditionally, the focus in schools has been on the individual; individual ability and differences have been emphasized, with measures being used to sort students into ability groups, tracks, and special education programs (Prawat, 1992, p. 9). As the importance of learning from others through scaffolding, discussion, cooperative learning, and consideration of multiple perspectives has become apparent, we see that the focus must be on group learning and building a community of learners. In an ideal community of learners, all students' contributions are valued. Activities and discussions are genuine because students feel that they are a valuable part of the learning community.

"Be firm but fair. Keep them busy. Don't smile until Thanksgiving." This was the kind of advice traditionally given to new teachers. Silence, order, and control were the signs of an effective classroom. Although there were group discussions and group projects, the focus was on individual achievement. After reviewing research by Vygotsky, among others, we now understand the power and importance of the social context of learning. In addition, as the United States has become more culturally diverse, it is now essential that teachers build communities of learning so that we learn from each other as we learn about each other (Peterson, 1992).

TABLE 14.2 Learning strategies and related instructional techniques

	Student's Learning Strategies	Teacher's Instructional Techniques
Preparational	Activating prior knowledge Previewing Predicting Setting purpose SQ3R	Brainstorming Discussion KWL DRA and DR-TA Discussing misconceptions Modeling Direct instruction Reciprocal teaching, ReQuest Think-alouds Responsive elaboration
Selecting/organizing	Selecting important or relevant details Main idea Summarizing Questioning Using graphic organizers SQ3R	Think-alouds DRA and DR-TA Modeling Direct instruction Reciprocal teaching KWL Discussing Study guide Responsive elaboration
Elaborational	Inferring Evaluating Applying Imaging SQ3R	Direct instruction DRA and DR-TA Modeling Think-alouds Reciprocal teaching Discussing Study guide KWL I-Search Responsive elaboration
Monitoring/metacognitive	Monitoring for meaning SQ3R Using fix-up strategies	Think-alouds Modeling Reciprocal teaching Direct instruction Study guide
Affective	Attending/concentrating Staying on task Self-talk	Think-alouds Modeling Discussing Encouraging

TABLE 14.2 (continued)

	Student's Strategies	Teacher's Instructional Techniques
Rehearsal/study	Using understanding	Modeling
	Using mnemonic devices	Think-alouds
	Rehearsing	Direct instruction
	SQ3R	
Word recognition	Using pronounceable word parts	Modeling
	Using analogies	Word building
	Sounding out words	Direct instruction
	Using context	Think-alouds
	Using morphemic analysis	Responsive elaboration
	Using syllabic analysis	
	Using the dictionary	
	Integrating word-attack skills	

Adapted from Jones, Palinscar, Ogle, & Carr, 1986.

Exemplary Teaching

Building a Sense of Community

Susan Moran wanted her students to realize that individual preferences in selecting literature were valid and that they had the right to express their viewpoints about works they had read. Moreover, she wanted students to realize that this applied to everyone, from the poorest to the most proficient readers. Adapting Nancy Atwell's (1987) concept of reading workshop, Moran ended the practice of having everyone read and discuss the same book and, instead, invited students to choose their own books, discuss them, and respond to the texts in a dialogue journal.

To start the workshop, students were asked to bring in their favorite books. The first person to volunteer was Matthew, a student who struggled with reading. Displaying a copy of *The Incredible Journey* (Burnford, 1961), a book that many students had read in an earlier grade, Matthew proclaimed, "It's the best book I've ever read. . . .

Actually . . . it's the only book I've ever read all the way through" (Prawat, 1992, p. 437). Fearing that some students might criticize Matthew's choice, Moran was relieved when the other students enthusiastically supported his selection and related how much they had enjoyed reading the book.

Moran was pleased with the class's sense of community and respect for each other. Moreover, her intention that students would be able to respond perceptively and knowingly to texts was confirmed:

> We were off and running. The classroom became . . . like a dining room table, where people could converse easily about books and poems and ideas. I could watch my students leave the classroom carrying on animated conversations about which book was truly Robert Cormier's best, why sequels are often disappointing, which books they planned to reread. (Prawat, 1992, pp. 437–439).

In an effective literacy program, the teacher focuses on building a community of learners.

To be as successful as possible, the literacy program must be carefully managed. The teacher has to think through the major management decisions he or she makes, as they will have both educational and psychological consequences. These decisions include allocating time, grouping and managing students, acquiring supplies and materials, and coordinating, monitoring, and evaluating the program.

Unfortunately, not all of the time set aside for instruction is put to good use—even in the classes that have allocated a time minimum. According to *What Works: A Report on Teaching and Learning* (U.S. Department of Education, 1986), the percentage of classroom time that elementary school teachers actually use for instruction ranges from 50 to 90 percent. The teacher's job is to get as close to that 90 percent figure as possible.

MANAGING A LITERACY PROGRAM

A teacher of literacy must be an efficient manager, determining how to handle physical set-up, materials, time, paid classroom assistants, and volunteers. The teacher must also coordinate his or her efforts with a number of specialists: the special education teacher, Title 1 personnel, the reading consultant, and the bilingual and ESL teachers. The teacher must consult with the school social worker, nurse, vice principal, principal, and supervisory personnel and enlist the support of parents.

USING TIME EFFICIENTLY

Research clearly indicates that the more time students spend engaged in learning activities and the more content they cover, the more they learn (Berliner, 1985; Brophy & Good, 1986; Rosenshine & Stevens, 1984). The amount of time spent on reading varies greatly; states or local districts often specify a minimum. In one study, time set aside for reading ranged from 47 to 118 minutes in second grade and from 60 to 127 minutes in fifth grade (Guthrie, 1980). Thus some students receive more than twice as much instruction as others.

PACING

Proper pacing plays a key role in literacy achievement (Barr, 1974; Clay, 1993b). Teachers must eliminate those activities that have limited or no value. They should critically examine every activity, asking whether it results in effective learning or practice. One way to make better use of time is to avoid teaching students what they already know and to stop having them practice skills they have already mastered. For instance, when introducing new words for a selection, do not spend time on those that are already familiar to your students. One study found that students already knew 80 percent of the words recommended for instruction in the basal materials (Stallman et al., 1990). In addition to omitting words that students know, consider the level of students' knowledge of unknown words. If they are words that students recognize when they hear them but do not know in print, do not waste time teaching the meanings. Emphasize the visual form of the words, which is the unknown element.

Also eliminate unnecessary seatwork. Use cooperative learning, have students read self-selected books, and have them work at learning centers. Well-planned centers can provide excellent opportunities for exploration and skills application. To be effective, each center should have a specific objective. The key is to arrange a sequence of valuable activities that students can perform without teacher direction. If some of the planned activities involve partners, students can obtain feedback and elaboration from each other. Table 14.3 describes two sample centers (Ford, 1994).

Carefully plan and regulate activities so time is not lost because of lack of direction or time-consuming transitions. This means creating a purposeful, focused program that has energy and vitality. Schoephoeister (1980) declared, "Teaching efficiently means conducting the instructional program with an urgency that can be sensed and shared by the students. This occurs when instruction is vital, when the teacher refuses to procrastinate, when every free moment is seized upon and put to good use" (p. 19).

TABLE 14.3 Two sample centers

Type	Objective	Sequence of Activities
Listening Post	Building fluency	1. Students listen to a taped story. 2. Students read along with the taped story. 3. Students listen to the taped story again. 4. Students read the story to each other. 5. Students again read along with the taped story.
CD-ROM Center	Building understanding	1. Students examine the title and illustration on the first frame and predict what the story might be about. 2. Students either read the story silently or have it read aloud. 3. Students discuss the story in light of their predictions. 4. Students take turns reading the story to each other. 5. Students fill out a response form, supplying their name, the title of the story, and a summarizing sentence that tells what the story is about.

Adapted from Ford, 1994.

In addition to being efficient, instruction should be conceptual and substantive. Four characteristics of high-quality, substantive instruction are promoting higher-order thinking, developing depth of knowledge, establishing connectedness to the world by having students relate what they have learned to what they actually know and apply that knowledge to their everyday lives, and fostering substantive conversation (Newmann & Wehlage, 1993). Substantive conversation consists of using questions and discussions to learn. It involves asking questions about key concepts, discussing issues, organizing information, forming generalizations, drawing conclusions, and evaluating information.

A fifth characteristic of high-quality instruction is providing social support. When a teacher provides social support, she or he has high expectations for the class and clearly conveys these expectations. There is a sense that learning is an adventure in which both the teacher and students are involved. The class is inclusive and cooperative. All students are members of the learning team and are expected to help each other and value each other's viewpoints.

The Matthew Effect (Stanovich, 1986) is very much in evidence in traditional grouping practices. Compared with brighter students, those in a low-achieving group read less, are asked fewer high-level questions, are given fewer prompts, and so fall even further behind. It is a classic example of the poor becoming poorer.

A major advantage of individualized reading and reading workshop is that they avoid the stereotyping and other pitfalls associated with grouping.

The **Joplin plan** is a form of grouping in which students of varying ages and grade levels are divided on the basis of achievement in reading. The groups assemble each day for reading instruction.

Silent reading is also suggested for transitions. An average school day has about thirty-one major transitions that account for as much as 15 percent or more of the day (Doyle, 1986). Still another source of added instructional time is out-of-school reading. Encourage all students to spend time each day reading voluntarily. Those who are falling behind or who are struggling with their reading can be given a choice of easy books or encouraged to reread books that have already been read in class so that their reading becomes automatic and effortless.

PROVIDING FOR INDIVIDUAL DIFFERENCES

What is the best way to handle the diversity that exists in the typical classroom? The answer for much of this century has been "three groups." Between 1920 and 1935, the practice of dividing a class into three groups—below average, average, and above average—became established (Otto, Wolf, & Eldridge, 1984). Individualized reading, whole language, literature-based reading, reading and writing workshops, and other innovations have made inroads in this traditional practice.

The three-group approach has several flaws. For one thing, three groups usually do not allow enough latitude for the diversity of reading abilities in a class. Often, the poorest readers end up with a text that is too difficult and the best readers are assigned one that is a bit too easy. In addition, groups tend to be rigid. Once students have been placed in a group, they tend to stay there. This is especially true of slow learners. One group of students who were tracked into the below-average group in kindergarten stayed there throughout their elementary school years (Rist, 1970). Finally, grouping can be harmful to self-esteem. Students who are placed in low-achieving groups see themselves as poor readers and so does everyone else, especially if the groups remain unchanged (Hiebert, 1983). Students in the low-achieving group are also deprived of peer models of high performance.

Because of the harmful effects of assigning students to groups and keeping them there, the Wisconsin Reading Association has issued a Position Statement for Grouping Practices for Reading in which it advocates the use of more than one kind of grouping, offering students the opportunity to participate in diverse groupings, balancing whole class instruction with small groups, and halting the practice of keeping students in a single group.

USING THE JOPLIN PLAN

One form of ability grouping, the **Joplin plan,** takes place among classes rather than within the classroom. Teachers exchange students during the reading period. If three teachers are involved, one might take the top readers, another the middle group, and a third the slower readers. In that way, the range of reading abilities is limited within each class. A teacher can, of course, also group within his or her class but may only need two groups. Sometimes, an entire school adopts the Joplin plan. At other times, an informal agreement may be worked out between two teachers: "You take my high group; I'll take your low group."

WHOLE CLASS GROUPING

Whole class instruction can be efficient and build a sense of community. Moreover, low achievers typically try harder when they are part of whole class instruction (Radencich, Beers, & Schumm, 1993). Reading aloud to students, shared reading, and introducing new concepts and strategies lend themselves to whole class instruction. Reading and writing workshops begin and end with whole class activities. As discussed in Chapter 9, some teachers also have their students read certain core texts or selections as a whole group.

A teacher must provide thorough preparation for a reading of the selection when using whole class grouping. Anticipating difficulties that students might have with the text, the teacher develops background knowledge, activates schema, builds vocabulary, sets a purpose, and creates interest in the selection. Although the initial preparatory instruction may be the same for all students, some read the text in different ways. Higher-achieving students read independently. Others can receive varying degrees of assistance. The teacher might spend additional time reviewing vocabulary, reading a portion of the selection to get the students started, or guiding students through the selection section by section. For children who have more serious reading problems, the teacher might use shared or assisted reading or allow them to listen to a taped version of the selection or view it on CD-ROM.

After the selection has been read, students can discuss it as part of a whole group. Having read and discussed a story together builds community among students. However, it should be emphasized that although the selection might have been easy or just slightly challenging for some students, it was probably very difficult for others. For this reason, whole group reading of selections should be used sparingly, and some teachers might not choose to use it at all. If used, whole group reading of selections should be balanced by providing lower-achieving students with opportunities to read on their instructional or independent levels.

Radencich (1995) suggests the use of two-tier instruction for students whose skills are so limited that they cannot read the core selection, no matter how much help the teacher provides. Operating in the top tier of a two-tier system, low-end students participate in the reading of the core selection by share-reading it with the teacher or by listening as the teacher or an aide reads the selection to them. Operating in the lower tier, low-end students read a selection that is on their instructional level and that addresses their needs. If possible, the lower-level text is related to the theme of the core selection. Through the two-tier system, students "maintain their membership in the classroom community. In addition, however, they regularly receive instruction and practice in easier texts, and on specific skills and strategies" (Radencich, 1995, p. 163).

Although whole class grouping is efficient and builds a sense of community, it does have certain disadvantages. Teaching tends to be teacher-centered, there is less opportunity to provide for individual differences, and students have less opportunity to contribute (Radencich, 1995).

OTHER TYPES OF GROUPS

A number of other grouping patterns can be effective in the typical elementary school classroom. Some can be used along with ability grouping, others instead of

Although a review of the research suggests that the Joplin plan is effective (Slavin, 1987a), the plan does have some disadvantages. Some time is lost when children move from class to class. In addition, it is necessary to start and stop the reading period at specific times to allow students to leave and then return to their regular classroom. This scheduling causes a loss of time flexibility; for example, the reading period cannot be extended, even though an interesting discussion is taking place. The opportunity to correlate reading with other subjects is also reduced, as it is often difficult to tie in reading instruction received outside of the homeroom with reading in the content areas.

Whole class instruction is the practice of teaching the entire class at the same time. However, assignments or tasks may be individualized.

Interest groups are groups formed on the basis of students' mutual interests.

Skills or strategies groups are temporary groups, sometimes known as *ad hoc* groups, that are formed for the purpose of learning a skill or strategy.

Cooperative learning is a way of acquiring skills or information in which students work together to help each other learn.

Jigsaw is a type of cooperative activity in which each student has responsibility for a portion of the topic or task. Ultimately, members of the group put all the pieces of the task together. Jigsaw is an excellent device for fostering interdependence because each member of the group must contribute her or his share in order for the group to complete its task.

Each member of a cooperative group may have a specific role, which the teacher assigns or the group member chooses. Possible roles include moderator or leader who manages the group, a recorder who writes down the group's response, an observer who notes the group's efforts and its use of group processes, a resource specialist who obtains and cares for resource materials, a researcher who obtains needed information, and an editor who checks the work for completeness and accuracy. A particularly important role is that of checker of understanding, who makes sure that each member of the group can explain how the group's conclusion was reached (Johnson & Johnson, 1994).

ability grouping. By employing several patterns, the teacher gives students the opportunity to mix with a greater variety of other students, and there is less of a chance that lower-achieving students will brand themselves as "slow" learners.

In **interest groups,** students who are interested in a particular topic, author, or genre join together. For example, groups can be set up to discuss particular categories of famous people, such as inventors, entertainers, sports figures, or scientists.

In **skills or strategies groups,** students are grouped based on the need for a particular skill or strategy. Once the skill has been mastered, the group is disbanded. For example, if a number of students are having difficulty monitoring their comprehension, you might group them for lessons and practice sessions on how to use strategies in this area. Make sure that skills or strategies groups provide for specials needs that high-achieving students have so that the groups are not stigmatized as being remedial (Radencich, 1995).

Pairs of students can work together in a variety of ways—for example, as reading partners who take turns reading to each other, as study buddies who work on an assignment together, or as peer editors who read and comment on each other's writttten pieces.

Other organizational patterns include individualized reading, reading and writing workshops, and literature circles. See Chapter 10 for a discussion of individualized reading and Chapter 9 for an explanation of literature circles.

Another way of grouping is through **cooperative learning.** Cooperative learning seems almost too good to be true. Not only do students improve in their subject matter areas (Slavin, 1987b), they also feel better about themselves and have the added satisfaction of working with and helping others (Johnson & Johnson, 1987). As a bonus, they learn the interpersonal skills necessary to become leaders and cooperative workers, skills that they will need both in school and in the wider world.

Although cooperative learning activities can take a variety of forms, two major types are jigsaw and study group. **Jigsaw** is an approach devised to promote understanding among diverse groups of students (Aronson, 1978). In the jigsaw, there are two types of subgroups: home and topic. Each member of a home group is provided with different information. For example, if a class is studying a selection on whales, the teacher might divide the selection into four parts: kinds of whales, habits of whales, whaling, and steps taken to save whales. Each member of a home group is assigned one topic and given a series of questions to guide his or her reading. Each student is to become an "expert" on his or her topic. After getting their assignments, students join a topic group. Each member of a topic group has the same assignment. For instance, all the students investigating kinds of whales join together. Topic group members help each other with hard words and other difficulties and go to the teacher for assistance only as a last resort. After students have read their assigned parts and shared their information in the topic groups, they rejoin their home groups. Then each member of a home group shares the piece of the jigsaw for which he or she was responsible. The members of the home group check to make sure that each team member understands all the subtopics and can put together all the information. A quiz is then given by the teacher.

Each home group may be assessed on the basis of its total score or on the degree of its improvement. The teacher initially makes sure that each group has a clear understanding of the assignment and knows what the criteria for successful performance are—for example, being able to answer eight out of ten questions about whales and being able to write an interesting, informative paper about whales. The teacher evaluates total performance of the group and each student's grasp of the information and then reteaches content or strategies as necessary. The teacher also evaluates group processes to see how well the members worked together. Using adaptations of the jigsaw model, the teacher may have students put on a puppet play or create a TV commercial, with each student assigned a distinct task.

In a **study group**, students help each other learn information in much the same way students have always gathered together to prepare for exams (Hotchkiss, 1990). The teacher presents the skill or information to be learned, provides guided practice, and then assigns students to heterogeneous groups to practice. Team members might work as a whole group or in pairs to complete the exercises. Later, students are given a quiz on the material.

Why does cooperative learning work? When one person explains information to another, both benefit. The speaker organizes, summarizes, elaborates on, and evaluates the information. The listener obtains information. Information obtained from a peer might be more credible and more understandable than that derived from the teacher. Even controversy, when properly conducted, fosters learning. It causes students to reflect upon and evaluate their views and possibly search for additional information or a better explanation, resulting in increased understanding and retention (Johnson & Johnson, 1994).

BALANCED GROUPING

Grouping patterns should be balanced. At times, it is best for the class to work as a whole; at other times, small groups work best, and students should also have some experience working individually. The foundation of flexible grouping lies in the building of a sense of community. Realizing that they are valued and have a common purpose, students are better able to work with each other.

CONTINUOUS MONITORING OF PROGRESS

A near universal finding of research on effective teaching is that it is essential to know where students are (Hoffman, 1991). **Monitoring** should be continuous and does not necessarily entail formal testing. Observing, periodically checking portfolios, and administering informal checks can provide knowledge about students' progress. Such continuous monitoring assumes that if something is lacking in the students' learning, the program will be modified. Skills and strategies that have been forgotten will be retaught; processes that have gone off on the wrong path will be rerouted. If materials prove to be too dull or too hard, substitutions will be made. If a child needs extra time to learn, it will be supplied. Such adjustments are especially important for slow learners.

A number of interpersonal and group-processing skills are needed to make cooperative learning work. Beginning skills include staying with the group, taking turns, doing your share, using quiet voices, and using each other's names. More advanced skills include listening to what is being said, criticizing ideas and not people, being an active and interested group member, respecting the viewpoints of others, and not changing one's mind unless convinced by reasons or proof (Johnson & Johnson, 1994).

A **study group** is a form of cooperative learning in which students work together to learn information or a skill.

Cooperative learning could be a welcome, effective alternative to seat work (Stevens, Madden, Slavin, & Farnish, 1987). Instead of completing worksheets that may not even be related to the selection being read, students can work on projects related to skills or strategies they have been taught or selections they have read. The projects might even be designed for voluntary reading activities.

When deciding on grouping patterns, pick configurations that are efficient but that also help build a sense of community. Also ask, "What is the best type of grouping for this particular activity?" And, of course, consider the impact of grouping on the individual student. How will it affect his or her self-esteem and sense of belonging? Grouping has to meet social as well as academic needs.

Monitoring refers to the assessment of students' progress to see whether they are performing adequately.

INVOLVING PARENTS

Parents have a right to be kept informed about their child's literacy program. As a practical matter, keeping them up to date, especially if the program is a new one, will forestall complaints due to misunderstanding and will build support.

"Parents are their children's first and most influential teachers. What parents do to help their children learn is more important to academic success than how well off the family is" (U.S. Department of Education, 1986, p. 7). Study after study shows that even the most impoverished and least educated parents have high aspirations for their children (Wingfield & Asher, 1984). Unfortunately, however, today's parents have less time to spend with their children. About 24 percent of U.S. families are headed by single parents, and more than 50 percent of mothers of school-age children work outside the home. According to one report, the average American mother spends less than half an hour a day talking or reading with her children; fathers spend less than fifteen minutes (U.S. Department of Education, 1986).

However, if systematic efforts are made, most parents will pitch in. Prior to changes made to improve the effectiveness of the program in an impoverished elementary school in Southern California, teachers falsely assumed that parents would lack the time, ability, or motivation to help their children (Goldenberg, 1994). Although the parents were not well educated, they had high aspirations for their children. The school sent home reading materials and suggestions for ways in which the materials might be used. Although parents were interested and supportive, merely making suggestions at the beginning of the year wasn't enough. The teachers found that it was important to use follow-up notes, phone calls, and regular homework assignments. With follow-through and monitoring, parents began providing assistance and students' achievement increased. The lesson is clear. The school must establish *and* maintain contact with parents. Quarterly report cards and PTA notices are a start, but more is necessary. Encourage students to take their papers home to show their parents, and to read to their parents from their basals and/or trade books. This is especially important for novice readers. After students have finished a level in their basals or completed a trade book, help them prepare a passage to read to their parents.

A key step in communicating with parents is to keep them informed about your program when changes are made. Parents may expect instruction to be the way it was when they were in elementary school. If they understand how a program works, they will be more inclined to support it, which helps ensure the program's success. The school might also hold open houses and special meetings to explain the program. Letters in which the teacher describes what students are studying and why and how parents can help should be sent home periodically. Parents want to help their children but may not know what to do. Provide suggestions specific to the current unit, as well as more general ones with more far-reaching consequences. For example, reading to a child is a powerful technique for developing language *and* for developing a close relationship with the child. Parents can also provide a place and a time for the child to study, even if it is just a relatively quiet corner in a small apartment. Psychological support is more important than physical space.

Refrain from suggesting to parents that it is their obligation to teach their children to read or to correct any reading deficiencies that they might have. Stress that their efforts on their children's behalf should be natural and unpressured. Parents should be informed if the child is having difficulty, however. They need to know what their options are, how the school can help, and other resources that are available. If they choose to help their child, give them some guidelines and suggestions.

Parents should also be encouraged to obtain books for their children and to take them to the library. As some parents may not have much knowledge of book selection, you may want to supply them with lists of suitable books. These lists should be personalized, geared to each student's ability and interests.

WORKING WITH OTHER PROFESSIONALS

Mirroring the trend toward cooperative and group learning activities, today's model of effective literacy instruction is one of cooperation and collaboration. The classroom teacher works closely with other classroom teachers, sharing expertise, experience, and resources. In many schools, teachers meet not only to plan programs but also to support each other and to explore new developments in the field. In some schools, for instance, teachers meet to discuss the latest children's books. With the emphasis on inclusion, classroom teachers are also working more closely with the special education teacher, the reading/language arts consultant, and other specialists.

Because of the emphasis on using children's books and technology in the literacy program, it is important for classroom teachers to work with the media specialist. A well-balanced reading program must have a continuous supply of children's books. Media specialists can hold story hours, teach library skills, conduct book talks, help students use computers that are housed in the library, arrange special displays, and help children find appropriate books. They may even be able to provide loans to the classroom library and can keep teachers informed about the latest children's books. Classroom teachers can assist by letting the media specialist know when they plan to ask students to obtain books on certain topics or suggest that students read books by a certain author, so that the necessary materials can be assembled.

LITERACY AND TECHNOLOGY

Because of the growing prevalence and importance of technology in the field of communication, this section is devoted to literacy and technology. Although other technologies are discussed, the major emphasis is on computers.

COMPUTERS

With advances in technology, there have been dramatic improvements in the quality of educational software. Two of the most significant changes have been the switch to more powerful computers and the increased use of **CD-ROM**. CD-ROM disks, which are essentially the same as the CDs used to store and play music, have extensive storage capacity. Because of this storage capacity, software publishers have been able to produce highly sophisticated, interactive programs and sell them for relatively modest prices. For instance, an entire encyclopedia

Brochures containing suggestions for parents for helping their children in a variety of literacy areas are available from the International Reading Association (800 Barksdale Road, Newark, DE 19714-8139) and the National Council of Teachers of English (1111 Kenyon Road, Urbana, IL 61801).

Despite your best efforts, some parents will stay uninvolved. Fredericks and Rasinski (1990) have recommended a positive approach. Instead of blaming parents for not being participants, keep them informed with a steady stream of information about the program. Telephone or visit them. Encourage their participation, but don't be judgmental. Try to schedule activities at times that might be most convenient to parents. Also, share good news with them; periodically, let them know about their child's accomplishments.

CD-ROM is a compact disc on which large amounts of computerized read-only information can be stored. (Read-only data can be accessed but cannot be added to.)

By the end of 1992, only 900,000 computer owners possessed CD-ROM drives. By the end of 1993, that number exceeded 10 million. Today, about one out of every eight computer owners possesses a CD-ROM drive (Shields, 1994). In fact, many computers now have one that is built in. As a result, there is a wealth of CD-ROM software. Some of these offerings are updated versions of floppy disks and include such venerable titles as the *Oregon Trail* (MECC) and *Bank Street Writer* (Scholastic). In fact, many of the most successful pieces of educational software are now available on CD-ROM.

 Computers are powerful literacy tools.

including film clips and sound effects can be placed on a single disk and might be priced under $100.

In terms of literacy instruction, computers have four major uses, which sometimes overlap. They provide practice, tutorial instruction, and simulations. They are also powerful communication tools for both students and teachers.

Cloze (Continental Press) is a good example of traditional reinforcement software, as is *Bailey's Book House* (Edmark). Both supply the kind of practice presented by workbooks but are more interesting, give knowledge of results, and are more interactive. *Cloze* keeps track of a student's progress and has an authoring tool so that the teacher can add passages. *Bailey's Book House,* which emphasizes basic decoding and sight-vocabulary skills, features lively graphics, sound effects, and high-quality speech. Students activate animated sequences that illustrate letter-sound elements and high-frequency words. They also create sight-word stories.

In tutorial software, the student is walked through a lesson with a series of questions and answers or activities. Active participation is required. After a skill is explained, reinforcement exercises are provided. One of the most extensive examples of tutorial software is the phonics component of *Writing to Read* (IBM), which explains and provides practice with letter-sound relationships.

A **simulation** is a type of computer program that presents activities giving the feel of a real experience.

One of the best instructional uses of software is the presentation of **simulations.** Students can travel back in time, take journeys across country, and perform experiments without leaving their computers. For example, in *Amazon Trail* (MECC), students travel up the Amazon to find a lifesaving medicine and deliver it to a hidden city X. In *Oregon Trail,* version 1.2 (MECC), students plan a trip west; in *Dino Park Tycoon* (MECC), students can use a database to access facts about nineteen different kinds of dinosaurs. As they manage Dino Park and learn about dinosaurs, students use a variety of math, reading, and writing skills. *A*

Navajo Vacation: Living in Two Worlds (Teacher Support) enables students to explore Navajo culture.

USING THE COMPUTER AS A TOOL

Computers are most powerful in literacy learning when they are used as a tool. They can help locate data, retrieve information, organize data, compose information, and present information.

Word Processing.   Computers are most frequently used as an aid to composition. The major advantage of word-processing software is that students can revise without rewriting or retyping the whole piece. Such software can also help with planning, checking spelling, and checking grammar and usage.

Bundling word-processing features, design, and illustration capabilities, desktop publishing (DTP) systems allow students to create newspapers, newsletters, brochures, and booklets. See Chapter 12 for additional information about word processing and DTP.

Telecommunications.   Telecommunications by computer involves using a modem to hook up the computer to a telephone line and using the proper software to communicate with another computer or a network of computers.

Using **electronic mail** or bulletin board systems, students can send and receive messages to and from students in the same building, other buildings, other states, or even other nations; there have been numerous electronic "keypal" projects. In a project sponsored by Technical Education Research Center, fourth- through sixth-graders in nine schools throughout the country shared information on acid rain. As they learned about acid rain, they learned about each other. Both science and communication skills were enhanced. An organization entitled I*LEARN matches students from a variety of countries on worthwhile projects. In one project, students built water pumps out of bicycle parts and sent them to villages in Nicaragua (Dyrli, 1994). One commercial service (Scholastic) offers students the opportunity to teleconference with favorite authors. Another service has created *Cyberkids,* an electronic magazine. Students can submit articles electronically and also receive the magazine electronically. A noncommercial network specifically designed for schools is the Global SchoolNet, which sponsors a wide variety of projects. Global SchoolNet offers access to a number of collaborative learning projects such as Newsday, in which students exchange news stories with other students from around the world; Gala, in which students exchange poems, plays, and other creations; and Animal Riddles, in which primary grade students are encouraged to make up riddles. For more information, contact Global SchoolNet Foundation, P.O. Box 243, Bonita, CA 91908, or info@acme.fred.org.

SELECTING SOFTWARE

The key to making effective use of the computer is to obtain high-quality software. The selection of software starts with your objectives; be sure that the program you choose is designed to help students meet them. The program must also do a better or more efficient job than the materials or techniques you now use. Teachers sometimes fall into the trap of obtaining software simply because it is

Electronic mail is the sending of notes or messages by means of computer.

Developed by the National Science Foundation, the Internet is a worldwide network of computer users that began as a means for researchers to share information. Because it is not commercially owned, the Internet is open to all. With more and more institutions, organizations, and individuals joining the Internet each day, it has become an incredibly rich and diverse source of information. However, because it is composed of a loose confederation of regional networks, the Internet can be difficult to use. You can connect to the Internet through an institutional connection (most universities have access to it), a regional provider, or one of the commercial online services such as America Online, CompuServe, or Prodigy. Through an Internet connection, students can even contact the President of the United States by typing in president@whitehouse.gov. The reply will not be a personal one, but it will be fast and will illustrate ways of obtaining additional information about matters of national concern (Dyrli, 1994).

fun or attractive, but fail to consider its educational value. Factors to be considered when evaluating software include the following (Cook, 1986):

- Does it help the attainment of an educationally valid objective?
- Are its activities consistent with the way I teach reading or writing?
- Does it make use of the special capabilities of the computer—providing immediate knowledge of results, learner participation, use of graphics, use of speech, keeping track of progress, and so on?
- Does the software include learning aids, such as pronouncing and/or defining difficult words on request and providing additional information or more practice if needed?
- Is the material presented accurately and on the proper level of readability?
- Is the software reasonably easy to use?
- Can it be modified to add customized examples or exercises?

Tool software and software that can be modified provide the most return on the dollar. They can be used over and over again.

A small sampling of available software is listed in Table 14.4. To get a more complete listing, consult *The Educational Software Selector* (TESS) from EPIE Institute (Hampton Bays, NY); it describes more than sixteen thousand pieces of software and videodiscs. TESS is available on CD-ROM. Software is regularly reviewed in the journals *Electronic Learning* and *Technology and Learning*.

GETTING THE MOST OUT OF COMPUTERS

Computer software, like other educational materials, requires teacher guidance. Students have to be prepared to complete the activity offered by the software. They must have their background knowledge activated, have a purpose for completing the assignment, and know how to read the material. Should they read it fast or slow? Should they read it in parts or as a whole? They also have to know how to use any learning aids that might be built into the program. Can they reread the directions, for instance, or get help with difficult vocabulary? When using some kinds of software, students may need teacher input. After students have completed the software activity, give them the opportunity to discuss what they have learned, clarify misconceptions, integrate new and old information, and extend and apply their learning.

In most schools, computer time is limited. To make the most of the time they have, students should be directed to complete necessary preparations before they sit down at the computer. Have students read the instructions until they understand what they are to do. A story or essay should be written on a piece of paper before it is entered into the word processor. Set up schedules so that everyone has equal time on the computer.

OTHER TECHNOLOGIES

Audio and audiovisual technologies can be used to motivate children to read or to expand children's understanding and appreciation of a selection. For poor readers, audiovisual aids may provide access to a piece of literature that they would not be able to read on their own.

The framework of a DRA or direct instruction might be used with computer software. The software, if it consists primarily of material to be read, functions as the reading portion of the lesson. Preparation, purpose setting, discussion, extension or direct instruction, guided practice, and application would have to be supplied.

Where feasible, students should work in pairs. Not only is this an efficient use of resources, but it also increases verbal interaction as students work on a project cooperatively (Balajthy, 1989). However, as with other cooperative learning situations, students must be taught how to work together, if best results are to be achieved.

In addition to acting as a means of reinforcement and a tool for learning for students, computers can be useful for teachers. Word-processing and DTP systems can be used to create attractive learning materials. Computers can even help teachers keep up-to-date professionally. By using the Internet, America Online, Prodigy, CompuServe, DIA-LOG, or other online service, you can access educational databases.

TABLE 14.4 Sampling of software for literacy programs

Software (Publisher)	Grade Level	Format	Description
Big Book Maker (Queue)	1–8	Mac; floppy	A series of programs, present visuals that can be used as a basis for creating posters or big books. Topics range from fairy tales and numbers and shapes to the rain forest.
Kid Pix Studio (Broderbund)	K–8	Mac, PC; CD-ROM	Provides digital puppets, film clips, songs, and sound effects so that students can create animated pictures and multimedia presentations.
First Connections: The Golden Book Encyclopedia for Windows (Hartley/Jostens)	1–6	Mac, PC, MPC; Floppy	In addition to containing 1500 articles, also features film clips, excerpts from famous speeches, and sound effects. Has voiced instructions and also can read text.
Microsoft Creative Writer 1.0 (Microsoft)	2–8	Mac, PC; CD-ROM	Includes graphics, formats for various kinds of writing, multiple typefaces, a spell checker, and a thesaurus. Also includes story starters, designs for posters and other projects, and a feature that creates random three-part sentences.
My First Incredible Amazing Dictionary (Multimedia)	K-2	Mac, PC; CD-ROM	Uses spoken words and illustrations to introduce children to 1000 words.
The New Kid on the Block (Broderbund)	2–4	Mac, PC; CD-ROM	Presents poems by Jack Prelutsky. Viewers hear the poems read aloud as text is displayed on the screen with accompanying animation. When words or phrases are clicked on, they are dramatized. (e.g., click on the word *sonata,* and one is played.) Excellent for building enjoyment of light verse and building reading skills and vocabulary.
The San Diego Zoo Presents . . . The Animals (Software Toolworks)	3–9	Mac; floppy	Presents more than 200 animals.
Storybook Weaver (MECC)	2–4	Mac; floppy	Includes 650 images from cultures around the world, which students can use to prompt or illustrate their writing. Also available in a Spanish version.
Superprint for the Macintosh (Scholastic)	K-8	Mac; floppy, CD-ROM	Can be used to create banners, posters, charts, big books, maps, and other visuals.
Wiggleworks (Scholastic)	K-2	Mac, PC; CD-ROM	Highlights text as children's books are read aloud. Children can record themselves reading the text and then see how they sound. Children can also write using a sentence starter, create their own books, and explore letters and sounds.

VIDEODISCS

A **videodisc,** also known as a laser disk, is a metallic disk on which large amounts of computerized data can be stored and accessed via a beam of laser light.

There is some evidence that use of videodiscs fosters confidence, improves attitudes toward learning, and can lead to higher achievement (Rock & Cummings, 1994).

A **videodisc** performs the same function as a videotape. However, the videodisc is more durable and produces a higher-quality image. Most important, any one of its fifty-four thousand frames can be accessed instantaneously. The videodisc also has two audio channels so that a question can be posed on one channel and a response can be received on the other.

Educational videodiscs are typically controlled by a barcode reader. Barcodes correspond to specific segments on the videodisc. A teacher's guide contains a listing of the videodisc's segments and their barcodes. If you wish to view a specific film clip or examine a certain chart, you access it by scanning the barcode in the manual with the barcode reader. Currently, videodiscs are most popular in the sciences because they do such an excellent job of showing scientific processes. However, language arts videodiscs are beginning to appear. For instance, *Channel R.E.A.D.* (Houghton Mifflin) is a series of fifteen thirty-minute videodiscs that reinforce a variety of reading strategies in an interactive format. At various points in each of the dramas presented, students use barcode readers or remote controls to build background, learn vocabulary, and respond to open-ended questions. The series is designed for grade 3 and up.

AUDIO TECHNOLOGIES

Audio versions of books have three advantages (Rickelman & Henk, 1990b). Although warmth and interaction are missing in an electronic reading, it can be played over and over by the student. In addition, it often includes sound effects, may be dramatized, and may even have been recorded by the author of the work. Because of their superior sound quality, CD versions are preferred to taped ones but may not be available for certain titles.

AUDIOVISUAL TECHNOLOGIES

Films and videocassettes are also available for a wide variety of children's books. There are hundreds of children's books on video, including *Frog and Toad Are Friends* (Churchill Media), *Cinderella* (Playhouse Video), *Mufaro's Beautiful Daughters* (Weston Woods), and *Following the Drinking Gourd* (SRA Group). For an extensive listing of high-quality children's videos, see *The Best of the Best for Children* (Donavin, 1992).

HYPERMEDIA AND HYPERTEXT

Hypermedia are works that combine several types of media.

Through the use of computer, video, audio, and videodisc technologies, **hypermedia** presentations that combine text, still pictures, filmclips, sound, oral commentary, and videotaped footage can be created. For instance, one of the special features of Compton's *Interactive Encyclopedia* is Editing Room. Using Editing Room, students can create their own multimedia presentations incorporating text from the encyclopedia and/or text they have created as well as sounds and pictures from the encyclopedia. If a microphone is available, students can also incorporate their own spoken comments or dramatizations. Another easy-to-use multimedia system is *Super Talk to Me* (Educational Activities), which allows teachers and students to create presentations composed of video images, text, spoken commentary, and sound effects.

Hypertext is information arranged in nontraditional or nonsequential ways using a computer. (Blanchard & Rottenberg, 1990). It is possible to arrange text, visual, and/or auditory segments in a variety of sequences or according to a number of themes. One could examine John F. Kennedy's presidency from a number of perspectives: by viewing his speeches on domestic issues, by viewing legislation proposed during his term in office that was not enacted, or by looking at his foreign policy statements.

Hypertext and hypermedia could change the way children learn. Visual and auditory images make text more memorable. Understanding of a person, event, or idea can be greatly enhanced if students are able to view the subject in a variety of ways. And their understanding would not just be fuller; it would also be more flexible. They would better understand the numerous causes and diverse solutions that many problems have. More flexible understanding (cognitive flexibility) is highly desirable, for with it, students are better able to apply the principles they learn and see applications that may not be immediately apparent (Spiro, 1990). Of course, we do not have to wait for hypermedia and hypertext to reach the elementary school before we start teaching for cognitive flexibility. We can start right now by helping students organize their knowledge in diverse ways and look at problems and possible solutions from many perspectives.

Hypertext is created by using a computer to search through and group pieces of information in a variety of ways.

LITERACY IN TODAY'S AND TOMORROW'S WORLD

Increasingly, literacy will include the ability to use computers and other high-technology devices. Students need to know how to use resources such as the

Increasingly, today's students will be using electronic card catalogues.

Technology is increasing the need for literacy, as we have access to much more information. With the use of databases and word-processing systems, we also have new tools for organizing and presenting information.

Internet and how to construct multimedia reports. They also need to understand how to get the most out of interactive encyclopedias and other sophisticated sources of information. Computer literacy still requires traditional skills: the ability to read with understanding, to write coherently, and to think clearly. However, today's technology also requires a higher level of literacy. Computer searches allow students to obtain greater amounts of data on a particular topic, including data published that day. Students need the skills to skim and scan data so that they can quickly select information that is relevant and important. A key reading skill for the era of the information superhighway is the ability to decide quickly and efficiently whether an article, study, or other document merits reading. With so much more information available, it is essential that time is not wasted reading texts that are not pertinent or worthwhile. Having more data to work with means that students must be better at organizing information, evaluating it, drawing conclusions, and conveying the essence of the information to others. They also need cognitive flexibility to make use of the growing amounts of information in proposing diverse solutions to the increasingly complex problems sure to arise in the coming years.

PROFESSIONAL DEVELOPMENT

To keep up with the latest development in the fields of reading and writing instruction, it is necessary to be professionally active—to join professional organizations, attend meetings, take part in staff-development activities, and read in the field. The International Reading Association (100 Barksdale Road, Newark, DE 19714) and the National Council of Teachers of English (1111 Kenyon Road, Urbana, IL 61801) are devoted to professional improvement in reading and the language arts. For elementary school teachers, the IRA publishes the widely read periodical *The Reading Teacher* and the NCTE publishes *Language Arts*. Both organizations have local and state chapters and sponsor local, state, regional, and national conferences.

As with any other vital endeavor, teachers should set both long-term goals and short-term professional objectives, asking such questions as the following:

- Where do I want to be professionally five years from now?
- What steps do I have to take to get there?
- What are my strengths and weaknesses as a teacher of reading and writing?
- How can I build on my strengths and remediate my weaknesses?
- What new professional techniques/skills or areas of knowledge would I most like to learn?

The answers should result in a plan of professional development.

The checklist is meant as a review of techniques and concepts, a device for self-evaluation, and a motivator for self-improvement.

Filling out the checklist in Figure 14.1 will help you create a profile of your strengths and weaknesses as a reading/writing teacher. The checklist covers the entire literacy program and incorporates the major principles covered in the text. As such, it provides a review of the book as well as a means of self-assessment.

Directions: To read each question, insert the phrase "Do I" before it (e.g., Do I read aloud regularly?). Then circle the appropriate response. If you are not in the teaching situation described, respond as though you were. When finished, analyze your answers. What are your strengths? What are some areas in which you might need improvement?

Teaching Practices: General	Never	Seldom	Often	Usually
Read aloud regularly	1	2	3	4
Directly teach key strategies and skills	1	2	3	4
Model reading and writing processes	1	2	3	4
Use think-alouds to make reading and writing processes explicit	1	2	3	4
Provide adequate guided practice	1	2	3	4
Provide opportunities for application	1	2	3	4
Integrate reading, writing, listening, and speaking	1	2	3	4

Teaching Practices: Comprehension/Study Skills				
Build background and activate prior knowledge	1	2	3	4
Set or encourage the setting of purposes	1	2	3	4
Present a variety of comprehension strategies	1	2	3	4
Teach monitoring/strategic reading	1	2	3	4
Provide adequate practice/application	1	2	3	4

Teaching Practices: Word Recognition				
Provide systematic instruction in major skill areas: phonics, context clues, syllabication, morphemic analysis, dictionary skills	1	2	3	4
Provide systematic instruction in use of major cueing systems: phonics, syntactic, semantic	1	2	3	4
Encourage the use of a variety of decoding strategies	1	2	3	4
Provide opportunities for students to read widely so skills become automatic	1	2	3	4

Content Area				
Use high-quality content area texts	1	2	3	4
Supplement content area texts with informational books and nonprint materials	1	2	3	4
Provide texts on appropriate levels of difficulty or make adjustments	1	2	3	4
Present skills and strategies necessary to learn from informational texts	1	2	3	4

Teaching Practices: Writing				
Encourage self-selection of topics	1	2	3	4
Use a process approach	1	2	3	4

(continued)

FIGURE 14.1 *(continued)*

	Never	Seldom	Often	Usually
Provide frequent opportunities for writing	1	2	3	4
Provide opportunities to compose in a variety of forms	1	2	3	4
Materials				
Use a variety of print materials	1	2	3	4
Children's books, fiction and nonfiction	1	2	3	4
Supplementary materials	1	2	3	4
Basal series	1	2	3	4
Periodicals	1	2	3	4
Real-world materials	1	2	3	4
Pamphlets, brochures	1	2	3	4
Pupil-written works	1	2	3	4
Use a variety of nonprint materials	1	2	3	4
Tape recorder	1	2	3	4
VCR	1	2	3	4
Videodiscs	1	2	3	4
Filmstrips	1	2	3	4
Computer	1	2	3	4
Games	1	2	3	4
Adapt materials to students' needs	1	2	3	4
Provide materials for slow as well as bright students	1	2	3	4
Evaluate materials before using them	1	2	3	4
Evaluation				
Set goals and objectives for the program	1	2	3	4
Collect formal and informal data to use as a basis for evaluating the program	1	2	3	4
Encourage self-assessment	1	2	3	4
Assess data-collection instruments in terms of validity and reliability	1	2	3	4
Assemble a portfolio for each student	1	2	3	4
Share assessment data with students and parents	1	2	3	4
Use assessment data to improve instruction for each student and to improve program	1	2	3	4
Organization/Management				
Provide for individual differences	1	1	3	4
Use a variety of grouping strategies	1	2	3	4
Use time and materials efficiently	1	2	3	4

	Never	Seldom	Often	Usually
Use positive reinforcement and other effective strategies to manage classroom behavior	1	2	3	4
Build self-esteem in students	1	2	3	4
Encourage students to be independent learners	1	2	3	4
Collaborate with special-education resource teachers, the reading specialist, Title 1 teachers, and other professionals	1	2	3	4
Work closely with media specialists	1	2	3	4
Involve parents in the program	1	2	3	4
Professional				
Set objectives for professional development and take steps to meet those objectives	1	2	3	4
Join professional organizations	1	2	3	4
Keep up with current research and practices	1	2	3	4
Attend professional meetings	1	2	3	4
Try out new methods and materials	1	2	3	4

After you have completed the checklist, add up your score. An average score is around 150. Note the areas in which you are strong (scores of 3 and 4) and those in which you are weak (1 and 2). Plan a self-improvement program that builds on your strengths and ameliorates your weaknesses.

SUMMARY

1. The construction of a reading program starts with consideration of the needs and characteristics of students, the parents' wishes, and the nature of the community. General goals and specific objectives are based on these factors. The teacher's goals, objectives, and philosophy, in turn, dictate materials and teaching strategies.

2. High-quality teaching, use of varied materials, continuous monitoring of students' progress, involvement of parents, and efficient management of time and resources are key elements in effective programs.

3. Time is a precious commodity in teaching. Through critical examination of activities, the teacher should choose those activities that are promising and eliminate activities that are ineffective or reteach material that is already known.

4. Parents should be kept informed about the program, not only because it is their right, but also because their support is needed. To encourage parental involvement, teachers should establish and maintain communication with the home.

5. An important part of the reading/language arts teacher's role is working with other professionals, including the librarian/media specialist. The media specialist can be invaluable in providing materials for classroom use and supporting the program.

6. Since students have diverse needs and abilities, there must be some provision for individual differences. This can be done through individualized reading, reading and writing workshops, or some sort of grouping. Alternatives to the traditional three groups include

cooperative learning, skills or interest grouping, and the Joplin plan. Grouping should be flexible and sensitive to the needs and feelings of students.

7. Whole class instruction can be an efficient way to teach. While whole class instruction can build a sense of community, it should be balanced with provision for individual differences.

8. Technology should be integrated into the literacy program. Computers provide practice, tutorial instruction, and simulations and are a powerful literacy tool.

Word-processing and DTP systems can help students present information. Telecommunications foster the exchange of information. Audio and audiovisual technologies can be used to motivate students.

9. Hypermedia and hypertext combine technologies and make it possible for students to view information from many perspectives. Although technology enhances the ability to obtain, organize, and present information, it also demands higher levels of literacy.

CLASSROOM APPLICATIONS

1. Set up goals and objectives for a reading/language arts program that you are now teaching or plan to teach. Discuss your goals and objectives with a colleague or classmate.

2. Complete the checklist in Figure 14.1. If you are not teaching now, answer it on the basis of how you believe you will conduct yourself when you are a

teacher. According to the results, what are your strengths and weaknesses?

3. Respond to the questions about professional goals and objectives on page 544. Based on these responses and your responses to the checklist in Figure 14.1, plan a series of professional development activities.

FIELD APPLICATIONS

1. For a week, keep a running record of the activities in your reading/language arts class. Which seem to be especially valuable? Which, if any, seem to have limited value or take up excessive amounts of time? Based on your observations, construct a plan for making better use of instructional time. If you are not teaching now, arrange to observe a teacher who has a reputation for

having a well-managed classroom. Note the strategies that the teacher uses to keep the class running smoothly and to make efficient use of time.

2. Assess the parental involvement component of your literacy program. Based on your assessment and the suggestions made in this chapter, make any changes that seem to be needed.

REFERENCES

PROFESSIONAL

Adams, M. J. (1990). *Beginning to read: Thinking and learning about print.* Cambridge, MA: MIT Press.

Adams, M. J. (1994). Modeling the connections between word recognition and reading. In R. B. Ruddell, M. R. Ruddell, & H. Singer (Eds.), *Theoretical models and processes of reading* (4th ed.) (pp. 838–863). Newark, DE: International Reading Association.

Adams, M. J., & Higgins, A. W. F. (1985). The growth of children's sight vocabulary: A quick test with educational and theoretical implications. *Reading Research Quarterly, 20,* 262–281.

Adoption Guidelines Project. (1990a). Beginning reading and decoding skills. In Adoption Guidelines Project, *A guide to selecting basal reading programs.* Urbana, IL: University of Illinois, Center for the Study of Reading.

Adoption Guidelines Project. (1990b). Comprehension I: The directed reading lesson. In Adoption Guidelines Project, *A guide to selecting basal reading programs.* Urbana, IL: University of Illinois, Center for the Study of Reading.

Adoption Guidelines Project. (1990c). Reading and writing instruction. In Adoption Guidelines Project, *A guide to selecting basal reading programs.* Urbana, IL: University of Illinois, Center for the Study of Reading.

Adoption Guidelines Project. (1990d). Workbooks. In Adoption Guidelines Project, *A guide to selecting basal reading programs.* Urbana, IL: University of Illinois, Center for the Study of Reading.

Afflerbach, P. (1990). The influence of prior knowledge on expert readers' main idea construction strategies. *Reading Research Quarterly, 25,* 31–46.

Afflerbach, P. P., & Johnston, P. H. (1986). What do expert readers do when the main idea is not explicit? In J. F. Baumann (Ed.), *Teaching main idea comprehension* (pp. 49–72). Newark, DE: International Reading Association.

Ahlmann, M. E. (1992). Children as evaluators. In K. S. Goodman, L. B. Bird, & Y. M. Goodman (Eds.), *The whole language catalog: Supplement on authentic assessment* (p. 95). Santa Rosa, CA: American School Publishers.

Allen, E. G., Wright, J. P., Laminack, I. I. (1988). Using language experience to ALERT pupils' critical reading skills. *The Reading Teacher, 41,* 904–910.

Allen, R. V. (1961). More ways than one. *Childhood Education, 38,* 108–111.

Allen, V. (1991). Teaching bilingual and ESL children. In J. Flood, J. M. Jensen, D. Lapp, & J. R. Squire (Eds.), *Handbook of research on teaching the English language arts* (pp. 356–364). New York: Macmillan.

Allen, V. G. (1994). Selecting materials for the reading instruction of ESL children. In K. Spangenberg-Urbschat & R. Pritchard (Eds.), *Kids come in all languages: Reading instruction for all ESL students* (pp. 108–131). Newark, DE: International Reading Association.

Allington, R. (1983). The reading instruction provided readers of differing reading ability. *Elementary School Journal, 83,* 548–559.

Altwerger, B., Edelsky, C., & Flores, B. M. (1987). Whole language: What's new? *The Reading Teacher, 41,* 144–154.

Alvermann, D. E., O'Brien, D. G., & Dillon, D. R. (1990). What teachers do when they say they're having discussions of content reading assignments: A qualitative analysis. *Reading Research Quarterly, 25,* 296–322.

Alvermann, D. E., & Phelps, S. F. (1994). *Content area reading and literacy: Succeeding in today's diverse classrooms.* Boston: Allyn & Bacon.

American Psychiatric Association. (1994). *Diagnostic and statistical manual of mental disorders* (4th ed.). Washington, DC: Author.

Ames, L. B. (1986). Ready or not: How birthdays leave some children behind. *American Educator, 10,* 30–33, 48.

Ames, L. B., Gillespie, C., Haines, C., & Ilg, F. L. (1979). *The Gesell Institute's child from one to six: Evaluating the behavior of the preschool child.* New York: Harper & Row.

Ames, L. B., Ilg, F. L., & Baker, S. M. (1988). *Your ten- to fourteen-year-old.* New York: Delacorte.

Anderson, C. W. (1987). Strategic teaching in science. In B. F. Jones, A. S. Palincsar, D. S. Ogle, & E. G. Carr (Eds.), *Strategic teaching and learning: Cognitive instruction in the content areas* (pp. 73–91). Alexandria, VA: ASCD.

Anderson, G., Higgins, D., & Wurster, S. R. (1985). Differences in the free-reading books selected by high, average, and low achievers. *The Reading Teacher, 39,* 326–330.

Anderson, L. (1981). *Student responses to seatwork: Implications for the study of students' cognitive processing* (research series no. 102). East Lansing: Michigan State University, The Institute for Research on Teaching.

Anderson, L. (1984). The environment of instruction: The function of seatwork in a commercially developed curriculum. In G. G. Duffy, L. R. Roehler, & J. Mason (Eds.), *Comprehension instruction: Perspectives and suggestions* (pp. 93, 96). New York: Longman.

Anderson, R. C. (1984). Role of the reader's schema in comprehension, learning, and memory. In R. C. Anderson, J. Osborn, & R. J. Tierney (Eds.), *Learning to read in American schools: Basal readers and content texts.* Hillsdale, NJ: Lawrence Erlbaum.

Anderson, R. C. (1990, May). *Microanalysis of classroom reading instruction.* Paper presented at the annual conference on reading research, Atlanta.

Anderson, R. C., & Au, K. (Directors). (1991). *Teaching word identification* (videocassette). Urbana, IL: University of Illinois, Center for the Study of Reading.

Anderson, R. C., Hiebert, E. H., Scott, J. A., & Wilkinson, I. A. G. (1985). *Becoming a nation of readers: The report of the commission on reading.* Washington, DC: National Institute of Education.

Anderson, R. C., Wilson, P. T., & Fielding, L. G. (1988). Growth in reading and how children spend their time outside of school. *Reading Research Quarterly, 23,* 285–303.

Anderson, T. H., & Armbruster, B. B. (1984). Studying. In P. D. Pearson, R. Barr, M. L. Kamil, & P. Mosenthal (Eds.), *Handbook of reading research* (pp. 657–679). New York: Longman.

Andre, M. E. D. A., & Anderson, T. H. (1978–1979). The development and evaluation of a self-questioning study technique. *Reading Research Quarterly, 14,* 605–623.

Anthony, H. M., Pearson, P. D., & Raphael, T. E. (1989). *Reading comprehension research: A selected review* (Tech. Rep. No. 448). Champaign, IL: University of Illinois, Center for the Study of Reading.

Anyon, J. (1980). Social class and the hidden curriculum of work. *Journal of Education, 162*(1), 67–92.

Applebee, A. N. (1978). *The child's concept of story: Ages two to seventeen.* Chicago: University of Chicago Press.

Applebee, A. N., Langer, J. A., & Mullis, I. V. S. (1988). *Who reads best? Factors related to reading achievement in grades 3, 7, and 11.* Princeton, NJ: Educational Testing Service.

Armbruster, B. B., & Anderson, T. H. (1981). *Content area textbooks* (Tech. Rep. No. 23). Champaign, IL: University of Illinois, Center for the Study of Reading.

Aronson, E. (1978). *The jigsaw classroom.* Beverly Hills: Sage.

Asch, S., & Nerlove, H. (1967). The development of double function terms in children: An exploratory investigation. In J. P. Cecco (Ed.), *The psychology of thought, language, and instruction* (pp. 283–291). New York: Holt, Rinehart & Winston.

Athey, I. (1985). Reading research in the affective domain. In H. Singer & R. B. Ruddell (Eds.), *Theoretical models and processes of reading* (3rd ed.) (pp. 527–557). Newark, DE: International Reading Association.

Atkinson, R. L., Atkinson, R. C., Smith, E. E., & Hilgard, E. R. (1987). *Introduction to psychology* (9th ed.). New York: Harcourt Brace Jovanovich.

Atwell, N. (1987). *In the middle.* Portsmouth, NH: Boynton/Cook.

Atwell, N. (1990). *Coming to know: Writing to learn in the intermediate grades.* Portsmouth, NH: Heinemann.

Au, K. H. (1994). Portfolio assessment: Experiences at the Kamehameha elementary education program. In S. W. Valencia, E. H. Hiebert, & P. P. Afflerbach (Eds.), *Authentic reading assessment: Practices and possibilities* (pp. 103–126). Newark, DE: International Reading Association.

Au, K. H., & Mason, J. M. (1981). Social organization factors in learning to read: The balance of rights hypothesis. *Reading Research Quarterly, 17,* 115–151.

Au, K. H., & Mason, J. M. (1989). Elementary reading programs. In S. B. Wepner, J. T. Feeley, & D. S. Strickland (Eds.), *The administration and supervision of reading programs* (pp. 60–75). New York: Teachers College Press.

Aukerman, R. (1984). *Approaches to beginning reading* (2nd ed.). New York: Wiley.

Aukerman, R. C. (1972). *Readers in the secondary school classroom.* New York: McGraw-Hill.

Austin, M. C., & Morrison, C. (1963). *The first R: The Harvard report on reading in elementary schools.* New York: Macmillan.

Australian Ministry of Education. (1990). *Literacy profiles handbook.* Victoria, Australia: Author.

Ausubel, D. P. (1959). Viewpoints from related disciplines: Human growth and development. *Teachers College Record, 60,* 245–254.

Ausubel, D. P. (1960). The use of advance organizers in the learning and retention of meaningful verbal material. *Journal of Educational Psychology, 51,* 267–272.

Baker, L., & Brown, A. L. (1984). Metacognitive skills and reading. In P. D. Pearson, R. Barr, M. L. Kamil, & P. Mosenthal (Eds.), *Handbook of reading research* (pp. 353–394). New York: Longman.

Balajthy, E. (1989). *Computers and reading: Lessons from the past and the technologies of the future.* Englewood Cliffs, NJ: Prentice-Hall.

Banks, J. A. (1994a). Transforming the mainstream culture. *Educational Leadership, 51*(8), 4–8.

Banks, J. A. (1994b). *An introduction to multicultural education.* Boston: Allyn & Bacon.

Barba, R. H. (1995). *Science in the multicultural classroom: A guide to teaching and learning.* Boston: Allyn & Bacon.

Barbe, W. B., & Abbott, J. L. (1975). *Personalized reading instruction.* West Nyack, NY: Parker.

Baron, N. S. (1992). *Growing up with language: How children learn to talk.* Reading, MA: Addison-Wesley.

Barr, R. (1974). Instructional pace differences and their effect on reading acquisition. *Reading Research Quarterly, 9,* 526–554.

Barron, R. R. (1969). Research for the classroom teacher: Recent developments on the structured overview as an advanced organizer. In H. L. Herber & J. D. Riley (Eds.), *Research in reading in the content areas: The first report* (pp. 28–47). Syracuse, NY: Syracuse University, Reading and Language Arts Center.

Barstow, B., & Riggle, J. (1995). *Beyond picture books: A guide to first readers* (2nd ed.). New York: Bowker.

Bartlett, F. C. (1932). *Remembering.* Cambridge: Cambridge University Press.

Bauman, G. A. (1990, March). *Writing tool selection and young children's writing.* Paper presented at the spring conference of the National Conference of Teachers of English, Colorado Springs, CO.

Baumann, J. F. (1986). The direct instruction of main idea comprehension ability. In J. F. Baumann (Ed.), *Teaching main idea comprehension* (pp. 133–178). Newark, DE: International Reading Association.

Baumann, J. F., & Serra, J. K. (1984). The frequency and placement of main ideas in children's social studies textbooks: A modified replication of Braddock's research on topic sentences. *Journal of Reading Behavior, 16,* 27–40.

Beach, R., & Hynds, S. (1991). Research on response to literature. In R. Barr, M. L. Kamil, P. Mosenthal, & P. D. Pearson (Eds.), *Handbook of reading research,* vol. II (pp. 453–489). New York: Longman.

Bear, D. (1995). *Word study: A developmental perspective based on spelling stages.* Paper presented at the annual meeting of the International Reading Association, Anaheim, CA.

Beck, I. L., & McKeown, M. G. (1983). Learning words well—a program to enhance vocabulary and comprehension. *The Reading Teacher, 36,* 622–625.

Beck, I. L., McKeown, M. G., & Omanson, R. C. (1987). The effects and uses of diverse vocabulary instructional techniques. In M. G. McKeown & M. E. Curtis (Eds.), *The nature of vocabulary acquisition* (pp. 147–163). Hillsdale, NJ: Lawrence Erlbaum.

Beck, I. L., Omanson, R. C., & McKeown, M. G. (1982). An instructional redesign of reading lessons: Effects on comprehension. *Reading Research Quarterly, 17,* 462–481.

Benét, W. R. (1987). *Benét's reader's encyclopedia* (3rd ed.). New York: Harper & Row.

Bereiter, C. (1980). Toward a developmental theory in writing. In L. Gregg & R. Steinberg (Eds.), *Cognitive processes in writing* (pp. 73–93). Hillsdale, NJ: Lawrence Erlbaum.

Bereiter, C., & Scardamalia, M. (1982). From conversation to composition: The role of instruction in a developmental process. In R. Glass (Ed.), *Advances in instructional psychology,* vol. 2 (pp. 1–64). Hillsdale, NJ: Lawrence Erlbaum.

Berkowitz, S. J. (1986). Effects of instruction in text organization on sixth-grade students' memory for expository text. *Reading Research Quarterly, 21,* 161–178.

Berlin, A. (1972). Hearing problems. In G. P. Cartwright & C. A. Cartwright (Eds.), *CARE: Early identification of handicapped children.* University Park, PA: Pennsylvania State University.

Berliner, D. C. (1981). Academic learning time and reading achievement. In J. T. Guthrie (Ed.), *Comprehension and teaching: Research reviews* (pp. 203–226). Newark, DE: International Reading Association.

Berliner, D. C. (1985). Effective classroom teaching: The necessary but not sufficient condition for developing exemplary schools. In G. R. Austin & H. Gartier (Eds.), *Research on exemplary schools.* New York: Academic Press.

Bishop, R. S. (Ed.). (1994). *Kaleidoscope, a multicultural booklist for grades K–8.* Urbana, IL: National Council of Teachers of English.

Bissex, G. L. (1980). *GNYS AT WRK.* Cambridge, MA: Harvard University Press.

Blachowicz, C. L. Z. (1977). Cloze activities for primary readers. *The Reading Teacher, 31,* 300–302.

Blachowicz, C. (1986). Making connections: Alternatives to the vocabulary notebook. *Journal of Reading, 29,* 643–649.

Blanchard, J. S., & Rottenberg, C. J. (1990). Hypertext and hypermedia: Discovering and creating meaningful learning environments. *The Reading Teacher, 43,* 656–661.

Bloom, B. (Ed.). (1957). *Taxonomy of educational objectives.* New York: McKay.

Bloom, B. (1976). *Human characteristics and school learning.* New York: McGraw-Hill.

Bloomfield, L. (1942). Linguistics and reading. *Elementary English Review, 19,* 125–130, 183–186.

Bloomfield, L., & Barnhart, C. (1961). *Let's read.* Detroit: Wayne State University Press.

Boehm, A. E. (1971). *Boehm test of basic concepts manual.* New York: Psychological Corporation.

Bond, G. L., & Dykstra, R. (1967). The cooperative research program in first-grade reading instruction. *Reading Research Quarterly, 2,* 5–142.

Bradshaw, G. L., & Anderson, J. R. (1982). Elaborative encoding as an explanation of levels of processing. *Journal of Verbal Learning and Verbal Behavior, 21,* 165–174.

Brandt, R. (1992). Yes, children are still at risk. *Educational Leadership, 50*(4), 3.

Bransford, J. D. (1994). Schema activation and schema acquisition: Comments on Richard C. Anderson's remarks. In R. B. Ruddell, M. R. Ruddell, & H. Singer (Eds.), *Theoretical models and processes of reading* (4th ed.) (pp. 483–495). Newark, DE: International Reading Association.

Bransford, J. D., & Stein, B. S. (1984). *The ideal problem solver: A guide for improving thinking, learning, and creativity.* New York: Freeman.

Bransford, J. D., Stein, B. S., Shelton, T. S., & Owings, R. A. (1981). Cognition and adaptation: The importance of learning to learn. In J. Harvey (Ed.), *Cognition, social behavior, and the environment.* Hillsdale, NJ: Lawrence Erlbaum.

Brewster, P. G. (Ed.). (1952). *Children's games and rhymes.* Durham, NC: Duke University Press.

Bridge, C. A., Winograd, P. N., & Haley, D. (1983). Using predictable materials vs. preprimers to teach beginning sight words. *The Reading Teacher, 36,* 884–891.

Brophy, J. E., & Good, T. L. (1970). Teachers' communication of differential expectations for children's classroom performance: Some behavioral data. *Journal of Educational Psychology, 61,* 365–375.

Brophy, J. E., & Good, T. L. (1986). Teacher behavior and student achievement. In M. E. Wittrock (Ed.), *Handbook of research on teaching* (pp. 328–375). New York: Macmillan.

Brown, A. L., (1985). *Reciprocal teaching of comprehension strategies: A natural history of one program for enhancing learning* (Tech. Rep. No. 334). Champaign, IL: University of Illinois, Center for the Study of Reading.

Brown, A. L., & Day, J. D. (1983). Macrorules for summarizing text: The development of expertise. *Journal of Verbal Learning and Verbal Behavior, 22*(1), 1–14.

Brown, C. S., & Lytle, S. L. (1988). Merging assessment and instruction: Protocols in the classroom. In S. M. Glazer, L. W. Searfoss, & L. M. Gentile (Eds.), *Reexamining reading diagnosis: New trends and procedures* (pp. 94–102). Newark, DE: International Reading Association.

Brown, H., & Cambourne, B. (1987). *Read and retell.* Portsmouth, NH: Heinemann.

Brown, J. J. (1988). *High impact teaching: Strategies for educating minority youth.* Lanham, MD: University Press of America.

Brown, R. (1973). *A first language: The early stages.* Cambridge, MA: Harvard University Press.

Bruner, J. (1975). The ontogenesis of speech acts. *Journal of Child Languages, 2,* 1–40.

Bruner, J. (1986). *Actual minds, possible worlds.* Cambridge, MA: Harvard University Press.

Burns, J. M., & Richgels, D. S. (1989). An investigation of task requirements associated with the invented spelling of 4-year-olds with above average intelligence. *Journal of Reading Behavior, 21,* 1–14.

Bush, C., & Huebner, M. (1979). *Strategies for reading in the elementary school* (2nd ed.). New York: Macmillan.

Byrne, B. (1992). Studies in the acquisition procedure for reading: Rationale, hypotheses, and data. In P. B. Gough, L. C. Ehri, & R. Treiman (Eds.), *Reading Acquisition* (pp. 1–35). Hillsdale, NJ: Lawrence Erlbaum Associates.

Calfee, R., & Hiebert, E. (1991). Classroom assessment of reading. In R. Barr, M. L. Kamil, P. Mosenthal, & P. D. Pearson (Eds.), *Handbook of reading research,* vol. II (pp. 281–309). New York: Longman.

California State Department of Education. (1986). *Recommended readings in literature, kindergarten through grade eight.* Sacramento, CA: Author.

Calkins, L. M. (1980, February). Punctuate! Punctuate? Punctuate. *Learning, 8*(3), 86–89.

Calkins, L. M., (1986). *The art of teaching writing.* Portsmouth, NH: Heinemann.

Calkins, L. M., & Harwayne, S. (1991). *Living between the lines.* Portsmouth, NH: Heinemann.

Carlsen, J. M. (1985). Between the deaf child and reading: The language connection. *The Reading Teacher, 38,* 424–426.

Carnine, D., Kameenui, E. J., & Coyle, G. (1984). Utilization of contextual information in determining the meaning of unfamiliar words. *Reading Research Quarterly, 19,* 188–204.

Carnine, D., Silbert, J., & Kameenui, E. J. (1990). *Direct instruction in reading.* Columbus, OH: Merrill.

Carr, E., Dewitz, P., & Patberg, J. P. (1989). Using cloze for inference training with expository text. *The Reading Teacher, 42,* 380–385.

Carr, E. M. (1985). The vocabulary overview guide: A metacognitive strategy to improve vocabulary, comprehension and retention. *Journal of Reading, 28,* 684–689.

Carr, K. S. (1983). The importance of inference skills in the primary grades. *The Reading Teacher, 36*, 518–522.

Carroll, J. B., Davis, P., & Richman, B. (1971). *The American Heritage word frequency book.* New York: American Heritage.

Cartwright, C. P., Cartwright, C. A., & Ward, M. E. (1989). *Educating special learners.* Belmont, CA: Wadsworth.

Carver, R. P. (1990). *Reading rate: A review of research and theory.* San Diego, CA: Academic.

Carver, R. P. (1992). Reading rate: Theory, research, and practical implications. *Journal of Reading, 36*, 84–95.

Castle, M. (l994). Helping children choose books. In E. H. Cramer & M. Castle (Eds.), *Fostering the love of reading: The affective domain in reading education* (pp. 145–168). Newark, DE: International Reading Association.

Caverly, D. C., & Orlando, V. P. (1991). Textbook study strategies. In D. C. Caverly & V. P. Orlando (Eds.), *Teaching reading and study strategies at the college level* (pp. 86–165). Newark, DE: International Reading Association.

Center for the Study of Reading. (1990). *Suggestions for the classroom: Teachers and independent reading.* Urbana, IL: University of Illinois Press.

Ceprano, M. A. (1981). A review of selected research on methods of teaching sight words. *The Reading Teacher, 35*, 314–322.

Chall, J. S. (1958). *Readability: An appraisal of research and application.* Columbus, OH: Bureau of Educational Research, Ohio State University.

Chall, J. S. (1967). *Learning to read: The great debate.* New York: McGraw-Hill.

Chall, J. S. (1983a). *Learning to read: The great debate* (rev. ed.). New York: McGraw-Hill.

Chall, J. S. (1983b). *Stages of reading development.* New York: McGraw-Hill.

Chall, J. S. (1987). Two vocabularies for reading: Recognition and meaning. In M. G. McKeown & M. E. Curtis (Eds.), *The nature of vocabulary acquisition* (pp. 7–17). Hillsdale, NJ: Lawrence Erlbaum.

Chall, J. S., & Conrad, S. S. (1991). *Should textbooks challenge students? The case for easier or harder books.* New York: Teachers College Press.

Chall, J. S., & Dale, E. (1995). *The new Dale-Chall readability formula.* Cambridge, MA: Brookline Books.

Chall, J. S., Jacobs, V. A., & Baldwin, L. E. (1990). *The reading crisis: Why poor children fall behind.* Cambridge: Harvard University Press.

Chall, J. S., Snow, C., Barnes, W. S., Chandler, V., Goodman, I. F., Hemphill, L., & Jacobs, L. (1982). *Families and literacy: The contribution of out-of-school experiences to literacy.* Final report to the National Institute of Education. Cambridge, MA: Harvard University Graduate School of Education (ERIC Document Reproduction Service No. ED 234 345).

Chamot, A. U., & O'Malley, J. M. (1994). Instructional approaches and teaching procedures. In K. Spangenberg-Urbschat & R. Pritchard (Eds.), *Kids come in all languages: Reading instruction for ESL students* (pp. 82–107). Newark, DE: International Reading Association.

Chard, N. (1990). How learning logs change teaching. In N. Atwell (Ed.), *Coming to know: Writing to learn in the intermediate grades* (pp. 61–68). Portsmouth, NH: Heinemann.

Children's books in print 1994–1995 (26th ed.). (1994). New York: Bowker.

Christenbury, L., & Kelly, P. (1983). *Questioning: A path to critical thinking.* Urbana, IL: National Council of Teachers of English.

Christie, J. F. (1990). Dramatic play: A context for meaningful engagements. *The Reading Teacher, 43*, 542–545.

Church, S. M. (1994). Is whole language really warm and fuzzy? *The Reading Teacher, 47*, 362–370.

Clarke, L. K. (1988). Invented vs. traditional spelling in first graders' writings: Effects on learning to spell and read. *Research in the Teaching of English, 22*, 281–309.

Clay, M. M. (1972). *Reading: The patterning of complex behavior.* Auckland, New Zealand: Heinemann.

Clay, M. M. (1982). *Observing young readers.* Portsmouth, NH: Heinemann.

Clay, M. M. (1985). *The early detection of reading difficulties* (3rd ed.). Auckland, New Zealand: Heinemann.

Clay, M. M. (1989). Concepts about print in English and other languages. *The Reading Teacher, 42*, 268–276.

Clay, M. M. (1991). *Becoming literate: The construction of inner control.* Portsmouth, NH: Heinemann.

Clay, M. M. (1993a). *An observation survey of early literacy achievement.* Portsmouth, NH: Heinemann.

Clay, M. M. (1993b). *Reading Recovery, a guidebook for teachers in training.* Portsmouth, NH: Heinemann.

Cline, R. K. J., & Kretke, G. L. (1980). An evaluation of long-term SSR in the junior high school. *Journal of Reading, 23*, 503–506.

Cohen, C. (1983). *Writers' sense of audience: Certain aspects of writing by sixth grade normal and learning-disabled children.* Unpublished doctoral dissertation, Northwestern University, Roseville, MN.

Cole, J. (Ed.). (1982). *Best-loved folktales of the world.* Garden City, NY: Doubleday.

Cole, J. (Ed.). (1984). *A new treasury of children's poetry.* Garden City, NY: Doubleday.

Collins, A., & Smith, E. (1980). *Teaching the process of reading comprehension* (Tech. Rep. No. 182). Urbana, IL: University of Illinois, Center for the Study of Reading.

Combs, M. (1987). Modeling the reading process with enlarged texts. *The Reading Teacher, 40*, 422–426.

Conoley, J. C., & Kramer, J. J. (Eds.). (1992). *The eleventh mental measurements yearbook.* Lincoln, NE: University of Nebraska Press.

Conrad, S. S. (1990, May). *Change and challenge in content textbooks.* Paper presented at the annual conference of the International Reading Association, New Orleans.

Cook, D. M. (1986). *A guide to curriculum planning in reading.* Madison, WI: Wisconsin Department of Public Instruction.

Cooper, C. R., & Odell, L. (1977). *Evaluating writing: Describing, measuring, judging.* Urbana, IL: National Council of Teachers of English.

Cooper, J. D. (1993). *Literacy: Helping children construct meaning* (2nd ed.). Boston: Houghton Mifflin.

Cox, C., & Many, J. E. (1992). Towards an understanding of the aesthetic stance towards literature. *Language Arts, 66*, 287–294.

Cox, C., & Zarillo, J. (1993). *Teaching reading with children's literature.* New York: Merrill.

Crafton, L. K. (1991). *Whole language: Getting started . . . moving forward.* Katonah, NY: Richard C. Owen.

Crawford, L. W. (1993). *Language and literacy learning in multicultural classrooms.* Boston: Allyn & Bacon.

Crawford, P., & Shannon, P. (1994). "I don't think these companies have much respect for teachers": Looking at teacher's manuals. In P. Shannon & K. Goodman (Eds.), *Basal readers: A second look* (pp. 1–18). Katonah, NY: Richard C. Owen.

Culyer, R. (1982). How to develop a locally relevant basic sight word list. *The Reading Teacher, 35*, 596–597.

Cummins, J. (1994). The acquisition of English as a second language. In K. Spangenberg-Urbschat & R. Pritchard (Eds.), *Kids come in all languages: Reading instruction for all ESL students* (pp. 36–62). Newark, DE: International Reading Association.

Cunningham, J. W., & Foster, E. O. (1978). The ivory tower connection: A case study. *The Reading Teacher, 31,* 365–369.

Cunningham, J. W., & Moore, D. W. (1986). The confused world of main idea. In J. F. Baumann (Ed.), *Teaching main idea comprehension* (pp. 1–17). Newark, DE: International Reading Association.

Cunningham, P. M. (1978). Decoding polysyllabic words: An alternative strategy. *Journal of Reading, 21,* 608–614.

Cunningham, P. M. (1980). Teaching *were, with, what,* and other "four-letter" words. *The Reading Teacher, 34,* 160–163.

Cunningham, P. M., & Allington, R. L. (1994). *Classrooms that work: They can all read and write.* Boston: HarperCollins.

Cunningham, P. M., & Cunningham, J. W. (1992). Making words: Enhancing the invented spelling-decoding connection. *The Reading Teacher, 46,* 106–115.

Curtis, M. E. (1987). Vocabulary testing and vocabulary instruction. In M. G. McKeown & M. E. Curtis (Eds.), *The nature of vocabulary acquisition* (pp. 37–51). Hillsdale, NJ: Lawrence Erlbaum.

Dahl, K. (1992). Kidwatching revisited. In K. S. Goodman, L. B. Bird, & Y. M. Goodman (Eds.), *The whole language catalog: Supplement on authentic instruction* (p. 50). Santa Rosa, CA: American School Publishers.

Dale, E., & Chall, J. (1948). *A formula for predicting readability.* Columbus, OH: Bureau of Educational Research, Ohio State University.

Dale, E., & O'Rourke, J. (1964). *Students' knowledge of roots and affixes.* Unpublished study, Ohio State University, Columbus.

Dale, E., & O'Rourke, J. (1971). *Techniques of teaching vocabulary.* Chicago: Field.

D'Arcy, P. (1989). *Making sense, shaping meaning: Writing in the context of a capacity-based approach to learning.* Portsmouth, NH: Boynton/Cook.

Dave, R. H. (1964). *The identification and measurement of environmental process variables that are related to educational achievement.* Unpublished doctoral dissertation, University of Chicago.

Davey, B. (1983). Think aloud: Modeling the cognitive processes of reading comprehension. *Journal of Reading, 27,* 44–47.

Davey, B., & McBride, S. (1986). Effects of question-generation training on reading comprehension. *Journal of Educational Psychology, 78,* 256–262.

Davies, P. (Ed.). (1986). *The American Heritage school dictionary.* Boston: Houghton Mifflin.

Davis, B. (1972). Significant factors in the migrant experience. In A. B. Cheyney (Ed.), *The ripe harvest: Educating migrant children* (pp. 3–21). Coral Gables, FL: University of Miami Press.

Davis, F. B. (1968). Reseach on comprehension in reading. *Reading Research Quarterly, 3,* 449–545.

Davis, Z. T., & McPherson, M. D. (1989). Story map instruction: A road map for reading comprehension. *The Reading Teacher, 43,* 232–240.

Day, K. C., Day, H. D., Spicole, R., & Griffin, M. (1981). The development of orthographic linguistic awareness in kindergarten children and the relationship of this awareness to later reading achievement. *Reading Psychology, 2,* 76–87.

DeFord, D. E. (1985). Validating the construct of theoretical orientation in reading instruction. *Reading Research Quarterly, 20,* 351–367.

Deighton, L. C. (1959). *Vocabulary development in the classroom.* New York: Columbia University Press.

Delpit, L. D. (1990, May). *A socio-cultural view of diversity and instruction.* Paper presented at the Annual Conference on Reading Research, Atlanta.

Denman, G. A. (1988). *When you've made it your own—Teaching poetry to young people.* Portsmouth, NH: Heinemann.

Devine, T. G. (1986). *Teaching reading comprehension: From theory to practice.* Boston: Allyn & Bacon.

Dewitz, P., Carr, E. M., & Patberg, J. P. (1987). Effects of inference training on comprehension and comprehension monitoring. *Reading Research Quarterly, 22,* 99–121.

Dias, P. (1990). A literary-response perspective on teaching reading comprehension. In D. Bogdan & S. B. Straw (Eds.), *Beyond communication: Reading comprehension and criticism* (pp. 283–299). Portsmouth, NH: Boynton/Cook.

Dillon, J. T. (1983). *Teaching and the art of questioning.* Bloomington, IN: Phi Delta Kappa.

DiLuglio, P., Eaton, D., & de Tarnowsky, J. (1988). *Westward wagons.* North Scituate, RI: Scituate School Department.

Dole, J. S., Duffy, G. G., Roehler, L. R., & Pearson, P. D. (1991). Moving from the old to the new: Research on reading comprehension. *Review of Educational Research, 61,* 239–264.

Donavin, D. P. (Ed.). (1992). *Best of the best for children.* New York: Random House.

Dorion, R. (1994). Using nonfiction in a read-aloud program: Letting the facts speak for themselves. *The Reading Teacher, 47,* 616–624.

Douglas, M. P. (1989). *Learning to read: The quest for meaning.* New York: Teacher's College Press.

Doyle, W. (1986). Classroom organization and management. In M. E. Wittrock (Ed.), *Handbook of research on teaching* (3rd ed.) (pp. 392–431). New York: Macmillan.

Duffelmeyer, F. A. (1985). Main ideas in paragraphs. *The Reading Teacher, 38,* 484–486.

Duffelmeyer, F. A., & Duffelmeyer, B. B. (1979). Developing vocabulary through dramatization. *Journal of Reading, 23,* 141–143.

Duffy, G. G., & Roehler, L. R. (1987). Improving reading instruction through the use of responsive elaboration. *The Reading Teacher, 40,* 514–520.

Duffy, R. (1994). It's just like talking to each other: Written conversation with five-year-old children. In N. Hall & A. Robinson (Eds.), *Keeping in touch: Using interactive writing with young children.* Portsmouth, NH: Heinemann.

Dunkeld, C. (1991). Maintaining the integrity of a promising program: The base of reading recovery. In D. E. Deford, C. A. Lyon, & G. S. Pinnell (Eds.), *Bridges to literacy: Learning from reading recovery* (pp. 37–53). Portsmouth, NH: Heinemann.

Durkin, D. (1966). *Children who read early.* New York: Teachers College Press.

Durkin, D. (1970). A language arts program for pre-first grade children: Two-year achievement report. *Reading Research Quarterly, 5,* 534–565.

Durkin, D. (1974). A six-year study of children who learned to read in school at age of four. *Reading Research Quarterly, 10,* 9–61.

Durkin, D. (1993). *Teaching them to read* (6th ed.). Boston: Allyn & Bacon.

Durrell, D. (1958). First grade reading success study: A summary. *Journal of Education, 140*(3), 1–24.

Durrell, D., & Catterson, J. (1980). *Durrell analysis of reading difficulty.* San Antonio, TX: Psychological Corporation.

Dykstra, R. (1974). Phonics and beginning reading instruction. In C. C. Walcutt, J. Lamport, & G. McCracken (Eds.), *Teaching reading: A phonic/linguistic approach to developmental reading* (pp. 373–397). New York: Macmillan.

Dyrli, O. E. (1994). Riding the Internet schoolbus. *Technology & Learning 15*(2), 33–38.

Early, M., & Sawyer, D. J. (1984). *Reading to learn in grades 5 to 12.* New York: Harcourt Brace Jovanovich.

Eckhoff, B. (1983). How reading affects children's writing. *Language Arts, 60,* 607–616.

Edelsky, C. (1994). Exercise isn't always healthy. In P. Shannon & K. Goodman (Eds.), *Basal readers: A second look* (pp. 19–34). Katonah, NY: Richard C. Owen.

Eeds, M. (1985). Bookwords: Using a beginning word list of high-frequency words from children's literature K–3. *The Reading Teacher, 38,* 418–423.

Ehri, L. C. (1991). Development of the ability to read words. In R. Barr, M. L. Kamil, P. Mosenthal, & P. D. Pearson (Eds.), *Handbook of reading research,* vol. II (pp. 383–417). New York: Longman.

Ehri, L. C. (1994). Development of the ability to read words: Update. In R. B. Ruddell, M. R. Ruddell, & H. Singer (Eds.), *Theoretical models and processes of reading* (4th ed.) (pp. 323–358). Newark, DE: International Reading Association.

Elkind, D. (1981). *The hurried child.* Reading, MA: Addison-Wesley.

Elkonin, D. B. (1973). Reading in the USSR. In J. Downing (Ed.), *Comparative reading* (pp. 551–579). New York: Macmillan.

Elley, W. B. (1989). Vocabulary acquisition from listening to stories. *Reading Research Quarterly, 24,* 174–187.

Emig, J. (1971). *The composing processes of twelfth-graders.* Urbana, IL: National Council of Teachers of English.

Erikson, E. H. (1963). *Childhood and society* (2nd ed.). New York: Norton.

Estes, T. H., Mills, D. C., & Barron, R. F. (1969). Three methods of introducing students to a reading-learning task in two content subjects. In H. L. Herber & R. F. Barron (Eds.), *Research in reading in the content areas: First-year report* (pp. 40–48). Syracuse, NY: Syracuse University, Reading and Language Arts Center.

Fader, D. (1977). *The new hooked on books.* New York: Berkley.

Fallon, I., & Allen, J. (1994). Where the deer and the cantaloupe play. *The Reading Teacher, 47,* 546–551.

Farnan, N., Flood, J., & Lapp, D. (1994). Comprehending through reading and writing: Six research-based instructional strategies. In K. Spangenberg-Urbschat & R. Pritchard (Eds.), *Kids come in all languages: Reading instruction for all ESL students* (pp. 135–147). Newark, DE: International Reading Association.

Farr, R. (1991). Current issues in alternative assessment. In C. P. Smith (Ed.), *Alternative assessment of performance in the language arts: Proceedings* (pp. 3–17). Bloomington, IN: ERIC Clearinghouse on Reading and Communication Skills and Phi Delta Kappa.

Farr, R., & Carey, R. F. (1986). *Reading: What can be measured?* Newark, DE: International Reading Association.

Farr, R., & Farr, B. (1990). *Integrated assessment system.* San Antonio, TX: Psychological Corporation.

Feitelson, D., Kita, B., & Goldstein, Z. (1986). Effects of reading series stories to first-graders on their comprehension and use of language. *Research on the Teaching of English, 20,* 339–356.

Fernald, G. M. (1943). *Remedial techniques in basic school subjects.* New York: McGraw-Hill.

Ferreiro, E. (1986). The interplay between information and assimilation in beginning literacy. In W. H. Teale & E. Sulzby (Eds.), *Emergent literacy* (pp. 15–49). Norwood, NJ: Ablex.

Ferreiro, E. (1990). Literacy development: Psychogenesis. In Y. M. Goodman (Ed.), *How children construct literacy* (pp. 12–25). Newark, DE: International Reading Association.

Ferreiro, E., & Teberosky, A. (1982). *Literacy before schooling.* Portsmouth, NH: Heinemann.

Fielding, L. G., Wilson, P. T., & Anderson, R. C. (1986). A new focus on free reading: The role of trade books in reading instruction. In T. E. Raphael (Ed.), *The contexts of school-based literacy* (pp. 149–160). New York: Random House.

Fields, M. W., Spangler, K., & Lee, D. M. (1991). *Let's begin reading right: Developmentally appropriate beginning literacy* (2nd ed.). New York: Macmillan.

Fillmore, L. W., & Valdez, C. (1986). Teaching bilingual learners. In M. E. Wittrock (Ed.), *Handbook of research on teaching* (pp. 648–685). New York: Macmillan.

Fisher, B. (1994). Response to basals. In P. Shannon & K. Goodman (Eds.), *Basal readers: A second look* (pp. 163–165). Katonah, NY: Richard C. Owen.

Fisher, C., & Natarelli, M. (1982). Young children's preferences in poetry: A national survey of first, second, and third graders. *Research in the Teaching of English, 16,* 339–355.

Fitzgerald, J. (1989). Research on stories: Implications for teachers. In K. P. Muth (Ed.), *Children's comprehension of text: Research into practice* (pp. 2–36). Newark, DE: International Reading Association.

Flavell, J. H. (1963). *The developmental psychology of Jean Piaget.* New York: Van Nostrand.

Flexner, S. B., & Hauck, L. C. (1994). *The Random House dictionary of the English language* (2nd ed., rev.). New York: Random House.

Flynt, E. S., & Cooter, R. B. (1995). *Reading inventory for the classroom* (2nd ed.). Scottsdale, AZ: Gorsuch Scarisbrick.

Ford, M. P. (1994). *Keys to successful whole group instruction.* Paper presented at the annual conference of the Connecticut Reading Association, Waterbury.

Fox, M. (1994). Hearts and minds and literacy: Lessons from ourselves. In P. Shannon & K. Goodman (Eds.), *Basal readers: A second look* (pp. 139–142). Katonah, NY: Richard C. Owen.

Franklin, E. A. (1988). Reading and writing stories: Children creating meaning. *The Reading Teacher, 42,* 184–190.

Fredericks, A. D. (1986). Mental imagery activities to improve comprehension. *The Reading Teacher, 40,* 78–81.

Freeland, D. (1986, April). Perfect bribery—or how Sgt. Slaughter made 8th graders read. *Learning 86, 14*(8), 52–55.

Freppon, P. A., & Dahl, K. L. (1991). Learning about phonics in a whole language classroom. *Language Arts, 68,* 190–197.

Fries, C. C. (1962). *Linguistics and reading.* New York: Holt, Rinehart & Winston.

Fries, C. C., Wilson, R., & Rudolph, W. (1986). *Merrill linguistic readers.* Columbus, OH: Merrill.

Fry, E. (1977a). *Elementary reading instruction.* New York: McGraw-Hill.

Fry, E. (1977b). Fry's readability graph: Clarifications, validity, and extension to level 17. *Journal of Reading, 21,* 242–252.

Fry, E. (1989). Readability formulas—maligned but valid. *Journal of Reading, 32,* 292–297.

Fry, E. (December 1993–January 1994). Commentary: Do students read better today? *Reading Today,* p. 33.

Frymier, J., & Gansneder, B. (1989). The Phi Delta Kappa study of students at risk. *Phi Delta Kappan, 71,* 142–146.

Gage, F. C. (1990, October). *An introduction to reader-response issues: How to make students into more active readers.* Paper presented at the annual meeting of the Connecticut Reading Conference, Waterbury.

Gallo, D. R. (1985). Teachers as reading researchers. In C. N. Hedley & A. N. Baratta (Eds.), *Contexts of reading* (pp. 185–199). Norwood, NJ: Ablex.

Gambrell, L. B. (1980). Think time: Implications for reading instruction. *The Reading Teacher, 34,* 143–146.

Gambrell, L. B., & Bales, R. J. (1986). Mental imagery and the comprehension monitoring performance of fourth- and fifth-grade poor readers. *Reading Research Quarterly, 21,* 454–464.

Gambrell, L. B., & Javitz, P. B. (1993). Mental imagery, text illustrations, and children's story comprehension. *Reading Research Quarterly, 28,* 264–276.

Gambrell, L. B., Wilson, R. M., & Gantt, W. N. (1981). Classroom observations of good and poor readers. *Journal of Educational Research, 24,* 400–404.

Gans, R. (1940). *Study of critical reading comprehension in intermediate grades, Teacher's College contributions to education* (No. 811). New York: Bureau of Publications, Teachers College, Columbia University.

García, G. E. (1990). *Response to "A socio-cultural view of diversity and instruction."* Paper presented at the annual Conference on Reading Research, Atlanta.

García, G. E., Pearson, P. D., & Jiménez, R. T. (1994) *The at-risk situation: A synthesis of reading research.* Champaign, IL: University of Illinois, Center for the Study of Reading.

Gardner, H. (1983). *Frames of mind: The theory of multiple intelligences.* New York: Basic Books.

Garner, R., Hare, V. C., Alexander, P., Haynes, J., & Winograd, P. (1984). Inducing use of a text lookback strategy among unsuccessful readers. *American Educational Research Journal, 21,* 789–798.

Garner, R., MacCready, G. B., & Wagoner, S. (1984). Readers' acquisition of the components of the text lookback strategy. *Journal of Educational Psychology, 76,* 300–309.

Gaskins, R. W., Gaskins, J. C., & Gaskins, I. W. (1991). A decoding program for poor readers—and the rest of the class, too! *Language Arts, 63,* 213–225.

Gates, A. I. (1917). Recitation as a factor in memorizing. *Archives of Psychology, 40,* 65–104.

Gates, A. I. (1937). The necessary mental age for beginning reading. *Elementary School Journal, 37,* 497–508.

Gelzheiser, L. M., & Meyers, J. (1990). Special and remedial education in the classroom: Theme and variation. *Reading, Writing, and Learning Disabilities, 6,* 419–436.

Gesell, A. L. (1925). *The mental growth of the preschool child.* New York: Macmillan.

Gibson, E. J., Gibson, J. J., Pick, A. D., & Osser, H. (1962). A developmental study of the discrimination of letter-like forms. *Journal of Comparative and Physiological Psychology, 55,* 897–906.

Gibson, E. J., & Levin, H. (1974). *The psychology of reading.* Cambridge, MA: MIT Press.

Gibson, L. (1989). *Literacy learning in the early years: Through children's eyes.* New York: Teachers College Press.

Gibson, S. (1989). *A pocketful of poetry.* Unpublished manuscript.

Gillingham, A., & Stillman, B. W. (1960). *Remedial training for children with specific difficulty in reading, spelling, and penmanship* (7th ed.). Cambridge, MA: Educators Publishing Service.

Gipe, J. P. (1980). Use of a relevant context helps kids learn. *The Reading Teacher, 33,* 398–402.

Glass, G. G. (1976). *Glass analysis for decoding only: Teacher's guide.* Garden City, NY: Easier to Learn.

Gold, J., & Fleisher, L. S. (1986). Comprehension breakdown with inductively organized text: Differences between average and disabled readers. *Remedial and Special Education, 7,* 26–32.

Goldenberg, C. (1994). Promoting early literacy development among Spanish-speaking children: Lessons from two studies. In E. H. Hiebert & B. M. Taylor (Eds.), *Getting reading right from the start* (pp. 171–200). Boston: Allyn & Bacon.

Golick, M. (1987). *Playing with words.* Markham, ONT: Pembroke.

Goodman, K. S. (1974). Miscue analysis: Theory and reality in reading. In J. E. Merritt (Ed.), *New horizons in reading* (pp. 15–26). Newark, DE: International Reading Association.

Goodman, K. S. (1984). Unity in reading. In A. C. Purves & O. Niles (Eds.), *Becoming readers in a complex society* (83rd Yearbook of the National Society for the Study of Education), part 1 (pp. 79–114). Chicago: University of Chicago Press.

Goodman, K. S. (1986). *What's whole in whole language?* Portsmouth, NH: Heinemann.

Goodman, K. S. (1992). A letter to teachers new to whole language. In K. S. Goodman, L. B. Bird, & Y. M. Goodman (Eds.), *The whole language catalog: Supplement on authentic assessment* (p. 10). Santa Rosa, CA: American School Publishers.

Goodman, K. S. (1994). Forward: Lots of changes, but little gained. In P. Shannon & K. Goodman (Eds.), *Basal readers: A second look* (pp. xiii–xxvii). Katonah, NY: Richard C. Owen.

Goodman, K. S., Bird, L. B., & Goodman, Y. M. (1991). *The whole language catalog.* Santa Rosa, CA: American School Publishers.

Goodman, K. S., & Goodman, Y. M. (1978). *Reading of American children whose language is a stable rural dialect of English or a language other than English.* Detroit: Wayne State University Press (ERIC Document Reproduction Service No. ED 182 465).

Goodman, Y. M. (1985). Kidwatching: Observing children in the classroom. In A. Jagger & M. T. Smith-Burke (Eds.), *Observing the language learner* (pp. 9–18). Newark, DE: International Reading Association.

Gordon, C. J. (1989a). Modeling inference awareness across the curriculum. *Journal of Reading, 28,* 444–447.

Gordon, C. J. (1989b). Teaching narrative text structure: A process approach to reading and writing. In K. P. Muth (Ed.), *Children's comprehension of text: Research into practice* (pp. 79–102). Newark, DE: International Reading Association.

Goswami, U. & Bryant, P. (1990). *Phonological skills and learning to read.* East Sussex, UK: Lawrence Erlbaum.

Gough, P. B. (1985). One second of reading: Postscript. In H. Singer & R. R. Ruddell (Eds.), *Theoretical models and processes of reading* (3rd ed.) (pp. 687–688). Newark, DE: International Reading Association.

Gough, P. B., Juel, C., & Griffith, P. L. (1992). Reading, spelling, and the orthographic cipher. In P. B. Gough, L. C. Ehri, & R. Treiman (Eds.), *Reading Acquisition* (pp. 35–48). Hillsdale, NJ: Lawrence Erlbaum.

Gough, P. B., & Walsh, M. A. (1991). Chinese, Phoenicians, and the orthographic cipher of English. In S. A. Brady & D. P. Shankweiler (Eds.), *Phonological processes in literacy: A tribute to Isabelle Y. Liberman* (pp. 199–210). Hillsdale, NJ: Lawrence Erlbaum.

Grasser, A., Golding, J. M., & Long, D. L. (1991). Narrative representation and comprehension. In R. Barr, M. L. Kamil, P. Mosenthal, & P. D. Pearson (Eds.), *Handbook of reading research,* vol. II (pp. 171–205). New York: Longman.

Grauer, N. A. (1994). *Remembered laughter: A life of James Thurber.* Lincoln, NE: University of Nebraska Press.

Graves, D. H. (1975). Examination of the writing processes of seven-year-old children. *Research in the Teaching of English, 9,* 221–241.

Graves, D. H. (1982). Break the welfare cycle: Let writers choose their topics. *Forum, 5,* 7–11.

Graves, D. H. (1983). *Writing: Teachers and children at work.* Exeter, NH: Heinemann.

Graves, D. H. (1985). All children can write. *Focus, 1,* 5–10.

Graves, M. F. (1987). Roles of instruction in fostering vocabulary development. In M. G. McKeown & M. E. Curtis (Eds.), *The nature of vocabulary acquisition* (pp. 165–184). Hillsdale, NJ: Lawrence Erlbaum.

Graves, M. F., & Hammond, H. K. (1980). A validated procedure for teaching prefixes and its effect on students' ability to assign meaning to novel words. In M. Kamil & A. Moe (Eds.), *Perspectives on reading research and instruction* (pp. 184–188). Washington, DC: National Reading Conference.

Gray, W. S., & Holmes, E. (1938). *The development of meaning vocabulary in reading.* Chicago: Publications of the University of Chicago.

Greenlaw, M. J. (1983). Reading interest research and children's choices. In N. Roser & M. Frith (Eds.), *Children's choices: Teaching with books children like* (pp. 90–92). Newark, DE: International Reading Association.

Griffith, P. L., & Olson, M. W. (1992). Phonemic awareness helps beginning readers break the code. *The Reading Teacher, 45,* 516–523.

Groff, P. (1986). The maturing of phonics instruction. *The Reading Teacher, 39,* 912–923.

Guild, P. (1994). The cultural learning style connection. *Educational Leadership, 51*(8), 16–21.

Gunning, T. (1975). *A comparison of word attack skills derived from a phonological analysis of frequently used words drawn from a juvenile corpus and an adult corpus.* Unpublished doctoral dissertation, Temple University, Philadelphia.

Gunning, T. (1977). *Basic reading units: Main idea: Teacher's guide.* Elizabethtown, PA: Continental Press.

Gunning, T. (1982). Wrong level test: Wrong information. *The Reading Teacher, 35,* 902–905.

Gunning, T. (1988a, May). *Decoding behavior of good and poor second grade students.* Paper presented at the annual meeting of the International Reading Association, Toronto.

Gunning, T. (1988b). *Teaching phonics and other word attack skills.* Springfield, IL: Charles C Thomas.

Gunning, T. (1989). *Learning to read and think, book G: Teacher's guide.* Providence, RI: Jamestown.

Gunning, T. (1990). *How useful is context?* Unpublished study, Southern Connecticut State University, New Haven.

Gunning, T. (1994). *Word building book B.* New York: Phoenix Learning Systems.

Gunning, T. (1995). Word building: A strategic approach to the teaching of phonics. *The Reading Teacher, 48,* 484–488.

Guthrie, J. T. (1980). Research views: Time in reading programs. *The Reading Teacher, 33,* 500–502.

Guthrie, J. T., Schafer, W., Wang, Y. Y., & Afflerbach, P. (1995). Relationships of instruction to amount of reading: An exploration of social, cognitive, and instructional connections. *Reading Research Quarterly, 30,* 8–25.

Gutkin, R. J. (1990). Sustained ____ reading. *Language Arts, 67,* 490–492.

Hackett, J. K., Moyer, R. H., & Adams, D. K. (1989). *Merrill science.* Columbus, OH: Merrill.

Hague, S. A. (1989). Awareness of text structure: The question of transfer from L1 and L2. In S. McCormick & J. Zutell (Eds.), *Cognitive and social perspectives for literacy research and instruction* (pp. 55–64). Chicago: National Reading Conference.

Hale-Benson, J. E. (1986). *Black children: Their roots, culture, and learning styles* (rev. ed.). Baltimore: Johns Hopkins University Press.

Hall, N., May, E., Moores, J., Shearer, J., & Williams, S. (1987). The literate home-corner. In P. K. Smith (Ed.), *Parents and teachers together* (pp. 134–144). London: Macmillan.

Halstead, J. W. (1988). *Guiding gifted readers.* Columbus, OH: Ohio Psychology.

Hamilton, H. (1976). TV tie-ins as a bridge to books. *Language Arts, 53,* 129–130.

Hansen, J. (1981). The effects of inference training and practice on young children's reading comprehension. *Reading Research Quarterly, 16,* 391–417.

Hansen, J., & Pearson, P. D. (1980). *The effects of inference training and practice on young children's comprehension* (Tech. Rep. No. 166). Urbana, IL: University of Illinois, Center for the Study of Reading.

Hansen, J., & Pearson, P. D. (1982). *Improving the inferential comprehension of good and poor fourth-grade readers* (Rep. No. CSR-TR-235). Urbana, IL: University of Illinois, Center for the Study of Reading (ERIC Document Reproduction No. ED 215–312).

Hardman, M. L. (1994). *Inclusion: Issues of educating students with disabilities in regular education settings.* Boston: Allyn & Bacon.

Hardman, M. L., Drew, C. J., Egan, M. W., & Wolf, B. (1993). *Human exceptionality* (4th ed.). Boston: Allyn & Bacon.

Hare, V. C., & Borchardt, K. M. (1984). Direct instruction of summarization skills. *Reading Research Quarterly, 20,* 62–78.

Harris, A. J., & Jacobson, M. D. (1982). *Basic reading vocabularies.* New York: Macmillan.

Harris, A. J., & Sipay, E. R. (1990). *How to increase reading ability* (9th ed.). New York: Longman.

Harste, J. (1991). Whole language and evaluation: Some grounded needs, wants, and desires. In C. P. Smith (Ed.), *Alternative assessment of performance in the language arts: Proceedings* (pp. 18–35). Bloomington, IN: ERIC Clearinghouse on Reading and Communication Skills and Phi Delta Kappa.

Harste, J. C., Short, K. G., & Burke, C. (1988). *Creating classrooms for authors: The reading-writing connection.* Portsmouth, NH: Heinemann.

Harste, J. C., Woodward, V. A., & Burke, C. L. (1984). *Language stories and literacy lessons.* Portsmouth, NH: Heinemann.

Hartman, D. K. (1994). The intertextual links of readers using multiple passages: A postmodern semiotic/cognitive view of meaning making. In R. B. Ruddell, M. R. Ruddell, & H. Singer (Eds.), *Theoretical models and processes of reading* (4th ed.) (pp. 616–636). Newark, DE: International Reading Association.

Hayes, D. A., & Tierney, R. J. (1982). Developing readers' knowledge through analogy. *Reading Research Quarterly, 17,* 256–280.

Head, M. H., & Readence, J. E. (1986). Anticipation guides: Meaning through prediction. In E. K. Dishner, T. W. Bean, J. E. Readence, & D. W. Moore (Eds.), *Reading in the content areas* (2nd ed.) (pp. 229–234). Dubuque, IA: Kendall/Hunt.

Heath, S. B. (1983). *Ways with words: Language, life, and work in communities and classrooms.* Cambridge, England: Cambridge University Press.

Heath, S. B. (1991). The sense of being literate: Historical and cross-cultural features. In R. Barr, M. L. Kamil, P. Mosenthal, & P. D. Pearson (Eds.), *Handbook of reading research,* vol. II (pp. 3–25). New York: Longman.

Heilman, A. W., Blair, T. R., & Rupley, W. H. (1982). *Principles and practices of teaching reading* (5th ed.). Columbus, OH: Merrill.

Heimlich, J. E., & Pittelman, S. D. (1986). *Semantic mapping: Classroom applications.* Newark, DE: International Reading Association.

Helper, S. (1989). A literature program: Getting it together, keeping it going. In J. Hickman & B. Culliman (Eds.), *Children's literature in the classroom: Weaving Charlotte's web* (pp. 209–220). Needham Heights, MA: Christopher-Gordon.

Henderson, E. H. (1981). *Learning to read and spell.* DeKalb, IL: Northern Illinois University Press.

Henderson, E. H. (1990). *Teaching spelling.* Boston: Houghton Mifflin.

Henry, M. K. (l990). Reading instruction based on word structure and origin. In P. G. Aaron & R. M. Joshi (Eds.), *Reading and writing disorders in different orthographic systems* (pp. 25–49). Dordrecht, Netherlands: Kluwer Academic Publishers.

Herber, H. L. (1970). *Teaching reading in content areas.* Englewood Cliffs, NJ: Prentice-Hall.

Herber, H. L., & Herber, J. N. (1993). *Teaching in content areas with reading, writing, and reasoning.* Boston: Allyn & Bacon.

Herman, J. L. (1992). What research tells us about good assessment. *Educational Leadership, 49*(8), 74–78.

Herman, J. L., & Winters, L. (l994). Portfolio research: A slim collection. *Educational Leadership, 52*(2), 48–55.

Herman, P. A., Anderson, R. C., Pearson, P. D., & Nagy, W. E. (1987). Incidental acquisition of word meanings from expositions with varied text features. *Reading Research Quarterly, 22,* 263–284.

Heward, W. L., & Cavanaugh, R. A. (l993). Educational equality for students with disabilities. In J. A. Banks & C. A. M. Banks (Eds.), *Multicultural education: Issues and perspectives* (2nd ed.). Boston: Allyn & Bacon.

Hidi, S., & Anderson, V. (l986). Producing written summaries: Task demands, cognitive operations, and implications for instruction. *Review of Educational Research, 56,* 473–493.

Hiebert, E. (1983). An examination of ability grouping for reading instruction. *Reading Research Quarterly, 18,* 231–255.

Hiebert, E. H. (1994). A small-group literacy intervention with Chapter 1 students. In E. H. Hiebert & B. M. Taylor (Eds.), *Getting reading right from the start* (pp. 85–106). Boston: Allyn & Bacon.

Hiebert, E. H., & Taylor, B. (1994). Interventions and the restructuring of American literacy instruction In E. H. Hiebert & B. M. Taylor (Eds.), *Getting reading right from the start* (pp. 201–217). Boston: Allyn & Bacon.

Hiebert, E. H., Valencia, S. W., & Afflerbach, P. P. (1994). Definitions and perspectives. In S. W. Valencia, E. H. Hiebert, & P. P. Afflerbach (Eds.), *Authentic reading assessment: Practices and possibilities* (pp. 6–25). Newark, DE: International Reading Association.

Hildreth, G. (1936). Developmental sequences in name writing. *Child Development, 7,* 291–303.

Hildreth, G. (1950). *Readiness for school beginners.* New York: World.

Hirsch, E. D. (1987). *Cultural literacy—what every American needs to know.* Boston: Houghton Mifflin.

Hoffman, J. V. (1991). Teacher and school effects in learning to read. In R. Barr, M. L. Kamil, P. Mosenthal, & P. D. Pearson (Eds.), *Handbook of reading research,* vol. II (pp. 911–950). New York: Longman.

Hoffman, J. V. (1992). Critical reading/thinking across the curriculum: Using I-charts to support learning. *Language Arts, 69,* 121–127.

Holdaway, D. (1979). *The foundations of literacy.* New York: Ashton Scholastic.

Holdaway, D. (1984). *Stability and change in literacy learning.* Portsmouth, NH: Heinemann.

Holt, J. (1983). *How children learn* (rev. ed.). New York: Delacorte.

Hornsby, P., Sukarna, P., & Parry, J. (1986). *Read on: A conference approach to reading.* Portsmouth, NH: Heinemann.

Hotchkiss, P. (1990). Cooperative learning models: Improving student achievement using small groups. In M. A. Gunter, T. H. Estes, & J. H. Schwab (Eds.), *Instruction: A models approach* (pp. 167–184). Boston: Allyn & Bacon.

Howell, G. C., & Woodley, J. W. (1992). Viewpoint: Self-evaluation in the whole language classroom: Lessons from values clarification. In K. S. Goodman, L. B. Bird, & Y. M. Goodman (Eds.), *The whole language catalog: Supplement on authentic assessment* (p. 87). Santa Rosa, CA: American School Publishers.

Huck, C. S. (1989). No wider than the heart is wide. In J. Hickman & B. E. Cullinan (Eds.), *Children's literature in the classroom: Weaving Charlotte's web* (pp. 252–262). Needham Heights, MA: Christopher-Gordon.

Huck, C. S., Helper, S., & Hickman, J. (1993). *Children's literature in the elementary school* (5th ed.). New York: Holt, Rinehart & Winston.

Hyman, R. T. (l978). *Strategic questioning.* Englewood Cliffs, NJ: Prentice-Hall.

Idol, L., & Croll, V. (1985). Story mapping training as a means of improving reading comprehension. *Learning Disability Quarterly, 10,* 214–229.

Ilg, F., & Ames, L. B. (1964). *School readiness.* New York: Harper & Row.

International Reading Association. (1988). *New directions in reading instruction.* Newark, DE: Author.

Irwin, P. A., & Mitchell, J. N. (1983). A procedure for assessing the richness of retellings. *Journal of Reading, 26,* 391–396.

Jenkins, J. R., Matlock, B., & Slocum, T. A. (1989). Approaches to vocabulary instruction. *Reading Research Quarterly, 24,* 215–235.

Jensema, C. (1975). *The relationship between academic achievement and demographic characteristics of hearing-impaired children and youth.* Washington, DC: Gallaudet College, Office of Demographic Studies.

Jett-Simpson, M. (Ed.). (l990). *Toward an ecological assessment of reading progress.* Schofield, WI: Wisconsin State Reading Association.

Jiganti, M. A., & Tindall, M. A. (1986). An interactive approach to teaching vocabulary. *The Reading Teacher, 39,* 444–448.

Johns, J. L. (1980). First-graders' concepts about print. *Reading Research Quarterly, 15,* 529–549.

Johns, J. L. (1994). *Basic reading inventory* (6th ed.). Dubuque, IA: Kendall/Hunt.

Johnson, D. D., Moe, A. J., & Baumann, J. F. (1983). *The Ginn word book for teachers: A basic lexicon.* Lexington, MA: Ginn.

Johnson, D. D., & Pearson, J. D. (1984). *Teaching reading vocabulary* (2nd ed.). New York: Holt, Rinehart & Winston.

Johnson, D. W., & Johnson, R. T. (1994). *Learning together and alone: Cooperative, competitive, and individualistic learning* (4th ed). Boston: Allyn & Bacon.

Johnson, M. S., & Kress, R. A. (1965). *Developing basic thinking abilities.* Unpublished manuscript, Temple University, Philadelphia.

Johnson, M. S., Kress, R. A., & Pikulski, J. J. (1987). *Informal reading inventories* (2nd ed.). Newark, DE: International Reading Association.

Johnson, R. T., & Johnson, D. W. (1987). How can we put cooperative learning into practice? *Science Teacher, 54,* 46–48, 50.

Joint Task Force on Assessment. (1994). *Standards for the assessment of reading and writing.* Newark, DE: International Reading Association and Urbana, IL: National Council of Teachers of English.

Jongsma, E. (1980). *Cloze instruction research: A second look.* Newark, DE: International Reading Association.

Juel, C., & Roper-Schneider, D. (1985). The influence of basal readers on first-grade reading. *Reading Research Quarterly, 20,* 134–152.

Kaissen, J. (1987). SSR/Booktime: Kindergarten and first grade sustained silent reading. *The Reading Teacher, 40,* 532–536.

Kameenui, E. J., Dixon, R. C., & Carnine, D. W. (1987). Issues in the design of vocabulary instruction. In M. E. McKeown & M. E. Curtis (Eds.), *The nature of vocabulary instruction* (pp. 129–145). Hillsdale, NJ: Lawrence Erlbaum.

Kang, H. (1994). Helping second language readers learn from context. *Journal of Reading, 37,* 646–652.

Kavanagh, J. F. (1986). *Otitis media and child development.* Parkton, MD: York.

Kawakami-Arakaki, A., Oshiro, M. & Farran, D. (1989). Research to practice: Integrating reading and writing in a kindergarten curriculum. In J. Mason (Ed.), *Reading and writing connections* (pp. 199–218). Boston: Allyn & Bacon.

Kennedy, D. M., Spangler, A., & Vanderwerf, B. (1990). *Science and technology in fact and fiction. A guide to children's books.* New York: Bowker.

Kesey, K. (1989, December 31). Remember this: Write what you don't know. *The New York Times,* Sec. 7, pp. 1, 21.

Kibby, M. W. (1989). Teaching sight vocabulary with and without context before silent reading: A field test of the "focus of attention" hypothesis. *Journal of Reading Behavior, 21,* 261–278.

Kibby, M. W. (1993). What reading teachers should know about reading proficiency in the U.S. *Journal of Reading, 37,* 28–40.

Kimmel, S., & MacGinitie, W. H. (1984). Identifying children who use a perseverative text processing strategy. *Reading Research Quarterly, 19,* 162–172.

Kintsch, W. (1989). Learning from text. In L. B. Resnick (Ed.), *Knowing, learning, and instruction: Essays in honor of Robert Glaser* (pp. 25–46). Hillsdale, NJ: Lawrence Erlbaum.

Kintsch, W. (1994). The role of knowledge in discourse comprehension: A construction-integration model. In R. B. Ruddell, M. R. Ruddell, & H. Singer (Eds.), *Theoretical models and processes of reading* (4th ed.) (pp. 951–995). Newark, DE: International Reading Association.

Kirk, S. A., & Gallagher, J. J. (1986). *Educating exceptional children* (5th ed.). Boston: Houghton Mifflin.

Klare, G. R. (1984). Readability. In P. D. Pearson, R. Barr, M. L. Kamil, & P. Mosenthal (Eds.), *Handbook of reading research* (pp. 681–784). New York: Longman.

Kobasigawa, A., Ranson, C. C., & Holland, C. J. (1980). Children's knowledge about skimming. *Alberta Journal of Educational Research, 26,* 169–182.

Kohl, H. (1967). *36 children.* New York: New American Library.

Koskinen, P. S., Gambrell, L. B., Kapinus, B. A., & Heathington, B. S. (1988). Retelling: A strategy for enhancing students' reading comprehension. *The Reading Teacher, 41,* 892–896.

Kruse, G. M., & Horning, K. T. (1991). *Multicultural literature for children and young adults* (3rd ed.). Madison, WI: Cooperative Children's Book Center, University of Wisconsin and Wisconsin Department of Public Instruction.

Laberge, D., & Samuels, S. J. (1974). Toward a theory of automatic information processing in reading. *Cognitive Psychology, 6,* 293–323.

Laminack, L. L. (1990). "Possibilities, Daddy, I think it says possibilities": A father's journal of the emergence of literacy. *The Reading Teacher, 43,* 536–540.

Landau, S. I. (1984). *Dictionaries: The art and craft of lexicography.* New York: Scribner.

Langer, J. A. (1981). From theory to practice: A prereading plan. *Journal of Reading, 25,* 152–156.

Langer, J. A., Applebee, A. N., Mullis, I. V. S., & Foertsch, M. A. (1990). *Learning to read in our nation's schools: Instruction and achievement in 1988 at grades 4, 8, and 12.* Princeton, NJ: Educational Testing Service.

Lapp, D., & Flood, J. (1994). Issues and trends. Integrating the curriculum: First steps. *The Reading Teacher, 47,* 416–419.

Lapp, D., Flood, J., & Tinajero, J. V. (1994). Issues and trends. Are we communicating? Effective instruction for students who are acquiring English as a second language. *The Reading Teacher, 48,* 260–264.

Lara, J. (1994). Demographic overview: Changes in student enrollment in American schools. In K. Spangenberg-Urbschat & K. Pritchard (Eds.), *Kids come in all languages: Reading instruction for all ESL students* (pp. 9–21). Newark, DE: International Reading Association.

Larter, S., & Donnelly, J. (1993). Toronto's benchmark program. *Educational Leadership, 50*(4), 59–62.

Laughlin, M. K., & Kardaleff, P. P. (1991). *Literature-based social studies: Children's books and activities to enrich the K–5 curriculum.* Phoenix, AZ: Onyx.

Learning Media. (1991). *Dancing with the pen: The learner as a writer.* Wellington, New Zealand: Ministry of Education.

Lenz, B. K., Clark, F. L., Deshler, D. D., & Schumaker, J. B. (1988). *The strategies instructional approach (preservice training package).* Lawrence, KS: University of Kansas Institute for Research in Learning Disabilities.

Leslie, L., & Caldwell, J. A. (1995). *Qualitative reading inventory.* Glenview, IL: Scott, Foresman/Little, Brown Higher Education.

Leung, C. B. (1992). Effects of word-related variables on vocabulary growth through repeated read-aloud events. In C. K. Kinzer & D. J. Leu (Eds.), *Literacy research, theory, and practice: Views from many perspectives* (pp. 491–498). Chicago: National Reading Conference.

Liberman, I. Y., & Shankweiler, D. (1991). Phonology and beginning reading: A tutorial. In L. Rieben & C. A. Perfetti (Eds.), *Learning to read: Basic research and its implications* (pp. 3–18). Hillsdale, NJ: Lawrence Erlbaum.

Lima, C. W., & Lima, J. A. (1993). *The A to zoo subject access to children's picture books* (4th ed.). New York: Bowker.

Linden, M., & Wittrock, M. C. (1981). The teaching of reading comprehension according to the model of generative learning. *Reading Research Quarterly, 17*, 44–57.

Lipson, M. Y. (1984). Some unexpected issues in prior knowledge and comprehension. *The Reading Teacher, 37*, 760–764.

Lipson, M. Y., Valencia, S. W., Wixson, K. K., & Peters, C. W. (l993). Integration and thematic teaching and learning. *Language Arts, 70*, 252–263.

Loban, W. (1976). *Language development: Kindergarten through grade twelve*. Urbana, IL: National Council of Teachers of English.

Lukens, R. J. (1995). *A critical handbook of children's literature* (5th ed.). New York: HarperCollins.

Maimon, E. P., & Nodine, B. F. (1979). Measuring syntactic growth: Errors and expectations in sentence-combining practice with college freshmen. *Research in the Teaching of English, 12*, 233–244.

Manning, G. L., & Manning, M. (1984). What models of recreational reading make a difference? *Reading World, 23*, 375–380.

Many, J. E. (1990). The effect of reader stance on students' personal understanding of literature. In J. Zutell & S. McCormick (Eds.), *Literacy theory and research: Analyses from multiple paradigms* (thirty-ninth yearbook of the National Reading Conference) (pp. 51–63). Chicago: National Reading Conference.

Many, J. E. (1991). The effects of stance and age level on children's literary responses. *Journal of Reading Behavior, 21*, 61–85.

Manzo, A. V., (1969). The ReQuest procedure. *Journal of Reading, 13*, 123–126.

Manzo, A. V., & Manzo, V. C. (1993). *Literacy disorders*. Fort Worth, TX: Harcourt Brace Jovanovich.

Manzo, A. V., & Manzo, V. C. (1995). *Teaching children to be literate: A reflective approach*. New York: Holt, Rinehart & Winston.

Marchbanks, G., & Levin, H. (1965). Cues by which children recognize words. *Journal of Educational Psychology, 56*, 57–61.

Maria, K. (1990). *Reading comprehension instruction: Issues and strategies*. Parkton, MD: York Press.

Maria, K., & MacGinitie, W. (1987). Learning from texts that refute the reader's prior knowledge. *Reading Research and Instruction, 26*, 222–238.

Marks, M., Pressley, M., Cooley, J. D., Craig, S., Gardner, R., DePinto, T., & Rose, W. (l993). Three teachers' adaptations of reciprocal teaching in comparison to traditional reciprocal teaching. *Elementary School Journal, 94*, 267–283.

Martin, J. H., & Friedburg, A. (1986). *Writing to read*. New York: Warner.

Martin, R. E., Sexton, C., Wagner, K., & Gerlovich, J. (1994). *Teaching science for all children*. Boston: Allyn & Bacon.

Martinez, M., & Teale, W. H. (1987). The ins and outs of a kindergarten writing program. *The Reading Teacher, 40*, 444–451.

Marzano, R. J., & Marzano, J. S. (1988). *A cluster approach to elementary vocabulary instruction*. Newark, DE: International Reading Association.

Mason, J. M., Peterman, C. L., & Kerr, B. M. (1988). *Fostering comprehension by reading books to kindergarten children* (Tech. Rep. No. 426). Champaign, IL: University of Illinois, Center for the Study of Reading.

Matthews, J. K. (1990). From computer management to portfolio assessment. *The Reading Teacher, 43*, 420–421.

May, F. B. (1990). *Reading as communication: An interactive approach*. Columbus, OH: Merrill.

McArthur, T. (Ed.). (1992). *The Oxford Companion to the English language*. New York: Oxford University.

McClure, A. A., Harrison, P., & Reed, S. (1990). *Sunrises and songs: Reading and writing poetry in an elementary classroom*. Portsmouth, NH: Heinemann.

McClure, A. A., & Kristo, J. V. (Eds.). (1994). *Inviting children's responses to literature*. Urbana, IL: National Council of Teachers of English.

McConnell, S. (1992–1993). Talking drawings: A strategy for assisting learners. *Journal of Reading, 36*, 260–269.

McCormick, S. (1992). Disabled readers' erroneous responses to inferential comprehension questions: Description and analysis. *Reading Research Quarterly, 27*, 55–77.

McCoy, K. M., & Pany, D. (1986). Summary and analysis of oral reading corrective feedback research. *The Reading Teacher, 39*, 548–554.

McCracken, R. A. (1989, May). *Whole language*. Paper presented at a meeting of the International Reading Association, New Orleans.

McGee, L. M., & Richgels, P. J. (1989). "K" is "Kristen's": Learning the alphabet from a child's perspective. *The Reading Teacher, 43*, 216–225.

McGee, L. M., & Tompkins, G. E. (1981). The videotape answer to independent reading comprehension activities. *The Reading Teacher, 34*, 427–433.

McGill-Franzen, A. (1994). Compensatory and special education: Is there accountability for learning and belief in children's potential? In E. H. Hiebert & B. M. Taylor (Eds.), *Getting reading right from the start: Effective early literacy interventions* (pp. 13–35). Boston: Allyn & Bacon.

MacGinitie, W. (1976). When should we begin to teach reading? *Language Arts, 53*, 878–882.

MacGinitie, W., & MacGinitie, R. (1989). *Manual for scoring and interpretation of the Gates-MacGinitie reading tests* (3rd ed.). Chicago: Riverside.

McKenna, M. C., & Kerr, D. J. (1990). Measuring attitude toward reading: A new tool for teachers. *The Reading Teacher, 43*, 626–639.

McKeown, M. G. (1993). Creating effective definitions for young word learners. *Reading Research Quarterly, 28*, 16–32.

McKeown, M. G., Beck, I. L., Sinatra, G. M., & Loxterman, J. A. (1992). The contribution of prior knowledge and coherent text to comprehension. *Reading Research Quarterly, 27*, 78–93.

McLane, J. B., & McNamee, G. D. (1990). *Early literacy*. Cambridge, MA: Harvard University Press.

McNamara, T. P., Miller, D. L., & Bransford, J. D. (1991). Mental models and reading comprehension. In R. Barr, M. L. Kamil, P. Mosenthal, & P. D. Pearson (Eds.), *Handbook of reading research*, vol. II (pp. 490–511). New York: Longman.

McNeil, J. D. (1987). *Reading comprehension: New directions for classroom practice* (2nd ed.). Glenview, IL: Scott, Foresman.

Medley, D. M. (1977). *Teacher competence and teacher effectiveness: A review of process-product research*. Washington, DC: American Association of Colleges for Teacher Education.

Meek, M. (l982). *Learning to read*. London: Bodley Head.

Melmed, P. J. (1973). Black English phonology: The question of reading interference. In J. L. Laffey & R. Shuy (Eds.), *Language differences: Do they interfere?* (pp. 70–85). Newark, DE: International Reading Association.

Menke, P. J., & Pressley, M. (1994). Elaborative interrogation: Using "why" questions to enhance the learning from text. *Journal of Reading, 37*, 642–645.

Meyer, B. J. F., & Rice, G. E. (1984). The structure of text. In P. D. Pearson, R. Barr, M. L. Kamil, & P. Mosenthal (Eds.), *Handbook of reading research* (pp. 319–351). New York: Longman.

Meyers, K. L. (1988). Twenty (better) questions. *English Journal, 77*(1), 64–65.

Mills, E. (1974). Children's literature and teaching written composition. *Elementary English, 51,* 971–973.

Mish, F. C. (1983). *Webster's ninth new collegiate dictionary.* Springfield, MA: Merriam-Webster.

Modiano, N. (1968). National or mother language in beginning reading: A comparative study. *Research in the Teaching of English, 2,* 32–43.

Moldofsky, P. B. (1983). Teaching students to determine the central story problem: A practical application of schema theory. *The Reading Teacher, 38,* 377–382.

Monahan, B. D., & Dharm, M. (1995). The Internet for educators: A user's guide. *Educational Technology, 15*(5), p. 44.

Montessori, M. (1964). *The Montessori method* (A. E. George, trans.). Cambridge, MA: Robert Bentley.

Moore, D. W., & Moore, S. A. (1986). Possible sentences. In E. K. Dishner, T. W. Bean, J. E. Readence, & D. W. Moore (Eds.), *Reading in the content areas: Improving classroom instruction* (2nd ed.) (pp. 174–179). Dubuque, IA: Kendall/Hunt.

Moore, D. W., Moore, S. A., Cunningham, P. M., & Cunningham, J. W. (1986). *Developing readers and writers in the content areas.* New York: Longman.

Moore, D. W., Readence, J. E., & Rickelman, R. J. (1989). *Prereading activities for content area reading and learning* (2nd ed.). Newark, DE: International Reading Association.

Morrow, L. M. (1985). Reading and retelling stories: Strategies for emergent readers. *The Reading Teacher, 38,* 871–875.

Morrow, L. M. (1988). Young children's responses to one-to-one story readings in school settings. *Reading Research Quarterly, 23,* 89–107.

Morrow, L. M. (1994). *Literacy development in the early years: Helping children read and write* (2nd ed.). Boston: Allyn & Bacon.

Mosenthal, J. H. (1990). Developing low-performing, fourth-grade, inner-city students' ability to comprehend narrative. In J. Zutell & S. McCormick (Eds.), *Literacy theory and research: Analyses from multiple paradigms* (thirty-ninth yearbook of the National Reading Conference) (pp. 275–286). Chicago: National Reading Conference.

Mountain, L., Crawley, S., & Fry, E. (1991, 1995). *The Jamestown heritage readers.* Providence, RI: Jamestown.

Mullis, I. V. S., Campbell, J. R., & Farstrup, A. E. (1993). *Executive summary of the NAEP 1992 reading report card for the nation and the states.* Princeton, NJ: Educational Testing Service.

Murphy, R. T., & Appel, L. R. (1984). *Evaluation of the right to read instructional system, 1982–1984.* Princeton, NJ: Educational Testing Service.

Murray, D. (1979). The listening eye: Reflections on the writing conference. *College English, 41,* 13–18.

Murray, D. M. (1989). *Expecting the unexpected: Teaching myself—and others—to read and write.* Portsmouth, NH: Boynton/Cook.

Muschla, G. R. (1993). *Writing workshop survival kit.* West Nyack, NY: Center for Applied Research in Education.

Muth, K. D. (1987). Teachers' connection questions: Prompting students to organize text ideas. *Journal of Reading, 31,* 254–259.

Nagy, W. E. (1988). *Teaching vocabulary to improve reading comprehension.* Newark, DE: International Reading Association.

Nagy, W. E., & Anderson, R. C. (1984). How many words are there in printed English? *Reading Research Quarterly, 19,* 304–330.

Nagy, W. E., Anderson, R. C., & Herman, P. A. (1987). Learning word meanings from context during normal reading. *American Educational Research Journal, 24,* 237–270.

Nagy, W. E., & Herman, P. A. (1987). Breadth and depth of vocabulary knowledge: Implications for acquisition and instruction. In M. G. McKeown & M. E. Curtis (Eds.), *The nature of vocabulary acquisition* (pp. 19–35). Hillsdale, NJ: Lawrence Erlbaum.

National Association of State Boards of Education. (1992). *Winners all: A call for inclusive schools.* Alexandria, VA: Author.

Nessel, D. (1987). The new face of comprehension instruction: A closer look at questions. *The Reading Teacher, 40,* 604–606.

Neu, H. C. (1989). Infectious diseases. In D. F. Tapley, T. Q. Morris, L. P. Rowland, & R. J. Weiss (Eds.), *The Columbia University College of Physicians and Surgeons complete home medical guide* (rev. ed.) (pp. 449–475). New York: Crown.

Newmann, F. M., & Wehlage, G. G. (1993). Five standards of authentic instruction. *Educational Leadership, 50*(7), pp. 8–12.

Nicholson, T., & Whyte, B. (1992). Matthew effects in learning new words while listening to stories. In C. K. Kinzer & D. J. Leu (Eds.), *Literacy research, theory, and practice: Views from many perspectives* (pp. 499–501). Chicago, IL: National Reading Conference.

Nisbet, J., & Shucksmith, J. (1986). *Learning strategies.* London: Routledge & Kegan Paul.

Nist, S. L., & Simpson, M. L. (1989). PLAE, a validated study strategy. *Journal of Reading, 33,* 182–186.

Noble, B. P. (1994, November 6). At work, still in the dark on diversity. *The New York Times,* p. F 27.

Noyce, R., & Christie, J. F. (1989). *Integrating reading and writing instruction in grades K–8.* Boston: Allyn & Bacon.

O'Brien, C. A. (1973). *Teaching the language-different child to read.* Columbus, OH: Merrill.

Ogle, D. M. (1989). The know, want to know, learn strategy. In K. D. Muth (Ed.), *Children's comprehension of text* (pp. 205–223). Newark, DE: International Reading Association.

Olson, J. L. (1987). Drawing to write. *School Arts, 87*(1), 25–27.

Olson, W. C. (1949). *Child development.* Boston: D. C. Heath.

O'Rourke, J. P. (1974). *Toward a science of vocabulary development.* The Hague: Mouton.

Osborn, J. (1984). The purposes, uses, and content of workbooks and some guidelines for publishers. In R. C. Anderson, J. Osborn, & R. J. Tierney (Eds.), *Learning to read in American schools: Basal readers and content texts* (pp. 51–67). Hillsdale, NJ: Lawrence Erlbaum.

Otto, W. (1990). Research: Getting smart. *Journal of Reading, 33,* 368–370.

Otto, W., Wolf, A., & Eldridge, R. G. (1984). Managing instruction. In P. D. Pearson, R. Barr, M. L. Kamil, & P. Mosenthal (Eds.), *Handbook of reading research* (pp. 799–828). New York: Longman.

Painter, H. W. (1970). *Poetry and children.* Newark, DE: International Reading Association.

Paivio, A. (1971). *Imagery and verbal processes.* New York: Holt, Rinehart & Winston.

Paivio, A. (1986). *Mental representations: A dual coding approach.* New York: Oxford University Press.

Palincsar, A. S., & Brown, A. L. (1986). Interactive teaching to promote independent learning from text. *The Reading Teacher, 39,* 771–777.

Palincsar, A. S., Winn, J., David, Y., Snyder, B., & Stevens, D. (1993). Approaches to strategic reading instruction reflecting different assumptions regarding teaching and learning. In L. J. Meltzer (Ed.), *Strategy assessment and instruction for students with learning disabilities: From theory to practice* (pp. 247–292). Austin, TX: Pro-Ed.

Paris, S. G., Wasik, B. A., & Turner, J. C. (1991). The development of strategic readers. In R. Barr, M. L. Kamil, P. Mosenthal, & P. D. Pearson (Eds.), *Handbook of reading research,* vol. II (pp. 609–640). New York: Longman.

Parker, R. P., & Morrow, L. M. (1994). Writing and literacy development. In L. M. Morrow (Ed.), *Literacy development in the early years: Helping children read and write* (2nd ed.). Boston: Allyn & Bacon.

Parsons, C. (1985). Seeds: *Some good ways to improve our schools.* Santa Barbara, CA: Woodbridge.

Parsons, L. (1990). *Response journals.* Portsmouth, NH: Heinemann.

Pauk, W. (1989). The new SQ3R. *Reading World, 23,* 386–387.

Pearson, P. D. (1985). Changing the face of reading comprehension instruction. *The Reading Teacher, 38,* 724–738.

Pearson, P. D., & Camperell, K. (1994). Comprehension of text structures. In R. B. Ruddell, M. R. Ruddell, & H. Singer (Eds.), *Theoretical models and processes of reading* (4th ed.) (pp. 448–568). Newark, DE: International Reading Association.

Pearson, P. D., & Gallagher, M. C. (1983). The instruction of reading comprehension. *Contemporary Educational Psychology, 8,* 317–345.

Pearson, P. D., & Johnson, D. D. (1978). *Teaching reading comprehension.* New York: Holt, Rinehart & Winston.

Perfetti, C. A. (1992). The representation problem in reading acquisition. In P. B. Gough, L. C. Ehri, & R. Treiman (Eds.), *Reading acquisition* (pp. 145–174). Hillsdale, NJ: Lawrence Erlbaum.

Peters, C. W. (1990). Content knowledge in reading: Creating a new framework. In G. G. Duffy (Ed.), *Reading in the middle school* (pp. 63–80). Newark, DE: International Reading Association.

Peters, E. E., & Levin, J. R. (1986). Effects of a mnemonic imagery strategy on good and poor readers' prose recall. *Reading Research Quarterly, 21,* 179–192.

Peterson, R. (1992). *Life in a crowded place: Making a learning community.* Portsmouth, NH: Heinemann.

Petty, W., Herold, C., & Stoll, E. (1968). *The state of the knowledge of the teaching of vocabulary* (Cooperative Research Project No. 3128). Champaign, IL: National Council of Teachers of English.

Pike, K., Compain, R., & Mumper, J. (1994). *New connections: An integrated approach to literacy.* New York: HarperCollins.

Platt, P. (1978). Grapho-linguistics: Children's drawings in relation to reading and writing skills. *The Reading Teacher, 31,* 262–268.

Prawat, R. S. (1989). Promoting access to knowledge, strategy, and disposition in students: A research synthesis. *Review of Educational Research, 59,* 1–41.

Prawat, R. S. (1992). From individual differences to learning communities—our changing forms. *Educational Leadership, 49*(7), 9–13.

Pressley, M. (1994). *What makes sense in reading instruction according to research.* Paper presented at the annual meeting of the Connecticut Reading Association, Waterbury.

Pressley, M., Borkowski, J. G., Forrest-Pressley, D., Gaskin, I. W., & Wiley, D. (1990). *Cognitive strategy instruction that really improves children's academic performance.* Cambridge, MA: Brookline Books.

Pressley, M., Johnson, C. J., Symons, S., McGoldrick, J. A., & Kurita, J. A. (1989). Strategies that improve children's memory and comprehension of what is read. *Elementary School Journal, 89,* 3–32.

Pressley, M., Levin, J. R., & McDaniel, M. A. (1987). Remembering versus inferring what a word means: Mnemonic and contextual approaches. In M. G. McKeown & M. E. Curtis (Eds.), *The nature of vocabulary acquisition* (pp. 107–127). Hillsdale, NJ: Lawrence Erlbaum.

Pressley, M., Levin, J. R., & Miller, G. E. (1981). How does the keyword method affect vocabulary comprehension and usage? *Reading Research Quarterly, 16,* 213–226.

Pritchard, R., & Spangenberg-Urbschat, K. (1994). Introduction. In K. Spangenberg-Urbschat & R. Pritchard (Eds.), *Kids come in all languages: Reading instruction for ESL students* (pp. 1–5). Newark, DE: International Reading Association.

Probst, R. (1988). Dialogue with a text. *English Journal, 77*(1), 32–38.

Purves, A. C. (1993). Toward a reevaluation of reader response and school literature. *Language Arts, 70,* 348–361.

Purves, A. C., & Monson, D. L. (1984). *Experiencing children's literature.* Glenview, IL: Scott, Foresman.

QuanSing, J. (1995). *Developmental teaching and learning using developmental continua as maps of language and literacy development which link assessment to teaching.* Paper presented at the annual meeting of the International Reading Association, Anaheim, Ca.

Quigley, S., & King, C. (1981). *Reading milestones.* Beavertown, OR: Dormac.

Radencich, M. C. (1995). *Administration and supervision of the reading/writing program.* Boston: Allyn & Bacon.

Radencich, M. C., Beers, P. G., & Schumm, J. S. (1993). *A handbook for the K–12 resource specialist.* Boston: Allyn & Bacon.

Raines, S., & Isbell, R. (1994). *Stories: Children's literature in early education.* Albany, NY: Delmar.

Raphael, T. E. (1984). Teaching learners about sources of information for answering questions. *The Reading Teacher, 28,* 303–311.

Raphael, T. E. (1986). Teaching question/answer relationships, revisited. *The Reading Teacher, 39,* 516–522.

Raphael, T. E., & Englert, C. S. (1990). Writing and reading: Partners in constructive meaning. *The Reading Teacher, 43,* 388–400.

Raphael, T. E., Englert, C. S., & Kirschner, B. W. (1989). Acquisition of expository writing skills. In J. M. Mason (Ed.), *Reading and writing connections* (pp. 261–290). Boston: Allyn & Bacon.

Rasmussen, D., & Goldberg, L. (1985). *Basic reading series.* Chicago: SRA.

Read, C. (1971). Pre-school children's knowledge of English phonology. *Harvard Educational Review, 41,* 1–34.

Readence, J. E., Bean, T. W., & Baldwin, R. S. (1992). *Content area literacy: An integrated approach* (4th ed.). Dubuque, IA: Kendall/Hunt.

Renzulli, J. (1978). What makes giftedness? Re-examining a definition. *Phi Delta Kappan, 60,* 361–363.

Reutzel, D. R., & Cooter, R. B. (1991). Organizing for effective instruction: The reading workshop. *The Reading Teacher, 44,* 548–555.

Reutzel, D. R., & Cooter, R. B. (1992). *Teaching children to read: From basals to books.* New York: Macmillan.

Reynolds, M. C., & Birch, J. W. (1988). *Adaptive mainstreaming: A primer for teachers and principals* (3rd ed.). New York: Longman.

Rhodes, L. K. (1990, March). *Anecdotal records: A powerful tool for ongoing literacy assessment.* Paper presented at the National Council of Teachers of English spring conference, Colorado Springs, CO.

Rhodes, L. K., & Dudley-Marling, C. (1988). *Readers and writers with a difference: A holistic approach to teaching learning-disabled and remedial students.* Portsmouth, NH: Heinemann.

Rice, M. L. (1989). Speech and language impaired. In E. L. Meyen & O. T. Skrtic (Eds.), *Exceptional children and youth* (3rd ed.) (pp. 233–261). Denver: Love.

Richardson, J. S., & Morgan, R. F. (1994). *Reading to learn in the content areas* (2nd ed.). Belmont, CA: Wadsworth.

Richek, M. A. (1977–1978). Readiness skills that predict initial word learning using two different methods of instruction. *Reading Research Quarterly, 13,* 200–222.

Richgels, D. S., McGee, L. M., & Slaton, E. A. (1989). Teaching expository text structure in reading and writing. In K. D. Muth (Ed.), *Children's comprehension of text* (pp. 167–184). Newark, DE: International Reading Association.

Rickelman, R. J., & Henk, W. A. (1990). Reading technology: Children's literature and audio/visual technologies. *The Reading Teacher, 43,* 682–684.

Rimer, S. (1990, June 19). Slow readers sparkling with a handful of words. *The New York Times,* pp. B1, B5.

Rinehart, S. D., Stahl, S. A., & Erickson, L. G. (1986). Some effects of summarization training on reading and studying. *Reading Research Quarterly, 21,* 422–438.

Rist, R. (1970). Student social class and teacher expectations. The self-fulfilling prophecy in ghetto education. *Harvard Educational Review, 40,* 411–451.

Robinson, F. P. (1970). *Effective study* (4th ed.). New York: Harper & Row.

Rock, H. M., & Cummings, A. (1994). Can videodiscs improve student outcomes? *Educational Leadership, 51*(7), 46–54.

Roller, C. (1990). Commentary: The interaction of knowledge and structure variables in the processing of expository prose. *Reading Research Quarterly, 25,* 79–89.

Rose, M. C., Cundick, B. P., & Higbee, K. L. (1983). Verbal rehearsal and visual imagery: Mnemonic aids for learning disabled children. *Journal of Learning Disabilities, 16,* 352–354.

Rosenblatt, L. (1978). *The reader, the text, the poem.* Carbondale, IL: Southern Illinois University Press.

Rosenblatt, L. (1991). Literature—S. O. S.! *Language Arts, 68,* 444–448.

Rosenshine, B., & Berliner, D. C. (1978). Academic engaged time. *British Journal of Teacher Education, 4,* 3–16.

Rosenshine, B., & Stevens, R. (1984). Classroom instruction in reading. In P. D. Pearson, R. Barr, M. L. Kamil, & P. Mosenthal (Eds.), *Handbook of reading research,* vol. II (pp. 745–798). New York: Longman.

Rosier, P. (1977). *A comparative study of two approaches introducing initial reading to Navajo children: The direct method and the native language method.* Unpublished doctoral dissertation, Northern Arizona University, Flagstaff.

Roth, K. J. (1991). Reading science texts forconceptual change. In C. M. Santa & D. E. Alvermann (Eds.), *Science learning: Process*

and applications (pp. 48–63). Newark, DE: International Reading Association.

Routman, R. (1991). *Invitations: Changing as teachers and learners K–12.* Portsmouth, NH: Heinemann.

Ruddell, M. R. (1994). Vocabulary knowledge and comprehension: A comprehension-process view of complex literacy relationships. In R. B. Ruddell, M. R. Ruddell, & H. Singer (Eds.), *Theoretical models and processes of reading* (4th ed.) (pp. 414–447). Newark, DE: International Reading Association.

Ruddell, R. B., & Boyle, O. F. (1989). A study of cognitive mapping as a means to improve summarization and comprehension of expository text. *Reading Research and Instruction, 29*(1), 12–22.

Ruddell, R. B., & Ruddell, M. R. (1995). *Teaching children to read and write: Becoming an influential teacher.* Boston: Allyn & Bacon.

Rumelhart, D. (1980). Schemata: The building blocks of cognition. In R. J. Spiro, B. C. Bruce, & W. F. Bruner (Eds.), *Theoretical issues in reading comprehension* (pp. 33–58). Hillsdale, NJ: Lawrence Erlbaum.

Rumelhart, D. (1984). Understanding understanding. In J. Flood (Ed.), *Understanding reading comprehension* (pp. 1–20). Newark, DE: International Reading Association.

Rye, J. (1982). *Cloze procedure and the teaching of reading.* London: Heinemann.

Sadow, M. K. (1982). The use of story grammar in the design of questions. *The Reading Teacher, 35,* 518–522.

Sadowski, M., & Paivio, A. (1994). A dual coding view of imagery and verbal processes in reading comprehension. In R. B. Ruddell, M. R. Ruddell, & H. Singer (Eds.), *Theoretical models and processes of reading* (4th ed.) (pp. 582–601). Newark, DE: International Reading Association.

Salinger, T. (1988). *Language arts and literacy for young children.* Columbus, OH: Merrill.

Samuels, S. J. (1967). Attentional processes in reading: The effect of pictures in the acquisition of reading responses. *Journal of Educational Psychology, 58,* 337–342.

Samuels, S. J. (1988). Characteristics of exemplary reading programs. In S. J. Samuels & P. D. Pearson (Eds.), *Changing school reading programs: Principles and case studies* (pp. 3–9). Newark, DE: International Reading Association.

Samuels, S. J. (1994). Toward a theory of automatic information processing in reading revisited. In R. B. Ruddell, M. R. Ruddell, & H. Singer (Eds.), *Theoretical models and processes of reading* (4th ed.) (pp. 816–837). Newark, DE: International Reading Association.

Santa, C. (1989, November). *Comprehension strategies across content areas.* Paper presented at the annual conference of the New England Reading Association, Newport, RI.

Santa, C. (1994, October). *Teaching reading in the content areas.* Paper presented at the International Reading Association's Southwest Regional Conference, Little Rock, AR.

Sartain, H. W. (1972). The place of individualized reading in a well-planned program. In A. J. Harris & E. R. Sipay (Eds.), *Readings on reading instruction* (pp. 193–197). New York: McKay.

Savin, H. B. (1972). What the child knows about speech when he starts to learn to read. In J. F. Kavanagh & I. G. Mattingly (Eds.), *Language by ear and by eye* (pp. 319–326). Cambridge, MA: MIT Press.

Scardamalia, M., & Bereiter, C. (1986). Research on written composition. In M. C. Wittrock (Ed.), *Handbook of research on teaching* (pp. 778–863). New York: Macmillan.

Scardamalia, M., Bereiter, C., & Goelman, H. (1982). The role of production factors in writing ability. In M. Nystrand (Ed.), *What writers know: The language, process, and structure of written discourse* (pp. 173–210). New York: Academic.

Schatz, E. K., & Baldwin, R. S. (1986). Context clues are unreliable predictors of word meanings. *Reading Research Quarterly, 21,* 439–453.

Schoephoeister, H. D. (1980). *Building a failure-proof reading program.* Boston: Houghton Mifflin.

Schulz, J. B. (l993). Teaching students with disabilities in the regular classroom. In J. A. Banks & C. A. M. Banks (Eds.), *Multicultural education: Issues and perspectives* (2nd ed.) (pp. 262–278). Boston: Allyn & Bacon.

Schunk, D. H., & Rice, J. H. (1987). Enhancing comprehension skill and self-efficacy with strategy value information. *Journal of Reading Behavior, 19,* 285–302.

Searfoss, L. W., & Readence, J. E. (1994). *Helping children learn to read* (3rd ed.). Boston: Allyn & Bacon.

Shade, B. J., & New, C. A. (1993). Cultural influences on learning: Teaching implications. In J. A. Banks & C. A. M. Banks (Eds.), *Multicultural education: Issues and perspectives* (2nd ed.) (pp. 317–331). Boston: Allyn & Bacon.

Shields, J. (l994). CD-ROM hits its stride. *Technology and Learning, 15*(1), 33.

Short, K. D., & Kauffman, G. (1988). Reading as a process of authorship. In J. C. Harste, K. G. Short, & C. Burke (Eds.), *Creating classrooms for authors* (pp. 105–115). Portsmouth, NH: Heinemann.

Short, K. G. (1990, March). *Using evaluation to support learning in process-centered classroom.* Paper presented at the spring conference of the National Council of Teachers of English, Colorado Springs, CO.

Shuy, R. (1973). Nonstandard dialect problems: An overview. In J. L. Laffey & R. Shuy (Eds.), *Language differences: Do they interfere?* (pp. 3–16). Newark, DE: International Reading Association.

Silberman, A. (1989). *Growing up writing: Teaching children to write, think, and learn.* New York: Times Books.

Simmons, J. (1990). Portfolios as large-scale assessment. *Language Arts, 67,* 262–268.

Sims, R. S. (Ed.). (1994) *Kaleidoscope, A multicultural booklist for grades K–8.* Urbana, IL: National Council of Teachers of English.

Sinatra, R. C., Stahl-Gemeke, J., & Berg, D. N. (1984). Improving reading comprehension of disabled readers through semantic mapping. *The Reading Teacher, 38,* 22–29.

Sinatra, R. C., Stahl-Gemeke, J., & Morgan, N. W. (1986). Using semantic mapping after reading to organize and write original discourse. *Journal of Reading, 30,* 4–13.

Singer, H., & Donlan, D. (1989). *Reading and learning from text* (2nd ed.). Hillsdale, NJ: Lawrence Erlbaum.

Singer, H., Samuels, S. J., & Spiroff, J. (1973–1974). The effect of pictures and contextual conditions on learning responses to printed words. *Reading Research Quarterly, 9,* 555–567.

Skolnick, S. (1963). *A comparison of the effects of two methods of teaching reading on the reading achievement of high and low anxious children.* Unpublished doctoral dissertation, University of Connecticut, Storrs.

Slater, W. H., & Graves, M. F. (1989). Research on expository text. Implications for teachers. In K. D. Muth (Ed.), *Children's comprehension of text* (pp. 140–166). Newark, DE: International Reading Association.

Slaughter, H. B. (1988). Indirect and direct teaching in a whole language program. *The Reading Teacher, 42,* 30–34.

Slavin, R. E. (1987a). Ability grouping and student achievement in elementary schools: A best-evidence synthesis. *Review of Educational Research, 57,* 293–336.

Slavin, R. E. (1987b). Cooperative learning and the cooperative school. *Educational Leadership, 45*(3), 7–13.

Slavin, R. E. (1990). IBM's writing to read: Is it right for reading? *Phi Delta Kappan, 72,* 214–216.

Slavin, R. E., Madden, N. A., Karweit, N. L., Dolan, L. J., & Wasik, B. A. (1994). Success for all: Getting reading right the first time. In E. H. Hiebert & B. M. Taylor (Eds.), *Getting reading right from the start* (pp. 125–148). Boston: Allyn & Bacon.

Sloan, G. D. (1984). *The child as critic* (2nd ed.). New York: Teachers College Press.

Smith, C. R. (1994). *Learning disabilities: The interaction of learner, task, and setting.* Boston: Allyn & Bacon.

Smith, E. L., & Anderson, C. W. (1984). Plants as producers: A case study of elementary science teaching. *Journal of Research in Science Teaching, 21,* 685–698.

Smith, F. (1983). Reading like a writer. *Language Arts, 60,* 558–567.

Smith, F. (1988). *Understanding reading: A psycholinguistic analysis of reading and learning to read.* Hillsdale, NJ: Lawrence Erlbaum.

Smith, J. L., & Johnson, H. (1994). Models for implementing literature in content studies. *The Reading Teacher, 48,* 198–209.

Smith, R. J. (1985). *Using poetry to teach reading and language arts: A handbook for elementary school subjects.* New York: Teachers College Press.

Smith, R. J., & Dauer, V. L. (1984). A comprehension monitoring strategy for reading content area materials. *Journal of Reading, 28,* 144–147.

Smith-Burke, M. T., & Jaggar, A. M. (1994). Implementing Reading Recovery in New York: Insights from the first two years. In E. H. Hiebert & B. M. Taylor (Eds.), *Success for all: Getting reading right the first time* (pp. 63–84). Boston: Allyn & Bacon.

Somers, A. B., & Worthington, J. E. (1979). *Response guides for teaching children's books.* Urbana, IL: National Council of Teachers of English.

Spache, G. S. (1974). *Good reading for poor readers* (9th ed.). Champaign, IL: Garrard.

Spearitt, D. (1972). Identification of subskills and reading comprehension by maximum likelihood factor analysis. *Reading Research Quarterly, 8,* 92–111.

Spencer, P. G. (1984). Booktalking seventeen hundred students at once—Why not? *English Journal, 73,* 86–87.

Spiro, R. (1990, May). *New computer environments for content area learning: Hypertext and hypermedia.* Paper presented at the annual conference on reading research, Atlanta.

Spirt, D. L. (1994). *Introducing bookplots 4: A book talk guide for use with readers 8–12.* New York: Bowker.

Squire, J. R. (1994). Research in reader response, naturally interdisciplinary. In R. B. Ruddell, M. R. Ruddell, & H. Singer (Eds.), *Theoretical models and processes of reading* (4th ed.) (pp. 637–652). Newark, DE: International Reading Association.

Stahl, S. A. (1990). *Responding to children's needs, styles, and interests*. Paper presented at the thirty-fifth annual convention of the International Reading Association, Atlanta.

Stahl, S. A., & Fairbanks, M. M. (1986). The effects of vocabulary instruction: A model-based meta-analysis. *Review of Educational Research, 56,* 72–110.

Stahl, S. A., & Miller, P. D. (1989). Whole language and language experience approaches for beginning reading: A quantitative research synthesis. Review *of Educational Research, 24,* 27–43.

Stahl, S. A., Osborne, J., & Lehr, F. (1990). *Beginning to read: Thinking and learning about print: A summary*. Urbana, IL: Center for the Study of Reading, University of Illinois at Urbana-Champaign.

Stahl, S. A., Richek, M. A., & Vandeiver, R. J. (1991). Learning meaning vocabulary through listening: A sixth-grade replication. In J. Zutell & S. McCormick (Eds.), *Learner factors/teacher factors: Issues in literacy research and instruction* (pp. 185–192). Chicago: National Reading Conference.

Stallings, J. A., & Stipek, D. (1986). Research on early childhood and elementary school teaching programs. In M. E. Wittrock (Ed.), *Handbook of research on teaching* (pp. 727–754). New York: Macmillan.

Stallman, A. C., Commeyras, M., Kerr, B., Reimer, K., Jiminez, R., & Hartman, D. K. (1990). Are "new" words really new? *Reading Research and Instruction, 29,* 12–29.

Stanovich, K. E. (1986). Matthew effects in reading: Some consequences of individual differences in the acquisition of literacy. *Reading Research Quarterly, 21,* 360–407.

Stauffer, R. G. (1969). *Directing reading maturity as a cognitive process*. New York: Harper & Row.

Stauffer, R. G. (1970, January). *Reading-thinking skills*. Paper presented at the annual reading conference at Temple University, Philadelphia.

Sternberg, R. J. (1987). Most vocabulary is learned from context. In M. G. McKeown & M. E. Curtis (Eds.), *The nature of vocabulary acquisition* (pp. 89–105). Hillsdale, NJ: Lawrence Erlbaum.

Sternberg, R. J., & Powell, J. S. (1983). Comprehending verbal comprehension. *American Psychologist, 38,* 878–893.

Stevens, R. J., Madden, N. A., Slavin, R. E., & Farnish, A. M. (1987). Cooperative integrated reading and composition: Two field experiments. *Reading Research Quarterly, 22,* 433–454.

Sticht, T. G., & James, J. H. (1984). Listening and reading. In P. D. Pearson, R. Barr, M. L. Kamil, & P. Mosenthal (Eds.), *Handbook of reading research* (pp. 293–317). New York: Longman.

Stoll, D. R. (1994). *Magazines for kids and teens*. Newark, DE: International Reading Association.

Stotsky, S. (1983). Research of reading/writing relationships: A synthesis and suggested directions. *Language Arts, 60,* 568–580.

Straw, S. B., & Sadowy, P. (1990). Dynamics of communication: Transmission, translation, and interaction in reading comprehension. In D. Bogdan & S. B. Straw (Eds.), *Beyond communication: Reading comprehension and criticism* (pp. 21–47). Portsmouth, NH: Boynton/Cook.

Strickland, D. S., & Taylor, D. (1989). Family storybook reading: Implications for children, curriculum, and families. In D. S. Strickland & L. M. Morrow (Eds.), *Emerging literacy: Young children learn to read and write* (pp. 27–33). Newark, DE: International Reading Association.

Sulzby, E. (1989). Assessment of writing and of children's language while writing. In L. Morrow & J. Smith (Eds.), *The role of assessment and measurement in early literacy instruction* (pp. 83–109). Englewood Cliffs, NJ: Prentice-Hall.

Sulzby, E., & Barnhart, J. (1992). The development of academic competence: All our children emerge as writers and readers. In J. W. Irwin & M. A. Doyle (Eds.), *Reading/writing connections: Learning from research* (pp. 120–144). Newark, DE: International Reading Association.

Sulzby, E., Barnhart, J., & Hieshima, J. A. (1989). Forms of writing and rereading from writing: A preliminary report. In J. M. Mason (Ed.), *Reading and writing connections* (pp. 31–50). Boston: Allyn & Bacon.

Sulzby, E., & Teale, W. (1991). Emergent literacy. In R. Barr, M. L. Kamil, P. Mosenthal, & P. D. Pearson (Eds.), *Handbook of reading research*, vol. II (pp. 727–757). New York: Longman.

Sulzby, E., Teale, W., & Kamberelis, G. (1989). Emergent writing in the classroom: Home and school connections. In D. S. Strickland & L. M. Morrow (Eds.), *Emerging literacy: Young children learn to read and write* (pp. 63–79). Newark, DE: International Reading Association.

Sundbye, N. (1987). Text explicitness and inferential questioning: Effects on story understanding and recall. *Reading Research Quarterly, 22,* 82–98.

Susskind, E. (1969). The role of question-asking in the elementary school classroom. In F. Kaplan & S. Sarason (Eds.), *The psychoeducational clinic*. Boston: Department of Mental Health.

Sutherland, Z., & Arbuthnot, M. H. (1986). *Children and books* (7th ed.). Glenview, IL: Scott, Foresman.

Sutton, C. (1989). Helping the nonnative English speaker with reading. *The Reading Teacher, 42,* 684–688.

Taba, H. (1965). The teaching of thinking. *Elementary English, 42,* 534–542.

Taylor, B. M., Strait, J., & Medo, M. A. (1994). Early intervention in reading: Supplemental instruction for groups of low-achieving students provided by first-grade teachers. In E. H. Hiebert & B. M. Taylor (Eds.), *Getting reading right from the start* (pp. 85–106). Boston: Allyn & Bacon.

Taylor, D., & Dorsey-Gaines, C. (1988). *Growing up literate, learning from inner-city families*. Portsmouth, NH: Heinemann.

Taylor, K. K. (1986). Summary writing by young children. *Reading Research Quarterly, 21,* 193–208.

Taylor, M. A. (1990, March). *Exploring mythology and folklore: The macrocosm and microcosm*. Paper presented at the spring conference of the National Council of Teachers of English, Colorado Springs, CO.

Teale, W. H., & Sulzby, E. (1986). *Emergent literacy: Writing and reading*. Norwood, NJ: Ablex.

Temple, C., Nathan, R., Temple, F., & Burris, N. A. (1993). *The beginnings of writing* (3rd ed.). Boston: Allyn & Bacon.

Terman, L. M. (1954). The discovery and encouragement of exceptional talent. *American Psychologist, 9,* 221–230.

Terry, A. (1974). *Children's poetry preferences*. Urbana, IL: National Council of Teachers of English.

Tetewsky, S. J., & Sternberg, R. J. (1986). Conceptual and lexical determinants of nonentrenched thinking. *Journal of Memory and Language, 25,* 202–225.

Thiessen, D., & Matthias, M. (Eds.). (1992). *The Wonderful World of Mathematics*. Reston, VA: National Council of Teachers of Mathematics.

Thomas, E. L., & Robinson, H. A. (1972). *Improving reading in every class: A sourcebook for teachers*. Boston: Allyn & Bacon.

Thomas, R. L. (1993). *Primaryplots 2: A book talk guide for use with readers 4–8*. New York: Bowker.

Thompson, A. (1990). Thinking and writing in learning logs. In N. Atwell (Ed.), *Coming to know: Writing to learn in the intermediate schools* (pp. 35–51). Portsmouth, NH: Heinemann.

Thorndike, R. L. (1973). Reading as reasoning. *Reading Research Quarterly, 9,* 135–147.

Thorndike, R. L., & Hagen, E. P. (1984). *Measurement and evaluation in psychology and education* (4th ed.). New York: Wiley.

Thorndyke, P. (1977). Cognitive structures in comprehension and memory of narrative discourse. *Cognitive Psychology, 9,* 77–110.

Tiedt, P. M., & Tiedt, I. M. (1990). *Multicultural teaching: A handbook of activities, information, and resources.* Boston: Allyn & Bacon.

Tierney, R. J., Carter, M. A., & Desai, L. E. (1991). *Portfolio assessment in the reading-writing classroom.* Norwood, MA: Christopher-Gordon.

Tierney, R. J., Readence, J. E., & Dishner, E. K. (1995). *Reading strategies and practices: A compendium* (4th ed.). Boston: Allyn & Bacon.

Tompkins, G. E., & Yaden, D. B. (1986). *Answering questions about words.* Urbana, IL: National Council of Teachers of English.

Touchstone Applied Science Associates. (1988). *Readability of textbooks* (8th edition). Brewster, NY: Author.

Tractenburg, P. (1990). Using children's literature to enhance phonics instruction. *The Reading Teacher, 43,* 648–654.

Treiman, R. (1992). The role of intrasyllabic units in learning to read. In P. B. Gough, L. C. Ehri, & R. Treiman (Eds.), *Reading acquisition* (pp. 65–106). Hillsdale, NJ: Lawrence Erlbaum.

Trelease, J. (1989). *The new read-aloud handbook.* New York: Penguin.

Trussell-Cullen, A. (1994). *Celebrating the real strategies for developing non-fiction reading and writing.* Paper presented at the annual meeting of the Connecticut Reading Association, Waterbury.

Tunnell, M. O., & Ammon, R. (Eds.). (1993). *Teaching history through children's literature.* Portsmouth, NH: Heinemann.

Tunnell, M. O., & Jacobs, J. S. (1989). Using "real" books: Research findings on literature-based reading instruction. The *Reading Teacher, 42,* 470–477.

Turbill, J. (1982). *No better way to teach writing!* Rozelle, Australia: Primary English Teaching Association.

Turner, I. (1972). *Cinderella dressed in yella.* New York: Taplinger.

Tuttle, D. W. (1988). Visually impaired. In E. M. Meyer & T. M. Skrtic (Eds.), *Exceptional children and youth* (3rd ed.) (pp. 351–385). Denver: Love.

Tyson, E. S., & Mountain, L. (1982). A riddle or pun makes learning words fun. *The Reading Teacher, 36,* 170–173.

U.S. Department of Education. *What Works: Research on teaching and learning* (1986). Washington, DC: Author.

Vacca, R. T., & Vacca, J. L. (1986). *Content area reading* (2nd ed.). Boston: Little, Brown.

Valencia, S. (1990). Assessment: A portfolio approach to classroom reading assessment: The whys, whats, and hows. *The Reading Teacher, 43,* 338–340.

Valencia, W. W., & Place, N. A. (1994). Literacy portfolios for teaching, learning, and accountability: The Bellevue literacy assessment project. In S. W. Valencia, E. H. Hiebert, & P. P. Afflerbach (Eds.), *Authentic reading assessment: Practices and possibilities* (pp. 134–156). Newark, DE: International Reading Association.

Van Dijk, T. A., & Kintsch, W. (1985). Cognitive psychology and discourse: Recalling and summarizing stories. In H. Singer & R. B. Ruddell (Eds.), *Theoretical models and processes of reading* (3rd ed.) (pp. 794–812). Newark, DE: International Reading Association.

Van Riper, C., & Emerick, L. (1984). *Speech correction: Principles and methods* (6th ed.). Englewood Cliffs, NJ: Prentice-Hall.

Vellutino, F. R., & Scanlon, D. M. (1988). Phonology and coding, phonological awareness, and reading ability: Evidence from longitudinal and experimental study. *Merrill-Palmer Quarterly, 33,* 321–363.

Venezky, R. L. (1965). *A study of English spelling-to-sound correspondences on historical principles.* Unpublished doctoral dissertation, Stanford University, Stanford, CA.

Vygotsky, L. S. (1962). *Mind and society: The development of higher psychological processes.* Cambridge, MA: MIT Press.

Vygotsky, L. S. (1978) *Thought and language.* Cambridge, MA: MIT Press.

Vygotsky, L. S. (1987). The development of scientific concepts in childhood. In R. F. Rieber & A. S. Carton (Eds.), *The collected works of L. S. Vygotsky,* vol. 1 (N. Mnick, trans.) (pp. 167–241). New York: Plenum.

Wade, S. E. (1983). A synthesis of the research for improving reading in the social studies. *Review of Educational Research, 53,* 461–497.

Wallace, G., & McLoughlin, J. A. (1988). *Learning disabilities: Concepts and characteristics* (3rd ed.). Columbus, OH: Merrill.

Walsh, D. S., Price, G. G., & Gillingham, M. G. (1988). The critical but transitory importance of letter naming. *Reading Research Quarterly, 23,* 108–122.

Warren, D. H. (1984). *Blindness and early childhood development* (2nd ed.). New York: American Foundation for the Blind.

Watson, A. J. (1984). Cognitive development and units of print in early reading. In J. Downing & R. Valten (Eds.), *Language awareness and learning to read* (pp. 93–118). New York: Springer-Verlag.

Watson, S. B. (1991). Cooperative learning and group education modules: Effects on cognitive achievement of high school biology students. *Journal of Research in Science Teaching, 28,* 141–146.

Weaver, B. (1992). *Defining literacy levels.* Charlotteville, NY: Story House.

Weaver, C. (1994). Understanding and educating students with attention deficit hyperactivity disorders: Toward a system-theory and whole language perspective. In C. Weaver (Ed.), *Success at last: Helping students with AD(H)D achieve their potential.* Portsmouth, NH: Heinemann.

Weaver, C. K., & Kintsch, W. (1991). Expository text. In R. Barr, M. L. Kamil, P. Mosenthal, & P. D. Pearson (Eds.), *Handbook of reading research,* vol. II (pp. 230–245). New York: Longman.

Weber, R., & Shake, M. C. (1988). Teachers' rejoinders to students' responses in reading lessons. *Journal of Reading Behavior, 20,* 285–299.

Weinstein, C., & Mayer, R. (1986). The teaching of learning strategies. In M. C. Wittrock (Ed.), *Handbook of research on teaching* (pp. 315–327). New York: Macmillan.

Wells, G. (1986). *The meaning makers: Children learning language and using language to learn.* Portsmouth, NH: Heineman.

White, T. G., Power, M. A., & White, S. (1989). Morphological analysis: Implications for teaching and understanding vocabulary growth. *Reading Research Quarterly, 24,* 283–304.

White, T. G., Sowell, J., & Yanagihara, A. (l989). Teaching elementary students to use word-part clues. *The Reading Teacher, 42,* 302–308.

Wilde, S. (1995). *Twenty-five years of inventive spelling: Where are we now?* Paper presented at the annual meeting of the International Reading Association, Anaheim, CA.

Williams, J. P. (1986a). Identifying main ideas: A basic aspect of reading comprehension. *Topics in Language Disorders, 8,* 1–13.

Williams, J. P. (1986b). Research and instructional development on main idea skills. In J. F. Baumann (Ed.), *Teaching main idea comprehension* (pp. 73–95). Newark, DE: International Reading Association.

Williams, P. L., Reese, C. M., Campbell, J. R., Mazzeo, J., & Phillips, G. W. (1995). *1994 NAEP reading: A first look.* Washington, DC: Office of Educational Research and Improvement, U.S. Department of Education.

Wilson, J. (1960). *Language and the pursuit of truth.* London: Cambridge University Press.

Wilson, P. (1986, April). *Voluntary reading.* Paper presented at the annual convention of the International Reading Assocation, Philadelphia.

Wilson, P. (1992). Among nonreaders: Voluntary reading, reading achievement, and the development of reading habits. In C. Temple & P. Collins (Eds.), *Stories and readers: New perspectives on literature in the elementary classroom* (pp. 157–169). Norwood, MA: Christopher-Gordon.

Wingfield, A., & Asher, S. R. (1984). Social and immigration influences on reading. In P. D. Pearson, R. Barr, M. L. Kamil, & P. Mosenthal (Eds.), *Handbook of reading research,* vol. II (pp. 423–452). New York: Longman.

Winne, R. H., Graham L., & Prock, L. (1993). A model of poor readers' text-based inferencing: Effects of explanatory feedback. *Reading Research Quarterly, 28,* 536–566.

Winograd, K. (1992). What fifth graders learn when they write their own math problems. *Educational Leadership, 50*(7), pp. 64–67.

Winograd, P. (1989). Introduction: Understanding reading instruction. In P. N. Winograd, K. K. Wixson, & M. Y. Lipson (Eds.), *Improving basal reading instruction* (pp. 1–17). New York: Teachers College Press.

Winograd, P. (1994). Reading assessment: Developing alternative assessments; six problems worth solving. *The Reading Teacher, 47,* 420–423.

Winograd, P. N. (1984). Strategic difficulties in summarizing text. *Reading Research Quarterly, 19,* 404–425.

Withers, C. (Ed.). (1948). *A rocket in my pocket: The rhymes and chants of young Americans.* New York: Holt.

Wixson, K. K. (1983). Questions about a text: What you ask about is what children learn. *The Reading Teacher, 37,* 287–293.

Wolf, W., King, M., & Huck, C. (1968). Teaching critical reading to elementary school children. *Reading Research Quarterly, 3,* 435–498.

Wong, B. Y. L. (1982). Understanding the learning-disabled student's reading problems: Contributions from cognitive psychology. *Topics in Learning and Learning Disabilities, 1*(4), 43–50.

Wright, J. W. (Ed.). (1991). *The universal almanac.* Kansas City, MO: Andrews & McMeel.

Yopp, H. K. (1988). The validity and reliability of phonemic awareness tests. *Reading Research Quarterly, 23,* 159–199.

Yopp, R. H., & Yopp, H. K. (1992). *Literature-based reading activities.* Boston: Allyn & Bacon.

Zarnowski, M. (1990). *Learning about biographies: A reading-and-writing approach for children.* Urbana, IL: National Council of Teachers of English.

Zarnowski, M., & Gallagher, A. F. (Eds.). (1993). *Children's literature and social studies: Selecting and using notable books in the classroom.* Washington, DC: National Council for the Social Studies.

Zinsser, W. (1988). *Writing to learn.* New York: Harper & Row.

Zorfass, J., Corley, P., & Remey, A. (l994). Helping students with disabilities become writers. *Educational Leadership, 51*(7), 62–66.

CHILDREN'S BOOKS AND PERIODICALS

Aardema, V. (1975). *Why mosquitoes buzz in people's ears: A West African folk tale.* New York: Dial.

Armento, B. J., Nash, G. B., Salter, C. L., & Wixson, K. K. (1991a). *America will be.* Boston: Houghton Mifflin.

Armento, B. J., Nash, G. B., Salter, C. L., & Wixson, K. K. (1991b). *From sea to shining sea.* Boston: Houghton Mifflin.

Armento, B. J., Nash, G. B., Salter, C. L., & Wixson, K. K. (1991c). *A message of ancient days.* Boston: Houghton Mifflin.

Armento, B. J., Nash, G. B., Salter, C. L., & Wixson, K. K. (1991d). *This is my country.* Boston: Houghton Mifflin.

Baldwin, D., & Lister, C. (1984). *Your five senses.* Chicago: Children's Press.

Bauer, C. (1984). *Too many books.* New York: Viking.

Blos, J. W. (1979). *A gathering of days: A New England girl's journal.* New York: Scribner's.

Blumberg, R. (l987). *The incredible journey of Lewis and Clark.* New York: Lothrop.

Bodecker, N. M. (1974). *Let's marry, said the cherry, and other nonsense poems.* New York: Atheneum.

Brenner, B. (1978). *Wagon wheels.* New York: Harper & Row.

Bridwell, N. (1972). *Clifford the small red puppy.* New York: Scholastic.

Brink, C. (1935). *Caddie Woodlawn.* New York: Macmillan.

Brown, D. P. (l985). *Sybil rides for independence.* New York: Whitman.

Brown, J. G. (1976). *Alphabet dreams.* Englewood Cliffs, NJ: Prentice-Hall.

Burnford, S. (1961). *The incredible journey.* Boston: Little, Brown.

Burton, L. L. (1942). *The little house.* Boston: Houghton Mifflin.

Byars, B. (1970). *Summer of the swans.* New York: Viking.

Byars, B. (1977). *The pinballs.* New York: Harper & Row.

Carle, E. (1973). *Have you seen my cat?* New York: Watts.

Carle, E. (1974). *All about Arthur (an absolutely absurd ape).* New York: Franklin Watts.

Carle, E. (1985). *The very busy spider.* New York: Philomel.

Cleary, B. (1983). *Dear Mr. Henshaw.* New York: Morrow.

Cooney, B. (1983). *Miss Rumphius.* New York: Viking.

Curie, E. (1937). *Madam Curie: A biography* (V. Sheehan, trans.). New York: Doubleday.

Curtis, F. (1977). The *little book of big tongue twisters.* New York: Harvey House.

Davis, B. (l976). *Black heroes of the American Revolution.* San Antonio, TX: Harcourt.

Degen, B. (1983). *Jamberry*. New York: Harper & Row.

dePaola, T. (1973). *Andy: That's my name*. Englewood Cliffs, NJ: Prentice-Hall.

Dickinson, T. (1988). *Exploring the sky by day: The equinox guide to weather and the atmosphere*. Camden East, Ontario: Camden House.

Douglas, B. (1982). *Good as new*. New York: Lothrop.

Duggleby, J. (1990). *Pesticides*. New York: Crestwood.

Eastman, P. D. (1960). *Are you my mother?* New York: Random House.

Epstein, S., & Epstein, B. (1968). *Harriet Tubman: Guide to freedom*. Champaign, IL: Garrard.

Folsom, M., & Folsom, M. (1986). *Easy as pie*. New York: Clarion.

Forbes, E. (1943). *Johnny Tremain*. Boston: Houghton Mifflin.

Friedman, I. (1984). *How my parents learned to eat*. New York: Houghton Mifflin.

Fritz, J. (1973). *And then what happened, Paul Revere?* New York: Coward.

Fritz, J. (1977). *Can't you make them behave, King George?* New York: Putnam.

Fritz, J. (1982). *Will you sign here, John Hancock?* New York: Coward.

Gág, W. (1928). *Millions of cats*. New York: Coward.

Galdone, P. (1973). *The three billy goats Gruff*. New York: Clarion.

Galdone, P. (1974) *Little Red Riding Hood*. New York: Clarion.

Galdone, P. (1975). *The gingerbread boy*. New York: Clarion.

Garten, J. (1964). *The alphabet tale*. New York: Random House.

Geisel, T. S. (Dr. Seuss). (1961). *The cat in the hat comes back*. New York: Random House.

Geisel, T. S. (Dr. Seuss). (1974). *There's a wocket in my pocket*. New York: Beginner.

Goodall, J. S. (1988). *Little Red Riding Hood*. New York: Macmillan.

Gramatky, H. (1939). *Little Toot*. New York: Putnam.

Gwynne, F. (1970). *The king who rained*. New York: Windmill.

Gwynne, F. (1988a). *Chocolate moose for dinner*. New York: Simon & Schuster.

Gwynne, F. (1988b). *A little pigeon toad*. New York: Simon & Schuster.

Hacker, R., & Kaufman, J. (1990). The president's playhouse. *Sports Illustrated for Kids, 2*(2), 42–47.

Hamilton, V. (1985). *The people could fly*. New York: Knopf.

Haskins, J. (1991). *Outward dreams: Black inventors and their inventions*. New York: Crowell.

Heilbroner, J. (1964). *Meet George Washington*. New York: Random House.

Henry, M. (1947). *Misty of Chincoteague*. New York: Rand McNally.

Hill, E. S. (1967). *Evan's corner*. New York: Holt, Rinehart & Winston.

Hoban, R. (1964). *Bread and jam for Frances*. New York: Harper & Row.

Hyman, T. S. (1983). *Little Red Riding Hood*. New York: Holiday House.

Ivimey, J. W. (1987). *The complete story of the three blind mice*. New York: Clarion.

Kane, J. N. (1981). *Famous first facts* (4th ed.). New York: Wilson.

Keats, E. J. (1964). *Whistle for Willie*. New York: Viking.

Kipling, R. (1912). *Just so stories*. New York: Doubleday.

Komori, A. (1983). *Animal mothers*. New York: Philomel.

Kraus, R. (1971). *Leo the late bloomer*. New York: Windmill.

Krauss, R. (1945). *The carrot seed*. New York: Harper.

Lambert, M. (1986). *Transportation in the future*. New York: Bookwright.

Lane, H. U. (Ed.). (1995). *The world almanac (1995)*. New York: Newspaper Enterprise.

L'Engle, M. (1962). *A wrinkle in time*. New York: Farrar, Straus & Giroux.

Levinson, R. (1985). *Watch the stars come out*. New York: Dutton.

Lewis, C. S. (1950). *The lion, the witch, and the wardrobe*. New York: Macmillan.

Lobel, A. (1970). *Frog and Toad are friends*. New York: Harper & Row.

Louie, A. (1982). *Yeh-Shen: A Cinderella story from China*. New York: Philomel.

Lowry, L. (1990). *Number the stars*. Boston: Houghton Mifflin.

MacLachlan, P. (1985). *Sarah, plain and tall*. New York: Harper & Row.

Martin, B., Jr. (1983). *Brown bear, brown bear, what do you see?* New York: Holt.

Mayerson, E. W. (1990). *The cat who escaped from steerage*. New York: Scribner's.

McCloskey, R. (1941). *Make way for ducklings*. New York: Viking.

McFarlan, D. (Ed.). (1995). *Guinness book of world records*. New York: Sterling.

Meltzer, M. (1987). *The American revolutionaries: A history in their own words*. New York: Crowell.

Musgrove, M. (1976). *Ashanti to Zulu*. New York: Dial.

Naylor, P. (1991) *Shiloh*. New York: Atheneum.

Nedobeck, D. (1981). *Nedobeck's alphabet book*. Chicago: Children's Press.

Neff, M. M. (1990). Legends: How Gordie Howe was a hockey star in his youth and also when he was a grandpa. *Sports Illustrated for Kids, 2*(2), 48.

Noble, T. H. (1980). *The day Jimmy's boa ate the wash*. New York: Dial.

O'Brien, R. C. (1971). *Mrs. Frisby and the rats of NIMH*. New York: Atheneum.

O'Neill, M. L. (1961, 1989). *Hailstones and halibut bones*. New York: Doubleday.

Oxenbury, H. (1971). *Helen Oxenbury's ABC of things*. New York: Delacorte.

Payne, E. (1944). *Katy no-pocket*. Boston: Houghton Mifflin.

Potter, B. (1908). *The tale of Peter Rabbit*. London: Warne.

Reigot, B. (1988). *A book about planets and stars*. New York: Scholastic.

Rolfer, G. (1990). Game day. *Sports Illustrated for Kids, 2*(8), 25.

Roop, P., & Roop, C. (1986). *Buttons for General Washington*. Minneapolis, MN: Carolrhoda.

Rylant, C. (1987). *Henry and Mudge, the first book*. New York: Bradbury.

Sanford, W. R., & Green, C. R. (1989). *The old English sheepdog*. New York: Crestwood.

Segal, L. (1973). *All the way home*. New York: Farrar, Straus & Giroux.

Sendak, M. (1963). *Where the wild things are*. New York: Harper & Row.

Sewall, M. (1986). *The pilgrims of Plimoth*. New York: Atheneum.

Sewall, M. (1990). *People of the breaking day*. New York: Atheneum.

Shaw, N. (1986). *Sheep in a jeep*. Boston: Houghton Mifflin.

Singer, I. B. (1966). *Zlateh the goat and other stories*. New York: Harper.

Sobol, D. (1961). *The Wright brothers at Kitty Hawk*. New York: Dutton.

Speare, E. (1958). *The witch of Blackbird Pond*. Boston: Houghton Mifflin.

Spier, P. (1980). *People*. New York: Doubleday.

Stevens, J. (1987). *The three billy goats Gruff*. New York: Holiday.

Stone, L. M. (1985). *Antarctica*. Chicago: Children's Press.

Tejima, K. (1987). *Owl lake*. New York: Putnam.

Waber, B. (1972). *Ira sleeps over*. Boston: Houghton Mifflin.

White, E. B. (1952). *Charlotte's web*. New York: Harper & Row.

Wilder, L. I. (1941). *Little house on the prairie*. New York: Harper & Row.

Wildsmith, B. (1982). *Cat on the mat*. New York: Oxford University Press.

Wildsmith, B. (1988). *Squirrels*. New York: Oxford University Press.

Williams, M. (1926). *The velveteen rabbit*. New York: Doubleday.

Worth, V. (1972). Zinnias. In V. Worth, *Small poems*. New York: Farrar, Straus & Giroux.

Yashima, T. (1955). *Crow boy*. New York: Viking.

Yolen, J. (1987). *Owl moon*. New York: Philomel.

Zajdler, Z. (1968). *Polish fairy tales*. Chicago: Follett.

Zion, G. (1956). *Harry the dirty dog*. New York: Harper & Row.

INDEX

A, B, See! (Hoban), 57, 88
A Is for Animals (Shirley), 57
A My Name Is Alice (Bayer), 64
A to Zoo: Subject Access to Children's Books (Lima & Lima), 56
Aardema, V., 344, 345
Aaron and Gayle's Alphabet Book (Greenfield), 56
Abbott, J. L., 387, 388
Abstract reading, 17
Abuela (Dorros), 37, 451
Acronym, as memory device, 317
Acrostic, as memory device, 317
Activation of prior knowledge, 197
Adams, D. K., 222, 292
Adams, M., 55, 78, 79, 102, 111, 125, 131
Adler, A., 478
Adler, D. A., 360
Adoption Guidelines Project, 374, 375
Adorjan, C., 356
Advanced organizer, 291
Adventuring with Books: A Booklist for Grades Pre-K-Grade 6 (Jensen & Roser), 385
Aesop's Fables, 379
Aesthetic judgment, developing, 341–342
Aesthetic stance, 10, 333–335, 337
Affix, 133
Afflerbach, P. P., 199, 202, 206, 364, 489
Ahlmann, M. F., 514
ALERT critical reading technique, 274
Alexander, S., 227, 356, 478
Aliki, 345
All About Arthur (An Absolutely Absurd Ape) (Carle), 62, 85
All Fall Down (Wildsmith), 130
All the Way Home (Segal), 32
Allen, E. G., 274
Allen, J., 51
Allen, V. G., 461
Allington, R. L., 106, 399, 400, 403, 405
Allison's Zinnia (Lobel), 64
Alpha Beta Chowder (Steig), 64
Alphabeasts (King Smith), 57
Alphabet, teaching of, 55–58

Alphabet books, 56–57
Alphabet Dreams (Brown), 63
Alphabet Puzzle (Downie), 88
Alphabet Tale, The (Garten), 86, 87
Alphabetic principle, 14
Alphabetics (MacDonald), 88
Altwerger, B., 408
Alvermann, D., 219, 220, 278, 318
Amazing Grace (Hoffman), 451
Amazing Writing Machine, The (Broderbund), 438
Amazon Trail (MECC), 538
American Heritage Word Frequency Book, The (Carroll, Davis, & Richman), 123
American Revolutionaries: A History in Their Own Words (Meltzer), 286
American Sports Poems (Knudson & Swanson), 350
American Tall Tales (Osborne), 346
America's Story (Bernstein), 283
Ames, L. B., 13, 25
Ammon, R., 309
Analogies, constructing, 300
Analogy strategy, 115–116, 137, 152
Analytic approach, to teaching phonics, 79–80
Analytic scoring, 516–517
And I Mean It, Stanley (Bonsall), 101, 130
And Then What Happened, Paul Revere? (Fritz), 286
Anderson, C. W., 307, 308
Anderson, G., 363
Anderson, J. R., 185
Anderson, L., 375
Anderson, R. C., 18, 30, 78, 137, 146, 163, 183, 194, 361, 362, 364, 371, 411
Anderson, T. H., 224, 243, 314, 326
Anderson, V., 210, 211, 213
Andre, M. E. D. A., 224
Andy: That's My Name (dePaola), 106
Anecdotal records, 511–512
Angelou, M., 37
Animal Babies (Hamsa), 101
Animal Mothers (Komori), 43
Animalia (Base), 64
Anna Banana: 101 Jump Rope Rhymes (Cole), 177

Annie's Pet (Brenner), 102
Anno, M., 310
Anno's Math Games (Anno), 310
Ant and the Dove, The (Wang), 100
Antarctica (Stone), 313
Antee, N., 100
Anthony, H. M., 228
Anticipation guide, 289–290, 308
Anyon, J., 453
Ape in a Cape (Eichenberg), 88
Appel, L. R., 406
Applebee, A. N., 18, 371, 394, 415, 453
Applebet: An ABC (Watson), 88
Arbuthnot, M. H., 343
Are You My Mother? (Eastman), 32, 37, 39, 43
Armbruster, B., 243, 314, 320, 326
Armento, B. J., 16, 17, 204
Arnold, C., 310
Arono, S., 456
Aronson, E., 534
As: A Surfeit of Similes (Juster), 426
Asch, S., 189
Ashanti to Zulu (Musgrove), 57
Asher, S., 426
Asher, S. R., 536
Assessment, 488, 502–503. *See also* Evaluation; Retelling; Think-Alouds
functional level, 506
Assumptions, detecting, 272
Aster Aardvark's Alphabet Adventures (Kellogg), 64
Athey, I., 19
Atkinson, R. C., 258, 315
Atkinson, R. L., 258, 315
At-risk students, 452–453. *See also* Economically disadvantaged children; Learning disability, children with; Linguistically and culturally diverse students; Mental retardation, students with; Physical disabilities, children with; Slow learners
Attention deficit disorder, 467–469
Atwell, N., 312, 313, 389, 395, 396, 397, 398
Au, K., 137, 457, 458, 518, 519, 525
Audio and audiovisual technologies, 542

Auditory perception, 84
Aukerman, A., 291, 370
Aunt Flossie's Hats (and Crabcakes Later) (Howard), 38
Austin, M., 394
Australian Ministry of Education, 505, 511
Ausubel, D., 25, 291
Authentic assessment, 488–489
Author's chair, 427
Author's circle, 430–431
Author's purpose, recognizing, 270–271
Automaticity, 122, 127–128
Aylesworth, J., 56, 59
Baer, E., 451
Bailey's Book House (Edmark), 538
Baker, L., 13, 225, 226, 227, 228
Balajthy, E., 540
Baldwin, L. E., 146, 455
Baldwin, R. S., 318
Bales, R. J., 221
Bandes, H., 64
Bank Street Writer (Scholastic), 538
Bank Street Writer for the MacIntosh (Scholastic), 437
Banks, J. A., 280, 450, 451, 452, 457
Barba, R. H., 279, 286
Barbe, W., 387, 388
Barkin, C., 426
Barnes-Murphy, F., 37
Barnhart, C. L., 156, 407
Barnhart, J., 40, 47, 50, 69
Baron, N. S., 3
Barr, R., 530
Barron, R. R., 291
Barstow, B., 465
Bartlett, F. C., 241
Basals, 371–376
Base, G., 64
"Base Stealer" (Francis), 349
Basic Reading Inventory (Johns), 510
Basic Reading Series (SRA), 407
Bauer, C. F., 33, 347
Bauman, G. A., 28
Baumann, J. F., 189, 200, 201
Bayer, J., 64
Be Good to Eddie Lee (Fleming), 478
Beach, R., 335
Bean, T. W., 318
Bear, D., 113, 114
Beck, I., 166, 167, 168, 180, 185, 196, 248, 261
Bedtime for Frances (Hoban), 37
Beers, P. G., 533
Beginning reading, 14–15
Benchmark, 504-505, 506

Benchmark Assessment Guide (Weaver), 505
Benchmark program, 137
Benet, W. R., 344
Benfield, C. M., 38
Bennett Cerf's Book of Riddles (Cerf), 177
Bereiter, C., 419, 420, 426, 439
Berenstain, J., 139
Berenstain, S., 139
Berg, D. N., 246
Berkowitz, S. J., 172, 214
Berliner, D. C., 19, 458, 529
Bernstein, J. E., 177
Best: High/Low Books for Reluctant Readers, The (Pilla), 466
Best of the Best for Children, The (Donavin), 542
Beyond Picture Books: A Guide to First Readers (Barstow & Riggle), 465
Big Big Alphabet, The (Spectrum, Holobyte), 90
Big book, 41, 42, 43. *See also* Shared reading
Big Book Maker (Queue), 541
Big Max (Platt), 102
Biggest Snowfall, The (Moncure), 139
Bilingual approach, 459–460
Bilingual learners, 459–464
Bingo, the Best Dog in the World (Siracusa), 102
Biographies from American History (Globe Fearon), 283
Biography, 359–361
Birch, J. W., 480
Bird, L. B., 22, 410
Bishop, R. S., 38, 344
Bissex, G. L., 46
Blachowicz, C. L. Z., 181, 266
Black Heroes of the American Revolution (Davis), 286
Blair, T. R., 75
Blanchard, J. S., 543
Bland, J., 356
Blends, 91
Blocksma, M., 101, 130
Bloom, B., 19, 249, 385
Bloomfield, L., 80, 407
Blos, J. W., 382
Blue Pages, Resources for Teachers from Invitations, The (Routman), 386
Blueberries for Sal (McCloskey), 33
Blumberg, R., 283
Bodecker, N. M., 124
Boehm, A. E., 209

Bogehold, B. D., 100
Bond, G. L., 411
Bonsall, C., 101, 130
Book About the Origins of Everyday Words and Phrases, A (Sarnoff & Ruffins), 176
Book About Planets and Stars, A (Reigot), 147
Book of Greek Myths (D'Aulaire & D'Aulaire), 345
Booklist, 385
Booth, B., 478
Borchardt, K. M., 210
Borkowski, J. G., 234
Borreguita and the Coyote: A Tale from Ayutla, Mexico (Aardema), 345
Bottom-up approach, to teaching reading, 10–11, 12
Boyden, P. C., 348
Boyle, O. F., 211
Bracemesseter, R., 348
Bradley, L., 59
Bradshaw, G. L., 185
Brainstorming, 417. *See also* Clustering
Brandt, R., 278, 279
Bransford, J. D., 194, 195, 208, 229, 315–316
Brazil (BFA), 181
Bread and Jam for Frances (Hoban), 33
Brenner, B., 101, 102
Brett, J., 37
Brian Wildsmith's ABC (Wildsmith), 57
Bridge, C. A., 126, 128
Bridwell, N., 74
Brink, C., 382
Brophy, J. E., 251, 529
Brown, A. L., 210, 212, 225, 226, 227, 228, 231, 233
Brown, C. S., 510
Brown, D. P., 283
Brown, H., 408, 511
Brown, J. G., 63
Brown, J. J., 458
Brown, M., 37
Brown, M. W., 130
Brown, R., 138
Brown Bear, Brown Bear, What Do You See? (Martin), 38, 44
Bruchac, J., 349
Bruner, J., 6
Bryant, P., 59, 102
Bugs (McKissack & McKissack), 99, 100

Bulletin of the Center for Children's Books, 385
Bunny Play, The (Leedy), 357
Burke, C., 45, 340, 379, 380, 430, 431
Burke, E., 385
Burnford, S., 530
Burns, D. L., 177
Burns, J. M., 113
Burris, N., 50, 115
Burton, L. L., 221, 222, 266, 379
Bush, C., 511, 512
Busy Buzzing Bumblebees and Other Tongue Twisters (Schwartz), 64
Busy Day: A Book of Action Words (Maestro & Maestro), 129
Buttons for General Washington (Roop & Roop), 286
Buzz Said the Bee (Lewison), 99, 100
Byars, B., 221, 222, 336, 351
Byrne, B., 81

Cache of Jewels and Other Collective Nouns, A (Heller), 177
Caddie Woodlawn (Brink), 382
Cake That Mack Ate, The (Robart), 101, 130
Caldwell, J., 510
Calfee, R., 503
California State Department of Education, 379
Calkins, L. M., 242, 313, 325, 349, 415, 416, 417, 424, 428, 443
Calmenson, S., 88
Cambourne, B., 408, 511
Cameron, P., 59
Campbell, J. R., 18, 361, 371, 375, 387, 459
Camperell, K., 196, 244
Canon, J., 37
Can't You Make Them Behave, King George? (Fritz), 286, 360
Care: Early Identification of Handicapped Children (Cartwright & Cartwright), 474
Carey, R. F., 488, 503
Carle, E., 32, 62, 85, 100, 129, 130, 461
Carlsen, J. M., 475
Carlstrom, N. W., 59, 88
Carnine, D. D., 10, 25, 146, 168
Carona, P., 310
Carr, E. M., 166, 215, 218, 264
Carr, J., 349
Carr, K. S., 216
Carroll, J. S., 122
Carrot Seed, The (Krauss), 35, 38

Carter, M. A., 518, 520
Cartwright, C. A., 469, 473, 474, 475
Cartwright, G. P., 469, 473, 474, 475
Castle, M., 366
Cat at Bat (Stambler), 102
Cat Games (Ziefert), 100
Cat in the Hat Comes Back, The (Geisel), 124
Cat on the Mat (Wildsmith), 100, 130, 461, 505
Cat Who Escaped from Steerage, The (Mayerson), 286
Catterson, J., 510
Cavanaugh, R. A., 450
Caverly, D. C., 319, 320
CD-ROM, 537–538
dictionaries on, 153, 159, 541
Cebulash, M., 130
Center for the Study of Reading, 365
Ceprano, M. A., 124
Cerf, B., 177
Chall, J. S., 13, 17, 78, 163, 183, 279, 281, 283, 410, 455
Chamot, A. U., 283, 461, 464
Channel R.E.A.D. (Houghton Mifflin), 542
Character analysis, 341–342, 351–355
Chard, N., 313
Charlotte's Web (White), 16, 146, 335, 354, 379
Checking, 226
Children's Books in Print (Bowker), 385
Children's Literature and Social Studies: Selecting and Using Notable Books in the Classroom (Zarnowski & Gallagher), 309
Children's Literature in the Elementary School (Huck, Helper, & Hickman), 385
Children's Writing and Publishing Center, The (Learning Company), 438
Chocolate Moose for Dinner (Gwynne), 188
Choi, S., 451
Christenbury, L., 251
Christie, J. F., 30, 312
Christopher, M., 7
Church, S. M., 410
Ciardi, J., 349
Cinderella (Playhouse Video), 542
Clark, E. C., 177
Clark, F. L., 193
Classifying, 199–200

Clay, M. M., 19, 20, 25, 45, 50, 55, 61, 62, 72, 73, 117, 482, 499, 500, 530
Cleary, B., 366, 371, 385, 445
Clifford the Small Red Puppy (Bridwell), 74
Clifton, L., 350
Cline, R. K., 18
Cloze, 264–267
Cloze (Continental Press), 538
Cluster, 91
Clustering, 318, 419. *See also* Brainstorming
Coarticulation, 58
Cognitive development, 46
Cognitive Strategy Instruction in Writing, 439–442
Cohen, C., 466
Cohen, N., 88
Cohen, P., 177
Cole, J., 64, 177, 339, 347
Collections for Young Scholars (Open Court), 94, 526
Collins, A., 226
Combs, M., 42
Commercial materials, in emergent literacy program, 67
Compain, R., 359, 405
Complete Story of the Three Blind Mice, The (Ivimey), 48
Composing, 420
Compound words, 138–139
Comprehension
applying strategies for, 230–234
process of, 193–196
strategies for, 196–230
Compton's Interactive Encyclopedia (Compton), 542
Computers, 537–540. *See also* Desktop publishing; Word processing
and students with physical disabilities, 473
Concepts, learning, 165–166
Concepts about Print Tests (Clay), 72–73,
Concepts of print, 26–27
Conceptual change, reading for, 307–308
Conceptual understanding, as memory device, 315–316
Concrete operations stage, of cognitive development, 5–6
Conferences
group reading, 390, 393
individual reading, 389–390

Conferences (*continued*)
  peer, 429–430
  writing, 428–429, 430–431
Connotations, 190
Conoley, J. C., 504
Conrad, S. S., 279, 281
Conserve, 5
Consonant clusters, 91
Consonant sounds, 62–65, 83–88
Consonants, 82–83
Content area literacy, 278
  choosing texts for, 281–283
  estimating readability of texts for,
    281-284
  multilevel texts for, 283, 285
  teacher's role in achieving, 278–279
  techniques for teaching principles
    of, 287–304
  using children's books and
    periodicals for, 308–311
  using literature and trade books for,
    286, 287
Content knowledge, teaching,
    306–307
Context clues, 146–150
Contextual analysis, 146–150. *See
  also* Corrective feedback
Cook, D. M., 13, 540
Cooley, J. D., 233
Cooney, B., 15
Cooper, C. R., 516
Cooper, P. D., 395, 396, 398
Cooperative learning, 230, 295, 301,
    358, 359, 376–377, 394, 408,
    452, 457, 461, 481–482, 530,
    534–535, 536
Cooter, R. B., 395, 399, 492
Corbett, P., 177
Core literature, 379
Corley, P., 437
Corrective cues hierarchy, 151–152
Corrective feedback, 150–153
Correspondence, 79
  troublesome, 92–93
Courlander, H., 344
Cox, C., 334, 335, 351, 379, 456
Cox, J., 189
Coyle, G., 146
Crafton, L., 409
Craig, S., 233
Crawford, J., 311
Crawford, L. W., 449
Crawford, P., 376
Crawley, S., 385
*Creative Fingerplays and Action
  Rhymes* (Defty), 177
Criterion-referenced tests, 502

Critical reading, 267–268
  scope and sequence of skills for,
    268–274
Croll, V., 239
Crossword Magic (L & S
    Computerware), 178
Crow Boy (Yashima), 351
Culyer, R., 123
Cummings, A., 542
Cummins, J., 461, 462
Cumulative tales, 380
Cundick, B. P., 240
Cunningham, J. W., 107, 199, 211,
    239
Cunningham, P. M., 106, 107, 131,
    135, 211, 399, 400, 403, 405
Curie, M., 323
Curtis, F., 64
Curtis, G., 37
Curtis, M. E., 184

Dahl, K. L., 72, 112
Dale, E., 138, 139, 164, 176, 178,
    190, 281, 282
D'Arcy, P., 52, 419
Dark Night, Sleepy Night (Ziefert),
    101
Dauer, V. L., 296
D'Aulaire, D., 345
D'Aulaire, P., 345
Dave, R. H., 453
Davey, B., 224, 295
David, Y., 226
*David Gantz Wacky World of
    Numbers, The* (Gantz), 311
Davies, P., 189
Davis, B., 286, 454
Davis, J., 513
Davis, P., 122
Davis, Z. T., 239
Day, H. D., 73
Day, J. D., 210, 212
Day, K. C., 73
Day Jimmy's Boa Ate the Wash, The
    (Noble), 444
de Angeli, M., 59
Dear Mr. Blueberry (James), 38
Dear Mr. Henshaw (Cleary), 373, 445
Decenter, 5
Decoding, 78, 81–82
Deford, D., 12
Defty, J., 177
Degen, B., 59
Delpit, L. D., 455
Demi, 88
Demi's Find the Alphabet A, B, C
    (Demi), 88

Denman, G. A., 348
Denotations, 190
dePaola, T., 37, 60, 106, 349
DePinto, T., 233
de Regniers, B. S., 349
Derivational suffixes, 141
Desai, L. E., 518, 520
Deshler, D. D., 193
Desktop publishing, 438–439, 540
Details
  comprehension of, 205–208
  important, 207
  supporting, 201, 203
  organizing of, 207–208
Devine, T. G., 245
Dewitz, P., 215, 218, 264
*Diagnostic and Statistical Manual of
    Mental Disorders* (American
    Psychiatric Association), 467
Dialects, 158
  acceptance of, 404–405, 458
  and the dictionary, 158–159
  and phonics, 82
Dialogue journals, 396–398
"Diary of Leigh Botts, The" (Cleary),
    373
Dias, P., 334, 341
Dickinson, T., 288
Dictation, 54
Dictionaries
  on CD-ROM, 153, 159, 541
  use of, 154–160
Digraphs, 91
Dillon, J. T., 250, 251, 278
DiLuglio, P., 381
Dino Park Tycoon (MECC), 538
Dinosaur Babies (Penner), 101
Dinosaur Days (Milton), 102
Dinosaur Days Plus (Pelican), 438
Dinosaur Time (Parish), 101, 252
Direct instruction, of skills and
    strategies, 389
Directed reading activity, 255–261,
    288, 376, 392, 526, 540
Directed reading-thinking activity
    (DRTA), 261–264, 288, 376, 526
Directions, comprehending, 208–210
Dishner, E. K., 263, 288, 299, 480,
    489, 512
Distributed practice, 319
Dixon, R. C., 168
Do You Want to Be My Friend?
    (Carle), 129
Dolan, L. J., 482
Dole, J. S., 202, 211, 216, 234
Domain knowledge, 306–307
Donavin, D. P., 542

Donkey's Tale, The (Oppenheim), 101
Donlan, D., 283
Donnelly, J., 506
Don't Forget the Bacon (Hutchins), 59
Dorion, R., 31
Dorothea Lange: Life Through the Camera (Meltzer), 360
Dorros, A., 37, 451
Dorsey-Gaines, C., 8, 9, 456
Douglas, B., 42
Douglas, M. P., 5
Downie, J., 88
Doyle, M. A., 40, 531
Dozen Dogs, A (Ziefert), 101, 130
Dr. Peet's Talk/Writer (Hartley), 56, 99, 436
Dr. Seuss. *See* Geisel, T. S.
Dr. Seuss's ABC (Geisel), 64, 88
Drafting, as stage of writing, 421
Dragon Dictate (Dragon Systems), 437
"Dragonfly" (Jaques), 350
Drama, 355–359
Dramatic play, 30
Drawing, as aid to writing, 44, 418
Dream Keeper and Other Poems, The (Hughes), 350
Dream Wolf (Goble), 345
Drew, C. J., 469, 470, 474, 475, 476
Dual coding theory, 220
Dudley-Marling, C., 435
Duffelmeyer, B. B., 174
Duffelmeyer, F. A., 174
Duffy, G. G., 202, 211, 216, 234, 254, 255
Duffy, R., 434–435
Duggleby, J., 144
Dunkeld, C., 482
Durkin, D., 25, 27, 66, 68
Durrell, D., 55, 510
Durrell Analysis of Reading Difficulty (Durrell & Catterson), 510
Dykstra, R., 78, 411
Dyrli, O. E., 539

"Eagle, The" (Tennyson), 348
Early, M., 321
Early intervention programs, 481–484. *See also* Reading Recovery
Earth Verses and Other Rhymes (Lewis), 350
Eastman, P. D., 32, 37, 39, 43
Easy as Pie (Folsom & Folsom), 85, 86

Eat Your Peas, Louise (Pigeen), 101
Eating the Alphabet (Ehlert), 56
Eating Fractions (McMillan), 311
Eaton, D., 381
Economically disadvantaged children, 453–456
    reading aloud to, 39
Edelsky, C., 375, 376, 408
Education for All Handicapped Children Act, The (PL94–142), 464, 467
Educational Software Selector, The (TESS), 540
Eeds, M., 124
Eek! There's a Mouse in the House (Wong), 60
Efferent stance, 10, 333–334
Egan, M. W., 469, 470, 474, 475, 476
Egocentric, 5
Ehlert, L., 56
Ehri, L. C., 80, 124
Eichenberg, F., 88
Elaboration, as comprehension strategy, 196, 197, 214–224
Eldridge, R. D., 531
Electronic Learning, 540
Electronic mail, 539
Elementary Reading Attitude Survey (McKenna & Kerr), 513
Elkind, D., 25
Elkonin, D. B., 58, 61, 62, 65
Elkonin phonemic segmentation technique, 61–62, 65
Elley, W. B., 184
Emergent literacy, 24
    essential skills and understandings in, 26–27
    fostering, 28–67
    issues in, 67–69
    monitoring, 69–75
    and observation guides, 70–71
Emergent reading, 13–14
Emergent storybook reading, 39–41
Emerick, L., 475
Emig, J., 416, 427
Englert, C. S., 439, 440
English as a second language (ESL) students, 2
    adapting instruction for, 89, 461, 462–464
    and classroom teacher's role, 460–461
    and language-experience approach, 404, 464
Enz, B., 492
Epstein, B., 286

Epstein, S., 286
Erickson, L. G., 211, 212
Erikson, E. H., 13, 16
ESL, 2, 460–464
Estes, T., 291, 299
Evaluation, 487–490. *See also* Assessment; Self-evaluation
    authentic, 488
    for placement, 490–500
    tests for, 500–502, 506
    of writing, 516–517
Evans Corner (Hill), 443
Exploring the Sky by Day (Dickinson), 288
Expository text, 242–248

Fables of Aesop, The (Barnes-Murphy), 37
Fader, D., 363
Fairbanks, M. M., 167
Fallon, I., 51
Famous First Facts (Kane), 366
Farejon, E., 348
Farnan, N., 281
Farnish, A. M., 536
Farr, B., 519
Farr, R., 488, 502, 503, 519
Farran, D., 51
Farstrup, A. E., 18, 361, 371, 375, 387
Favorite Nursery Tales (dePaola), 37
Feed Me! (Hooks), 101
Feitselson, D., 34
FELS questioning technique, 251–253, 254
Fernald, G. M., 112
Ferreiro, E., 25, 26, 27, 45, 46
Field, R., 348
Fielding, L. G., 18, 361, 362, 364
Fields, M. W., 20, 33, 34, 35
Figurative language, 189, 348
Fillmore, L. W., 459, 460
"Firefly" (Roberts), 350
First Connections: The Golden Book Encyclopedia for Windows (Hartley/Jostens), 541
Fisher, B., 373
Fisher, C., 347
Fitzgerald, J., 238
Fix-up strategies, 226–230
Flash cards, as memory device, 317–318
Flavell, J. H., 13
Fleisher, L. S., 201
Fleming, V., 478
Flexner, S. B., 94, 163
Flood, J., 281, 283, 382, 449

Flores, B. M., 408
Flynt, E. S., 492
Flynt-Cooter Reading Inventory for the Classroom (Flynt & Cooter), 492
Foertsch, M. A., 371, 394, 453
Folklore, 343–346
Folktales, 343
Follow Me (Ziefert), 101
Following the Drinking Gourd (SRA Group), 542
Folsom, Marcia, 85, 86
Folsom, Michael, 85, 86
For Reading Out Loud! A Guide to Sharing Books with Children (Kimmel & Segal), 38
Forbes, E., 286
Ford, M. P., 351, 379, 531, 532
Formal operations stage, of cognitive development, 6
Forrest-Pressley, D., 234
Foster, E. O., 239
"Foul Shot" (Hoey), 348
Fox, M., 37, 334
Fox Be Nimble (Marshall), 102
Fox on Wheels (Marshall), 102
Francesca, M., 345
Franklin, E. A., 444
Fredericks, A. D., 223, 537
Free writing, 419
Freedman, R., 360
Freeland, D., 367
Freeman, P. A., 139
Freppon, P. A., 112
Friedburg, A., 405, 406
Friedman, I., 456
Fries, C. C., 407
Fritz, J., 286, 360
Frog and Toad Are Friends (Churchhill Media), 542
Frog and Toad Are Friends (Lobel), 383
From Apple to Zipper (Cohen), 88
Frustration level, of informal reading inventory, 488
Fry, E., 19, 20, 122, 385
Fry Readability Graph, 284–285
Frymier, J., 452
Functional level, of assessment, 506
Functional reading, 470–472
Functional Reading: A Resource Guide for Teachers (Maryland State Department of Education), 471, 472

Gág, W., 34
Gage, F., 390

Galdone, P., 35, 43, 89, 380
Gallagher, A. F., 287, 308, 309, 476, 478
Gallagher, M. C., 19
Gallo, D., 365
"Galoshes" (Bracemesseter), 348
Gambrell, L., 220, 221, 240, 241, 242, 250
Gansneder, B., 452
Gantt, W. N., 19
Gantz, D., 311
Garcia, G. E., 453, 455, 460, 461
Gardner, H., 227, 279
Gardner, R., 233
Gardner, T., 311
Garner, R., 227, 228
Garten, J., 86, 87
Gaskins, I. W., 137, 234
Gaskins, J. C., 137
Gaskins, R. W., 137
Gates, A. I., 25, 319
Gathering of Days, A (Blos), 382
Geisel, T. S., 64, 65, 88, 124
Gelman, R. G., 101, 130
Gelzheiser, L. M., 481
Generalization approach, to teaching syllabication, 133–135
Gerlovich, J., 282
Gesell, A., 25
Gibson, E. J., 45, 55, 415
Gibson, J. J., 55
Gibson, L., 68
Gibson, S., 45
Gifted or talented students, 479–480
Giftedness, 479
Gillespie, S. T., 13
Gillingham, A., 112
Gillingham, M. G., 55
Gingerbread Boy, The (Galdone), 35, 44, 89
Ginn Word Book (Johnson, Moe, & Baumann), 189
Giovanni, N., 350
Gipe, J. P., 166, 167
Glass, G., 110
Global SchoolNet, 539
Goble, P., 345
Gods and Goddesses of Olympus, The (Aliki), 345
Goelman, H., 420
Gold, J., 201
Goldberg, L., 407
Goldenberg, C., 456, 483, 536
Golding, J. M., 241, 242
Goldstein, E. L., 34
Golick, M., 117
Good, T. L., 251, 529

Good as New (Douglas), 41
Good Bad Cat, The (Antee), 100
Good Night, Owl (Hutchins), 130
Goodall, J., 380
Goodman, K. S., 11, 12, 22, 111, 151, 374, 410, 411, 458
Goodman, Y. M., 22, 72, 410, 458, 511
Goodnight, Goodnight (Rice), 139
Gordon, C. J., 196, 217
Gordon, S., 130
Gorilla/Chinchilla and Other Animal Rhymes (Kitchen), 177
Goswami, U., 102
Gough, P., 12, 78, 82, 124
Grade equivalent score, 504
Graham, L., 215, 216
Gramatky, H., 443
Grand Slam Riddles (Bernstein & Cohen), 177
Grandfather's Journey (Say), 451
Grandma's Baseball (Curtis), 37
Grandpa's Great City Tour (Stevenson), 64
Graphic aids, in textbooks, 281, 282. *See also* SQ3R; Survey technique; Typographical aids in textbooks
Graphic organizers, 169, 245–246, 247, 300. *See also specific types* creating, 300–302
Grasser, A., 241, 242
Grauer, N. A., 422
Graves, D. H., 416, 417, 418, 423, 424
Graves, M. F., 139, 163, 243
Greenfield, E., 37, 56, 349, 350
Greenlaw, M. J., 362
Gregorich, B., 100
Greydanus, R., 100, 104
Griffin, M., 73
Griffith, P. L., 59, 78, 82
Grimm's Fairy Tales, 379
Groff, P., 80
Grouping, 531–535. *See also* Author's circle; Cooperative learning; Literature circles
Guild, P., 457
Guiness Book of World Records (McFarlan), 366
Gum on the Drum, The (Gregorich), 100
Gunning, T., 91, 92, 93, 102, 104, 109, 110, 115, 135, 136, 146, 200, 272, 506
Guppies in Tuxedos: Funny Eponyms (Terban), 176
Guthrie, J. T., 364, 530

Gutkin, R. J., 364
Gwynne, F., 188

Hacker, R., 148
Hackett, J. K., 222, 292
Hagen, E. P., 75
Hague, S. A., 243
Haiku, 347
"Hailstones and Halibut Bones"
     (O'Neil), 348
Haines, C., 13
Hale-Benson, J. E., 457
Haley, D., 126, 128
Hall, N., 30
Halmoni and the Picnic (Choi), 451
Halstead, J. W., 362
Hamilton, H., 367
Hamilton, V., 344
Hammond, D., 139
Hamsa, B., 101
Hansen, J., 216, 217, 248
Hardman, M. L., 469, 470, 474, 475,
     476, 480
Hare, V. C., 210, 227
Harriett Tubman: Guide to Freedom
     (Epstein & Epstein), 286
Harris, A., 356
Harris, A. J., 93, 132, 140, 141, 142,
     151, 189, 227, 249, 283, 362
Harrison, P., 346, 347, 350
Harry the Dirty Dog (Zion), 38
Harste, J., 45, 340, 379, 380, 430,
     431, 490
Hartman, D. K., 194
Harwayne, S., 242, 325, 417
Haskins, J., 286, 360
Hauck, L. C., 94, 163
Have You Seen My Cat? (Carle), 32,
     130, 461
Have You Seen My Duckling?
     (Tafuri), 130
Haviland, V., 345
Hawkins, C., 100
Hawkins, J., 100
Hayes, D. A., 300
Haynes, J., 227
Hearing loss, students with, 473–475
*Hearing Measurement: A Book of
     Readings* (Ventry, Chaiklin, &
     Dixon), 289
Heath, S. B., 7, 250, 251
Heathington, B. S., 240, 241, 242
Heilbroner, J., 286
Heilman, A. W., 75
Heimlich, J. E., 169
Helen Oxenbury's ABC of Things
     (Oxenbury), 85, 88

Heller, R., 139, 177
Helper, S., 13, 383, 385
Henderson, E. H., 46, 52, 128
Hennessy, B. G., 60
Henry (Cleary), 366
Henry, M., 137, 144, 221, 263, 384
Henry and Mudge: The First Book
     (Rylant), 15–16, 102
Herber, H. L., 279–280, 281, 299
Herber, J. N., 279–280
Herman, J. L., 489, 503, 520
Herman, P. A., 146, 183
Hero tales, 345–346
Herold, C., 184
Heward, W. L., 450
Hickman, J., 13, 385
Hidi, S., 210, 211, 213
Hiebert, E., 20, 30, 78, 371, 411,
     489, 503, 532
Hieshima, J. A., 47, 69
Higbee, K. L., 240
Higgins, D., 131, 363
High-frequency words, 123. *See also*
     Sight words
High/Low Handbook (Liberetto), 466
Hildreth, G., 25, 58
Hilgard, E. R., 258, 315
Hill, E. S., 443
Hillinger, M. L., 124
Hirsch, E. D., 17, 39
Hoban, R., 33, 37
Hoban, T., 57, 88, 129
Hoberman, M., 349
Hoey, E., 348
Hoff, S., 101, 130
Hoffman, J. V., 327, 525, 535
Hoffman, M., 451
Holdaway, D., 39, 41, 42, 43, 45,
     112
Holiday Plays Round the Year
     (Kamerman), 357
Holistic approach, to teaching
     reading, 10
Holistic scoring, 516
Holland, M., 225,
Holt, J., 152
Holton, C., 427
Homographs, 156, 188–189, 190
Homophones, 188
*Honey Hunters: A Traditional African
     Tale* (Francesca), 345
Honey, I Love (Greenfield), 37
Hong, L., 38
Hooks, W. H., 101
Hooray for Snail! (Stadler), 101
Hopkins, L. B., 102, 347, 349
Horn Book, The, 385

Horning, K. T., 38, 344
Hornsby, P., 266, 392
Hotchkiss, P., 536
Houghton Mifflin Social Studies series
     (Armento et al.), 16, 17, 204
How Do Octopi Eat Pizza Pie?
     (Crawford), 311
How Much Is a Million? (Schwartz),
     311
How My Parents Learned to Eat
     (Friedman), 456
How to Be a Better Writer (Ryan),
     427
*How to Be School Smart: Secrets of
     Successful Schoolwork* (James &
     Barkin), 426
Howard, E., 38
Howell, G. C., 514
Huck, C., 13, 267, 333, 385
Hudson, W., 350
Huebner, M., 511, 512
Hughes, L., 350
Hungry, Hungry Sharks (Wynne),
     101
Hutchins, P., 59, 130
Hyman, R. T., 252
Hyman, T. S., 380
Hynds, S., 335
Hyperactivity, 467, 468–469
Hypermedia, 542–543
Hypertext, 543

"I Can't" Said the Ant (Cameron), 59
I-charts, 327–329
"I Like Bugs" (Brown), 350
I Love Cats (Matthias), 101, 130
*I Never Saw a Purple Cow and Other
     Nonsense Rhymes* (Clark), 177
Idea maps, 214
Idiomatic expressions, 189
If You Give a Mouse a Cookie
     (Numeroff), 38
If You Made a Million (Schwartz),
     311
Ilg, F., 13, 25
Imaging, 220–223
Impulsivity, 467, 468–469
Incidental learning, 185
Inclusion, 20, 473, 480–481
Incredible Journey, The (Burnford),
     530
*Incredible Journey of Lewis and
     Clark, The* (Blumberg), 283
Independent level, of informal reading
     inventory, 491
Individual differences, providing for,
     531. *See also* Grouping

Individualized reading, 387
   adapting, 395
   advantages and disadvantages of, 394–395
   and conferences, 389–392
   implementing, 388–389
   materials for, 387
   organizing, 388
Individuals with Disabilities Education Act (IDEA) (PL 101–476), 464–465, 467
Inferences, 215–220
Inflectional suffixes, 141
Informal reading inventory, 465, 490
   administering, 492–496
   analysis of miscues in, 496–499
   group, 283
   interpreting, 496
   levels of, 491–492
Information processing, 234
Informational books, 361
Inside, Outside, Upside Down (Berenstain & Berenstain), 139
Instructional level, of informal reading inventory, 491
Interactionists, 10, 11–12, 13
Interactive writing, 433–435
Interest groups, 534
International Reading Association, 537, 544
Internet, 539
Interviews, 514
Introducing Book Plots 4 (Spirt), 384
Invented spelling, 43, 47, 49, 50, 52, 53, 57, 69, 72, 113, 115
Inviting Children's Responses to Literature (McClure & Kristo), 384
Ira Sleeps Over (Waber), 33
It Begins with an A (Calmenson), 88
Ivimey, J. W., 44

Jacob K. Javits Gifted and Talented Students Education Act (PL 100–297), 479
Jacobs, J. S., 18
Jacobs, V. A., 455
Jacobson, M. D., 132, 140, 141, 142, 189
Jake Baked the Cake (Hennessey), 60
Jamberry (Degen), 59
James, E., 426
James, J. H., 491
James, S., 38
Jamestown Heritage Readers, The (Mountain, Crawley, & Fry), 385

Jason's Bus Ride (Ziefert), 101
Javitz, P. B., 220
Jen the Hen (Hawkins & Hawkins), 100
Jenkins, J. R., 146
Jennings, C. A., 356
Jensema, C., 473
Jensen, J. M., 385
Jensen, P., 130
Jesse Bear, What Will You Wear? (Carlstrom), 59
Jett-Simpson, M., 505, 514
Jiganti, M. A., 176
Jigsaw group, 534–535
Jiménez, R. T., 453, 455, 460, 461
John Henry (Lester), 345
Johnny Appleseed: A Tall Tale (Kellogg), 345
Johnny Tremain (Forbes), 286
Johns, J. L., 73, 510
Johnson, C. J., 210
Johnson, D. D., 169, 171, 189, 250
Johnson, D. W., 535, 536
Johnson, H., 286
Johnson, M. S., 200, 283, 491, 499
Johnson, R. T., 535, 536
Johnston, P. H., 199, 206
Joint Task Force on Assessment, 503, 506
Jonas, A., 45
Jongsma, E., 265
Joplin plan, 532
Joshua James Likes Trucks (Petrie), 99, 100, 130
Journals, 418, 514. *See also* Dialogue journals; Response journals
Juel, C., 78, 82, 99
Junior Great Books, 480
Just Like Me (Neasi), 100
Just So Stories (Kipling), 384
Juster, N., 426

Kaissen, J., 364
Kaleidoscope, a Multicultural Booklist for Grades K8 (Bishop), 38, 344
Kamberelis, G., 54
Kameenui, E. J., 10, 25, 146, 168
Kamerman, S. E., 356, 358
Kang, H., 281
Kapinus, B. A., 240, 241, 242
Kardaleff, P. P., 309
Karweit, N. L., 482
Katy No Pocket (Payne), 15
Kauffman, J., 392
Kaufman, J., 129, 148
Kavanagh, J. F., 473

Kawakami-Arakaki, A., 51
Keats, E. J., 33, 34, 38
Keegan, M., 451
Kellogg, S., 64, 345
Kelly, P., 251
Kennedy, D. M., 309
Kerr, B. M., 35–36
Kerr, D. J., 513
Kessler, L., 139
Key word approach, 186–187, 317
Kibby, M., 20, 124
Kid Works II (Davidson), 438
Kids' Stories (Storm), 438
Kimmel, M. M., 38, 201
King, C., 475
King, M., 267
King-Smith, D., 57
King Who Rained, The (Gwynne), 188
Kintsch, W., 195, 196, 275, 307
Kipling, R., 384
Kirk, D., 60
Kirk, S. A., 476, 478
Kirshner, B. W., 439
Kitchen, B., 177
Klare, G. R., 281
Know Your World Extra (Field), 466
Knudson, R. R., 350
Knutson, K., 64
Koala Lou (Fox), 37
Kobasigawa, A., 225
Kohl, H., 180
Komori, A., 43
Koskinen, P. S., 240, 241, 242
Kramer, J. J., 504
Kraus, R., 100, 130, 384
Krauss, R., 35, 38
Kress, R. A., 200, 283, 491, 499
Kretke, G. L., 18
Kristo, J. V., 340, 341
Kruse, G. M., 38, 344
Kurita, J. A., 210
KWL Plus (Know, Want to Know, Learn), 281, 304–305, 306, 308, 376

Laberge, D., 122
Laminack, L. L., 24, 274
Landau, S. I., 153, 163
Langer, J. A., 18, 288, 371, 394, 453
Langston Hughes: American Poet (Walker), 360
Language and speech disorders, students with, 475–476
Language Arts (NCTE), 544

Language development, role of school in, 65–67
Language-experience approach, 44–45, 399
adapting, 406
advantages and disadvantages of, 406
in content areas, 405
and dialects, 404–405
and ESL students, 404, 464
as a group approach, 400–402
high-tech version of, 405–406
as an individual approach, 402–403
introducing skills and strategies for, 403–404
personalizing, 402
word banks and, 402, 403
Language learning, conditions of, 408–409
Lapp, D., 281, 382, 449
Lara, J., 459
Larter, S., 506
Laughlin, M. K., 309
Lear, E., 177
Learning centers, 530
Learning disability, children with, 464–467. *See also* Attention deficit disorder
Learning environment, 234, 274–275
Learning logs, 312–313, 514
Learning Media, 375, 377
Learning styles, 457
Lee, D. M., 20, 33, 34, 35
Leedy, L., 358, 426
Legends, 345–346
Lehr, F., 78, 111
L'Engle, M., 384
Lenz, B. K., 193
Leo the Late Bloomer (Kraus), 100, 384
Leslie, L., 510
Lester, J., 345
Let's Get a Pet (Greydanus), 100, 104
" 'Let's Marry,' Said the Cherry" (Bodecker), 124
Letter knowledge, 55–58
Leung, C. B., 184
Levin, H. A., 45, 415
Levin, J. R., 186, 317
Levinson, R., 286
Lewis, C. S., 221, 222
Lewis, J., 350
Lewison, 99, 100
Liberman, A., 58
Libretto, E. V., 466
Libson, E. R., 38

Life and Death of Martin Luther King, Jr., The (Haskins), 360
Liggett, T. C., 38
Lincoln: A Photobiography (Freedman), 360
Linden, M., 214
Linguistic approach, to reading, 406–407
Linguistically and culturally diverse students, 456–464
Lion, the Witch, and the Wardrobe, The (Lewis), 221
Lipson, M. Y., 289, 380, 381
Listening capacity level, of informal reading inventory, 491
Literacy, 2
atmosphere fostering, 28–29
in tomorrow's world, 543–544
Literacy Profiles, 508
Literacy program, 525–537
building a sense of community, 527, 530
choosing materials for, 526
continuous monitoring of progress in, 535
involving parents in, 68–69, 536–537
managing, 530–535
pacing in, 530–532
providing for individual differences within, 532–535
selecting techniques and strategies for, 526–527
setting goals for, 525–526
using time efficiently in, 530
working with other professionals on, 537
Literacy 2000, 377
Literature. *See also* Biography; Drama; Folklore; Informational books; Poetry
experiencing, 333–335
principles of teaching, 341–342
Literature-based approach, 378
adapting, 386–387
advantages of, 386
choosing materials for, 385–386
creating literature guides for, 383–384
disadvantages of, 386
making the transition to, 376–377
organizing, 379–383
sample program for, 384–385
Literature-Based Social Studies: Children's Books and Activities to Enrich the K-5 Curriculum (Laughlin & Kardaleff), 309

Literature circles, 340–341
Literature for the Young Child (Burke), 385
Literature guides, 383–384
Little Book of Big Tongue Twisters, The (Foley), 64
Little House, The (Burton), 221, 266, 379
Little Pigeon Toad, A (Gwynne), 188
Little Red Riding Hood (Galdone), 380
Little Red Riding Hood (Hyman), 380
Little Toot (Gramatky), 443
Livingston, M. C., 426
Lobel, A., 34, 60, 64, 102, 383
Logical conclusions, 271
London, J., 349
Long, L. D., 241, 242
Long vowels, 94
Lookback strategy, 227–228
Louie, A., 380
Lowry, L., 379
Loxterman, J. A., 196
Lukens, R. J., 333, 341, 342
Lytle, S. L., 510

Maberry, D. L., 426
McArthur, T., 144
McBride, S., 224
McCloskey, R., 33, 38, 181, 182, 384
McClure, A. A., 340, 341, 346, 347, 350, 384
McConnell, S., 223
McCord, D., 349,
McCormick, S., 195, 220
McCoy, K. M., 151
McCracken, R. A., 11, 112
McDaniel, M. A., 186
MacDonald, S., 88
McGee, L. M., 55, 239, 244
McGill-Franzen, A., 482
MacGinitie, R., 25, 289, 502
MacGinitie, W., 201, 502
McGoldrick, J. A., 210
McKenna, M. C., 513
McKeown, M. G., 166, 167, 168, 180, 185, 196, 248, 261
McKissack, P. C., 99, 130
MacLachlan, P., 340, 382, 383
McLane, J. B., 9, 38, 68
McLenighan, V., 129
McLoughlin, J. A., 465, 479
McMillan, B., 311
McNamara, T. P., 194, 195, 208
McNamee, G. D., 9, 30, 68
McNeil, J. D., 225

McPhail, D., 38
McPherson, M. D., 239
MacCready, G. B., 228
Macrostructure, 195
Madden, N. A., 482, 536
Maestro, B., 129
Maestro, G., 129
Magazines for Kids and Teens (Stoll), 309
Mahey, M., 345
Maimon, E. P., 424
Main idea, 199–206
Mandy (Booth), 478
Manning, G. L., 363, 365
Manning, M., 363, 365
Manual for Scoring and Interpretation of the Gates-MacGinitie Reading Tests (MacGinitie & MacGinitie), 502
Many, J. E., 334, 335, 337
Manzo, A. V., 253, 254, 411
Manzo, V. C., 253, 254, 411
Marguerite de Angeli's Book of Nursery and Mother Goose Rhymes (de Angeli), 59
Maria, K., 221, 289, 454
Maris, R., 130
Markle, S., 311
Marks, B., 358
Marks, M., 233
Marshall, E., 102
Martha Speaks (Meddaugh), 177
Martin, B., 38, 60, 446
Martin, J. H., 405, 406
Martin, R. E., 282
Martinez, M., 50
Mary McLeod Bethune: Voice of Black Hope (Meltzer), 360
Maryland State Department of Education, 471, 472
Marzano, J. S., 60, 172
Marzano, R. J., 172
Marzollo, J., 60
Mason, J. M., 35–36, 48, 49, 457, 458, 526
Massed practice, 319
Math in Science and Nature (Gardner), 311
Math Mini-Mysteries (Markle), 311
Mathematics, children's books in, 310–311
Mathias, C., 101, 129
Matlock, B., 146
Matthews, J. K., 520
Matthias, M., 130, 310
May, E., 30
May, F. B., 362

Mayer, R., 197, 316
Mayerson, E. W., 286
Mazzeo, J., 459
Meagher, J., 422
Measurements: Fun, Facts, and Activities (Arnold), 310
Meddaugh, S., 177
Medley, D. M., 248
Medo, M. A., 482
Meek, M., 24
Meet George Washington (Heilbroner), 286
Melmed, P. J., 458
Meltzer, M., 286, 360
Memory, 313–314. *See also* Key word approach; Rehearsal
conceptual understanding and, 315–316
devices, 315–318
distributed versus massed practice and, 319
and metacognitive awareness, 318–319
principles of, 315
Menke, P. J., 255
Mental models, 194–195, 196
Mental retardation, students with, 469
functional reading curriculum for, 470–472
Merrill Linguistic Readers (Fries, Wilson, & Rudolph), 407
Merrill Science (Hackett, Moyer, & Adams), 292
Merry-Go-Round (Heller), 139
Mess, The (Jenssen), 130
Messages in the Mailbox (Leedy), 426
Metacognition, 225–228
strategies for, 228–230
Metacognitive awareness, 225
Metalinguistic awareness, 27
Meyer, B. J. F., 243
Meyers, J., 338, 339, 481
Microsoft Creative Writer (Microsoft), 541
Microsoft Word (Microsoft), 437
Mike Fink (Kellogg), 345
Miles, B., 345
Miller, D. L., 194, 195, 208
Miller, G. E., 186
Miller, P. D., 411
Millions of Cats (Gág), 34
Mills, D. C., 291
Mills, E., 443
Milton, J., 102
Miscue, 496
Miscue analysis, 496–497

Miss Rumphius (Cooney), 15
Miss Spider's Tea Party (Kirk), 60
Misty of Chincoteague (Henry), 221, 263, 384
Mnemonics, 316. *See also* Memory
Modeling, of revising, 423
Modiano, N., 459
Moe, A. J., 189
Moldofsky, P. B., 205
Mollel, T. M., 346
Mom Can't See Me (Alexander), 478
Moncure, J., 100, 139
Monitoring, 197, 210. *See also* Metacognition
Monjo, F. N., 360
Monson, D. L., 13, 338
Montessori, M., 112, 405
Moon Boy (Brenner), 101
Moore, D. W., 182, 199, 211
Moore, E., 182, 211, 349
Moores, J., 30
Mora, P., 451
Moran, S., 530
More Spaghetti I Say (Gelman), 101, 130
Morgan, N. W., 246
Morgan, R. F., 314, 318, 320
Morning message, 51–52
Morpheme, 138. *See also* Prefixes; Root words; Suffixes
Morphemic analysis, 137–145
Morris the Moose (Wiseman), 101
Morrison, C., 394
Morrow, L. M., 28, 29, 37, 39, 50, 240, 241, 242
Mosenthal, J. H., 274–275
Mountain, L., 178, 385
Moyer, R. H., 222, 292
Mrs. Brice's Mice (Hoff), 101, 130
"Mrs. Peck Pigeon" (Farejon), 348
"Mud" (Boyden), 348
Mufaro's Beautiful Daughters (Weston Woods), 542
Mullins, P., 57
Mullis, I. V. S., 18, 361, 371, 375, 387, 394, 453
Multicultural education, 450–452
Multicultural Literature for Children and Young Adults (Kruse & Horning), 38, 344
Multicultural Teaching (Tiedt & Tiedt), 344
Mumper, J., 359, 405
Murphy, R. T., 406
Murray, D. M., 417, 428, 429
Muschla, G. R., 419, 425, 433
Musgrove, M., 57

Muth, K. D., 246
My Book (Maris), 130
My First Incredible Amazing Dictionary (Multimedia), 541
My Friend Leslie (Rosenberg), 478
My Media Text Workshop (Wings), 438
My New Boy (Phillips), 101, 130
My Painted House, My Friendly Chicken, and Me (Angelou), 37
My Song Is Beautiful (Hoberman), 349
My Teacher Sleeps at School (Weiss), 33
Myths, 344–345

Nagy, W., 146, 163, 166, 174, 183
Nash, G. B., 16, 17, 204
Natarelli, M., 347
Nathan, R., 50, 115
National Assessment of Educational Progress, 18
National Association of State Boards of Education, 481
National Council of Teachers of English, 537, 544
Navajo Vacation: Living in Two Worlds (Teacher Support), 539
Naylor, P., 379
Neasi, B., 100
Nedobeck, D., 62, 85, 86
Nedobeck's Alphabet Book (Nedobeck), 62, 63, 86–87
Neff, M. M., 148
Nessel, D., 198
Neu, H. C., 473
New, C. A., 449, 458
New House for Mole and Mouse, A (Ziefert), 101, 130
New Kid on the Block (Broderbund), 181, 541
New Read Aloud Handbook, The (Trelease), 38
New Treasury of Children's Poetry: Old Favorites and New Discoveries, A (Cole), 339, 347
New View, A (McGraw-Hill), 373
Newmann, F. M., 279, 532
Nicholson, T., 184
Nicky Upstairs and Down (Ziefert), 100, 130
Night on Neighborhood Street (Greenfield), 349
Nine Men Chase a Hen (Gregorich), 100
Nisbet, J., 329
Nist, S. L., 322

No! No! Word Bird (Moncure), 100
Nobel, B. P., 449
Noble, T. H., 444, 449
Nodine, B. F., 424
Norm-referenced scores, 504
Norm-referenced tests, 489, 500–502
Normal curve equivalents, 504
North American Legends (Haviland), 345
"Not Now!" Said the Cow (Oppenheim), 102
Notetaking, 324–326
Novels, 350–355
Noyce, R., 312
Number the Stars (Lowry), 379
Numbers (Carona), 310
Numdroff, L., 38

O'Brien, C. A., 462, 463
O'Brien, D. G., 278
O'Brien, R. C., 16
Observation, 511–513
Observation Survey in Early Literacy Achievement, An (Clay), 73, 499
Odell, L., 516
Ogle, D., 304, 305
Old Black Fly (Aylesworth), 56
Old Turtle's Riddle and Joke Book (Kessler), 139
Olson, J. L., 418
Olson, M. W., 59
Olson, W. C., 387
O'Malley, J. M., 283, 461, 464
Omanson, R. C., 166, 167, 168, 184, 248, 261
One Bad Thing About Father, The (Monjo), 360
One Crow, A Counting Rhyme (Aylesworth), 59
101 Words and How They Began (Steckler), 176
One Light, One Sun (Raffi), 130
O'Neil, M., 348
Onset, 102, 103
Oppenheim, J., 100, 101, 102
Oregon Trail (MECC), 538
Organizational strategy, 196, 197, 198–214
Orlando, V. P., 319, 321
O'Rourke, J., 137, 138, 139, 141, 142, 163, 176, 178, 190
Osborne, M., 78, 111, 346
Oshiro, M., 51
Osser, H., 55
Otfinoski, S., 426
Otitis media, 473
Otto, W., 313, 531

Outlining, 326–327
Outward Dreams: Black Inventors and Their Inventions (Haskins), 286
Over, Under and Through (Hoban), 129
Overlearning, 315
Over-Under (Mathias), 129
Owings, R. A., 229
Owl and the Pussycat, The (Lear), 177
Owl at Home (Lobel), 102
Oxenbury, H., 85, 88
Oxford Treasury of Children's Poems (Harrison & Stuart-Clark), 347

Pablo's Tree (Mora), 451
Painter, H. W., 349
Paivio, A., 179, 220
Palincsar, A. S., 226, 231, 233
Pany, D., 151
Parent's Guide to the Best Books for Children (Libson), 38
Parents, involving, 68–69, 536–537
Paris, S. G., 230, 439
Parish, P., 101, 188
Parker, F., 50
Parry, J., 266, 392
Parsons, C., 395
Parsons, L., 339, 390
Pass It On: African American Poetry for Children (Hudson), 350
Pass the Poetry, Please! (Hopkins), 347
Pat the Cat (Hawkins & Hawkins), 100
Patberg, J. P., 215, 218, 264
Patriotic and Historical Plays for Young People: One-Act Plays and Programs about the People and Events That Made Our Country Great (Kamerman), 357
Pattern approach, to teaching syllabication, 135–137
Pauk, W., 321
Paul Bunyan (Kellogg), 345
Payne, E., 15
Pearson, P. D., 19, 169, 171, 183, 196, 202, 211, 216, 217, 228, 234, 244, 248, 250, 453, 455, 460, 461
Pelican Press for the Macintosh (Pelican), 438
Penner, R., 101
People (Spier), 456
People Could Fly, The (Hamilton), 344

People of the Breaking Day (Sewall), 283
Percentile rank, 504
Perfetti, C. A., 82
Perry, M., 36
Pesticides (Duggleby), 144
Pet for Pat, A (Snow), 100, 104
Peterman, C. L., 35–36
Peters, C. W., 306, 380, 381
Peters, E. E., 317
Peterson, R., 527
Petrie, C., 99, 130
Petty, W., 184
Phelps, S. F., 219, 220, 318
Philip, N., 346
Phillips, J., 101, 130
Phoneme, 58
Phonemic awareness, 65. *See also* Phonological awareness
Phonic elements, 79, 90, 91, 102, 103. *See also* Consonants; Vowels
Phonic generalizations, 93, 109–110
  consonant, 93
  vowel, 109–110
Phonic programs
  Benchmark, 137
  word building, 102, 465
Phonics, 78–79
  approaches to teaching, 79–80, 102–105, 108
  in children's books, 85–88
  consonant correspondences and, 83–90, 117–118
  and context, 116
  integrated approach to, 111–112
  in language-experience approach, 403–404
  patterns and, 100–104, 106–108, 117–118
  scope and sequence of, 94–99
  and spelling, 112–115
  strategy instruction in, 115–116
  variability strategy of, 93–94, 110–111
  vowel correspondences and, 99–102, 117–118
Phonological awareness, 58–65
Physical disabilities, children with, 473–479
Piaget, J., 4–6, 13
Pick, A. D., 55
Pictorial maps, 172, 173
Picture Book of Eleanor Roosevelt, A (Adler), 360
Picture Book of Helen Keller, A (Adler), 478

Pigeen, S., 101
Pigs Aplenty, Pigs Galore (McPhail), 38
Pike, K., 359, 405
Pikulski, J. J., 283, 491, 499
Pilgrims of Plimoth, The (Seewall), 283
Pilla, M. A., 466
Pinballs, The (Byars), 336
Pittleman, S. D., 169
Place, N. A., 518
Placement, of students. *See* Informal reading inventory
Planned program, 184–185
Platt, K., 102
Platt, P., 44
Plays, 357
Plays Children Love (Jennings & Harris), 357
Plays Children Love Vol. II (Jennings & Harris), 357
Plays of Black Americans (Kamerman), 357
Playtime Treasury, The (Corbett), 177
Plot, 342, 352, 353
  chart, 357
Pocketful of Poetry (Gibson), 350
Poem-Making: Ways to Begin Writing Poetry (Livingstone), 426
Poetry, 346–350
Poetry Break, The (Bauer), 347
Polar Bear, Polar Bear, What Do You Hear? (Martin), 60
Polish Fairy Tales (Zajdler), 344
Pomerantz, C., 130
Portfolios, 515, 518, 521–522
  reading samples for, 519
  reviewing of, 435–436, 519–520
  writing samples for, 435–436, 518–519
Possible sentences, 182–183
Potter, B., 216
Pourquoi tales, 344–345
Powell, J. S., 146
Power, M. A., 138
Practice, 319
Prawat, R. S., 225, 527, 530
Predictable books, 128–131
Predicting, 198
Predictionaries, 153
Predict-o-gram, 181
Prefixes, 139–140, 145–146
Prelutsky, J., 347
Preoperational stage, of cognitive development, 5
PReP (Prereading Plan), 288–289

Preparational strategy, 196, 197–198
Preschool reading, 67–68
Pressley, M., 186, 210, 233, 234, 235, 255, 307
Pretend You're a Cat (Marzollo), 60
Previewing, 198
Prewriting, 416–420
Price, D. S., 55
Pride of Puerto Rico: The Life of Roberto Clemente (Walker), 361
Primary Plots 2 (Thomas), 384
Print conventions, 43. *See also* Concepts of print
Prior knowledge, 196
  activating, 197
Probst, R., 335, 336
Process approach, to writing, 416
Prock, L., 215, 216
Professional development, 544–547
Progress, monitoring of, 535–536
Promise to the Sun: An African Story, A (Mollel), 346
Prompts, for corrective feedback, 152–153
Pronounceable word part strategy, 115–116, 137, 152
Pronunciation keys, use of, 157–159
Propaganda, 272
  techniques for detecting, 272–274
Proposition, 195
Propositional theory, of comprehension, 195–196
Publishing, 427–428
Pueblo Boy: Growing Up in Two Worlds (Keegan), 451
Puppet Plays and Puppet-Making: The Plays–The Puppets–The Production (Marks), 357
Purpose, setting of, 197
Purves, A. C., 13, 334, 335, 338, 351
Push-Pull, Empty-Full (Hoban), 129
Put Your Foot in Your Mouth and Other Silly Sayings (Cox), 189

QAR (Question-Answer Relationship), 218–220
Qualitative Reading Inventory (Leslie & Caldwell), 510
QuanSing, J., 117
Questionnaires, 513
Questions
  and Bloom's taxonomy, 249–250, 385
  and classroom atmosphere, 251
  and comprehension, 248
  generation of, 223–224
  for novels, 352

for program evaluation, 490
techniques using, 251–255
types of, 248, 249–250
and wait time, 250–251
"why," 255
Quigley, S., 475

Radencich, M. C., 533, 534
Raffi, 101, 130
Rainbow of My Own, A (Freeman), 139
Ramona (Cleary), 366
Random House Book of Mother Goose, The (Lobel), 60
Random House Book of Poetry for Children, The (Prelutsky), 347
Random House Dictionary of the English Language, The (Flexner & Hauck), 94, 163
Ransom, C. C., 225
Raphael, T. E., 218, 219, 228, 248, 439, 440
Rasinski, T. V., 537
Rasmussen, D., 407
Rasorisky, Y., 356
Ratings, 512–513
Rattigan, J., 177
Raw score, 504
Read, C., 25, 45
Readability, estimating, 281–283
Readability formulas, 282–283, 284–285
Readability of Textbooks (Touchstone Applied Science Associates), 281
Readence, J. E., 193, 252, 263, 288, 289, 290, 480
Reader response, 335–336. *See also* Literature, experiencing; Response journals
sample lesson for, 338–339
steps in eliciting, 336–337
transaction, 335
transactional theory, 9–10
transmission of information, 9
Reader's theater, 358–359
Reader's Theater Script Service, 359
Readiness, 25–26. *See also* Emergent literacy
Reading
aesthetic, 10, 333–335, 337
to children, 30–39
and culture, 79
efferent, 10, 333–334
and experience, 67
and language, 34
role of cognitive development in, 46

stages of development of, 13–17
theories of teaching, 10–13. *See also* Whole language
and writing, 443–445
Reading logs, 516
Reading Milestones (Quigley & King), 475
"Reading Rainbow," 367
Reading Rainbow Guide to Children's Books (Liggett & Benfield), 38
Reading Recovery, 20, 61, 481, 482, 499
Reading Recovery: A Guidebook for Teachers in Training (Clay), 482
Reading Teacher, The, 544
Reading to learn, 15–17
Reading workshop, 395–399
Ready to Read, 377
Reciprocal teaching, 230–234
Reed, S., 346, 347, 350
Reese, C. M., 459
Regulating, 226
Rehearsal, 196–197, 316
Rehearsing, as part of prewriting process, 420
Reigot, B., 147
Reliability, 502–503
Remedial programs, 481. *See also* Early intervention programs
Remey, A., 437
Renzulli, J., 479
Repairing, 226–228
ReQuest, 253–254
Response Guides for Teaching Children's Books (Somers & Worthington), 384
Response journals, 339–340, 516
Responsive elaboration, 254–255
Retelling, 240–241
as assessment device, 507–509
evaluating, 508, 509
steps in teaching, 241–242
written, 508–509
Retention, 314–319
Reutzel, D. R., 395, 399
Revising, 422–424
Reynolds, M. C., 480
Rhodes, L. K., 435, 512
Rhyme, 59–61
Rice, E., 139
Rice, G. E., 243
Rich, J. H., 230, 314
Richard Scarry's Best Word Book Ever (Scarry), 129

Richard Scarry's Busytown (Paramount Interactive), 125
Richard Scarry's Find Your ABC (Scarry), 57
Richardson, J. S., 314, 318, 320
Richek, M. A., 122, 184
Richgels, P. J., 55, 113, 244
Richman, P., 122
Riddles, 177, 178
Riggle, J., 465
Rimer, S., 190
Rimes, 102, 103, 104
Rinehart, S. D., 211, 212
Ringgold, F., 451
Rist, R., 532
Robart, R., 101, 130
Robber Baby, The (Rockwell), 346
Roberts, E. M., 350
Robin Hood: His Life and Legend (Miles), 345
Robinson, F., 319, 320, 321
Robinson, H. A., 321
Roby, C., 478
Rock, H. M., 542
Rocket in My Pocket, A (Withers), 90
Rockwell, A., 346
Roehler, L. R., 202, 211, 216, 234
Rolfer, G., 148
Roller, C., 244
Rookie Read-About Science (Children's Press), 285
Roop, C., 286
Roop, P., 286
Root, 141–145
Rope-Schneider, D., 99
Rose, M. C., 240
Rose, W., 233
Rosenberg, M., 478
Rosenblatt, L., 9, 10, 333, 334, 335, 336, 337
Rosenbloom, J., 177
Rosenshine, B., 529
Ross, D. D., 12
Roth, K. J., 307
Rothermich, J., 268
Rottenberg, C. J., 543
Routman, R., 377, 380, 381
Rubric, 506, 507, 516
Ruddell, M. R., 52, 185
Ruddell, R. B., 52, 211
Ruffins, R., 176
Rumelhart, D., 193, 194
Running records, 499–500, 501
Rupley, W. H., 75
Russo, A. M., 33
Ryan, E. A., 427
Rye, J., 265

Rylant, C., 15, 102

Sadowski, M. K., 179, 220
Sadowy, P., 9
SAE (Still Acquiring English), 459.
    See also ESL
Salinger, T., 34
Salter, C. L., 16, 17, 204
Samuels, S. J., 12, 122, 124, 125,
    127, 168, 525
San Diego Zoo Presents . . . the
    Animals, The (Software
    Toolworks), 541
Santa, C., 172, 313, 351
Sarah, Plain and Tall (MacLachlan),
    340, 382, 383
Sarnoff, J., 176
Sartain, H., 394
Sawyer, D. J., 321
Say, A., 451
Scaffolding, 6
Scaled score, 504
Scardamalia, M., 419, 420, 426,
    439
Scarry, R., 57, 129
Schade, S., 101
Schafer, W., 364
Schema, 193
Schema theory, of comprehension,
    193–194, 196
Schoephoeister, H., 531
Scholastic Guide to Putting It in
    Writing, The (Otfinoski), 426
Scholastic Sprint, 466
School Library Journal, 385
Schulz, J. B., 475
Schumaker, J. B., 193
Schumm, J. S., 533
Schunk, D. H., 230, 314
Schwa, 96
Schwartz, A., 64
Schwartz, D. M., 311
Science and Technology in Fact and
    Fiction: A Guide to Children's
    Books (Kennedy, Spangler, &
    Vanderwerf), 309
Science in Action Series (Globe
    Fearon), 285
Scott, Foresman Beginning Dictionary
    (Thorndike & Barnhart), 156
Scott, J. A., 30, 371, 411
Searfoss, L. W., 193, 252
Segal, L., 32
Segmenting, of sounds in words,
    61–62
    Elkonin technique for, 61–62, 65
Self-evaluation, 514–515

Self-selection, of books, 383, 389,
    396
Semantic feature analysis, 172, 174,
    175, 353, 355
Semantic Mapper, The (Teacher
    Support Software), 172
Semantic maps, 169–172
Sendak, M., 221, 384
Sensorimotor stage, of cognitive
    development, 4–5
Sequence, of details, 207–208
Serra, J. K., 201
Sesquipedalian words, 178–179
Setting, of purpose and goals, 197
Setting, of story, 342, 352
Seven Chinese Brothers (Mahey), 345
Sewall, M., 283
Sexton, C., 282
Shade, B. J., 449, 458
Shake, M. C., 250
Shake My Sillies Out (Raffi), 101
Shankweiler, D., 58
Shannon, P., 376
Shared book experience, 41
Shared reading, 41–44
Shared writing, 405
Shaw, N., 59, 60, 79, 101, 108
Shearer, J., 30
Sheep in a Jeep (Shaw), 59, 100, 108
Sheep in a Shop (Shaw), 59
Sheep on a Ship (Shaw), 59
Sheep Take a Hike (Shaw), 60
Shelton, T. S., 229
Shields, J., 538
Shiloh, (Naylor), 379
Shirley, G. C., 57
Short, K., 340, 379, 380, 392, 430,
    431
Short vowels, 94
Show and Tell Frog, The
    (Oppenheim), 101
Shucksmith, J., 329
Shuy, R., 405, 458
Sight words, 122. *See also*
    Automaticity
    in children's books, 128–131
    in high-frequency list, 123
    in language-experience approach,
    403
    in predictable books, 128–129
    reinforcement activities for, 132
    strategy for teaching to disabled
    learners, 131
    teaching of, 126–127
Silberman, A., 422, 427
Silbert, J., 10, 25
Silverstein, S., 385

Simmons, J., 511, 518
Simpson, M. L., 322
Sims, R. S., 286
Simulations, 538–539
Sinatra, R., 196, 246
Sincerely Yours: How to Write Great
    Letters (James & Barkin), 426
Sing a Song of Popcorn: Every Child's
    Book of Poems (de Regniers et
    al.), 349
Singer, H., 124
Singer, I. B., 16
Sipay, E. R., 93, 151, 227, 249, 283,
    362
Siracusa, C., 102
Six Sick Sheep (Cole), 64
Ska-tat (Knutson), 64
Skills or strategies groups, 534
Skolnick, S., 394
Slanted writing, 271
Slaton, E. A., 244
Slaughter, H. B., 412
Slavin, R. E., 534, 536
Sleepy Dog (Ziefert), 101
Sleepy River (Bandes), 64
Sloan, G. D., 348
Slocum, T. A., 146
Slow learners, 472–473
Small Plays for Special Days
    (Alexander), 357
Smith, C. R., 465
Smith, E., 226
Smith, E. E., 258, 315
Smith, E. L., 307
Smith, F. E., 11, 445
Smith, J. L., 286
Smith, R. J., 350
Smith-Burke, M. T., 482
Snakes Alive! (Burns), 177
Snow, P., 100, 104
Snowy Day, The (Keats), 33, 34, 38
Snyder, B., 226
Sobol, D., 147, 148
Software, computer, 537–540. *See*
    also CD-ROM
    examples of, 541
Somers, A. B., 384
"Something Told the Wild Geese"
    (Field), 348
"Song of the Train" (McCord), 349
Sorting. *See* Phonics, and spelling;
    Spelling, sorting in
Soto, G., 452
"Sound of Water" (O'Neil), 348
Sources, critical reading of, 271, 272
Sowell, J., 140, 141
Spache, G. S., 283

Spangler, A., 20, 309
Spangler, K., 33, 34, 35
Speare, E., 146
Spearitt, D., 270
Special Learners (Cartwright, Cartwright & Ward), 474
Special Writer Coach (Tom Snyder), 90, 436, 437
Speech and language disorders, 475–476
Spelling, 45–47, 52. *See also* Invented spelling
  sorting in, 113–115
Spencer, P., 367
Spicole, R., 73
Spier, P., 456
Spiro, R., 543
Spiroff, J., 124
Spotlight on Reader's Theater (Phoenix Learning Resources), 359
SQ3R, 290–291, 319–321
Squire, J. R., 359
Squirrels (Wildsmith), 312
Stadler, J., 101
Stage Plays from the Classics (Bland), 357
Stages of reading development, 13–17
Stages of word knowledge, 164
Stahl, S. A., 65, 78, 111, 167, 211, 212, 411
Stahl-Gemeke, J., 246
Stallings, J. A., 454
Stallman, A. C., 530
Stambler, J., 102
Stance, of reader, 10, 333–335, 337
Standardized tests. *See* Tests, norm-referenced
Stanine, 504
Stanovich, K., 533
Stauffer, R. G., 261, 262
Steck Vaughn Social Studies (Steck Vaughn), 285
Steckler, A., 176
Steig, J., 64
Stein, B. S., 229, 315
Stellaluna (Canon), 37
Sternberg, R. J., 146, 148, 185, 188, 536
Stevens, D., 226
Stevens, R., 529
Stevenson, J., 64
Sticht, T. G., 491
Stillman, B. W., 112
Stipek, D., 454
Stoll, E., 184, 309
Stone, L., 313

Stop-Go, Fast-Slow (McLenighen), 129
Story Box, 377, 378
Story elements map, 261, 262
Story grammar, 239
Story map, 239–240. *See also* Story elements map
Story of Ourselves: Teaching History Through Children's Literature, The (Tunnell & Ammon), 309
Story schema, 238–240
  activities for exploring, 239–242. *See* Retelling
Story theater, 358
Storybook Weaver (MECC), 439, 541
Strait, J., 482
Strategies, comprehension. *See also* Reciprocal teaching
  activating prior knowledge, 197
  constructing the main idea, 201–205
  determining relative importance of information, 205–214
  following directions, 208–219
  imaging, 220–223
  making inferences, 215–220
  question generating, 223–224
  setting purpose and goals, 197
  summarizing, 210–212
Strategies, metacognitive
  checking, 226
  monitoring, 224–225
  regulating, 226
  repairing, 226–227
  using lookbacks, 227–228
Strategies, student
  for applying SQ3R, 320
  for applying variability to consonant correspondences, 93–94
  for applying variability to vowel correspondences, 110–111
  for attacking multisyllabic words, 137
  for constructing main idea, 201–202
  for following directions, 209–210
  for judging sources, 272
  for using ALERT, 274
Strategies, word recognition
  analogy, 115–116, 137, 152
  contextual analysis, 146–150
  corrective cues hierarchy, 151–152
  morphemic analysis, 137–145
  pronounceable word part, 115–116, 137, 152
  syllabic analysis, 137

Strategies or skills groups, 534
Strategy, 196
Straw, S. B., 9
Strega Nona (dePaola), 37
Strickland, D. S., 32, 36
Structural analysis. *See* Syllabication
Structured overview, 291–292, 293, 300–301, 302
Stuart-Clark, C., 347
Study groups, 535
Study guides, 297–300
  steps in creating, 297
Study habits, 323–324
Study skills, expressive. *See* I-charts, Notetaking; Outlining
Studying, strategies for
  clustering, 318
  and conceptual understanding, 315–316
  flash cards, 317–318
  metacognitive, 329–330
  mnemonic devices, 316–317
  rehearsal, 316
  SQ3R, 319–321
  and test taking, 322
Style, author's, 342, 352
Suffixes, 141, 142
Sukarna, P., 266, 392
Sulzby, E., 13, 24, 25, 26, 40, 47, 48, 49, 50, 54, 69, 415
Summarizing, 210–214
Summer of the Swans (Byars), 221, 351, 354
Sundbye, N., 248
Sunshine series, as reading program, 377
Super Talk to Me (Educational Activities), 543
Superdupers: Really Funny Real Words (Terban), 176
Superprint for the Macintosh (Scholastic), 541
Surprises (Hopkins), 102, 349
Survey technique, 290–291
Survival signs, 471
Susskind, E., 250
Sustained Silent Reading (SSR), 363–364
Sutherland, Z., 343
Sutton, C., 461, 462
Swenson, M., 350
Sybil Rides for Independence (Brown), 283
Syllabication, 132–137
Symons, S., 210
Synthetic approach, to teaching phonics, 80–81

Taba, H., 251, 253
Tafuri, N., 130
Tale of Peter Rabbit, The (Potter), 216
Tale of Sir Gawain, The (Philip), 346
Talented students, 479–480
Tar Beach (Ringgold), 451
Tarnowsky, J., 381
Taxonomy, 249
  of questions (Bloom), 249–250, 385
Taylor, B., 20, 482
Taylor, D., 8, 9, 32, 36
Taylor, K. K., 210, 211, 212, 214
Teaching lessons
  anticipation guide for, 289–290
  by sorting initial consonants, 114–115
  by summarizing, 212–214
  using context clues, 149
  using directed reading activity, 259–261
  using directed reading-thinking activity, 262–263
  using Elkonin phonemic segmentation technique, 62
  using important details, 207
  using inferences, 217–218
  using initial consonants, 84–85
  using key word approach, 186–187
  using language-experience approach, 400
  using main idea and supporting details, 203
  using making words, 107
  using outlining, 326–327
  using predictable books to teach sight words, 128–129
  using prefixes, 139–140
  using PReP, 288–289
  using QAR (Question-Answer Relationship), 219
  using reader response, 338
  using reciprocal teaching, 231–233
  using ReQuest, 253–254
  using retelling, 241
  using semantic feature analysis, 172–173
  using semantic mapping, 170–171
  using sight words, 125–126
  using syllabication and the generalization approach, 134–135
  using syllabication and the pattern approach, 135–136
  using think-alouds, 295–297

using vowel correspondence, 99
using word-building pattern, 103–104
Teale, W., 13, 24, 25, 26, 50, 54
Teberosky, A., 25
Technology, and literacy, 537–543. *See also* Computers; Videodiscs
Technology and Learning, 540
Telecommunications, 539
Tell Me About Yourself: How to Interview Anyone from Your Friends to Famous People (Maberry), 426
Temple, C., 50, 115
Temple, F., 50, 115
Tennyson, A. L., 348
Tenth Mental Measurements Yearbook (Conoley & Kramer), 504
Terban, M., 176
Terman, L. M., 479
Terry, A., 346, 348
Tests
  basal, 506
  criterion-referenced, 502
  norm-referenced, 489, 500–502
  reliability of, 502–503
  validity of, 503
Tetewsky, S. S., 188
Text sets, 379–380
Text structure, 240
  expository, 242–248
  and graphic organizers, 245–246, 247
  narrative, 238–240
  teaching of, 244–248
  types of, 243–244
Thematic unit, 380–383
Theme, of literary piece, 342, 352
There's a Wocket in My Pocket (Geisel), 65
Think-alouds, 295–297
  as assessment devices, 509–510
Thirteen Moons on Turtle's Back (Bruchac & London), 349
This Is the Way We Go to School (Baer), 451
Thomas, E. L., 321
Thomas Jefferson: Father of Our Democracy (Adler), 360
Thompson, A., 312
Thorndike, R. L., 75, 156, 168
Thorndyke, P., 239
Three Billy Goats Gruff, The (Brown), 37
Thurber, J., 422
Tiedt, I. M., 344, 464

Tiedt, P. M., 344, 464
Tierney, R., 263, 288, 290, 300, 403, 489, 518, 520
Tindall, M. A., 176
Tinajo, J. V., 283
Title 1, 481, 482
Toad on the Road (Schade), 101
Tomie dePaola's Book of Poems (dePaola), 349
Tomie dePaola's Mother Goose (dePaola), 60
Tompkins, G. E., 144, 239
Too Many Books (Bauer), 33
Too Many Tamales (Soto), 452
Top-down approach, to teaching reading, 10, 11
Town Mouse, Country Mouse (Brett), 37
Trachtenburg, P., 108
Transaction, 335
Transactional theory, 9–10
Transitional classes, 25
Treiman, R. 102
Trelease, J., 33, 38, 39
Trophy series (Harper), 286
Truman's Ant Farm (Rattigan), 177
Trussell-Cullen, A., 243
Tunnel, M. O., 18, 309
Tunnis, J., 7
Turbill, J., 428, 444
Turner, I., 90
Turner, J. C., 230
Tuttle, D. W., 477
Two Bad Ants (Van Allsburg), 373, 374
Typographical aids in textbooks, 28, 204, 282. *See also* Graphic aids in textbooks
Tyson, E. S., 178

"Uh-oh!" Said the Crow (Oppenheim), 101
Unit, 380–383
U.S. Department of Education, 536

V for Vanishing: An Alphabet of Endangered Animals (Mullins), 57
Vacca, J. L., 321
Vacca, R. T., 321
Valdez, C., 459, 460
Valencia, S., 380, 381, 489, 518, 519
Validity, 503
Van Allen, R., 399
Van Allsburg, C., 373
Vandeiver, R. J., 184
Vanderwerf, B., 309

Van Dijk, T. A., 196
Van Riper, C., 475
Vaughn, J., 299
Velveteen Rabbit, The (Williams), 221
Venezky, R., 93, 109
Venn diagram, 174, 175
Very Busy Spider, The (Carle), 32
Videodiscs (laser discs), 181, 542
Visual impairments, students with,
    476–477
Visualizing. *See* Imaging
Vocabulary
    building, 163–191
    incidental learning of, 184–185
    need for instruction in, 163
    planned program of, 184–185
    principles of, 165–169
    teaching special features of words
        in, 187–191
    techniques for remembering,
        185–187
    techniques for teaching, 169–184
Voluntary reading, 361. *See also*
    Sustained Silent Reading
    determining interests for, 362
    importance of, 361
    obtaining materials for, 362–363
    setting aside time for, 364
    use of, 364–367
Vowels, 94–99
Vygotsky, L. S., 4, 6, 420, 424, 527

Waber, B., 33
Wade, S., 281
Wagner, K., 282
Wagoner, S., 228
Wait time, 250–251
Wake Up, Baby (Oppenheim), 100
Walker, A., 360
Walker, P. R., 361
Wallace, G., 465, 479
Walsh, D. S., 124
Wang, M. L., 100
Wang, Y. Y., 364
Ward, M. E., 469, 473, 474, 475
Warren, D. H., 476
Wasik, B. A., 230, 482
Watch the Stars Come Out
    (Levinson), 286
Watson, A. J., 65
Watson, C., 88
Watson, S. B., 279
Weaver, B., 129, 505
Weaver, C. K., 54, 195, 275, 307,
    467
Web, 172, 174, 204. *See also*
    Semantic maps

Weber, R., 250
Wehlage, G. G., 279, 532
Weinstein, C., 197, 315
Weiss, L., 33
Wells, G., 3, 4, 31, 32, 66
What a Dog! (Gordon), 130
What a Tail! (Wildsmith), 130
*What Works: A Report on Teaching
    and Learning* (U.S. Department
    of Education), 530
What's Whole in Whole Language
    (Goodman, Bird, & Goodman),
    22
When Learning Is Tough (Roby), 478
Where Do You Get Your Ideas?
    (Asher), 426
Where Have You Been? (Brown), 130
Where the Wild Things Are (Sendak),
    221, 384
Where's the Bear? (Pomeranz), 130
Whistle for Willie (Keats), 34
White, E. B., 16, 146, 335, 353, 379
White, M. M., 141, 349
White, S., 138
White, T. G., 138, 140, 141
Who Is Who? (McKissack), 100, 130
Whole class instruction, 533–534. *See
    also* Author's circle; Cooperative
    learning; Literature circles
Whole language, 11, 13, 371,
    408–411
    activities for, 409–410
    adapting, 411
    advantages and disadvantages of,
        411
    basic principles of, 408
    rationale for, 11, 408
Whole Language Catalog, The
    (Goodman, Bird, & Goodman),
    410
Whole-part-whole approach, 108
Whose Mouse Are You? (Kraus), 130
*Why Mosquitoes Buzz in People's
    Ears: A West African Folktale*
    (Aardema), 344
Whyte, B., 184
Wide reading, 17–18
    effect on vocabulary of, 183–184
Wiggleworks (Scholastic), 541
Wilde, S., 52
Wilder, L. I., 148
Wildsmith, B., 57, 100, 130, 312,
    461, 505
Wile, D., 234
Wilkinson, I. A., 30, 78, 371, 411
Will You Sign Here, John Hancock?
    (Fritz), 286

Williams, J. P., 196, 200, 202
Williams, M., 221
Williams, R. L., 459
Williams, S., 30
Williams, W. C., 347
Willie's Wonderful Pet (Cebulash),
    130
Wilson, J., 18, 19, 268
Wilson, P., 363
Wilson, P. T., 361, 362, 363, 364,
    365
Wingfield, A., 536
Winn, J., 226
Winne, R. H., 215, 216
Winograd, P., 126, 128, 212, 227,
    374, 487, 520
Winters, L., 520
Wisconsin Reading Association, 532
Wiseman, B., 101
Witch of Blackbird Pond, The
    (Speare), 146
Withers, C. 90
Wittrock, M. E., 214
Wixson, K. K., 16, 17, 204, 248, 380,
    381
WKID: Easy Radio Plays (Rasorisky),
    357
Wolf, A., 531
Wolf, B., 474, 475, 476
Wolf, W., 267
*Wonderful World of Mathematics,
    The* (Thiessen & Matthias), 310
Wonders of Science, The (Gottlieb),
    285
Wong, E. Y., 60
Woodley, J. W., 514
Woodward, V. A., 45
Word Attack Three (Davidson), 181
Word banks, 402, 403
Word Bird Makes Words with Cat
    (Moncure), 100
Word Bird Makes Words with Pig
    (Moncure), 100
Word building, 102–105, 465
Word histories, 176
Word knowledge, stages of, 164
Word play, 58–59
Word processing, 436–437, 539, 540,
    541. *See also* Desktop publishing
Word recognition, integrated
    approach to, 160–161. *See also*
    Strategies, word recognition
Word walls, 403
Words
    enjoying, 176–178
    multiple uses of, 189–190,
        268–269

Words (Kaufman), 129
Workbooks, 375–376
World Almanac, The (Lane), 366
World History (Hart), 285
Worth, V., 338
Worthington, S., 384
Wright, J. W., 274, 453
Wright Brothers at Kitty Hawk, The
        (Sobol), 147
Writing
    activities, 445–446
    and author's circle, 430–431
    children's books on, 426–427
    and classroom setup, 432–433
    composing, 420–422
    conferences, 428–431
    dictation in, 54
    early stages of, 45
    editing, 424–427
    emergent, 46–47
    evaluation of, 516–517
    and focusing on audience, 421
    process approach to, 416

and publishing, 427–428
and reading, 443–445
revising, 422–424
sharing of, 432
stages of, 415–416
and teaching form, 439–445
and technology, 436–439
Writing process, 416
Writing to learn, 311–313. *See also*
        Learning logs
Writing to Read (IBM), 405–406, 538
Writing workshop, 431–433. *See also*
        Cognitive Strategy Instruction in
        Writing; Interactive writing
Written conversation, 433–435
Wurster, S. R., 363
Wynne, P., 101

Yaden, D. B., 144
Yanagihara, A., 140, 141
Yashima, T., 351, 443
*Yeh-Shen: A Cinderella Story from
        China* (Louie), 380

Yonas, P., 45
Yoo hoo, Moon! (Blocksma), 101,
        130
Yopp, H. K., 59, 242
Yopp, R. H., 242
You Are Much Too Small (Bogehold),
        100
You Read to Me, I'll Read to You
        (Ciardi), 349
Young Discovery Library, 286
Your Child's Vision Is Important
        (Beverstock), 477

Zajdler, Z., 344
Zarillo, J., 351, 379, 456
Zarnowski, M., 287, 308, 309,
        360
Ziefert, H., 100, 101, 130
"Zinnias" (Worth), 338
Zinsser, W., 311
Zion, G., 38
Zone of proximal development, 6
Zorfass, J., 437